INSPIRE / PLAN / DISCOVER / EXPERIENCE

INDIA

INDIA

CONTENTS

This page: Marigolds at a market in Kolkata
Previous page: Cockle pickers, Vembanad Lake, Kerala
Front cover: The Green Gate at Jaipur's City Palace

DISCOVER 6

EXPERIENCE 78

NEED TO KNOW 598

DISCOVER

The glistening lake at sacred Pushkar

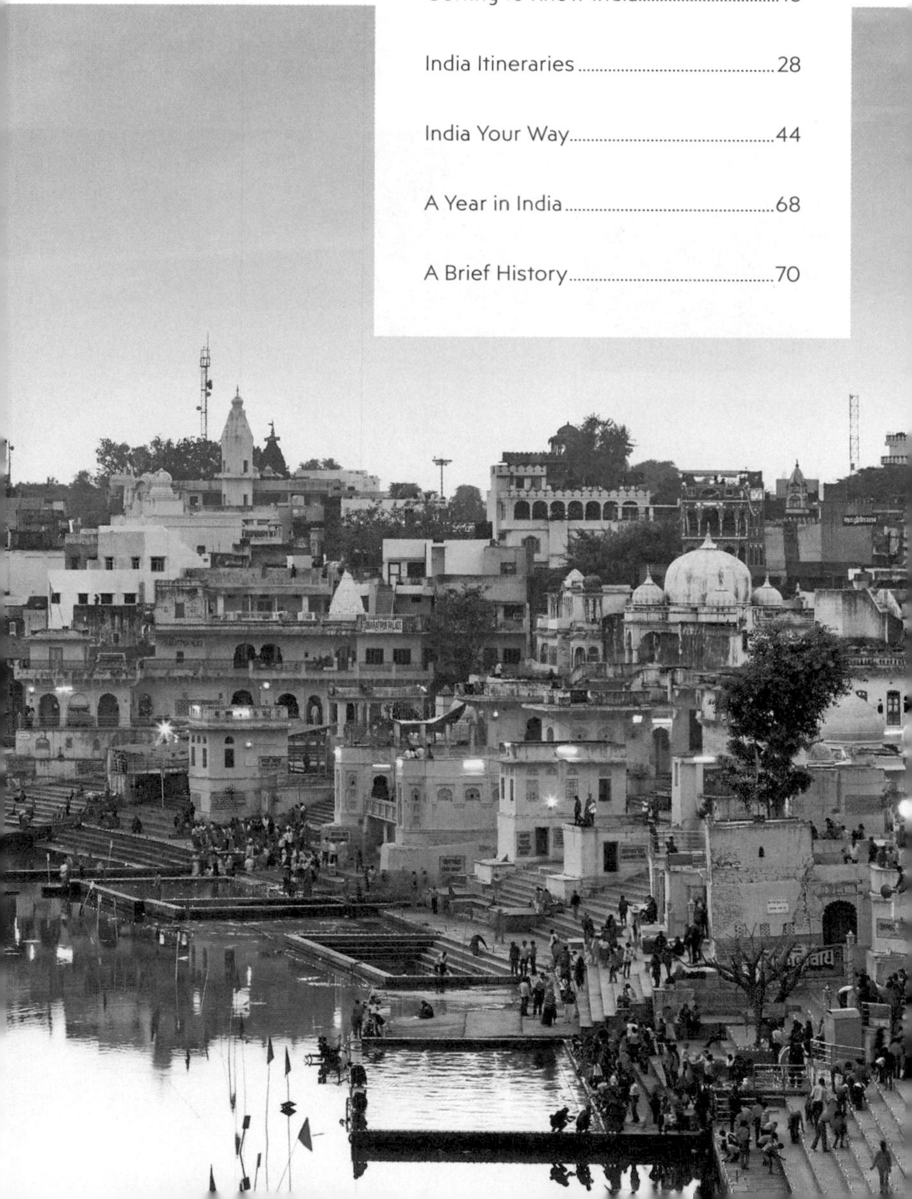

WELCOME TO
INDIA

Ancient and awe-inspiring, India has been captivating visitors for millennia. It's not hard to see why, as this country is endlessly enticing: in a single day you'll encounter sizzling street food, dazzling architecture and riotous religious festivals. Whatever sights your dream trip includes, this DK Eyewitness Travel Guide is the perfect companion.

1 Kerala's lush green hills.

2 Delhi's Baha'i Temple.

3 Frothy chai served with a dusting of cinnamon.

4 A woman gazing over the pavilions on Sagar Lake in Udaipur.

An epic country, India is bordered in the north by the peaks of the Himalayan mountains and extends down through the diverse jungles, rivers and deserts of the plains to the Indian Ocean in the south. In these landscapes, wild elephants gather at waterholes, one-horned rhinos roll in the mud, tigers prowl, and innumerable species of birds caw and crow.

India's urban jungles are just as fascinating as its natural world. Take the capital, Delhi. Here, modern skyscrapers and centuries-old mosques push up against each other, representative of a country where past and present blend in a way that never ceases to capture the imagination. Although the crush of major cities like Delhi and Mumbai may seem overwhelming at first, take a few days to relax to the pace, and you'll soon find yourself hailing down rickshaws

and ordering a stuffed paratha like a seasoned hand. And you'll need to be used to the crowds to brave India's exuberant religious festivals. In this deeply spiritual country, huge numbers of people take to the streets to throw coloured powder at the start of spring for Holi, to feast at the end of Eid, and to parade at the beginning of Catholic Lent.

With so much to see and do in India, it can be hard to know where to start. We've broken the country down into easily navigable chapters, with detailed itineraries, expert local knowledge, and colourful, comprehensive maps to help you plan the perfect visit. Whether you're staying for a weekend, a week, or longer, this Eyewitness guide will ensure that you make the most of all that the country has to offer. Enjoy the book, and enjoy India.

REASONS TO LOVE
INDIA

India is big in every way: size, population, personality, and, of course, big-ticket attractions like the Taj Mahal. Here are some reasons why you won't be able to resist the heady pace of this ancient land.

1 DEVOTIONS AT DUSK

Join the thousands of pilgrims who line the holy Ganges in colourful Varanasi *(p176)* to light candles and float them on the water, an act of devotion that sets the river aflame.

SUNDOWNERS IN GOA 2

Goa's golden beaches are lined with shacks where you can order a feni cocktail – a spirit made from cashews – to sip as the sun slips into the endless horizon of the Arabian Sea.

3 COLOURFUL CELEBRATIONS

India is a country that loves to party, whether it is rejoicing over spring or a god's birthday. Wear your oldest clothes to Holi, where colourful powder is thrown over the crowds.

4 IMMORTAL ROMANCE

It's unmissable, unmistakable and undeniably beautiful. The Taj Mahal *(p166)*, the famous monument to romantic love, is best visited at sunrise, although it's breathtaking at any hour.

TERRIFYINGLY TERRIFIC TIGERS 5

India is home to the world's largest population of tigers. Here, walk on the wild side and attempt to spot a big cat on a safari in one of the country's protected tiger reserves.

FOOD FOR THE SOUL 6

The streets of towns across India are heady with the aroma of spices and sizzling food. Each area has its own flavour and dishes, so be sure to bring an appetite as big as the country.

FANTASTICAL FORTS *7*

The sheer stone walls of Rajasthan's imposing hill forts hide palaces that have fallen straight out of a fantasy, with thrones of gold and sparkling bedrooms decorated in crystals.

HIMALAYAN HEIGHTS *8*

It's not just the altitude that will take your breath away in the beautiful Himalayas. Here, monasteries cling to mountains, narrow roads cross gorges and ancient markets do brisk trade.

9 SPIRITUAL HEALING

India is home to some of the oldest wellbeing practices in the world. Find your centre at a yoga school in Goa, a meditation retreat in the Himalayas or an Ayurvedic detox in Kerala.

10 ANCIENT CIVILIZATIONS

Walk in the footsteps of time – this is where some of the world's great religions and civilizations were founded and where ancient rulers built majestic cities and temples.

TEA TIME 11

Assam, Darjeeling... India is where some of the world's favourite tea is grown. In the hilly town of Darjeeling, taste the first leaves of that season's harvest with a "first flush" brew.

BEDAZZLING BOLLYWOOD 12

The world's biggest movie industry, Bollywood is full of big dance numbers, bigger songs and even bigger panache. Go on a tour of Film City *(p415)* in Mumbai to see it in action.

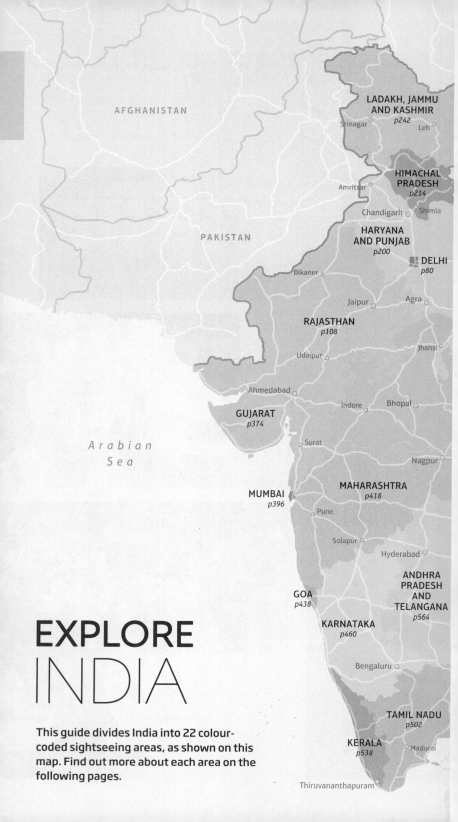

AFGHANISTAN

LADAKH, JAMMU
AND KASHMIR
p242

Srinagar   Leh

HIMACHAL
PRADESH
p214

Amritsar

Chandigarh   Shimla

PAKISTAN

HARYANA
AND PUNJAB
p200

DELHI
p80

Bikaner

Jaipur   Agra

RAJASTHAN
p108

Udaipur   Jhansi

Ahmedabad

GUJARAT
p374

Indore   Bhopal

*Arabian
Sea*

Surat

Nagpur

MAHARASHTRA
p418

MUMBAI
p396

Pune

Solapur

Hyderabad

ANDHRA
PRADESH
AND
TELANGANA
p564

GOA
p438

KARNATAKA
p460

EXPLORE
INDIA

This guide divides India into 22 colour-
coded sightseeing areas, as shown on this
map. Find out more about each area on the
following pages.

Bengaluru

TAMIL NADU
p502

KERALA
p538

Madurai

Thiruvananthapuram

UZBEKISTAN
KYRGYZSTAN
TURKMENISTAN
TAJIKISTAN
IRAN
AFGHANISTAN
CHINA
PAKISTAN
BHUTAN
NEPAL
U.A.E
INDIA
MYANMAR
SAUDI
ARABIA
OMAN
BANGLADESH
LAOS
VIETNAM
THAILAND
CAMBODIA
PHILIPPINES
Arabian
Sea
Bay of
Bengal
SRI
LANKA
MALAYSIA
MALDIVES

CHINA

NEPAL

Lucknow

BHUTAN

Siliguri

ASSAM
AND THE
NORTHEAST
p358

UTTAR PRADESH AND
UTTARAKHAND
p158

Guwahati

Patna

Bhagalpur

BIHAR AND
JHARKHAND
p258

BANGLADESH

Silchar

WEST BENGAL
AND SIKKIM
p324

MADHYA PRADESH
AND CHHATTISGARH
p274

Ranchi

KOLKATA
p306

MYANMAR

Raipur

ODISHA
p342

Bhubaneswar

Jagdalpur

Visakhapatnam

Vijayawada

Bay of
Bengal

CHENNAI
p486

Puducherry

Port Blair

ANDAMAN
ISLANDS
p588

SRI
LANKA

GETTING TO KNOW
INDIA

India: its name conjures images of crowded streets, colourful spices and textiles, ancient temples and forts, and a country that embraces its past while hurtling into the future. The regions across this epic land - from the mountainous hills covered with temples in the northern states to the bustling beaches and lively nightlife of the south coast - have their own culture and rich histories that entice visitors to return again and again.

DELHI

PAGE 80

A sprawling, constantly expanding metropolis, Delhi's noise and fast pace can at first seem overwhelming, but settle into the city's rhythms and you'll discover a remarkable place. India's capital is – and has always been – constantly evolving, and the outstanding architecture of monuments such as the Red Fort and Mehrauli Archaeological Park reveals this history in stone and mortar. You can also taste it on the streets: head to the famous Parathe Wali Gali in the Chandi Chowk bazaar in Old Delhi for fried paratha, long the dish of choice among the locals.

Best for
Architectural, cultural and culinary gems

Home to
Red Fort, Jama Masjid, Mehrauli Archaeological Park, Qutb Minar, Humayun's Tomb

Experience
Listening to haunting qawwalis at the medieval Nizamuddin Complex, one of the holiest shrines in Sufi Islam

RAJASTHAN

PAGE 108

The crown jewel of India, Rajasthan has it all. The myriad attractions here feel like they could have fallen out of the storybooks: picture the glittering palaces of the old kingdoms of Jaipur, Jodhpur, Jaisalmer and Udaipur, and the rainbow-coloured birds of Keoladeo Ghana and Ranthambhore national parks. Witness the hubbub of one of Asia's largest cattle fairs at the pilgrimage town of Pushkar or find some quiet in the wide expanses of the Thar Desert, complete with roving camels. Only a short distance from Delhi, Rajasthan is justifiably one of India's most popular destinations.

Best for
Magical forts and palaces

Home to
Jaipur, Amber Fort, Keoladeo Ghana National Park, Jodhpur, Jaisalmer, Udaipur, Ranthambhore National Park

Experience
Taking a safari across the Thar Desert

UTTAR PRADESH AND UTTARAKHAND

PAGE 158

Take a deep breath and dive in; between them, these neighbouring states have some of the biggest attractions in India, and the crowds to prove it. Uttar Pradesh is home to one of the world's greatest expressions of human love – Agra's Taj Mahal – as well as the divine, as pilgrims come to bathe in the holy waters of the Ganges at Varanasi. Mountainous Uttarakhand moves at a different pace, attracting pilgrims and yoga devotees looking to meditate at the country's best known yoga hub, Rishikesh.

Best for
History, heritage and religion

Home to
Agra, Fatehpur Sikri, Corbett National Park, Varanasi, Lucknow

Experience
Watching pilgrims and priests conduct their daily arti (rituals) at the Ganges in Varanasi

→

PAGE 200

HARYANA AND PUNJAB

These twin states share a single capital city, Chandigarh, a modernist classic designed by architect Le Corbusier. Divided during Partition, Punjab has more to offer visitors than Haryana: it is the birthplace of Sikhism and home to its most important monument, the glittering Golden Temple in Amritsar. Nearby is the Wagah border crossing, where Indian and Pakistani soldiers stage highly coordinated evening ceremonies, accompanied by cheers from their respective country-men and women. The region's food, centred around the tandoor, is another highlight.

Best for
Sikh culture and Modernist architecture

Home to
Golden Temple, Wagah Border

Experience
Eating dal at the Golden Temple, whose kitchen serves up to 100,000 free meals a day

PAGE 214

HIMACHAL PRADESH

Situated in the soaring, breath-stealing peaks of the Himalayas, Himachal Pradesh is a site of pilgrimage for many people. They come to pay homage to the Dalai Lama at Dharamsala, home to the Buddhist leader and the Tibetan government-in-exile; take on some of the best hikes in the country in the heart-stopping and isolated Spiti Valley; and escape the sweltering heat of the low country at cool, Raj-era hill stations, such as Shimla.

Best for
Himalayan hikes and Tibetan culture

Home to
Spiti Valley, Tabo Monastery, Shimla, Dharamsala, Bhimakali Temple

Experience
Walking the kora at the Dalai Lama's residence

PAGE 242

LADAKH, JAMMU AND KASHMIR

In the far north of India, the state of Jammu and Kashmir has staggeringly beautiful Himalayan scenery. Following a dip in popularity due to its unsettled political situation – both Pakistan and India lay claim to the land – tourism is rising again. With alpine scenery and Buddhist monasteries, the most spectacular area is Ladakh, which is also the start point of one of the world's most exhilarating (and occasionally deadly) drives along the Leh-Manali Highway.

Best for
Expansive Himalayan landscapes

Home to
Alchi Monastery, Leh

Experience
Spending a night on a houseboat on the shimmering waters of Dal Lake

PAGE 258

BIHAR AND JHARKHAND

Two of the poorest states in India, Bihar and Jharkhand are rich in history. Patna, on the banks of the Ganges, is Bihar's capital and one of the oldest continuously inhabited cities on earth. It makes a good base for the nearby Sonepur Mela, a huge cattle fair held towards the end of every year. Most visitors, though, come to experience two key Buddhist sites in Bihar: Bodh Gaya, where the Buddha attained enlightenment, and Nalanda, an ancient Buddhist university.

Best for
Buddhist culture and practice

Home to
Patna, Mahabodhi Temple, Nalanda

Experience
Sitting in quiet contemplation under the Bodhi tree in Bodh Gaya, the spot where the Buddha found enlightenment

→

MADHYA PRADESH AND CHHATTISGARH

PAGE 274

Landlocked, densely forested and culturally rich, the neighbouring states of Madhya Pradesh and Chhattisgarh are right in the centre of India. The former features an incredibly varied collection of attractions: Kiplingesque tiger reserves, imposing forts, overgrown and semi-ruined palaces, Buddhist stupas and ancient temples covered with sensuous art. If you really want to get off the beaten track, head to Chhattisgarh, home to myriad indigenous communities.

Best for
World-class tiger reserves

Home to
Bhopal, the Great Stupa, Mandu, Kanha National Park, Khajuraho, Orchha, Gwalior Fort, Bandhavgarh National Park

Experience
An amble through the picturesque royal city of Orchha, home to the many-layered Jahangir Mahal palace

KOLKATA

PAGE 306

Forget its reputation – Kolkata (formerly Calcutta) is one of the most beguiling cities in Asia. Set on the banks of the Hooghly, the capital of West Bengal is a welcoming, sophisticated and utterly Bengali place. The culture infuses every-day life here, from the city's rich literary traditions – including its second-hand book market – to its cuisine. Among Kolkata's many attractions are museums, such as the Victoria Memorial, and livelier spots, including Eden Gardens, one of India's finest cricket grounds.

Best for
Bengali culture and culinary delights

Home to
Victoria Memorial, Kalighat, Kumartuli

Experience
Following the Durga Puja processions through the streets during Kolkata's biggest festival worshipping the mother goddess

PAGE 324

WEST BENGAL AND SIKKIM

Beyond its busy capital, Kolkata, the state of West Bengal is most famous for its diverse range of landscapes, from the central lowlands – home to the terracotta temples of Bishnupur – to the cool tea estates of Darjeeling in the foothills of the Himalayas. Meanwhile, tiny Sikkim is a place of red pandas, rhododendron forests, monasteries and mountains – a landscape best explored on one of the numerous trekking routes.

Best for
Mangrove cruises, tea-tasting and treks

Home to
The Sundarbans, Shyama Raya Temple, Darjeeling

Experience
Sampling a cup of "first flush" tea at a plantation in the hill station of Darjeeling

PAGE 342

ODISHA

On the east coast of India facing the Bay of Bengal, Odisha is famed for its magnificent temples. There are more than 500 medieval mandirs in the capital Bhubaneswar alone – though the highlight is the glorious Sun Temple at Konark. The state also hosts an array of religious festivals, notably the extravagant Rath Yatra celebrations in Puri. A state enriched by its numerous indigenous communities, Odisha is also home to several wonderful nature reserves, including Bhitarkanika, where tens of thousands of Olive Ridley turtles nest each year.

Best for
Temples and turtles

Home to
Bhubaneswar, Konark Sun Temple

Experience
A cruise around the mangrove forests, islands, creeks and beaches of the wildlife-rich Bhitarkanika reserve

$\rightarrow$

PAGE 358

ASSAM AND THE NORTHEAST

Known as the Seven Sisters, the states of northeast India are off the beaten track with plenty to reward the adventurous traveller. The biggest of the seven is Assam, home to tea estates, the impressive Kaziranga National Park and Majuli, the world's largest inhabited river island. Arunachal Pradesh offers remarkable Himalayan vistas, Nagaland is rich in indigenous cultures and Meghalaya, one of the rainiest places in the world, has some incredible natural bridges formed from rubber plant roots.

Best for
Indigenous cultures and tea estates galore

Home to
Guwahati, Kaziranga National Park

Experience
Crossing one of Meghalaya's "living root bridges", which seem straight out of the imagination of J R R Tolkien

PAGE 374

GUJARAT

Reaching out into the Arabian Sea, Gujarat is the westernmost state in India. It is indelibly linked with independence leader Mahatma Gandhi, who was born in the city of Porbander and based his Sabarmati Ashram in the state capital, Ahmedabad. Elsewhere you'll find a diverse array of attractions including the lions of Gir National Park, the 1,000-year-old Sun Temple at Modhera, the finely detailed stepwell of Adalaj Vav and the isolated Kutch region, where strong craft and textile traditions persist amid a harsh but beautiful landscape.

Best for
Independence history and exquisite textiles

Home to
Ahmedabad, Adalaj Vav, Modhera Sun Temple, Little Rann of Kutch

Experience
Strolling through Ahmedabad's old city, a beguiling mix of temples, mosques and bazaars

PAGE 396

MUMBAI

A vast, cosmopolitan, pulsing metropolis, it's not hard to see why Mumbai was famously dubbed "maximum city" by writer Suketu Mehta. Mumbai (formerly Bombay) is synonymous with Bollywood, the world's biggest film industry, and there's plenty in the city to make you break into song and dance: here you are almost guaranteed to find some of the best cultural, food, shopping and night-life experiences in the country. Beyond the pulsating street life, there are more traditional attractions, including one of the country's finest art galleries at Chhatrapati Shivaji Maharaj Vastu Sangrahalaya.

Best for
City life and cultural delights

Home to
Chhatrapati Shivaji Terminus, Chhatrapati Shivaji Maharaj Vastu Sangrahalaya, Elephanta Island, the Gateway of India

Experience
Soaking up the ocean views and Art Deco architecture along Marine Drive with a cone of bhelpuri, a savoury tamarind-chutney-infused snack

$\rightarrow$

PAGE 418

MAHARASHTRA

Maharashtra is dominated by Mumbai, but there's far more to the state than its sprawling capital. Amid rugged hills and mountains, expansive plateaus and a long coastline, you'll find ancient monuments, niche and emerging vineyards, tranquil beach resorts and stately Mughal architecture. Maharashtra's main draws are the rock-cut caves, shrines and temples of Ellora and Ajanta, which are both UNESCO World Heritage sites, but the sophisticated city of Pune, Hindu temples of Nasik and the charming hill station of Matheran are also must-visits.

Best for
Ancient cave art, monasteries and temples

Home to
Ellora Caves, Ajanta Caves

Experience
Riding the toy train up to the picturesque hill station of Matheran

PAGE 438

GOA

Whether you want to stay up late dancing or get up early and complete a vinyasa flow on the beach, Goa will deliver. This small state moves to a different pace than the rest of India, but even though visitors are undoubtedly drawn here by the string of gorgeous beaches, Goa's history has just as much to enchant. Once occupied by the Portuguese, it still displays a strong European influence in its religious beliefs, cuisine and the crumbling colonial architecture of its capital.

Best for
Sunbathing and sundowners

Home to
Panaji, Old Goa, Braganza House

Experience
Learning to surf or stand-up paddleboard at one of Goa's many beach clubs, stretched out along 106 km (66 miles) of pristine coast

PAGE 460

KARNATAKA

Karnataka is a remarkable mix of the old and the new, the urban and the rural. Its capital Bengaluru (formerly Bangalore) is a fast-growing mega-city at the centre of India's flourishing tech industry. But the state is also home to the ancient temples of Pattadakal and Badami, and the atmospheric ruined city of Hampi. On the coast, Gokarna is a lower-key alternative to the beaches of neighbouring Goa, while the mountains and forests of the Western Ghats are some of the most biodiverse places on earth.

Best for
Ancient temples and rural escapes

Home to
Bengaluru, Badami, Hampi, Pattadakal

Experience
Climbing great granite boulders at the UNESCO World Heritage Site of Hampi, a spectacularly preserved ruined city

PAGE 486

CHENNAI

Tourists tend to zip through laid-back Chennai (formerly Madras) en route to other destinations but if you stick around a few days, you'll find the city steadily grows on you. The capital of Tamil Nadu and the biggest city in southern India, Chennai has some well-preserved colonial-era buildings, one of India's longest beaches and the excellent Government Museum Complex. But one of the greatest appeals of Chennai is the chance to sample authentic south India cuisine, particularly masala dosa, known locally as food for the soul.

Best for
Seaside strolls and classic architecture

Home to
The Marina

Experience
Buying a fire-roasted corn-on-the-cob from a street vendor on the Marina

$\rightarrow$

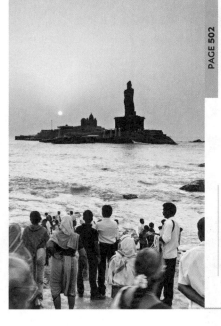

PAGE 502

TAMIL NADU

Whatever you're looking for in India, you'll probably find it in the south-eastern Tamil Nadu. The state has an array of temple towns, including historic Madurai – once known as the "Athens of the East" – and Thanjavur. Former French colony Puducherry has a distinct Gallic ambience, while the stone-carved Mamallapuram is a UNESCO World Heritage Site. For a taste of nature, Tamil Nadu has a long stretch of coastline and a large section of the lush Western Ghats.

Best for
Temple towns and ancient monoliths

Home to
Mamallapuram, Puducherry, Thanjavur, Madurai, Chettinad

Experience
Enjoying a croissant or coq au vin in one of Puducherry's French-style cafés or restaurants

PAGE 538

KERALA

Nicknamed "God's Own Country", Kerala is where people come seeking escape down the endless waterways. Even though it has several appealing cities, the countryside is the main draw here, an interior rich with tea and spice plantations, as well as protected areas like Periyar Wildlife Sanctuary. Beyond a maze of languid backwaters, there are attractive beach resorts like Varkala and, offshore, the coral atolls of the Lakshadweep islands. Kerala is also a centre of Ayurvedic medicine, the dance-drama of Kathakali and a delectable seafood-focused cuisine.

Best for
Rolling hills and serene backwater cruises

Home to
Kochi, Thiruvananthapuram, Padmanabhapuram Palace, Periyar Wildlife Sanctuary, Lakshadweep

Experience
Exploring the meandering Keralan backwaters on board a traditional kettuvallam

ANDHRA PRADESH AND TELANGANA

PAGE 564

Rich in both monuments and artisan culture, Andhra Pradesh and Telangana were one state until 2014, and still share a capital, Hyderabad. The city is home to the dramatic Golconda Fort, impressive Islamic monuments, a lucrative tech hub and the finest biryanis in India. Elsewhere you'll discover some of the most important Hindu sites in south India, including the Shri Venkateshvara Temple in Tirupati, which attracts up to 100,000 Hindu pilgrims a day.

Best for
Fortified cities and revered temples

Home to
Hyderabad, Golconda Fort

Experience
Watching the sunset at Golconda Fort, a great citadel on the edge of Hyderabad

PAGE 588

ANDAMAN AND NICOBAR ISLANDS

Located around 1,000 km (621 miles) east of the mainland, these islands have a different vibe to the rest of India, with a tropical landscape and a strong indigenous presence – although they share a similar colonial history. The lush archipelago is famed for its sandy beaches, crystal-clear waters and pristine coral reefs, a haven for snorkellers and scuba divers. If you're after a tranquil escape from the rest of the world, this is the place to come.

Best for
Beach life and scuba diving

Home to
Mahatma Gandhi Marine National Park

Experience
Scuba diving off Cinque Island, perhaps the most beautiful part of the Andaman and Nicobar Islands archipelago

←

1 Delhi's grand Jama Masjid.

2 Chand Baori stepwell.

3 Birdlife at Keoladeo Ghana National Park.

4 Detail of fabulous crystal in Sheesh Mahal in Amber.

From the heights of the Himalayas to the sandy shores of the Keralan coast, a journey through India is as varied as the country itself. These itineraries will help you make the most of your trip, whether it involves racing around dusty cities by rickshaw or wandering through ancient temples at dawn.

14 DAYS
in the Golden Triangle

Day 1

Wake up with breakfast in Parathe Wali Gali, at the heart of Old Delhi's Chandni Chowk. Take a rickshaw ride to explore the bustling district, and stop at Chor Bizarre at Hotel Broadway (p103) for lunch; it serves the best Kashmiri food in town. Hop on another rickshaw to some of Delhi's big sights: the imposing Red Fort (p86) and Jama Masjid (p88). From here, it's a short taxi ride to Gurudwara Bangla Sahib; a sunset stroll around the Sikh temple is not to be missed. Tonight, have dinner at the award-winning Indian Accent (p98).

Day 2

Start your day in the National Gallery of Modern Art (p94). After a few hours, head to Connaught Place (p104) for a thali at Saravana Bhavan and a browse of the eco-wares at People Tree (p104). Mughal-era Humayun's Tomb (p92) is one of Delhi's major sites – catch a taxi there, and stay for sunset at the nearby Nizamuddin shrine (p98). Make sure you've booked for dinner at Olive Bar and Kitchen (6-8 Kalka Das Marg New Delhi), a taxi ride away.

Day 3

Grab breakfast on your way to Hazrat Nizamuddin in Delhi's south to jump on the Gatimaan Express. The train leaves Delhi at 8:10am and arrives in Agra (p162) two hours later. First stop is Agra Fort (p162), a fascinating complex that has views of the Taj Mahal (p166). That afternoon, take a tour with Agrawalks (p164); your guide will regale you with stories from the city's history. For dinner, Esphahan (Oberoi Amarvilas, Taj East Gate Rd) plates up Mughal delicacies accompanied by music.

Day 4

The Taj Mahal opens at sunrise – arrive then, as it's your best chance to see it without as many of the crowds. Spend a few magical hours here, then pick up a rental car and drive to Keoladeo Ghana National Park (p128), known for its birdlife. After lunch at Sunbird (p128), take a rickshaw around the park. The afternoon will fly by and, before you know it, it'll be time for dinner. Eat at your accommodation, the Bagh hotel (p128), on the outskirts of the park.

Day 5

It's a three-hour drive to Jaipur, so enjoy breakfast in the hotel gardens before hitting the road, and break your journey at the Chand Baori stepwell. In Jaipur, head to Peacock (p113) for a relaxed lunch before meeting your guide from Virasat Experiences (p112). On this walking tour, you'll snack on street food and feast on the sights of bazaars, havelis and temples. Tonight, dinner is in the gardens at the former royal abode of Diggi Palace (Shivaji Marg C-Scheme), now a hotel.

Day 6

The old capital of Amber (p124) is a short drive outside Jaipur; here, you'll find the decadent Sheesh Mahal, with an interior made of crystal. Head back to the city and visit the Anokhi flagship store (p120), where you can purchase locally made textiles to take home, before eating at the store's café. Spend an hour or two at Jaipur's City Palace (p114), now a museum. As the sun fades, make tracks to Tiger Fort, whose views over Jaipur are best enjoyed at sunset. Treat yourself to a nightcap at the ornate Palladio bar (p113). →

Day 7

Leave early for Bundi *(p152)*, an oasis around three hours' drive away. Take your time on the highway: you'll spot camels, decorated trucks and pretty villages. In Bundi, the main attraction is Raniji-ki-Baori, otherwise known as the queen's stepwell. The impressive Taragarh Fort overlooking Bundi is also worth a visit for its interior, beautifully decorated with murals. After a leisurely exploration of the fort, wander back into town for a delicious dinner at the family-run Bundi Vilas *(p152)* in a 300-year-old haveli, where you can also stay for the night.

Day 8

On your drive from Bundi to Udaipur *(p140)*, the romantic river city, detour to Chittorgarh *(p156)*, whose fort has been overtaken by jungle. In Udaipur, spend the day exploring the city, including its rooftops, many of which are home to restaurants: why not try one for lunch or another for an afternoon snack? Save room for dinner, as Ambrai has the best views of the City Palace and serves up delectable traditional Rajasthani dishes.

Day 9

Beat the crowds with an early morning exploration of the exceptional City Palace *(p142)*. Having worked up an appetite, make your way to Jagat Niwas *(23-25 Lalghat)* for lunch on the rooftop. That afternoon, take a boat trip to Jag Mandir island in the middle of Lake Pichola, but make sure you're back in time for an early evening dance and music performance at Bagore ki Haveli, where dancers balance fire on their heads. Dinner tonight is at Upre 1559 AD *(P P Singhal Marg)*, which serves local dishes at its lakeside villa.

Day 10

Hop in the car and head for Rajasthan's mystical blue city, Jodhpur *(p130)*, a four-hour direct drive away. On your trip there, stop off at Ranakpur *(p155)* to admire the soaring turrets of the Jain temple and have lunch at the heritage hotel of Rawla Narlai *(Narlai village)*. Once you arrive in Jodhpur, spend the afternoon strolling around the labyrinthine streets of the pretty blue houses of the old city, following your nose – and your camera – down the numerous alleyways. Treat yourself to

1 Chittorgarh Samadhisvara.

2 Traditional dancers at Bagore Ki Haveli.

3 Colourful murals at Taragrah Fort.

4 Intricate columns at Ranakpur.

5 Looming Mehrangarh Fort.

6 Sam Sand Dunes near Jaisalmer.

a saffron lassi from the stall near the clocktower before dinner at the Raas (p131) hotel in the shadow of the old fort.

Day 11

You can easily spend the whole day at the atmospheric Mehrangarh Fort (p132). As well as the ornate Phool Mahal and Moti Mahal, it has a well-curated museum. After a day of exploring, head to Indique, the rooftop restaurant at Pal Haveli (p131), for a dinner, plus music and dance performances, fit for a royal.

Day 12

The drive to Jaisalmer (p134) crosses the Thar Desert; watch out for loping camels on the side of the highway, and make a stop – or two – for chai. After arriving, get your bearings by exploring the narrow alleyways in the oldest part of this desert city, with its characteristic and ornate havelis. Head to the terrace at KB Café for lunch before a visit to the ornate Patwon ki Haveli (p134), a traditional merchant's house. Come evening, watch the sun go down and Jaisalmer Fort (p136) light up

from the rooftop restaurant of the lovingly restored Nachana Haveli hotel (p135), as musicians play Rajasthani folk music.

Day 13

Jaisalmer Fort crowns a hill overlooking the town. Get an early start and head up to the fort, stopping for coffee near the entrance at Jaisal Italy (Gopa Chowk, Jaisalmer), which serves the best brew in town. Spend the morning and early afternoon wandering the fort's streets. In the late afternoon, take a trip out to the Sam Sand Dunes for supper at Desert Springs Resort (www.desertsprings.in). Spend the night at the resort in one of their regal tents.

Day 14

Before you head back to Delhi, stop in the desert town of Nagaur (p153). The fort here belongs to the Maharaja of Jodhpur, and is being spectacularly restored after years of neglect. In the fort is the boutique Ranvas hotel (p153), one of the best hotels in Rajasthan. Take a dip in the pool and then have a leisurely dinner. You'll end up feeling like a maharaja.

←

1 Mumbai's iconic Gateway of India.

2 The remains of Shaniwar Wada palace in Pune's old town.

3 Enjoying the wines at Sula Vineyard near Nasik.

4 A Buddhist cave at Ajanta.

6 DAYS

in Mumbai and Maharashtra

Day 1

Start your day in Mumbai at the Gateway of India *(p406)* before taking a boat over to Elephanta Island *(p404)*, with its Shiva temple hewn out of the rock. Back in town, lunch on the berry pulao at Britannia & Company *(p408)*, then explore Chhatrapati Shivaji Maharaj Vastu Sangrahalaya *(p402)*, a museum with artifacts from around India. Head past the grand Chhatrapati Shivaji Terminus *(p400)* to Chowpatty Beach *(p413)* for a sunset stroll and a cone of local favourite bhelpuri. Treat yourself to dinner at seafood restaurant Trishna *(p408)*, before finishing the night with a Bollywood hit at one of the many Art Deco cinemas.

Day 2

Pick up a rental car and drive to Nasik *(p432)*, one of four hosts of the Kumbh Mela, the largest religious festival on earth. The city's two most significant Hindu sites are the Ramkund bathing tank and Kala Rama Temple – visit both before heading out into the surrounding countryside, the heart of India's wine industry. Indulge in a tasting session at the award-winning Sula Vineyards *(www.sulawines.com)* before dinner at its restaurant, Little Italy *(p433)*.

Day 3

It will take most of the morning to drive from Nasik to Aurangabad *(p434)*, particularly as there are two major stops along the way: the forbidding 14th-century Daulatabad Fort *(p434)* and the nearby walled village of Khuldabad *(p435)*, which was home to several Sufi saints. After arriving in town, grab a quick lunch and head out to explore the centre, starting off at the Bibi ka Maqbara, a mausoleum

from 1678 that was inspired by the Taj Mahal. Finish the day with a spot of shopping at the Himroo Factory *(www. himroofabrics.com)*, which sells textiles made using local fabric, before a hearty vegetarian thali at Naivedya *(Jalna Rd)*.

Day 4

A stunning complex of temples carved out of a rocky cliff-face, the Ellora caves *(p422)* really need to be seen to be believed – luckily, they are only a short drive from Aurangabad. Factor in a full day's exploration at the site, but head back to Aurangabad in time for dinner at Latitude in the Vivanta hotel *(www. tajhotels.com)*. If the weather is cool enough, take a seat on the dining terrace and order one of the local specialties.

Day 5

Get up early to drive to another of the state's UNESCO World Heritage sites, Ajanta *(p424)*, a series of precipitous rock-cut 3rd-century BC Buddhist caves. After a day exploring Ajanta, head to the city of Jalgaon, where you will leave the car and board an overnight train (book ahead) to Pune *(p430)*, an engaging city that has been dubbed the "Oxford of the East".

Day 6

Spend the morning exploring Pune's streets with their wooden *wadas* (mansions) and the looming Shaniwar Wada palace. Afterwards, cross the Mula river to the Aga Khan Palace, where Gandhi was imprisoned by the British. Sample Pune's foodie scene at Koregaon Park; don't miss dinner at Malaka Spice *(www.malakaspice. com)*, perfect for your last night in town.

7 DAYS
in Goa and Karnataka

▎ *Day 1*

There's no better place for sun, sand and surf than north Goa. Start your week in paradise with a surf lesson at Vaayu Waterman's Village in Ashwem *(p452)*, followed by a healthy lunch at Prana Café *(Ashwem-Mandrem Beach Road)*. Relax into the local pace by finding a hammock for the afternoon. Come early evening, take a long beach walk that finishes at the award-winning La Plage restaurant *(p455)* on the beach at Ashwem; grab a seat on the sand for a supper of French fare and seafood. This part of the state is known for its nightlife, so join the crowds at the beachside club Soma Life *(Gawde Wada Rd, Morjim)* and dance the night away.

▎ *Day 2*

Wake up your body with a hatha yoga session at Ashiyana Mandrem *(Junas Waddo, Mandrem)*, a yoga retreat on a quieter beach. After your class, pay a bit extra and enjoy the delicious buffet breakfast here. Tropical Goa is infused with Portuguese influences; catch a taxi to the inland village of Assagao *(p453)*, where many of

the beautiful Portuguese houses have been turned into restaurants and shops. One of these is Project Café Goa *(Mazzal Waddo)*, a design-led hotel which serves a delicious lunch. Have a relaxing afternoon on the beach before hitting Curlies *(curliesgoa.com/anjuna-beach-parties. html)*, an Anjuna beach club that plays Goa Trance, a local and extremely popular style of dance music.

▎ *Day 3*

Have an early breakfast at a beachfront café before heading into Old Goa *(p444)*, the state's former capital. This atmospheric town has crumbling Portuguese churches and the majestic Basilica de Bom Jesus *(p446)*. Light a candle here before travelling onto the state's new capital, Panaji, in time for lunch of local dishes at Viva Panjim *(p443)*. After a traditional siesta, start your exploration of the city in the cool of the later afternoon. Wander around the Latin Quarter, where colourful Portuguese villas line the streets, then head up the hill to pay homage at Maruti Temple, dedicated to

1 Popular Palolem Beach.

2 Beachside dining at La Plage in Goa.

3 Intricate stone work in Hampi.

4 The flashy gold altar at the Basilica
de Bom Jesus in Old Goa

5 A yoga session overlooking
beautiful Om Beach in Gokarna.

Hanuman. Finally, pop into Gitanjali Gallery *(31st January Road)* to see some modern art. It's been a big day; top it off with a drink of local craft gin at tiny speakeasy Joseph's Bar *(Gomes Pereira Rd)*.

Day 4

Jump on the slow train and sip chai as you cross into Karnataka on your way to historic Hampi *(p468)*, where temples are hidden in a famously rocky landscape. Head straight to the site and spend the rest of the day exploring. Don't miss the multitiered Virupaksha Temple and the spectacular view from Matanga Hill.

Day 5

Hampi has been attracting climbers for decades – rise early to try your hand on the walls here before it gets too hot. Most hotels have gear, or you can go on a guided tour. Afterwards, make sure you see the rest of Hampi's big hitters: the stepwell at Queen's Bath, the majestic elephant stables and the Vitthala Temple, perhaps the most famous site in Hampi.

Day 6

Say goodbye to Hampi and head back to the Arabian Sea, this time to beautiful Gokarna *(p483)*, more laid-back than the Goan beach hubs. The town itself is full of temples, the best example of which is the 4th-century Mahabaleshwar Temple, which allows non-Hindus to explore everything apart from the inner sanctum. Head to the beach for the rest of the day.

Day 7

Wake up early for a stroll along Om Beach before the heat descends, and drop in for a yoga class and breakfast at Namaste Yoga Farm *(Kudle Beach Rd)*. Continue along the coastline on the neighbouring Kudlee Beach, before settling into a hammock for an hour or two. Have lunch with a sea view at the popular White Elephant *(www.whiteelephanthampi.com/gokarna)*. Soothe weary muscles with an Ayurvedic massage at the Swaswara Wellness Resort *(Om Beach)* before an indulgent final dinner at beachside Chez Christophe *(Main Beach)*, which serves some of the best French food in India.

7 DAYS
in Kerala

Day 1

Fly into Thiruvananthapuram *(p546)* and pick up a hire car. From here, head to Ariya Niwas *(Aristo Junction, Manorama Rd)* where the hearty vegetarian breakfast is a great welcome to Kerala. Afterwards, drive inland to the Padmanabhapuram Palace *(p548)*; the distinctive wooden architecture here is unique to Kerala. Explore the secrets of the palace before heading to the beach resort of Kovalam *(p554)*, where the headland is watched over by a red-and-white lighthouse. Eat dinner at Fusion Café *(Light House Beach)*, which offers fantastic seafood and lovely views.

Day 2

Get up early for a wander along the waterfront towards the lighthouse; if you are lucky, you might spot a few dolphins frolicking in the bay. For a fresh local breakfast try the German Bakery *(Light House Beach)*. Spend a happy hour or two here before heading to the beach and renting a hammock. There is nothing else on this morning's agenda apart from lolling about, so bring a book and a towel with you. Kerala has its own style of Ayurvedic medicine; in the afternoon, try a few treatments at Somatheeram Ayurveda Village *(www.somatheeram.in)*. For dinner, meander up to the hilltop Leela Palace hotel *(p465)* and nab a seat on the terrace for an al fresco meal.

Day 3

Drive up the coast to Alappuzha *(p557)*, the gateway to Kerala's famous back-waters. Over a thousand houseboats ply the waterways here and, this afternoon, your own boat will be among them. Before boarding, tuck in to a fish curry lunch at Chakara at the Raheem Residency *(Beach Rd)*, in a converted heritage house. Hop on your boat – you've booked an overnight tour, and the package includes a chef. So there's nothing for you to do but relax on a recliner and enjoy the serenity as the villages and jungles float past. For dinner, your chef will whip up Keralan dishes. At night, moor away from other houseboats for a tranquil night.

1 The Padmanabhapuram Palace.
2 The striking Kovalam Lighthouse.
3 Traditional Keralan food served in an Alappuzha houseboat.
4 A mural in Mattancherry Palace.
5 Fishing nets at Fort Kochi.
6 Tea plantations at Munnar.

Day 4

After you're dropped back in Alappuzha, drive to the port city of Kochi (p542), around an hour away. Pop into Caza Maria (p543) in Mattancherry for a Keralan lunch of curries and chutneys. This city is ripe for exploration, from the Jewish quarter with its synagogue and old antique shops – don't miss Ethnic Passage (p543) – to the Mattancherry (Dutch) Palace with its stunning murals. Head to Fort House (No 2/6A, Calvathy Rd) for dinner with a water view – what could be better?

Day 5

Jump on a commuter ferry from Fort Kochi (p544) to Vypeen Island and back. You can hop off at any stop to explore the town's waterways. After your return to dry land with your stomach rumbling, park yourself in the Kashi Arts Café (Burgher Street) in the fort area for lunch and to check out their current art exhibit. Stroll along the water's edge to see the Chinese fishing nets and head into the fort's back streets, where the heady aroma of spices fills the air. For dinner, the Malabar Junction hotel (p543) in an old Keralan house is a special experience.

Day 6

From Kochi, a winding road takes you up into the hills past rolling plantations to the cool hill station of Munnar (p558). Spend the the day walking through the peaceful tea estates and visiting the lively market in the small town. Check into the Windermere Estate (p556), which has stunning views of the undulating landscape.

Day 7

On your final day take a trip to Top Station, the highest point in Munnar, for vistas of hills and plunging valleys spanning the border of Kerala and Tamil Nadu. Travel back down to Munnar and try the delicious parathas at Rapsy restaurant (Main Bazaar, Mosque Road) in the market – it's a popular lunchtime haunt. From here, you could head home. Or it's only a hop over the border into Tamil Nadu (p42).

←

1 Shimla's alpine scenery.

2 A crowd of worshippers in Haridwar.

3 The elusive Indian tiger.

4 A vibrant Beatles mural at Rishikesh.

14 DAYS

in the Himalayas

Day 1

Get an early start in Delhi and hop on the long bus to the town of Ramnagar, the gateway to Corbett National Park (p174), India's oldest nature reserve. Once you've arrived at your resort, take a stroll in the forest, before the main event starts. It's an evening safari, where, if you're lucky, you'll spot the king of the jungle – a tiger.

Day 2

Take an early morning safari back into the park, once more on the trail of the big cat. Return to your resort for breakfast, before heading to the watchtower of Dhikala for stunning forest views. The Jim Corbett Museum at Kaladhungi, in the conservationist's former home, offers an insight into the park and the effort to save the tiger. Relax back at the resort with dinner.

Day 3

If you still haven't seen a tiger, try your luck at another morning safari. After breakfast, check out of your resort and take the bus from Ramnagar to the city of Haridwar (p189), where the Ganges enters the plains. Soak up the atmosphere watching worshippers performing rituals at the Ganges river. Catch the sunset from the hilltop Manasa Devi Temple – you can hike up or catch the cable car – before heading to your overnight stop of Rishikesh (p188) Dinner is a vegetarian feast at Atali (Badrinath Road).

Day 4

Engage in some yoga and have an ayurvedic breakfast at Sanskriti Vedic Retreat next to the river (Ram Jhula). Rishikesh is where the Beatles came seeking enlightenment, so visit the ashram where they spent time with Maharishi Mahesh Yogi. For a more adventurous afternoon, try whitewater rafting with Camp Silver Sands (Devprayag Rd). Afterwards, check out one of the evening ceremonies at the neon-lit ashrams, then eat naans and curried veg at Chotiwala (Swarg Ashram; (0135) 243 4070).

Day 5

Buy snacks for the long bus ride from here to the hill station of Shimla (p222), a heritage town that was once the summer capital of the British Raj. Take a sunset stroll along The Ridge and admire the buildings – Christ Church is probably the most famous – before checking out the Mall and dining at the Café Sol (Combemere Hotel; (0177) 252 2242).

Day 6

Start your day with a hike up Jakhoo to pay homage to the statue of the monkey god of war, Hanuman. Head back to town and pick up your 4WD – you'll need your own set of wheels to explore the more spectacular Himalayan regions. Drive east towards Sarahan, stopping for lunch at the New Himalayan Dhaba (0178) 224 2426) in Narkanda before weaving above the River Sutlej. Spend the night in Sarahan, home to the Bhimakali temple-cum-palace (p228).

Day 7

Drive to Sangla (p240) in the Baspa Valley, a small town backed by the snowy peaks of Kinner-Kailash near the border with Tibet. After lunch, carry on to the village of Chitkul and explore the meadows behind the village. Return to Sangla for an evening meal of Tibetan dumpling at the Tibetan Café on the main street bazaar. →

Day 8

Double back via the heritage town of Reckong Peo *(p241)*, stopping to look at the busy bazaar, before visiting picturesque Kalpa on the mountainside above. Amble around the sprawling village and apple orchards, admiring the sweeping vistas of Kinner-Kailash and visiting the small temple. Eat at the convivial restaurant of the Blue Lotus Guest House *(0178) 622 6001)* – and why not stay for the night as well?

Day 9

It's a long drive from here to Kaza via Nako, in the remote Spiti Valley *(p218)*, so get an early start. The road takes you across precipitous mountain passes and past stunning Tibetan monasteries that sit like mini kingdoms on top of hills. There are no more apple orchards here – the terrain becomes increasingly rugged and barren the further you go into the valley, and is often compared to a moonscape. Be sure to visit the exquisite monastery at Tabo *(p220)*, with its spectacular thangkas – intricate Buddhist religious art painted on fabric.

Day 10

Visit one or two of Kaza's brightly painted monasteries before getting back on the road to complete the dramatic circuit of the Spiti Valley. Don't miss the Buddhist gompa at Kibber; the monastery is one of the highest settlements of the planet at 4,200 m (13,780 ft). The road to Manali *(p234)* in the Kullu Valley takes you via the infamous Rohtang Pass – stop for a chai and take a few deep breaths before tackling this precipitous road with its majestic views. Soak up the laid-back vibe of Old Manali village and eat at one of the travellers' hangouts, some of which stock beer.

Day 11

Spend today exploring the Kullu *(p239)* and Parvati valleys, starting by visiting the riverside town of Manikaran *(p238)*, a site of pilgrimage for its Sikh gurdwara and hot springs. Take a quick dip in the allegedly curative waters here before heading to the nearby outpost of Kasol. Stop for lunch of grilled trout at Ragini Hotel Rooftop *(p234)* in Naggar and visit the excellent Nicholas Roerich Gallery, which showcases the art of the Russian

1 The cliffside village of Kalpa.

2 Monks at the Tabo Monastery.

3 A Buddha statue in one of Kaza's monasteries.

4 Tibetan Institute of Performing Arts.

5 The small Baijnath Temple.

6 Painting at Norbulingka Tibetan Crafts and Education.

painter. Take a dip in the natural hot baths in Vashisht as darkness descends, then return to Old Manali for Italian or Mexican food at Moon Dance garden café.

Day 12

It's the final leg of your week-long 4WD trip – and today you're heading into lush Kangra Valley, home to numerous Buddhist and Hindu temples, and the tea-growing region around the pretty hill station of Palampur (p235), on your way to Dharamsala (p224). Stop to pay your respects at the stone complex of Baijnath Temple, dedicated to Lord Shiva. The drive takes around seven hours – without stops – so hit the road early to arrive in the famous hill station by early evening. In Dharamsala, most people stay in the Tibetan enclave of McLeod Ganj.

Day 13

You might forget you're in India here – Dharamsala is where many Tibetans fled after the Chinese occupation of Tibet, and the McLeod Ganj district is rich with Tibetan culture. The most famous resident is, of course, the Dalai Lama, who lives at the Tsuglagkhang Complex. Complete the *kora*, a ritual circuit around the complex, along with Buddhist pilgrims, before heading the Namling Monastery, which has a fascinating museum. For a different sort of pilgrimage, head to St John in the Wilderness, a 19th-century church dedicated to St John the Baptist. After a dinner of *momos* (dumplings), catch a Tibetan dance and music programme at the Tibetan Institute of Performing Arts (*www.tipa.asia*).

Day 14

You've traversed the most spectacular regions of the Tibetan Himalayas – so spend your final day in the region relaxing. Stroll through the slopes to Dharamkot and back via hillside village of Bhagsu, which has a bathing tank in the village and waterfall beyond it. Take an afternoon trip out to the Norbulingka Tibetan Crafts and Education (*www.norbulingka.org*), where you can try your hand at traditional Tibetan arts. Enjoy a splendid last meal of cuisine from Tibet or Bhutan at the wonderful Tibet Kitchen (*p225*).

7 DAYS
in Tamil Nadu

Day 1

A fascinating jumble of labyrinthine streets, Madurai *(p518)* is a city worth getting lost in. Wander around the old town on your way to riotous, colourful Meenakshi Temple, which is often crowded with devotees. After paying homage here, pick up some street food for lunch on your way to the Thirumalai Nayakkar Palace, southeast of the temple. It has a wonderful museum with Pandyan, Jain and Buddhist sculptures where you can easily spend an hour or two. End the day with a thali dinner at Sree Sarabees *(56A West Perumal Maistry St; (0452) 437 9037)*, where you can enjoy endless refills of items served on a section of banana leaf.

Day 2

Wake up and smell the roses at Madurai's flower market before heading to the Gandhi Museum *(Tamukkam Palace)*, dedicated to the icon. Afterwards, ask your hotel to call you a taxi for a trip to the Chettinad region *(p522)*, known for its towns full of idiosyncratic mansions, as well as for its cuisine. Stop for lunch and a

demonstration of tamarind-flavoured Chettinad cooking at the Bangala in Karaikudi *(p523)*. Spend the afternoon exploring the streets of Kanadukatham, home to the Chettinadu Mansion. Return to Karaikudi for an evening browse of the antique shops lining Koil Street and dinner at a local café.

Day 3

After a morning stroll around Karaikudi admiring the mansion houses, get a taxi to Thanjavur *(p514)*, a two-hour drive away. Here, follow the example of the locals and make a picnic with a few local delicacies to enjoy in the grounds of the Brihadishvara Temple *(p516)*, where you can spend the afternoon relaxing. After watching the atmospheric early evening puja (prayer ritual) at the temple, listen to some live Carnatic music over dinner at Thillana restaurant *(Trichy Rd)*.

Day 4

Following a south Indian breakfast of crispy masala dosa at Sri Krishna Bhavan

1 Madurai's Meenakshi Temple.

2 A French-style church in Puducherry.

3 A distinctive Chettiar mansion.

4 A riotous puja at Nataraja Temple.

5 Mamallapuram's annual dance festival.

6 Sunset at the Marina in Chennai.

(68A VAC Nagar), take a look around the impressive Royal Palace compound (p514), which houses the Rajaraja Museum and Art Gallery – don't miss the exquisite Chola bronzes on display. Hop on a local train to Chidambaram (p526), towards the coast in the north-east of the state. Arrive in time to witness the incredible evening puja ceremony at the colourfully cacophonous Nataraja Temple (p526).

Day 5

Catch the bus to the former French colony of Puducherry (p510). Stop at Auroville Bakery (Kuilapalayam Main Rd) to pick up croissants before heading into the Botanical Gardens to admire its array of flora. Afterwards, visit the Aurobindo Ashram, one of India's most famous yoga centres, and then weave your way south through the streets of the old French Quarter. Take advantage of Puducherry's low alcohol tax with a few drinks over dinner at La Terrasse (p510), then check out a performance of traditional dance at Aurodhan, a guesthouse which puts on some of the best cultural events in town.

Day 6

Take an early bus to Mamallapuram (p506), where your first stop is the huge rock-cut shrines of the Pancha Rathas (p508) and the nearby artisan stalls. Mainly known for its heritage, the town is also a growing surfing centre; after lunch in one of the many cafés, book in for a surfing lesson. Dry off and watch the sunset behind the famous Shore Temple, before feasting on fresh fish at Seashore Garden Beach Restaurant (on the beach; 99403 19642) for a memorable dinner.

Day 7

On your final day in Tamil Nadu, head to the underrated capital, Chennai (p486). Take a taxi into town, and ask them to drop you at the Government Museum (p496), with its vast collection of artifacts. After an hour or two here, stroll around Fort St George (p492), the first British foothold in India, before heading to the popular Marina (p490) for the best people watching in Chennai. After the sun sets, head to Annalakshmi (p494) for a vegetarian feast – a fitting end to your trip.

Spot a Rare One-Horned Rhino

At the end of the twentieth century, the one-horned rhino was on the brink of extinction, with fewer than 200 left in the wild. But thanks to conservation efforts, the species has staged an incredible comeback and there are now 3,500 of these rhinos in the world, with roughly a third at Kaziranga National Park *(p362)*, a UNESCO World Heritage Site and the best place to spot the animal.

A pair of one-horned rhinos in Kaziranga ↑

INDIA FOR
WILDLIFE ENCOUNTERS

India packs a continent's worth of wildlife into a single country: this is a place where rhinos, elephants, deer, colourful birds and tigers still gather around the waterhole. Whether you want to track down a tiger or spot an elephant, India offers plenty of opportunities for up-close encounters.

Earn Your Tiger-Spotting Stripes

Seeing a tiger in the wild is a once-in-a-lifetime experience – and, with 70 per cent of the 3,900 big cats that survive outside captivity, India is the place to do it. You're most likely to catch a big cat in the wild at Bandhavgarh *(p198)* and Kanha *(p286)*, a pair of national parks that look like they've emerged from the pages of *The Jungle Book*. The guides at Shergarh, a camp near Kanha, offer safaris.

Did You Know?

The Asiastic lion is endangered – and now can only be spotted in the wild at Gir National Park *(p391)*.

A tiger prowling in Bandhavgarh National Park ↑

High-Altitude Wildlife Encounters

In the southeast corner of Ladakh, close to the Tibetan border, are a pair of glistening, green-blue lakes which act as a mirror for the surrounding Himalayan peaks and glaciers: Panggong Tso (p250) and Tso Moriri (p250). It feels like you're on the roof of the world, yet remarkably a diverse range of creatures thrive in this high-altitude environment, from the Instagram-level-adorable Himalayan marmot, the black-necked crane, and herds of yak.

→

Yaks near the high-altitude Pangong Lake

Terrific Twitching

From king vultures to kingfishers, hoopoes to hornbills, there are around 1,200 species of birds in India and almost a third of them can be spotted in a single place: Keoladeo Ghana National Park (p128). Located in Rajasthan, this is one of the best places to go twitching in Asia. Visit at the end of monsoon season to see the park at its best, when it is home to hundreds of year-round residents, as well as migratory birds.

←

A chattering band of painted storks in Keoladeo Ghana National Park

Animal-Spotting in the Mangroves

The Sundarbans (p328) is the world's biggest mangrove forest, a place where tigers swim between islands, fierce saltwater crocodiles grow up to 8 metres (26 ft) in length and graceful, Gangetic dolphins navigate despite being virtually blind. Take a trip to explore the wildlife here with ethically run tour operator Help Tourism (www.helptourism.com).

→

A crocodile lurking in the waters at the Sundarbans

Conscious Communities

For those seeking utopia, Auroville outside of Puducherry *(p511)* is a planned community with the lofty goal of creating a more harmonious and eco-friendly future. Here, there are organic farms, forested areas, creative hubs and sustainable business like the Auroville Bakery. But the most striking feature is the Matrimandir temple, a golden orb in the middle of the city where you can book time in for meditation.

←
Dawn meditation in front of Auroville's Matrimandir

INDIA FOR
CONSCIOUS LIVING

Home to some of the world's oldest wellbeing practices, India is where everyone from the Beatles to Elizabeth Gilbert have come to seek enlightenment. Perfect your vinyasa flow at a beachside yoga school or detox at an ayurvedic centre – it's all part of the journey.

Breathe Deep

Take a deep breath – India offers an almost overwhelming array of yoga schools and retreats where you can meditate and stretch your way to a more harmonious self. There are many different schools of yoga; seek and you will find one that appeals to you, whether that's Iyengar yoga at the Osho International Meditation Resort in Pune *(p430)* or Goa's relaxing Purple Valley Yoga Retreat *(www.yogagoa.com)*.

→
Yoga by the waves in Goa

Holistic Heritage

Founded thousands of years before holistic was a buzzword, ayurveda is a system that uses diet, yoga, astrology and herbal medicine to encourage wellbeing. Take a two-week *pancha-karma* (detox programme) at the award-winning Ananda *(www.anandaspa.com)*, an old palace turned health retreat nestled above quirky Rishikesh *(p188)*, or relax under Kerala's palms at the Somatheeram Ayurveda Village *(www.somatheeram.in)*.

↑ Relaxing massage at Ananda and (inset) one of the private pools

EAT

Birdsong Organic Café

This popular café serves Middle Eastern flavours, burgers and family favourites in a trendy space with brick walls.

⌂ Hill Road, Bandra West, Mumbai
☎ (022) 26422323

₹₹₹

Zest

Wholesome yet still delicious, Zest serves raw, vegan and vegetarian dishes at the beach.

⌂ Main Road, Palolem, Goa ☎ (0) 8806607919
🕒 Late Apr-Sep/Oct

₹₹₹

Kolkata's Victoria Memorial at sunset ↑

British Imperial Pomp

Delhi's Presidential Palace (p94) was built as a monument to the pomp and power of the British Raj – but now forms the heart of India's democracy. Book ahead to go on a tour (rashtrapatisachivalaya.gov.in/rbtour). Many other towns across India are marked by buildings from this imperial interlude, from Mumbai, with its grand railway terminus (p400), to Kolkata, with its Victoria Memorial (p310).

INDIA FOR
ARCHITECTURE

Look around you: India's history is written on its streets. Here, you'll find a riot of garish gopurams, fairy-tale forts, colonial churches and multitiered monasteries, which all tell the story of India as a place where some of the world's oldest religions were founded, and mighty kingdoms rose and fell.

Maharajas' Palaces

Be amazed by the opulent lifestyle of India's maharajas on a tour of one of their lavish forts, which loom over most towns in Rajasthan. Here you'll see bedrooms gilded in gold, elephant stables and courtyards adorned with priceless mosaics. Want to feel like a maharaja yourself? Spend the night in a lake-view suite at the magical Lake Palace in Udaipur.

↑ An exquisite room in the City Palace, Jaipur

Erotic Architecture

Look closer at Shekhawati's colourful *havelis* and you might be surprised: along with everyday activities, they also depict erotic acts – see the Podar Haveli Museum in Nawalgarh (p148) for excellent examples. Similarly, many Hindu temples have carved friezes that illustrate an array of sexual positions – most famous are those on Khajuraho's temples (p288).

← Colourful mural at the Podar Haveli Museum

One of the country's exuberantly decorated Hindu temples ↑

Godly Gopurams

Wander through the streets of most major towns in south India, with their riotously multicoloured gopurams, and you might think you've stumbled into a fever dream. These traditional towering entrances to the region's Hindu temples are unrestrained and joyous architectural acts of devotion, decorated with an array of finely carved and painted gods, goddess and mythological scenes. Among the oldest and most beautiful are those on the temple at Chidambaram *(p526)*, but the temples at Madurai *(p520)* and Srirangam *(p534)* also have outstanding examples.

STAY

Lake Palace
Spectacularly situated on a lake in Udaipur, this might be India's best heritage hotel.

🏠 Udaipur, Rajasthan
🌐 tajhotels.com

₹₹₹

Palace Belvedere
Lovely lake views from the beautiful summer palace of the Rajas of Awagarh.

🏠 Nainital, Uttarakhand
🌐 thepalace belvedere.com

₹₹₹

Neemrana Fort Palace
Carved into a hillside, this hotel's elegant rooms offer amazing countryside views.

🏠 Neemrana, Alwar, Rajasthan
🌐 neemranahotels.com

₹₹₹

↑ A woman admiring the elegant exterior of the iconic Taj Mahal

Marvellous Mausoleums

No trip to India would be complete without a visit to the Taj Mahal *(p166)*, the most famous - and most romantic - building in the world. But its builder, Shah Jahan, wasn't the only Mughal ruler who built epic tombs: this architectural tradition extended across the hundreds of years of Mughal reign in northern India. From Aurangabad's Bibi Ka Maqbara *(p434)* to Humayun's Tomb in Delhi *(p92)*, the palatial architecture of these tombs is life affirming.

Evening Eats for Ramzan

During the holy month of Ramzan (Ramadan), Muslims fast till nightfall, when the feasting starts. Head for any Muslim part of town to join the festivities, like in Old Delhi (p82), Ajmer (p152), Lucknow (p184) and Hyderabad (p568). Kebabs and kurmas are followed by sweets and cakes, and the dining continues until just before dawn. In Mumbai (p396), head to Mohammed Ali Road. Popular foods here include *malpua* (a kind of fried pancake), *firni* (an aromatic rice pudding) and *mawa jalebi* (swirls of deep-fried batter soaked in syrup).

→

A group at the Jama Masjid in Delhi, praying before the evening meal during Ramadan

INDIA FOR
RELIGION

The birthplace of Hinduism, Buddhism, Sikhism and Jainism, religion is woven into the fabric of everyday life in India. Whatever your creed, don't miss the chance to visit some of the country's holy sites or take part in its sacred festivals.

Dal with the Devout

Every Sikh gurudwara gives out free food: called *langar*, this is not just an act of charity, but promotes equality for all, regardless of religion, caste or social class. Everyone – rich and poor, Sikh and non-Sikh, Brahmin and Dalit – sits on the floor together to eat the same simple meal (usually rice and dal). Join the crowds of devout at the most famous Sikh temple of all, the Golden Temple in Amritsar (p204).

→

Communal meals at the Golden Temple

SACRED LIFE

Espousing non-violence and holding all life sacred, Jains go well beyond normal vegetarianism. Strict Jains will not even eat root vegetables such as onions or potatoes, as uprooting them kills the plant and may hurt tiny insects living in the soil.

Kaleidoscopic Celebrations

India is awash with countless colourful religious festivals. The biggest in the calendar and celebrated across the country in October or November, Diwali marks the triumph of good over evil with the lighting of oil lamps and huge fireworks displays. Heralding the start of spring, Holi is a major event where revellers throw handfuls of coloured powder at each other on the streets. One of the best celebrations is in Vrindavan *(p188),* where the festivities, and throwing of powder, starts forty days early.

← Lighting lamps during Diwali

Pilgrim's Path

Pilgrimage is big in India, and a whole pantheon of religious sites attracts the devoted year round. The most famous is, without a doubt, the holy city of Varanasi, perched on the Ganges *(p176),* where millions of pilgrims travel to bathe in the river's sacred waters and wash away their sins. Another big-hitter is Krishna's birthplace in the temple-filled town of Mathura *(p169),* its riverbank lined with an abundance of colourful ghats. It was in India, as well, that Buddha found enlightenment – the spot is marked by the carved temple at Mahabodhi *(p264).*

→

A pilgrim bathing in the holy waters of the Ganges at Varanasi

Did You Know?

Addas are Bengali literary salons where people gather to discuss books over endless cups of chai.

Lost in a Good Book Market

Book lovers unite every Sunday at the Daryaganj book market in Old Delhi *(p80)*, a haven for secondhand books and even the odd first edition. In Hyderabad *(p568)*, visit the city's popular Sunday Book Bazaar, then lift the cover on its streets in Koti, home to an underground book market that specializes in educational tomes. Kolkata *(p306)* is a city imbued with literary tradition, and the makeshift stalls on College Street *(p316)* have some of the best book bargains in the country.

→

Piles of books lining Kolkata's College Street

INDIA FOR
LITERATURE

Follow the footsteps of Rama in his mythological wanderings; immerse yourself in William Dalrymple's City of Djinns in Delhi; visit the house of Nobel Prize-winning authors. Stories are inscribed across the land of India, and here are some of the best ways to discover them.

Scribble Sessions

The most famous literary festival in India is undoubtedly in Jaipur, where local and international writers descend upon beautiful Diggi Palace every January *(www.jaipur literaturefestival.org)*. But there are a number of other book-focused festivals across India, from Mumbai to Kerala. One of the best is the soulful and uplifting Jashn-e-Rekhta in Delhi *(www.jashnerekhta.org)*, a festival of Urdu literature complete with Sufi poetry, ghazals and qawwali singing.

←

Visitors arriving at Diggi Palace to take part in Jaipur's famous literary festival

Fictional Footsteps

Dive into the bustle of Bombay as described in Gregory David Roberts' *Shantaram* on the Shantaram Tour *((0) 9869682817)*. Meet your guide, Kishore Khare – the brother of one of the protagonists – before strolling past Leopold Café and Bar *(p411)* on your way to Sassoon Docks. Or jump in a canoe and take a self-guided tour into the multigenerational saga of Arundhati Roy's *The God of Small Things*, set in Aymanam village in the backwaters of Kerala *(p540)*.

← The iconic Leopold Café and Bar in Mumbai, featured in Shantaram

The Poetic Heart

The streets of Kolkata, capital of West Bengal, are rich with poetry, which is at the heart of Bengali culture. Visit the house of one of the region's most lauded poets, Nobel Prize-winning Rabindranath Tagore *(p320)*, to discover more about this literary culture or head north to hear the popular poetic form of *ghazals* being sung at the World Sufi Spirit Festival in Jodhpur *(www.worldsacred-spiritfestival.org)*.

→ Rabindranath Tagore's home, Jorasanko

TOP 3 CRAFT MUSEUMS

Calico Museum, Ahmedabad
This unique museum (p378) showcases India's rich array of traditional textiles.

Anokhi Museum of Handprinting, Amber
The art of Rajasthani block-printing fabric is celebrated here (p124).

Crafts Museum, Delhi
A charming museum focusing on India's indigenous crafts (p94).

INDIA FOR
ARTISTS AND ARTISANS

With a rich history of miniature paintings and ornately sculpted temples, intricate brocade saris and embossed silverware, India comes alive through the vision of its artists and artisans. Every corner of the country offers different styles of textiles, jewellery, sculpture and handicrafts to discover.

Tamil Nadu's Stone Sculptors

Wander down a street in Mamallapuram in Tamil Nadu (p502) and you'll see exquisite sculptures of all shapes and sizes being crafted by expert artisans, who draw inspiration from as far back as the 7th century. While you might not fit the larger sculptures in your carry-on, feel tempted to take home a handcrafted goddess or the elephant-headed god Ganesha. You can also see sculptors in Kumartali in Kolkata (p306); here, the streets are lined with godly pantheons made of clay.

↑ Expert stone carvers at work in Mamallapuram in Tamil Nadu

Here Comes The Street Art

From the roads of Delhi to the walls of the Beatles Ashram near Rishikesh *(p188)*, street art is being used to transform public spaces across India. The Beatles Ashram, which the Fab Four visited in 1969 for peace, quiet and transcendental meditation, was abandoned in the 1990s, but has now become a site of pilgrimage for artists (and fans). The ashram reopened to the public in 2015: visit to see walls adorned with murals of the band, and abstract meditative art by both local artists and global street artists like Miles Toland. In Delhi *(p80)*, St+art India *(st-artindia.org)* is a not-for-profit arts foundation that runs an annual street art festival in Lodi Colony – watch international and local artists transforming the streets, all with the aim of making Delhi more walkable.

←

One of the colourful wall murals found at the Beatles Ashram near Rishikesh

Paint the Streets

Every December, the streets of Panaji *(p442)* in Goa come alive with the pop-up Serendipity Arts Festival *(www.serendipityartsfestival. com)* that gets art out of the galleries and into public spaces across the city. Heritage buildings, plazas, city bus stations and more are used to showcase works from a rich mix of both local and international artists. Similar festivals liven up the streets in Mumbai and Delhi.

→

An outdoor art installation at the pop-up Serendipity Arts Festival

Tribal Handicrafts

From a bedspread showing local flowers to printing using natural dyes, tribal handicrafts across India tell the story of those who made them. Go on a craft expedition into the Kutch in Gujarat *(p374)*, where the over 900 villages each has its own unique craft culture. Or in Rajasthan try your hand at traditional block printing at the Anokhi Museum of Hand Printing *(p124)*.

←

Embroidery at Dhrang village in the Kutch

Scour the Salt Pans of the Rann of Kutch

The starkly beautiful Kutch, reaching out into the Arabian Sea in the far west of India, is about as far as you can get from the Golden Triangle. Base yourself at Bhuj House (*www.thebhujhouse.com*), a heritage homestay in the Kutchi capital, and explore the region's villages producing traditional crafts, as well as the Little Rann of Kutch (*p384*), one of the world's largest salt flats – a strange and appealing place.

↑ Footsteps marking the incredibly isolated salt flats of Kutch

INDIA FOR
OFF THE BEATEN TRACK

The second most populous nation on earth, India is renowned for being vibrant, chaotic – and extremely crowded. But step away from the major sites and you'll find it's easier to escape from the crowds than you'd expect, as well as uncover some little-known, rarely visited and truly tranquil spots.

Hike Through Sikkim

A tiny state bordering Nepal, Tibet and Bhutan, Sikkim (*p324*) encompasses a remarkable array of landscapes, from deep valleys to Kanchenjunga, the third highest mountain on earth. Here, you can explore the state via scores of little-trod routes that take you past Buddhist monasteries, remote villages, river valleys and spectacular rhododendron forests. If you're lucky, you may even spot an endangered red panda. Yangsum Heritage Farm (*www.yangsumheritagefarm. com*) offers guided hikes in West Sikkim.

> 💬 INSIDER TIP
> ### Ascent Acclimitization
>
> Altitude sickness can be an issue in parts of Arunachal Pradesh and Sikkim: ascend slowly and in stages, and avoid strenuous activity until you've acclimatized.

Celebrate the Tibetan New Year at Tawang

Tucked away amid the peaks of remote Arunachal Pradesh, the Buddhist monastery at Tawang *(p367)* is the largest of its kind in India. Home to over 500 monks, the fortress-like building can only be accessed by the spectacular 4,300 m (14,000 ft) Sela Pass. Take a tour to this and other remote monasteries with local specialists Himalayan Holidays *(www.himalayan-holidays.net)*; plan your visit to coincide with the incredible Tibetan new year celebrations.

→

The remote Tawang Monastery, home to over 500 monks

Swap Goa for Gokarna

If you're looking for a pristine beach but without the crowds of ever-popular Goa, head to Gokarna *(p483)* in the neighbouring state of Karnataka. A centre for Hindu pilgrims for more than 2,000 years, the town has a string of gorgeous sandy beaches sprinkled with palm trees and framed by the lush green hills of the Western Ghats. Two of the most peaceful stretches of sand are Half Moon and Paradise, around 4 km (2 miles) south of town.

←

The enticing sandy expanses of the coastline in Gokarna, Karnataka

Lose Yourself in the "Hidden Place"

Close to Khajuraho *(p288)* but attracting only a fraction of the visitors, Orchha *(p294)* means the Hidden Place – and it more than lives up to its name. The palaces, shrines, temples, tombs and gardens here date back to the 1500s and are ripe for exploration. Stay at the atmospheric Sheesh Mahal hotel *(www.mptourism.com)*, and spend a day or two in the ruins.

→

The spires of Orchha on the banks of the Betwa river

↑ Spotting peaks on a hike through Yumthang Valley, North Sikkim

Spice Up Your Life

For most people, the smell and taste of chilli and spices are synonymous with Indian food. In fact, chilli only arrived in the Indian subcontinent from South America in the 1500s. Dive into the country's spicy history on a guided walk at Tropical Spice Plantation in Goa (*p459*). Alternatively, explore Delhi's markets with Saffron Palate *(www.saffronpalate.com)*, then learn how to add spices to your cooking and create delicious vegetarian dishes.

→

A zesty display at Goa's spice market

INDIA FOR
FLAVOUR

Infused with the tang of citrus and vinegar, pungent with the scent of gently toasted spices, seering with eye-watering chillis – every mouthful of India's amazing food bursts with a different flavour. Let your tastebuds be tempted all across the country.

Hit the Streets

Convenient, delicious and cheap to boot, India's legendary street food can't be beat. Join Delhi Food Walks *(www. delhifoodwalks.com)* to seek out golden spiral *jalebi* sweets and *aloo paratha* in Old Delhi. In Hyderabad, get up early for yummy dosas in Pragati Gully, renowned for its breakfasts, and chai served with buttery *nankahtai* biscuits from a handcart in Pather Ghatti Street. Later, hit up the Sindhi Colony area for a taste of the city's famous biryani.

←

Sampling freshly fried fare at Chandni Chowk, Delhi

Tradition With a Twist

From reinventing street food to pulling from India's rich food history, the country's top chefs are dedicated to cooking up new variations on traditional favourites. Sample some of the best at Indian Accent in the heart of New Delhi *(p99)*, where chef Manish Mehrotra's tasting menu mixes flavours such as Kashmiri morel mushrooms with chilli lotus root or pork belly tikka. Then follow your tastebuds south to Assago, Goa, home to celebrity chef Christopher Saleem Agha Bee's Sublime *(House No 481, Bouta Waddo)* restaurant. Our favourite is the chef's signature dish of Goan chorizo-encrusted sea bass.

←

Chef Manish Mehrotra's perfectly prepared *phulka* lamb curry

DRINK

Here are two of the best places to drink chai.

Amritsar

Pick up cups of piping hot fennel-infused chai outside the gates of the Golden Temple *(p204)* every morning at 6am. It's a warming – and free – way to greet the day.

⌂ **Golden Temple**

₹₹₹

Pushkar

Street vendors serve cups of chai in delicate clay vessels. Sip to the sound of drummers honouring the sun setting on another day.

⌂ **Sunset Point, Choti Basti**

₹₹₹

International Influencers

In Goa, Portuguese colonizers left behind more than just ornate churches. Here, many popular dishes mix the flavours of Europe and India – like spicy vindaloo, which uses vinegar. The British, meanwhile, hit the sweet spot in West Bengal with their desserts, where caramel custards are still a popular treat. In the northern states, distinctly Tibetan dishes are on the menu, particularly in Dharamsala, known as "Little Tibet". Pile up a plate of delicious *momos* (Tibetan dumplings) from a street stall, then learn to make them yourself with Lhamo *((0) 98164 68719)*, who moved here as a refugee from Tibet and runs classes at his home in Mcleod Ganj.

→

Portioning perfect parcels of Tibet *momos*, sealed with their distinctive twist, best served with tomato chutney

REGIONAL FOOD OF INDIA

Food across India showcases not only the variety of local produce, landscape, methods of cooking and climate, but also its history. In more tropical southern India, you can expect lighter foods made with coconut, fish and spice; while in the north, visitors will find richer curries, warming dals and tandoor meats.

NORTHERN FLAVOURS

In the north, wheat is the staple, and a variety of breads are baked in a tandoor. Rich curries, legacy of centuries of Mughal rule, are prepared across Delhi and the Punjab, as is the post-Partition cuisine of butter chicken and tikkas. Rajasthan's cuisine stems from its desert landscape, and uses a mix of cereals and lentils. The influence of non-violent Jain and Hindu religions is evident in Gujarati cuisine, which features complex vegetarian dishes. **Specialities**: *Aloo puri*, rogan josh, dal, gulab jamuns, *gatta curry*, *sulas*

BENGAL AND BEYOND

This region, watered by the rivers of the Gangetic Delta and the sea, is a land of plenty, with an abundance of fresh vegetables, coconut and fish. The region produces a wide variety of rice, which is a staple of many dishes. Bengali specialities include *ilish machher jhol* (hilsa fish curry). In Sikkim, food is influenced by Tibet. **Specialities**: *Momos*, prawn *malai* curry

SOUTHERN INSPIRATIONS

Rice dominates the food in south India: rice flour is used to make delicious dosa (pancakes served with a spiced potato filling) and myriad coconut and coriander chutneys. Despite commonalities, each state's cuisine has its own flavour – Tamil Nadu and Andhra Pradesh use sour spices like tamarind, and Mughal-influenced Telangana has savoury mutton dishes and biryanis. In Kerala, coconut and an abundance of spices is used in the preparation of most dishes. **Specialities**: *Appams* and stew, *bagara baigan*, *meen moilee*

GOA AND THE SOUTHWEST

Fish, coconut and rice are ubiquitous here, with the exception made for the major metropolis of Mumbai, where dishes reflect its diverse population. Of the coastal states, Goan dishes still show the colonial Portuguese influence, such as in vindaloo, one of the spiciest dishes in Indian cuisine, which is a robust mix of chilli (initially imported from South America) and vinegar. In Maharashtra and Karnataka, rice, lentils, maize and millet form the basis of most diets. **Specialities**: *Akuri*, vindaloo, *fugad*, *bisibele huliyana*

> **Rich curries, legacy of centuries of Mughal rule, are prepared across Delhi and the Punjab**

← A chef at Bukhara restaurant in Delhi preparing tikka

1 A woman eating Kerala's dosa pancake, which is served alongside a range of chutneys.

2 One of northern India's most popular desserts, gulab jamun are deep-fried milk-and-flour balls flavoured with rosewater and cardamom.

3 A Goan vindaloo is one of the spiciest dishes in Indian cuisine, and uses a unique combination of chilli and vinegar, influenced by Portuguese colonization.

4 *Momos*, Tibetan dumplings, are either filled with meat or vegetables and feature in northeast Indian cuisine.

Trek Through the Himalayas

Perched dramatically between the Himalayas and the Karakoram mountain range, Ladakh *(p242)* and the neighbouring region of Zanskar *(p254)* are the sort of epic trekking destinations that serious hikers dream of. Dozens of routes – some of them dating back millennia – cross this extreme, high-altitude, sparsely populated landscape. The main trekking season runs from June to September, and highlights include the six- to eight-day Markha Valley circuit and the demanding 10- to 12-day Padum to Lamayuru trek. Guided hikes and expeditions along both these routes – and many others – are offered by Spiritual Trek *(www.spiritualtrekladakh.com)*.

Did You Know?

At 3,500 m (11,480 ft), the Ladakh Marathon is one of the world's highest and toughest marathons.

A hiker admiring a vertiginous gorge in the Zanskar range ↑

INDIA FOR
ADVENTURERS

Look beyond the myriad cultures, world-class cuisines and dazzling array of wildlife, and you'll find one of the world's best under-the-radar destinations for thrill-seekers. Here, adventure lies around every corner, from jaw-dropping drives to epic treks across the Himalayas.

Scuba Dive off the Andaman Islands

Located in the middle of the Bay of Bengal, the Andaman and Nicobar Islands *(p588)* have crystal-clear waters and pristine coral reefs incredibly rich in life – making them the country's best place to dive. Here, you'll find hundreds of species of fish, loggerhead turtles, reef sharks and manta rays. See how many you can spot on a dive with Barefoot Scuba *(www.barefootscuba.in)*.

←

A diver exploring the multicoloured coral reefs of the Andaman Islands

Whitewater Raft in Rishikesh

Better known as a spot for those seeking spiritual enlightenment', Rishikesh *(p188)*, on the bank of the Ganges, is also a sinfully good spot to try whitewater rafting. With rapids ranging from Grades 1 to 4, there's something suitable for all levels of experience. Take a paddle with Snow Leopard Adventures *(www.snow leopardadventures.com)*.

→

Rafting the whitewater rapids of the Ganges at Rishikesh

Motor down the DIA Highway

One of the highest roads in the world, the Manali-Leh Highway is the most spectacular in India and reaches a breathless height of 5,328 m (17,480 ft) at the Tanglang pass. Thrill-seekers will have to contend with the altitude, gusting winds and bitterly cold temperatures along the 485-km- (300-mile-) long road. The rewards, however, are immense – not least the scenery.

←

Riding along the epic Manali-Leh Highway

Time Out at the Taj Mahal

Once described as a "teardrop on the face of eternity" by Nobel Prize-winning poet Rabindranath Tagore, the Taj Mahal is obvious, but unmissable (p166). Built in the 1600s by Mughal Emperor Shah Jahan in tribute to his late wife, Mumtaz Mahal, it stands as a monument to romantic love and its loss. The crowds are unavoidable: arrive early to find a vantage spot, and watch the mausoleum gradually change from pale dawn grey to soft evening pink.

Did You Know?

It is said Shah Jahan planned to build himself a black Taj opposite, but was deposed before he could start it.

Sunrise at the iconic Taj Mahal, the world's most beautiful building ↑

INDIA FOR
ROMANTICS

Home to the most beautiful building on earth and source of the book of love – the Kama Sutra – India has something to melt even the iciest hearts, from island palaces straight out of fairy tales to temples covered with erotically charged art.

Ancient Erotica

Entertainment for the gods; a how-to Kama Sutra guide; a depiction of Shiva and Parvati's wedding celebrations; or the work of a tantric cult – no one knows for sure why the ancient temples of Khajuraho (p288) are covered with eye-opening erotic sculptures. Whatever the reason, they are a truly remarkable and inspiring sight.

→

Wonderfully restored erotic artworks adorning the Khajuraho temples

Fairy-Tale Forts

Udaipur, with its unfeasibly gorgeous island palaces, rows of elegant whitewashed *havelis* and a backdrop of undulating hills, is the most romantic city in India *(p140)*. Even if your budget doesn't stretch to a night at the exclusive Lake Palace hotel *(www.tajhotels.com)*, gazing across the water as the sun sets will live long in the memory. Many of Rajasthan's romantic forts have been converted into hotels, such as the pastel Deogarh Mahal *(www.deogarhmahal. com)*; stay the night to feel like a royal.

↑ The glittering gold Sheesh Mahal suite at Deogarh Mahal, now a luxury hotel

Honeymoon at a Hill Station

Founded under the British Raj to allow perspiring officials to escape the summer heat, today hill stations make popular honeymoon destinations, affording temperate climes, panoramic views and charming hotels. The most famous is Shimla *(p222)*, summer capital of the Raj, but Mount Abu *(p154)*, Darjeeling *(p332)*, and Munnar *(p558)* are gorgeous spots.

← Lush forest surrounding Munnar hill station

Backwater Bliss

Kerala's lush Kuttanad region *(p539)* is a maze of rivers, lagoons and canals, best explored by traditional *kettu vallam*. Dreamy cruises on these converted rice barges are are run by local companies such as Lakes & Lagoons *(lakeslagoons.com)*. On board, you can relax into a more chill pace of life, as wildlife-rich coconut groves and small seemingly unchanged villages drift by.

↑ Floating through Kerala backwaters on a gentle *kettu vallam* cruise

Strike a Pose

Every region has its own dance style and tradition – and the best way to experience these is at India's numerous classical dance festivals. In February alone, catch performances at the Nishangandhi Festival, witness the pageantry of Mumbai's Kala Ghoda Arts Festival or visit the Vasantahabba festival in Bengaluru – the "Woodstock" of Indian classical dance. For those tempted to try a twirl or two, the Kala Ghoda Festival has fun free workshops *(www. kalaghodaassociation.com)*.

→

Performing a traditional Kathak dance at the Nishangandhi Festival

INDIA FOR
SPECTACULARS

With its ancient religions, a storytelling culture rich in dance and music, and a natural bounty that changes dramatically with the seasons, India always has something to celebrate. Here, almost every day is marked by a religious or social festival, and there is only one thing for a visitor to do – join in.

Religious Revellers

Holi is one of the country's most famous Hindu celebrations, but India's 50 faiths give rise to a vast number of other religious fests. In March, Jamshed-e-Navroz (Persian New Year) is marked with sandalwood offerings, and the Hindu festival of Diwali illuminates autumn with candles and fireworks. Don't miss Bakr-Id, a Muslim festival when devotees dine out on mutton biryani or kurma.

→

Celebrating Holi, the joyous Hindu festival of spring

Flowering Festivities

India is truly a country in bloom, and there are no shortage of festivals that celebrate its bounty of flowers and fruits. Gangtok in Sikkim is the place to go in May, when the International Flower Festival exhibits some of the state's rare and exotic flowering plants, including almost 500 varieties of orchid. In January and August, the Glass House in Bengaluru's Lalbagh Gardens is the scene of the twice-yearly Lalbagh Flower Show. For something to really sink your teeth into, Delhi's International Mango Festival in July has over 500 varieties of India's favourite sweet and juicy fruit *(p199)*.

← Floral display at the Lalbagh Flower Show

THE GREAT EPICS

Many classical dances in India tell the story of the two great Sanskrit epics, the *Ramayana* and the *Mahabharata*. The *Ramayana* is the story of the ideal hero, Rama, and his adventures in exile, while the *Mahabharata* recounts the rivalry between the Pandavas and the Kauravas. Both stories are a font of wisdom about human behaviour, emotions and moral dilemmas. Though known in oral form since at least the 9th century BC, they were only put into writing around the 4th century AD.

↑ The Indian cricket team playing at Eden Gardens stadium

Sporting Extravaganzas

In India, cricket could well be a religion – and the place to worship is at Eden Gardens in Kolkata *(p317)*, the nation's oldest cricket ground. It's generally easy to get tickets to a local or test match, or even a Twenty20 international; tickets go on sale at the stadium's booking office around two weeks before a game. If you don't have the stamina for a six-hour game, there are other speedier sports, like the vintage car rallies in Delhi and Mumbai, or the thrilling Nehru Trophy Boat Race in Kerala.

A YEAR IN
INDIA

JANUARY

Makar Sakranti *(mid-Jan)*. In Gujarat, Hindus fly kites in honour of the sun god Surya.

△ **Pongal** *(mid-Jan)*. Tamil harvest festival notable for its bright pavement rangolis.

Republic Day *(26 Jan)*. Colourful parades fill the streets in major cities and towns as the country celebrates becoming a republic in 1950.

FEBRUARY

Losar *(dates vary)*. Tibetan New Year festivities.

Sufi Festival *(late Feb)*. Spiritual music and dance performances in Jodhpur.

△ **Khajuraho Dance Festival** *(late Feb)*. Classical dance against the backdrop of the ancient temples in Khajuraho.

MAY

△ **Buddha Jayanti** *(dates vary)*. A big party for Buddha's birthday, held across east Asia.

Ooty Summer Festival *(all month)*. Hill station Ooty comes to life with flower and fruit shows.

Thrissur Pooram *(Apr–May)*. A loud festival featuring Keralan drumming and parades.

JUNE

△ **Saga Dawa** *(all month)*. Rituals mark the Buddha's birth, enlightenment and death in northern India.

Shimla Summer Festival *(Jun)*. Folk music shows.

Yuru Kabgyat *(Jun/Jul)*. Lively Buddhist festival at Lamayuru Monastery in Ladakh.

SEPTEMBER

Ganesh Chaturti *(Aug/Sep)*. Elaborate statues of Ganesh paraded then immersed in the sea.

△ **Muharram** *(Aug/Sep)*. Hazrat Imam Hussain's martyrdom commemorated by Muslims.

Dussehra *(dates vary)*. Colourful parades take place across the country marking the gathering and victories of the Hindu gods.

OCTOBER

△ **Gandhi Jayanti** *(2 Oct)*. Mahatma Gandhi's birthday observed nationwide.

Durga Puja *(dates vary)*. Huge idols of the goddess Durga are paraded in the streets.

Diwali *(Oct/Nov)*. Atmospheric festival of lights, fireworks and family feasts.

MARCH

△ **International Yoga Festival** *(first week)*. Thousands descend on Rishikesh to practise yoga.

Maha Shivratri *(Feb/Mar)*. All night solemn temple vigil for Lord Shiva, a principal Hindu deity.

Holi *(dates vary)*. The start of spring is celebrated by throwing multi-coloured powder.

APRIL

Easter *(dates vary)*. Christians celebrate Jesus' resurrection with church services and parades.

△ **Vaisakhi** *(mid-Apr)*. Sikh New Year and the spring harvest marked in the Punjab region.

Puthandu *(13/14 Apr)*. Families gather and houses are cleaned in advance of Tamil New Year.

JULY

Rath Yatra *(Jun/Jul)*. Legendary temple chariot festival through Puri's streets in Odisha.

△ **Hemis Tsechu** *(Jun-Jul)*. Ladakhis throng to Hemis Monastery for mask dances commemorating the renowned Guru Padma Sambhav.

Ladakh Polo Festival *(mid-Jul)*. Players compete on the highest plateau in India.

AUGUST

Independence Day *(15 Aug)*. Large parades across the country, especially in Delhi, celebrate independence from Britain.

△ **Onam** *(Aug/Sep)*. Keralan Hindus and Christians mark the beginning of the harvest.

Janmashtami *(Aug/Sep)*. Nocturnal performances of hymns and dance honour Krishna's birth.

NOVEMBER

△ **Guru Nanak Jayanti** *(dates vary)*. A sacred festival celebrating the Sikh founder's birthday.

Pushkar Camel Fair *(dates vary)*. A livestock trading bonanza on an epic scale in Rajasthan.

India Surf Festival *(mid-Nov)*. Surfing competition on the coast of Puri in Odisha.

DECEMBER

Hornbill Festival *(1–10 Dec)*. Nagaland in northeast India hosts a variety of cultural events.

Chennai Music Festival *(all month)*. Delightful musical events in Chennai region.

△ **Christmas Day** *(25 Dec)*. The birth of Jesus is celebrated around world.

1

A BRIEF
HISTORY

One of the world's oldest civilizations, India is one of its youngest nations, having become a sovereign country in 1947. Its natural boundaries have fostered a remarkable cultural unity, despite the area's size and diversity and a history marked by the rise and fall of powerful empires.

Ancient Civilizations

People have been living on this land for over 250,000 years, with the first sophisticated urban civilization emerging in 3300 BC. Known as the Indus Valley Civilization, this culture stretched across large swathes of north India. Around 1500 BC, a group known as the Aryans moved into the Indus region. Their Vedic religion contained caste division, which put the Brahmins (priestly class) at the top of the social hierarchy, followed by Kshatriyas (warriors), Vaishyas (traders) and Shudras (labourers). It was partly as a reaction to this that new religious movements emerged, including Buddhism and Jainism.

14
—
dharmic rock edicts were recorded by Mauryan emperor Ashoka across his empire.

Timeline of events

3300–1700 BC
Harappan culture flourishes in the Indus Valley.

1500 BC
Aryans migrate into northwest India; the next 500 years form the Rigvedic period.

1000 BC
The use of iron becomes widespread during the Later Vedic Age..

566 BC
Siddhartha Gautama, who became the Buddha, is born in Lumbini.

467 BC
Mahavira, the founder of the Jain religion, dies.

The Mauryan Empire

The first major dynasty in India, the Mauryan Empire was established in 322 BC when Chandragupta Maurya defeated the ruling Nanda dynasty of Magadha. Chandragupta's grandson Ashoka (269–232 BC) became one of India's greatest rulers, eventually expanding the Mauryan Empire from southeast Iran to Assam in the east. After his bloody conquest of Kalinga, Ashoka gave up violence and became a great patron of Buddhism. He had his ethical code recorded in Prakrit, Greek and Aramaic on rocks and pillars all over his vast empire.

Invasions from the West and Central Asia

In 326 BC, the forces of Alexander the Great invaded the Indus Valley, reaching as far as the Beas River in what is now Himachal Pradesh, while from the northwest a series of invaders from Central Asia established successive dynasties. These included the Indo-Greeks from Bactria (200–80 BC), the nomadic Indo-European Scythians or Sakas (from 80 BC), the Parthians from what is now Iran (1st century AD) and the Kushanas, Indo-Europeans from Bactria (AD 50–300).

1 An 18th-century map depicting the Indian subcontinent.

2 The ruins of Lothal, an Indus Valley Civilization city first inhabited in 3700 BC.

3 An illustration depicting an envoy of Emperor Ashoka declaring peace after the great War of Kalinga in 262 BC.

4 Artwork showing Alexander the Great invading northern India.

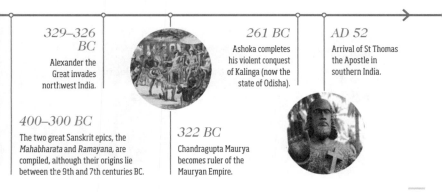

329–326 BC

Alexander the Great invades northwest India.

400–300 BC

The two great Sanskrit epics, the *Mahabharata* and *Ramayana*, are compiled, although their origins lie between the 9th and 7th centuries BC.

322 BC

Chandragupta Maurya becomes ruler of the Mauryan Empire.

261 BC

Ashoka completes his violent conquest of Kalinga (now the state of Odisha).

AD 52

Arrival of St Thomas the Apostle in southern India.

1

2

After the Mauryans

The decline of the Mauryans led to the rise of the Kushanas, whose empire linked the Indian Ocean to the Silk Road. Kanishka, the greatest Kushana king, was almost as great a patron of Buddhism as Ashoka had been. As the Kushanas declined, the Gupta empire (AD 320–500) emerged and presided over a great cultural flowering, including the establishing of the university at Nalanda. The Guptas were superseded by the Vardhanas, based at Kanauj; their most famous king was Harsha (AD 606–647). In central India, the Mauryans were supplanted by empires like the Satavahanas (100 BC–AD 220), based at Paithan in Maharashtra, and the Ikshvakus (AD 225–310) to the east, under whom Buddhist stupas were built at Amaravati. Many of the superb sculptures and paintings at Ajanta were made under the Vakatakas (AD 250–550), while a subsequent dynasty, the Chalukyas, built temples at Badami and Pattadakal.

The Rise of the Rajputs

In the 8th century, Harsha's old capital Kanauj became the site of a three-way power tussle between the Pratiharas, who ruled

SHANKARACHARYA

South Indian theologian and philosopher Adi Shankaracharya (788-820) consolidated the philosophical doctrine of Advaita Vedanta. This holds that atman (the self) is the same as the highest metaphysical reality known as Brahman, while all material objects are mere illusions (maya).

Timeline of events

606–647
Harsha reigns over a period of peace and prosperity.

608–642
Pulakeshin II, king of the Chalukyas, reigns over much of peninsular India.

476
Birth of Aryabhata, great astronomer, mathematician and physicist.

736
Dhillika (present day Delhi) is founded by Tomar king Anangpal.

320–500
The Gupta dynasty seizes power from the Kushanas.

Gujarat and Rajasthan, the Rashtrakutas who ruled Karnataka and Maharashtra, and the Palas, a Buddhist dynasty from Bengal. Finally, in around 836, the Pratiharas – who were one of a group of warlords known as the Rajputs – prevailed. Other Rajput dynasties included the Paramaras in Malwa (Madhya Pradesh), the Solankis in Gujarat, the Chauhans in Ajmer and the Tomars in Delhi. These dynasties fought frequent wars with each other, but between wars, the rulers lived in great luxury, in grand forts and richly ornamented palaces.

Southern Dynasties

In the south, the Pallavas, based in Tamil Nadu, rose to power in the 6th century. In 642, their ruler Narasimha Varman I defeated and killed the Chalukya king Pulakeshin II, and the great Chalukya kingdom fell apart. In the late 9th century, the Cholas defeated the Pallavas, Mysore's Western Ganga dynasty and the Pandyas of Madurai to establish supremacy in the south. International trade flourished, despite the constant wars. From the 7th century, reforms in Hinduism rejecting the caste system led to its resurgence and the wane of Buddhism's influence.

1 One of the temples built by the Chalukyas in Pattadakal. ↑

2 Fresco depicting royal Rajput women.

3 The Pallava ruler Narasimha Varman I defeating Pulakeshin II.

Did You Know?

The origin of the term Rajput is the word *rajaputra,* which translates to "son of a king".

740–973
The Rashtrakutas rule in central India and the Deccan, a vast plateau spanning southern and western India.

871
The long-ruling Chola Empire is founded and based in Thanjavur, Tamil Nadu.

900
The Western Gangas, builders of Shravana Belagola, begin their reign; they were later defeated by the Cholas.

916
The Chandelas build Khajuraho and reign until 1203.

The Arrival of Islam

In 1001, the Muslim Afghan sultan Mahmud of Ghazni invaded northern India, and by 1008 he had annexed the Punjab and turned the other Rajput kingdoms into vassal states. In 1192, skirmishes between Muslim Punjab and the Rajput rulers of Delhi and Ajmer prompted Muhammad of Ghur to seize those kingdoms. When he died, one of his generals, Qutbuddin Aibak, founded the Delhi Sultanate, whose rule spread across much of northern India, although its nobles and vassal states sometimes rebelled and declared independent kingdoms.

The Rise of the Mughals

In 1526 Babur, a central Asian prince who was a brilliant military campaigner, marched into India and overthrew the Delhi Sultanate's rulers at the battle of Panipat and established the Mughal Empire. Meanwhile, in Punjab, Guru Nanak (1469–1539) founded the Sikh religion. Mughal rule was briefly interrupted when Babur's son Humayun was overthrown in 1540 by an Afghan chieftain, Sher Shah Suri. Humayun regained his throne in 1555, and his son, Akbar, expanded the Mughal empire.

1 A depiction of Mahmud of Ghazni's invasion.

2 The soaring red Qutb Minar.

3 Maharaja Ranjit Singh, ruler of the Sikh Empire.

4 A Portugese fleet captures Diu, Gujarat.

Did You Know?

Mughal India was the world's largest economic power in the 17th century.

Timeline of events

1001
Mahmud of Ghazni, an Afghan sultan, invades northern India.

1206
The expansive Delhi Sultanate is founded by Qutbuddin Aibak.

1469
Guru Nanak, the founder of Sikhism, is born.

1556
Akbar the Great becomes emperor of the Mughals.

1498
Portuguese explorer Vasco da Gama reaches Calicut in Kerala.

4

The Decline of the Mughals

Aurangzeb, the last great Mughal, alienated the population with his religious intolerance. His persecution of the Sikhs led them to carve out a state for themselves in the Punjab. But the most serious backlash against Aurangzeb was the rise of the Maratha Confederacy. Founded in 1674 as a Hindu insurgency against Mughal rule in Maharashtra, the Marathas gradually expanded their territories until, by the mid-18th century, they were the main power in India. Mughal governors in places like Bengal and Hyderabad established independent states.

The Arrival of the Europeans

Europeans began to arrive in the 16th century, setting up a number of trading posts and acquiring land. They fought wars against one another and against local rulers; the Portuguese, who had been one of the first to arrive, lost most of their territories to the Dutch and English by the end of the 17th century. The 18th century saw major conflicts between the French and Britain's East India Company, involving Indian powers on both sides. Ultimately, the British were the victors.

THE MUGHALS

Babur (1526–30): Founded the empire.
Humayun (1530–56): Consolidated and expanded the empire.
Akbar (1556–1605): Promoted culture and religious tolerance.
Jahangir (1605–27): Neglected politics and focused on pleasure.
Shah Jahan (1628–58): Founded Old Delhi and built the Taj Mahal.
Aurangzeb (1658–1707): Supported Islamic orthodoxy.

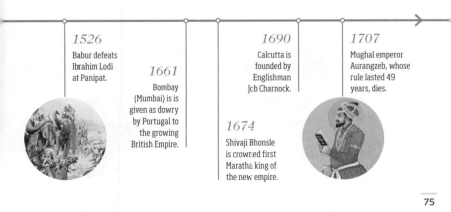

1526
Babur defeats Ibrahim Lodi at Panipat.

1661
Bombay (Mumbai) is is given as dowry by Portugal to the growing British Empire.

1674
Shivaji Bhonsle is crowned first Maratha king of the new empire.

1690
Calcutta is founded by Englishman Job Charnock.

1707
Mughal emperor Aurangzeb, whose rule lasted 49 years, dies.

The Rise of the British

The British East India Company continued to expand their territories, fighting the nawabs of Bengal and subjugating the Marathas through a series of wars between 1784 and 1818. Despite opposition from rulers such as Mysore's Haider Ali and Tipu Sultan, the Company controlled most of India by the mid-19th century. In 1857, an uprising now known as the War of Independence surged across north India. The Indian forces took Delhi and tried to restore Mughal rule, but the British managed to put down the rebellion, amid much brutality on both sides.

The Road to Independence

After 1857, the British abolished the East India Company and ruled India directly as a Raj (empire), but opposition continued to grow. In 1885, the Indian National Congress was founded to demand self-government. By 1920, Mohandas Gandhi, a Gujarati lawyer, was leader of the independence movement, whose demands Britain continued to ignore. Meanwhile, the Muslim League was demanding a separate Muslim state. After World War II, Britain no longer had the strength to enforce its

↑ Tipu Sultan, ruler of the Kingdom of Mysore and a foe of the British

Timeline of events

1757
The British defeat Siraj-ud-daulah, Nawab of Bengal, at the Battle of Plassey.

1853
The first commercial railway is built from Bombay to Thane.

1885
The Indian National Congress is founded.

1857
The War of Independence takes place against the British in north India.

1920
The Non-Cooperation Movement is launched by Mahatma Gandhi.

rule, and acceded to Indian demands for independence. On 14 August 1947, the new nation of Pakistan was born, with India following on 15 August. This was accompanied by a mass cross-migration of Hindus and Muslims into the new nations.

India Today

Jawaharlal Nehru, India's first prime minister, laid the foundations of a modern nation state, with his Congress Party dominating parliament. After Nehru died in 1964, his daughter Indira Gandhi continued his socialist policies, but became increasingly authoritarian. She was assassinated by her Sikh bodyguards in 1984, and her son Rajiv took over on a wave of sympathy. He was assassinated by a Sri Lankan Tamil separatist during the 1991 election campaign. In 1998 the Hindu nationalist Bharatiya Janata Party (BJP) took power, holding it until 2004 and regaining it in 2014. Today, with literacy rates having risen to 74 per cent and major economic reforms having boosted the rise of a huge middle class with significant spending power, India is the world's fastest-growing trillion-dollar economy, and is projected to become the fifth-largest economy by 2020.

1 Artwork depicting the 1857 uprising against the British.

2 A parade celebrating independence in 1947.

3 Indira Gandhi addressing the public.

4 Children at school.

Did You Know?

Indira Gandhi was voted "Woman of the Millennium'" in a 1999 public poll by the BBC.

1947
India becomes independent and Partition takes place; Mahatma Gandhi is assassinated a year later.

1992
The destruction of the Babri Masjid leads to communal riots.

2013
The Mars Orbiter Mission is launched successfully by India.

2007
Pratibha Patil is the first woman to become the president of India.

2019
Narendra Modi and the BJP win a decisive mandate for a second term in government.

EXPERIENCE

The Festival of Kites in Ahmedabad, Gujarat

Autorickshaws lining the crowded, bustling streets of Delhi

DELHI

The capital of India, Delhi is also its third-largest city, with a population of about 19 million. Its strategic location has given it a focal position in Indian history, and many great empires have been ruled from here. The monuments and ruins of these are scattered throughout the city, often cheek by jowl with modern structures and highrise towers. The vast urban sprawl of contemporary Delhi is, in fact, a conglomeration of several distinct enclaves. Chief among these are Old Delhi, with its 16th- and 17th-century Mughal-built monuments and congested souk-like bazaars, and New Delhi, with its wide avenues, grand vistas and colonial mansions, built by the British in the 1930s as their imperial capital. The picturesque 12th-century ruins of citadels built by the first Islamic rulers can be seen in the Qutb-Mehrauli area, and the affluent middle-class suburbs of South Delhi lie close by. Adding to Delhi's fascinating diversity is the fact that it is largely a city of migrants. After the violent Partition of India and Pakistan in 1947, millions of refugees, mainly from west Punjab, flocked here in search of a new life. Since then there has been a steady influx of people from all over India. Yet each regional community has retained its distinct cultural identity, making Delhi less a melting pot than a thali (platter), whose offerings may be savoured singly or in various interesting combinations.

DELHI

Must Sees

1. Red Fort
2. Jama Masjid
3. Mehrauli Archaeological Park
4. Qutb Complex
5. Humayun's Tomb

Experience More

6. National Gallery of Modern Art
7. Rashtrapati Bhavan
8. Rajpath
9. Raisina Hill
10. Crafts Museum
11. Jantar Mantar
12. Lakshmi Narayan Mandir
13. Nehru Memorial Museum and Library
14. Lodi Gardens
15. Purana Qila
16. Baha'i House of Worship
17. Sanskriti Museums
18. Nizamuddin Complex
19. Tughlaqabad
20. Feroze Shah Kotla
21. Around Kashmiri Gate
22. Coronation Memorial
23. Raj Ghat
24. Connaught Place
25. Safdarjung's Tomb
26. The Ridge
27. National Museum
28. National Rail Museum
29. Hauz Khas
30. Kingdom of Dreams
31. Jahanpanah

Eat

1. Indian Accent
2. Bukhara
3. Naivedyam

Stay

4. The Imperial
5. Haveli Hauz Khas
6. Hotel Broadway

Shop

7. Play Clan
8. Anokhi

0 kilometres 1

0 miles 1

N

RED FORT

D1 **Chandni Chowk** **Lal Quila, Chandni Chowk** **Complex: sunrise-sunset Tue-Sun; Son et Lumière: Feb-Apr, Sep & Oct: 8:30-9:30pm daily; Nov-Jan: 7:30-8:30pm daily; May-Aug: 9-10pm daily** **Mon & public hols** **delhitourism.gov.in**

Red sandstone battlements give this imperial citadel its name, Lal Qila, or Red Fort. Commissioned by Shah Jahan in 1639, it took nine years to build and was the seat of Mughal power until 1857, when the last Mughal emperor, Bahadur Shah Zafar, was dethroned and exiled. It was here that the national flag was hoisted for the first time when India became an independent nation on 15 August 1947.

One of Delhi's most famous and visited monuments, the Red Fort is iconic. Entry to the complex is through one of two main gates: the Delhi Gate and the Lahore Gate. The latter leads to the covered bazaar of Chatta Chowk, filled with paintings and trinkets, through which visitors walk to get to many of the fort's most spectacular sites. One of the most photographed is the Diwan-i-Aam, a 60-pillared red sandstone hall. The emperor, sitting underneath a lavishly carved stone canopy, gave audiences to the public here. This is in contrast to the Diwan-i-Khas, constructed entirely of white marble, which was an exclusive pavilion designed for private audiences with the emperor's most trusted nobles. The walls and pillars here were inlaid with gems. The Rang Mahal, part of the women's quarters, hides a similarly ornate room – the Shish Mahal, or Hall of Mirrors, where the walls and ceilings are decorated with pieces of reflective glass.

The white, ornamental Khas Mahal was the emperor's private residence. Inside this building is the Tosh Khana, or Robe Room, notable for its superb marble jali screen carved with the scales of justice (a motif seen in many miniature paintings). Close by lie the Hamams (Royal Baths), with inlaid marble floors and three enclosures, and the elegant Moti Masjid (Pearl Mosque), built in 1659.

THE LAST OF THE MUGHAL EMPERORS

The Red Fort was the seat of power of the Mughal Empire until its fall in 1857. Historian William Dalrymple tells the tale of the empire's final days in *The Last Mughal*. The emperor, Bahadur Shah Zafar II, was a gifted poet and calligrapher, who had reluctantly taken on the mantle of King of India just as the Mughal Empire was failing. His reign ended after the Siege of Delhi, part of the 1857 War of Independence, as he had supported forces opposing the British Empire in the ultimately doomed uprising. The book is a fantastic, gory and insightful read.

↑ The battlements of the Delhi Gate, one of the fort's main gateways

→ Brass relief of a figure riding an elephant on one of the Red Fort's doors at the Delhi Gate

PICTURE PERFECT
Pretty Pillars

Every angle provides a great photo op in the Diwan-i-Aam, the majestic public audience hall of the Red Fort. Head there late afternoon for exquisitely sculpted archways and long shadows.

↑ The intricately carved red sandstone arches of the Diwan-i-Aam

②

JAMA MASJID

📍D2 🚇Off Netaji Subhash Marg Ⓜ Chawri Bazar, Jama Masjid
🕐Sunrise–sunset daily 🚫To visitors during prayer hours

This grand mosque was constructed on the orders of the Emperor Shah Jahan, a prolific builder whose most famous commission was the Taj Mahal. An imposing structure with three black-and-white marble domes and twin minarets framing its great central arch, the Jama Masjid took six years and 5,000 workers to construct. Finally completed in 1656, the emperor's final architectural flourish is still considered India's largest and finest mosque.

Did You Know?

It took a whopping million rupees to build the Jama Masjid.

A magnificent flight of sandstone steps leads to the arched entrances of the Jama Masjid (also known as the Friday Mosque). The huge square courtyard can accommodate up to 25,000 devotees at the communal Friday prayer sessions and at Eid, the celebration at the end of Ramadan, when a sea of worshippers fills out the vast space.

Perched on top of a hillock, the mosque was also given the name Masjid e Jahan Numa, suitably meaning "mosque with a view of the world". Entry can made through either of the north, south or east gates. Ensure that you cover up appropriately before attempting to enter, and remove your shoes (unofficial "shoe minders" will offer look after them for a fee). The south minaret is popular with visitors for its great view; however, women who climb the structure must be accompanied by a man.

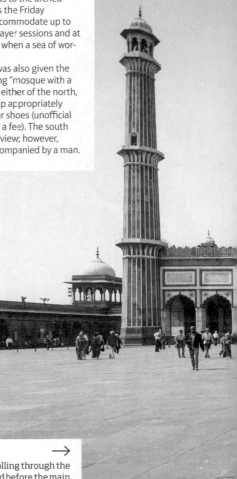

TOP 5 ARCHITECTURE FEATURES

Foundation stone
This was laid on Friday 6 October 1650.

Sundials
Two in the central courtyard show prayer times.

Central arch
Inscribed on the central arch are the words "Ya Hadi" (one who shows the right path).

Motifs
The mosque is decorated with a lotus flower motif.

Domes
Three domes in black-and-white marble strips adorned with gold top the mosque.

→
Strolling through the courtyard before the main façade of Jama Masjid

Huge crystal chandelier hanging inside the central dome →

GREAT VIEW
South Minaret

The south minaret has one of the best views in the city – visitors who climb the 120 steps to the top are rewarded with a panoramic look over both the new and old cities of Delhi. Particularly worth spotting are Connaught Place and Parliament.

← High cusped arches above the mosque's prayer hall

MEHRAULI ARCHAEOLOGICAL PARK

**⊙ A2 ⌂ Anuvrat Marg, Mehrauli Ⓜ Qutab Minar ⊙ Sunrise-sunset daily
ℹ Conservation Assistant's Office; www.delhitourism.gov.in**

Surrounded by lush forest, the Mehrauli Archaeological Park is a spectacular collection of ancient ruins, imposing tombs and striking stepwells. There are over 400 historic buildings scattered throughout this expansive park, which span the Sultanate, Mughal and British periods.

Now the most historically rich area in Delhi, Mehrauli was established as an archaeological park in 1997. The earliest buildings here date from the Rajput era, although more significant buildings are from the 12th century, when this area was the centre of the Delhi Sultanate, a kingdom founded by Qutbuddin Aibak, who also started building the neighbouring Qutb Minar (p88). Later, Mughal princes came here to hunt, and they also built tombs and shrines here. During the British Raj in the 19th century, British officials built weekend houses in Mehrauli, attracted by its orchards, ponds and game. Now a popular place for an evening stroll, Mehrauli can also be explored on a guided walking tour.

The spectacular Jamali-Kamali Mosque and Tomb surrounded by trees ↑

METCALFE'S FOLLY

Mehrauli witnessed one of the stranger episodes in Anglo-Indian history when Sir Thomas Metcalfe (1795-1853), British Resident at the Mughal Court, decided to establish a summer residence in the area. Rather than build a new house, Metcalfe made the decision to convert the tomb of Quli Khan into an English-style country residence, which he christened Dilkusha (Heart's Delight), although it is generally known as Metcalfe's Folly. He also built a string of Indian-style follies around it. As fate would have it, Metcalfe's love of all things Mughal did him little good: he died slowly, allegedly poisoned by one of the emperor's queens.

Park Highlights

Must See

Jahaz Mahal

Venue of the Phoolwalon ki Sair (a colourful flower procession), this square pleasure pavilion, built during the Lodi era (1451-1526), seems to float on the Hauzi-Shamsi tank, a reservoir built in the 11th century.

Dargah Qutb Sahib

Both the 13th-century dargah of Sufi saint Qutbuddin Bakhtiyar and the nearby Moti Masjid ("Pearl Mosque") attract many pilgrims.

Madhi Masjid

▷ Surrounded by bastions and a high wall, this fortress-like mosque, dating back to 1200, has a large open courtyard and a three-arched, heavily ornamented prayer hall.

Jamali-Kamali Mosque and Tomb

◁ The tomb of Jamali (the court poet during the late Lodi and early Mughal age) is inscribed with some of his verses. Its well-preserved interior has coloured tiles and richly decorated painted plasterwork.

Balban's Tomb

The 13th-century tomb of Balban, Qutbuddin's successor, lies in a square rubble-built chamber.

Rajon ki Baoli

This dramatic three-storeyed stepwell is also known as Sukhi Baoli (dry well). Nearby is the five-storeyed Gandhak ki Baoli, named after its strong sulphur *(gandhak)* smell. These baolis once supplied fresh water to the area.

Adham Khan's Tomb

▷ The son of Emperor Akbar's wet nurse, Adham Khan murdered a rival and was executed by the emperor for his crime. Akbar later built this large tomb for mother and son.

89

Did You Know?

The Iron Pillar next to the Qutb Minar grants wishes - if you can get your arms around it backwards.

The towering Qutb Minar, soaring high above the surrounding ruins ↑

④ 〈🏃〉 〈M〉 〈🍴〉

QUTB COMPLEX

◉ A2 🏠 Mehrauli, Delhi-Gurgaon Rd Ⓜ Qutab Minar 🕐 Sunrise-sunset daily 🌐 delhitourism.gov.in

One of the most spectacular sites in Delhi, the Qutb Complex houses a number of historical buildings, including the city's oldest mosque. It is, however, most famous for the Qutb Minar, an impressive sandstone-and-marble minaret standing 73 m (240 ft) high, a monument to Islamic victory in Delhi.

Qutbuddin Aibak, founder of the Delhi Sultanate, started to build the Qutb Complex in the late 12th century to celebrate his victory over Delhi's last Hindu kingdom. The two main structures of the complex are the Quwwat-ul-Islam ("Might of Islam") Mosque and the Qutb Minar, which were built using elements of razed temples that had previously stood here. The mosque is a fusion of decorative Hindu panels from the destroyed temples, and Islamic domes and arches. The Qutb Minar, also known as Victory Tower, is a five-storey monument that was completed in the reign of Aibak's successor, Iltutmish. Subsequent sultans continued to add more structures to the area. One such building is the Alai Darwaza, the complex's gateway, erected in 1311 by the sultan Alauddin, which established a new Islamic architectural style, marked by arches and panels carved with verses from the Qur'an.

↑ Intricate wall carvings at the complex

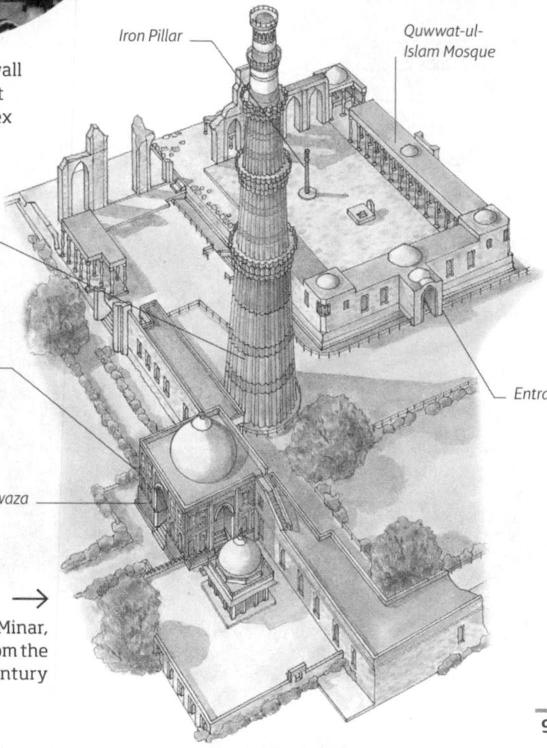

Iron Pillar

Quwwat-ul-Islam Mosque

Qutb Minar

Carved panels

Entrance

Alai Darwaza

→ The Qutb Minar, dating from the 12th century

5 ⟨✎⟩ ⟨▭⟩

HUMAYUN'S TOMB

📍E5 **🏠Off Mathura Rd, Bharat Scout Guide Marg** **Ⓜ JLN Stadium**
🕐Sunrise-sunset daily **🌐humayunstomb.com**

This magnificent tomb – the final resting place of Humayun, the second Mughal emperor – rises spectacularly above the surrounding palm-fringed gardens. The first great example of a Mughal garden tomb, it was the inspiration for several later monuments, including the incomparable Taj Mahal.

Built between 1565 and 1572 by Persian architect Mirak Mirza Ghiyas, the tomb was commissioned by Humayun's senior widow, Haji Begum. The monument is often called the "Dormitory of the Mughals", as the tomb complex houses over 150 of Humayun's Mughal family members. The graves in the tomb's chambers include those of Humayun's wives and Dara Shikoh, Shah Jahan's scholarly son. Also found in the complex are the octagonal tomb and mosque of Isa Khan, a 16th-century nobleman; the tomb of Humayun's favourite barber; and the impressive Arab ki Sarai, a rest house for the Persian masons who built the tomb. The monument is now a UNESCO World Heritage Site.

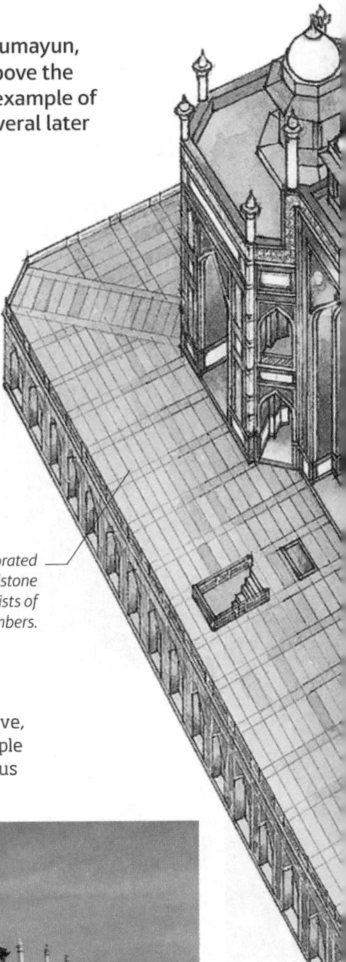

The plinth is decorated with red sandstone arches and consists of multiple chambers.

← The emperor's grave, underneath a simple marble sarcophagus

↑ The imposing exterior of Humayun's Tomb, one of the finest Mughal tombs

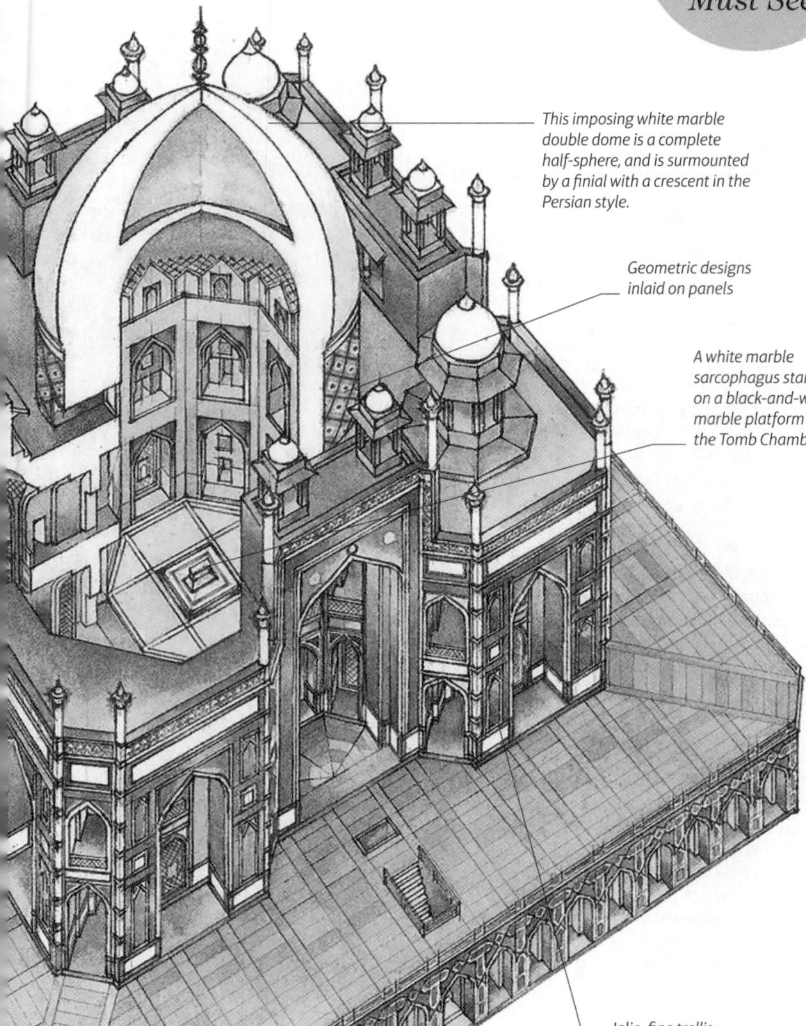

This imposing white marble double dome is a complete half-sphere, and is surmounted by a finial with a crescent in the Persian style.

Geometric designs inlaid on panels

A white marble sarcophagus stands on a black-and-white marble platform in the Tomb Chamber.

Jalis, fine trellis work in stone, became a key tomb feature.

↑ An illustration of Humayun's Tomb, showing the central tomb chamber

HAJI BEGUM

Of Persian descent, Haji Begum came to India in the mid-1550s as the wife of Emperor Humayun and the Empress Consort of the Mughal Empire. Initially called Bega Begum, she became known as Haji Begum after she went to Mecca for the Haj pilgrimage. After her husband's death, she decided to build a magnificent tomb to house his body and commissioned the Persian architect Mirak Mirza Ghiyas. Humayun's Tomb was the first majestic mausoleum in Islamic India; it was this elegant tomb, alongside others, that instigated a legacy of Mughal mausoleums.

EXPERIENCE MORE

6

National Gallery of Modern Art

♀D4 **⌂Jaipur House, near India Gate** **Ⓜ Khan Market** **⊘11am–6:30pm Tue–Fri; 11am–8pm Sat & Sun** **ⓦngmaindia.gov.in**

Jaipur House, the grand former residence of the maharajas of Jaipur, is now one of India's largest museums of modern art. Its collection covers the period from the mid-1800s to the present day and includes works by Indian painters such as Jamini Roy, Raja Ravi Varma and Amrita Shergil, as well as contemporary artists from Ram Kumar to Anjolie Ela Menon. Also on display are classical works by British painters such as Thomas Daniell.

> 💬 **INSIDER TIP**
> **Old Delhi Tour**
>
> Take a tour of Old Delhi with the knowledgeable Surekha Narain *(delhi metrowalks.com/home. htm)*. On her tours, you'll experience great street food, visit the best perfumery and see where sweets are made.

7

Rashtrapati Bhavan

♀B4 **⌂Raisina Hill** **ⓂCentral Secretariat** **⊘Changing of Guard: 15 Mar–14 Nov: 8am Sat, 5:30pm Sun; 15 Nov–14 Mar: 10am Sat, 4:30pm Sun** **ⓦrashtrapati sachivalaya.gov.in/rbtour/**

Designed by Sir Edwin Lutyens as the British Viceroy's Palace, Rashtrapati Bhavan is a huge, elegant beige and red sandstone building. Now the official residence of the President of India, it has a vast copper-clad cupola; Durbar Hall, situated beneath the dome, is where all important state ceremonies are held. Guided tours are held Thursdays to Sundays. To the west are the lovely terraced **Mughal Gardens**.

Mughal Gardens
⊘Opening hours vary, check website **ⓦrb.nic.in**

8

Rajpath

♀C4 **ⓂCentral Secretariat**

Running east of Vijay Chowk is Rajpath, a 3-km (2-mile) landscaped avenue used for

↑ Celebrating Independence Day in front of Rashtrapati Bhavan on Raisina Hill

parades, lined with fountains, canals and lawns. It is also the site of major museums: the **National Archives** houses a collection of state records and private papers; and, opposite, the **Indira Gandhi National Centre for the Arts** holds rare manuscripts and exhibitions.

At Rajpath's eastern end is India Gate, a massive red sandstone arch that was built to commemorate the Indian and British soldiers who died in World War I, and those who fell in battle in the North-West Frontier Province and the Third Afghan War. An eternal flame burns in memory of the soldiers who died in the 1971 India-Pakistan War.

National Archives
⌂Janpath **ⓂCentral Secretariat** **⊘10am–5:30pm Mon–Fri** **⊗Public hols** **ⓦnationalarchives.nic.in**

↑ Works on display at Delhi's National Gallery of Modern Art

Indira Gandhi National Centre for the Arts
Janpath 9am–5:30pm Mon–Fri ignca.nic.in

9

Raisina Hill

B4 Central Secretariat

The area around Raisina Hill was selected by the British to be the location of their new capital. The hill itself, with its dominant vantage point, was the site of government buildings such as the twin North and South blocks of the Secretariat, two virtually identical buildings which now sit on the top of Raisina Hill. These were designed by Sir Herbert Baker, who also designed the grand circular Sansad Bhavan (Parliament House) to the north of Vijay Chowk. Access is limited, and the galleries of Sansad Bhavan can be visited only with an official pass and a letter from an Indian MP.

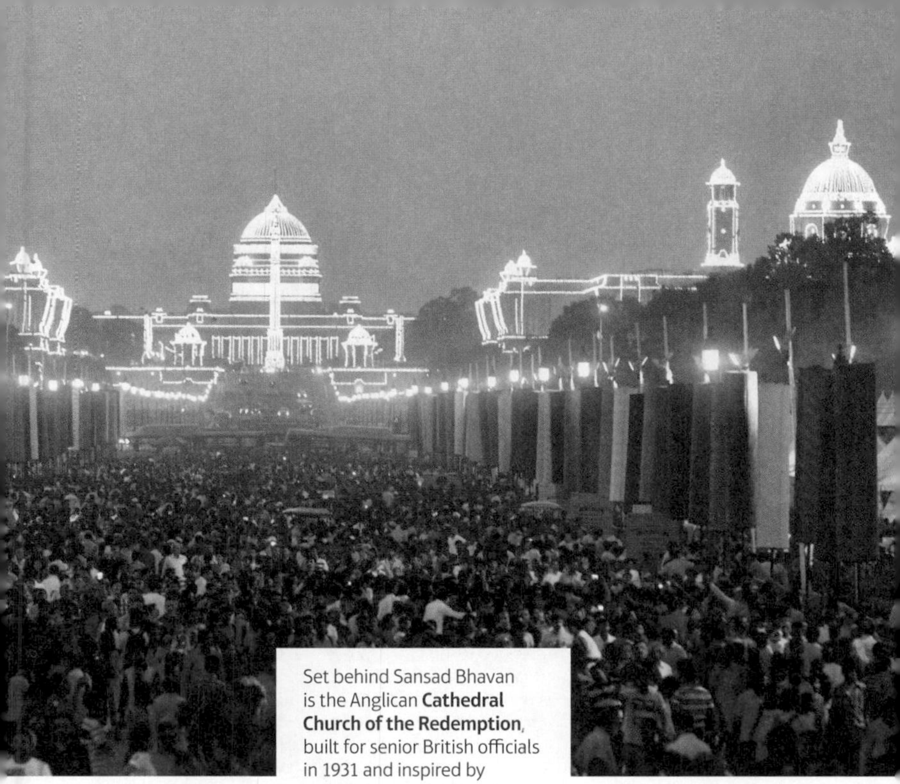

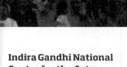

Set behind Sansad Bhavan is the Anglican **Cathedral Church of the Redemption**, built for senior British officials in 1931 and inspired by Palladio's graceful Church of Il Redentore in Venice.

Cathedral Church of the Redemption
Central Secretariat
9am–6pm daily theredemptionchurch.org

10

Crafts Museum

D4 Bhairon Marg Pragati Maidan 10am–5pm Tue–Sun nationalcraftsmuseum.nic.in

Located in a sprawling building designed by Charles Correa, the Crafts Museum is also charmingly surrounded by traditional village dwellings. It honours India's indigenous crafts – from intricate tribal folk paintings and delicate embroideries, to exquisitely carved stonework and bronze figures of Shiva. Highlights among the museum's 20,000 pieces include the life-sized wooden Bhuta figures from Karnataka and the beautiful architecture of the Kulla house.

REPUBLIC DAY PARADE

Ever since 1950, when India became a republic, this lively parade on 26 January has always attracted large crowds. Soldiers and sailors, war veterans and school children, and even elephants and camels, march down Rajpath. Especially popular are the folk dancers and the floats representing each state of the country. A flypast by the Indian Air Force signals the end of the colourful parade.

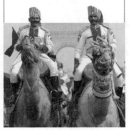

↑ The giant, fixed instruments making up the 18th-century observatory at Jantar Mantar

⑪ Jantar Mantar

📍 C3 🚪 Sansad Marg Ⓜ Janpath ⏰ 6am-6pm daily 🌐 delhitourism.gov.in

Sawai Jai Singh II of Jaipur, a keen astronomer, built this observatory – one of the five he constructed – in 1724 to calculate planetary positions and alignments, in order to perform sacred rituals at propitious moments.

Jantar Mantar's instruments are large and fixed, making them resistant to vibration and therefore more exact. The Samrat Yantra, a right-angled triangle whose hypotenuse is parallel to the earth's axis, is a gigantic sundial, with two brick quadrants on either side of it to measure the sun's shadow. The Ram Yantra reads the altitude of the sun, and the Jai Prakash Yantra, which was invented by Jai Singh II himself, verifies the time of the spring equinox.

⑫ Lakshmi Narayan Mandir

📍 B3 🚪 Mandir Marg Ⓜ RK Ashram Marg ⏰ 4:30am-9pm daily (closes for lunch)

This remarkable temple, built in 1938 by the industrialist

B D Birla, was one of the first to do away with caste restrictions – Mahatma Gandhi attended its first puja (prayer ritual). The Birla Mandir, as it is popularly known, features images of Vishnu and his wife Lakshmi in its main shrine. Subsidiary shrines around the courtyard are inscribed with verses from sacred Hindu texts and decorated with scenes from the great epics, the *Mahabharata* and *Ramayana*.

⑬ Nehru Memorial Museum and Library

📍 B5 🚪 Teen Murti Marg Ⓜ Lok Kalyan Marg ⏰ 9am-5:30pm Tue-Sun 🔒 Public hols 🌐 nehru memorial.nic.in

Originally built in 1930 as the residence of the Commander-in-Chief of the British Indian Army, this beautiful building became the residence of Jawaharlal Nehru, India's first prime minister, in 1947. It was converted into a museum and library after his death in 1964. Nehru's bedroom and study, still exactly as he left them, reflect his austere yet elegant personality and his eclectic taste in books.

The grounds are also home to the **Nehru Planetarium** and the square, three-arched

Kushak Mahal, a 14th-century hunting lodge built by Sultan Feroze Shah Tughlaq.

On the roundabout in front of the house stands the Teen Murti ("Three Statues"), a memorial dedicated to the Indian soldiers who died in World War I.

Nehru Planetarium
📞 (011) 2301 4504 ⏰ Shows: 11:30am & 3pm Tue-Sun 🔒 Public hols

⑭ Lodi Gardens

📍 C5 🚪 Entrance on Lodi Rd & South End Rd Ⓜ Jor Bagh ⏰ Sunrise-sunset daily

Landscaped at the behest of Lady Willingdon, the vicereine, in 1936, the park acts as a "green lung" for the people of Delhi. Its tree-lined pathways, well-kept lawns and flower-beds are laid out around the imposing 15th-century tombs of the Sayyid and Lodi dynasties, Delhi's last sultans. Many of them still have traces of the original turquoise tilework and calligraphy.

Many of these tombs are charmingly graceful, such as that of Muhammad Shah (r 1434–45), the third ruler of the Sayyid dynasty, said to be the oldest tomb in the garden. The largest of the structures is the dominant Bara Gumbad ("Big Dome") with an attached mosque built in 1494, and a guesthouse.

15 ⊘

Purana Qila

◉ D4 🏛 Mathura Rd
Ⓜ Pragati Maidan ⏱ 7am–5pm daily 🌐 delhitourism.gov.in

Purana Qila, literally "Old Fort", stands on an ancient site that has been continuously occupied since 1000 BC. The brooding ramparts of the fort now enclose the remains of the sixth city of Delhi, Dinpanah (p105), which was begun by the second Mughal emperor, Humayun, who ascended the throne in 1530. But this stage of his reign was short: in 1540 he was overthrown by the Afghan chieftain Sher Shah Suri. Sher

Shah added several new structures and renamed the citadel Shergarh ("Lion's Fort"). After Sher Shah's death and numerous battles, Humayun regained the throne. Of the many palaces, barracks and other edifices built by these two rulers, only two remain standing today. The mosque, Qila-i-Kuhna, was built by Sher Shah in 1541, and is an elegantly proportioned structure with fine decorative inlay work in red and white marble and slate. Humayun's library, south of the mosque, is a double-storeyed octagonal tower of red sandstone. The building is crowned by an elaborate *chhatri* (open pavilion), which is supported by eight pillars. This was the tragic spot where the devout emperor, hurrying to kneel on the steps for the evening prayer, missed his footing, tumbled, struck his head and died in January 1556. He is now buried in

The ramparts of Purana Qila and (inset) the fort's ↓ Bara Darwaza gate

💬 INSIDER TIP
Sunset at Lodi Gardens

While visitors may come to Lodi Gardens for the majestic Mughal tombs, local Delhites instead descend on the gardens for a sunset walk around the running track.

Delhi's remarkable Humayun's Tomb (p92), which was built by the emperor's chief wife in his memory. The tomb can be seen from the southern gate of the complex.

The ramparts of the Purana Qila have three gateways, of which the imposing Talaagi Darwaza on the western wall is the main entrance.

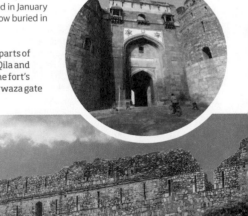

The innovative, lotus-inspired architecture of the Baha'i House of Worship

16

Baha'i House of Worship

📍B2 🏛Bahapur, Kalkaji Ⓜ Kalkaji Mandir 🕐Apr-Sep 9am-6pm Tue-Sun (to 5pm Oct-Mar) 🚫Public hols 🌐bahaihouseofworship.in

More commonly known as the Lotus Temple, the beautiful Baha'i House of Worship was designed by the Iranian architect Fariburz Sahba and completed in 1986. The building looks like a lotus – hence the name – with 27 white marble petals forming the exterior. The edifice is circled by nine pools and 92 ha (227 acres) of green lawns. Followers of all faiths are invited to attend the daily 15-minute services (at 10am, noon, 3pm and 5pm) in the lofty auditorium.

17

Sanskriti Museums

📍A2 🏛Anandgram, Mehrauli-Gurgaon Rd Ⓜ Arjan Garh 🕐10am-5pm Tue-Sun 🚫Public hols 🌐sanskritifoundation.org

These three unusual museums respectively focus on textiles, terracotta and everyday art.

Set amid spacious, beautifully landscaped grounds, exhibits are displayed in the garden and in specially constructed rural huts. The collections celebrate Indian crafts: from objects that demonstrate the utilitarian beauty of everyday art including combs, lamps, toys, kitchenware and foot-scrubbers to terracotta objects from all over India, including pots made with techniques unchanged for centuries and figures of South Indian village deities. The purpose of the charitable trust that runs the museums is to showcase local art and artisans.

> 💬 **INSIDER TIP**
> **Qawwali Performances**
>
> Visit the Nizamuddin Complex at sunset (5-9:30pm Fri-Wed) and head to the shrine to catch breathtaking and uplifting performances of sacred Sufi singing, called qawwali.

> **Nizamuddin belonged to a fraternity of Sufi mystics, the Chishtis, respected for their austerity, piety and disdain for material desires.**

18

Nizamuddin Complex

📍D5 🏛Old Nizamuddin Bazaar, Nizamuddin East Ⓜ Jangpura 🕐Dargah: 5am-10:30pm daily 🌐nizamuddinaulia.org

This medieval settlement, or *basti*, is named after Sheikh Hazrat Nizamuddin Auliya, whose grave is located here. Nizamuddin belonged to a fraternity of Sufi mystics, the Chishtis, respected for their austerity, piety and disdain for material desires. His daily assemblies drew both the rich and the poor, who believed that he was a "friend of God", who would intercede on their behalf on Judgement Day. He died in 1325, but his disciples call him a *zinda pir* (living spirit), who continues to heed their pleas. A three-day Urs is observed, and moving qawwalis sung, on the anniversary of his death.

Within the settlement, a busy and winding alley leads to the saint's grave (dargah). It is

crowded with mendicants and lined with stalls selling flowers, *chadars* (ceremonial cloths) and prints of Mecca. The main congregational area is a marble pavilion (rebuilt in 1562). Women are denied entry beyond the outer verandah but may peer through *jalis* into the small, dark chamber where the saint's grave lies draped with a rose petal strewn cloth and surrounded by imams, who continuously recite verses from the Qur'an.

Across the western side of the open courtyard is the Jama't Khana Mosque, built in 1325. To its north is a stepwell, which was constructed in secret while the fort of Tughlaqabad was being built, as the then ruler of Delhi, Ghiyasuddin Tughlaq, had banned building elsewhere.

The early-16th-century Tomb of Atgah Khan is to the north. A powerful minister in Emperor Akbar's court, he was murdered by Adham Khan, a political rival. The open marble pavilion, Chaunsath Khamba ("64 pillars"), is close by and just outside is an enclosure

→

Praying outside the tomb of Sheikh Hazrat Nizamuddin Auliya, Nizamuddin Complex

containing the grave of Mirza Ghalib (1786–1869). The verses of Ghalib, one of Delhi's greatest poets, are still recited.

19

Tughlaqabad

B2 **Off Mehrauli-Badarpur Rd** **Govind Puri** **Daily**

The third of Delhi's early capitals (p105), Tughlaqabad is dominated by its spectacular fort, built by Ghiyasuddin Tughlaq in the early 1300s. The fort's rubble-built walls, following the contours of the hill, survive intact all along the 7-km (4-mile) perimeter. Rising from the citadel to the right of the main entrance are the ruins of the Vijay Mandal ("Tower of Victory").

The smaller, adjoining Adilabad Fort was built by Muhammad bin Tughlaq, who is said to have killed his father Ghiyasuddin only five years into his reign by contriving to have a gateway collapse on him. Both are buried in Ghiyasuddin's Tomb, attached to the Tughlaqabad Fort by a causeway that crosses the dammed waters of a lake. This squat building is inlaid with white marble and has sloping walls, a pioneering and distinctive style that marks Tughlaq architecture.

EAT

Indian Accent
Award-winning celebrity chef Manish Mehotra serves up fusion food like wild mushroom kofta, chicken-tikka meatballs and tamarind crab.

D5 **The Lodhi, Lodi Road, New Delhi** **indianaccent.com**

₹₹₹

Bukhara
A hardy perennial of the Delhi dining scene, Bukhara offers hearty food from the northwestern frontier.

A4 **ITC Maurya, Sardar Patel Marg, Chanakyapuri** **itchotels.in**

₹₹₹

Naivedyam
A beautiful south Indian restaurant with columns and murals.

A2 **1 Hauz Khas Village** **naivedyam restaurants.in**

₹₹₹

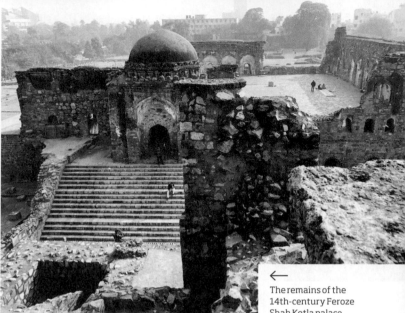

← The remains of the 14th-century Feroze Shah Kotla palace

20

Feroze Shah Kotla

📍 D3 🚌 Bahadur Shah Zafar Marg Ⓜ Pragati Maidan 🕙 10am–7pm daily

Now an atmospheric ruin, Feroze Shah Kotla was the palace complex of Ferozabad, Delhi's fifth city (p105) and was built by Feroze Shah Tughlaq, an indefatigable builder.

Entry is from the gate next to the Indian Express Building. At one end of a walled enclosure stand the roofless ruins of the Jama Masjid, which was once Delhi's largest mosque. According to popular legend, Timur, the Mongol conqueror who sacked Delhi in 1398, came here to say his prayers.

Next to the mosque are the remains of a pyramidal structure, topped by one of the Mauryan emperor Ashoka's polished stone pillars. Brought from the Punjab, it was placed here in 1356 by Feroze Shah, who built Delhi's fifth city. It was from the inscriptions on this pillar that James Prinsep deciphered the Brahmi script, a forerunner of the modern Devanagari, in 1837.

Opposite the ruins of Feroze Shah Kotla is Khuni Darwaza (the "Bloodstained Gate"), which was built by Sher Shah Suri as one of the gates to his city, Delhi's sixth (p105). This was where the Emperor Bahadur Shah Zafar's sons were shot by Lieutenant Hodson after the 1857 War of Independence.

21

Around Kashmiri Gate

📍 C1 🚌 Between Nicholson Rd, Ramlal Chandok Marg & Church Rd Ⓜ Kashmiri Gate

Some of the most bitter fighting of the War of Independence in 1857 (p76) was fought in the short stretch between this landmark and the Old Delhi General Post Office (GPO) when the city of Delhi lay under siege by the British. A final assault on 14 September 1857 led to the blasting of the gate by British engineers and miners, who won this battle. A plaque on the gate's western side marks this significant event. In the 1920s, this area was a favourite haunt of the British residents living in nearby Civil Lines.

The historic **St James' Church**, Delhi's oldest, was consecrated in 1836 by Colonel James Skinner. A flamboyant adventurer of mixed parentage who was rejected by the British Army, Skinner raised his own cavalry regiment who eventually joined the army and fought with distinction. Once, when Skinner lay dying on a battlefield, he vowed to build a church if he survived. St James' Church is the result, an unusual structure in the shape of a cross, topped by an imposing eight-leafed dome.

St James' Church
🏛 Lothian Rd 🕙 Church: 9:30am–12:45pm & 2:30–4:30pm daily; services in English: 8:30am Sun (summer), 9am Sun (winter) 🌐 stjameschurchdelhi.com

22
Coronation Memorial

A1 **S of NH1 Bypass** **GTB Nagar**

The memorial marks the spot where the Royal Durbar was held in 1911 to proclaim the accession of George V as King-Emperor of India. More than 100,000 people thronged to see the King-Emperor and Queen-Empress sit beneath a golden dome mounted on a crimson canopy. A large sandstone obelisk commemorates this coronation, but it is now a dusty and forlorn spot, surrounded by statues of former viceroys, including Lords Hardinge and Willingdon (known for their role in the construction of New Delhi). Towering over them all is the huge statue of the King-Emperor himself, which was removed from the Statue Canopy at India Gate and installed here in the 1960s.

About 3 km (2 miles) southeast is a forested area known as the Northern Ridge, cut through by Ridge Road and Rani Jhansi Road. At its southern end lies the Mutiny Memorial (known locally as Ajitgarh), a Victorian Gothic tower dedicated to both British and Indian soldiers who died in the 1857 War for Independence. It has panoramic views of Old Delhi.

Running parallel to the Northern Ridge is the Delhi University area; the distinguished St Stephen's College was designed by Walter George, who also worked on New Delhi, in 1938.

THE OLD SPICE MARKET IN DELHI

The spice market of Khari Baoli, which spreads around a mosque built by one of Emperor Shah Jahan's wives, is the oldest and largest wholesale spice market in India, where visitors can find spices from all over the country. It has been running since the 17th century and many stalls have been in the same families for generations.

23
Raj Ghat

D2 **Mahatma Gandhi Rd** **Delhi Gate** **6am-7pm daily (prayer meetings 5pm Fri)**

India's most potent symbol of nationhood, Raj Ghat is the site of Mahatma Gandhi's cremation. A black granite platform inscribed with his last words, *He Ram!* ("Oh God") now stands here. The only splash of colour comes from the garlands of orange marigolds draped over the platform. On Gandhi's birthday (2 October) and the anniversary of his death (30 January), the nation's leaders gather here for prayer meetings.

Just across the road, the **National Gandhi Museum** is filled with memorabilia, including Gandhi's letters and diaries. A plaque on the wall sets out his simple philosophy: "Non-violence is the pitting of one's whole soul against the will of the tyrant… it is then possible for a single individual to defy the might of an unjust empire."

National Gandhi Museum
9:30am–5:30pm Tue-Sun Public hols gandhimuseum.org

24
Connaught Place

C3 **Rajiv Chowk**

Opened in 1931, and named after the Duke of Connaught, this shopping complex, with its Palladian archways and stuccoed colonnades, was designed by Robert Tor Russell as a deliberate contrast to the chaos of an Indian bazaar. Its arcades and pavements spill over with *paan* kiosks, book stalls and shoeshine boys, while the eclectic mix of shops, normally open 10:30am until 8pm Monday to Saturday, is interspersed with eateries and cinema halls where you can escape from the city's heat. Though no longer Delhi's premier shopping area, its shaded arcades are pleasant to stroll through. The nearby Central Park features an amphitheatre, 21 fountains and plush lawns.

←

The towering Gothic lines of the Mutiny Memorial, erected in 1863

Safdarjung's Tomb reflected in the water, and *(inset)* the central chamber

25

Safdarjung's Tomb

◉ B5 **☖ Aurobindo Marg** **Ⓜ Jor Bagh** **◷ Sunrise-sunset daily** **ⓦ delhi tourism.gov.in**

This is the last of Delhi's garden tombs, built in 1754 for Safdarjung, the prime minister of Muhammad Shah, the Mughal emperor between 1719 and 1748. The marble used to build Safdarjung's Tomb was allegedly stripped from the tomb of Abdur Rahim Khan-i-Khanan in Nizamuddin. Approached by an ornate gateway, the top storey of which houses the library of the Archaeological Survey of India (ASI), the tomb has an exaggerated dome and stands in a garden cut by water channels into four parts. Its façade is ornamented with plaster carving and the central chamber has some fine stone inlay work on the floor.

26

The Ridge

◉ A4 **☖ Upper Ridge Rd** **Ⓜ Central Secretariat** **◷ Sunrise-sunset daily**

Delhi's ridge, the last outcrop of the Aravalli Hills extending northwards from Rajasthan, is a lush green area that runs across the city from southwest to northeast. The area was originally developed by Feroze Shah Tughlaq in the late 14th century as his hunting resort. The ruins of his many lodges can still be seen here. This green belt of undulating, rocky terrain is covered by dense scrub forest consisting mainly of laburnum *(Cassia fistula)*, kikar *(Acacia arabica)* and flame of the forest *(Butea monosperma)*, interspersed with colourful splashes of bougainvillea.

A large area in the centre is now the **Buddha Jayanti Park**, a well-manicured enclave with paved paths, where pipal *(Ficus religiosa)* trees abound. On a small ornamental island is a simple sandstone pavilion shading the large gilt-covered statue of the Buddha, installed by the 14th Dalai Lama in 1993. An inscription nearby quotes the Dalai Lama: "Human beings have the capacity

> **An inscription nearby quotes the Dalai Lama: "Human beings have the capacity to bequeathe to future generations a world that is truly human".**

the Royal Academy's Burlington House. After its return, it was housed in Rashtrapati Bhavan's Durbar Hall until the present building, built of the same beige and pink stone as the imposing new capital, was completed in 1960. The large museum's collection of Indus Valley relics and Central Asian treasures from the Silk Route is considered among the finest in the world.

28 🗺️ 🏛️

National Rail Museum

📍 A2 🏠 Chanakyapuri
🕐 10am–5pm Tue–Sun
🌐 nrmindia.com

India's railway network boasts some astonishing statistics. It has a route length of 64,460 km (40,054 miles) and tracks that cover 113,994 km (70,833 miles). There are about 7,500 stations, and 25 million people travel daily on the 12,600 passenger trains across the country.

This museum encapsulates the history of Indian railways. Steam locomotive enthusiasts will appreciate the collection that traces the development of the Indian railways from 1853, when the first 34 km (21 miles) of railway between Bombay (now Mumbai) and Thane were laid. Items on display inside include the skull of an elephant that collided with a mail train at Golkara in 1894, and a realistic model of an 1868 first-class passenger coach with separate compartments for servants.

to bequeathe to future generations a world that is truly human". Every year in May, large crowds of Buddhist devotees celebrate Buddha Jayanti here.

Buddha Jayanti Park
🕐 Sunrise–sunset daily

27 🗺️ 🗓️ 🖥️ 🏛️

National Museum

📍 C4 🏠 Janpath Ⓜ️ Udyog Bhawan 🕐 10am–6pm Tue–Sun 🚫 Public hols 🌐 nationalmuseumindia. gov.in

Five millennia of Indian history can be seen at the National Museum, which has a collection of more than 200,000 pieces of Indian art. A core collection of about 1,000 artifacts was sent to London in 1948–9 for an exhibition at

→

Vintage, flaming-red locomotive on display at the National Rail Museum

STAY

The Imperial
With exceptional restaurants and art collections on site, this elegant hotel captures the history of the city.

📍 C3 🏠 Janpath
🌐 theimperialindia.com

₹₹₹

───

Haveli Hauz Khas
This stylish boutique hotel is in a residential area of Delhi, close to Hauz Khas village.

📍 A2 🏠 P5 Hauz Khas Enclave
🌐 havelihauzkhas.com

₹₹₹

───

Hotel Broadway
Characterful rooms in the heart of Old Delhi, plus a Kashmiri restaurant with delightfully eccentric decor.

📍 D2 🏠 4/15 A Asaf Ali Road
🌐 hotelbroadway delhi.com

₹₹₹

Outside are several steam locomotives built in England in the late 19th century, and the salon that carried the Prince of Wales (later King Edward VII) on his travels during the 1876 Royal Durbar.

29

Hauz Khas

Q A2 **A** W of Aurobindo Marg **M** Hauz Khas

Once the site of Delhi's oldest university (*madrasa*), Hauz Khas village is a vibrant and, unlike most places in the city, easy-to-navigate area. Wander the labyrinthine streets to find gems like the Delhi Art Gallery, housing modern art from across India, and an ever-changing global restaurant scene. The deer park comes alive with joggers, yogis and drum circles in the early morning and at sunset. The ruins of the university buildings are also well worth a visit.

30

Kingdom of Dreams

Q A2 **A** Sector 29, Gurugram **M** IFFCO Chowk **C** 12:30pm–midnight Tue–Sun **W** kingdomofdreams.in

An immersive theatre experience, the Kingdom of Dreams offers a year-round *mela* (carnival) atmosphere. There are 14 state pavilions, live arts and crafts, themed village restaurants and dance

performances on street corners – it is a Bollywood-flavoured Disneyland. Here you can visit all corners of India without ever leaving the city, experiencing backwater Keralan vibes and Goan taverns. The main auditorium seats over 800 people, and there are regular Bollywood-style shows here and in another, smaller, amphitheatre. Book ahead for a variety of shows, including *Zangoora* – the first original live Bollywood musical, telling the tale of a gypsy who falls in love with a princess.

31

Jahanpanah

Q B2 **A** S of Panchsheel Park **M** Hauz Khas

In the heart of Jahanpanah, Muhammad bin Tughlaq's capital, stands Begumpuri Mosque, which was thought to have been built by Khan-i-Jahan Junan Shah. (Ask specifically for the old mosque, as a new one is located nearby.) The mosque is remarkable for its 44 domes that surmount the cloisters surrounding the central courtyard; although mainly well preserved, parts are now rubble. This mosque

has also functioned as a treasury, a granary and a general meeting place. To the north is the palace of Bijay Mandal, from where, according to the 14th-century Arab traveller Ibn Batuta, Muhammad bin Tughlaq reviewed his troops. The upper platform offers a grand view of Delhi, encompassing Qutb Minar to Humayun's Tomb.

← Visitors at Kingdom of Dreams, renowned for its live Bollywood shows

↑ The Red Fort, the centre of power in Shahjahanabad, Delhi's seventh city

THE SEVEN CITIES OF DELHI

Delhi's famous "seven cities" range from the 12th-century Qila Rai Pithora, built by Prithviraj Chauhan, to the imperial Shahjahanabad, constructed by the Mughals in the 17th century. Each of these cities comprised forts erected by powerful sultans, and the settlements that grew up around them. Today, Delhi is a medley of the ruins of these cities, and an ever-expanding, modern concrete jungle.

QILA RAI PITHORA

Qila Rai Pithora, the first of Delhi's seven cities, was erected by the Chauhans in about 1180. In 1192, it was captured by Qutbuddin Aibak.

SIRI

Delhi's second city, situated near the Siri Fort Auditorium and the adjacent Shahpur Jat village, was constructed by Alauddin Khilji around 1303.

↑ The ruined walls of Delhi's first city, Qila Rai Pithora

TUGHLAQABAD

Tughlaqabad, a dramatic fort on the foothills of the Aravallis, was Delhi's third city, built during Ghiyasuddin Tughlaq's four-year reign (r 1320–24).

JAHANPANAH

Jahanpanah was built by Muhammad bin Tughlaq (r 1325–51) as a walled enclosure to link Qila Rai Pithora and Siri. The ruins stand near Chiragh.

FEROZABAD

Stretching north from Hauz Khas to the banks of the Yamuna, Ferozabad is Delhi's fifth city, established by Feroze Shah Tughlaq (r 1351–88).

↑ The well-preserved remains of Siri, near Hauz Kaus

DINPANAH

Purana Qila, the citadel of the sixth city, Dinpanah, was founded by Humayun, but captured by Afghan chieftain, Sher Shah Suri (r 1540–45).

SHAHJAHANABAD

Delhi's seventh city was built from 1638 to 1649 by Shah Jahan and became the Mughal capital.

↑ The striking main gate to the sixth city's fortress

A SHORT WALK
CHANDNI CHOWK

Distance 2 km (1 mile) **Nearest Metro** Chandni Chowk
Time 30 minutes

Once the most elegant boulevard in the Mughal capital of Shahjahanabad, Chandni Chowk ("Moonlit Square"), laid out in 1648, had a canal running through it, and was lined with grand shops and mansions. Today, Chandni Chowk is the heart of Old Delhi, which built up around it. It is a bustling area where religious and commercial activity mix easily. At the entrance to Chandni Chowk is the Digambar Jain Temple. Built in 1656, it is the first of many shrines along the boulevard's length.

*There is a box for donations at the **Bird Hospital**.*

*In 1675, Guru Tegh Bahadur, the ninth Sikh guru, was beheaded at **Sisganj Gurdwara**.*

START

CHANDNI CHOWK

Sunehri Masjid (*"Golden Mosque"*), built in 1722, is famous for its three gilt domes. On 22 March 1739, Persian invader Nadir Shah stood on its roof as Delhi's citizens were massacred.

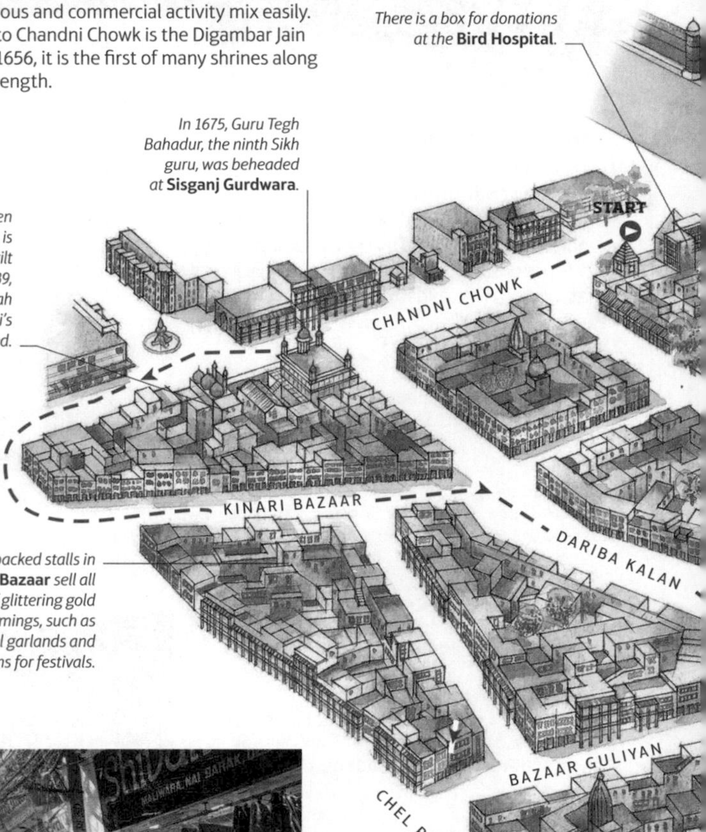

KINARI BAZAAR

DARIBA KALAN

*Tightly packed stalls in **Kinari Bazaar** sell all manner of glittering gold and silver trimmings, such as braids, tinsel garlands and turbans for festivals.*

BAZAAR GULIYAN

CHEL PURI

Shiv Temple

← A rickshaw driving past textile shops in bustling Chandni Chowk market

Locator Map
For more detail see p82

↑ Old Delhi's iconic Jama Masjid, thronging
with visitors and the devoted

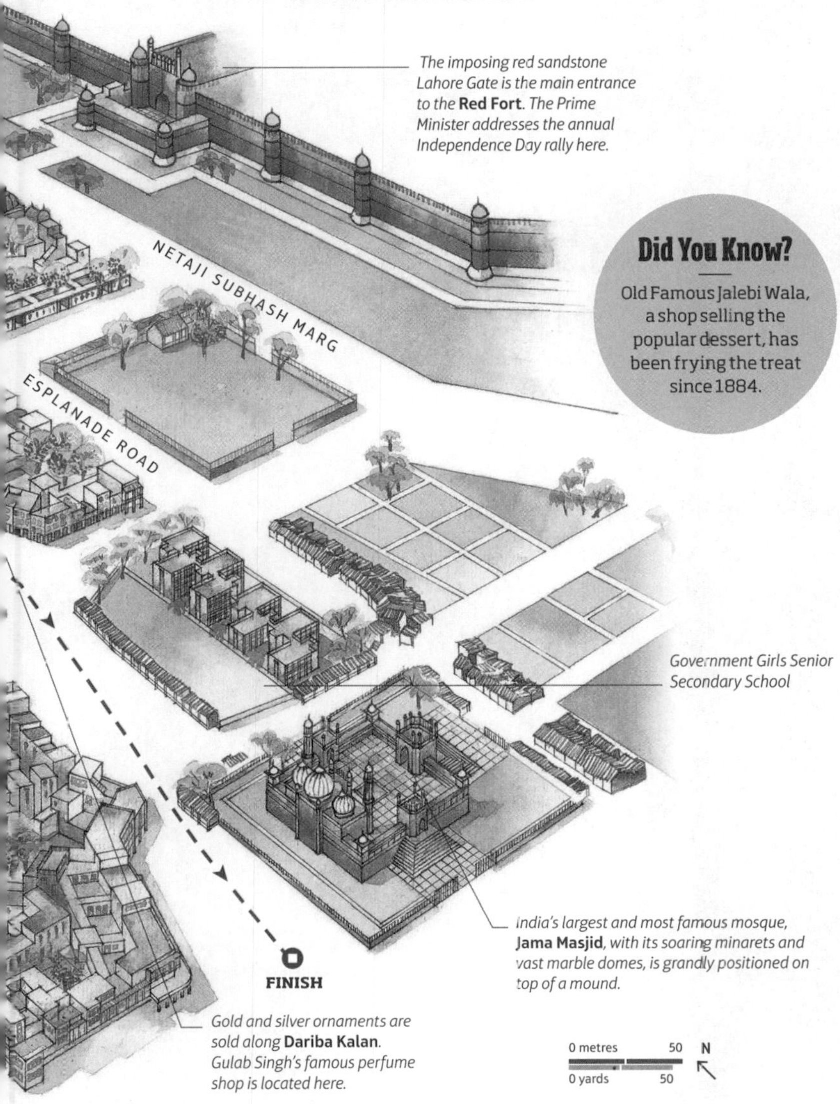

The imposing red sandstone
Lahore Gate is the main entrance
to the **Red Fort**. The Prime
Minister addresses the annual
Independence Day rally here.

NETAJI SUBHASH MARG

ESPLANADE ROAD

Did You Know?

Old Famous Jalebi Wala,
a shop selling the
popular dessert, has
been frying the treat
since 1884.

Government Girls Senior
Secondary School

FINISH

India's largest and most famous mosque,
Jama Masjid, with its soaring minarets and
vast marble domes, is grandly positioned on
top of a mound.

Gold and silver ornaments are
sold along **Dariba Kalan**.
Gulab Singh's famous perfume
shop is located here.

0 metres   50   N
0 yards   50

Looking over the city of Jodhpur from the cenotaph of Jaswant Thada

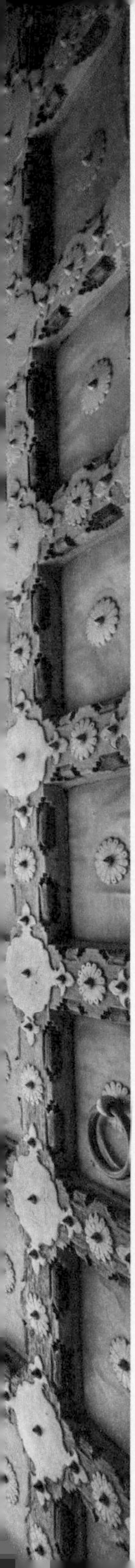

RAJASTHAN

This is a place where history comes to life. No state in India has so many magnificent palaces and forts, colourful festivals and bazaars as Rajasthan. It was one of the cradles of the early Indus Valley Civilization, but the richest period of this state's story can be seen in the three great kingdoms of Jaisalmer, Jodhpur and Bikaner, who ruled the endless stretches of the Thar Desert in the state's west for hundreds of years. In the 15th and 16th centuries these Hindu kingdoms faced increasing incursions from successive Mughal rulers, and many of the state's forts eventually fell to invaders. While the British gained control here in the 19th century, they allied with local rulers, who remained on their thrones until the modern day state of Rajasthan was formed after India gained independence from Britain in 1947. Today, many of the descendents of the maharajas still occupy old palaces and forts, and the rich tapestry of this history lives on.

RAJASTHAN

Must Sees

1. Jaipur
2. Amber Fort
3. Keoladeo Ghana National Park
4. Jodhpur
5. Jaisalmer
6. Udaipur
7. Ranthambhore National Park

Experience More

8. Pushkar
9. Deeg
10. Alwar
11. Shekhawati
12. Sariska National Park
13. Phalodi
14. Bikaner
15. Ajmer
16. Bundi
17. Nagaur
18. Kumbhalgarh
19. Mount Abu
20. Ranakpur
21. Kota
22. Chittorgarh
23. Dungarpur

GUJARAT
p374

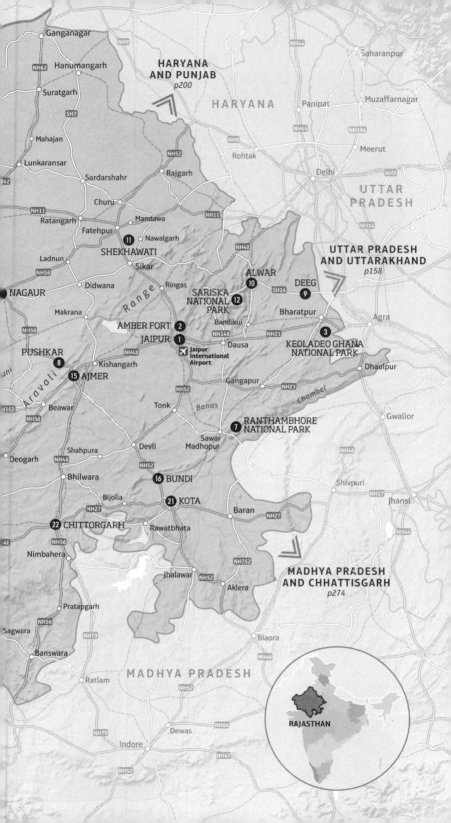

❶

JAIPUR

🏠 Jaipur district; 270 km (170 miles) S of Delhi ✈ 15 km (9 miles) S of city centre 🚃 🚌 ℹ Paryatan Bhavan, Mirza Ismail Rd; www.tourism.rajasthan.gov.in/jaipur.html

A labyrinth of bazaars, opulent palaces and historic sights, Jaipur is known as the Pink City because of the rosy hue of its buildings. One of the most popular destinations in Rajasthan, its old walled city contains jewels such as the City Palace and the Hawa Mahal.

① Govind Dev Temple

🏠 Jaleb Chowk (at City Palace) ⏰ 4:30am-9:30pm daily 🌐 govinddevji.net

The flute-playing Lord Krishna (also known as Govind Dev) is worshipped at this unusual temple. The image of this god originally came from the Govindeoji Temple in Vrindavan (p188), but was brought to Amber (p124), then the capital of Jaipur's ruling family, in the late 17th century to save it from the zeal of the Mughal emperor Aurangzeb, who was known for his religious intolerance.

It is believed this temple was once a garden pavilion called Suraj Mahal, where Sawai Jai Singh II lived while his dream-city, Jaipur, was being built. Legend has it that one night the king awoke from his sleep to find himself in the presence of Krishna, who asked that his *devasthan* ("divine residence") be returned to him, so Jai Singh moved to the Chandra Mahal, at the opposite end of the garden, and installed the image in the temple as the guardian deity of Jaipur's rulers. The temple has seven artis throughout the day where pilgrims can worship this incarnation of Krishna.

Just behind the temple is the 18th-century Jai Niwas Bagh, a Mughal-style garden with fountains and water channels. Towards the north is the Badal Mahal, a lovely hunting pavilion.

② 🎨 🎭 Hawa Mahal

🏠 Sireh Deori Bazaar ⏰ 9am-5pm daily 🚫 Public hols

The pink façade of the fanciful Hawa Mahal ("Palace of Winds") has become the icon of Jaipur. Erected in 1799 by Sawai Pratap Singh (r 1778–1803), the five-storey-high structure is only one room deep with walls not more than 20 cm (8 inches) thick, designed to enable the ladies of the harem to watch the lively streets below while remaining unseen. Dedicated to Lord Krishna, the tiered Baroque-like structure was meant, when seen from afar, to look like the crown that often adorns the god's head.

> 💬 INSIDER TIP
> **Find Hidden Jaipur**
>
> Explore Jaipur on a wonderful walking tour with Virasat Experiences (www.virasatexperiences.com), who take visitors to see hidden temples, taste the best samosas and meet skilled crafts-men and jewellers.

Hawa Mahal, a whimsical addition to the state's architectural vocabulary

from *chaugan*, a Persian form of polo played with a curved stick. The area, once used for festival processions and wrestling matches, still hosts major festivals.

④
Albert Hall Museum

🏛 Ram Niwas Bagh 🕐 9am–5pm & 7–10pm daily 🚫 Public hols 🌐 alberthall jaipur.gov.in

The most imposing treasure at this grand museum is one of the world's largest Persian garden carpets (dating from 1632), which can be viewed on request in the Durbar Hall. The museum also has an extensive collection of paintings dating back to the 1500s.

③
Chaugan Stadium

🏛 Gangori Bazaar Road, Tripolia Bazaar

This large open area near the City Palace derives its name

Must See

EAT

Palladio
With an opulent interior reminiscent of a maharaja's palace, Palladio serves food and drinks inspired by Italy.

🏛 Narain Niwas Palace Hotel, Kanota Bagh 🌐 bar-palladio.com

₹₹₹

Peacock
This popular rooftop restaurant has great views and serves dishes from around the world.

🏛 Hotel Pearl Palace, 51 Hathroi Fort, Ajmer Rd 🌐 hotelpearl palace.com

₹₹₹

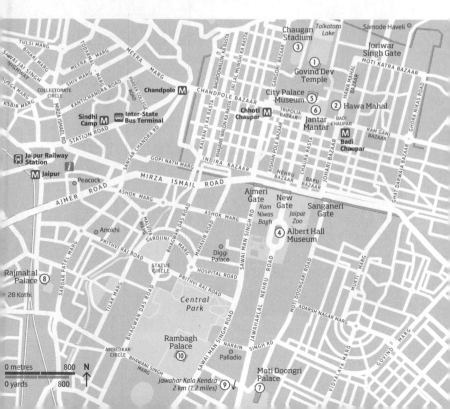

CITY PALACE MUSEUM

📍 **City Palace Complex** 🕐 **9:30am–5:30pm daily** 🚫 **Second day of Holi** 🌐 **royaljaipur.in**

EXPERIENCE Rajasthan

The Maharaja Sawai Man Singh II Museum, popularly known as the City Palace Museum, occupies Jaipur's City Palace. Built between 1729 and 1732 during the reign of Maharaja Sawai Jai Singh II, the palace lies at the heart of the city and has been home to the rulers of Jaipur since the 19th century. The sprawling complex is a superb blend of Rajput and Mughal architecture, with open, airy Mughal-style public buildings leading to private apartments.

The City Palace Museum's treasures are divided across five galleries – the Textile Gallery, Sabha Niwas (also called the Diwan-i-Aam), Sarvato Bhadra, Sileh Khana, and the Painting and Photography gallery – and provide a splendid introduction to Jaipur's princely past, and its fascinating arts and crafts. In the Textile Gallery are ornate garments, including extravagant medieval saris. The former ceremonial hall, Sabha Niwas, displays rare Mughal and Rajput miniature paintings, while Sarvato Bhadra is home to two giant, Guinness-World-Record-breaking silver urns. Sileh Khana houses a fine collection of antique weapons. In the Painting and Photography gallery, the illustrated manuscripts detailing the famous Hindu story of the Durga Saptashati and Bhagvata Puran are the star of the show. Also within the complex is the wonderfully opulent Chandra Mahal palace.

Visitors enter the palace's brightly coloured, arcaded courtyard via the Rajendra Pol gateway *(inset)*

RAJASTHANI MINIATURES

The vivid, intricate paintings of Rajasthan's princely states grew out of illustrated Jain and Hindu sacred texts. Originally, they depicted mainly religious themes, in bold lines and bright primary colours. During the 17th and 18th centuries, the lines became more delicate, and the range of colours and themes wider. Several distinct schools of style evolved, usually showing human figures in profile and in different colours, while seasons, flowers and animals are used symbolically to express moods.

← The finely painted Peacock Gate, representing autumn and dedicated to Lord Vishnu

→ Blue and white flourishes decorating the City Palace's walls and pillars

Did You Know?

The descendents of maharajas of Jaipur still reside in the seven-storey Chandra Mahal.

⑥ 🏛 🏃

JANTAR MANTAR

🏛 Chandni Chowk, outside City Palace 🕘 9am–4:30pm daily 🚫 Public hols
🌐 tourism.rajasthan.gov.in/jantar-mantar.html

A strange collection of circles, walls and stairs, Jantar Mantar is an early observatory. It was built by Sawai Jai Singh II in the early 18th century in order to predict the movements of the sun, moon and planets with the human eye; he had five of these structures built across his kingdom, but the one in Jaipur is the largest and best preserved.

Built between 1728 and 1734, the impressive Jantar Mantar observatory has been described as "the most realistic and logical landscape in stone", its 19 instruments, or yantas (meaning a machine for calculating), resembling a giant sculptural composition. It was constructed on the orders of Sawai Jai Singh II, a keen astronomer who kept abreast of the latest astronomical studies from around the world. Some of the instruments are still used to forecast how hot the summer months will be, as well as the expected date of arrival, duration and intensity of the monsoon, and the possibility of floods and famine.

→

The Krantivrtta, which measured the longitude and latitude of objects in the sky

TOP 5 CALCULATION INSTRUMENTS

Rashivalaya Yantra
This *yantra* is composed of 12 pieces, one for each zodiac sign, and is used by astrologers to draw up horoscopes. It is the only one of its kind.

Ram Yantra
This instrument's readings determine the celestial arc from horizon to zenith, as well as the altitude of the sun.

Laghu Samrat Yantra
This "small sundial" calculates local time to within 20 seconds.

Samrat Yantra
The largest machine on site, this 27-m- (89-ft-) high sundial forecasts the year's crop prospects.

Chakra Yantra
These two circular metal instruments can be used to calculate the angles of stars and planets from the equator.

↑ Rashivalaya Yantra's 12 pieces set in front of the tall Samrat Yantra

←
Illustration of Leo, one of the signs of the Zodiac, at the Rashivalaya Yantra

→
The Narivalaya Yantra, representing the two hemispheres and calculating time according to the solar cycle

⑦
Moti Doongri Palace

🏠 Jawaharlal Nehru Marg
🚫 To the public

A large walled fort astride a hill, Moti Doongri owes its exterior, which resembles a British castle, to Sawai Man Singh II (r 1922–49), who converted the old fort here into a palace. In 1940 he married Princess Gayatri Devi of Cooch Behar, and this palace became the venue for the couple's glittering parties. At the foot

---

of the hill is Lakshmi Narayan Temple, with its beautiful, elaborate carvings.

---

⑧
Rajmahal Palace

🏠 Sardar Patel Marg
🌐 sujanluxury.com

Now a grand hotel, this palace was built in 1739 for Sawai Jai Singh II's favourite queen, Chandra Kumari Ranawatji, who used it as a summer resort. In 1821, it became the official home of the British Resident in Jaipur – but the most memorable phase of its history came when Jaipur's last maharaja, Man Singh II, and his wife Gayatri Devi moved here in 1956. Among the celebrities they entertained were Prince Philip and Jackie Kennedy.

---

⑨ 🖼️
Jawahar Kala Kendra

🏠 Nehru Marg   🕐 Daily
🌐 jawaharkalakendra.rajasthan.gov.in

Designed by the noted Indian architect Charles Correa, this

arts centre is a remarkable example of contemporary Indian architecture. The building was inspired by Jaipur's famous grid system, where the city is organized into nine squares; it has eight connecting buildings (the ninth is a courtyard). The gallery displays a range of textiles, handicrafts and weaponry. Its open-air plaza is used for performances of traditional Rajasthani music.

---

⑩ 🍴
Rambagh Palace

🏠 Bhawani Singh Rd
🌐 tajhotels.com

The Rambagh Palace, now a splendid hotel, was built in 1835 as a small garden pavilion for Ram Singh II's wet nurse. Later, Madho Singh II, Ram Singh II's son, transformed it into a royal playground with a polo field and an indoor pool, surrounded by lush gardens. In 1933, it became the official residence of Madho Singh's heir, Man Singh II, who added a red-and-gold Chinese room, black marble bathrooms and Lalique crystal chandeliers. It became a hotel in 1957.

The splendid lobby of the Rambagh Palace, now a heritage hotel ↑

JAIPUR JEWELLERY

Be it the fabulous rubies and emeralds sported by former maharajas and their queens or the splendid silver and bone ornaments worn by peasants, jewellery is an integral part of Rajasthani culture. Even camels, horses and elephants have specially designed anklets and necklaces. Jaipur is one of the largest ornament-making centres in India, and *meenakari* (enamel work) and *kundankari* (inlay work with gems) are the two traditional techniques for which it is most famous.

STONE CUTTING

Jaipur is a centre of lapidary, specializing in cutting emeralds and diamonds from Africa, South America and various regions of India, which are used in refined *kundankari* work. Gem-cutters learn their skill by cutting garnets.

STONE SETTERS

The skill of stone-setting can be seen in the crowded alleys of Haldiyon ka Rasta, Jadiyon ka Rasta and Gopalji ka Rasta. An inherited art, the jewellery trade is in the hands of artisans' guilds.

STYLES OF JEWELLERY

Kundankari uses highly refined gold as a base, inlaid with lac and set with precious and semiprecious stones to provide colour and design. *Meenakari* is the art of enamelling gold and can be used to embellish the obverse side of *kundan* jewellery.

AMRAPALI MUSEUM

Showcasing a collection of over 4,000 pieces of jewellery, the privately owned Amrapali Museum *(www.amrapalimuseum. com)* in Jaipur aims to preserve and educate about Indian craftsmanship. While the pieces on display come from all over India, the museum highlights the specialities of local artisans.

Pieces of Jewellery

Chandbali earrings

Known for the crescent moon design style, these earrings originated in Rajasthan, but became popular across India.

Sarpech

A cypress-shaped turban ornament, the *sarpech* was introduced by the Mughal emperors in the early 17th century and used to display their finest gems. Rajput rulers sported dazzling pieces such as this one, enamelled with gold.

Kundan Pendant

This pendant was often made with diamonds and gold using the traditional, intricate *kundankari* technique.

A SHORT WALK
BADI CHAUPAR

Distance 2 km (1 mile) **Nearest Bus Station** Badi Chaupar
Time 30 minutes

Near Jaipur's biggest attractions of the City Palace and Hawa Mahal, the Badi Chaupar ("Large Square") is at one end of the colourful Tripolia Bazaar. The area is a hub of activity, rich with pungent smells and vibrant colours, with temple bells adding to the cacophony of street sounds, and narrow pedestrian lanes branching out from the main streets. Wander down these to find artisans fashioning handi-crafts in tiny workshops, and the *havelis* of former eminent citizens, now used as schools and shops. As few changes have been made to the original 18th-century street plan, walking these streets is a stroll through history.

Did You Know?

Jaipur was the first planned city in India, organized into nine square grids that still remain.

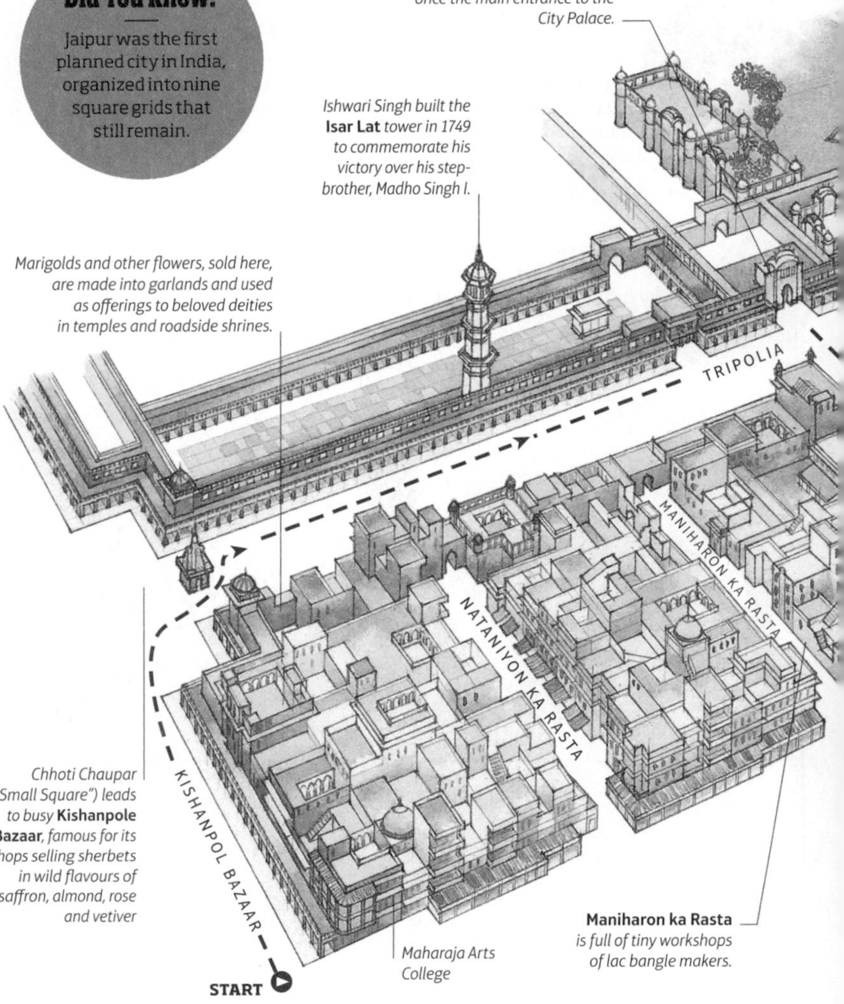

*Constructed in 1734, the impressive **Tripolia Gate** was once the main entrance to the City Palace.*

*Ishwari Singh built the **Isar Lat** tower in 1749 to commemorate his victory over his step-brother, Madho Singh I.*

Marigolds and other flowers, sold here, are made into garlands and used as offerings to beloved deities in temples and roadside shrines.

TRIPOLIA

MANIHARON KA RASTA

NATANIYON KA RASTA

*Chhoti Chaupar ("Small Square") leads to busy **Kishanpole Bazaar**, famous for its shops selling sherbets in wild flavours of saffron, almond, rose and vetiver*

KISHANPOL BAZAAR

Maharaja Arts College

START

Maniharon ka Rasta *is full of tiny workshops of lac bangle makers.*

← Bustling and colourful Tripolia Bazaar, one of the most popular sights in Badi Chaupar

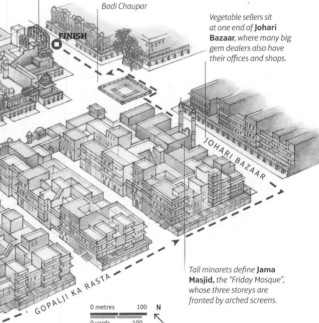

Jantar Mantar, Jai Singh II's observatory, looks like a series of futuristic sculptures.

A view of **Hawa Mahal**'s *unusual rear façade can be seen from the City Palace.*

Badi Chaupar

FINISH

Vegetable sellers sit at one end of **Johari Bazaar**, *where many big gem dealers also have their offices and shops.*

JOHARI BAZAAR

...AZAAR

CHAURA RASTA

GOPALJI KA RASTA

Tall minarets define **Jama Masjid,** *the "Friday Mosque", whose three storeys are fronted by arched screens.*

0 metres	100
0 yards	100

N

Tarkeshwar Temple

Large terracotta urns, pots of all sizes, bells, statues, foot-scrapers and oil lamps made by craftsmen are sold at this excellent **pottery shop**.

→ Looking over the rooftops of Badi Chaupar from Hawa Mahal

by the dynasty's founder, Duleh Rai (r 1093–1135), who also built a temple dedicated to the goddess Jamvai Mata. Ramgarh Lodge, on the banks of a man-made lake, was built in 1931 for the royal family. It was designed to look like a French villa and is now a hotel. Even though the lake, which was used for water-based sports during the 1982 Asian Games is now dry, and the polo ground no longer operational, the hotel remains popular due to its proximity to Jaipur.

JAIPUR: OUTER SITES

⑪
Sanganer

🏠 Jaipur district; 15 km (9 miles) S of Jaipur

This colourful town, famous for its blockprinted cotton, owes its success to a rivulet whose waters have a mineral content that fixes dyes. Sanganer is also a centre of handmade paper, as well as where Jaipur's renowned Blue Pottery – vases and tiles handpainted with delicate Persian, Turkish and Indian designs – are made. Tucked away in the old walled town is the impressive 11th-century Jain Sanghiji Temple, lavishly decorated with carvings.

⑫
Galta

🏠 Jaipur district; 10 km (6 miles) E of Jaipur

This picturesque gorge cradles Galta Kund, an 18th-century religious site with two main temples and a few smaller shrines. Seven sacred tanks here, fed by a natural spring, are said to have curative powers. Two pavilions on either side of the complex have lovely frescoes. The Surya Temple, high on the ridge, has spectacular views of Jaipur.

⑬
Sisodia Rani ka Bagh

🏠 Jaipur district; 6 km (4 miles) E of Jaipur
📞 (0141) 261 8862
🕐 8am–5pm daily

This terraced garden was laid out in the 18th century for Sawai Jai Singh II's second wife, who married him on the condition that her son would succeed to the throne. The garden is overlooked by a two-storeyed palace, which features lively murals. This building, located outside of the walled city, was where the queen moved to escape royal intrigue. The palace and the gardens are today a popular film location.

⑭
Ramgarh

🏠 Jaipur district; 40 km (25 miles) NE of Jaipur

Ramgarh is the site of one of the earliest Kachhawaha fortresses. The fort was built

⑮
Gaitor

🏠 Jaipur district; 8 km (5 miles) NE of Jaipur 🕐 10am–5:30pm daily 🚫 Public hols

The marble cenotaphs of the Kachhawaha kings are

↑ Looking out towards the Jal Mahal palace, rising out of Man Sagar lake

enclosed in a walled garden just off the Amber road. This area was chosen by Sawai Jai Singh II as the new cremation site after Amber *(p126)* was abandoned. Ornate carved pillars support the marble *chhatris* erected over the platforms where the maharajas were cremated. One of the most impressive cenotaphs in the complex is that of Jai Singh II himself. It is a large tomb with 20 marble pillars carved with mythological and religious scenes and is topped by a white marble dome.

---

⑯ ⊘
Jaigarh

🏠 Jaipur district; 12 km (7 miles) NE of Jaipur
📞 (0141) 267 1848 ⏰ 9am–4:30pm daily 🚫 Public hols

The legendary "Victory Fort", Jaigarh, watches over the old capital of Amber from a nearby hill. Connected to Amber Fort, this was a defensive structure that once housed the capital's treasury. One of the few surviving cannon foundries is located here, and contains the monumental 50-tonne Jai Van, said to be the world's largest cannon on wheels.

⑰
Jal Mahal

🏠 Jaipur district; 8 km (5 miles) NE of Jaipur

During the monsoon, water fills the Man Sagar lake, and the Jal Mahal ("Water Palace") seems to rise from it like a mirage, although multiple levels remain underwater. Built in the mid-18th century by Madho Singh I, it was inspired by the Jag Niwas Palace *(p140)* at Udaipur, where the king spent his childhood. It was later used for royal duck-shooting parties, and a variety of water birds still populate the lake. The terraced garden, enclosed by arched passages, has elegant towers capped by cupolas in each corner. The palace is not open to visitors.

⑱ ⊘
Nahargarh

🏠 Jaipur district; 9 km (6 miles) N of Jaipur
📞 (0141) 513 4038 ⏰ 10am–5:30pm daily 🚫 Public hols

The forbidding hill-top fort of Nahargarh ("Tiger Fort") stands in what was once a densely forested area near

Ranthambhore National Park. The fierce Meena tribe ruled this region until they were defeated by the Kachhawahas. Within the looming walls are multiple palaces and courtyards, added by successive rulers. The lavish and ornate Madhavendra Bhavan palace was added by Madho Singh II for his nine queens. Laid out in a maze of terraces and courtyards, it has a cool, airy upper chamber from which the ladies of the court could view the city. Its walls and pillars are an outstanding example of *arayish*, a form of plasterwork that is hand-polished with a piece of agate to produce a marble finish. Now beautifully renovated, the palace houses a gallery showcasing contemporary Indian sculpture.

> 🏔 GREAT VIEW
> **Sunset at Nahargarh**
>
> Nahargarh offers epic views over Jaipur at sunset. Get there in plenty of time to visit the Sculpture Park *(www.thesculpture-park.in)* inside the Madhavendra Bhavan.

② ⌦ ⌧ ⌸ ⌹

AMBER FORT

⌂ Jaipur district; 11 km (7 miles) N of Jaipur ⌚ 8am–5:30pm & 6:30–9pm daily ⌦ Public hols ⌨ tourism.rajasthan.gov.in/amber-palace.html

A grandiose and dramatic reminder of a time when Rajasthan was split into different kingdoms ruled by maharajas, Amber Fort – pronounced "Amer" – was the centre of what became the Jaipur state from 1037 until 1727, when the capital moved to Jaipur.

Located in the Aravalli Hills, Amber Fort was a monument to the power of the Kachwaha Rajputs and was home to the maharajas and their families. The complex is spectacularly opulent, with splendid mosaics and frescoes, halls decorated with inlaid mirrors, and a particularly glorious set of moulded silver doors.

The existing citadel was established in 1592 by Man Singh I, one of the members of the ruling Kachwaha dynasty, on the remains of an 11th-century fort – but the numerous buildings added by Jai Singh I (r 1621–67) form the most magnificent part of the palace.

Looming above Amber Fort, but connected to it by an underground tunnel, is Jaigarh Fort (p123); this heavily fortified building housed the state treasury and was also where the rulers would retreat if Amber came under attack.

In 1727, the capital moved from Amber to nearby Jaipur, but successive rulers continued to come here on important occasions to seek the blessings of the family deity, Shila Devi. An epic structure, Amber Fort is recognized as one of the finest examples of a hill fort in Jaipur, and, along with five other forts in Rajasthan, is protected as a UNESCO World Heritage Site.

→ The imposing walls of Amber Fort, protecting palaces and gardens

↑ Kesar Kyari Bagh, a garden of saffron in Maota Lake, sprawling under the fort

→ The elegant arches, and light and airy courtyard of Amber Fort

BLOCK PRINTING IN JAIPUR

India has been exporting cloth since the 6th century BC, and its fabric is notable for its hand-printed block designs. Most states have their own distinctive style. In Rajasthan, the centre of the textile trade has always been around Jaipur. Here, artisans dye cotton and use different blocks to create hundreds of unique patterns. The Anokhi Museum in Amber *(Chanwar Palkiwon ki Haveli, near the fort)* showcases both local and country-wide textile traditions.

The Fort Complex

A steep hike from the town below, Amber Fort's main entrance is the imposing Suraj Pol ("Sun Gate"), so called because it faces the direction of the rising sun, the Kachwaha family emblem. The gate leads into a huge courtyard, Jaleb Chowk, lined on three sides with shops. From here, a flight of steps leads to the Shila Devi Temple, which has silver doors, silver oil lamps and grand pillars carved to look like banana trees, and contains the Kachwaha family deity, a stone (shila) image of the goddess Kali. The next courtyard is the Diwan-i-Aam, the space for public audiences. Near it is the Sattais Katcheri, a colonnade of 27 (sattais) pillars where scribes once sat to record revenue petitions. Magnificent Ganesh Pol is the gateway to three graceful pleasure palaces, each with special features, built around a Mughal-style garden. The oldest end of the fort was converted into the women's quarters, with screens and covered balconies for the seclusion of the royal ladies in purdah. Faint traces of frescoes are still visible on the walls here. In the centre of the courtyard is the Baradavi Pavilion, which has 12 pillars.

On Maotha Lake below the palace, the Kesar Kyari Bagh has star-shaped flower beds once planted with saffron flowers; Dilaram Bagh, also on the lake, was built in 1568 as a resting place for Emperor Akbar on his way to Ajmer.

WHAT ELSE TO SEE IN AMBER

The Chand Pol ("Moon Gate"), directly opposite Suraj Pol, leads to the old town outside the fort. The beautiful Jagat Shiromani Temple, with its remarkable torana (gateway), is one of the many temples that lie along this route. To the east lies Sagar, a popular picnic spot with two lakes. The Jaipur-Delhi Highway cuts across the town, and Amber's main market and bus stand are located on this road. Further north is the Akbari Mosque, built in 1569, while towards the east is Bharmal ki Chhatri, a walled enclosure containing a group of memorials.

Jas Mandir, the Hall of Private Audience, has latticed windows and an elegant alabaster-and-glass ceiling.

Aram Bagh was the palace's pleasure garden.

Aram Bagh, Amber Fort's famous pleasure garden, with its pool

The flame of a single candle, reflected in the tiny mirrors embedded in Sheesh Mahal, transforms the chamber into a starlit sky.

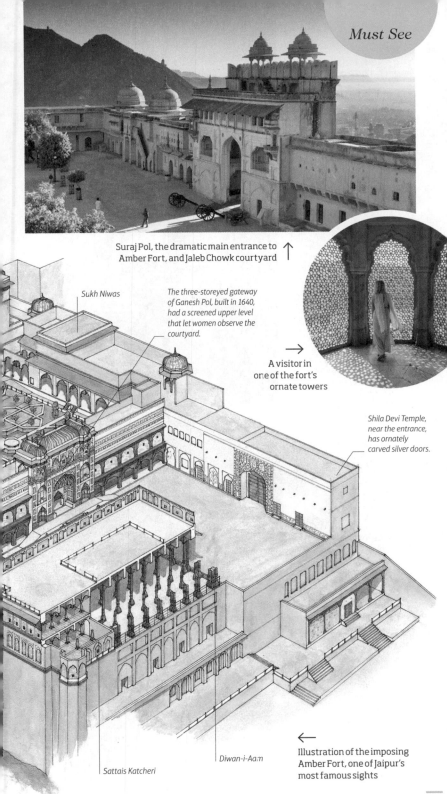

Suraj Pol, the dramatic main entrance to Amber Fort, and Jaleb Chowk courtyard ↑

Sukh Niwas

The three-storeyed gateway of Ganesh Pol, built in 1640, had a screened upper level that let women observe the courtyard.

→

A visitor in one of the fort's ornate towers

Shila Devi Temple, near the entrance, has ornately carved silver doors.

Sattais Katcheri

Diwan-i-Aam

←

Illustration of the imposing Amber Fort, one of Jaipur's most famous sights

TOP **3**

ANIMALS TO SPOT

Cormorants
With the arrival of the monsoon, thousands of birds, such as greater cormorants, set up nesting colonies. As many as 60 noisy nests on one tree may be seen during this season.

Painted Storks
These birds can usually be seen between July and October, when the trees become nesting sites for nearly 5,000 pairs of storks.

Nilgai (Blue Bull)
The largest of all Asiatic antelopes, these avid crop grazers are protected against hunting because of their resemblance to the holy cow.

3

KEOLADEO GHANA NATIONAL PARK

🏠 Bharatpur district; 196 km (122 miles) E of Jaipur 🚉🚌 Bharatpur
🕐 Summer: 6am–6pm daily; winter: 6:30am–5pm daily 🛈 Deputy Chief Wildlife Warden, (05644) 222 777; RTDC Hotel Saras, Bharatpur, www.tourism.rajasthan.gov.in/keoladeo-ghana-national-park.html

This UNESCO World Heritage Site, one of the world's most important animal sanctuaries, is a mosaic of wetlands, woodlands, grass and scrub. It is most known for its incredibly diverse bird population; there are 375 species in the park, which include birds such as the world's tallest stork.

Keoladeo Ghana derives its name from a temple to the Hindu god Shiva (Keoladeo) within a dense forest (*ghana*). This once-arid scrubland was first developed by Bharatpur's rulers in the mid-18th century by diverting the waters of a nearby irrigation canal to create a private duck reserve. Today, the park spreads over 29 sq km (11 sq miles) and attracts a wide variety of migrant and water birds, which fly in each winter from as far as Siberia. Expert boatmen will navigate the wetlands for you, and bicycles and cycle rickshaws are available for the forest paths. The park is also home to nilgai (blue bull), whose broad backs offer comfortable resting places for birds.

Did You Know?

The Sarus crane mates for life, and attracts its partner with an elaborate dance.

↑ A flamboyant flock of flamingos wading through the wetlands

Lucky onlookers spotting nilgai slipping gracefully into the water ↑

→ A pair of spotted owls nestling up against each together in the safety of a tree

STAY

The Bagh
Luxurious rooms with stunning gardens; perfect for visiting nearby Keoladeo Ghana National Park.

⌂ Bharatpur
🖥 thebagh.com

₹₹₹

Sunbird
Just a few hundred metres from the gates of Keoladeo Ghana National Park, with comfortable rooms and a great restaurant.

⌂ Bharatpur
🖥 hotelsunbird.com

₹₹₹

4

JODHPUR

Jodhpur district; 331 km (206 miles) W of Jaipur
5 km (3 miles) S of city centre 🚗🚌 ℹ High Court Rd;
www.tourism.rajasthan.gov.in/jodhpur.html

With the majestic Mehrangarh Fort towering over opulent palaces and colourful bazaars, Jodhpur epitomizes all the feudal splendour of Rajasthan. Now the second-largest city in the state, Jodhpur was founded in 1459 by Rao Jodha, ruler of the kingdom of Marwar. Strategically located on the overland trade route, it soon became a flourishing trade centre.

1 Sadar Bazaar

Clustered around a 1912 clock tower in the old town near the fort (p132), this fascinating bazaar has little shops selling silver jewellery, lacquer bangles, tie-dyed fabrics, decadently soft camel-leather shoes, puppets, clay figurines and colourful heaps of sweets and spices. The pavements are lined with henna artists who decorate women's palms with intricate, lacy patterns.

The bazaar is surrounded by interesting buildings – one of the best is the early-17th-century Taleti Mahal, which has carved balconies supported by temple pillars, built for a favourite royal concubine.

2 Jaswant Thada

⏱ 9am–5pm daily

An elegant pillared marble structure with fine lattice carving, the lakeside cenotaph of Maharaja Jaswant Singh II (r 1873–95) is a stunning memorial to the maharaja, whose innovative irrigation schemes brought water and prosperity to this parched land. Local people believe that the maharaja has retained his healing touch, and come regularly to offer prayer and flowers at his shrine. The cenotaphs of subsequent rulers and members of the royal family are also here, though earlier rulers have their memorials at Mandore.

3 Umaid Bhawan Palace

This immense palace, built of creamy-pink sandstone and marble, has 347 rooms, including eight dining halls, two theatres, a ballroom and a vast underground swimming pool. A 60-m (197-ft) dome covers the cavernous central hall, which, at its inauguration, seated 1,000 people for dinner. The palace, commissioned by Maharaja Umaid Singh, fuses Rajput, Jain and European Art

BHOPA BALLADEERS

The Bhopa tribe of western Rajasthan is known for its tradition of storytelling through song and dance. The Bhopa unrolls a painted scroll crammed with images depicting dramatic events in the life of a brave Marwar warrior, and narrates the story through songs, while his wife brings the tale to life with dance sequences. These performances draw enthusiastic crowds at fairs and festivals across the Marwar region.

← Panoramic sunset view over Jodhpur, also known as the Blue City

Deco styles. Begun in 1929, it took 3,000 men 15 years to complete; 19 km (12 miles) of railway tracks were also laid to bring the sandstone from the quarry.

Umaid Singh's grandson still lives in a section of the palace, making it the largest private residence in the world, while the rest of the building has been turned into a luxury hotel. A museum displays decorated weapons, watches and clocks, paintings, French furniture and porcelain.

④ Mandore

🏠 6 km (4 miles) N of Jodhpur

Mandore was the capital of the Rathore kings of Marwar until the 15th century, when Rao Jodha built a new capital at Jodhpur. Set around a terraced garden on a hillside are the red sandstone cenotaphs of Jodhpur's earlier rulers. The most imposing is that of Ajit Singh with its towering, temple-like spire. When he died in 1724, his six wives and 58 concubines committed *sati* on his funeral pyre. The Hall of Heroes has 15 life-size statues of religious deities and folk heroes. Further up the hill are the queens' cenotaphs (Raniyon ki Chhatri) and the tall and narrow 17th-century Ek Thamba Mahal Palace.

⑤ Marwar Craft Villages

🏠 20 km (12 miles) S of Jodhpur

The craft villages south of Jodhpur offer a fascinating insight into tribal life and the tribes' relationship with their environment. The Bishnois see themselves at one with nature, believing that if the native blackbuck deer remains unharmed, they will be reborn as one. This connection to nature is reflected in motifs running through their crafts – indigenous flora and fauna appear in woven rugs and on terracotta pots.

STAY

Raas
An elegant hotel in a stunning modern building.

🏠 Makrana Mohalla, Gulab Sagar
🌐 raasjodhpur.com

₹₹₹

Pal Haveli
This converted *haveli* has lovely rooms and a rooftop restaurant.

🏠 Gulab Sagar, near the clock tower
🌐 palhaveli.com

₹₹₹

Singhvi's Haveli
Pretty, simple rooms in a restored *haveli*.

🏠 Navchokiya, Ramdeo Ji Ka Chowk
🌐 singhvihaveli.com

₹₹₹

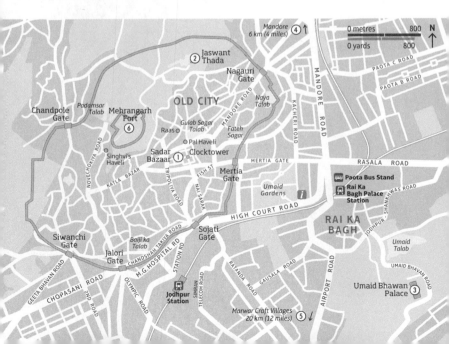

⑥ 🏛 🍴 🛍

MEHRANGARH FORT

🏠 Jodhpur 🚉 🕙 9am–5pm daily 🚫 Public hols

Described by an awe-struck Rudyard Kipling as "the creation of angels, fairies and giants", Mehrangarh is perhaps the most majestic of Rajasthan's forts. Rising sheer out of a 125-m-(410-ft-) high rock, Mehrangarh's forbidding ramparts are in sharp contrast to the flamboyantly decorated palaces within, where rooms are inlaid with gold and jewels.

Founded by Rao Jodha in 1459, the sandstone fort was added to by later rulers, mostly between the mid-17th and mid-19th centuries. The royal apartments within the fort now form part of an outstanding museum, justly regarded as the finest palace museum in Rajasthan. Its rich and varied collection includes a golden throne, fine miniature paintings, traditional costumes and fascinating weapons. Particularly magnificent are the skilfully restored royal chambers, which present a vivid picture of princely life in Rajasthan. The museum also has a fine collection of Rajasthani turbans and folk music instruments.

The ramparts, parts of which are hewn out of the rock, are in places 24-m (79-ft) thick and 40-m (131-ft) high.

The magnificent Moti Mahal was the Hall of Private Audience. Its ceiling is decorated with mirrors and gold leaf.

The courtyard of Shringar Chowk displays the coronation throne of the Jodhpur rulers.

Did You Know?

Jhanki Mahal (Peeping Palace) refers to the secluded women of the fort who would spy on the courtyards below.

→ An overview of Mehrangarh Fort, once home to Jodhpur's rulers

↑ The looming walls of Mehrangarh Fort, giving little clue to the ornate buildings inside

→ The gold walls and inlaid jewels of the richly gilded Phool Mahal

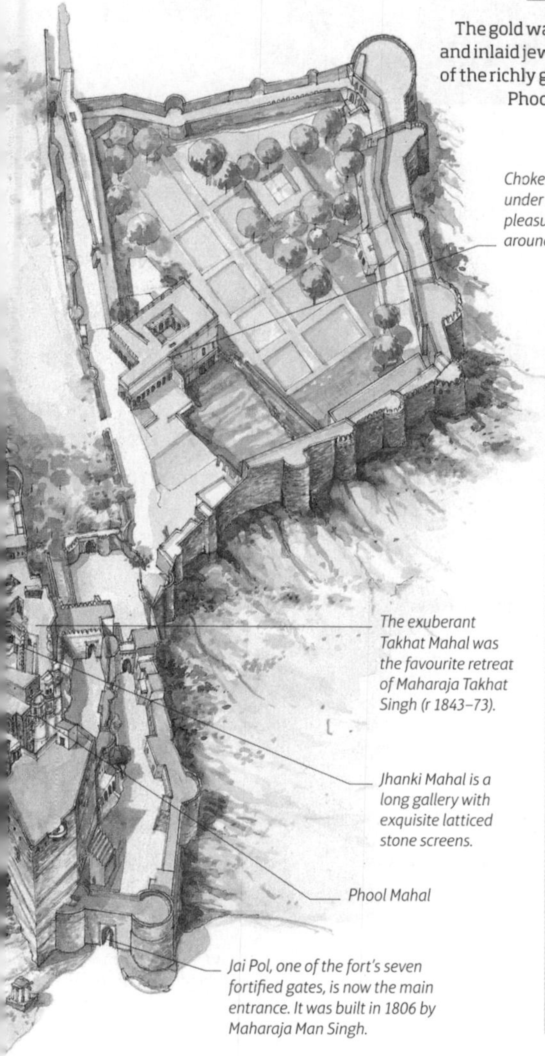

Chokelao Palace, now under restoration, was a pleasure palace built around a sunken garden.

The exuberant Takhat Mahal was the favourite retreat of Maharaja Takhat Singh (r 1843–73).

Jhanki Mahal is a long gallery with exquisite latticed stone screens.

Phool Mahal

Jai Pol, one of the fort's seven fortified gates, is now the main entrance. It was built in 1806 by Maharaja Man Singh.

MUSICAL JODHPUR

Mehrangarh Fort provides a dramatic backdrop to two rather fantastic music festivals each year: the World Sacred Spirit Festival in February *(www.world sacredspiritfestival.org)* and the Rajasthani International Folk Festival in October *(www.jodhpur riff.org)*. The spirit festival showcases a range of traditional Indian instruments like the sitar and tabla, as well as more unconventional offerings like the *algoza* double flute. Don't miss the melodies of the qawwali performances from the Sufi tradition and the sounds of the Persian oud and the Indian santoor from international guests (you might even hear classical guitar from Argentina). Later on, DJs spin fusion dance music into the night.

⑤
JAISALMER

🏠 Jaisalmer district; 285 km (177 miles) W of Jodhpur 🚗🚌
ℹ Station Rd; www.tourism.rajasthan.gov.in/jaisalmer.html

Today a remote outpost in the Thar Desert, Jaisalmer, founded in the 12th century, was once a busy trade centre on the caravan route to Central Asia. Its rulers grew rich by looting the caravans, but by the 1500s Jaisalmer had become a peaceful town, its wealthy inhabitants vying with each other to beautify their austere desert surroundings with splendid palaces.

①
Badal Vilas

🏠 Near Amar Sagar Gate
🕐 Daily

This palace, built in the late 19th century, is distinguished by its multi-tiered tower in the shape of a *tazia*, a decorated tower of wood, metal and coloured paper carried by Shia Muslims at Muharram, the first month of the Islamic calendar and a time of mourning. The Tazia Tower of Badal Vilas, built in the mid-20th century, was a parting gift to the maharaja from the town's Shia stone-carvers, many of whom moved to Pakistan after independence.

②
Manik Chowk

At the entrance to the fort (p136), this bazaar, often crowded with desert nomads and their camels, has shops selling camel-hair blankets and embroidered textiles.

③
Patwon ki Haveli

🏠 E of Nathmalji's Haveli
🕐 9am–5pm daily

This enormous *haveli* was built between 1805 and 1855 by Guman Chand Patwa, one of Jaisalmer's richest merchants.

This towering mansion has five adjoining apartments for each of his sons, and 66 balconies. The curved eaves on the balconies suggest a fleet of sailing boats, and the latticed windows are carved with breathtaking intricacy.

④
Salim Singh's Haveli

🏠 Near the fort entrance

This *haveli* was built in 1815 by a prime minister of Jaisalmer. Narrow at the base, its six storeys grow wider at each level, and all its 38 balconies have different designs; carved peacocks dance between the arches on the topmost balcony, and blue cupolas cap the roof. Local guides can arrange visits for a fee.

⑤
Nathmalji's Haveli

🏠 Near Gandhi Chowk

Built in 1855 by another prime minister of Jaisalmer, the particular charm of this five-storeyed mansion is that the two sides of its façade were

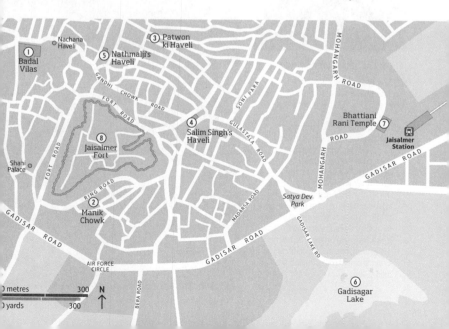

← Boats moored by a ghat on Gadisagar Lake at sunrise

carved by two craftsman brothers, Hathu and Lallu. Though at first glance they seem identical, the details on each side are actually quite different. Besides the usual floral, geometric and animal patterns, this *haveli*'s motifs also reflect new influences – a European-style horse and carriage, bicycles and steam engines. Local guides can arrange visits for a fee.

⑥ Gadisagar Lake

🏛 SE of the city walls

This rainwater reservoir, built in 1367, was once the city's sole source of water. Lined with ghats and temples, it comes alive during the Gangaur festival (March/April), when the maharawal leads a procession here. The gateway leading to the tank was built by a royal courtesan, Telia, whose audacity so enraged the queens that they demanded its demolition. The quick-witted Telia had a statue of Krishna installed on top, thereby ensuring that the gateway would stand.

⑦ Bhattiani Rani Temple

🏛 2 km (1 mile) S of fort
🕐 Daily

This secluded Hindu shrine was built in honour of a 19th-

century Jaisalmer princess who committed *sati* on the funeral pyre of her brother-in-law. A clan of Muslim musicians, the Manganiyars, are now the caretakers of the temple, and recount this story in their soulful ballads about Jaisalmer's history.

Must See

STAY

Nachana Haveli
Enjoy a warm welcome at this stunning sandstone *haveli* run by the descendants of the founder of Jaisalmer.

🏛 Gandhi Chowk
🌐 nachanahaveli.com

₹₹₹

Shahi Palace
This hotel offers simple but beautiful rooms and fantastic views from its rooftop restaurant.

🏛 Shiv Road
🌐 shahipalacehotel.com

₹₹₹

(8) 🏷️ 🍴 🛍️

JAISALMER FORT

📍 Jaisalmer Fort ⏰ Fort: 9am–6pm daily; Jain temples: 8am–12pm daily; museum: 8am–6pm daily ℹ️ Station Rd; www.tourism.rajasthan.gov.in/jaisalmer.html

Jaisalmer Fort rises like a fabulous mirage out of the sands of the Thar Desert, the awesome contours of its 99 bastions softened by the golden hue of the stone. Built in 1156 by Maharawal Jaisal, and added to by his successors, this citadel stands on the peak of the 80-m- (262-ft-) high Trikuta Hill. The ramparts, with an inner parallel wall, have huge cannonballs perched on top, ready to crush invaders.

In medieval times, Jaisalmer's entire population lived within the fort, and even now, thousands of people reside here, making it India's only living fort. Royal palaces, mansions and shops are all contained within its walls, along with a cluster of exquisitely carved 15th- and 16th-century Jain temples that were built by the town's wealthy traders. The seven-storey palace complex consists of several interconnected palaces, built between the 16th and 19th centuries. The mid-18th-century palace Sarvottam Vilas is decorated with brilliant blue tiles and glass mosaic work.

JAISALMER IN JEOPARDY

The growth of tourism together with attempts to green the nearby desert have, ironically, posed a threat to the fort. Built for an arid climate that hardly ever experienced rainfall, the fort had no provision for water supply or drainage. Now, with rising groundwater levels in the area and the introduction of piped water in the fort, seepage has made the golden stone crumble in places. Conservation efforts by Indian and international organizations are now under way to save this unique fort and town.

→ Graceful walk-ways lining a pleasure garden

← Pilgrims inside one of the Jain temples in the fort

Must See

EAT

Kuku Coffee Shop
This popular stop for coffee in the walls of the fort has spectacular views over the town from the rooftop tables. The coffee is freshly brewed, and there are sweets and thali on offer. Don't miss the delicious lassi.

⌂ Near Hari Om Jewellers
☎ 94608 06672

₹₹₹

↑ Aerial view across the top of the fort towards Jaisalmer city

JAISALMER: OUTER SIGHTS

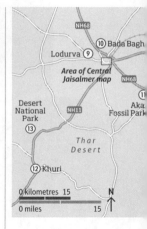

⑨ Lodurva

🏠 15 km (9 miles) NW of Jaisalmer

The capital of the Bhatti Rajputs before they built Jaisalmer Fort, Lodurva was abandoned after it was sacked by Muslim invaders in the 11th century. A group of incredibly intricate Jain temples dominates this site, and the remains of many other fine buildings lie concealed here beneath the desert sands. A beautiful *torana* leads to the main temple, which is topped by a metal sculpture of the Kalpavriksha ("Celestial Tree"), which is believed to have wish-fulfilling powers.

⑩ Bada Bagh

🏠 7 km (4 miles) N of fort

The royal cenotaphs, with elaborately carved ceilings and equestrian statues of the rulers, are set in a green oasis.

Next to them is the temple of the god Bhaironji, where childless women offer silver girdles to the deity in the hope that he will cure their infertility.

⑪ Akal Fossil Park

🏠 17 km (11 miles) SE of Jaisalmer 🕐 9am–5pm daily

The extraordinary fossilized tree trunks, some of them 180 million years old, protected in this park bear witness to the fact that the barren expanses of the Thar Desert were once covered with dense forest. Friendly emus roam freely around the area.

⑫ Khuri

🏠 40 km (25 miles) SW of Jaisalmer

Set among sand dunes, this little village is an excellent example of desert architec-

ture. Functional as well as beautiful, the village houses have thick mud walls that provide protection against the fierce desert heat and winds, while the paintings that decorate their exteriors bring colour and beauty to the brown, parched environs.

⑬ Desert National Park

🏠 43 km (27 miles) W of Jaisalmer ℹ️ For permission, contact Collector's Office, (02992) 25 2201

This park, a UNESCO World Heritage Site, is spread over 3,162 sq km (1,221 sq miles) of the Thar Desert close to the border with Pakistan. While still populated with villages, it also protects the unique flora and fauna of this region. The star attraction is the great Indian bustard (*Choriotis nigriceps*), a large bird that had been almost hunted to extinction. Only about 1,000 remain now, but this park is the most likely place to spot them. Other wildlife includes sand grouse, falcons and vultures, desert fox, and *chinkara* (Indian gazelle).

← Bada Bagh's complex of splendidly ornate royal cenotaphs

↑ *Havelis* lining the streets in the oldest part of the golden city of Jaisalmer

THE JAISALMER HAVELI

After the fort, Jaisalmer's *havelis* are its greatest attraction, with their golden stone façades so finely carved that they could be made of lace. Built in the 19th century by the town's merchants and ministers, these mansions dominate its labyrinthine lanes. Several generations of an extended family lived together in these huge mansions.

JALIS

Jalis, or latticed stone screens, display a rich variety of patterns. They keep out the harsh desert sun but let in fresh air. They also enabled women to observe street life without being seen, a feature also seen on Rajasthani palaces.

JHAROKHAS

Jharokhas, or projecting balconies, have curved *bangaldar* eaves. Their purpose was more decorative than functional, and they gave the stonemasons an opportunity to display the full range of their creativity and skill.

INNER COURTYARDS

A *haveli* traditionally has two courtyards: the outer was more public, whereas the inner courtyard was a protected place for children to play in, and for women to attend to their daily chores in privacy.

↑ Patwon Ki Haveli, a famous example of the style

↑ Yellow sandstone showing intricate carving

The picture-perfect city of Udaipur, surrounding Lake Pichola

⑥
UDAIPUR

🏠 Udaipur district; 269 km (167 miles) S of Jodhpur ✈ 25 km (16 miles) E of city centre 🚌 🚕 ℹ️ Rajasthan Tourism, Suraj Pol; www.tourism.rajasthan.gov.in/udaipur.html

With its marble palaces and lakes surrounded by a ring of hills, Udaipur was founded by Maharana Udai Singh in 1559, and became the capital of Mewar in 1567. The city is dominated by the massive City Palace, which overlooks Lake Pichola. Picturesque *havelis*, ghats and temples line the lake front, with the lively bazaars of the old walled city stretching behind them.

① Jag Mandir

🏠 Lake Pichola ⏰ 10am–6pm daily 🚤 City Palace Jetty

The enchantingly lovely island palace of Jag Mandir, with its lush gardens and marble chambers exquisitely inlaid with coloured stone, was built in 1620. Eight stone elephants stand guard at its entrance; it is now a hotel, as is the nearby **Jag Niwas**, or Lake Palace. This former royal summer retreat, built between 1734 and 1751, is a luxurious escape and serves as a popular location for film shoots.

Jag Niwas
📞 📱 (0294) 252 8016

② Jagdish Mandir

🏠 Moti Chhohta Rd ⏰ 4am–8pm daily

This 17th-century temple has a vast black stone image of Vishnu in its profusely carved main shrine. A bronze image of Garuda (the mythical bird who is Vishnu's vehicle) stands in front of the temple.

Nearby, the 18th-century **Bagore ki Haveli** is now a museum of traditional arts and crafts, with daily music and dance performances.

In the old walled city, east of the Jagdish Mandir, are the Bapu and Bara bazaars.

Bagore ki Haveli
♿ 🏠 Gangaur Ghat

③ Fateh Sagar Lake

🏠 Fateh Sagar Rd

Overlooking Fateh Sagar Lake, Moti Magri Hill has a statue of Udaipur's great 16th-century warrior Maharana Pratap, and his valiant steed, Chetak.

④ Saheliyon ki Bari

🏠 Saheli Marg ⏰ 8am–8pm daily

This charming retreat was built for a queen whose dowry included 48 maids (its name means "Garden of the Maids of Honour") in the north of the city. It has ornamental fountains, a lotus pool and a rose garden.

Did You Know?

Maharana Udai Singh met a sage while hunting who told him to build a city here, as the site was auspicious.

⑤ Ahar

🏠 Ashok Nagar Rd

Ahar has the cenotaphs of 19 Mewar rulers, and a small archaeological **museum**.

Museum

♿ 📞 (0294) 247 0004
🕐 10:30am–4pm Sat–Thu
🚫 Public hols

⑥ Eklingji

🏠 22 km (14 miles) NE of Udaipur

Eklingji is a complex of 108 temples and shrines dedicated to Lord Shiva. The main temple dates to the 16th century. Built of marble and granite, it includes an impressive pillared hall and a four-faced image of Shiva crafted in black marble, with a silver Nandi facing it.

⑦ Nathdwara

🏠 48 km (30 miles) NE of Udaipur

One of Rajasthan's main pilgrimage sites is the 18th-century Shrinathji Temple at Nathdwara. The main deity is Lord Krishna, known locally as Shrinathji. The temple's black stone Shiva was brought from Mathura to save it from destruction by the Mughal

emperor Aurangzeb in the 17th century. Beautiful painted cloth hangings known as *pichhwais* are hung behind it. Non-Hindus cannot enter the temple, but Nathdwara town's picturesque bazaar, with its *pichhwai* painters at work, is worth a visit. *Pichhwais* all depict 24 scenes from the Krishna legend, each linked with a particular festival or holy day. At the centre of each painting is a stylized image of Lord Krishna against a background of foliage, skyscapes, animals and birds. Arrayed around the deity are cows, milkmaids and devotees.

EAT

Upre by 1559AD
Elegant rooftop eatery with lake views serving Rajasthani delicacies.

🏠 Lake Pichola Hotel, Hanuman Ghat
🌐 1559ad.com

₹₹₹

STAY

The Oberoi Udaivillas
The deserving winner of the best hotel in India offers luxurious suites and a stunning pool.

🏠 Haridasji Magri
🌐 oberoihotels.com

₹₹₹

Kankarwa Haveli
A lovingly restored *haveli* on the lakeside with comfortable rooms.

🏠 Lal Ghat
🌐 kankarwahaveli.com

₹₹₹

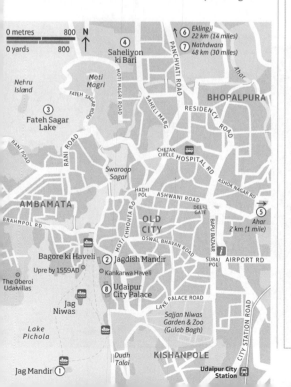

UDAIPUR CITY PALACE

(8) ⊘ ⊛ ⊟ ⊡

🏠 City Palace Complex 🕑 9:30am–5:30pm daily 🅦 Fateh Prakash & Shiv Niwas: hrhhotels.com

Beautifully situated on the shores of Lake Pichola, the Udaipur City Palace is an iconic monument in this waterside city. The palace was the centre of power of Mewar, the kingdom ruled by the Sisodia dynasty. Behind the fortified walls, with their rows of arched windows and intricate turrets, lies a maze to explore.

The City Palace complex is a miniature kingdom of royal apartments, reception halls and court-yards, linked to each other by narrow passages and steep staircases.

The main attraction within the complex is the superb City Palace Museum. Spread out over several palaces, the museum is entered through the imposing Tripolia Gate, built in 1713. Beyond this is the Ganesh Deorhi Gate, where entrance tickets for the museum are checked. It leads into a courtyard decorated with frescoes of horses and elephants, and a dazzling marble relief of the god Ganesha.

The next courtyard is the Rajya Angan Chowk, from where steps lead to the Chandra Mahal, built in 1620. One of the loveliest palaces in the complex, it has beautiful columns and striking marble reliefs of Rajput women. There is a magical view of Lake Pichola and its island palaces from here. Another flight of steps leads to the charming Bari Mahal, built in 1699. Perched 27 m (89 ft) above the ground, it is built on a terraced hillside that is completely enclosed within the palace walls. Halls with receding rows of carved arches open into an enchanting courtyard with a marble pool in the middle, surrounded by tall neem trees.

The Bari Mahal leads to two remarkable chambers – the Kanch Burj, inlaid with red-and-silver glass, and the Krishna Niwas, which exhibits outstanding miniature paintings.

To the left of this palace is the ornate Moti Mahal, the chamber of the Maharana Jawan Singh (r 1828–38), who once promised a

↑ Stunningly multicoloured Mor Chowk, known as the Peacocks' Gallery

💬 INSIDER TIP
Water Views

Once dubbed the Venice of the East, Udaipur looks beautiful from the water. Boat trips around Lake Pichola run every hour, and take a turn around the lake and visit Jag Mandir Island. Tickets are available from City Palace gates.

danc ng girl half his kingdom if she could walk a tightrope across the lake. The girl had almost managed it when the maharana's alarmed courtiers cut the rope. Still further left is the Mor Chowk with its mosaics of three dancing peacocks.

The southern end of the City Palace complex has three other opulent palaces – Shambhu Niwas, where the descendants of the rulers now live, and Fateh Prakash and Shiv Niwas, which are now luxury hotels, but are open to visitors for tours and meals.

↑ Dazzlingly gold Moti Mahal *(inset)* in Udaipur City Palace, next to Lake Pichola

⑦ 🌀 🅜 🛍

RANTHAMBHORE NATIONAL PARK

📍 Sawai Madhopur district; 150 km (93 miles) SE of Jaipur
🚌 🚘 🕐 Oct–Jun ℹ Project Tiger, (07462) 220 479; RTDC
Hotel Vinayak, Sawai Madhopur; www.tourism.rajasthan.
gov.in/ranthambore.html

Once a hunting ground for the royals of Jaipur, Ranthambhore is now one of India's most beloved national parks. It is a haven for an array of wildlife, but most people visit here seeking a glimpse of a tiger.

Ranthambhore National Park lies in the shadow of the Aravalli and Vindhya mountain ranges and covers a core area of 392 sq km (151 sq miles). Its razor-sharp ridges, deep boulder-filled gorges, lakes and jungles are the habitat of carnivores such as caracals, panthers, jackals and hyenas, numerous species of deer, and a rich variety of resident and migratory birds. The most famous resident, however, is the endangered tiger – the park was established to protect this predator. Their numbers have recently increased to around 70 thanks to preservation efforts. Only jeeps hired from the Project Tiger office are allowed in the park.

STAY

Khem Villas
Get intimate with nature in this stylish wilderness camp, where you can watch an abundance of birds from your veranda.
📍 Sherpur Khiljipur
🌐 khemvillas.com
₹₹₹

A majestic Bengal tiger prowling through the tall grass by a lake

↑ The cenotaph of Hamir Dev Chauhan, one of many historic buildings in the park

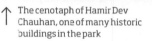

→ A proud peacock putting on a fine-feathered display for the park's peahens

TIGER WATCH

Set up by the former director of the national park, Tiger Watch exists to monitor and help protect the park's tigers. It warns that villagers pose as much of a threat as poachers, as locals graze cows during monsoon season, which degrades the vegetation. However, tiger numbers are on the up; some have even been taken to repopulate nearby Sariska, which lost all of its tigers to poaching in the 2000s.

Did You Know?

Thanks to conservation efforts, there are now over 2,500 Bengal tigers across the world.

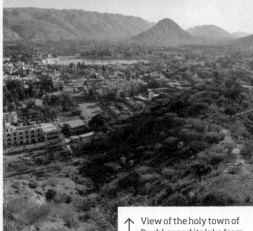

↑ View of the holy town of Pushkar and its lake from a hillside temple

EXPERIENCE MORE

8
Pushkar

🏠 Ajmer district; 144 km (89 miles) SW of Jaipur 🚌 ℹ️ www.tourism.rajasthan. gov.in/pushkar.html

A holy town of temples, ghats and whitewashed homes, Pushkar is arrayed around the banks of Lake Pushkar, which is said to have formed when the god Brahma threw a lotus flower to the ground. From bells chiming at dawn to the colourful bazaars, it is a vibrant place to visit; pilgrims are drawn by the town's Brahma Temple, considered the auspicious to visit. The town also hosts the Pushkar Camel Fair (Oct–Nov); thousands descend upon Pushkar.

> 💬 **INSIDER TIP**
> ## Pushkar's Savitri Temple
>
> Take a late-afternoon stroll up the hill to Savitri Temple, a simple building dedicated to Brahma's first wife Savitri. Here you can watch the sun set over Lake Pushkar and enjoy amazing views.

9
Deeg

🏠 Bharatpur district; 36 km (22 miles) N of Bharatpur 🚌 ℹ️ RTDC Hotel Saras, Bharatpur; (05644) 223 790

Once the capital of the Jat kings of Bharatpur, Deeg rose to prominence after the decline of the Mughal Empire in the 18th century. Its fort and town, once filled with grand mansions and gardens, now lie unkempt and forlorn. One of the dynasty's great rulers, Raja Suraj Mal, and his son, Jawahar Singh, were keen builders of pleasure palaces. The most remarkable of these is the **Deeg Water Palace**, a summer retreat for the Jat kings. Inspired by the magic of the monsoon, the palace is a lyrical fantasy of sandstone and marble pavilions ornamented with gardens and pools. A cooling system drew water from a reservoir and used a number of innovative special effects to simulate monsoon showers and even produce rainbows. The coloured fountains are now used only during the Jawahar Mela.

Deeg Water Palace
🕐 9am–5pm Sat–Thu
🚫 The day after Holi (Mar)

10
Alwar

🏠 Alwar district; 150 km (93 miles) NE of Jaipur 🚆🚌 ℹ️ RTDC, Nehru Marg; www.tourism. rajasthan.gov.in/alwar.html

The former princely state of Alwar is now a dusty provincial town, visited by few tourists except those on their way to the Sariska National Park. Nevertheless it has some remarkable monuments, built by its wealthy rulers in the 18th century, that are worth seeing. The most significant of these is the **City Palace**, whose architectural features include a profusion of curved bangaldar roofs and chhatris (pavilions) as well as delicate Mughal floral tracery and jalis. The palace, built in 1793, now houses the District Collectorate and Police Headquarters, and is best viewed from the central courtyard with its lovely marble pavilions. The lavishly decorated Durbar Hall and the Sheesh Mahal, on the first floor, can only be viewed with special permission, but a door to the right of the courtyard leads to the **City Palace Museum**, open to visitors and spread over three halls on the palace's upper storey.

Its treasures, which bear witness to the opulent lifestyles of Alwar's maharajas, include rare and exquisite copies of the Persian poet Sa'adi's Gulistan (written in 1258) and the Babur Nama or "Memoirs of Babur" (1530), superb Mughal and Rajput miniatures and an awesome armoury. Particularly intriguing is a macabre coil called *nagphas*, used for strangling enemies. Another decadent exhibit is a silver dining table with dividers, through which shoals of metal fish can be seen swimming.

The cenotaph of Maharaja Bakhtawar Singh (r1790–1815) lies behind the palace, across a magnificent *kund* (tank). It is locally known as **Moosi Maharani ki Chhatri**, after his mistress who committed *sati* here after he died. An elegant monument that blends brown sandstone with white marble, its ceilings are adorned with gold leaf paintings.

On a steep hill above the town is the rugged **Bala Qila**, a fort with extensive ramparts, massive gateways and some spectacular views. Built in the 10th century, the mud fort was added to by the Mughals and Jats, and captured by Pratap Singh of Alwar in 1775. Also visible are the ruins of the Salim Mahal, named after Jahangir (Salim), the heir of Mughal emperor Akbar, who was exiled here after he plotted to kill Abu'l Fazl, the emperor's historian. The **Tomb of Fateh Jang**, one of Emperor Shah Jahan's ministers, was built in 1647. This five-storeyed structure is dominated by an enormous dome, and its walls and ceiling have plaster reliefs.

Company Bagh, a garden with a greenhouse, offers visitors to Alwar some much needed respite from the heat.

City Palace
⊛ Ⓐ Near Collectorate
🕐 10am–4:30pm Sat-Thu

City Palace Museum
⊛ 🕐 10am–5pm Tue-Sun
🚫 Public hols

Moosi Maharani ki Chhatri
⊛ 🕐 Daily 🚫 Public hols

Bala Qila
🚫 Daily (written permission needed from Police Superintendent, City Palace)

Tomb of Fateh Jang
Ⓐ Near railway station
🕐 Sunrise-sunset daily

Alwar's ornate Moosi Maharani ki Chhatri cenotaph, and *(inset)* its gold-decorated ceiling

EAT

Pink Floyd Cafe
This quirky rooftop restaurant run by ardent Pink Floyd fans boasts beautiful river views and is a great place to relax as evening descends.

Ⓐ Chotti Basti, near Marwar Bus Stand, Pushkar
📞 (0145) 277 2317

₹₹₹

Madeena Hotel
A popular, unassuming spot that serves tasty mutton curry, including an excellent korma, and freshly baked breads.

Ⓐ Opposite Railway Station, Ajmer
📞 (0145) 262 5115

₹₹₹

Sunset Café
Don't miss sunset at this rooftop restaurant, which serves an array of international dishes.

Ⓐ Choti Basti, Pushkar Lake
📞 (0145) 277 2725

₹₹₹

⑪ Shekhawati

📍 Sikar & Jhunjhunu districts; Nawalgarh, 140 km (87 miles) NW of Jaipur 🚌 🌐 www.tourism.rajasthan.gov.in/shekhawati.html

Named after its 15th-century ruler Rao Shekha, this region is known for its fascinating small towns with intricately painted *havelis*. These sprawling, colourful mansions were built between the late 18th and early 20th centuries by local merchants who had migrated to Mumbai and Kolkata to seek their fortunes. With their subsequent wealth, they built these magnificent ancestral buildings in their hometowns. While the frescoes across the *havelis* have similar themes, each family tried to outdo the others using the profusion of paint colours that became available in the 19th century. The small towns of Mandawa

↑ Elaborate paintings in the inner courtyard of a *haveli* in Shekhawati

and Nawalgarh are good starting points for exploring the region, since they have a range of hotels and guesthouses and are quite easy to navigate. Mandawa has been described as an al fresco art gallery, with ornate paintings adorning buildings such as Sewaram Saraf Haveli and Hanuman Prasad Goenka Haveli. In Nawalgarh, visit the charming Dr Ramnath A Podar Haveli Museum, with its 750 plus restored frescoes.

From here, visit the painted towns of Ramgarh and Fatehpur – equally beautiful but with fewer places to stay. Of note in Ramgarh is the town's largest mansion house, Sawalka Haveli, while in Fatehpur, Haveli Nadine Le Prince has been carefully restored. You can also visit the restored forts at Bissau, Mahansar and Dundlod, which are all now heritage hotels.

Although not technically part of the Shekhawati region, Churu, farther out into the desert, has many stunning painted *havelis*. One of them is Malji Ka Kamra, now a

SHEKHAWATI'S PAINTED HAVELIS

The style and content of the frescoes decorating Shekhawati's mansions are a telling comment on the urbanization of a classic genre. The local artists still followed the one-dimensional realism of traditional Rajput painting *(p54)*, but among gods, goddesses and martial heroes are the symbols of the industrial society that was emerging in the late 19th century: brass bands, trains, motorcars, aeroplanes, gramophones and telephones.

hotel. The owners organize a fascinating walking tour of the town, which is a charming place, despite many of the buildings falling into disrepair. Some of the murals are not so traditional – check out Banthia Haveli for an image of Jesus smoking a cigar – while some depict local folklore and Shekhawati's own Romeo and Juliet, Dhola and Maru.

STAY

Apani Dhani Ecolodge

Guests stay in ochre-coloured huts and dine on organic produce from the garden.

⌂ Nawalgarh
🌐 apanidhani.com

₹₹₹

Hotel Mandawa Haveli

Lovingly restored, this *haveli* features intricately painted murals in the central courtyard.

⌂ Mandawa
🌐 hotelmandawa haveli.com

₹₹₹

Malji Ka Kamra

This stunning mansion fuses Mughal architecture with an Italian Art Deco vibe.

⌂ Churu
🌐 maljikakamra.com

₹₹₹

Hill Fort Kesroli

Perched on a rocky outcrop, this 14th-century fort offers elegant rooms.

⌂ Kesroli, near Alwar
🌐 neemranahotels.com

₹₹₹

Sariska National Park

⌂ Alwar district; 37 km (23 miles) SW of Alwar 🚌
⏱ 6–10am & 3–6pm daily; limited access Jul–Sep
ℹ Field Director, Project Tiger Sanctuary, Sariska; (0144) 284 1333

Designated a Tiger Reserve under Project Tiger *(p174)* in 1979, Sariska National Park, formerly the private hunting ground of the princely state of Alwar, sprawls some 866 sq km (334 sq miles), with a core area of 497 sq km (192 sq miles). The Aravalli Range branches out at Sariska, forming low plateaux and valleys that harbour a wide spectrum of wildlife. The tiger population at Sariska is now believed to be 14 and sightings are rare. Forest guides keep track of where a tiger was last seen and can sometimes lead visitors to spot this predator.

For those seeking wildlife encounters, the watering holes throughout the park at Pandupol, Bandipol, Slopka, Kalighati and Talvriksha draw hordes of animals at sunset, come to quench their thirst. Among those to watch out for are the gentle chital or spotted deer, while the *chausingha* (four-horned antelope), unique to the national park, can be spotted

A majestic tiger, a rarely seen resident of Sariska National Park ↓

INSIDER TIP
Village Safari

Take a jeep ride into the desert and villages around Churu at sunrise. Malji Ka Kamra *(maljikakamra.com)* organizes tours with breakfast – flasks of hot chai and parathas – at an interesting site.

around the atmospheric Pandupol watering hole. Other species that can often be seen here range from jackals and hyenas, panthers and black-faced langur monkeys to nilgai (blue bulls), wild boars and porcupines.

Among the birds that can be spotted are the crested serpent eagle, the great Indian horned owl, woodpeckers, kingfishers and partridges.

The dry deciduous forests of Sariska come to life during the brief spring and early summer when the flowering *dhak (Butea monosperma)* and laburnum bloom. The date palm begins to bear fruit, while berries known locally as *kair (Capparis decidua)* appear on the bushes.

Sariska is also marked by human history: the Kankwari Fort, dating to the 17th century, and temple ruins, such as Pandupol Temple, lie within the park. The Sariska Palace, built at the end of the 19th century as a hunting lodge for Alwar's rulers, is now a luxury hotel, with a collection of vintage hunting photos.

← An elegant demoiselle crane on the shores of the lake at Khichan village, near Phalodi

13
Phalodi

📍 Jodhpur district; 150 km (93 miles) SW of Bikaner 🚌

This large town mainly attracts those interested in visiting the lovely hamlet of Khichan, 4 km (2 miles) to its east. Khichan is famous for the demoiselle cranes that gather around its lake between September and March. The birds migrate here from the Mongolian steppes for the winter. Every day, the villagers spread grain on the fields for the birds, and as a result the number of cranes that come here has increased substantially over the years. At last count, 7,000 cranes spent the winter at Khichan.

14
Bikaner

📍 Bikaner district; 361 km (224 miles) NW of Jaipur 🚉🚌
ℹ www.tourism.rajasthan.gov.in/bikaner.html

Along with Jodhpur and Jaisalmer, Bikaner was one of the three great desert kingdoms of Rajasthan and, like them, prospered because of its location on the overland caravan trade route to Central Asia and China. It was founded

Did You Know?

Rao Bika built his low bed after his grandfather was drugged and murdered in his sleep.

in 1486 by Rao Bika, the younger son of Rao Jodha, the ruler of Jodhpur. It remains a fascinating place to visit, from its old walled town to its many temples and palaces – especially its magnificent fort.

The town's most significant landmark, **Junagarh Fort** was constructed between 1587 and 1593 by the third ruler of Bikaner, Rai Singh. The fort is protected by a 986-m- (3,235-ft-) long sandstone wall with 37 bastions, a moat and, most effectively of all, by the forbidding expanse of the Thar Desert. Not surprisingly, it has never been conquered, a fact that explains its excellent state of preservation. Within the fort's austere stone walls are no fewer than 37 profusely decorated palaces, temples and pavilions, built by its successive rulers over the centuries, though in a harmonious continuity of style. The most outstanding is the Anup Mahal, built by Maharaja Anup

Singh in 1690 as his Hall of Private Audience. It was then sumptuously decorated between 1787 and 1800 by Maharaja Surat Singh. In an ingenious imitation of Mughal *pietra dura* work at a fraction of the cost, the lime-plaster walls of the Anup Mahal have been polished to a high lustre. They are covered with red-and-gold lacquer patterns, further embellished with mirrors and gold leaf.

Two other gorgeous, heavily decorated palaces are the 17th-century Chandra Mahal ("Moon Palace") and Phool Mahal ("Flower Palace"). The museum in the latter contains Rao Bika's small, low bed with curved silver legs, on which he slept with his feet touching the ground. The bed was so designed to enable Rao Bika to jump quickly to his feet and fight off murderous intruders. The Chandra Mahal, which was the queens' palace, has carved marble panels depicting the legend of the great romance between Radha and Krishna, and both palaces have superb stone carving and *jalis*.

The blue-and-gold Badal Mahal ("Cloud Palace") is covered with paintings of clouds, yellow streaks of lightning and rain showers – a favourite fantasy in this arid land. The oldest palace in the fort is Lal Niwas, dating to 1595 and decorated with floral motifs in red and gold. The newest palace is the huge Durbar Niwas ("Coronation Palace"), built in the early 20th century by Bikaner's most progressive ruler, Sir Ganga Singh (r 1887–1943), who gave Bikaner its railway link and built the Ganga Canal, which brought precious irrigation water to his kingdom. The Durbar Niwas now houses the fort museum, whose armoury section includes such fascinating exhibits as a 56-kg (123-lb) suit of armour, a dagger with a pistol built into it, and swords with lion-shaped handles. Other exhibits include a curious half-spoon for soup, used by the maharaja to ensure that his luxuriant moustache remained pristine during mealtimes.

In the old walled town, entered through Kote Gate, is the bazaar, where local handicrafts, such as rugs and carpets, painted lampshades made of camel hide, and beautiful miniatures in the Bikaneri style, can be found. Savoury snacks (bhujias) are another local speciality, and Bikaneri bhujias are renowned throughout India, as are local sweets made of camel's milk.

The grand 17th- and 18th-century havelis of Bikaner's wealthy merchants line the narrow lanes in the vicinity around Rampuria Street. Two of the most ornate are the Rampuria and Kothari havelis; the former is now a delightful heritage hotel. In the south-western corner of the walled town are two Jain temples, the Bhandeshwar and Sandeshwar temples, dating from the early 16th century. The interiors of

> **The blue-and-gold Badal Mahal ("Cloud Palace") is covered with paintings of clouds, yellow streaks of lightning and rain showers - a favourite fantasy in this arid land.**

both are ornately carved and embellished with frescoes and mirrorwork and have intricate gold-leaf scrollwork.

Lalgarh Palace, outside the walled town, is a sprawling extravaganza of carved friezes, *jalis*, pillars and arches in the local reddish-pink sandstone (which resulted in Bikaner being dubbed the "Red City"). Constructed between 1902 and 1926, it was designed by Sir Samuel Swinton Jacob in a style that combines Rajput and Renaissance European features with Art Nouveau decor inside. Part of it has been converted into a hotel, and another section into a museum with vintage photographs and wildlife trophies.

The **National Research Centre on Camels** was set up in 1975 and breeds nearly half the camels found in India. The farm is best visited in the late afternoon, when the camels return from grazing.

Gajner, 30 km (19 miles) northwest of Bikaner, is known for Gajner National Park, home to blackbucks, wild boars, foxes and a large number of migratory birds. Also worth a visit is the 17th-century **Karni Mata Temple**, known as the Rat Temple. This is because of the thousands of rats that swarm around the temple and its precincts. The rats are considered sacred and to be good luck and are fed sweets and milk by the priests and visitors, who believe that they are reincarnated holy men.

Junagarh Fort
◈ ◈ ⏱10am–4:30pm Sat–Thu

Lalgarh Palace
◈ 🚩 N of city centre
📞 (0151) 254 0201
⏱10am–5pm Mon–Sat

National Research Centre on Camels
◈ 🚩 9km (6 miles) SE of Bikaner ⏱Hours vary, check website 🌐nrccamel.icar.gov.in

Karni Mata Temple
🚩 30 km (16 miles) SE of Bikaner ⏱Sunrise–sunset daily

Bikaner's monumental Junagarh Fort, built in the distinctive local red sandstone ↓

15

Ajmer

🏛 Ajmer district; 135 km (84 miles) SW of Jaipur 🚂🚌 ℹ RTDC Hotel Khadim; **www.tourism.rajasthan. gov.in/ajmer.html**

Ajmer is famous for the holy Muslim shrine of Dargah Sharif, the tomb of the great Sufi saint Khwaja Moinuddin Chishti (1143–1235). The saint's majestic marble-domed tomb is at the heart of the expansive Dargah complex, which includes a bazaar and two marble mosques.

Millions of pilgrims come to Ajmer for the saint's annual Urs (death anniversary) in the seventh month of the Islamic lunar calendar, when spirited Sufi musicians sing the saint's praises in front of his tomb.

West of the shrine is the Adhai-Din-ka-Jhonpra, or "Hut of Two-and-a-Half Days", a 13th-century mosque complex whose name is said to derive from the duration of a religious fair that used to be held here. Although it is now in ruins, this complex remains impressive, its main glory an exquisite seven-arched screen in front of the colonnaded hall. Each arch is different, and the columns have elaborate carvings.

↑ Muslim women gathering in prayer at the Dargah Sharif shrine in Ajmer

In the southeast corner of Ajmer is Mayo College, one of India's best public schools. An excellent example of Indo-Saracenic architecture, which was a Gothic style inspired by Mughal architecture favoured during the Raj, it was set up in 1875 by the viceroy Lord Mayo as an "Eton of the East". Its early students were often accompanied by family retainers and tutors, and some, like the prince of Alwar, even brought along their own elephants. Behind the 19th-century Nasiyan Temple, in the heart of the old city, is the Svarna Nagari Hall, vividly decorated with coloured-glass mosaics and gilded wooden figures, recreating scenes from Jain mythology.

The **Ajmer Government Museum**, also in the old city, is located in the legendary Emperor Akbar's fortified palace. Its exhibits include sculptures dating from the 4th to the 12th centuries.

Ajmer Government Museum

⊗ 🏛 Near bus stand 🕘 9am–5:30pm Sat–Thu

⛰ GREAT VIEW
Hidden Haveli

In the shadow of the Garh Palace, the Bundi Vilas is a welcoming family-run hotel in a converted *haveli* with some of the best views – and probably the best lunch – in the town from its rooftop restaurant.

16

Bundi

🏛 Bundi district; 215 km (134 miles) S of Jaipur 🚂🚌 ℹ **www.tourism.rajasthan. gov.in/bundi.html**

Surrounded on three sides by the rugged, thickly forested Aravalli Hills, this walled town has an appealing historic character, with two of the state's most famous palace complexes – Taragarh Fort and Garh Palace – crowning the steep hill that overlooks the town.

The state of Bundi was founded in 1341 by Rao Deva of the "fire-born" Hada Chauhan Rajput clan; the massive, square Taragarh Fort dates to his reign, whereas work on the Garh Palace, often called Bundi's jewel, began in the 16th century and was added to by successive rulers over the next 200 years. Unlike most other palaces in Rajasthan, there is very little Mughal influence in its architecture and it instead represents a rare example of the pure Rajput style, with curved roofs topping pavilions and kiosks, a profusion of temple columns and ornamental brackets, and typically Rajput motifs such as elephants and lotus flowers. Unusually, the palace is not built of sandstone, but of a green-tinged serpentine stone, quarried locally. Since this stone does not lend itself to fine carving, Garh Palace was embellished by paintings.

The palace is entered through the imposing Hathia Pol ("Elephant Gateway"), flanked by two towers topped by a pair of painted elephants. The most spectacular parts of the complex are the smaller lake palace of Chattar Mahal (built in 1660), and the gracious Chitrashala, an arcaded gallery (built between 1748 and 1770) overlooking a hanging garden. The murals in these portray scenes from religious ceremonies, hunting scenes and other princely amusements.

Bundi has over 50 stepwells, of which the most beautiful is the 46-m- (151-ft-) deep Rani-ki-Baori, which is in the centre of town. Built in the 17th century, the stepwell has

richly decorated archways and sculptures of Vishnu's avatars.

Bijolia, 50 km (31 miles) southwest of Bundi, has three beautiful 13th-century temples dedicated to the god Shiva. Menal, 20 km (12 miles) further along the same road, is a delightful wooded spot with 11th-century temples located near a gorge.

Tonk, 113 km (70 miles) north of Bundi, was once the capital of the only Muslim princely state in Rajasthan. Its main attraction is the splendid Sunehri Kothi ("Golden Mansion") within the palace complex, which has a stunning interior covered with gold leaf, lacquerwork and mirrorwork.

---

⑰

Nagaur

📍 Nagaur district; 137 km (85 miles) NE of Jodhpur 🚌 🌐 www.tourism.rajasthan. gov.in/nagaur.html

A little desert town between Jodhpur and Bikaner, Nagaur is dominated by the stunning Ahhichatragarh Fort, which dates from the 12th century. Innovative in its day, the fort has an ingenious system of air ducts conducting cool breezes around the inner buildings, and beautifully decorated water channels. The fort has had several facelifts, starting in the

middle of the 18th century when the ruler of Jodhpur, gifted it by the Mughals, turned the building into a pleasure palace. Over time, the fort's frescoes fell into disrepair, but under the guidance of Maharajah Gaj Singh of Jodhpur, and with several international grants, these are being restored to their former exquisite glory. The project has also been commended for training craftsmen in the restoration process. One wing of the fort – the Apartments of the Nine Wives – has been turned into Ranvas, a boutique hotel with only nine rooms and an excellent restaurant.

↑ Vibrant, elaborate murals decorating the Chitrashala gallery, in Bundi's Garh Palace

18

Kumbhalgarh

Rajsamand district; 63 km (39 miles) N of Udaipur **Kankroli, 35 km (21 miles) SE of Kumbhalgarh, then bus**

The ramparts of Kumbhalgarh Fort wind along the rugged contours of the Aravalli Hills for 36 km (22 miles). This massive 15th-century fort, located at a height of 1,050 m (3,445 ft) along the border between Marwar (Jodhpur region) and Mewar (Udaipur region), was known as "The Eye of Mewar", because it offered a commanding view of the countryside for miles. Built by Maharana Kumbha (r 1433–68), who also built the great fort of Chittorgarh (p156), Kumbhalgarh was said to be the most impregnable fort in Rajasthan. Its ramparts are wide enough for six horsemen to ride abreast, and seven fortified gates, studded with threatening spikes, lead to the entrance. The crenellated walls of the fort enclose the smaller fortress of Kartargarh, several palaces and temples now in ruins, fields, water reservoirs and stables. Standing at the highest point inside the fort is the Badal Mahal, a 19th-century

INSIDER TIP
Divine Dancing

At the end of the year, crowds descend upon Kumbhalgarh for its annual classical dance festival. Beyond performances of traditional Rajasthani folk dances, there is classical music and fun activities.

palace with airy chambers and fine wall paintings of hunting scenes. The 15th-century Neelkantha Temple, which lies within the fort, has a huge Shiva *linga* and is still in use.

Outside of the fort, in a gorge to the east of Kartargarh, is Navachoki Mamdeva Temple. This interesting site contains several slabs of black granite inscribed with the history of Mewar, with the earliest slab dating to 1491. Next to it is the cenotaph of Maharana Kumbha, a former ruler of Mewar..

The Kumbhalgarh Wildlife Sanctuary covers 578 sq km (223 sq miles) of the Aravalli Hills, west of the fort, on the leeward side. Panthers, flying squirrels, wolves and many bird species can be seen here.

The charming little town of Deogarh, 55 km (34 miles) north of Kumbhalgarh, is a popular base for horse safaris and has a bright yellow fort, now a luxury hotel.

19

Mount Abu

Sirohi district; 185 km (115 miles) W of Udaipur **Abu Rd, 20 km (12 miles) SE of town centre, then bus** **www.tourism.rajasthan.gov.in/mount-abu.html**

Rajasthan's only hill station, Mount Abu has one of India's most spectacular sights – the **Dilwara Jain Temples**. This group of five marble temples sits on a hill 3 km (2 miles) northeast of the town. The two most outstanding are the Vimala Vasahi Temple and the Luna Vasahi Temple. The sculptural details on the doorways, archways, pillars and ceilings of both these temples are simply breathtaking, and the marble is worked so finely that in places it is almost translucent.

The Vimala Vasahi Temple, dedicated to the first Jain *tirthankara*, or spiritual leader, Adinath, was built in 1031 by Vimala Shah, a wealthy prime minister of the Solanki kings of Gujarat. A statue of him seated on an elephant is in a pavilion to the right of the entrance. Inside, graceful nymphs and musicians, spirited horses and elephants adorn the arches and pillars and the superb 11-tiered domed ceiling in the main hall. The inner sanctum has a

Traditional dancers performing below Kumbhalgarh Fort ↓

↑ Visitors among the pillars in Adinath Temple in Ranakpur, and *(inset)* an example of the temple's elaborate carvings

statue of Adinath in tranquil meditation, while 52 carved niches contain images of the other *tirthankaras*. The Luna Vasahi Temple, dedicated to Neminath, the 22nd Jain *tirthankara,* dates from 1231 and is even more ornately carved. Its glorious main hall has a magnificent lotus-shaped, tiered pendant carved from a single block of marble, hanging from its domed ceiling. Behind the main shrine is the fascinating Hall of Donors, which has a series of figures mounted on elephants, some in black marble. There are also life-size statues of the donors and their wives, with every detail of their dress and jewellery exquisitely carved. Visitors cannot take leather items inside the temples.

Aside from the temples, the focal point of Mount Abu town is Nakki Lake, ringed by colonial mansions and the summer palaces of Rajput rulers.

Achalgarh, 8 km (5 miles) beyond Dilwara, has the ruins of a 15th-century fort, and a Shiva temple with a statue of Nandi, the sacred bull, made

from over 4,000 kg (8,818 lbs) of gold, silver, brass and copper. A short walk from the temple is Guru Shikhar, Rajasthan's highest point.

Dilwara Jain Temples
🕑 Noon–5pm daily

20

Ranakpur

📍 Rajsamand district; 90 km (56 miles) NW of Udaipur 🚍 🕑 Noon–5pm daily

Set in a secluded, wooded valley of the Aravalli Hills, the 15th-century Ranakpur temple complex, dominated by the great Adinath Temple, is one of the five great holy places of the Jain faith. The grand scale and sheer architectural complexity of

this white marble temple distinguish it as perhaps the single most impressive example of Western Indian temple architecture. The temple has an unusual four-sided plan, with four separate entrances. Each entrance leads through a veritable forest of columns, and a number of beautifully ornamented halls and chapels, to the central sanctum containing a four-faced image of Adinath.

Each of the temple's 1,444 pillars is carved with different patterns of floral motifs, and the play of light and shadow on the pillars, as the sun moves from east to west each day, is one of the special parts of this monument. This craftsmanship continues throughout, from the superb filigree carving on the concentric ceiling pendants to the exuberantly graceful sculptures of the goddesses who form the support brackets. Visitors cannot take leather items inside and photographs are not allowed; lockers are provided for visitors' cameras.

> Its glorious main hall has a magnificent lotus-shaped, tiered pendant carved from a single block of marble, hanging from its domed ceiling.

The vast Chittorgarh
Fort complex, site of
many dramatic events

Did You Know?

In legend, the Rajput
ruler of Chittorgarh
heard about Rani
Padmini's beauty from
a talking parrot.

21 Kota

🏛 Kota district; 261 km
(162 miles) S of Jaipur 🚉🚌
ℹ Hotel Chambal; www.
tourism.rajasthan.gov.in/
kota.html

The imposing façade of Kota's
City Palace, which dates back
to 1625, stretches along the
banks of the Chambal river,
recalling the princely past of
this now heavily industrialized
city. Every available surface in
the palace apartments is
covered with miniature
paintings, mirrorwork, murals
and mosaics. Particularly
resplendent is the Durbar
Hall, with its ebony-and-
ivory doors, and paintings
depicting Kota's history. Many
of the royal apartments now
form part of the excellent **Rao
Madho Singh
Museum**,
which has a
fine collection
of weapons and
royal regalia.
On Kishorsagar Lake, in
the middle of the town, is
the charming Jag Mandir, an
island palace built in the 18th
century by a Kota queen who
yearned for her childhood
home in Udaipur (p140).
Bardoli, 55 km (34 miles)
southwest of Kota, has one of
Rajasthan's most beautiful
Hindu temple complexes.
The 9th-century Ghateshwar
Mahadev temple has an
outstanding sculpture of
Nataraja (the dancing Shiva)
on the door of its sanctum.

Rao Madho Singh Museum
⊘ ⏲ 10am–5pm daily
🚫 Public hols

22 Chittorgarh

🏛 Chittorgarh district;
115 km (71 miles) NE of
Udaipur 🚉🚌 ℹ Janta Avas
Graha, Station Rd; www.
tourism.rajasthan.gov.in/
chittorgarh.html

The tragic history of the great,
battle-scarred Chittorgarh
Fort epitomizes the valour,
romance, chivalry and strict
death-before-dishonour code
glorified in Rajput myths and
legends. Sprawling across
280 ha (692 acres), atop a steep
rocky hill, the fort's ruined
palaces, temples and towers
bear witness to its illustrious
and turbulent past, when it
was the capital of the Sisodia
rulers of Mewar between the
12th and 16th centuries.
Rajasthan's mightiest fort,
Chittorgarh was the target of
successive invaders. The first
siege, in 1303, was by Sultan
Alauddin Khilji, whose goal
was to capture not only the
fort but also the queen, Rani
Padmini, whose beauty was
legendary. When defeat
seemed inevitable, Rani
Padmini – along with
13,000 local women –
committed *jauhar*, a ritual
form of mass suicide by
immolation, practised by

Stone elephant at the
entrance gate of the
City Palace of Kota

Rajput women to escape dishonour at the hands of their enemies. It is said that 50,000 Rajput warriors died in the battle. After their victory, the Sultan's army sacked the fort and destroyed many of its buildings. But within a few years the Sisodia dynasty had regained the fort.

In 1535, the fort was again attacked, this time by Sultan Bahadur Shah of Gujarat. The Queen Mother, Rani Jawaharbai, led a cavalry charge and died on the battlefield along with large numbers of Rajput men. Once again, thousands of women inside Chittorgarh committed *jauhar*.

The third and final assault on the city was led by the Mughal emperor Akbar, who was able to capture it in 1567. Chittorgarh was abandoned and the Sisodias moved their capital to Udaipur *(p140)*.

Seven massive spiked gates lead to the fort. The first building to the right is Rana Kumbha's Palace (which was built between 1433 and 1468), probably the earliest surviving example of a Rajput palace. Its northern side has a profusion of richly carved balconies, and a unique stepped wall.

The public areas of the fort include both elephant stables and a council chamber, while the private apartments are a maze of small rooms. Near it are graceful **Fateh Prakash Palace**, which now houses a museum displaying sculptures found on the site; the Kumbha Shyam Temple, dating to the 15th century, with a fine sculpture of Vishnu in his Varaha (boar) incarnation; and the Meerabai Temple, built in 1440 by Meerabai, another remarkable Mewar queen. A mystic and a poet, she defied the conventional role for Rajput women and instead devoted her life to the worship of Lord Krishna.

The main street in the fort runs south of this temple towards the nine-storeyed Vijay Stambh ("Victory Tower"), built by Maharana Kumbha between 1458 and 1468 to commemorate his victory over Sultan Mahmud of Malwa. The view from the top of this extraordinary 36-m- (118-ft-) high sandstone structure, richly carved with gods and goddesses, is magnificent. This street continues further south past some noblemen's mansions to the Gaumukh Reservoir, fed by an underground spring, and the 16th-century Kalika Mata Temple, built over the original Sun Temple, which was destroyed during the devastating siege of 1303.

Opposite this temple stands the 19th-century reconstruction of Padmini's Palace, with an atmospheric lake pavilion adjacent to it.

Fateh Prakash Palace
⊘ ⏰ 10am–4:30pm Sat-Thu

㉓
Dungarpur

🏠 Dungarpur district; 110 km (68 miles) S of Udaipur 🚌
ℹ www.tourism.rajasthan.gov.in/chittorgarh.html

This remote town boasts some unexpected artistic treasures, like the seven-storeyed Juna Mahal, built in the 13th century on a large rock. The interior of this complex, in contrast to its rather battered exterior, glows with exuberant ornamentation and contains some remarkably well-preserved frescoes, such as a series of erotic paintings from the *Kama Sutra* in the ruler's bedroom.

The 19th-century Udai Vilas Palace, beside the lake, blends Rajput and Mughal styles. Rising from the centre of its courtyard is a fantastic four-storeyed pavilion with cusped arches, densely carved friezes, and a profusion of canopies and balconies.

↑ The vibrantly decorated throne room at the ancient palace of Dungarpur

Flower offerings to the sacred Ganges river

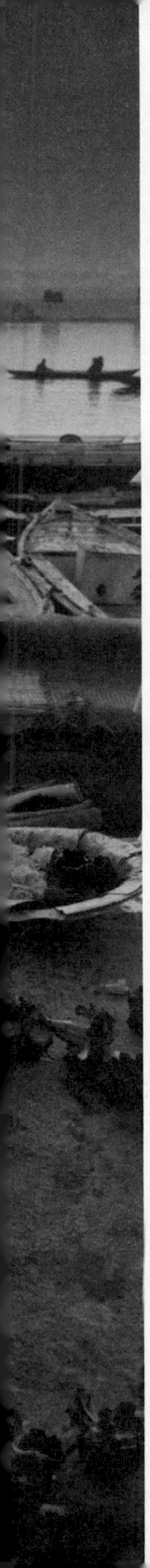

UTTAR PRADESH AND UTTARAKHAND

Stretching from the Himalayas to the Indo-Gangetic Plains, Uttar Pradesh and Uttarakhand cover a vast area of 294,000 sq km (113,514 sq miles), with a population of almost 214 million. The state of Uttarakhand was formed in 2000, acknowledging its difference from lowland Uttar Pradesh. Uttar Pradesh has a wealth of monuments that speak to its long history. The initial Buddhist stupas at Sarnath were built in the 4th century BC during the reign of Ashoka, the Mauryan emperor famous for his military exploits who then became a Buddhist and spread the religion far and wide. This area has long been written into India's history; the city of Mathura even features in the early Hindu epic, the *Mahabharata*. Similarly, the state has featured in most of the key empires that have ruled over India, from the early Hindu dynasties, such as the Guptas, before occupation by Muslim invaders starting with the Delhi Sultanate and, subsequently, the Mughals. It is here that the Mughals built some of their most spectacular monuments, including the Taj Mahal, a symbol to lasting romantic devotion. The British annexed both states to become part of their Raj, and built charming hill station retreats in the cool hills of Uttarakhand. This area was one of the main areas of rebellion against the British during the War of Independence in 1857; their ambition for an independent India was achieved in 1947, and the state of Uttar Pradesh was proclaimed in 1950.

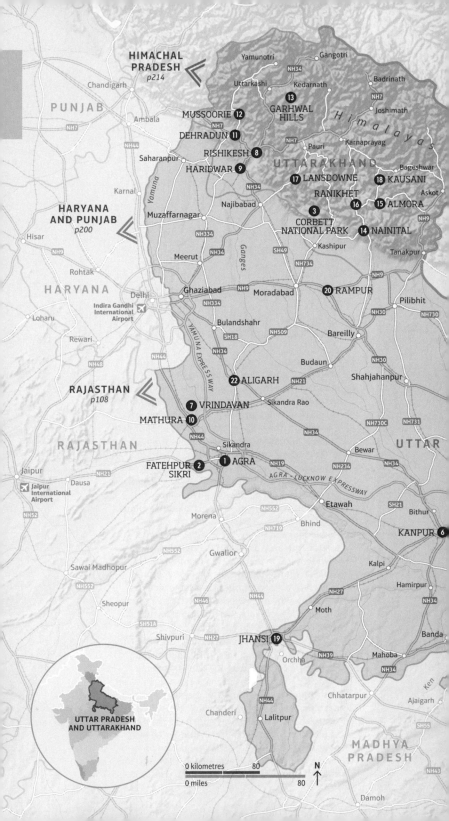

UTTAR PRADESH AND UTTARAKHAND

Must Sees

1 Agra
2 Fatehpur Sikri
3 Corbett National Park
4 Varanasi
5 Lucknow

Experience More

6 Kanpur
7 Vrindavan
8 Rishikesh
9 Haridwar
10 Mathura
11 Dehradun
12 Mussoorie
13 Garhwal Hills
14 Nainital
15 Almora
16 Ranikhet
17 Lansdowne
18 Kausani
19 Jhansi
20 Rampur
21 Dudhwa National Park
22 Aligarh
23 Sarnath
24 Prayagraj (Allahabad)
25 Ayodhya
26 Kalinjar Fort
27 Jaunpur
28 Chitrakoot

Agra Fort, an impressive red-brick complex that stands alongside the river ↑

① AGRA

📍 Agra district, Uttar Pradesh; 201 km (125 miles) SE of Delhi ✈ Kheria, 8 km (5 miles) SW of city 🚉 Agra Cantonment, Raja ki Mandi, Fort 🚌 Idgah ℹ UPSTDC, 64 Taj Rd; UPSTDC, Agra Cantt; ITDC, 191 Mall Rd; www.uptourism.gov.in/article/Agra-Fatehpur-Sikri

Agra was the seat of the imperial Mughal court during the 16th and 17th centuries, before the capital was shifted to Delhi. The city flourished under the patronage of the emperors Akbar, Jahangir and Shah Jahan. With the decline of the Mughals, Agra was captured by the Jats, the Marathas and, finally, the British, early in the 19th century.

① Agra Fort

🕐 Fort: 6am–6pm daily; Son et Lumière: 7pm daily 🌐 agrafort.gov.in

Situated on the west bank of the Yamuna, Agra Fort was built by Emperor Akbar between 1565 and 1573. Its imposing red sandstone ramparts form a crescent along the riverfront, and encompass an enormous complex of courtly buildings, ranging in style from the early eclecticism of Akbar to the sublime elegance of Shah Jahan. The barracks to the north are 19th-century British additions. A deep moat, once filled with water from the Yamuna, surrounds the fort.

The impressive Amar Singh Gate, to the south, leads into the fort. To its right is the so-called Jahangiri Mahal, the only major palace in the fort that dates back to Akbar's reign. This complex arrangement of halls, courtyards and galleries was the zenana or main harem. Along the riverfront are the Khas Mahal, an elegant marble hall with a vividly painted ceiling, characteristic of Shah Jahan's style of architecture, and two golden pavilions with *bangaldar* roofs

📷 PICTURE PERFECT
Archways at Agra Fort's Diwan-i-Am

With nine ornate arches along its west-facing side, the Diwan-i-Am makes for a perfect landscape shot. It is best taken in the late afternoon, when the steadily descending sun gleams on it.

(curved roofs derived from Bengali huts). The Sheesh Mahal and royal baths are to the northeast, near Musamman Burj, a double-storeyed octagonal tower with clear views of the Taj, where Shah Jahan, imprisoned by his son Aurangzeb, spent the last years of his life. Mina Masjid, probably the smallest mosque in the world and intended for the emperor only, is nearby.

② St John's College

📍 Mahatma Gandhi Rd 🕐 Mon–Sat 🔒 Public hols 🌐 stjohnscollegeagra.in

St John's College consists of a group of red sandstone

buildings, including a hall and library, arranged around a quadrangle, all designed in a quasi-Fatehpur Sikri (p170) style by Sir Samuel Swinton Jacob, who perfected the Indo-Saracenic style of architecture. Started by the Church Missionary Society in 1850, the college is now affiliated to Agra University and continues to be one of Agra's most prestigious institutions.

③ Roman Catholic Cemetery

⌂ Opp Civil Courts ⏲ Daily

Towards the north of the town stands the Roman Catholic Cemetery – the oldest European graveyard in North India – established in the 17th century by an Armenian merchant, Khoja Mortenepus. A number of Islamic-style gravestones, with inscriptions in Armenian, survive today; they include those of the cannon expert, Shah Nazar Khan, and Khoja Mortenepus himself. There are also tombs of European missionaries, traders and adventurers such as the 18th-century French freebooter Walter Reinhardt. The largest tomb is that of John William Hessing, a British commander in the army of the Scindias, the rulers of Gwalior (p296). Hessing's red sandstone tomb, built after his death in 1803, is modelled on the lines of the Taj Mahal. One of the oldest tombs belongs to the English merchant John Mildenhall, envoy of Elizabeth I, who arrived at the Mughal court in 1603 seeking permission to trade. He was the first Englishman buried in India.

STAY

The Oberoi
Stylish and elegant, the Oberoi is a short walk from the Taj Mahal.

⌂ Taj East Gate Road, Paktola �W oberoihotels. com/hotels-in-agra-amarvilas-resort

₹₹₹

Hotel Taj Plaza
The best rooms here have good views of the Taj.

⌂ 23-24 Taj East Gate Road, Paktola W hoteltajplazaagra.com

₹₹₹

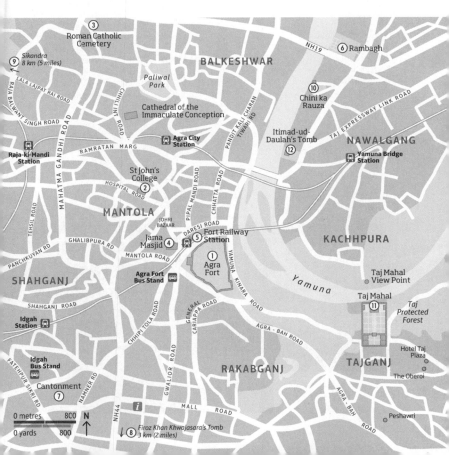

④

Jama Masjid

🕓 Sunrise-sunset daily
🕙 To non-Muslims during prayer times

A magnificently proportioned building in the heart of the historic town, the "Friday Mosque" was sponsored by Shah Jahan's favourite daughter, Jahanara Begum, who also commissioned several other buildings and gardens, including the canal that once ran down Chandni Chowk (p106) in Delhi. Built in 1648, the mosque's sandstone and marble domes with their distinctive zigzag chevron pattern dominate this section of the town. The eastern courtyard

> **INSIDER TIP**
> **Explore Agra**
>
> To get a real insight into Agra's history and life, take one of Agrawalks' fascinating three-hour guided culture tours, or learn about local cuisine with their food tour (www.agrawalks.com).

wing was demolished by the British in 1857. Of interest are the tank with its *shahi chirag* (royal stove) for heating water within the courtyard, and the separate prayer chamber for ladies.

The area around Jama Masjid was once a vibrant meeting place, famous for its kebab houses and lively bazaars. A stroll through the narrow alleys offers glimpses of an older way of life, reminiscent of Mughal Agra. This is also the city's crafts and trade centre where a vast array of products such as jewellery, *zari* embroidery, inlaid marble objects, durries, dried fruit, sweets, shoes and kites are available. Quieter lanes such as Panni Gali have many fine buildings, with imposing gateways leading into secluded courtyards, where the thriving workshops of master craftsmen still exist.

⑤

Fort Railway Station

This memorable Raj building was constructed in 1891 as a stopping-off point for colonial tourists visiting Agra's many

monuments. The octagonal bazaar chowk that originally connected the Delhi Gate and Agra Fort to the old city and the Jama Masjid was demolished, and this station, with its French château-style slate-roofed platforms, was built. It is still in use today. Agra's two other railway stations are located in the cantonment and at Raja ki Mandi.

⑥

Rambagh

🏠 3 km (2 miles) N of Itimad-ud-Daulah's Tomb 🕓 Daily

Further upriver from Agra Fort, the quiet, tree-shaded Rambagh or Aram Bagh ("Garden of Rest") is thought to be the earliest Mughal garden, laid out by Babur, the first Mughal emperor, in 1526. The garden also served as his temporary burial place, before his body was moved to Kabul. The large walled garden, divided by walkways that lead to a raised terrace with open pavilions overlooking the river, was further developed by the empress Nur Jahan.

The Jama Masjid, built in 1648, with its spacious courtyard

GOLD THREAD AND BEAD ZARDOZI

Agra's flourishing traditional craft of elaborate gold thread (*zari*) and bead embroidery is called *zardozi*. Central Asian in origin, the technique came to the region with the Mughal emperors. Local craftsmen in the old city developed refinements and complex new patterns to make garments and accessories for the imperial court. With the decline of court patronage, the skill almost vanished. It owes its revival to encouragement from modern fashion designers.

---

⑦
Cantonment

📍 **Enclosed by Mahatma Gandhi Rd, Grand Parade Rd & Mall Rd**

The pleasant, tree-shaded army cantonment area, with its own railway station and orderly avenues, has many interesting public buildings, churches, cemeteries and bungalows in a medley of styles dating from colonial times. St George's Church (1826) is a plastered, ochre-coloured building designed by Colonel JT Boileau, architect of Shimla's famous Christ Church (*p222*). Havelock Memorial Church, constructed in 1873 in a "trim Classical style", commemorates one of the British generals involved in the War of Independence of 1857.

---

⑧
Firoz Khan Khwajasara's Tomb

📍 **S of Agra, on Gwalior Rd**
🕐 **Daily**

A signpost on the Gwalior Road indicates the turning to this unusual 17th-century octagonal structure, standing on the edge of a lake. This marks the spot where Firoz Khan Khwajasara, a eunuch and the custodian of Shah Jahan's palace harem, is buried. The red sandstone edifice stands on a high plinth and has a gateway attached to the main building. Steps lead to the upper storey, where a central pavilion containing the grave is located. If the tomb is closed, the watchman from the village will open the gate.

---

⑨
Sikandra

📍 **Agra district; 8 km (5 miles) NW of Agra** 🚍🚉

The Mughal Emperor Akbar is buried in this small village on the outskirts of Agra. It is believed that Akbar designed and started the construction of his own **mausoleum** (free on Fridays), which was modified and completed by his son Jahangir. The result is this impressive, perfectly symmetrical complex, with the tomb located in the centre of a vast walled garden. On each corner are four graceful marble minarets, considered to be the forerunners of those of the Taj Mahal (*p166*).

The large enclosed garden, where monkeys frolic, is in the *charbagh* style – divided in four (representing the four quarters of life) by a system of raised walkways, sunken groves and water channels.

The main tomb is a distinct departure from the conventional domed structure of the tomb of Akbar's father, Humayun, in Delhi (*p92*). The first three storeys of its majestic four tiers consist of red sandstone pavilions.

Mausoleum
⊗ 📞 **(0562) 264 1230** (for permission to go to the tomb terrace) 🕐 **Sunrise-sunset daily**

↑ The magnificent, colourfully tiled ceiling of Chini ka Rauza

⑩
Chini ka Rauza

📍 **1 km (0.6 miles) N of Itimad-ud-Daulah's Tomb**
🕐 **10am–5pm daily**

Chini ka Rauza (literally "China Tomb", after its tiled exterior), was built by Afzal Khan, a poet-scholar from Shiraz (Persia). The surface of this Persian-style square structure was once covered with tiles from Lahore and Multan, interspersed with calligraphic panels.

EAT

Peshawri
One of Agra's top restaurants, specializing in the meat-based dishes of the North-West Frontier, many cooked in a tandoor.

📍 **ITC Mughal Hotel, Taj Ganj** 🌐 **itchotels.in**

₹₹₹

⑪ ⊘ Ⓜ

TAJ MAHAL

🏠 Tajganj 🚌 🛺 🕐 Taj Mahal: 6am-7pm Sat-Thu; museum:
10am-5pm Sat-Thu 🚫 Taj Mahal: Fri; museum: public hols
🌐 tajmahal.gov.in

One of the world's most famous buildings, the Taj Mahal
("Crown of Palaces") was built by the Mughal emperor
Shah Jahan in memory of his wife, Mumtaz Mahal. Its
perfect proportions and exquisite craftsmanship have
been described as "a vision, a dream, a poem, a wonder".

This sublime garden-tomb, an image of the Islamic garden of
paradise, took 20,000 labourers around 15 years to build and
was completed in 1648. Its four minarets, each 40 m (131 ft)
high and crowned by a *chhatri* (an open octagonal pavilion),
frame the tomb, highlighting the perfect symmetry of the
complex. Inside the mausoleum, the octagonal chamber in the
centre houses Mumtaz Mahal's cenotaph, which is raised on a
platform and placed next to Shah Jahan's. The actual graves,
in a dark crypt below, are closed to the public.

THE TAJ GETS
A FACIAL

Over the years, the Taj's
marble surface has been
ravaged by pollution and
grubby insects, and by
the turn of the 21st
century it was looking
quite yellow. The fix
has been a natural
treatment long used by
Indian women: a *multani
mitti* mudpack, which
has left the treated
areas looking cleaner,
younger and healthier.

TOP 5 DECORATIVE ELEMENTS

Pietra Dura
Semiprecious and precious stone inlays, often in the form of ornate flowers.

Jali Screens
Filigree screens carved from stone slabs, casting mosaic-like shadows on the tomb.

Carved Reliefs
Intricate floral bas-reliefs, expertly carved out of polished marble or sandstone.

Calligraphy
Arabic verses and passages from the Qur'an, typically inlaid using black marble.

Incised Painting
Carved incisions filled with thick paint or stucco plaster, which is then delicately scraped off to leave the design.

←
The perfectly proportioned Taj Mahal in the morning, as captured by a drone

₹15 million

The eventual cost of building the Taj Mahal, equivalent to nearly £600 million today.

1 Panels of exquisite Arabic calligraphy reach up and over the entrance arches to the mausoleum. The text increases in size as it gets higher, creating the optical illusion of uniform script.

2 Much of the red sandstone of the mosque is carved with rich, delicate reliefs representing a variety of flowers.

3 Inspired by the paradise garden, intricately carved floral designs inlaid with precious stones embellish the austere white marble surface to give it the look of a bejewelled casket.

Exploring the Taj Mahal

Surrounded by landscaped gardens, the elegant towers and graceful domes of the Taj are an awe-inspiring sight. The interior, decorated with precious stones, calligraphic panels and intricate filigree screens, is just as spectacular.

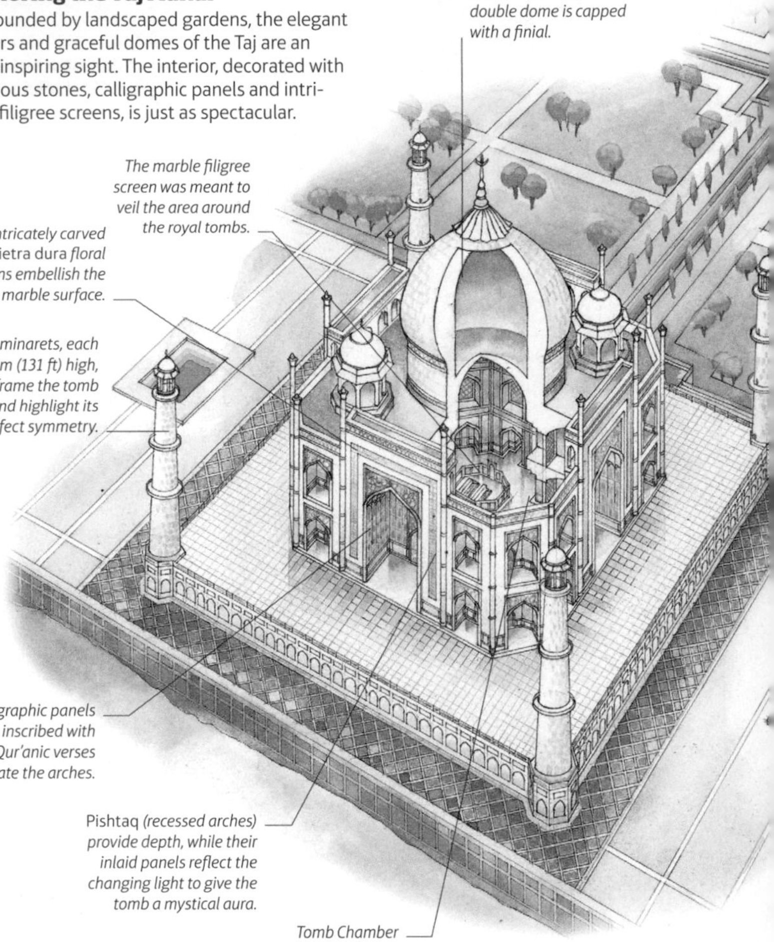

The 44-m- (144-ft-) double dome is capped with a finial.

The marble filigree screen was meant to veil the area around the royal tombs.

Intricately carved pietra dura floral designs embellish the white marble surface.

Four minarets, each 40 m (131 ft) high, frame the tomb and highlight its perfect symmetry.

Calligraphic panels inscribed with Qur'anic verses decorate the arches.

Pishtaq (recessed arches) provide depth, while their inlaid panels reflect the changing light to give the tomb a mystical aura.

Tomb Chamber

Timeline

1631

▼ Mumtaz Mahal, the favourite wife of Mughal Emperor Shah Jahan, dies in Burhanpur.

1632

Shah Jahan orders a mausoleum to be built along the Yumana's banks; work begins.

1908

▼ The Taj - after centuries of neglect - is restored under the orders of British Viceroy Lord Curzon.

1648

The white marble mausoleum and many of the surrounding buildings are completed.

1666

▲ Shah Jahan, who had been overthrown and imprisoned by his son, dies. He is interred next to Mumtaz Mahal in the Taj Mahal.

⑫ ✍

ITIMAD-UD-DAULAH'S TOMB

⌂ E bank of Yamuna, 4 km (2 miles) upstream from the Taj Mahal ⏰ Sunrise-sunset daily

Lyrically described as a "jewel box in marble", the small yet elegant garden-tomb of Mirza Ghiyas Beg, titled Itimad-ud-Daulah, a Grand Vizier in the Mughal court, was built by his daughter Nur Jahan, the favourite wife of Mughal emperor Jahangir.

Begun in 1622, it took six years to complete this tomb, which is beautifully made of white marble, coloured mosaic, stone inlay and lattice work. The most stylistically innovative Mughal building of this era, it marks the transition in Mughal architecture from robust, red standstone structures to more intricate and delicate buildings – of which the most famous example is the Taj Mahal. Itimad-ud-Daulah's square two-storeyed tomb stands in the centre of a *charbagh (p156)*. At the corners of the platform on which the tomb sits are four squat minarets. The polished marble exterior is covered in stone inlay, the first time the *pietra dura* technique had been extensively used. But the main glory of this tomb is its interior, covered in mosaics and painted-and-gilded stucco and stalactite patterns.

The charbagh garden was irrigated with water from the Yamuna river.

← Illustration of the Taj Mahal, showing its interior and surrounds

→ Mosaics and stuccowork lining the interior of Itimad-ud-Daulah's tomb

1983

△ The building is named a UNESCO World Heritage Site for being "a jewel of Muslim art" and an internationally renowned masterpiece of the world's architectural heritage.

↑ The marble tomb, with its unusual square dome and surrounding gardens

2 🏛 🎨 🍴 🛍 🏛

FATEHPUR SIKRI

📍 Agra district, Uttar Pradesh; 37 km (23 miles) W of Agra
🕐 Sunrise-sunset daily 🌐 fatehpursikri.gov.in

One of the greatest examples of Mughal architecture in India, Fatehpur Sikri is a well-preserved example of the might of this once-powerful empire – and so beautiful it could have fallen out of a storybook. Its immense yet elegant mosque, the Jama Masjid, is still a major site of pilgrimage.

Built by Emperor Akbar, one of the empire's most famous rulers, between 1571 and 1585, this sprawling city complex was the Mughal capital for 14 years. A magnificent example of a Mughal walled city, Fatehpur Sikri had defined private and public areas and imposing gateways. Its architecture was a blend of Hindu and Islamic styles, which reflected Akbar's secular vision as well as his style of governance.

After the city was abandoned, many of its treasures were plundered, until the British viceroy Lord Curzon, a legendary conservationist (he also ordered the preservation of the Taj Mahal), made efforts to protect and restore it. It is now a UNESCO World Heritage Site.

Did You Know?

The city was built on the site inhabited by the hermit who predicted that Akbar would have a son.

↑ The lovely pool of Anoop Talao, outside Akbar's private chambers

← The soaring arches of the Jama Masjid, built in Akbar's favourite sandstone

→ The grand Diwan-i-Khas (Hall of Private Audience), showing the balcony where Akbar sat

THE GREAT AKBAR

The greatest of the Mughal emperors, Akbar (r 1556–1605) expanded his territory to stretch all the way from Afghanistan to Bengal and down to Maharashtra. A Sunni Muslim, Akbar was well known for his religious tolerance. He had Hindu, Buddhist and Christian philosophers at court, and took a keen interest in the mystical Sufi side of Islam. He also allowed his Hindu wives to freely practise their religion. He died from an attack of dysentery, probably brought on from drinking dirty water.

← Buland Darwaza, the
entrance to the grand
Jama Masjid mosque

and Jain architecture with the elegant domes
and arches of Islamic buildings, showing the
diversity of Akbar's kingdom.

The gate opens into the cloistered courtyard
of the Diwan-i-Aam, where Akbar sat on a
balcony and gave public audiences. A passage
behind it leads into the inner citadel. This
contains the Diwan-i-Khas, Khwabgah and
Anoop Talao, along with the treasuries and the
Abdar Khana, where water and fruit for the
royal household were stored.

The Haram Sara, or harem complex, was a
maze of interconnected buildings. Its massive
and austere exterior leads to a collection of
palaces and a mosque, and form the outermost periphery of the palace complex.
Beyond the royal complex, the most well-
known building here is the Jama Masjid,
the grand open mosque that
contains the tomb of the
Sufi mystic, Salim
Chishti.

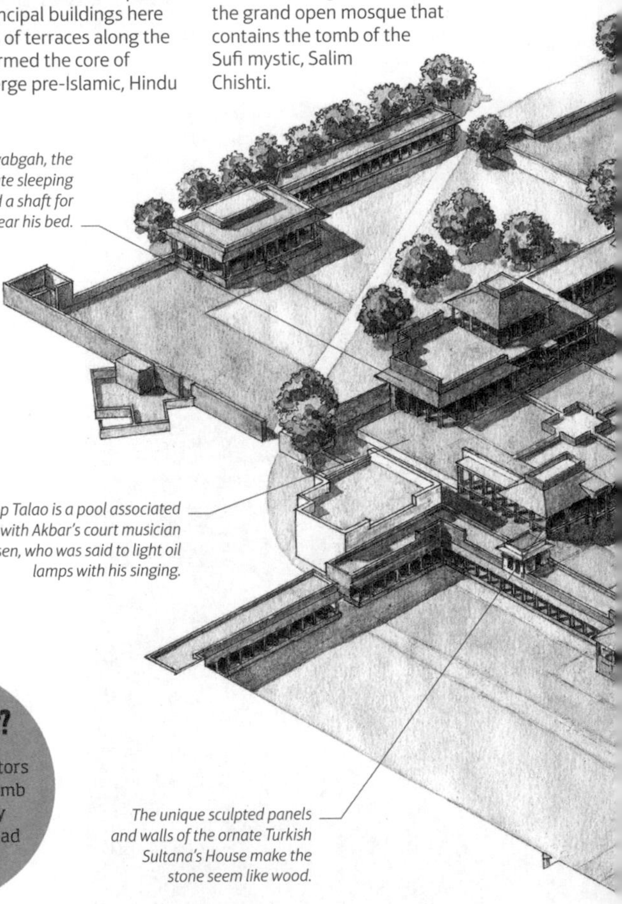

Exploring Fatehpur Sikri

Even today, access to the city is via a straight
road built by the emperor, which was once
lined with bazaars. It leads visitors through the
Agra Gate to the triple-arched Naubat Khana,
where the emperor's entry was announced by
a roll of drums. Leading off from the Naubat
Khana is the western entrance to the imperial
palace complex. The principal buildings here
are clustered on a series of terraces along the
sandstone ridge, and formed the core of
Akbar's capital. They merge pre-Islamic, Hindu

*The Khwabgah, the
emperor's private sleeping
quarters, had a shaft for
ventilation near his bed.*

→ An overview of the
palace complex at
Fatehpur Sikri

*Anoop Talao is a pool associated
with Akbar's court musician
Tansen, who was said to light oil
lamps with his singing.*

Did You Know?

It is tradition for visitors
to Salim Chishti's tomb
to make a wish by
tying a cotton thread
to its screen.

*The unique sculpted panels
and walls of the ornate Turkish
Sultana's House make the
stone seem like wood.*

The white marble tomb of Salim Chishti, within the Jama Masjid ↑

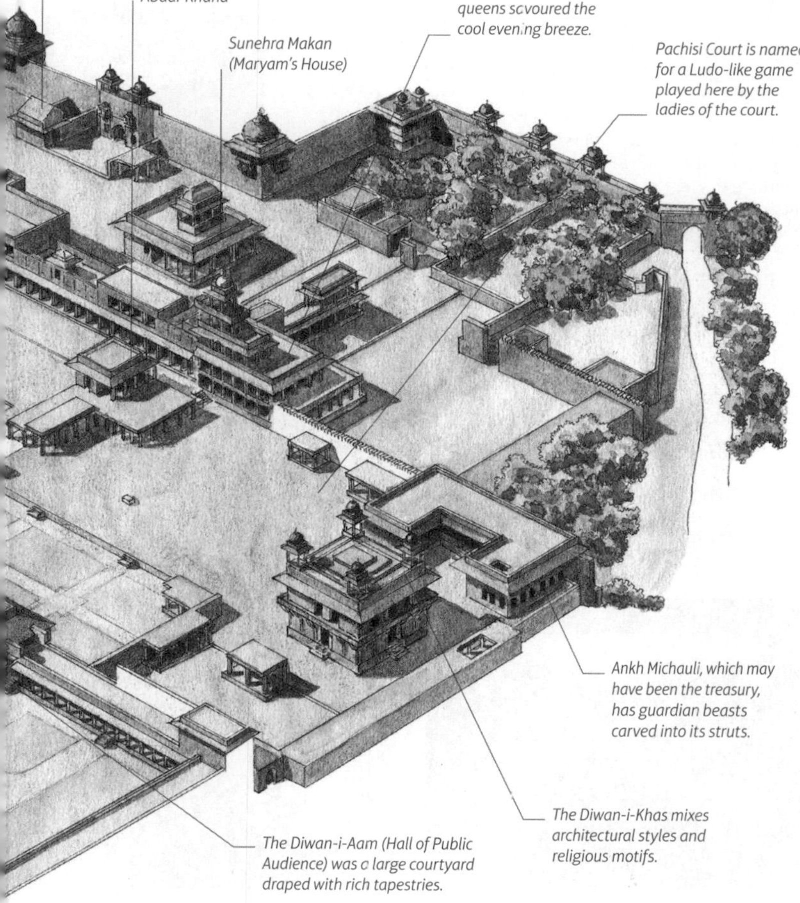

Haram Sara

Abdar Khana

Sunehra Makan (Maryam's House)

The five-storeyed open pavilion of *Panch Mahal* is where Akbar's queens savoured the cool evening breeze.

Pachisi Court is named for a Ludo-like game played here by the ladies of the court.

Ankh Michauli, which may have been the treasury, has guardian beasts carved into its struts.

The Diwan-i-Khas mixes architectural styles and religious motifs.

The Diwan-i-Aam (Hall of Public Audience) was a large courtyard draped with rich tapestries.

173

3

CORBETT NATIONAL PARK

Pauri Garhwal & Nainital districts, Uttarakhand; 436 km (271 miles) NW of Lucknow; entry points at Dhangarhi & Kalagarh ⏰Hours vary, check website ℹ️Tourist Rest House, Ramnagar; www.corbettonline.uk.gov.in (for permits)

This national park was India's first, and is home to a spectacular array of wildlife, including elephants, tigers and more than 600 species of birds, in an equally diverse natural setting.

Situated along the valley of the Ramganga river and fringed by the Himalayan foothills in the north, the park encompasses varied terrain, from savannah grasslands to hilly ridges of deciduous forest with chir pine and sal *(Shorea robusta)*. It is considered one of India's finest wildlife sanctuaries, and is one of the most popular places in Uttarakhand, mainly visited by people on safari hoping to catch a glimpse of an elusive tiger.

The 1,288-sq-km (497-sq-mile) reserve was a hunter's paradise during the British Raj. In 1936, it became India's first national park, largely due to the efforts of the great British hunter-turned-conservationist Jim Corbett, after whom the park is named. Corbett advocated for the establishment of a national park, photographed local animals and educated people about conservation – although he never stopped shooting tigers. Today, the park is renowned for its remarkable variety of wildlife.

Did You Know?

Jim Corbett shot the Champawat Tiger, which was responsible for killing at least 436 people.

PROJECT TIGER

Launched in Corbett National Park in 1973, Project Tiger is a government-backed programme to save India's tigers from extinction using a network of protected reserves. From nine reserves when it started, the project now has over 50. It has had to surmount all kinds of problems, particularly poaching. Despite this, the project has been very successful, and has seen India's tiger population increase from fewer than 1,500 in 2006 to around 3,000 today.

1

2

3

1 The sambar deer is native to India, and is now considered a vulnerable species.

2 There are five zones within Corbett National Park, only one of which is open to visitors on safari tours. This group has just spotted a tiger in the wild.

3 The colourful Indian roller bird is one of hundreds of bird species in the park.

↑ Elephants drinking from a waterhole in the national park

④

VARANASI

🏛 Uttar Pradesh; 286 km (178 miles) SE of Lucknow
✈ 22 km (14 miles) NW of the city 🚉🚌 ℹ Chaukaghat;
www.uptourism.gov.in/article/varansi-sarnath

Also known as Kashi ("the City of Light") and Benares, Varanasi is situated on the west bank of the Ganges and is India's holiest Hindu city, with a spiritual and religious legacy that goes back nearly 3,000 years. Here, visitors experience rituals of both life and death, which make up day-to-day existence in Varanasi.

This is the city of Shiva, foremost among the 12 places where the god burst into the sky in a pillar of light (*jyotirlinga*) to test Brahma and Vishnu. Sanctified by Shiva's presence and the sacred Ganges, the 90 or so ghats along the river define the life and identity of Varanasi, and stretch for more than 6 km (4 miles) from the southern Assi Ghat to the northern Adi Keshava Ghat, close to the Malviya Bridge. Lined with temples and shrines, the ghats reverberate with the endless cycle of Hindu religious practice, both the daily and the profound.

↑ A pipal tree at Assi Ghat, southernmost ghat in Varanasi

One of Varanasi's oldest sites, Tulsi Ghat (earlier known as Lolarka Ghat) was renamed after the poet-saint Tulsidas.

Bhadami Ghat

Vaccharaj Ghat

Rewa Ghat

Brick-red steps distinguish Janki Ghat, in keeping with the Varanasi tradition of each ghat having its own distinctive colour.

Founded by the Bengali saint Anandamayi Ma, Anandamayi Ghat draws thousands of devotees.

Ganga Mahal Ghat

A linga stands beneath a pipal tree on Varanasi's southernmost ghat, Assi Ghat, which marks the confluence of the Asi and Ganges rivers.

RAMLILA

A cycle of plays telling the story of the *Ramayana*, the Ramlila is the tale of Lord Rama, who was exiled from his kingdom for 14 years. The Ramlila tradition was started in Varanasi by Tulsidas, author of the *Ramcharitmanas* (a popular version of the epic). Street performances take place in the evenings at different venues in September/October, attracting thousands of spectators. The performance at Ramnagar Fort is by far the most spectacular of these.

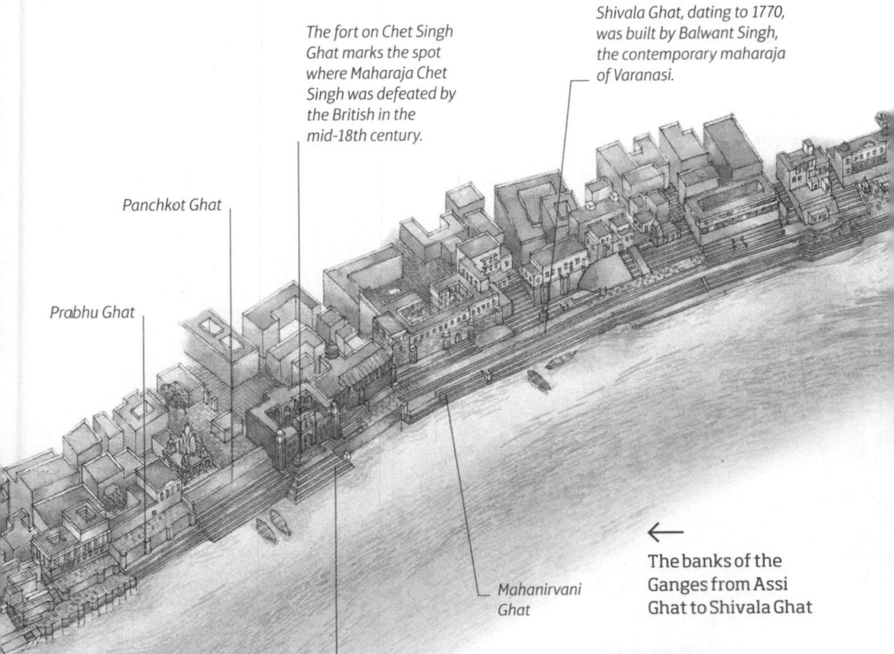

Panchkot Ghat

Prabhu Ghat

The fort on Chet Singh Ghat marks the spot where Maharaja Chet Singh was defeated by the British in the mid-18th century.

Shivala Ghat, dating to 1770, was built by Balwant Singh, the contemporary maharaja of Varanasi.

Mahanirvani Ghat

Niranjani Ghat

Jain Ghat

← The banks of the Ganges from Assi Ghat to Shivala Ghat

→ A sadhu, a wandering Hindu mystic, at the holy city of Varanasi

Multitudes of devotees praying and bathing on the Ganges at sunrise ↑

Varanasi: Digpatiya Ghat to Mir Ghat

The centrally located ghats along this stretch of the Ganges are the city's most sacred, and many of them were built under the patronage of India's erstwhile princely states, such as Darbhanga, Jaipur and Indore. One of Varanasi's two cremation ghats, Harishchandra Ghat lies just to the south. Behind the holy Dasashvamedha Ghat meanders a winding lane known as Vishwanath Gali, lined with a multitude of shops that sell all manner of religious objects. It leads to the city's principal shrine, the Vishwanath Temple, said to be over a thousand years old.

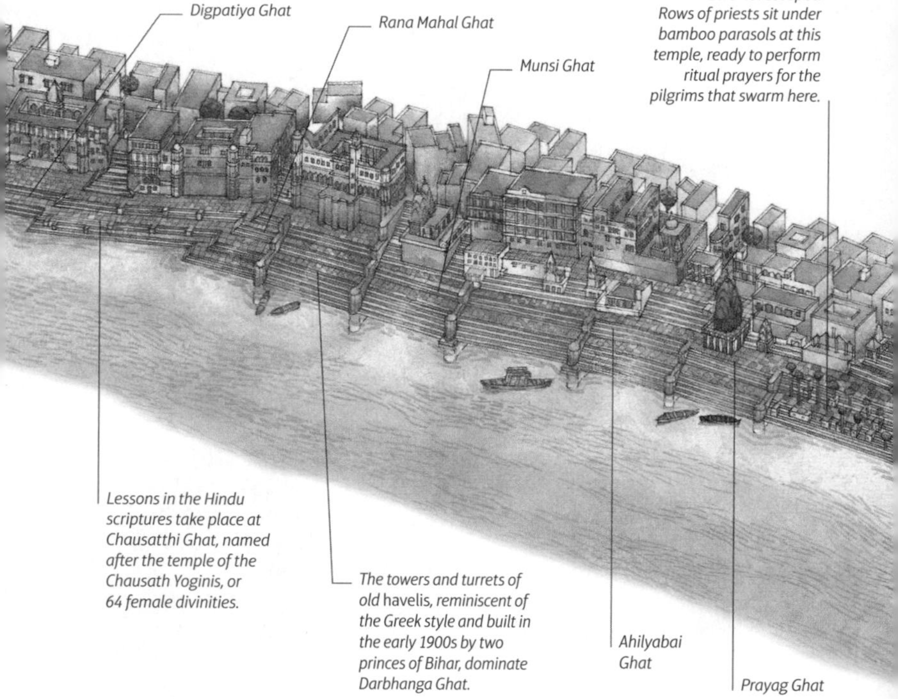

Digpatiya Ghat

Rana Mahal Ghat

Munsi Ghat

The centrally located Dasashvamedha Ghat is Varanasi's holiest spot. Rows of priests sit under bamboo parasols at this temple, ready to perform ritual prayers for the pilgrims that swarm here.

Lessons in the Hindu scriptures take place at Chausatthi Ghat, named after the temple of the Chausath Yoginis, or 64 female divinities.

The towers and turrets of old havelis, *reminiscent of the Greek style and built in the early 1900s by two princes of Bihar, dominate Darbhanga Ghat.*

Ahilyabai Ghat

Prayag Ghat

BOAT RIDES

The highlight of a trip to Varanasi is a boat ride at sunrise, when the temples along the riverfront are bathed in soft light. The people of Varanasi trickle out of the labyrinthine lanes and head for the ghats at dawn. Here, they wash clothes, perform yoga asanas, offer flowers and incense to the river, and take a ritual dip. The most fascinating ride is from Dasashvamedha to Manikarnika Ghat. Dozens of rowing boats ply up and down the river, and can be hired by the hour. Rates are negotiable, so fix the price before hiring one.

The daily evening arti ceremony at Dasashvamedha Ghat

→ A flower offering floating on the Ganges

Must See

EAT

Raga Korean Café
This cosy spot serves great Korean food.

⌂ 10/53 Lahori Tol, behind Manikarnaka Ghat ☎ 0542 240 2945

₹₹₹

Pizzeria Vaatika
Pizzas, salads and the best apple pie in town.

⌂ B1/178, Panch Mandir, Assi Ghat
🌐 pizzeriavaatika.in

₹₹₹

Jai Singh II of Jaipur built one of his four Jantar Mantars above Raja Man Singh's palace in 1710. Its sundial is visible from the Man Mandir Ghat.

Tripura Bhairavi Ghat

Mir Ghat

↑ Digpatiya Ghat to Mir Ghat, lined with temples and *havelis*

Did You Know?

Dasashvamedha Ghat is named after the ten simultaneous horse sacrifices performed by Brahma.

The Palace of the Dom Raja, the king of the Doms. The Doms are a caste who have exclusive rights over the cremation ghats. They sell wood and collect the ashes.

Varanasi: Nepali Ghat to Panchaganga Ghat

Along this stretch is the famed Manikarnika Ghat, one of the city's two cremation ghats. Dying in Varanasi is a cause of celebration for Hindus, as it is believed to bestow instant salvation or moksha (liberation from the cycle of birth and death). It is said that Shiva whispers into the ears of the dying, and the old and infirm, sages and ordinary people, all come here to breathe their last.

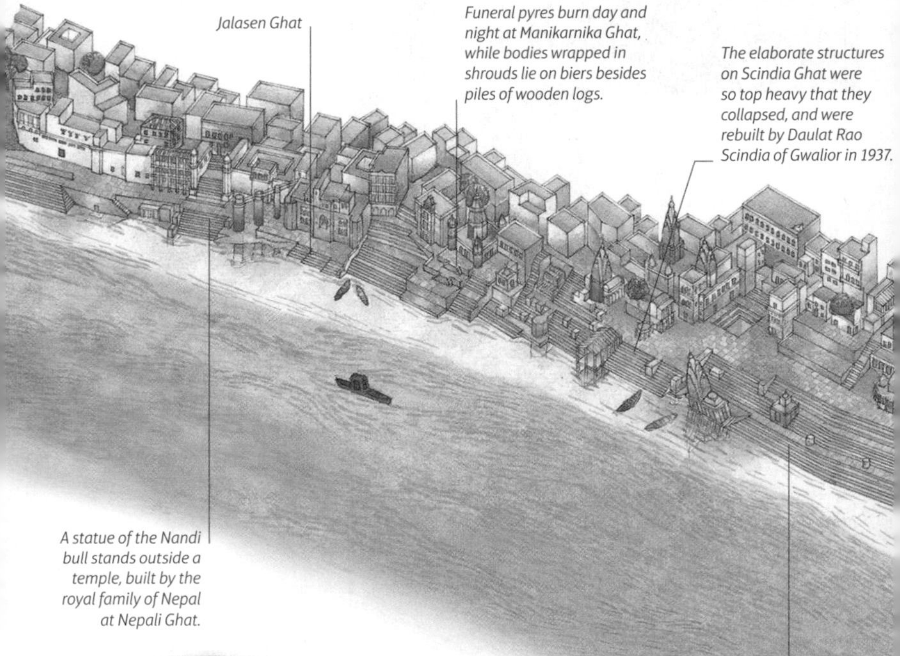

Jalasen Ghat

Funeral pyres burn day and night at Manikarnika Ghat, while bodies wrapped in shrouds lie on biers besides piles of wooden logs.

The elaborate structures on Scindia Ghat were so top heavy that they collapsed, and were rebuilt by Daulat Rao Scindia of Gwalior in 1937.

A statue of the Nandi bull stands outside a temple, built by the royal family of Nepal at Nepali Ghat.

A stone sculpture, full of personality, on a temple at Scindia Ghat

Sankatha Ghat

An arti ceremony, performed nightly at Manikarnika Ghat

WHAT ELSE TO SEE IN VARANASI

At the heart of Varanasi lies the Old City, with temples at every turn. The most famous is the Vishwanath Temple. The current structure was built in the 18th century by Ahilyabai *(p303)* of Indore, and is known as the Golden Temple thanks to its 800 kg (1,763 lb) of gold plating. Five km (3 miles) south, the campus and museum of the Benaras Hindu University are a retreat from the bustle.

↑ Women congregating on the banks of the Ganges at Ganga Mahal Ghat

Ganga Mahal Ghat was built by the king of Gwalior in the early 19th century.

Bhonsle Ghat

Mehta Ghat

Jatar Ghat

Aurangzeb's mosque, built on the site of a Hindu temple that was destroyed, is a grand structure that dominates the skyline.

Panchaganga Ghat marks the mythical meeting place of five sacred rivers, and features images of the five river goddesses.

↑ Nepali Ghat to Panchaganga Ghat, where the five rivers met

THE GANGES

Although there are over 700 temples in Varanasi, none are more sacred than the river itself. The Ganges is worshipped as a living goddess, with the power to cleanse all earthly sins, and thousands come to this sacred city every day to bathe in its holy waters. The government has officially declared the Ganges India's national river.

MYTHS OF THE GANGES

The Ganges is a goddess, named Ganga, which is also the name of the river in Hindi. According to legend, Vishnu scratched a hole in the fabric of the universe with his toenail when he was measuring it with his feet, which allowed the waters of the great cosmic ocean to come through. Shiva caught the sacred waters in his hair to tame their flow and prevent them destroying the earth - which is why depictions of Ganga often show her standing in Shiva's hair. In some versions of the myth, Ganga is constantly falling from the heavens and being tamed by Shiva.

> Bathing in the water of the Ganges is believed to wash away your sins, and the riverbanks are also the most auspicious place to be cremated.

↑ Shiva catching Ganga in his hair, stopping her sacred waters from flooding the world

↑ The bustling ghats of Varanasi lining the banks of the Ganges

SACRED RITUALS

The daily arti rituals, conducted at dawn and dusk, are salutations to the river. Oil lamps are offered and bells rung while sacred mantras are chanted. Offerings of flowers and diyas floating down the river are a common and pretty sight. Bathing in the water of the Ganges is believed to wash away your sins, and being cremated on the river banks or immersing the ashes in the holy waters are ways to gain salvation.

POLLUTION AND CLEANING UP

Sullied by industrial and human waste, the Ganges is the world's sixth most polluted river. In Varanasi, some 40,000 dead bodies are cremated on its banks every year then placed in the river. The water is unfit for drinking, bathing and even agricultural purposes. Various clean-up schemes have been launched, few with any success. In 2014, the government announced an initiative with 37 billion rupees in funding, but a schoogirl's Freedom of Information request revealed that barely half of that had been spent, with zero results.

↑ The daily arti ceremony at Rishikesh on the Ganges

→ Bathing in the Ganges, surrounded by offerings of colourful flowers

5

LUCKNOW

Uttar Pradesh; 335 km (208 miles) E of Agra Amausi; 15 km (9 miles) SW of Lucknow Alambagh, (0522) 245 5477 Regional Tourist Office, C-13, Vipin Khand, Gomti Nagar; www.uptourism.gov.in/article/lucknow

As the Mughal Empire fell, independent kingdoms such as Avadh were established. Its capital, Lucknow, rose to prominence when Asaf-ud-Daula, the fourth nawab, shifted his court here from Faizabad in 1775.

① Bara Imambara

Hussainabad Sunrise-sunset Sat-Thu Fri

Lucknow's most distinctive architectural structures are the *imambaras*, or ceremonial halls, used during the Islamic mourning of Muharram. The Bara ("Great") Imambara, built by Asaf-ud-Daula in 1784, was essentially a famine relief project that provided much-needed employment to the local people. Elaborate gates lead to this sprawling, low edifice. The most remarkable feature here is a large hall, 50 m (164 ft) long and 15 m (49 ft) high, totally unsupported by pillars.

Within is the *bhulbhulaiya*, a labyrinth of corridors. The Asafi Mosque (also known as Shahi Masjid) and a stepwell also lie in the compound.

② Qaiser Bagh Palace

Qaiser Bagh Daily

Once the most magnificent palace in Lucknow, Qaiser Bagh was built by Wajid Ali Shah (r 1847–56), the last nawab. Under his reign, Lucknow witnessed an artistic flowering. An aesthete who was not very interested in governance, Wajid Ali Shah instead devoted himself to poetry and music and is believed to have introduced the *thumri* (a form of classical music). He was deposed by the British in 1856 and exiled to Calcutta (Kolkata). When the British recaptured

Lucknow, they demolished many of the complex's more fanciful structures, with their florid sculptures of mermaids and cherubs. However, the remaining buildings, although in ruins, hint at their former splendour. The ornate, red Lal Baradari now houses a fine arts academy and the archaeological section of the State Museum; the Bhatkhande Music Institute Deemed University is used as a school for Hindustani music; and the Safaid Baradari, where the nawab, dressed as a fakir (religious ascetic), once held court, is now an office building.

③ Sikandar Bagh

Sikandar Bagh 6am–8pm daily

Named after Nawab Wajid Ali Shah's favourite queen, Sikandar Bagh was the royal pleasure garden. In the 1857 War of Independence, British troops led by Sir Colin Campbell lifted the siege of the British Residency complex here. The National Botanical Gardens and Research Centre are now located in its grounds.

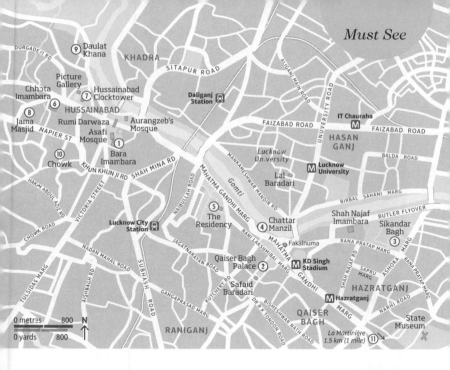

9 Daulat Khana

DURGADE/I RD

KHADRA

SITAPUR ROAD

ALIGAN MAIN ROAD

Picture Gallery

Chhota Imambara **6** **7** Hussainabad Clocktower

HUSSAINABAD

Daliganj Station

FAIZABAD ROAD

IT Chauraha **M**

FAIZABAD ROAD

UNIVERSITY ROAD

8 Jama Masjid

Rumi Darwaza

Asafi Mosque **1**

Aurangzeb's Mosque

NAPIER ST

HASAN GANJ

Lucknow University

BALDA ROAD

10 Chowk

Bara Imambara

KHUN KHUN JI RD SHAH MINA RD

HAK/MABDUL AZIZ RD

VICTORIA STREET

NADAN MAHAL ROAD

MAHATMA GANDHI MARG

NAIBULLAH ROAD

Gomti

Lucknow University **M** Lucknow University

Lal Baradari

BIRBAL SAHANI MARG

CHOWK ROAD

Lucknow City Station

5 The Residency

JAGATNARAYAN ROAD

MANAMESHWAR MANDIR RD

RANI LAKSHMIBAI MARG

4 Chattar Manzil

Fakalnuma

Shah Najaf Imambara

BUTLER FLYOVER

Sikandar Bagh **3**

RANA PRATAP MARG

TULSIDAS MARG

AISHBAGH RD

SUBHASH ROAD

GANGAPRASAD MARG

Qaiser Bagh Palace **2**

KUTCHERY MARG

Safaid Baradari

KD Singh Stadium

MAHATMA GANDHI MARG

SHAH NAAF RD

SAPRU MARG

ASHOKA MARG

RANA PRATAP MARG

HAZRATGANJ

DR R K TONDON ROAD

BISHESHWAR NATH ROAD

Hazratganj **M**

NARHI ROAD

0 metres 800
0 yards 800
N

RANIGANJ

QAISER BAGH

La Martinière 1.5 km (1 mile) **11**

State Museum

4

Chattar Manzil

🏛 **NW of Qaiser Bagh**
🕐 **Daily**

Built during Saadat Ali Khan II's reign (1798–1814), the Chattar Manzil ("Umbrella Palace") derives its name from its umbrella-shaped gilt dome (*chattar*). The building now houses the state's depart-ment of archaeology.

5

The Residency

🏛 **NW of Qaiser Bagh**
📞 **(0522) 232 8220**
🕐 **Sunrise-sunset daily**

Lucknow's most haunting monuments are the desolate ruins of the Residency. This complex of buildings, which grew around the large brick home of the Resident, was an exclusive British enclave, protected by fortifications. In 1857, all the city's British citizens took refuge here during the five-month siege. Sir Henry Lawrence, who was the commander of the troops, expected relief to arrive within 15 days. But it was 87 days before a force led by Sir

← View of the Asafi Mosque from one of the balconies at the Bara Imambara

Henry Havelock broke through the ranks of Indian soldiers, only to find themselves trapped inside. For the next seven weeks they faced constant bombardment, until Sir Colin Campbell retook the Residency on 17 November. By then, almost 2,000 people had died, either from bullet wounds or from cholera and typhoid.

LOCAL MUSIC

At the shrine of the Sufi saint Waris Ali Shah at Dewa Sharif, 35 km (22 miles) east of town, devotees maintain a constant harmony of devotional qawwali music, particularly moving at dusk. Visitors of all faiths are warmly welcomed here.

Ghazal – originally an Arabic poem form – is a type of song that is popular in India. Nightly ghazal perfor-mances are held at the Fakalnuma restaurant in the Hotel Clarks Avadh – don't miss it.

⑥
Chhota Imambara

🏠 Husainabad Road
🕐 6am–5pm Sat-Thu

Also called the Hussainabad Imambara, this gem-like structure is surmounted by a delicate gold dome, and its outside walls are engraved with superb calligraphy. The interiors are adorned with gilt-edged mirrors, ornate chandeliers, silver pulpits and colourful stucco decorations.

EAT

Falaknuma
This is the best place in town to sample the succulent, slow-cooked Awadhi cuisine of the Lucknow region.

🏠 Hotel Clarks Avadh, 8 Mahatma Gandhi Marg, Hazratganj
🌐 hotelclarks.com/avadh-lucknow

₹₹₹

---

⑦
Hussainabad Clocktower

🏠 Hussainabad Road
🚫 To visitors

Erected in 1887, this 67-m-(220-ft-) high Gothic tower was built to mark the arrival of Sir George Cooper, Avadh's first lieutenant governor. To its west lies the 19th-century Baradari, which was built by Muhammed Ali Shah (the eighth nawab), whithin which is the Picture Gallery. Splendid life-sized portraits of the ten nawabs, painted between 1882 and 1885, are on display here.

---

⑧
Jama Masjid

🏠 Near Unity College 🕐 5am–9pm daily

This striking structure was built by Muhammed Ali Shah in the early 19th century. Its walls are heavily ornamented, and its arches covered with stucco work.

---

⑨
Daulat Khana

🏠 NW of the Jama Masjid, Daulatganj

Formerly the palace of Asaf-ud-Daula, the Daulat Khana was constructed in the late 1780s and includes numerous Indo-European buildings. The most prominent among them is the elegant Asafi Kothi.

---

⑩
Chowk

🏠 S of Hardoi Rd

Lucknow's main market is in the Chowk, the city's

← The 19th-century Hussainabad Clocktower

↑ The stunning Chhota Imambara under clear blue skies

atmospheric old quarter. Stretching from Gol Darwaza to Akbari Darwaza, this maze of narrow *galis* (lanes) is lined with shops and wholesale markets selling a range of goods from colourful kites to *paan* to Lucknow's famed *chikankari*, where fine muslin is delicately embroidered with threadwork. The Chowk is also a great place to sample some authentic local cuisine, especially the many varieties of succulent kebabs.

⑪
La Martinière

🏛 Kalidas Marg
🚫 To visitors

The extraordinary La Martinière was built by Major General Claude Martin, a French soldier of fortune and, in 1793, the richest European in Lucknow. A fanciful Gothic château, it has four enormous octagonal towers. The exterior is decorated with animals and mythological figures. Martin died in 1800 and is buried in the basement. In 1845, the building, in accordance with Martin's will, became a school for boys.

EXPERIENCE MORE

⑥
Kanpur

🏛 Kanpur district, Uttar Pradesh; 79 km (49 miles) SW of Lucknow 🚉 Kanpur Central ☎ 🛈 www.uttar pradesh.gov.in

One of British India's largest garrisons was at Kanpur, or Cawnpore, as it was then known. It witnessed some of the bloodiest episodes in the War of Independence in 1857. Large numbers of British soldiers and civilians were killed when Nana Sahib, the Maratha ruler, defeated the British forces at the town. When British reinforcements arrived, equally ferocious reprisals occurred against Indian soldiers and locals.

Today, Kanpur is a busy industrial city with leather, oil and cotton as its main products. The old garrison, still in use by the Indian army, has some interesting relics of the Raj. Among them are the All Souls' Memorial Church, a grand Gothic-style structure with an intricate stained-glass window, and, east of the church, the pretty Memorial Garden with a statue of an angel surrounded by a Gothic screen. This statue commemorates a terrible massacre in Bibighar, where British women and children were murdered in the town's centre in 1857. Northeast of the church, Sati Chaura Ghat, along the Ganges, is the spot where Indian forces killed 500 British soldiers and civilians. The Military Cemetery on the edge of the cantonment has many interesting graves.

Bithur, 25 km (16 miles) west of Kanpur, boasts a fort built by the Peshwas. It is also the legendary birthplace of Lav and Kush, the twin sons of Hindu dieties Rama and Sita.

→ Carved Gothic arch leading to the angel statue at the Memorial Garden, Kanpur

People covered in ↑ colourful powder celebrating the festival of Holi in Vrindavan

Did You Know?

In Vrindavan, Holi is celebrated for 40 days, and both powder and flowers are showered on devotees.

7

Vrindavan

🏠 Mathura district, Uttarakhand; 68 km (42 miles) NW of Agra 🚌 ℹ️ www.uptourism.gov.in/article/vrindavan

Situated along the Yamuna river, Vrindavan ("Forest of Fragrant Basil") is an important pilgrim centre for devout Hindus, who believe that the young Krishna once lived here as a humble cowherd and romanced the beautiful milk-maid Radha. Their love is widely celebrated in dance, art and literature. Vrindavan's numerous temples, ashrams and ghats were mainly built by Hindu kings and rich merchants. Many Hindu widows live in ashrams here, devoting their lives to the worship of Krishna.

At the edge of the town is the historic Govindeoji Temple, built in 1590 by Raja Man Singh I of Amber. Across is the 19th-century Sri Ranganathji Temple, with a gold-plated ritual pillar and an interesting museum of temple treasures.

Amid the narrow streets of the old town are the sacred walled groves of Seva Kunj. This is said to be where Krishna dances with Radha every night, a ritual known as the Raslila or raas leela. Other temples in Vrindavan include the red sandstone Madan Mohan Temple, built in 1580 on a hill by the river, the Banke Bihari Temple, near the main bazaar, and the 16th-century Jugal Kishore Temple.

8

Rishikesh

🏠 Dehradun district, Uttarakhand; 228 km (142 miles) NE of Delhi 🚌 Yatra bus station ℹ️ Shail Vihar; www.uttarakhandtourism.gov.in/rishikesh

Located at the confluence of the Chandrabhaga and the Ganges, Rishikesh is one of the most famous destinations for yoga and "alternative" travel in India. It has several famous ashrams, including Sivanand, Shanti Kunj and Purnanand, which offer courses in India's ancient knowledge systems. Rishikesh's prime location at

YOGA: PATH TO HEALTH AND ENLIGHTENMENT

Yoga is a system of physical and mental exercises linked to an ancient Hindu philosophy, with a number of famous gurus. Its practice in India is particularly associated with religious ascetics, but yoga was popularized in the west for its *asanas*, which are physical exercises and body postures used to heighten mindfulness and increase suppleness. Today, many come to India to practise yoga. Rishikesh claims to be its world centre, and a yoga festival *(p68)* is held here every March.

STAY

Rainforest House
A simple place surrounded by forest, with a waterfall nearby.

🏠 32 Brahmpuri, Badarinath Road, Rishikesh 🌐 rainforest-house.com

₹₹₹

Ananda in the Himalayas
Try ayurvedic-based health programmes at this upscale spa resort.

🏠 The Palace Estate, Narendra Nagar, Garhwal 🌐 anandaspa.com

₹₹₹

Haveli Hari Ganga
This riverside hotel has a wellness spa and its own private ghat.

🏠 21 Pilibhit House, Ram Ghat, Haridwar 🌐 havelihariganga.com

₹₹₹

the foothills of the Himalayas also attracts those seeking adventure sports. Just north of Rishikesh, the town of Muni-ki-Reti ("Sand of the Sages") is said to be a blessed site, since ancient sages meditated at here. It is also the starting point for the Char Dham pilgrim route.

---

❾ Haridwar

🏠 Haridwar district, Uttarakhand; 214 km (133 miles) NE of Delhi 🚃🚌 ℹ️ Rahi Motel; www. uttarakhandtourism.gov. in/haridwar

The Ganges descends from the Himalayas and begins its long journey through the plains at Haridwar. This gives the town a unique status, and making a pilgrimage to Haridwar is every devout Hindu's dream.

Haridwar's main "sight" is the Ganges itself, lined with bathing ghats, tanks and temples. The main ghat, Har-ki-Pauri, is named after a supposed imprint of Vishnu's feet at the site. Hundreds attend the daily evening arti at this ghat, when leaf boats are filled with flowers, lit with lamps and set adrift on the Ganges. Further south, a ropeway connects the town to the Mansa Devi Temple on a hill across the river, which has panoramic views of Haridwar.

The riverside bazaar is lined with eateries and stalls full of ritual paraphernalia – small mounds of vermilion powder, coconuts wrapped in red-and-gold cloth, brass idols and jars. These are used to carry back a key ingredient of Hindu rituals: water from the Ganges (Gangajal), which, the faithful believe, remains ever fresh.

---

❿ Mathura

🏠 Mathura district, Uttarakhand; 62 km (39 miles) NW of Agra 🚃🚌 ℹ️ mathura.nic.in

Mathura, on the west bank of the Yamuna river, is revered as the birthplace of Lord Krishna – a room in the Sri Krishna Janmabhoomi Temple, on the periphery of the city, is said to be the actual site of his birth. Along the river front, 25 ghats form a splendid network of temples, pavilions, trees and stone steps leading down to the water. The Jama Masjid, with its striking tilework, lies behind the riverfront.

The **Government Museum** has a superb collection of sculptures dating from about the 5th century BC until the 4th century AD, when Mathura was a major Buddhist centre, including a Standing Buddha.

Government Museum
♿ 🏠 Dampier Nagar 🕐 10:30am–4:30pm Tue-Sun 🚫 Public hols and alternate Sat

⓫ Dehradun

📍 Dehradun district, Uttarakhand; 256 km (159 miles) NE of Delhi ✈ Jolly Grant, 24 km (15 miles) SE of town centre 🚉🚌 ⓘ UTDB, Patel Nagar; www.uttarakhandtourism.gov.in/dehradun

Fringed by the Shivalik Hills, Dehradun lies in the pretty Doon Valley, flanked by the Ganges to the west and the Yamuna to the east, an area known for its fragrant rice and mango orchards. The provisional capital of the state of Uttarakhand, formed in 2000, the town is also the gateway to the Garhwal Hills. A number of prestigious institutions have their headquarters here, such as the Survey of India and the Forest Research Institute. One of India's most privileged private colleges,

↑ Bathers having fun at Kempty Falls, near the town of Mussoorie

Doon School, and the Indian Military Academy, are also here. Rajpur Road, the main link to the hills, is lined with bakeries and restaurants and has the old Clock Tower, the town's principal landmark, at one end.

The picturesque wildlife sanctuary of Rajaji National Park is 5 km (3 miles) southeast of Dehradun. Open from November to June, it is known for its birdlife and elephants.

About 7 km (4 miles) west of town is a house known as Everest House. This was the home of Sir George Everest, the legendary Surveyor-General who completed the mapping of India and mapped Mount Everest.

EAT

Ramana's Garden Organic Cafe

Enjoy great vegetarian and vegan food. The profits support a local school and orphanage.

📍 Laxman Jhula Road, Tapovan, Rishikesh 🌐 facebook.com/ Ramanas organiccafe

₹₹₹

Sitting Elephant

A rooftop restaurant with mountain views serving Garhwali and North Indian dishes.

📍 Ell Bee Ganga View Hotel, Palika Nagar, Rishikesh 🌐 ellbeehotels.com

₹₹₹

⓬ Mussoorie

📍 Uttarkashi district, Uttarakhand; 35 km (22 miles) N of Dehradun 🚌 ⓘ UTDB; www. uttarakhandtourism. gov.in/mussoorie

Perched on a ridge above the Doon Valley at a height of 1,920 m (6,299 ft), Mussoorie is inundated with visitors in summer. The Mall, the main thoroughfare, is lined with shops and eating places. The town's small Tibetan community is settled in Happy Valley, close to Convent Hill. The Tibetan Market, below The Mall, sells woollens. A ropeway from The Mall leads up to Gun Hill, which, on a clear day, has fine views of many Greater Himalayan peaks, including Nanda Devi, Kedarnath and Badrinath. Kempty Falls, lying 12 km (7 miles) northwest of town, is a popular picnic spot.

⓭ Garhwal Hills

📍 Uttarkashi and Chamoli districts, Uttarakhand; 148 km (92 miles) NE of Rishikesh to Uttarkashi 🚌 TGMA Bus Station ⓘ UTDB, Uttarkashi; www. uttarakhandtourism.gov.in

The northern stretches of Garhwal (Uttarakhand's western hills) are strewn with pilgrim towns, ancient shrines and snowbound peaks. The main town, Uttarkashi, lies 148 km (92 miles) north of Rishikesh (p188), and is an important starting point for treks to the upper reaches of Garhwal. A leading climbing school, the Nehru Institute of Mountaineering, is situated in this town.

This region also includes an area known as Dev Bhoomi ("Abode of the Gods"). The Char Dham, or four major places of pilgrimage, Gangotri,

Yamunotri, Kedarnath and Badrinath, are all situated here at altitudes over 3,100 m (10,171 ft) – Hindus believe that visiting all four is a step towards salvation.

Yamunotri, situated 209 km (130 miles) north of Rishikesh, is the source of the Yamuna. It is a 13-km (8-mile) walk from Hanuman Chatti Temple, which was rebuilt in the 20th century after the earlier one was destroyed by floods.

Gaumukh, the source of the River Ganges, lies 18 km (11 miles) upstream of the village of Gangotri, below the soaring Bhagirathi peaks, and can be reached via a path that follows the lovely river valley. At this point, the river is known as the Bhagirathi, and only becomes the Ganges proper after it joins the Alaknanda river at Devprayag. The impressive Kedarnath peaks form the backdrop for the pilgrim town of Kedarnath, sacred to Shiva, and 223 km (139 miles) northeast of Rishikesh. A beautifully carved stone temple, said to be 800 years old, lies 14 km (9 miles) north of the road head at Gaurikund. The most visited of all the Char Dham shrines, Badrinath is 298 km (185 miles) northeast of Rishikesh. Its colourfully painted temple is usually packed with pilgrims.

At the confluence of the Dhauli Ganga and Alaknanda rivers at Vishnuprayag, 250 km (155 miles) northeast of Rishikesh, Joshimath is one of the four *mathas* (seats of learning) established by the great 9th-century sage Adi Shankaracharya The town is a gateway to the Nanda Devi

Pilgrims at the Shiva temple in Kedarnath, in the Garhwal Hills, and *(inset)* holy men en route to Gaumukh

TREKKING IN GARHWAL AND KUMAON

Relatively easy to access, the Garhwal and Kumaon ranges provide a great introduction to hiking in the Himalayan hills. The best seasons are February–May and September–November. Among many trails, of different lengths and difficulties, one of the most popular is the 23-km (14-mile) path from Kalyani along the Asi Ganga river valley to Doital.

Sanctuary and the ski slopes of Auli, reached via road or cable car from Joshimath. The trek to the Sikh shrine of Hemkund Sahib and the Valley of Flowers National Park begins 20 km (12 miles) north of Joshimath, from Ghangaria. The Valley of Flowers, best visited between June and September, is a carpet of flowers and other alpine flora.

⑭

Nainital

🏠 Nainital district, Uttarakhand; 322 km (200 miles) NE of Delhi 🚉 Kathgodam, 35 km (22 miles) S of Nainital, then taxi or bus 🚌 ℹ️ KMVN, Om Park; www.uttarakhand tourism.gov.in/nainital

This pretty hill station, nestled in the Kumaon Hills, is named after the emerald green eyes of Parvati, Shiva's consort. A temple dedicated to the goddess stands on the northern shore of the large freshwater lake (tal). The lake is encircled by the Mall Road, and the "flats", a large field that is a popular promenade. Nainital was the summer capital of the British Raj's United Provinces, and its many attractive colonial buildings include the governor's summer residence (built in 1899), St Joseph's School, the old Secretariat (now the Uttarakhand High Court) and the Municipal Library. Nainital also has some beautiful walking trails, one of

which leads up from the flats through the densely wooded Ayarpata Hill, to Tiffin Top and Dorothy's Seat. These lookout points offer panoramic views of the lakeside. The Upper Cheena Mall leads to Naina Peak, which has mountain views. Visitors can also take the cable car up to the viewing platform at Snow View.

The area around Nainital is often described as India's Lake District, with a number of lakes and forests. Within easy reach of Nainital are Bhim Tal, 22 km (14 miles) east of the hill station; Naukuchiya Tal, just 4 km (2 miles) from Bhim Tal, is a lake with nine corners and rich in birdlife; and Sat Tal, a conglomeration of seven lakes, is found 21 km (13 miles) northeast of Nainital. Located 30 km (19 miles) northeast of Nainital, Mukteshwar is one of the most beautiful spots in the area, along with the orchards at Ramgarh, close by.

> The area surrounding Nainital is often described as India's Lake District, with a number of serene lakes and thick forests.

Did You Know?

Legend has it that Nainital Lake formed from the fallen eye of Parvati, Shiva's wife.

⑮

Almora

🏠 Almora district, Uttarakhand; 380 km (236 miles) NE of Delhi 🚉 Kathgodam, 90 km (56 miles) S, then taxi or bus 🚌 ℹ️ KMVN, Holiday Home; www.uttarakhandtourism. gov.in/almora

The large, hilly market town of Almora is the headquarters of the surrounding district, and offers expansive views of the spectacular Greater Himalayan Range. Almora

→
Rowing boats for hire on the mountain-fringed lake in Nainital

Bells lining a path in the Chitai Temple, set in a pine forest near Almora

has a distinctive architectural style: tall, narrow houses with delicately carved wooden façades. The bustling bazaar, with its cobbled street, is where locally crafted *tamta* products (hand-beaten copper and brass utensils plated with silver) are sold, along with the town's famous confectionery, the *bal mithai*, a type of chocolate fudge.

The historic Almora Jail, probably one of the few in the country in such picturesque surroundings, once held important political prisoners such as Mahatma Gandhi and Jawaharlal Nehru. A number of temples dot the landscape; the most popular of these are the Chitai Temple and the Ucyotchandeshwar Temple.

Binsar, some 34 km (21 miles) northeast of Almora, at an altitude of 2,412 m (7,913 ft), is a great spot from which to view the Himalayas.

16 Ranikhet

⌂ Almora district, Uttarakhand; 367 km (228 miles) NE of Delhi
🚌 ℹ www.uttarakhand tourism.gov.in/ranikhet

Primarily a cantonment town, Ranikhet is home to the renowned Kumaon Regiment. Not surprisingly, the army is the town's most visible presence. Ranikhet's many red-roofed bungalows spread across the wide "Queen's Field", a literal translation of

the town's name. Chaubatia, once a British sanatorium, now houses the Government Fruit Garden, which grows 200 varieties of fruit. Ranikhet's true allure, however, lies in the spectacular views of nearly 350 km (217 miles) of the Greater Himalayan Range.

17 Lansdowne

⌂ Almora district, Uttarakhand; 240 km (149 miles) NE of Delhi
🚉 Kotdwar, 45 km (28 miles) SW, then taxi or bus 🚌
ℹ www.uttarakhand tourism.gov.in/lansdowne1

The cantonment town of Lansdowne is one of the few hill stations that has managed to remain largely unchanged. A loosely spread-out jumble of bungalows and shops, the town is set on gentle forested slopes of pine, deodar and silver oak. The Army's Garhwal Rifles have their regimental centre here, and a visit to the regimental mess is a must. Tip-n-Top, 3 km (2 miles) from town, is a lookout point with excellent mountain views.

→

Sculpture of the goddess Varahi in the town of Bageshwar, near Kausani

18 Kausani

⌂ Almora district, Uttarakhand; 431 km (268 miles) NE of Delhi
🚌 ℹ Tourist Reception Centre; www.uttarakhand tourism.gov.in/kausani

After a stay at the Anashakti Yoga Ashram in mountainous Kausani in 1929, Gandhi remarked on how unnecessary it was for Indians to visit the European Alps when they had the beauty of this town nearby. Perfect evidence for this is provided by the 400-km (249-mile) uninterrupted panorama of the Nanda Devi Range from the old Circuit House.

Baijnath, 20 km (12 miles) north of Kausani, is known for a now-ruined cluster of temples built in the 11th century. The main attraction is the Parvati Temple, with a 2-m- (7-ft-) high image of the goddess dating from the 12th century.

Bageshwar, 41 km (25 miles) east of Kausani, lies at the confluence of the Gomti and Saryu rivers, and was once a major trading post between Tibet and Kumaon. With its stone temples dedicated to Shiva, it is also an important pilgrimage centre. Nila Parvat (the "Blue Mountain") stands between the two rivers, and locals believe that it is home to all the 330 million deities of the Hindu pantheon. Many visitors to Bageshwar are en route to the Pindari Glacier.

19 Jhansi

⌂ Jhansi district, Uttar Pradesh; 301 km (187 miles) SW of Lucknow 🚗🚆
ℹ Regional Tourist Office, Hotel Virangna; www.uptourism.gov.in/article/jhansi-deogarh

Most famous for the role that its queen, Rani Lakshmibai, played during the Indian War of Independence in 1857, Jhansi is a key transit point for visitors travelling from Delhi to the temples of Khajuraho (p288). The main site of interest is Shankar Fort, built in 1613 by Raja Bir Singh Deo, which features 9-m- (30-ft-) high walls built in rings around its centre.

Located just outside the fort on the road back to town, the **Government Museum** displays medieval Hindu sculpture, royal artifacts and some prehistoric tools.

Government Museum

♦ 🕾 (0510) 233 0035
🕐 10am–5pm Tue–Sun
🗓 2nd Sat

20 Rampur

⌂ Rampur district, Uttar Pradesh; 310 km (193 miles) NW of Lucknow 🚗🚆

Earlier a stronghold of the Afghan Rohilla chieftains (highlanders from Peshawar), Rampur became a princely state under the British. It was ruled by a dynasty of Muslim nawabs, who were great connoisseurs of the arts. They drew hundreds of scholars and artists to their court, whose books and paintings became part of the state collection. They also established a famous *gharana* (school) of classical music. The Hamid Manzil, built by Nawab Hamid Ali

RANI LAKSHMIBAI OF JHANSI

India's Joan of Arc, Rani Lakshmibai single-handedly defied the British when her husband, Raja Gangadhar Rao, died in 1853, leaving no adult heir. She wished to rule as Regent, but the British invoked the infamous Doctrine of Lapse, and she was driven from her kingdom. While the War of Independence of 1857 brewed in the north, the queen and her general, Tantia Tope, captured Gwalior Fort. She died defending it in 1858. According to the historian Christopher Hibbert, "she died dressed as a man, holding her sword two-handed and the reins of her horse in her teeth". She remains one of India's best-loved heroines.

The imposing walls of the historic Shankar Fort, overlooking Jhansi

Khan Bahadur, who came to the throne in 1896, now houses the renowned **Raza Library**, which boasts a collection of almost 5,000 Mughal miniatures, over 60,000 books, numerous rare manuscripts, and portraits dating from the 16th to 18th centuries.

Hamid Ali Khan was also responsible for renovating many of Rampur's palaces, including the sprawling palace and fort complex to the northwest of the town.

Rampur is a maze of bazaars and was once known for its fine cotton *khes* (damask). Traces of its Rohilla warrior ancestry are visible in the famous daggers, always on sale, and in the touches of Pashto (the native tongue of Peshawar), which pepper the Urdu that is spoken here.

The town of Moradabad, lying around 37 km (23 miles) west of Rampur, is a small 17th-century settlement, best known for its brass and metalware industries. The town's fort and mosque are almost hidden by the many tenements and bazaars.

Raza Library

🏠 Hamid Manzil Qila Rampur ⏰ 10am–5pm Sat–Thu 🚫 Public hols 🌐 razalibrary. gov.in

㉑ 🖊️

Dudhwa National Park

🏠 Lakhimpur-Kheri district, Uttar Pradesh; 220 km (137 miles) N of Lucknow 🚍🚌 ⏰ Hours vary, check website 🌐 dudhwatiger reserve.com

Located close to the border with Nepal, Dudhwa National Park covers some 680 sq km (263 sq miles) of densely wooded plains. Its forests have some of the finest specimens of *sal* trees in India, but most people visit to try and spot a tiger. In 1977, Dudhwa was recognized as a Tiger Reserve, mainly thanks to the efforts of Billy Arjan Singh, a renowned environmentalist. Arjan Singh is best remembered for hand-rearing the tigress Tara; he returned her to the wild in 1978.

Today, the reserve is home to more than 30 tigers. Dudhwa is also well known for its herds of swamp deer (*Cervus duvauceli*). Better known as *barasingha* (literally, 12-antlered), these deer find their ideal habitat in the grassy wetlands in the southern reaches of the park.

Other species in the reserve include leopards, sloth bears and a small herd of rhinos, brought here from Assam and Nepal in an attempt to re-introduce the species into Dudhwa. The park also provides a habitat for nearly 400 species of birds, many of them on the endangered list, such as the Bengal florican and the black stork, plus swamp partidges, lesser floricans and hornbills. The park's lakes attract waterfowl such as fishing eagles.

㉒

Aligarh

🏠 Uttar Pradesh; 371 km (231 miles) NW of Lucknow 🚍🚌 🌐 Aligarh Muslim University: amu.ac.in

Located in an agriculturally rich region, Aligarh was a Rajput stronghold from the end of the 1100s onwards, until it was wrested by the Mughals. Its 16th-century fort fell to the British under Lord Lake in 1803. One of the town's foremost citizens, Sir Syed Ahmed Khan founded the Aligarh Muslim University in 1875. The sprawling campus has many imposing buildings, such as a mosque that is an exact replica of the Jama Masjid (*p86*) in Delhi, only one-third its size.

↑ The façade of Aligarh Muslim University, founded in the late 19th century

23

Sarnath

🏛 Varanasi district, Uttar Pradesh; 10 km (6 miles) NE of Varanasi 🚌 ℹ www.uptourism.gov.in/article/varansi-sarnath

To Buddhists, Sarnath is as sacred as Varanasi is to Hindus. The Buddha came to the deer park here in 528 BC, to preach the Dharmachakra, or the Wheel of Law, his first major sermon after gaining enlightenment (p271). Sarnath was then one of ancient India's greatest centres of learning, visited by Chinese travellers Fa-Hsien and Hiuen Tsang, who wrote of its flourishing Buddhist monasteries.

The central monument of the existing complex is the 5th-century Dhamekh Stupa, which is built at the site where the Buddha is believed to have delivered his sermon to five disciples. To its west are the remains of the remarkable Dharmarajika Stupa, built by the Mauryan emperor Ashoka to preserve the Buddha's relics. The complex also has several smaller monasteries and temples, as well as a Bodhi tree, planted in 1931, and the statue of Anagarika Dharmapala, the founder of the society that returned Sarnath and Bodh Gaya (p271) from Hindu to Buddhist control.

The **Archaeological Museum** exhibits a superb collection

of Buddhist artifacts. The highlight of the display is the Ashokan lion capital.

Archaeological Museum
⊛ 🕘 9am–5pm Sat–Thu
🌐 sarnathmuseumasi.org

24

Prayagraj (Allahabad)

🏛 Allahabad district, Uttar Pradesh; 204 km (141 miles) SE of Lucknow 🚉🚌 ℹ 35 MG Marg, Civil Lines; www.uptourism.gov.in/article/allahabad-chitrakoot-explore

Prayagraj, formerly known as Allahabad, has a sacred location at the confluence (sangam) of three rivers – the Ganges, the Yamuna and the mythical Saraswati – which has given it cultural and religious importance for nearly 3,000 years.

Occupied by various rulers throughout its history, in the 16th century the town was captured by the Mughals, who renamed it Allahabad. Later, the British had a large military presence here and established the law courts and the university. Jawaharlal Nehru (p77), who became India's first prime minister, was born here in 1889; the town later became a major centre of the independence Movement. The town was controversially renamed by the Bharatiya Janata Party (BJP). Today it is a quietly prosperous provincial centre, the broad, tree-lined avenues of the Civil Lines area contrasting with the congested bustle of the old city.

Allahabad Fort was built in 1583 by Akbar, who had a 3rd-century BC Ashokan pillar brought here from Kausambi. On the fort's eastern side is a temple complex with the Akshaivata, a famously undying banyan tree. Legend has it that anyone who leapt from its branches would achieve salvation from the endless cycle of rebirths. After too many such attempts, the tree was fenced off, and a special permit is required from the local tourist office to view it.

Khusro Bagh, a tranquil Mughal garden on the western edge of town, is named after Emperor Jahangir's eldest son, who led an unsuccessful rebellion against his father and was later murdered during the battle over succession with his brother, Shah Jahan, in 1622. His tomb lies next to those of his sister and his mother. The latter, a Rajput princess from Jaipur, distraught by the war between her husband and son, took an overdose of opium. The chhatris on her tomb show Rajput influence.

Anand Bhavan, ancestral home of the Nehru-Gandhi family, now houses a museum of Nehru memorabilia and chronicles the high points of

← Dhamekh Stupa, anchoring the Sarnath complex, which is sacred to Buddhists

the Independence Movement. Close by, in the Civil Lines area, is the fantastically arched and turreted Muir College (now part of Allahabad University), built in 1870 and a fine example of Indo-Saracenic architecture. Some glazed blue and white tiles still cling to the dome and a single tower soars to a height of 60 m (197 ft).

To the west, the **Allahabad Museum** has an interesting collection of terracottas from

Ornate decoration of a tomb, and *(inset)* a building in its garden surrounds, Khusro Bagh, Prayagraj

Kausambi and some 10th- to 13th-century sculptures from the Chandela era. Across Civil Lines to the west stands the All Saints' Cathedral, built in 1877 and designed by William Emerson, architect of Kolkata's Victoria Memorial *(p310)*. It is lined with Jaipur marble inside.

Kausambi is 63 km (39 miles) from Prayagraj on the eastern bank of the Yamuna. The ruins of a stupa, a palace and extensive ramparts lie within a 2-km (1-mile) radius. Local legend holds that the city was built by the Pandavas, heroes of the *Mahabharata,* but excavations reveal that a Buddhist community lived here between 600 BC and AD 600. The site contains the remains of a paved road, small houses, each with a ceramic drain, and the stump of an Ashokan pillar dating to the 3rd century BC.

THE KUMBH MELA

Hindu legend has it that the gods and demons once warred over an urn *(kumbha)* holding the nectar of immortality. To prevent the demons from seizing the urn, a divine carrier flew off with it, spilling a drop each on Nasik *(p433)*, Ujjain *(p303)*, Haridwar *(p189)* and Prayagraj. A mela (fair) is held at each spot every few years. Pilgrims converge from all over, making this the world's largest gathering - 120 million people attended the 2019 mela at Prayagraj. The next Kumbh Mela at Prayagraj will be in 2025.

Allahabad Fort
🚫 Only with permit from tourist office

Anand Bhavan
♿ 📞 (0532) 246 7096
🕐 9:30am–5:30pm daily

Allahabad Museum
♿ 📍 Chandrashekhar Azad Park, Kamla Nehru Rd
🕐 10am–5:30pm Tue–Sun

↑ Colourful decorated arch at Ayodhya's Hanuman Garhi, a temple dedicated to the monkey god

25

Ayodhya

🏛 Faizabad district, Uttar Pradesh; 127 km (79 miles) E of Lucknow 🚌 (05278) 232 067 🛈 Ayodhya Tourist Information Centre; www.uptourism.gov.in/article/ayodhya

Located on the banks of the Sarayu river, Ayodhya is said to be the birthplace of Rama, the divine hero of the *Ramayana* (p67). Dozens of temples in this small pilgrim town commemorate his birth. Whether this is a historical fact or simply part of oral tradition, for devout Hindus Ayodhya remains inextricably linked with the legend of Rama. As a result, when the Mughal emperor Babur built a mosque near the supposed spot of Rama's birthplace in 1526, he left behind a bitterly contested site. Known as the Babri Masjid ("Mosque of Babur"), it was a long-simmering source of tension between Hindus and Muslims. In 1992, a mob of Hindus tore down the mosque, leading to rioting all over the country. Security personnel now guard the site. A makeshift temple outside the security ring still attracts pilgrims, particularly during the full moon night of Kartik Purnima. One of the more renowned temples, among the hundreds of shrines on the river bank, is the Hanuman Garhi. Built within the walls of an old fort, it is dedicated to the monkey god, Hanuman.

Faizabad, Ayodhya's twin town, lying 6 km (4 miles) to its west, has a sizeable Muslim population and was Avadh's first capital before it was shifted to Lucknow in 1775. In the town's centre is the Jama Masjid, built by the later Mughals, while the 18th-century tomb of Bahu Begum, the wife of Avadh's third nawab, is an austere structure built in marble. Faizabad has a pretty rose garden.

26

Kalinjar Fort

🏛 Banda district, Uttar Pradesh; 205 km (127 miles) SW of Prayagraj 🚉 Banda, 62 km (39 miles) N of Kalinjar Fort, then bus 🚌 🛈 UP Government Assistant Tourist Office, Chitrakoot; (05198) 224 219/ 222 218

One of India's oldest forts, Kalinjar was called Kanagora by Ptolemy, the 2nd-century AD Greek geographer. Its strategic location on the route between North and South India made it a coveted target for many rulers. It has thus had a very turbulent history, and was successively occupied by many medieval rulers, until it fell to the Afghan ruler Sher Shah Suri (p74) in 1545.

Seven gateways, named after planets and lined with sculptures and carvings, lead to the fort. These include a giant Shiva with 18 arms and a dancing Ganesha. The Neelkanth Temple, inside the fort, is dedicated to Shiva. The temple's inner sanctum contains an ancient linga, which is still worshipped.

27

Jaunpur

🏛 Jaunpur district, Uttar Pradesh; 250 km (155 miles) SE of Lucknow 🚉🚌

Though largely bypassed by visitors, Jaunpur has a

→ Worshippers performing their ablutions along the Mandakini river, Chitrakoot

wealth of medieval Islamic architecture. Located along the Gomti river, the city was established by Feroze Shah Tughlaq in the late 14th century and soon grew into an important trading post. It was subsequently ruled by the independent Muslim rulers of the Sharqi dynasty, who held sway for much of the 15th century, until Ibrahim Lodi conquered the city in 1479. It eventually fell to the Mughals in the early part of the 16th century.

Jaunpur's numerous rulers each left their distinct architectural stamp on the city. The Mughal emperor Akbar, for example, ordered the construction of the great Shahi Bridge, which still stands across the river. To its north is the Old Shahi Fort, which dates back to the Tughlaq era. It contains a mosque, built with yellow-and-blue enamelled bricks, and an exact replica of a traditional Turkish bath or *hamam*. The most striking mosque in Jaunpur, the Atala Masjid, located just outside the fort, dates to the Sharqi period. It is embellished with recessed arches and ornamental fringes, with square courts surrounding the central structure. Though built on a grander scale, the 15th-century Jama Masjid borrows its basic architectural inspiration from the Atala Masjid.

THE MANGO

The Mughal emperor Babur called the mango *(aam)* the "finest fruit of Hindostan", and there are over 500 varietals grown across the country. Mango leaves, considered auspicious, are used as bunting at festive occasions. Of the hundreds of varieties grown all over the subcontinent, few are as aromatic and juicy as the mangoes of Jaunpur. The *langra* is arguably the best among the varieties grown here. It is fleshy, juicy and sweet, with a distinct tangy flavour. It sells at a premium country wide and is widely exported to the Middle East and Europe. The *dussehri* from Lucknow and the *chausa* from the Rampur region are also popular varieties, with the raw *chausa* considered ideal for making into spicy chutneys and pickles.

28

Chitrakoot

🏠 **Chitrakoot district, Madhya Pradesh; 125 km (78 miles) SW of Prayagraj** 🚉 **Karwi, 8 km (5 miles) NE, then taxi or bus** 🚌 ℹ️ **www.uptourism.gov.in/article/allahabad-chitrakootexplore**

Though in neighbouring Madhya Pradesh, this pilgrim town on the banks of the Mandakini river is most easily accessed from Prayagraj. Chitrakoot, literally "the Hill of Many Wonders", refers to the forested Kamadgiri Hill, where according to the *Ramayana*, Rama, Sita and Lakshman spent a portion of their 14-year exile. Below the hill lies Hanuman Dhara, a natural spring that flows over a delightful image of the monkey god, Hanuman, placed in a recess. Dotted with numerous temples, and full of sadhus, the town has a unique charm. Boat rides from the attractive Ramghat, the town's main ghat, provide an impressive view of the temples along the river bank.

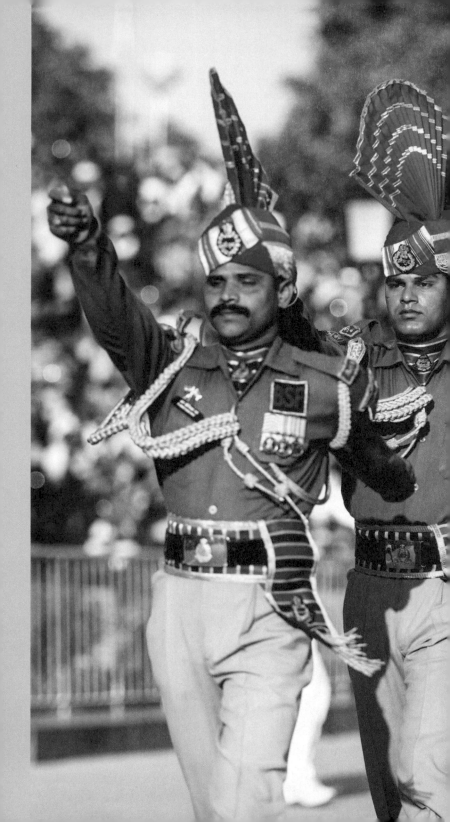

HARYANA AND PUNJAB

The neighbouring states of Haryana and Punjab cover the vast plains that stretch between the River Indus and the Gangetic belt. This area has a long history of human occupation; one of the earliest recorded cultures in India, the Indus Valley Civilization, established cities here. After their decline, the Vedic civilization emerged in the 16th century BC, and dominated for around a thousand years. The subsequent kingdoms that ruled are a who's who of major Indian civilizations, starting with the Mauryan Empire, and followed by the Gupta Empire, the Delhi Sultanate, the Mughals and the British Raj. But this region diverges from other states controlled by the same invading groups in one notable way – Amritsar in Punjab is where the Sikh religion was founded in the 15th century. The followers of this anti-caste belief system emerged as a political force in the time of the Mughals, and subsequently ruled parts of Punjab in the 18th and 19th century.

When northern India was split into Hindu-majority India and Muslim-majority Pakistan after independence from Britain in 1947, the border-territory of Punjab was the site of horrific massacres on both sides. Although there is occasional tension along the border, the area is now mainly peaceful. It was split into Sikh-dominated Punjab and Hindu-majority Haryana in 1966.

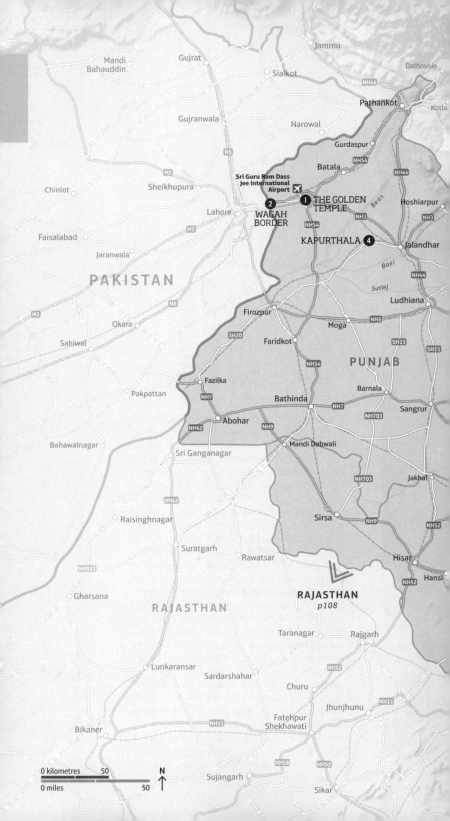

Mandi
Bahauddin

Gujrat

Jammu

Sialkot

Dalhousie

NH44

Pathankot

Kotla

Narowal

Gurdaspur

Gujranwala

Batala

NH54

NH44

Chiniot

M2

Sheikhupura

Sri Guru Ram Dass
Jee International
Airport

✈ ① THE GOLDEN
TEMPLE

Hoshiarpur

Beas

NH3

Lahore

② WAGAH
BORDER

NH54

NH3

Faisalabad

M3

KAPURTHALA

④

Jalandhar

Jaranwala

PAKISTAN

Baei

NH44

Sutlej

Ludhiana

N5

Firozpur

Moga

NH5

Okara

Faridkot

SH13

SH11

Sahiwal

SH20

NH54

PUNJAB

Pakpattan

Fazilka

Barnala

M3

NH7

Bathinda

Sangrur

Bahawalnagar

NH62

Abohar

NH9

NH7

NH703

Mandi Dabwali

Sri Ganganagar

Jakhal

NH703

NH62

Sirsa

NH9

NH52

Raisinghnagar

Gharsana

Suratgarh

Rawatsar

RAJASTHAN
p108

Hisar

Hansi

NH52

RAJASTHAN

Taranagar

Rajgarh

Lunkaransar

Sardarshahar

NH52

Churu

Jhunjhunu

NH11

Bikaner

NH11

Fatehpur
Shekhawati

NH58

NH52

0 kilometres   50

0 miles   50

N

Sujangarh

Sikar

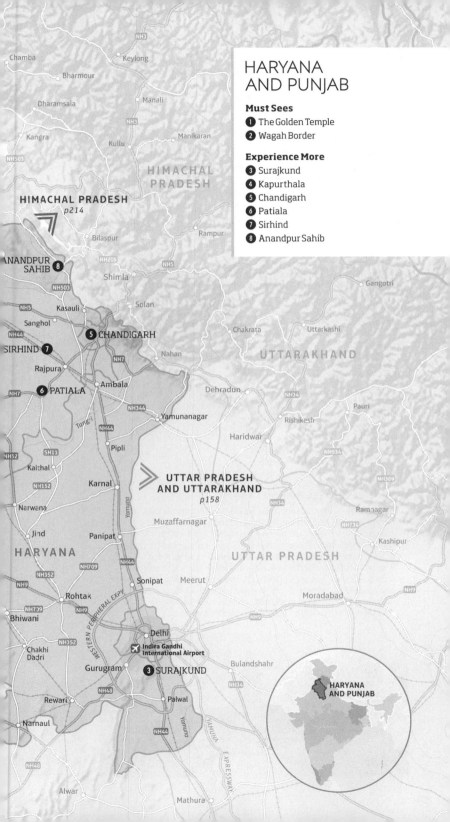

HARYANA AND PUNJAB

Must Sees
1 The Golden Temple
2 Wagah Border

Experience More
3 Surajkund
4 Kapurthala
5 Chandigarh
6 Patiala
7 Sirhind
8 Anandpur Sahib

HIMACHAL PRADESH
p214

**UTTAR PRADESH
AND UTTARAKHAND**
p158

HARYANA
AND PUNJAB

❶

THE GOLDEN TEMPLE

🏠 Circular Rd, Amritsar, Punjab; 227 km (141 miles) NW of Chandigarh 🕐 Sunrise–sunset daily
🌐 sgpc.net/sri-harmandir-sahib/

The spiritual centre of the Sikh religion, the Golden Temple is one of the holiest places in India, visited by thousands of pilgrims daily. Built between 1589 and 1601, it is a superb synthesis of Islamic and Hindu styles of architecture.

In keeping with the syncretic tradition of those times, the foundation stone of the Golden Temple was laid by a Muslim saint, Mian Mir. The temple was virtually destroyed in 1761 by an Afghan invader, Ahmed Shah Abdali, but was rebuilt in 1764 by Jassa Singh Ahluwalia. In the early 19th century, Maharaja Ranjit Singh, ruler of Punjab, covered the dome in gold and embellished the interiors with lavish decoration. In 1984, parts of the temple were badly damaged during an army operation ordered by then-president Indira Gandhi to flush out separatist extremists hiding inside, but the building has now been restored.

WHAT ELSE TO SEE IN AMRITSAR

A few other shrines are found just outside the Temple complex. These include a shrine dedicated to Guru Hargobind Singh, as well as the nine-storeyed Baba Atal Tower, which marks the spot where Atal Rai, son of Hargobind, attained martyrdom. Lying 2 km (1 mile) northeast of the Golden Temple, the 16th-century Durgiana Temple, visited by Hindus, is dedicated to Durga. Jallianwala Bagh, also a short distance from the Golden Temple, is the site of an infamous massacre that took place in 1919. Hundreds of unarmed demonstrators were gunned down in this enclosed garden on the orders of General Reginald Dyer. A memorial to those killed stands at the eastern end.

PICTURE PERFECT
Golden Glow

At sunrise, the sun hits the Golden Temple. At this hour, the temple is reflected in the waters of Amrit Sarovar, which is the ideal time to snap a photo.

↑ The Golden Temple, covered in gold leaf and *(inset)* reading the sacred Guru Granth Sahib

Exploring the Golden Temple

Surrounded by a maze of lanes and 18 fortified gateways, the Golden Temple complex is a city within a city. The main entrance is through its northern gateway, the Darshani Deor, from where steps lead down to the Parikrama (marble pathway), which encircles the Amrit Sarovar ("Pool of Nectar") and the main shrine, the golden domed Harmandir Sahib ("Temple of God"). Among the sites lining the Parikrama is a tree shrine called the Gurdwara Dukh Bhanjani Ber, said to have the miraculous power to heal diseases, and the Ath-Sath Tirath, which represents 68 of the holiest Hindu pilgrim shrines. The Parikrama continues on to the Sri Akal Takhat Sahib, the seat of the Sikh religious order. It was built in 1606 by the sixth guru, Guru Hargobind.

As part of the daily ritual, the holy book of the Sikhs, the Guru Granth Sahib, is carried out of the Sri Akal Takhat Sahib to the Harmandir Sahib at daybreak. The head priest then opens it for the vaq, the message for the day. From dawn till late at night the temple echoes with the music of ragis, musicians employed by the temple trust to sing verses from the Guru Granth Sahib. No visit is considered complete without a meal at the Guru ka Langar, a free kitchen where visitors are fed a simple meal of dal-roti (lentil curry and bread). Prayers end by 9:45pm, when the holy book is carried in a silver palanquin back to the Sri Akal Takhat Sahib.

Visitors to the Temple must remove their shoes, wash their feet and cover their heads before entering. Note also that alcohol and tobacco are forbidden within the complex.

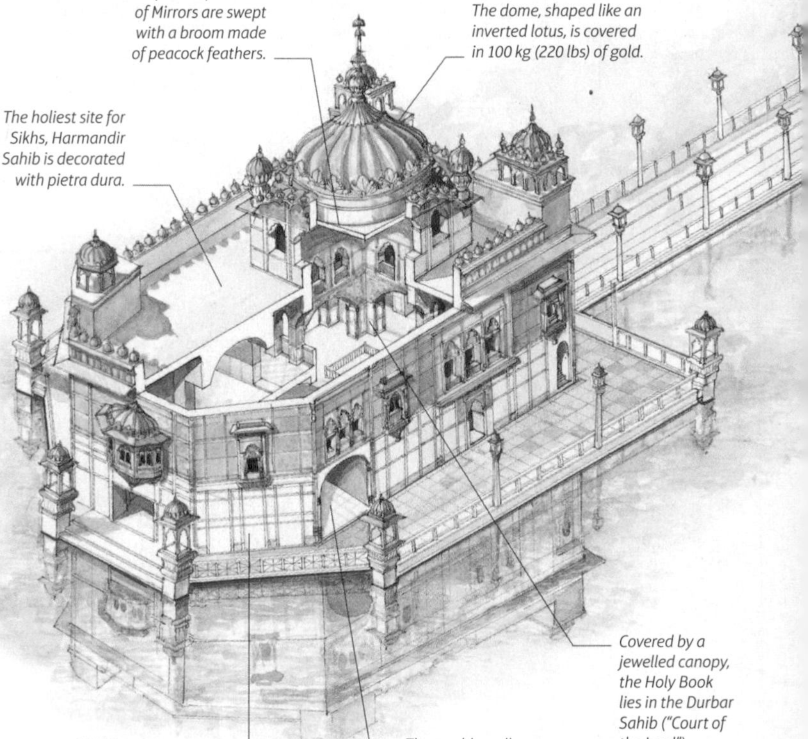

The floors of the Hall of Mirrors are swept with a broom made of peacock feathers.

The dome, shaped like an inverted lotus, is covered in 100 kg (220 lbs) of gold.

The holiest site for Sikhs, Harmandir Sahib is decorated with pietra dura.

Covered by a jewelled canopy, the Holy Book lies in the Durbar Sahib ("Court of the Lord").

The marble walls of the first floor have pietra dura inlay and decorative plasterwork.

The lower wall of the temple is made of white marble.

↑ The Golden Temple, the holiest site in the Sikh religion

Did You Know?

Every visitor entering the Harmandir Sahib is given a dollop of sweet *prasad* (holy offering).

The seat of the supreme governing body of the Sikhs, Sri Akal Takhat Sahib houses the holy book at night.

Darshani Deor is a gateway to the temple's inner sanctum. It has two silver doors and sacred verses carved on its walls.

Amrit Sarovar, the pool where Sikhs are baptized, was built in 1577 by the fourth guru.

The 60-m- (197-ft-) long causeway is flanked by 18 gilded lamps.

↑ Devotees walking down the marble causeway towards the Harmandir Sahib

↑ Floral pattern inlaid into the marble floor of the Golden Temple

SIKHISM

The Sikh religion is a reformist faith, founded by Guru Nanak in the 15th century. Strongly opposed to idol worship, rituals and the caste system, it believes in a formless God. Sikhism is also called Gurmat, meaning "the Guru's Doctrine", and Sikh temples are called gurdwaras, literally "doors to the guru". Nanak, the first of ten gurus, chose his successor from among his most devout disciples. Gobind Singh (1666–1708), the tenth and last guru, reorganized the community in 1699 as a military order, the Khalsa, to combat religious persecution by the Mughals. He gave the Sikh community a distinctive religious identity, as well as physical markers in the form of the Khalsa's five symbols: uncut hair, undergarment, dagger, comb and steel bangle.

Crowds watching the lowering of the flags on the Pakistan and India border ↑

2

WAGAH BORDER

📍 Pakistan-India border, Amritsar district, Punjab; 29 km (18 miles) W of Amritsar 🚌 From Amritsar 🕐 Sunset daily except in times of border tension

The Changing of the Guard at the Wagah Border is one of the most spectacular rituals in India. It takes place every day at sunset on the Pakistani border and is a poignant reminder of the 1947 Partition, when the modern nations of India and Pakistan were formed amid horrific bloodletting.

At this very popular ceremony, crowds sit on specially erected stands on both sides of the border to watch the simultaneous lowering of the flags of each nation every night. As the buglers sound the last post, two splendidly uniformed and mustachioed guards, one from Pakistan and one from India, goose-step to the flagpoles by the border gate to lower their respective flags simultaneously. The guards' steps are matched so perfectly that it is like watching a mirror image of the same exercise. While the ceremony is good natured, there are still times of heightened border tensions, when public attendance may occasionally be suspended. Frequent autos and minibuses make the run from Amritsar nightly.

> As the buglers sound the last post, two splendidly uniformed and mustachioed guards, one from Pakistan and one from India, goose-step to the flagpoles.

THE PARTITION OF INDIA

When British India was split into Hindu and Muslim republics in 1947, Britain divided its largest provinces - Punjab and Bengal - between the two. The job went to Cyril Radcliffe, a British civil servant who knew little about India. He split Punjab according to which religious group was the local majority, but when independence came, all too many people found themselves on the wrong side of the line. As huge numbers tried to flee, violence mounted and thousands were massacred. The communal displacement and killings went on for months.

→ Two guards, one from Pakistan and one from India, perform their elaborate steps

The distinctive ↑ uniform of the Indian border guards

↑ Crowds at the bustling crafts fair held every February in Surajkund

EXPERIENCE MORE

③

Surajkund

⌂ Faridabad district, Haryana; 21 km (13 miles) S of Delhi ▣ ⓘ 36 Janpath, New Delhi; www.haryanatourism.gov.in/destination/surajkund

Also known as the Lake of the Sun, this reservoir, built between the 10th and 11th centuries by King Surajpal of the Rajput Tomar dynasty, is now a popular picnic spot. The original embankment of stone terraces surrounding the tank, built to trap rainwater, still exists. Nearby, a man-made lake has boating facilities. The area comes alive in the first two weeks of February, when a crafts *mela* is held here, with artisans from all over India selling their wares. Puppets from Rajasthan, bell metal beasts from Odisha and mirrorwork from Gujarat are displayed alongside a variety of food stalls, while musicians and folk dancers weave through the crowds, giving the fair a joyous, carnival air.

④

Kapurthala

⌂ Kapurthala district, Punjab; 165 km (103 miles) NW of Chandigarh ▣ ▣ ⓘ www.punjabtourism.gov.in

This former princely state is a pocket of extraordinary architecture – which is all owed to the eccentric ruler

---

EAT

Elevens

One of Chandigarh's best restaurants, Elevens offers North Indian non-veg dishes and Indian-style Chinese cuisine in comfortable surrounds.

⌂ The Kaptain's Retreat, 303-304, Sector 35-B, Chandigarh ⓒ (0172) 466 1111

₹₹₹

Did You Know?

A colourful figure, Maharaja Jagatjit Singh scandalized society by marrying a Spanish dancer.

Maharaja Jagatjit Singh, who created, amid the agricultural fields of Punjab, a corner that looks more like France than India. In 1906 this passionate Francophile commissioned a French architect to build him a palace modelled on Versailles, with features from the Louvre and Fontainebleau added on. This amazing structure, which he grandly named the Elysée Palace – now the **Jagatjit Palace** – sits amid ornate gardens and is surrounded by villas modelled on those that were in vogue in the suburbs of Paris in the late 19th century.

After this palace was built, the maharaja went through a Spanish phase, which found expression in the Buena Vista Hunting Lodge. Located on the outskirts of the town, it is occupied by his descendants. Another impressive sight is the town's Moorish Mosque, which was inspired by the grand Qutubiya Mosque in Marrakesh – and designed by another French architect employed by Jagatjit Singh. Its inner dome has been beautifully painted by Punjabi artists.

Jagatjit Palace
⊘ ⏰ With prior permission

⑤ Chandigarh

🏛 Chandigarh district, Haryana/Punjab; 248 km (154 miles) N of Delhi 🚆 8 km (5 miles) S of city centre 🚌🚋 ℹ️ Interstate Bus Terminal, Sector 17; www.punjabtourism.gov.in

The state capital of both Haryana and Punjab, this city was built in the early 1950s by a team of architects following the masterplan of internationally renowned designer Le Corbusier. It is considered the first modern city of independent India.

Le Corbusier conceived the city along the lines of a modular man. Laid out on a grid divided evenly into 57 blocks or sectors, the Capitol Complex, which includes the dramatic concrete sculptural buildings of the Secretariat, Assembly and High Court, is the "head" of the city. The main shopping area, Sector 17, is the "heart" of Le Corbusier's plan, and is set around a central plaza and fountain, lined with shops

that reflect the affluence of this city and its residents. Adjoining this sector is a stretch of green, the city's "lungs", with an enormous Rose Garden that is at its best in February. Over a thousand varieties of colourful roses bloom amid winding paths, fountains and sprawling, beautifully tended lawns.

The city's large residential sectors make up its "torso", with neat houses and gardens showing impressive evidence of the residents' green fingers. Each road is lined with a different species of flowering tree, adding vibrant and joyous colour to the often-concrete cityscape.

Chandigarh's **Museum and Art Gallery** houses one of the country's finest collections of Gandharan sculpture, which was an ancient civilization mentioned in Buddhist texts, and miniature paintings, many from northern India. Among the exhibits are a serene 6th-century Standing Bodhisattva, and a rare 11th-century statue of Vishnu holding a conch shell from Kashmir. The miniatures section has a comprehensive display of Pahari paintings from the Kangra, Basohli and Guler schools, while modern art includes mountainscapes by the Russian painter Nicholas Roerich *(p234)*.

A short distance away is the man-made Sukhna Lake, where a pleasant promenade attracts joggers and walkers. This is one of Chandigarh's prettiest areas, especially in the evenings, when visitors can enjoy dramatic sunsets

THE ROCK GARDEN OF CHANDIGARH

Opposite the Capitol Complex, the Rock Garden is Chandigarh's most popular tourist spot. Created illegally on waste ground as a hobby by road inspector Nek Chand, it was discovered by the authorities in 1975. Recognizing it as a work of art, the city council allowed Chand to continue, and the garden now covers 1.6 ha (4 acres). Its serried ranks of sculptures are crafted from such unlikely materials as discarded neon lights, fuse switches, broken crockery and glass.

and views of the twinkling lights of the beautiful nearby hill station, Kasauli *(p230)*. The Pinjore Gardens, 22 km (14 miles) north of Chandigarh, were designed in the 17th century by Fidai Khan, foster brother of the Mughal emperor Aurangzeb. They are terraced in the Mughal style and dotted with domed pavilions, fountains and water chutes. Sanghol, 40 km (25 miles) west of Chandigarh, has an excavated site of a 2nd-century Buddhist stupa with an interesting museum of Kushana sculptures.

Museum and Art Gallery
⊘ 🏛 Sector 10 📞 (0172) 274 0261 ⏰ 10am–4:30pm Tue–Sun

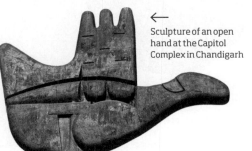

← Sculpture of an open hand at the Capitol Complex in Chandigarh

BAISAKHI FESTIVAL

The Sikh new year, Baisakhi, falls on 13 or 14 April and is celebrated as the solar new year by Hindus, too. For Sikhs it marks the foundation of the Khalsa (Sikh community) by Guru Gobind Singh in 1699. In Punjab it has always been a harvest festival, marked with fairs, processions and *bhangra* dancing, but all over the country Sikhs gather to bathe communally and recite the scriptures.

6

Patiala

⌂ Patiala district, Punjab; 63 km (39 miles) SW of Chandigarh 🚌🚆 🛈 www.punjabtourism.gov.in

Patiala, situated between the Sutlej and Ghaggar rivers, was formerly a princely state, led by a string of flamboyant rulers in the 19th century who made its name a byword for everything decadently over-sized. Thus, the "Patiala Peg" is a whopping measure of whisky and the Patiala *salwar* is three times the width of an ordinary one. Its rulers were also enthusiastic patrons of the arts and sports.

The present city has grown around the Qila Mubarak, a fort built in 1763. Its oldest part, Qila Androon, though now derelict, has traces of fine wall paintings. The **Durbar Hall**, added later, is used as a museum; it has a beautifully ornamented ceiling and well-preserved murals. The hall houses a spectacular display of cannons and arms, including the sword of the Persian ruler Nadir Shah, who invaded India in 1739. In the lively bazaar around the fort, the city's famous hand-crafted leather shoes (*juttis*), tasselled silken braids (*pirandis*) and brightly embroidered *phulkari* fabric are on sale.

The enormous and grand **Old Moti Bagh Palace**, completed in the early years of the 20th century, has as many as 15 dining halls. One of the largest residences in Asia, it is set amid terraced gardens and water channels inspired by Mughal designs. The terraces lead to the Sheesh Mahal, where the art gallery displays miniature paintings, rare manuscripts, *objets d'art*, and hunting trophies from the former royal collection. This gallery overlooks a large tank flanked by two towers, with a rope suspension bridge to connect them. The main palace is now home to the National Institute of Sports, and the large pleasure pool, where the maharaja once lounged and watched dancing girls cavorting, has been turned into a wrestling pit.

Durbar Hall Museum
⊗ 🕘 9am–12pm Tue–Sun

Old Moti Bagh Palace
⊗ 🕘 Tue–Sun

7

Sirhind

⌂ Fatehgarh Sahib district, Punjab; 55 km (34 miles) SW of Chandigarh 🚌🚆 🛈 Punjab Tourism; www.punjabtourism.gov.in

The town of Sirhind was one of the most important settlements in north India between the 16th and 18th centuries. Once the capital of the Pathan Sur sultans, the ruins of whose massive fort can still be seen, Sirhind was also a favourite stop for the Mughal emperors on their

→ The Kesgarh Sahib Gurdwara, one of the main seats of Sikhism, and *(inset)* a temple shrine

annual journeys to Kashmir. In the 11th century, Afghani king Mahmud of Ghazni expanded his extensive empire up to this area, thus giving the town its name, which in Persian means "Frontier of India".

The Mughals constructed several beautiful buildings here, in the area now called **Aam Khas Bagh**, which they had designed for both civilian and royal use. While much of the site is in ruins, it is well worth a visit, particularly for the Royal Hamam, a structure for hot and cold baths that uses water drawn from wells nearby through an intricate system of hand pulleys. Close to the baths are the remains of Shah Jahan's double-storeyed palace, the Daulat Mahal, and the better-preserved Sheesh Mahal, whose walls still have traces of the original tilework and decorative plaster.

To the north of Aam Khas Bagh is the white Fatehgarh Sahib Gurdwara, standing in the midst of bright yellow mustard fields, which bloom in January. It was built to honour the memory of the younger sons of the tenth Sikh guru, Gobind Singh, who were buried

alive in a wall at this spot by Mughal emperor Aurangzeb in 1705, for refusing to convert to Islam.

Adjacent to the gurdwara is an important pilgrimage site for Muslims, the tomb-shrine of the Sufi saint and theologian Shaikh Ahmad Faruqi Sirhindi, who is also known as Mujaddad-al-Saini ("The Reformer of the Millennium"). This magnificent octagonal structure, its dome covered in glazed blue tiles, was built in the 16th century. Also known as the Rauza Sharif, it is considered as holy as the Dargah Sharif in Ajmer (p152).

Aam Khas Bagh
Shamsher Nagar 6am–7pm Tue–Sun

8

Anandpur Sahib
Rupnagar district, Punjab; 73 km (45 miles) NW of Chandigarh www.punjabtourism.gov.in

Guarded by the Shivalik Hills and a ring of imposing forts, Anandpur Sahib is a

complex of historic Sikh gurdwaras. It was here that the severed head of the ninth guru, Tegh Bahadur, was brought to be cremated, at a site now marked by the Sisganj Sahib Gurdwara. The gurdwara also stands on the place where the tenth and last guru, Gobind Singh, founded the Khalsa, or "Army of the Pure", in 1699, along with five volunteers to help him defend the faith. The Kesgarh Sahib Gurdwara, which was built to commemorate this event, is one of the five *takhts* or main seats of the Sikh religion; the others are at Amritsar (p204), Nanded in Maharashtra, Talwandi Sabo in Punjab and Patna (p262) in Bihar. Built to mark the 300th anniversary of the Khalsa, the Virasat-e-Khalsa is a museum on the history of Sikhism.

Forts surround Anandpur Sahib on all sides. Lohagarh Fort was used as the armoury of the Khalsa army; Fatehgarh Fort guarded the road from Delhi to Lahore; and Taragarh Fort protected the complex from attacks by the hill states lying to the north.

Anandpur Sahib comes to life every year during the Hola Mohalla festival, when the blue-robed Nihang Sikhs, descendants of the gurus' personal guards, display their martial and equestrian skills.

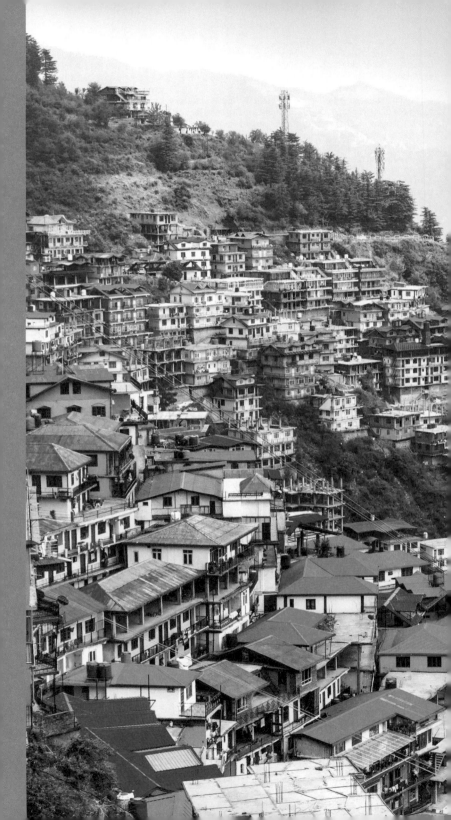

The multicoloured houses of Shimla, Himachal Pradesh's capital

HIMACHAL PRADESH

Himachal, the "Abode of Snow", covers over 56,000 sq km (21,622 sq miles) of the western Himalayan mountains, from the Shivalik range bordering the plains of Punjab, to the peaks fringing Ladakh and Tibet. The united state of Himachal Pradesh has only existed since 1971, but, much like the rest of northern India, the hilly regions that comprise it have a long history marked by invasion and occupation. The numerous hill kingdoms here were subject to multiple invasions by the Mughals, who ruled in Delhi, and most of the state was eventually captured by the Kingdom of Nepal. Once the British arrived and annexed the state, they established Himachal Pradesh's now capital, Shimla, as their summer headquarters, because it offered a cool relief from the intense heat of the plains. The neighbouring country of Tibet was annexed by China in 1951, and, under rising political pressure, the 14th Dalai Lama, symbolic head of the Tibetan government, fled to India. He established the Tibetan government-in-exile in Dharamsala, where he continues to live. The town consequently has a significant Tibetan influence and flavour.

HIMACHAL PRADESH

Must Sees

1 Spiti Valley
2 Tabo Monastery
3 Shimla
4 Dharamsala
5 Bhimakali Temple

Experience More

6 Chail
7 Narkanda
8 Kasauli
9 Kinnaur
10 Mandi
11 Lahaul Valley
12 Nahan
13 Manali
14 Kangra Valley
15 Chamba
16 Dalhousie
17 Bharmour
18 Parvati Valley
19 Great Himalayan National Park
20 Kullu Valley

NH3

Meroo

Indus

Chumathang

Pang

NH3

Tso Moriri

Chumar

Zanskar Range

Hansa

Kunjam Pass

Key Gompa

SPITI VALLEY 1

Kaza

Dhankar Gompa

Khirganga National Park

Pin

Pin Valley National Park

NH505

2 TABO MONASTERY

Himalayas

HIMACHAL PRADESH

Nako Chokhor

Khab

Diyaxiang

19

GREAT HIMALAYAN NATIONAL PARK

NH5

CHINA

Kalpa

9 KINNAUR

Rekong Peo

Sutlej

5 BHIMAKALI TEMPLE

Sangla

Baspa

Rampur

Chitkul

Chirgaon

NH705

Sawra

Range

Chaupal

UTTAR PRADESH AND UTTARAKHAND

p158

Gangotri

Chakrata

Uttarkashi

NH34

UTTARAKHAND

Mussoorie

Dehradun

NH7

Rishikesh

Pauri

NH34

Haridwar

HIMACHAL PRADESH

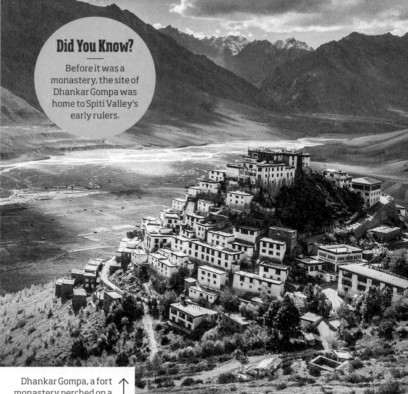

Did You Know?

Before it was a monastery, the site of Dhankar Gompa was home to Spiti Valley's early rulers.

Dhankar Gompa, a fort monastery perched on a cliff far above the valley ↑

❶

SPITI VALLEY

🏠 Lahaul and Spiti district; 170 km (106 miles) N from Shimla to Keylong via Kunjam Pass ℹ️ www.himachaltourism.gov.in/destination/spiti-valley

The heart of Himachal's cold desert, Spiti is a land of fascinating contrasts. Monasteries and prayer flags are dotted along the banks of glacial streams, while blue sheep and ibex graze amid sparse pastures sprinkled with marine fossils.

Once part of a West Tibetan kingdom, Spiti submitted to Ladakhi rule in the 17th century and became a part of British India in the 19th century. Unlike the lush meadows of the Kullu Valley, this is a barren land of rocky massifs, enclosed by the Himalayas to the north, the Pir Panjal to the south, and international borders. Though now part of Himachal Pradesh, forming part of the Lahaul and Spiti district, it has retained its Tibetan character and is an important preserve of ancient Buddhist heritage, and many of the hills here are marked by dramatic Buddhist monasteries.

This dramatic landscape is marked by mountains and lakes such as Chandra Tal, or the "Moon Lake", which lies at the entrance to Spiti when approached from Lahaul. Oval in shape, with deep blue waters, it is overlooked by craggy peaks and hanging glaciers.

Marking the border between Lahaul and Spiti, Pin Valley National Park is an untrammelled pastureland in the shadow of virgin snowcapped peaks. It surrounds the upper reaches of the Pin river and its tributary, the Paraiho. Ibex, foxes and snow wolves are common, while the snow leopard is more elusive.

Key Gompa

▶ Dramatically perched on a windy hilltop, 16th-century Key Gompa is not only the largest monastery in Spiti but a prime example of Tibetan architecture. Having survived seemingly endless violent attacks, fires and even earthquakes, the monastery is still inhabited by a community of lamas. It also has a series of assembly halls, containing numerous musical instruments, icons, manuscripts and *thangkas* (Tibetan Buddhist paintings).

Sakya Tangyud

◀ This modern yet attractive monastery on the edge of a canyon serves as the main place of worship for the growing number of inhabitants in the town of Kaza, the administrative headquarters of Spiti. Brightly painted in the trademark primary colours of Tibetan Buddism, there is a large main prayer hall and a huge courtyard in front of the building for people to gather and socialize.

Dhankar Gompa

Built into a precipitous cliff face (the word *dhankar* literally translates as "cliff fort"), and thus affording magnificent vistas of the Spiti Valley and surrounding peaks, this monastery is probably best known for its wonderfully vivid murals, most likely painted in the 17th century. These depict various scenes from the life of the Buddha, and compensate for the dilapidated state of the buildings.

Nako Chokhor

▶ In the far southeastern corner of the valley, high above the river, Nako's 11th-century monastery is said to have been founded by Rinchen Zangpo (a prolific translator of Buddhist texts). Although much of it is in disrepair, Serkhang (Golden Hall) is a sight to behold, and its murals rival those of Alchi in quality.

↑ Capturing the splendour of Spiti from on high

↑ Prayer flags streaming through the mountains

TABO MONASTERY

🏠 Lahaul and Spiti district; 380 km (236 miles) NE of Shimla 🚌 🕐 May–Oct 🛈 Permits required to travel to Tabo via Shimla (Kinnaur); foreign tourists may go via Manali (Kaza) without a permit; apply at Shimla's District Collectorate or Rekong Peo's SDM Office; www.himachaltourism.gov.in/destination/spiti-valley

One of the most important Buddhist centres in Spiti, Tabo Monastery was founded in the 11th century by Rinchen Zangpo, a legendary scholar. Under the patronage of Tibetan king Ye-she-od, he encouraged a resurgence of Buddhism by translating religious texts and promoting prodigious temple building.

The *gompa* (monastery) at Tabo is one of the largest monasteries built during this resurgence. The squat mud structures of Tabo are enclosed within a mud wall about 84 m by 75 m (276 ft by 246 ft) and appear quite unimpressive from the outside. It is the exquisite wall paintings inside, however, that make Tabo one of the most significant art treasures of the Tibetan Buddhist world. The earliest paintings in the *dukhang* (assembly hall) are from the 10th and 11th centuries and depict scenes from the life of the Buddha. The hall also contains imposing clay sculptures of the chief deities from the Buddhist pantheon. One of the shrines houses a huge clay idol of a sitting Maitreya (the Future Buddha).

Tabo is a favourite retreat of the Dalai Lama, but this monastery is difficult to access and travel is restricted due to the proximity of the border with Tibet.

↑ Monks praying at the shrine inside richly decorated Tabo Monastery

↑ Scenes from the life of the Buddha along the interior walls of the monastery

THANGKAS

Thangkas are religious art that adorn the walls of many Tibetan Buddhist monasteries in India, from Thiksey Gompa in Ladakh to the Kalachakra Temple in Dharamsala, the town where His Holiness the Dalai Lama resides. Thangkas are delicate paintings on fabric depicting Buddhist deities like the Buddha or Green Tara, mandalas and the Wheel of Life. You can see thangkas being painted at the beautiful Norbulingka Institute an hour's drive from Dharamsala. The institute's aim is to preserve Tibetan arts and culture, and they also host workshops.

24

stupas (or chortens in Ladakh) of various sizes are dotted around the Tabo Monastery.

↑ The colourful exterior of the stupa, amid the squat buildings of the historic monastery *(inset)*

SHIMLA

⌂ Shimla district; 375 km (233 miles) N of Delhi
✈ 23 km (14 miles) W of Shimla 🚂🚌 ℹ Apply for permits at the District Collectorate; www.himachaltourism.gov.in/destination/shimla

The fast-growing capital of Himachal Pradesh, Shimla became the summer headquarters of the British government in India in 1864. Today this hill station still retains much of its heritage charm.

① The Ridge

⌂ Mall Road

A popular promenade and the centre of Shimla's cultural scene, the Ridge, at a height of 2,230 m (7,316 ft), is an open stretch of land on the western shoulder of Jakhu Hill. It offers views of the Himalayan peaks.

② Christ Church

☎ (0177) 265 295 ⌚ 8am-6pm daily (call ahead)

Dominating the eastern end of the Ridge is the Gothic Christ Church, built in 1846 and one of the first churches in north India. Its fine stained-glass windows and organ were acquired in the 19th century.

---

③ 🍴 🖥 🛍

The Mall

This 7-km (4-mile-) long thoroughfare runs from Boileauganj in the west to Chhota Shimla in the south-east. The central section, flanked by rows of half-timbered buildings, has a profusion of restaurants, bars and upmarket shops, and cars are not permitted to drive here. The Mall's highest spot, Scandal Point, is marked by a statue of the freedom fighter Lala Lajpat Rai. The so-called "scandal" may refer to the reputed abduction of an

English lady in the late 19th century from this spot by a maharaja of Patiala. Nearby are the timber-framed Post Office and the jewel-like Gaiety Theatre, opened in

← People enjoying a stroll through the snow in the hill station of Shimla

1887, and still a popular venue for amateur dramatics. A favoured local pastime is to stroll along The Mall from Scandal Point to Combermere Bridge. Further ahead on this stretch lies the mock-Tudor Clarkes Hotel.

④ 🍴 🥤 🛍️
Lower Bazaar

Below the central section of The Mall is the Lower Bazaar, the option of cheaper wares and less fashionable hostelries and eating places. Lower still is the Ganj, a congested bazaar where the town's wholesale trade in groceries takes place.

⑤ 🏷️
State Museum

🏠 Chaura Maidan Rd
📞 (0177) 265 4589
🕐 10am-5pm Tue-Sun
🚫 Public hols

The State Museum houses a collection of almost 10,000 artifacts, including stone sculptures dating from the 6th to 11th centuries and a collection of Kangra miniatures based on the seasons (*Baramasa*), musical modes (*Ragamala*) and episodes from the *Gita Govinda*, a devotional poem. Most impressive, however, is a spectacular series of mid-19th-century wall paintings from Chamba.

⑥
Jakhu Hill Temple

🏠 Jakhu Hill 🚠 To the temple 🕐 6am-8pm daily

The forested dome of Jakhu Hill, at 2,450 m (8,038 ft), is the highest point in Shimla. At its peak stands a temple dedicated to the monkey god, Hanuman. According to the epic *Ramayana*, the god rested here during his journey to fetch the Sanjivini herb from the Himalayas to save the wounded Lakshman's life. A steep 2 km (1 mile) climb from the Ridge to the summit through deodar and oak forests offers panoramic views of Shimla and its suburbs. Monkeys are a common sight all over Shimla, but Jakhu is their kingdom. Visitors should watch out for simian hands rifling through their pockets and belongings.

Must See

Did You Know?

The Monkey King in Chinese epic *Journey to the West* is said to have been inspired by Hanuman.

⑦ 🏷️
Viceregal Lodge

🏠 The Mall 📞 (0177) 283 1376 🕐 9am-5pm Tue-Sun (later hours in summer)

Situated atop Observatory Hill, this grey stone structure was built in 1888 as a summer residence for the viceroys of India. Well-maintained gardens surround the stately mansion on three sides. The interior is as impressive, with two rows of balconies overlooking the magnificent teak-panelled entrance hall. A bronze plaque behind the building lists the peaks visible at a distance. The Lodge now houses the Indian Institute of Advanced Study, and only the entrance hall, a couple of rooms on the ground floor, a picture gallery and the gardens are open to the public.

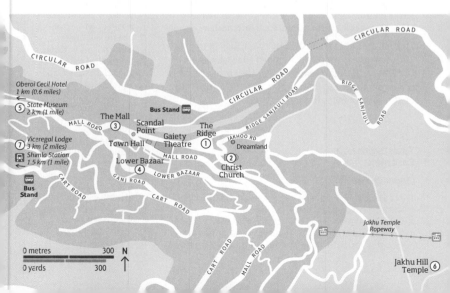

← Shoppers walking along the colourful high street in McLeod Ganj

4

DHARAMSALA

⌂ Kangra district; 238 km (148 miles) NW of Shimla
✈ Gaggal, 11 km (7 miles) S 🚉 Pathankot, 80 km (50 miles)
NW of Dharamsala, then bus or taxi 🚌 🛈 McLeod Ganj;
www.himachaltourism.gov.in/destination/dharamshala

This hill station, established by the British in the mid-19th century, is today the home of the Dalai Lama and the Tibetan Government-in-Exile. The town consists of two sections; the upper town, McLeod Ganj, is the destination of most foreign visitors.

①
Tsuglagkhang Complex

🕐 5am–8pm daily

The focal point of the upper town, called McLeod Ganj, this complex is at the southern edge and contains the residence of the Dalai Lama (not open to visitors), the Namgyal Monastery, where monks can be seen debating in the afternoons, and the important Tsuglagkhang Temple. A simple hall, painted in yellow, the temple has a raised dais from where the Dalai Lama holds discourses, and three beautiful images from the Buddhist pantheon –

LITTLE TIBET

When the 14th Dalai Lama, Tenzin Gyatso, fled Tibet in 1959 after the Chinese occupation, McLeod Ganj in Dharamsala became his home, as well as the base of the Tibetan Government-in-Exile. The town is today often called Little Tibet, and it preserves Tibet's religious and cultural heritage, keeps the Tibetan cause alive internationally, and serves as the focal point for the 100,000 Tibetans scattered in refugee settlements all over India. Dharamsala also attracts Buddhists from across the world, such as Hollywood actor Richard Gere.

Sakyamuni (the Historical Buddha), Avalokitesvara and Padmasambhava. The Dalai Lama is believed to be an incarnation of Avalokitesvara. Another temple in the complex has an intricate mural of the Kalachakra ("Wheel of Time") and beautiful sand mandalas, painstakingly created by the monks over a period of time and then ritually destroyed. Pilgrims often come to the complex and walk the Kora, which is a ritual walk clockwise around a holy place, at the Dalai Lama's residence.

② Nechung Monastery

🕑 9am–3pm daily

The Nechung Monastery is the seat of the Tibetan State Oracle, whose predictions on major events in the coming year carry great weight in the Tibetan community.

③ Gangchen Kyishong

🕑 Daily

This administrative centre of the Tibetan Government-in-Exile is midway between the upper and lower towns. The complex includes the excellent Library of Tibetan Works and Archives, a museum on the first floor with bronze images and *thangkas*, as well as the Institute of Tibetan Medicine.

④ Tibetan Institutes

📍 Dharamkot Rd
🕑 For performances

Situated at the northern edge of town on the way to the village of Dharamkot are the Tibetan Institute of Performing Arts and the beautiful Norbulingka Institute, where traditional arts and crafts are promoted.

⑤ Bhagsu

📍 7 km (4 miles) N of Dharamsala

Immediately below sleepy Dharamkot, the livelier village of Bhagsu attracts hordes of domestic tourists, who bathe in the temple tank and hike up to the nearby waterfall.

⑥ Church of St John in the Wilderness

📍 1.5 km (1 mile) W of McLeod Ganj 🕑 9am–5pm daily

On the road to Kotwali Bazaar is this picturesque church, a grey stone structure built in 1852. Brass plaques and colourful Belgian stained-glass windows can be seen inside. The tomb of Lord Elgin, the British viceroy, lies here.

EAT

Tibet Kitchen
Excellent restaurant spread over three floors serving Tibetan, Indian and Chinese cuisine.

📍 Just off Main Chowk
📞 97362 54543

₹₹₹

Jimmy's Italian Kitchen
Hip first-floor café, decorated with movie posters, where you can enjoy pizza, pasta, salads, desserts and good coffee.

📍 Jogiwara Rd
📞 98162 97093

₹₹₹

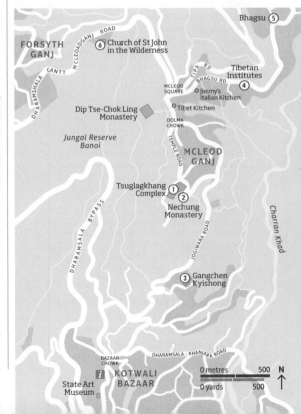

BUDDHISM

It was in India that Siddhartha Gautama found enlightenment and became the Buddha ("awakened one") in the 6th century BC. His subsequent anti-caste religion spread rapidly throughout the country, aided by powerful followers such as the Mauryan king Ashoka in the 3rd century BC. The most common form seen in modern India is Tibetan Buddhism, which emphasizes the role of reincarnated teachers (lamas), most notably the Dalai Lama.

PLACES OF WORSHIP

It was the exile of the Dalai Lama from Tibet in 1959 and establishment of the Tibetan Government-in-Exile at Dharamsala in Himachal Pradesh that reinvigorated the Buddhist faith in India. The monastery where the Dalai Lama lives, Namgyal Temple (often called Dalai Lama Temple) is an important pilgrimage site for Buddhists. The religion is the majority faith in Ladakh, parts of Sikkim and Himachal Pradesh, plus there are sizeable communities as far south as Karnataka. In all these areas there are places of worship ranging from small temples to huge monastery complexes. Common features are brightly painted worship halls, Buddha statues and stupas of various sizes. The Buddha spent most of his time in India in Bihar and Jharkhand, and there are now temples on many important sites.

> **The monastery where the Dalai Lama lives, Namgyal Temple (often called Dalai Lama Temple) is an important pilgrimage site for Buddhists.**

DALAI LAMA

Renowned worldwide for his smile, tireless campaigns for peace and endless shows of compassion, Tenzin Gyatso, the 14th Dalai Lama, is based in Dharamsala but spends a lot of time on tour. Private audiences are rare, but visitors can attend his occasional public lectures.

← A colourful Buddha statue in the hall at Tawanga Monastery

TOP 5 BUDDHIST RITUAL ITEMS

Prayer Wheels
These can be handheld wheels or massive drums. Turning the wheels releases written prayers into the air.

Prayer Flags
Strings of colourful triangular flags flutter prayers into the wind.

Thangkas
Embroidered or painted fabric hangings with images of the Buddha or Bodhisattvas.

Sand Mandalas
Symbolizing the universe, these are meticulously created and then ceremonially destroyed with fire, which is meant to help the monks meditate.

Singing Bowls
These metal bowls sound a constant note when struck.

MONASTIC RITUALS

Saffron- and maroon-robed monks engage in daily rituals at all monasteries, often early morning or late afternoon. These include lighting yak butter candles, rhythmically chanting "Om mane padme hum" and blowing rasping blasts through long brass horns.

DEVOTEE PRACTICES

Ordinary Buddhists regularly partake in practices such as meditating, chanting, turning prayer wheels at temples and circumambulating holy places, always in a clockwise direction. The most famous of these walks is the circuit around the residence of the Dalai Lama in Dharamsala, a ritual known as the Kora.

↑ Turning prayer wheels at a monastery

← The residence of the Dalai Lama in India, Namgyal Monastery

5

BHIMAKALI TEMPLE

📍 Sarahan, Shimla district; 198 km (123 miles) NE of Shimla 🚌 🕐 Sunrise-sunset daily

Situated in the small town of Sarahan, Bhimakali Temple has a unique architectural design that blends elements of Buddhist and Hindu architecture – all against the stunning backdrop of epic mountains and apple orchards.

Sarahan was once the summer capital of the Bushahr kings, and the Bhimakali Temple complex was their temple-cum-palace; the family lived here, and it was also where they housed their deity, as per feudal tradition. The Bushahrs worshipped Bhimakali, one of the myriad forms of the goddess Kali, whose image is housed on the first-floor of the pagoda-style building. This image of Kali is still worshipped at the annual Dussehra Festival. Although the exact age of Bhimakali is not known, it is associated with events dating to the 7th century, while parts of it are 800 years old.

The temple-palace has a unique architectural style, with many intricate details such as the exquisitely carved panels on the overhanging balconies. Its layout consists of a series of courtyards connected by gateways. This area is prone to earthquakes, and the temple was built to withstand these events.

↑ The Leaning Tower, the former main shrine of the temple

WHAT ELSE TO SEE IN SARAHAN

Perched high above the left bank of the Sutlej at the height of 2,165 m (7,103 ft), the town of Sarahan has a pleasant climate enhanced by vistas of the Srikhand Range across the valley, with the prominent twin peaks of Gushu-Pishu and the holy mountain of Srikhand Mahadev. It also has a short nature trail leading to a pheasantry; the many pheasants here include the colourful Himalayan monal *(left)* and the near-extinct Western Himalayan tragopan.

The marble walls of the first floor are decorated with pietra dura and plasterwork of animal and flower motifs covered in gold leaf.

The main entrance is an elaborately decorated metal door that opens into the first courtyard.

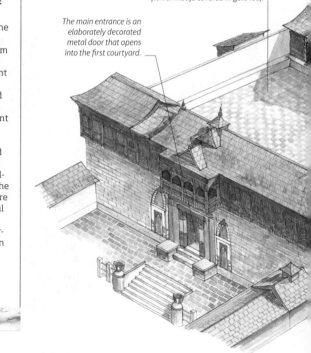

The uppermost storey of the renovated temple is fringed by overhanging balconies.

↑ Bhimakali Temple, with the Srikhand Range looming behind

The golden finials represent the deity and royal patrons.

The Leaning Tower was the main temple until it was damaged in 1905. The adjoining tower has since become the main shrine.

1905

The year the Leaning Tower was damaged in an earthquake – and got its name.

The silver doors to the second courtyard have panels depicting Hindu gods. They were added during the reign of King Padam Singh (1914–47).

↑ Bhimakali Temple, the former home of the Bushahr kings

EXPERIENCE MORE

❻ Chail

🏠 Solan district; 45 km (28 miles) SE of Shimla 🚌
ℹ️ The Palace Hotel; (0114) 242 3100

A tiny hill station on a ridge at a similar altitude to Shimla (p222), pretty Chail was developed as the summer capital of the Patiala maharajas in the 1920s, and their residence, Chail Palace, a stone mansion occupying a hilltop amid beautiful orchards and gardens, is now a deluxe hotel. The cricket pitch, near the top of a hill, is said to be one of the highest in the world. Walks through the deodar forests of the Chail Wildlife Sanctuary are the best way to discover Chail's natural beauty.

❼ Narkanda

🏠 Shimla district; 64 km (40 miles) N of Shimla 🚌

At a height of 2,750 m (9,022 ft), Narkanda stands on the HT Road as it winds along the edges of the ridge-line which divides the Sutlej and Yamuna catchments. From here, the great Himalayan peaks feel enticingly close and the walks through dense temperate forests, where spruce, fir and high-altitude oak take over from the deodar and blue pine, are quite spectacular. The best walk is the 6-km (4-mile) hike to Hatu Peak (3,300 m/10,827 ft), which is crowned by a temple dedicated to Hateshwari Devi. The area around Narkanda is lush with apple orchards. In winter, the slopes are ideal for skiing.

❽ Kasauli

🏠 Solan district; 77 km (48 miles) SW of Shimla 🚌

The closest hill station to the plains, Kasauli offers the charm of quiet walks shaded by chir pine, oak and horse chestnut trees. It is at its best just after the monsoon, when colourful dahlias cover the hillsides. The town remains delightfully intact, with old-fashioned buildings with gable roofs and wooden balconies lining the Upper and Lower Malls, the two main streets that run right through the town. Monkey Point, the highest spot in Kasauli, is 4 km (2 miles) from the bus station. From here there are clear views of Shimla hill station, the meandering Sutlej river and Chandigarh.

> 💬 INSIDER TIP
> **Go Fruit Picking in the Hills**
>
> Narkanda, known as the "Gateway to the Apple Country" is famous for its orchards. You can visit many orchards on a picking tour - Stokes Farm, close to town, is an excellent option.

❾ Kinnaur

🏠 Kinnaur district; 244 km (152 miles) NE from Shimla to Rekong Peo 🚌 ℹ️ Travel permits required for areas close to the Chinese border; himachaltourism.gov.in/destination/kinnaur

The remote northeastern corner of Himachal Pradesh fringing the Tibetan Plateau, Kinnaur is a region of awesome grandeur. The dramatic variations of terrain, climate, vegetation and wildlife have broadly divided this region into Lower, Middle and Upper. Lower Kinnaur is arrayed on both banks of the gorge-like Sutlej river. The picturesque left bank has mountain slopes, terraced fields and tightly packed rows of houses clinging to the hillsides; the right bank has higher peaks but a smaller population, apart from in the main town, Rekong Peo.

Middle Kinnaur is much more rugged. Dominating its heart are the majestic heights of the Kinner Kailash Range, while to its south is the gentle valley of the Baspa, one of the Sutlej's largest tributaries. The highest region, Upper Kinnaur,

← Green, flower-dotted meadows on Hatu Peak, a short hike from Narkanda

The village of Sangla, in the Baspa Valley of the Kinnaur region, near the border with Tibet ↑

is located in the Zanskar peaks, a cold desert country of stark mountains dotted with the occasional village and irrigated fields.

Rekong Peo, the district headquarters, is a bustling little township on the right bank of the Sutlej river, with some shops and adequate transport connections. About 13 km (8 miles) higher up on the same mountain is Kalpa, the former headquarters. With its view of the Kinner Kailash Range, Kalpa is a must in any Kinnaur itinerary. The choice of walks include one to the upland pastures through deodar and *chilgoza* pine (*Pinus gerardiana*) forests.

About 20 km (12 miles) from Rekong Peo, the Baspa river joins the Sutlej at its left bank. Apart from a furious rush in the last stretch of its course, the Baspa river ambles along a wooded valley surrounded by gneiss faces and forests of deodar, pine and birch reaching up to long swards of pasture and snowy

peaks. The Baspa Valley is better known as the Sangla Valley after the largest village in Kinnaur. A road trip through it, which takes two to three days (p240), is the best way to experience the dramatic transition in landscape. The tour begins at Kafour village, whose Hirma Temple, dedicated to a local mother goddess, stands out amid the slate rooftops. From the road at Tranda, further away, there are striking views of sheer rock walls falling 500 m (1,640 ft) to the river. On the other side, cliffs of equal magnitude enclose the Sutlej in a narrow, impenetrable gorge. The route then passes the temple at Sungra Maheshwar, with its pagoda-like roof and fine wooden carvings. The next village, Sapni, has a tower temple that contains some of the finest examples of wooden sculpture in Kinnaur. The Kamroo Narayan Temple is the next point of interest. The temple's tower commands a picturesque

view of the valley. Fields and orchards slope down to the Baspa on one side of the river, while on the other side, thick forests rise up to pasture-lands. Nearby is Sangla, the largest among the valley villages. The tour ends at the village of Chitkul, just before the pastures of the Upper Baspa Valley. Both Sangla and Chitkul provide basic accommodation. Every village along the route from Sangla to Chitkul offers glorious walks and a choice of festivals to celebrate with the local people.

Buddhism holds complete sway throughout Upper Kinnaur. Fluttering prayer flags and mud-walled temples with clay images and wall paintings dot the region, reflecting its proximity to Tibet. Many temples are credited to the 11th-century scholar Rinchen Zangpo, revered in Tibetan Buddhism as the Lotsawa (Translator) who initiated the mammoth task of translating Indian texts into Tibetan and supposedly built 108 monasteries in one night. During the rains (June–September), Upper Kinnaur is ideal for trekking, as it is shielded from monsoon showers.

> **The highest region, Upper Kinnaur, is located in the Zanskar peaks, a cold desert country of stark mountains.**

10 Mandi

⊠ Mandi district; 156 km
(97 miles) N of Shimla
🚉 Joginder Nagar, 53 km
(33 miles) NW of Mandi,
then taxi or bus 🚌
ℹ himachaltourism.gov.
in/destination/mandi

Often referred to as the gateway to the Kullu Valley (p239), the small market town of Mandi is situated at the confluence of the Beas river with a small rain-fed tributary. The capital of the erstwhile princely state of Mandi, it was once a vital link between the hill communities on either side of it but is now visited for its busy market, found in a sunken garden in the centre of town, and its palaces and temples. In the town centre, the former residence of the Mandi kings, built in the colonial style, is now the heritage Rajmahal Palace Hotel. Several wonderful 16th- to 17th-century temples with beautiful stone carvings – such as the Madho Rai Temple, Tarna Devi Temple and Bhootnath Temple, where the Shivratri festival is celebrated – can be found all over town.

Rewalsar, a bustling village at a height of 360 m (1,181 ft), is 24 km (15 miles)

In the town centre, the former residence of the Mandi kings, built in the colonial style, is now the heritage Rajmahal Palace Hotel.

southeast of Mandi. Arrayed around the shores of the Rewalsar Lake, the village is notable for its three Buddhist monasteries, three temples and a gurdwara commemorating the month-long stay of the tenth Sikh guru, Gobind Singh, in 1738. It is said that Padmasambhava, the 8th-century Indian apostle credited with bringing Buddhism to Tibet, used his legendary powers to fly from here to Tibet. His spirit is said to reside in the tiny floating reed islands on the lake.

---

11 Lahaul Valley

⊠ Lahaul and Spiti district;
170 km (106 miles) N of
Shimla 🚌

With an average altitude of 2,750 m (9,022 ft), Lahaul, bordering Tibet and Ladakh's Zanskar Valley, comprises

one of the trans-Himalayan regions of western Himachal Pradesh. This is a barren land of rocky massifs and hanging glaciers, with the Himalayas to the north and the Pir Panjal to the south. Rainfall is scarce, and the region is dependent upon glacial melt for the cultivation of its main crops.

Although the neighbouring Spiti Valley (p218) is beautiful, the difficult terrain inhibits some travellers – Lahaul is more accessible. Upper Lahaul is a land where mountains line the valleys of the Chandra and Bhaga rivers, while Lower Lahaul lies below the town of Tandi, where the two rivers form the Chandrabhaga.

Today, Lahaul's population comprises both Buddhists and Hindus, reflecting the close ties with Tibet, Ladakh and Kullu.

←

Statue of Padmasambhava
on the shores of Rewalsar
Lake, near Mandi

The district headquarters and principal town, Keylong, is located on the Bhaga river. With many basic facilities, it is widely used as a stopover by travellers en route to Leh *(p248)* or as a base for treks. Across the river, opposite Keylong, a steep, tree-shaded pathway leads to Drugpa Kardang Gompa, the largest monastery *(gompa)* in Lahaul. It has a fine collection of *thangkas (p220)*, musical instruments and old weapons. Nearby is the 16th-century Shashur Gompa This monastery is renowned for its 4.5 m (15 ft) *thangka*.

On the road to Manali *(p234)*, about 16 km (10 miles) south of Keylong, the eight-storeyed tower of the Gondhla chiefs dominates the landscape. The oldest monastery in Lahaul, the 800-year-old Guru Ghantal Gompa at Tandi, 11 km (7 miles) southwest of Keylong, is believed to have been established by Guru Padmasambhava, the founder of Tibetan Buddhism.

⑫

Nahan

 Sirmaur district; 100 km (62 miles) S of Shimla 🚌

Lying in the lower Shivalik Hills close to the plains, Nahan nestles on a low wooded ridge at 930 m (3,051 ft). The old town is a charming jumble of narrow cobbled streets with an interesting bazaar that dates to the 17th century. Other attractions include the Ranzore Palace facing the Chaugan (the royal polo

> 💬 INSIDER TIP
> **Traditional Twirls**
>
> Normally held in June – although dates vary according to the Tibetan calendar – the Tsheshu Festival is a summer celebration at Shashur Gompa where monks perform *chaam*, or masked dances.

↑ A monk looking out over Lahaul from Shashur Gompa

ground), the lively Jagannath Temple in the bazaar and the chir pine forests on the Villa Round.

Lying 42 km (26 miles) east of Nahan is the sacred Renuka Lake. The lake is named for the Hindu myth of Renuka, who was the wife of the sage Jamdagni and mother of Parasurama, an incarnation of Lord Vishnu. She was killed by her son at his father's order, and miraculously came back to life, only to disappear again, leaving behind an imprint in the shape of her body that now forms the shoreline of the lake. At the far end of Renuka Lake is a wildlife park that houses lions, Himalayan black bear and antelope. Nearby, below the smaller Parasurama Tal lake, is an open area where the Renuka Fair is held every year in November to celebrate the harvest.

EAT

The Johnson's Café
The garden café in this plush hotel is the spot for expertly grilled trout and other culinary delights.

⌂ Johnson Hotel, Old Manali Road
☎ (0190) 225 3023

₹₹₹

Moon Dance
The menu at this convivial garden restaurant overlooking the river includes Italian and Mexican options.

⌂ Old Manali
☎ 98162 01046

₹₹₹

Ragini Hotel Rooftop
Enjoy the views while sampling grilled trout in garlic lemon sauce or decent Mexican cuisine.

⌂ Naggar
☎ (0190) 224 8185

₹₹₹

⑬
Manali

⌂ Kullu district; 210 km (130 miles) N of Shimla 🚍
ℹ himachaltourism.gov.in

The picturesque hill station of Manali, along the west bank of the Beas river, is surrounded by incredible natural beauty, and visitors are often drawn to the town for its variety of scenic walks and treks. Although the downtown is now overrun by shops and hotels, the town's unique flavour can still be found.

Located 1.5 km (1 mile) north of the main bazaar is the sacred Hadimba Temple, shaded by a grove of stately deodars. This four-tiered wooden temple with its pagoda-style roof was built in 1553 around a small natural cave enshrining the footprints of the demoness turned goddess Hadimba, wife of Bhima, the mighty Pandava brother.

Particularly charming is the original village, about 3 km (2 miles) north of the main bazaar, with its temple dedicated to Manu, the Hindu sage after whom Manali is named. Also 3 km (2 miles) north of the bazaar, on the left bank of the Beas, is the village of Vashisht, where hot sulphur springs are piped into Turkish-style baths. Further up, the

↑ The big prayer wheel of Khardung Gompa, one of the must-see sights in Manali

Solang Valley, 14 km (9 miles) from downtown Manali, is the scene of most of the area's outdoor activities. Treks lead up to the pastures of Dhumti and the small snow-fed lake of Beas Kund. Paragliding, a popular activity, takes place on the nearby slopes, which also attract skiers in the winter.

Rohtang Pass, the perilous pass crossing into Lahaul at an altitude of 3,980 m (13,058 ft), is 52 km (32 miles) north of Manali. It is a full day's excursion from Manali, with a brief halt at the Rahalla Falls along the way. The pass is closed in winter.

The first capital of the Kullu kings, Jagatsukh is 6 km (4 miles) south of Manali, on the left bank of the Beas. The two *shikhara*-style stone temples here may date back to the 6th century. Naggar, further south, on the same

The formidable, snow-covered Himalayan mountains surrounding the town of Manali ↑

Baijnath Temple, built in the 9th century near Palampur and entitled to Shiva

side of the river, succeeded Jagatsukh as the capital until it was moved to Kullu (p239) in the 17th century. Now a hotel with fine views of the Beas Valley, the 15th-century Naggar Castle is an excellent example of traditional local architecture, with walls made of alternate layers of wooden beams and evenly hewn stone. Nearby is the **Nicholas Roerich Art Gallery,** displaying the work of the Russian painter Nicholas Roerich. Lying across the river from Naggar is scenic Katrain, surrounded by orchards. Trout fishing is popular here.

The remote and unique village of Malana, beyond Chanderkhani Pass, is 25 km (16 miles) southeast of Naggar. Malana's isolated people live by their own code of conduct and shun contact with outsiders. Their culture, language and system of government set them apart from the rest of the valley. Visitors should enter the village only if invited.

Nicholas Roerich Art Gallery
⊗ Naggar ⊙ 10am– 5pm daily

⑭

Kangra Valley

Kangra district; 222 km (138 miles) NW of Shimla
Gaggal, 10 km (6 miles) N
Joginder Nagar & Una
himachaltourism.gov.in

In the western part of Himachal Pradesh, spread between the Shivalik foothills and the Dhauladhar Range, the Kangra Valley is a beautiful land where expanses of tea gardens and terraced paddy fields are crisscrossed by snow-fed rivulets. Kangra is the most populated district of Himachal Pradesh, and is well connected with the plains as it is situated along the border with Punjab.

The valley derives its name from the ancient town of Kangra, even though Dharamsala (p224) is the present district headquarters. The history of the town goes back 3,500 years, when it was called Nagarkot and was the capital of the kingdom of Trigartha. In 1620, Kangra and its fort were captured by Emperor Jahangir, after which it became a Mughal province. Dominating the town today are the ruins of the Kangra Fort, perched on a steep cliff overlooking the Banganga and Majhi rivulets. Within the fort's compound are two Hindu temples dedicated to Ambika Devi (a local goddess) and Lakshmi Narayan, and a Jain temple with a stone image of Adinath. Behind the crowded bazaar is the Brajeshwari Devi Temple, whose fabled riches were plundered by Mahmud of Ghazni (p74) in 1009. The present structure was built in 1920, after the terrible earthquake of 1905 destroyed the city and original temple.

Some 40 km (25 miles) southwest of Kangra town are the 15 monolithic rock-cut temples of Masroor, dating to the 10th century and carved in a style similar to those at Ellora (p422). The picturesque Jwalamukhi Temple, 35 km (22 miles) southwest of Kangra, is one of north India's most important pilgrimage sites.

Further east of Kangra, the tea garden country unfolds around Palampur, 45 km (28 miles) away. East of this town are the 9th-century stone Baijnath Temple, dedicated to Shiva; Bir, with its Tibetan Buddhist monastery; and Billing, a take-off point for paragliding over the valley.

About 40 km (25 miles) southeast of Palampur, on the right bank of the Beas, is the fortress of Sujanpur-Tira. Built in the early 18th century, it was the favoured residence of Raja Sansar Chand, the renowned patron of Kangra miniature painting. At the far end of the Kangra Valley is Jogindernagar, 55 km (34 miles) south of Palampur, and the terminus of a narrow-gauge railway line that winds up the valley from Pathankot in the west.

The Maharana Pratap Sagar Lake, to the southwest of Kangra, is a stopover for birds migrating from Central Asia.

15

Chamba

🏠 Chamba district; 378 km (235 miles) NW of Shimla 🚌
🛈 Apply for permits at the District Collectorate; himachaltourism.gov.in

This town was chosen as the capital of the princely state of Chamba in the 10th century, when Raja Sahil Varman moved here from Bharmour. He named it after his favourite daughter, Champavati, also called Chameshni, who legend says sacrificed herself to provide water for the parched city. During the Sui festival, women and children sing her praises in the town's many temples, of which the distinctive and central Champavati Temple is the main site for pilgrims.

A bridge over the Ravi river leads up to the town, situated on the ledge of a mountain, overlooking the right bank of the river. In the town's centre is the Chaugan, a huge expanse of meadow that is the focal point of its cultural and social life. Clustered around it are a number of imposing buildings, including the old Akhand Chandi Palace, part of which is now a college. The Chaugan is also the main marketplace with shops that sell a variety of merchandise, ranging from traditional silver jewellery with enamelled clasps to embroidered Chamba *chappals* (sandals) that may look flimsy but are excellent for walking up hillsides.

💬 INSIDER TIP
Chamba's Celebrations

Chamba is famous for its festivals, which often happen on the Chaugan. The most popular is the annual Mijar Mela, which starts in July and runs for seven days, culminating in a parade through the town.

Chamba's towering stone temples are some of the finest in the region. The most important are the six North Indian *shikhara*-style temples that comprise the Lakshmi Narayan Temple complex, to the west of the Chaugan. Of these, three are dedicated to Vishnu and three to Shiva. The white marble image of Lakshmi Narayan, in the main temple, was brought from central India in the 10th century. The carved panels on the temple walls illustrate mythological scenes as well as animal and floral motifs.

Other temples include the Madho Rai Temple, near the palace, with a bronze image of Krishna, and further up, the Chamunda Temple.

A glimpse of Chamba's rich heritage can be seen at the **Bhuri Singh Museum**, set up in 1908 by the king of Chamba at the time. It has an excellent collection that includes Pahari paintings, murals, inscribed fountain slabs, carved-stone panels and other artifacts, such as Chamba *rumals*, metal masks, copper plates and silver jewellery.

Bhuri Singh Museum
◈ 🏠 S of Chaughan
📞 (01899) 222 590
🕐 10am–5pm Tue–Sun

16

Dalhousie

🏠 Chamba district; 336 km (209 miles) NW of Shimla 🚌
🛈 Geetanjali Hotel, Moti Tiba; himachaltourism.gov.in/destination/dalhousie

Sprawling over five hills that range in height from 1,525 m to 2,378 m (5,003 ft to 7,802 ft), historic Dalhousie has well-preserved buildings from the British Raj – from spacious, gable-roofed bungalows to churches – flanking its leafy lanes. Originally conceived as a health sanatorium for the expatriate population rather than as a fashionable summer retreat, the town was founded in 1853 and named after Lord Dalhousie, the governor-general of British India between 1848 and 1856.

The most popular walks are the twin rounds of Garam Sarak ("Warm Road") and Thandi Sarak ("Cold Road"), so called because one path is sunnier than the other. A shorter walk from the Circuit House to Gandhi Chowk – the central part of town, where a school, church and the post office are situated – offers spectacular views of the Pir Panjal Range. From Gandhi Chowk, another pleasant ramble, about 3 km (2 miles) long, leads south to the pretty picnic spot of Panjpula or "Five Bridges".

As well as historic houses, the town has an old British cemetery that can be reached via a track leading off to the right from the main bus stand. One of the two small churches here has stained-glass windows and sandstone arches.

A scenic road through dense forests of pine, deodar, oak, horse chestnut and rhododendron leads to the **Kalatope Wildlife Sanctuary**. With prior permission from the forest department at Chamba it is possible to take a diversion at Bakrota and drive to a rest house deep inside the sanctuary.

About 26 km (16 miles) east of Dalhousie is Khajjiar, situated at a height of 2,000 m (6,562 ft). This saucer-shaped expanse of green meadow, bordered by towering deodars, has a picture postcard beauty, comparable with the finest views in Kashmir or even in Switzerland. The centre has a small lake, and the glade is flanked by a temple dedicated to the local deity, Khajjinag.

Kalatope Wildlife Sanctuary

⊛ 🏠 8 km (5 miles) E of Dalhousie 🚹 For permission contact: Forest Department, Chamba; (01899) 222 639

Did You Know?

After taking a dip in Manimahesh Lake to wash away their sins, pilgrims walk around the lake three times.

⑰ Bharmour

🏠 Chamba district; 64 km (40 miles) SE of Chamba 🚌

The Bharmour region, homeland of the semi-nomadic, sheep-herding Gaddis and the first capital of the Chamba rulers, spreads right across a steep mountainside, high above Budhil, a tributary of the Ravi river. Bharmour's main attraction is the fascinating Chaurasi (literally, "Eighty-Four") Temple complex, built in the 10th century under Raja Sahil Varman to honour the 84 saints who visited Bharmour. The major shrines here are dedicated to Narasimha, Ganesha, and the local deities Manimahesh and Larkana Devi. The intricate wooden carvings on the temple lintels and the images of the main deities are outstanding, and it is said that the sculptor's hands were cut off to prevent him from replicating such remarkable work.

At a height of 3,950 m (12,959 ft), Manimahesh Lake, 35 km (22 miles) from Bharmour, is the area's most sacred lake, as its holy waters are believed to cleanse all sins. In August/September, thousands of pilgrims converge here to participate in the annual Manimahesh Yatra. The main motor road continues up to Hadsar, 16 km (10 miles) beyond Bharmour, and from there the *yatra* (procession) ascends in two stages via Dhanchho to the lake, nestling at the base of the Manimahesh Kailasa.

For the adventurous, Bharmour also offers a five-day trek over the Kugti Pass (5,040 m/16,535 ft) to Lahaul (*p232*). Holi, 26 km (16 miles) away in the main Ravi Valley, is the base for a number of trails over the Dhauladhar Range to the Kangra Valley. Down the course of the Ravi, on the road to Chamba, the Chatrari Temple with its exquisite bronze image of Shakti Devi, is also worth a stop.

↑ The forested hills surrounding the lake at Khajjiar, near Dalhousie

STAY

The Himalayan Village

Built in traditional Kathakunia style and located amid a tranquil deodar forest, this enchanting resort has huge detached cottages which are lavishly furnished.

🏠 Between Jari and Kasol
🌐 thehimalayan village.in

₹ ₹ ₹

Naggar Castle

Now a state-run hotel, this atmospheric 16th-century castle – which looks more like a timber mansion – has a splendid flagstone courtyard. It offers visitors comfortable rooms and vistas of the Kullu Valley.

🏠 Naggar
🌐 hptdc.in

₹ ₹ ₹

18

Parvati Valley

🏠 Kullu district; 180 km (112 miles) NE of Shimla
🚌 ℹ HP Tourism, near Maidan, Kullu; (01902) 222 349

The scenic Parvati Valley, with its green, terraced rice fields and apple orchards, draws an increasing number of visitors. However, because of illegal marijuana cultivation in the surrounding countryside, the Parvati Valley has gained notoriety as a centre for the narcotics trade, and some foreign visitors have gone missing from the area. It is advisable to take guides and porters, available from Naggar (p234) and Manikaran, for treks in this region.

The main settlement in the Parvati Valley is Manikaran. This town is renowned for its hot springs, which have an interesting origin myth. In the tale, a serpent stole the earrings of Parvati, the consort of Lord Shiva, and disappeared with them into a deep burrow. Shiva became terribly angry, and the snake, witnessing this, was too terrified to come out of its hole. Instead, it managed to snort the earrings out through the earth, creating vents from which the hot

> The main settlement in the Parvati Valley is Manikaran, renowned for its hot springs. It is also the starting point for a number of treks.

springs bubble out. A bath here is said to be good for the body and the soul, and local people sometimes boil rice in the geothermal steam. Aside from the hot springs, the town is known for nearby treks.

The Rama Temple and the Shiva Temple, next to a Sikh gurdwara, are always thronged with holy men.

19

Great Himalayan National Park

🏠 Kullu district; 205 km (127 miles) N of Shimla (via Jalori Pass); entry points at Sainj and Gushani
🚌 Shamshi, 15 km (9 miles) S of Kullu, then jeep
🌐 greathimalayan nationalpark.org

The great Himalayan National Park, covering an area of 754 sq km (291 sq miles),

←

The riverfront Sikh gurdwara at Manikaran, the main settlement in the Parvati Valley

ranges in altitude from 1,300 m (4,265 ft) to 6,100 m (20,013 ft), and abuts the cold desert region of Pin Valley National Park *(p218)*. The variety of flora and fauna found here represents the entire Western Himalayas, from subtropical species to alpine grasslands covered with edelweiss and oak forests, and musk deer to the elusive snow leopard. Among the 300-odd species of birds, there are at least six different kinds of pheasant. There are a number of trekking trails and forest huts in the buffer zone.

20

Kullu Valley

🏠 Kullu district; 240 km (149 miles) N of Shimla 🚌 Bhuntar, 10 km (6 miles) S of Kullu town ☷ ℹ HP Tourism, near Maidan; apply for permits at the District Collectorate; himachaltourism.gov.in/ destination/kullu-2

Cut through by the Beas river, the Kullu Valley in central Himachal Pradesh, known locally as "Valley of the Gods", is a spectacular alpine region perhaps most famous for its annual Gathering of the Gods (Dussehra) festival, when the icons of 360 gods worshipped at different temples in the region are brought here.

Unlike the areas around the British-built hill stations in the Himalayas, Kullu remained relatively unknown to the outside world until it was "discovered" in the 1960s by hippies, who were enchanted as much by its hillsides covered with marijuana plants *(Cannabis sativa)*, as by its gentle beauty, glorious mountain vistas and amiable people. The men of

the Kullu Valley usually wear the distinctive Kullu *topi*, a snug woollen cap with a colourful upturned flap. The women weave thick shawls with striking geometric designs on their borders, the sale of which is now a flourishing local industry. The attractive town of Kullu, with its charming houses rising above green meadows, is the district headquarters and the largest settlement in the valley. On the right bank of the Beas, the town's chief attraction is the 17th-century Raghunath Temple, which is dedicated to Rama and Sita, whose richly adorned images lead the processions at the Dussehra festival.

At the northern end of the town, the Akhara Bazaar is famous for its handicrafts shops, selling shawls and traditional silver jewellery. At the southern end of town is the large green open space called Dhalpur Maidan, where the colourful Dussehra festivities take place.

A number of temples, all with superb stone carvings, lie in the vicinity of Kullu town – the Vaishno Devi Cave Shrine is 4 km (2 miles) to the northeast; the Jagannathi Devi Temple at Bekhli, 5 km (3 miles) to the north; and the Vishnu Temple at Dayar, 12 km (7 miles) to the west. The pyramidal Basheshwar Mahadev Temple at Bajaura, 15 km (9 miles) to the south, has superb images of Vishnu, Ganesha and Durga. The Bijli

Mahadev Temple, dedicated to the "Lord of Lightning", lies 14 km (9 miles) to the southeast, on a high spur on the left bank of the river. This temple has an 18-m- (59-ft-) high staff, which attracts lightning during thunderstorms, especially in spring. This is regarded as a divine blessing, even though it shatters the Shiva linga in the sanctum of the temple. The stone fragments are then painstakingly put together again with a mortar of clarified butter and grain, by the head priest.

↑ A misty sunrise over the lushly forested hillsides of the Kullu Valley

A DRIVING TOUR
SANGLA VALLEY

Length 180 km (110 miles) **Stopping-off points** Sarahan, Sungra and Sangla **Difficulty** Windy, steep roads, at times without safety railings; tarmac occasionally in poor condition

The largest village in the Kinnaur region of Himachal Pradesh, Sangla often lends its name to the whole Baspa Valley. A drive through this area over two to three days can encapsulate a dramatic transition in landscape, from the spectacular river gorge at the entrance to Kinnaur to alpine valley pastures. It takes in awesome mountain scenery and mixed forests of oak and rhododendron, before reaching charming slate-roofed villages that nestle amid orchards and fields.

*From the road at Tranda there are striking views of the **Sutlej Valley**, where sheer rock walls fall 500 m (1,640 ft) to the river.*

*Strung out along a spur below the road, **Kafour** is home to the Hirma Temple, dedicated to a local mother goddess.*

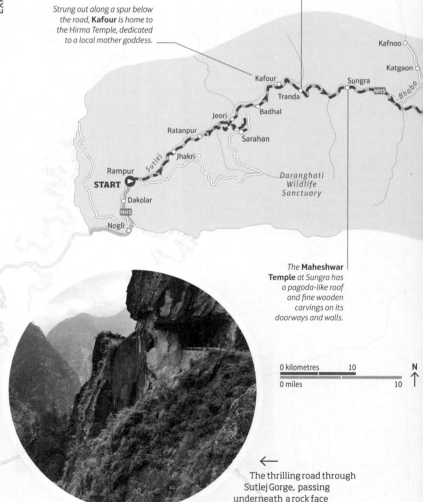

*The **Maheshwar Temple** at Sungra has a pagoda-like roof and fine wooden carvings on its doorways and walls.*

0 kilometres 10
0 miles 10
N

← The thrilling road through Sutlej Gorge, passing underneath a rock face

← Thick forests and mountains surrounding Chitkul town

Locator Map
For more detail see p216

The tower of the **Kamroo Narayan Temple** *commands a picturesque view of the valley's fields and orchards, forests and pasturelands.*

The largest among the villages that dot the valley, **Sangla** *has some beautiful walks where you can stretch your legs after a day's drive.*

The tour ends at the village of **Chitkul**, *just before the pastures of the Upper Baspa Valley.*

Reckong Peo

Kalpa

Tapri　Chooling

Sutlej

Sutlej

NH5

Sapni

Baspa

Kamroo

Sangla　　Batseri

Rakchham

Chitkul
FINISH

Sapni *village has a tower temple that contains fine examples of local wooden sculptures.*

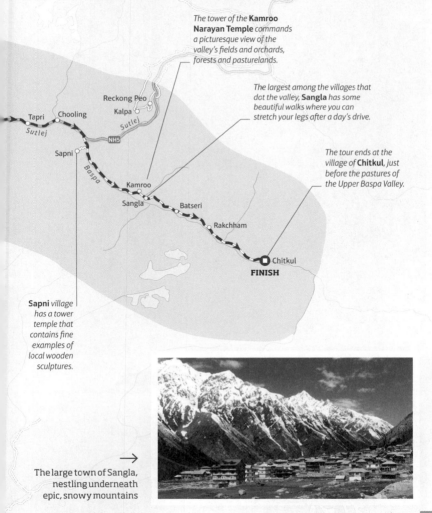

→ The large town of Sangla, nestling underneath epic, snowy mountains

LADAKH, JAMMU AND KASHMIR

Lying across six major mountain ranges, and covering an area of some 222,000 sq km (85,715 sq miles), Jammu and Kashmir is India's northernmost state, bordering Pakistan and China's Tibetan Plateau. It has three distinct regions – Ladakh, Jammu and Kashmir. Sparsely populated Ladakh, which accounts for two-thirds of the state's area, is a high altitude desert. Buddhism was introduced to this area in the 3rd century BC by Mauryan emperor Ashoka and Ladakh has ancient monasteries that still attract people to this harsh land. Jammu, encompassing plains and mountains, features the shrine of Vaishno Devi, an important pilgrimage site for Hindus. The predominantly Muslim Kashmir is a mosaic of forests, ricefields and waterways. This land was ruled by a succession of Hindu dynasties until it was conquered by Muslim invaders in the 14th century, before being annexed by Maharaja Ranjit Singh's Sikh empire in 1808. The 1846 Treaty of Amritsar then established the princely state of Jammu and Kashmir under the suzerainty of the British. After the countries of India and Pakistan were created in 1947, the maharaja of Kashmir voted to join India over Pakistan. Pakistan disputed this and sent in troops – as did India. A ceasefire was called in 1949, and the state partitioned between the two countries. This temporary measure still exists, and Kashmir remains one of India's most volatile regions, with clashes still an occasional occurrence.

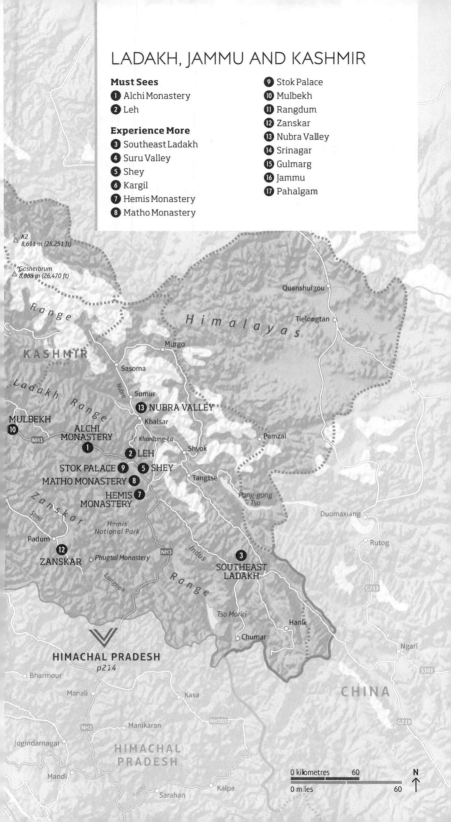

LADAKH, JAMMU AND KASHMIR

Must Sees
1. Alchi Monastery
2. Leh

Experience More
3. Southeast Ladakh
4. Suru Valley
5. Shey
6. Kargil
7. Hemis Monastery
8. Matho Monastery
9. Stok Palace
10. Mulbekh
11. Rangdum
12. Zanskar
13. Nubra Valley
14. Srinagar
15. Gulmarg
16. Jammu
17. Pahalgam

K2
8,611 m (28,251 ft)

Gasherbrum
8,068 m (26,470 ft)

Quanshuizou

Tielongtan

Himalayas

KASHMIR

Murgo

Sasoma

Ladakh Range

Nubra

Sumur

NUBRA VALLEY 13

Khalsar

MULBEKH
10 NH1

ALCHI MONASTERY 1

Khardung-La

Shyok

Pamzal

2 **LEH**

STOK PALACE 9 5 **SHEY**

MATHO MONASTERY 8

Tangtse

Pang-gong Tso

HEMIS MONASTERY 7

Duomaxiang

Zanskar

Stod

Hemis National Park

Rutog

Padum

12 NH3

ZANSKAR Phugtal Monastery

Indus

Lungnak

Range

3

SOUTHEAST LADAKH

Tso Moriri

Hanle

Ngari

S301

HIMACHAL PRADESH
p214

Bharmour

Chumar

CHINA

Manali

Kasa

G219

Jogindarnagar

NH3 Manikaran

NH505

HIMACHAL PRADESH

Mandi

Sutlej

Kalpa

Sarahan

0 kilometres   60

0 miles   60

N

❶ ⟨ℬ⟩

ALCHI MONASTERY

📍 Leh district; 70 km (43 miles) W of Leh on the Leh-Kargil Highway ⏱ Daily;
book ahead for a guide from Leh 🌐 jktourism.org/index.php/alchi-monastery

Founded in the early 12th century, Alchi is the jewel among Ladakh's monasteries. Unknown to the outside world until 1974, it is now one of the area's major attractions, renowned as a great centre of Buddhist art. The entire Mahayana Buddhist pantheon of deities is represented within its five temples.

Abandoned in the 16th century, Alchi Monastery has a remarkably well-preserved collection of 12th- and 13th-century paintings, which are undimmed by the soot from butter lamps and incense sticks. Of the five temples here, the finest murals are in the two oldest, the Dukhang assembly hall and the Sumtsek. These have been executed with great skill by master painters who were probably from Kashmir.

The Dukhang, is the oldest temple and holds some of Alchi's greatest treasures, including the beautiful central image of Vairocana, the main Buddha of Meditation, and six elaborate mandalas (spiritual symbols) painted on the walls. The three-storeyed Sumtsek has spectacular images and paintings, notably the gigantic images of Avalokitesvara, Manjushri and Maitreya that stand in alcoves in its walls. Only their legs and torsos are visible from the ground floor, while their heads protrude into the upper storey – take a torch to examine their incredible detail.

← Pilgrims wandering under the prayer flags amid the low-lying temple buildings

The low-lying monastery of Alchi has five temples, each hiding spectacular examples of early Buddhist art ↑

GREEN TARA

There are several exquisite images of this goddess, variously identified as Green Tara, the Saviour, and Prajnaparamita (the Perfection of Wisdom) in the complex's second-oldest temple, Sumtsek. Five of them are to the left of the gigantic Avalokitesvara statue, opposite his leg. The Green Tara seems to have held a special place in Alchi, since the goddess is not given such importance in other monasteries. One of the most popular Buddhist goddesses, Tara is compassionate, and aims to ease human suffering.

The Lhakhang Soma painting symbolizes the union of opposites.

← The Alchi Monastery, renowned for its Buddhist art

Avalokitesvara is a huge statue whose legs are covered with paintings.

Chortens containing holy relics are dotted around the complex.

A mural in the Dukhang shows details of royal dress and hairstyles.

Dukhang is a serene image of the Vairocana Buddha.

The façade of Sumtsek temple is in the style of Kashmiri temple architecture.

Lotsawa Lhakhang

A rare portrait of Rinchen Zangpo, an influential Tibetan saint.

Manjushri Lhakhang, one of the five temples, contains a large image of Manjushri.

②

LEH

📍 Leh district; 1,077 km (669 miles) N of Delhi ✈ 11 km (7 miles) S of town centre 🚌 🌐 jktourism.org/destinations/ladakh

From the 17th century until 1949, Ladakh's main town, Leh, was the hub of the caravan trade between Punjab and Central Asia, and between Kashmir and Tibet. The old town offers a maze of narrow alleys dotted with Buddhist *chortens* and *mani* walls, and clusters of flat-roofed houses constructed of sun-baked bricks.

①

Leh Palace

📞 (01982) 252 297 🕐 7am–4pm daily

Leh is dominated by the nine-storeyed Leh Palace, built in the 1630s by Sengge Namgyal, Ladakh's most famous king. The palace's massive inward-leaning walls are in the same architectural tradition as Lhasa's famous Potala Palace, but the solidity of its exterior belies the dilapidation inside, although some repair work is now being done. Visitors can go up to the open terrace on the level above the main entrance.

②

Main Bazaar

Much of Leh's charm lies in exploring its interesting streets, particularly its large Main Bazaar in the heart of town. Its broad kerbs are lined with eateries and curio shops selling precious stones and ritual religious objects such as prayer wheels. The Jokhang, a rare modern ecumenical Buddhist establishment, was built in 1957 in the bazaar and is considered the spiritual centre of town; the local mosque is nearby. The Dalai Lama has visited the Jokhang, as well as the rural monastery of the same name.

③

Namgyal Tsemo

📞 (0194) 247 2449 🕐 7–9am and 5–8pm daily

On the peak above the town are the small fort and monastery complex of Namgyal Tsemo (mid-16th century), believed to be the earliest royal residence in Leh. Next to its now-ruined fort are a *gonkhang* (Temple of the Guardian Deities) and a

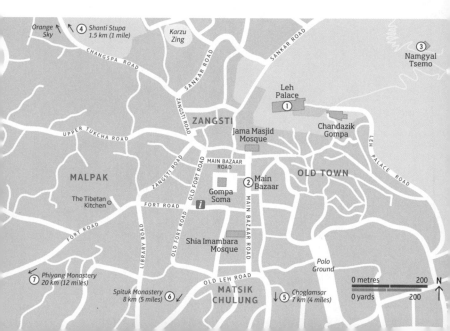

← View over the distinctive flat-roofed houses in the old town of Leh

temple to Maitreya (the Future Buddha), both of which have vibrant murals. Those inside the *gonkhang* include a court scene with a portrait believed to be that of King Tashi Namgyal (mid-16th century), the founder of the complex.

④ Shanti Stupa

📍 4 km (2 miles) N of Leh

The gleaming white Shanti Stupa ("Peace Pagoda"), founded in the 1980s under the sponsorship of Japanese Buddhists, is situated on a hilltop west of the city.

Down the hill in the village of Skara, the massive mud walls of the 19th-century Zorawar Fort catch the eye. A lovely walk is up past the Moravian Church to the serene village of Changspa, with its ancient *chorten*. From here a road turns towards the beautifully maintained 19th-century **Sankar Monastery**, with its impressive images of Avalokitesvara and of Vajra Bhairav, Guardian of the Gelugpa order.

Sankar Monastery
🕉 🕐 7–10am and 5–7pm daily

⑤ Choglamsar

📍 10 km (6 miles) S of Leh

Choglamsar, outside of Leh, is Ladakh's main Tibetan refugee settlement. It includes the Dalai Lama's prayer ground, an SOS Children's Village, the Central Institute of Buddhist Studies and workshops that promote Tibetan handicrafts.

⑥ 🕉 Spituk Monastery

📍 7 km (4 miles) NW of Leh
📞 (01982) 260 036 🕐 7am–7pm daily

On a hilltop perilously close to the airport is this monastery, which is the oldest establishment of the Gelugpa sect in Ladakh. It houses the library of Tsongkapa, the sect's founder, and a shrine devoted to the goddess Tara (*p247*).

⑦ 🕉 Phiyang Monastery

📍 19 km (12 miles) NW of Leh 🕐 6am–6pm daily

Situated in the charming village of Fiang, this is one of

only two monasteries of the Drigungpa sect. It was founded by Ladakh's 16th-century ruler, Tashi Namgyal, supposedly as an act of atonement for the violence by which he came to the throne. Its treasures include a large collection of Kashmiri bronzes of Buddhist deities, dating back to the 13th century, or possibly earlier.

EAT

The Tibetan Kitchen
People flock to this place for the best Tibetan food in town, especially the delicious *momos* and mutton *thukpa*.

📍 Off Fort Rd
📞 9697811510

💰💰💰

Orange Sky
Outdoor restaurant with fire pits, cushioned areas and (often) live rock music.

📍 Changspa Lane
📞 8492057100

💰💰💰

EXPERIENCE MORE

3

Southeast Ladakh

🏛 Pang-gong Tso: Leh district, 150 km (93 miles) SE of Leh; Tso Moriri: Leh district, 220 km (137 miles) SE of Leh 🛈 Apply for Inner Line Permits (ILP) online at lahdclehpermit.in or at the District Collectorate; only groups of two or four tourists with a certified travel agent can apply; www.jktourism.org

Southeast Ladakh, on the sensitive international border with Tibet, is a region with a series of beautiful lakes. The two main ones, Pang-gong Tso and Tso Moriri, are accessible by road, although visitors must arrange their own transport.

The biggest of the lakes is the narrow Pang-gong Tso. It is 130 km (81 miles) in length and lies at an altitude of 4,420 m (14,500 ft), extending far into western Tibet. Visitors may go as far as Spangmik, 7 km (4 miles) along the lake's southern shore, from where there are spectacular views to the north of the Chang-

> The lake and its freshwater inlets are breeding areas for species of migratory birds such as the black-necked crane, bar-headed geese and the great crested grebe.

chenmo Range. Above Spangmik rise the glaciers and snowcapped peaks of the Pang-gong Range.

Tso Moriri, 365 km (227 miles) to the south of Pang-gong Tso is a 140-sq-km (54-sq-mile) expanse of remarkably intense blue water. At an altitude of 4,600 m (15,092 ft), it is set among rolling hills behind which lie epic snow-covered mountains. The isolated region's only permanent settlement, Karzok, is on the lake's western shore and comprises a handful of houses and a monastery whose barley fields are among the highest cultivated areas in the world. The lake and its freshwater

Did You Know?

For centuries, Ladakh was the centre of caravan trade between Punjab and central Asia.

inlets are breeding areas for species of migratory birds such as the black-necked crane, bar-headed geese and the great crested grebe. Wild asses, marmots and foxes can also be spotted in the region.

Southeast Ladakh is sparsely inhabited. Among the people who live there are nomadic herders known as Changpa, who brave extreme cold (-40° C/-40° F in winter, and freezing nights even in summer) throughout the year, living in their black yak-hair tents. They raise yak and sheep, but their main source of income is the coat of the pashmina goat. The severe cold of winter stimulates the goats to grow an undercoat of soft warm fibre, which they shed at the beginning of summer. This fibre, known as *pashm*, is the raw material for Kashmir's renowned shawl industry and is, in fact, the unprocessed form of the region's internationally famous cashmere wool. The lucrative trade in *pashm* from Ladakh's high-altitude pastures, as well

Tranquil Pang-gong Tso, an alpine lake in southeast Ladakh ↓

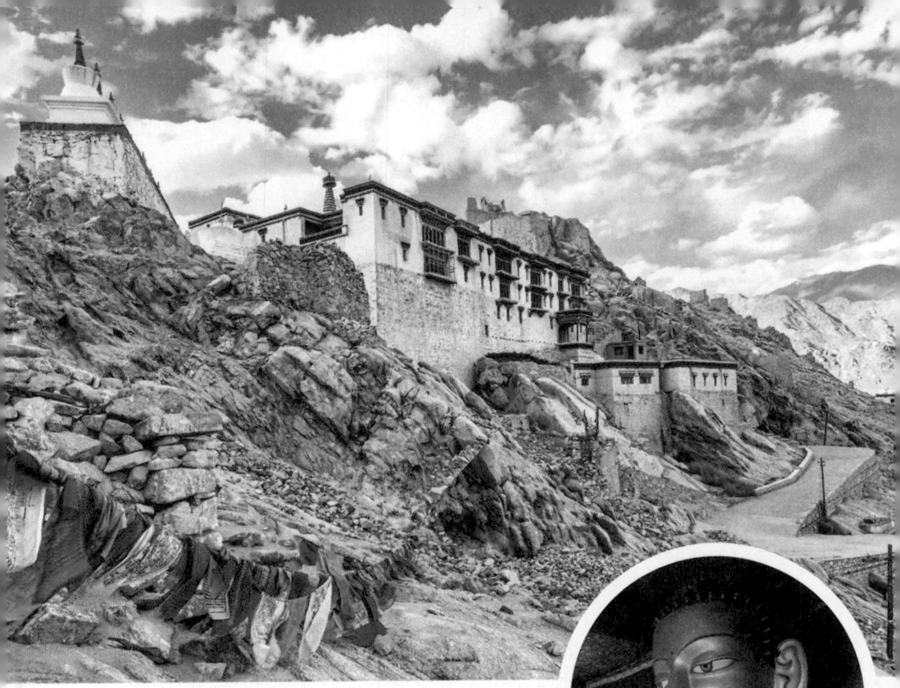

Shey Palace, clinging to a rocky hill, and *(inset)* the Buddha statue inside ↑

as from western Tibet, was the main motivation behind Ladakh's annexation by the Maharaja of Kashmir in 1834.

④ Suru Valley

📍 Kargil district; 19 km (12 miles) S of Kargil 🚌 To Sankhu 🌐 www.jktourism. org/index.php/suru-valley

One of Ladakh's loveliest regions, the Suru Valley runs for 100 km (62 miles) south-east from its head at Kargil. It boasts rolling alpine pastures, mud-walled villages and views of snowcapped peaks. Water from melting snows gives the Suru Valley rich harvests of barley and plantations of willow and poplar, especially around Sankhu village. Close to Sankhu are the ruins of ancient forts, together with rock engravings of Maitreya and Avalokitesvara from the valley's pre-Islamic past. The upper valley is dominated by the peaks, ridges and glaciers of the Nun-kun massif, which is 7,135 m (23,409 ft) high. Expeditions to the mountain start from the picturesque village of Panikhar, whose pastures are covered with alpine flowers in June and July.

⑤ Shey

📍 Ladakh district; 15 km (9 miles) SE of Leh 🚌 🛈 Leh Tourist Office; (01982) 252 094/297

The ancient capital of Ladakh, Shey was abandoned by the state's rulers in the 19th century. They left behind the Shey Palace, now partially ruined. It contains a temple with a gigantic image of Buddha, surrounded by murals painted in rich colours. Another beautiful Buddha image is housed in a nearby temple. Just below the palace are huge 11th-century rock carvings of the Five Buddhas of Meditation.

Shey Palace
📍 Daily

⑥ Kargil

📍 Kargil district; 230 km (143 miles) NW of Leh and NE of Srinagar 🚌 🛈 Apply for Inner Line Permits (ILP) online at lahdcleh permit.in or at the District Collectorate; www.jktour ism.org/destinations/ ladakh/kargil

The second-largest urban centre in Ladakh, Kargil is considered a good base for travellers exploring the region. The town is also the start for expeditions to the Suru Valley, Zanskar *(p254)* and Nun-kun.

Kargil's apricots are famous, and its orchards are a lovely sight in bloom in May and in July, when the fruit is ripe. While Kargil suffered shelling during the conflict between India and Pakistan in 1999, the last conventional war between the two, it is now stable.

↑ Monks rehearsing a dance for the annual festival at Hemis Monastery

7

Hemis Monastery

🏛 Leh district; 43 km (27 miles) SE of Leh 🚌
🕐 7am–6pm daily

Tucked away up a winding glen in the mountains south of the Indus, Hemis is the largest and the richest of the central Ladakh monasteries.

THE MONASTIC DANCE-DRAMAS OF LADAKH

The dance-dramas performed at Ladakh's annual monastery festivals constitute a link between popular and esoteric Buddhism. Attended by high lamas and novice monks in their ceremonial robes and hats, as well as by local families dressed in their traditional regalia, these events are a vibrant expression of age-old cultural and religious values. They also provide people from far-flung Ladakhi villages with an eagerly awaited opportunity to meet and exchange news and views.

It was founded in the 1630s by King Sengge Namgyal, and was the most favoured monastery throughout the Namgyal dynasty. There are several temples here, but the most rewarding is the *tshog-khang*, a secondary assembly hall that contains a fine image of the Buddha in front of a huge silver chorten set with flawless turquoise gems.

Hemis is also renowned for its spectacular annual festival, dedicated to Guru Padmasambhava, the 8th-century apostle who took Buddhism to Tibet. A unique feature of this festival, which is held in the summer and attracts huge crowds, is the 12-yearly unveiling of the monastery's greatest treasure – a three-storey thangka of Padmasambhava, embroidered and studded with pearls and semiprecious stones. The last unveiling of the thangka took place in 2016.

8

Matho Monastery

🏛 Leh district; 30 km (19 miles) SE of Leh 🚌
🕐 6am–6pm daily

The only monastery in Ladakh of the Sakyapa sect, Matho, built in the early 16th century, is also one of the few that continues to attract large numbers of new entrants. Its main importance, however, lies in its Oracles – two monks who, after months of purification by fasting and meditation, are possessed by a deity. This event takes place during Matho's annual festival, held between February and March. The drama of the occasion is tremendous as the Oracles traverse the topmost parapet of the monastery blindfolded, despite the 30-m (98-ft) drop onto the rocks below. The Oracles answer questions put to them about public and private affairs, and great faith is reposed in their predictions. Matho also has a small museum with a rare collection of 16th-century thangkas and costumes.

9

Stok Palace

🏛 Ladakh district; 14 km (9 miles) SW of Leh
🚌 🌐 stokpalaceheritage.com

Ladakh became independent in 1843, and its former rulers, the Namgyals, moved to Stok

TOP 5 OTHER MONASTERIES IN LADAKH

Thiksey
📍 16 km (10 miles) SE of Leh
A 15th-century gem with a Maitreya temple.

Chemrey
📍 24 km (15 miles) SE of Leh
Buddhist scriptures with gold lettering are the prize treasure here.

Stakna
📍 24 km (15 miles) SE of Leh
A 17th-century building with vivid murals.

Likir
📍 56 km (35 miles) NW of Leh
Likir has fine thangkas and images.

Lamayuru
📍 115 km (70 miles) NW of Leh
From the 11th-century, it has fine thangkas.

Palace, where the family still resides. Part of the palace has been converted into a museum of the dynasty and its history. Its collections include a set of 35 thangkas representing the life of the Buddha, said to have been commissioned by the 16th-century King Tashi Namgyal. Images and ritual religious objects, such as the bell and *dorje* (thunderbolt), are of unsurpassed workmanship. Secular objects include fine jade cups, the queens' jewellery, including a spectacular headdress, the kings' turban-shaped crown, and ceremonial robes. There is also a sword with its blade twisted into a knot, said to have been contorted by the enormous strength of Tashi Namgyal. Six rooms in the palace have now been converted into a luxury hotel, and visitors can chat with the owners over dinner.

🔟 Mulbekh

📍 Kargil district; 190 km (118 miles) NW of Leh 🚌 ℹ️ Kargil Tourist Office; (01985) 232 721

The pretty village of Mulbekh is spread over the broad green valley of the Wakha river. It marks the point at which the proselytizing tide of Islam, spreading towards central Ladakh, lost its impetus. As a consequence, Mulbekh is rare here in that it has a mixed population of Buddhists and Muslims, and supports a mosque as well as a monastery, which is perched on a crag above the village. Its main attraction, however, is a giant engraving of Maitreya,

↑ The giant statue of Maitreya Buddha carved into the rock at Mulbekh

the Future Buddha who will bring complete enlightenment, on a huge free-standing rock by the roadside. This magnificent sight is believed to date back to the 8th century.

🔟 Rangdum

📍 Kargil district; 110 km (68 miles) SE of Kargil 🚌 ℹ️ Kargil Tourist Office; (01985) 232 721

The village of Rangdum is a popular overnight stop between Kargil (*p251*) and Zanskar. Situated on a wide, flat plateau at 3,800 m (12,467 ft), crisscrossed by water courses and framed by snow peaks and dramatic hills of curiously striated rock, Rangdum has a wild, desolate beauty. Though it is geographically part of the Suru Valley, which has a mainly Muslim population, Rangdum is largely Buddhist and has an imposing monastery, the fortress-like 18th-century Gelugpa. Built on a hillock, this complex has a small temple which has a fantastic wall painting of a battle scene, which features fierce warriors wearing traditional Mongolian-looking armour and battle dress.

↑ Dramatic lighting over the mountains surrounding the monumental palace at Stok

12

Zanskar

◻ Kargil district; 230 km (143 miles) SE from Kargil
🚌 To Padum 🖪 www.jktourism.org/destinations/ladakh/zanskar

There is a certain mystique about Zanskar. This is no

doubt due to its remoteness and altitude, between 3,350 m (10,991 ft) and 4,400 m (14,436 ft), and the fact that the region is hard to access – the only road into the valley is usually open from around early June to mid-October. But Zanskar's reputation as a Shangri-la also derives from the grandeur of its landscapes, the simplicity of life in its villages, and the serene ambience in its *gompas*, often built around ancient cliff-top meditation caves.

Zanskar contains the valleys of two rivers, the Stod and the Lungnak, which join to become the Zanskar river. This continues north through a gorge in the Zanskar Range, eventually joining the Indus.

The western arm of Zanskar, the Stod Valley, and its central plain, are fertile and well watered – villages form green pockets, and the virtual absence of trees contributes to an extraordinary sense of space. The inhabitants of this region are mostly agricultural farmers, growing barley, wheat and peas in the lower villages, and raising livestock – yaks, sheep and dzos (a hybrid between cows and yaks) – in the higher villages. In winter, many farmers trek for six gruelling days across the frozen Zanskar river to sell

> **In winter, many farmers trek for six gruelling days across the frozen Zanskar river to sell their highly prized yak butter in Leh.**

their highly prized yak butter in Leh. In contrast to the fertile western arm and central plain, the eastern arm of Zanskar – the Lungnak Valley – is a forbidding and stony gorge, with few villages to be found in the vicinity.

The main gateway to Zanskar is the Pensi-la (4,400 m/14,436 ft), about 130 km (81 miles) southeast of Kargil. There are spectacular views from the top of this pass, before the road then continues down to Padum, 230 km (143 miles) southeast of Kargil, at an altitude of 3,500 m (11,483 ft). Padum is Zanskar's main village and administrative headquarters. This is the only place in the region with basic facilities, including accommodation, transport and a few shops. It is also the starting point for a number of treks in the region. Padum itself has few sites of interest, except for a rock engraving of the Five Dhyani Buddhas in

---

EAT

Zan-Khar
In the town's main bazaar, this simple restaurant serves tasty Tibetan dishes.

◻ Main Bazaar, Padum
📞 91 194 246 1111

💲💲💲

Latitude
This restaurant, perched high above Srinagar, has great views and serves international dishes.

◻ Vivanta Dal View, Srinagar
📞 94190 25612

💲💲💲

←

Trekking on the partially frozen river Zanskar as it snakes through the namesake gorge

the centre of the village, and a mosque. Within easy reach on foot is the village of Pipiting, which has a temple and chorten (stupa) on top of a mound of glacial debris, and a pavilion that was specially constructed for the Dalai Lama's prayer assemblies.

Sani, 8 km (5 miles) northwest of Padum, is one of the oldest religious sites in the Western Himalayas. Within the monastery walls stands the Kanika Chorten, its name possibly linking it to the Kushana ruler Kanishka, whose empire stretched from Afghanistan to Varanasi in the 1st and 2nd centuries AD. The monastery itself is said to have been founded by Padmasambhava in the 8th century, and its main temple has some fine murals. Even more interesting is another small temple in the complex, which has unique, beautifully painted stucco bas-relief decorations.

The buildings of the Gelupga monastery of Karsha, 10 km (6 miles) northeast of Padum, seem to spill down the mountainside west of the main valley. This site includes ancient rock engravings, and the murals in its Avalokitesvara temple, just outside the main complex, seem to put it in the same period as Alchi (p246). Tradition, however, attributes the monastery's foundation to Padmasambhava. Karsha has a large community of resident monks and holds its colourful annual festival between July and August.

Stongde, on the opposite side of the valley, 12 km

(7 miles) from Padum, is perched on a ridge, high above the mosaic of the village's fields. Believed to have been founded in the 11th century, it houses no fewer than seven temples, some of them containing exquisite murals.

The villages of Sani, Karsha and Stongde are connected by motor transport, though the monasteries in the Lungnak Valley are less accessible. The narrow footpath leading up the valley winds along unstable scree slopes high above the river, and the walk is strenuous. It takes a sharp climb on foot or on horseback to reach Bardhan and Phugtal monasteries.

Bardhan, 9 km (6 miles) southeast of Padum, sits atop a crag jutting out from the mountain and rising some 100 m (328 ft) sheer out of the river. It has fine wall paintings dating back to the time of the monastery's foundation in the early 17th century. Of all Ladakh's many monasteries, however, none can rival Phugtal, 60 km (37 miles) southeast of Padum, for the grandeur and drama of its location. Its main temples are constructed inside a huge cave on the mountainside above the Tsarap river, at a point where the drop to the water is almost sheer. Yet below the temples the monks' dwellings have somehow been built on or into the cliff face, and the whole complex is linked by a system of ladders and walkways. The style of Phugtal's paintings links

INSIDER TIP
Whitewater Wonderland

One of the best agencies to operate whitewater rafting trips from Leh to the wild river Zanskar is Aquaterra Adventures, which also boasts eco-conscious credentials (www.aquaterra.in).

it with Tabo Monastery in Spiti (p220) and the traditions established by the Tibetan scholar Rinchen Zangpo (p220) in the 11th century.

13

Nubra Valley

Leh district; 150 km (93 miles) N of Leh
Apply for Inner Line Permits (ILP) online at lahdclehpermit.in or at the District Collectorate; www. jktourism.org/destina tions/ladakh/nubra

Entering the remote Nubra Valley via the Khardung La pass is like descending into another world, as the villages dotted along the gradually diverging Nubra and Shyok rivers have a definite Central Asian feel. On the Shyok are Diskit, with some impressive temples, and Hundur, where Bactrian camels amble across the sand dunes. To the east, along the Nubra, sleepy Sumur has the region's most important monastery. There are hot springs at Panamik.

Large statue of the Buddha at the monastery in Diskit, a village in the Nubra Valley

⑭

Srinagar

🏛 Srinagar district; 700 km (435 miles) NW of Delhi ✈ 8 km (5 miles) S of city centre 🚌 ℹ www.jk tourism.org/destinations/ kashmir/srinagar

The summer capital of Jammu and Kashmir, Srinagar is a city of lakes and waterways, gardens and wooden architecture. The old quarters of the city sprawl over both sides of the Jhelum river, crossed by seven bridges. At the city's edge are the idyllic Dal and Nagin lakes, which are linked by a network of backwaters.

Srinagar's mosques and shrines are among the city's most attractive features. These are typically built of wood, intricately carved in geometric patterns and, instead of a dome, they are surmounted by a pagoda-like steeple. The most striking examples are the Mosque of Shah Hamadan in the old city, and the Shah Makhdum Sahib Shrine on the slopes of Hari Parbat hill. Two conventional stone mosques, the Patthar Mosque and the

Mosque of Akhund Mulla Shah, date from the 17th century. In an altogether different style is the Hazratbal Mosque, with its dazzling white dome and single slender minaret. Rebuilt in the Saracenic style after a fire in the 1960s, it contains Kashmir's most sacred relic, a hair from the beard of the Prophet Muhammad.

The Mughal emperors enhanced Kashmir's beauty by introducing the stately *chinar* tree (*Platanous orientalis*) to the Kashmir Valley. They also created terraced hillside gardens that were designed around fountains and water courses, formed by channelling water from natural springs or streams. Of the 777 Mughal gardens that reportedly once graced the Kashmir Valley, not many survive. There are three, however, within easy reach of Srinagar, on the eastern shore

of the Dal Lake – **Chashma Shahi, Nishat** and **Shalimar Gardens**. Above the pretty Chashma Shahi Garden, and rising tier upon tier on the mountainside, are the ruins of a 17th-century religious college. Built by a Mughal prince for his teacher, it is somewhat incongruously known as Pari Mahal or "Palace of the Fairies". From this vantage point, there are views of Dal Lake and the snowy ridge of the Pir Panjal Range.

Vestiges of Kashmir's pre-Islamic past can be seen in the ruins of magnificent Hindu temples at Avantipora, 28 km (17 miles) southeast of the capital, and Martand, 60 km (37 miles) southeast of Srinagar. The Sun Temple at Martand is believed to date from the 8th century, while the two Avantipora temples are from the 9th century.

Chashma Shahi Garden
◇ ⏰ 10am–6pm daily

Nishat Gardens
◇ ⏰ 9am–7pm daily

Shalimar Gardens
◇ ⏰ 9am–7pm daily

700

houseboats of various categories and sizes are moored on Dal Lake.

→ A traditional boat on the tranquil waters of picturesque Dal Lake at dusk, Srinagar

⑮
Gulmarg

🏠 Srinagar district; 58 km (36 miles) W of Srinagar
🚌 𝒊 www.jktourism.org/destinations/kashmir/gulmarg1

Gulmarg, or the "Meadow of Flowers", at an altitude of 2,730 m (8,957 ft), was developed by the British around a meadow on the northern flank of the Pir Panjal Range. Together with Khilanmarg, some 300 m (984 ft) higher up in the mountains, it is among India's few ski resorts.

⑯
Jammu

🏠 Jammu district; 500 km (311 miles) NW of Delhi
🚉 8 km (5 miles) SW of city centre 🚌 𝒊 www.jktourism.org/destinations/jammu/jammu-city

The winter capital of Jammu and Kashmir state, the city of Jammu sits on a bluff of the Shivalik Range, overlooking the northern plains. The **Amar**

↑ Skiers on the snowy slopes around Gulmarg, one of the few ski resorts in India

Mahal Museum, once the residence of the maharajas, now houses a museum with artifacts relating to the region's culture and history. Jammu is also the base for the pilgrimage to the cave shrine of the goddess Vaishno Devi in the Trikuta mountains, 50 km (31 miles) away.

Amar Mahal Museum
⊘ 🏠 Off Srinagar Rd
🕘 9am–5pm Tue–Sun

⑰
Pahalgam

🏠 Srinagar district; 96 km (60 miles) E of Srinagar
🚌 𝒊 www.jktourism.org/destinations/kashmir/pahalgam

In the valley of the Lidder river, Pahalgam is on the southern slope of the Great Himalayas. It is the base for several treks to Kishtwar and the Suru Valley *(p251)*, and for the pilgrimage to the holy cave of Amarnath, the destination of several thousand Hindu pilgrims, every August.

Pahalgam also offers trout fishing, golf and expeditions into the nearby mountains. The road from Srinagar to Pahalgam passes by Pampore, famous for its fields of saffron *(Crocus sativus)*, which has been cultivated in Kashmir since the 10th century. The saffron flower blooms in late autumn.

Prayer flags strung across a lake in Bodh Gaya

BIHAR AND JHARKHAND

The name Bihar derives from the Sanskrit word vihara, or monastery – an apt title for a state that was the birthplace of Buddhism. It was here that the Buddha came and found enlightenment at Bodh Gaya; other major Buddhist sites were subsequently established, such as the university at Nalanda, a centre of learning renowned across the ancient world. As with most states in India, Bihar and Jharkhand have an incredibly rich history, with sites of importance relating to many religions and dynasties. The hills surrounding Rajgir were not just where the Buddha gave a number of his best-known sermons, but also where Mahavira, the founder of Jainism, spent many months meditating.

Ancient kingdoms, such as the Mauryan and Gupta empires, dominated this region, and Bihar's capital of Patna was a city of major importance. The Mughals also conquered the area, and one of their most famous rulers, Sher Shah Suri, who established one of Delhi's seven capitals, is buried at Sasaram. After the decline of the Mughals, the Nawabs of Bengal took control, before the British annexed the territory. The state is famous for its role in the independence movement – it was in Bihar that Gandhi launched his movement of civil disobedience in 1916 and the state produced many of the movement's leaders. In 1947, India gained independence from Britain and the new state of Bihar was declared. In November 2000, the southern part of Bihar became the new state of Jharkhand.

BIHAR AND JHARKHAND

Must Sees
1 Patna
2 Mahabodhi Temple
3 Nalanda

Experience More
4 Sasaram
5 Sonepur
6 Vaishali
7 Munger
8 Deoghar
9 Jamshedpur
10 Rajgir
11 Parasnath
12 Hazaribagh National Park
13 Gaya
14 Netarhat
15 Palamau Wildlife Sanctuary
16 Ranchi

UTTAR PRADESH
AND UTTARAKHAND
p158

MADHYA PRADESH
AND CHHATTISGARH
p274

1

PATNA

🏠 Patna district, Bihar; 1,092 km (678 miles) SE of
Delhi ✈ 6 km (4 miles) SW of the city centre 🚉 🚌
ℹ bihartourism.gov.in

Stretching along the Ganges, Bihar's capital is a modern
city with ancient roots. During the reign of the Maurya
and Gupta empires Patna, then known as Pataliputra,
was one of Asia's great cities, but today it is better
known for its urban sprawl. West Patna has stately
mansions, while the old city in the east is a warren of
old monuments and bustling bazaars.

①

Golghar

🕐 Tue-Sun

Patna's signature landmark,
the Golghar (literally "round
house") is an extraordinary
dome that resembles a giant
beehive. Built in 1786 by
Captain John Garstin as a
silo to store grain during
the famines that occurred
frequently in those days, the
Golghar was never actually put
to use. The structure is 125-m
(410-ft) wide at the base and
gradually tapers up to a height
of 29 m (95 ft). Two external
staircases spiral upwards along
its sides, with platforms to rest
on along the way. The idea was
to haul the grain up, and pour
it down a hole at the top into
the dome's pit. A remarkable
echo can be heard inside the
structure. The dome's summit
offers excellent views of the
Ganges, which are particularly
impressive during the
monsoon season, when the
river can swell to a width of
8 km (5 miles).

②

Khuda Bakhsh Library

🕐 Sat-Thu 🌐 kblibrary.bih.
nic.in

Opened in 1891, this library
has a renowned collection
of rare Persian and Arabic
manuscripts, including a
group of beautiful illuminated
medieval Qur'ans, and superb
Mughal miniature paintings.
Its rarest exhibits are volumes
salvaged from the sacking of
the Moorish University in
Cordoba, Spain, in the 11th
century, though how they
found their way to India
still remains a mystery.

③

Harmandir Sahib

🕐 Sunrise-sunset daily

This historic Sikh gurdwara
marks the birthplace of the
firebrand tenth guru, Gobind

← Sun setting over the bustling streets around Patna's train station

Singh, who was born in Patna in 1666. Regarded as one of the four holiest Sikh shrines, this marble temple, with its ornate white exterior, was built in the 19th century and houses the guru's relics.

↑ Hazrat Makhdum Yahya Maneri's mausoleum, in Maner

④
Jalan Museum

☎ (0612) 264 1121 ⊙ By appt

Also known as Quila ("Fort") House, this museum has an eclectic collection that includes Chinese paintings, Mughal jade and silverware, Napoleon III's bed and Marie-Antoinette's Sèvres porcelain. Quila House itself is an interesting structure, built on the ruins of a 16th-century fort constructed by the ruler Sher Shah Suri.

⑤ 🏛
Kumrahar

⊙ 9am–5pm Tue–Sun

Excavations on this site have unearthed the ancient city of Pataliputra; there are ornately carved wooden ramparts, polished sandstone pillars and the remains of a vast Mauryan assembly hall. A museum displays some of these finds, which date from an era when Patna was described by a Greek envoy as "a city of light, where even wooden walls shine bright as glass".

⑥
Maner

📍 30 km (19 miles) W of Patna

Maner is a major centre of Islamic learning, and contains the fine 16th-century mausoleum of the Sufi saint Hazrat Makhdum Yahya Maneri. It is also famous for *laddoos*, a confection made of gram flour and molasses.

⑦
Old Opium Warehouse

📍 Gulzarbagh ⊙ Mon–Fri

Located in a walled compound on the riverbank, the opium warehouse of the East India Company is now the Government Printing Press. Opium was packaged in the three long, porticoed buildings and sent by boat to Kolkata.

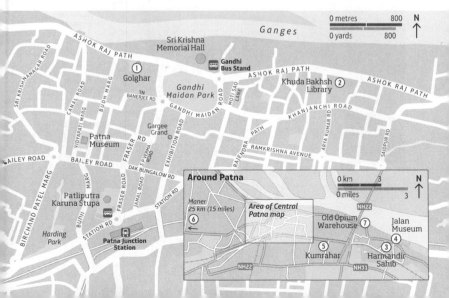

Ganges

0 metres 800
0 yards 800
N ↑

ASHOK RAJ PATH

Sri Krishna Memorial Hall

Gandhi Bus Stand

① Golghar

TN BANERJEE RD

Gandhi Maidan Park

ASHOK RAJ PATH

Khuda Bakhsh ② Library

ASHOK RAJ PATH

SRI KRISHNANAGAR ROAD

CANAL ROAD

BUDH MARG

VIDYAPATI MARG

MOTI SAO LANE

GANDHI MAIDAN ROAD

KHANJANCHI ROAD

ARYA KUMAR RD

SAIDPUR RD

Gargee Grand

EXHIBITION ROAD

RAJENDRA PATH

RAMKRISHNA AVENUE

Patna Museum

FRASER RD

S PVERMA ROAD

BAILEY ROAD

BAILEY ROAD

FRASER ROAD

JAMAL ROAD

DAK BUNGALOW RD

Patliputra Karuna Stupa

BIRCHAND PATEL MARG

BUDH MARG

STATION RD

Harding Park

STATION RD

Patna Junction Station

Around Patna

0 km 3
0 miles 3
N ↑

Maner 25 km (15 miles) ⑥ ←

Area of Central Patna map

NH22

Old Opium Warehouse ⑦

Jalan Museum

⑤ Kumrahar

③ Harmandir Sahib ④

NH22 NH31

2

MAHABODHI TEMPLE

🏠 Gaya district, Bihar; 115 km (71 miles) S of Patna 🚉 Gaya, 13 km (8 miles) N of town centre, then taxi or bus 🚌 🕐 Daily ℹ Temple Office; www.bihartourism.gov.in

The Mahabodhi Temple marks the site where, more than 2,500 years ago, Prince Siddhartha meditated on the causes of human suffering, found the answers under the Bodhi tree and became the Buddha – the Enlightened One.

The holiest Buddhist site in the world, the original temple was built by Mauryan emperor Ashoka in the 3rd century BC, rebuilt in the 7th century AD, severely damaged by Muslim invaders in the 12th century and restored in the 14th century. The site was then flooded and effectively "lost" until it was excavated in the late 19th century. It is now a major site of pilgrimage, especially for three weeks during the winter, when thousands of monks and pilgrims congregate here for the Monlam Chenmo Prayers, often presided over by the Dalai Lama. The best time to visit the temple is at dusk, when countless oil lamps bathe it in golden light, and the sound of prayers fills the air.

The soaring pyramidal spire of Mahabodhi Temple, dominating the landscape of Bodh Gaya ↑

← Monks gathering around the sacred Bodhi tree, where Prince Siddhartha attained enlightenment

The Sacred Bodhi Tree

According to lore, the original Bodhi tree (*Ficus religiosa*) was cut down by Emperor Ashoka's wife because she was jealous of the time he spent at his Buddhist devotions. The emperor revived the tree and built a stone railing around it. The tree that stands today is said to come from the same stock as the original. Ashoka's son Mahinda took a sapling to Sri Lanka on one of his proselytizing missions. The tree flourished and was brought back to be planted at Bodh Gaya after the original tree died.

↑ Statues of the meditating Buddha lining the walls inside the temple

WHAT ELSE TO SEE IN BODH GAYA

Today, Bodh Gaya flourishes as an international centre for Buddhism. Temples and monasteries built by various countries dot the town. The Thai temple is the most picturesque, while the modern Japanese temple is remarkable for its 25-m- (82-ft-) high Buddha statue. The Bhutanese and Tibetan monasteries are filled with colourful murals and prayer wheels, and both are always thronged by red-robed monks. Across the street from Mahabodhi Temple, the Archaeological Museum has fragments of the original 3rd-century BC temple railing, and 8th–12th century bronze and stone images excavated during the restoration of the temple.

3 ⬮

NALANDA

⌂ Nalanda district, Bihar; 90 km (56 miles) SE of Patna ⊙ Complex: 9am–5pm daily; museum: 9am–5pm Sat–Thu ℹ Bihar Tourism, Nav Nalanda, near bus station; www.bihartourism.gov.in

EXPERIENCE Bihar and Jharkhand

Regarded as the oldest university in the world, the Buddhist University of Nalanda was founded in the 5th century AD. The well-preserved ruins here, spread over 23 hectares (57 acres), are a testament to the 800 years where people came to learn and study, as are the references to the university in numerous ancient documents.

Once the most prestigious centre of learning in Asia, the Buddhist University of Nalanda had over 5,000 international students and teachers, and a library of nine million manuscripts. Built on a hallowed site where the Buddha had often stayed, Nalanda flourished, most notably under the Gupta Empire, as a monastic and educational institution – it is a testament to the development of the Buddhist religion. Nalanda was looted and destroyed in AD 1199 by the Turkish raider Bakhtiyar Khalji. The evocative ruins of its monasteries and temples, now a much-visited UNESCO World Heritage Site, still convey a vivid impression of the serene and ordered life of contemplation and learning that prevailed here.

> **The Buddhist University of Nalanda had over 5,000 international students and teachers, and a library of nine million manuscripts.**

HIUEN TSANG IN NALANDA

The great Chinese scholar-monk Hiuen Tsang travelled across deserts and mountains to come to Nalanda in the early 7th century AD. He was dazzled by Nalanda's "soaring domes and pinnacles, pearl-red pillars carved and ornamented..." and spent 12 years studying and teaching here. On his return to China he translated into Chinese the Buddhist scriptures he had brought back with him from Nalanda.

The ruin of the main temple at Nalanda, offering a glimpse of its former glory ↑

A group of monks exploring one of the ruined courtyards at Nalanda

INSIDER TIP
Pink Prayers

Don't miss the elegant and colourful Wat Thai Nalanda temple and the salmon pink edifice of the Nava Nalanda Mahavihara college of Pali and Buddhist studies, a short walk south of Nalanda's archaeological site.

Architectural details on the mossy ruins of a building

EXPERIENCE MORE

④ Sasaram

⌂ Rohtas district, Bihar; 158 km (98 miles) SW of Patna 🚉🚌

The dusty town of Sasaram, on the historic Grand Trunk Road, is famous for the mid-16th-century Mausoleum of Sher Shah Suri, the great Afghan ruler.

Set in the middle of an artificial lake, the pyramidal sandstone structure rises in five tiers to a height of 45 m (148 ft). The first two tiers comprise a stepped basement and a high terrace that seem to emerge from the water, with a pavilion at each corner. The octagonal tomb is set on this plinth, and tapers towards the dome in three layers of arches, crenellated parapets and small pillared kiosks. All these elements combine to create a superbly proportioned structure that appears to float above the lake. The mausoleum's Indo-Islamic design is the work of Aliwal Khan, who also covered the structure in brilliant yellow and blue tiles; some of these

→
The elegant Mausoleum of Sher Shah Suri in Sasaram

are still in place today. Nearby is the tomb of Sher Shah's father, Hasan Sur, built by the same architect.

---

⑤ Sonepur

⌂ Saran district, Bihar; 25 km (16 miles) N of Patna 🚌 ⓘ Bihar Tourism, Patna; www.bihartourism.gov.in

Across the Ganges from Patna is the little town of Sonepur, known for its annual *mela*, reputedly the largest livestock fair in Asia. The famous month-long fair begins on the full moon of Kartik Purnima, which usually falls in November or December. The *mela* site is a sandy bank at the confluence of the Ganges and Gandak rivers, and attracts millions of sadhus, pilgrims and local rural families, as well as livestock traders from all over India. On sale are elephants, camels, horses and cows, and an array of exotic birds.

A sideshow to the buying and selling of animals, grain and fodder are several troupes of folk singers and magicians, *nautanki* (vaudeville) groups, dance bands, wrestlers and gymnasts, all exhibiting their skills on the sands and performing for the many attendees. In between trading and entertainment, everyone takes a holy dip in the river during this most auspicious period in the Hindu calendar. The state tourism department sets up a tourist village a week in advance of the fair, and cottages and tents can be booked at their office in Patna. Even if buying livestock is not on your holiday agenda, the Sonepur Mela, with its colourful combination of religion, entertainment and commerce, is an unforgettable experience.

MADHUBANI PAINTING

Painted on the walls of village homes by women, Madhubani art is native to this area of Bihar and features motifs and themes inspired by Hindu mythology, nature, festival and daily life. The vibrant colours used are made of vegetable and mineral dyes, and the paintings are drawn with thin bamboo sticks. Madhubani paintings are now also created on paper and fabric, and are widely available for sale in many Indian cities.

6

Vaishali

 Vaishali district, Bihar; 32 km (20 miles) NE of Patna 🚌 ℹ️ Tourist Information Centre, Vaishali; 94710 06730

Set in the lush landscape of north Bihar, dotted with groves of banana and lychee trees, Vaishali is an important religious site. Mahavira, who founded the Jain faith, is said to have been born here in 599 BC. It is also the place where the Buddha preached his last sermon. Around this time, Vaishali was a flourishing city under the rule of the Lichhavi dynasty, who established one of the world's first city republics here. A stone pillar, a remnant of the Mauryan Empire that spread across most of India in the 3rd century BC, with a life-size lion sitting atop it, is located 4 km (2 miles) west of the Tourist Lodge.

Close to the pillar are the Abhishek Pushkarni, the ancient coronation water tank, and the Monkey Tank. According to legend, the latter was dug by monkeys, who offered the hungry Buddha a bowl of honey here – a scene often depicted in Buddhist sculpture and painting. Also

near the pillar are the ruins of a 5th-century BC brick stupa. It is believed to have been built by the Lichhavi rulers soon after the Buddha's death to enshrine his ashes.

7

Munger

 Munger district, Bihar; 180 km (112 miles) E of Patna 🚌 ℹ️ Tourist Information Centre, Fort Area, Munger; 94710 06733

Picturesquely located on the banks of the Ganges, Munger is home to the famous and controversial Bihar School of Yoga, one of the early modern schools of the practice, located within the 15th-century Munger Fort. The fort was successively occupied by the Mughals, various regional rulers and the British. Near the north gate of the fort is an 18th-century British cemetery with ornate pyramid-shaped tombs.

8

Deoghar

 Deoghar district, Jharkhand; 250 km (155 miles) SE of Patna 🚌🚌 ℹ️ Tourist Information Centre; 95700 74424

Deoghar's Baidyanath Dham temple is said to mark the spot where the heart of Shiva's consort Sati fell as part of the

famous Shakhi Peeths. Sati immolated herself to protest insults against her husband; after death, Vishnu cut her body into 51 pieces which all fell to the ground. An object of special worship is the linga inside the temple, one of Shiva's 12 *jyotirlingas*, believed to have miraculously materialized out of light. The month-long annual *mela* draws over 100,000 pilgrims daily.

9

Jamshedpur

 East Singbhum district, Jharkhand; 130 km (81 miles) SE of Ranchi 🚆🚌🚌 ℹ️ Tourist Information Centre, Bistupur; (0657) 243 2892

A major industrial centre, Jamshedpur is surrounded by lakes, rivers and the Dal Hills. It was established in 1908 by the Parsi tycoon Jamsetji Tata, who set up the Tata Iron and Steel Company here. The Tata Empire funded a garden, gallery and a zoological park here, among other buildings, which are open to visitors.

←

The life-size lion statue topping the Mauryan stone pillar in Vaishali

EAT

Mayur
Local and international vegetarian dishes are served in this stylish hotel restaurant.

 4th Floor, Hotel Baidyanath, Castair Town, Deoghar
📞 92048 52030

₹₹₹

⑩ Rajgir

🏛 Nalanda district, Bihar; 110 km (68 miles) SE of Patna 🚌🚆 ℹ️ Bihar Tourism, Kund Market; 9471006728

Surrounded by five holy hills, the picturesque little town of Rajgir is important for Buddhists as well as Jains. Both the Buddha and Mahavira, founder of Jainism, spent many months meditating and preaching here. The hills around are dotted with Jain temples, the ruins of monasteries and meditation caves. Dominating Rajgir is the large Japanese-built Vishwa Shanti Stupa on Ratnagiri Hill, with its four gilded statues of the Buddha. The 38-m- (125-ft-) high stupa was built in 1969 by the Nipponzan Myohoji Buddhist sect. Visitors can go up to the stupa by chairlift. From

here, a path leads to the adjoining Griddhakuta Hill ("Vulture's Peak"), a site much venerated by Buddhists. Two rock-cut caves here were a favourite retreat of the Buddha, and it was on this hill that he preached two of his most famous sermons. The incident of the Buddha subduing a wild elephant, a scene often depicted in Buddhist art, also took place in Rajgir. To the west of Griddhakuta Hill is Vaibhara Hill, at the foot of which are hot sulphur springs, crowded with people seeking a medicinal dip. On top of the hill are the seven Saptaparni Caves where the First Buddhist Council met soon after the Buddha's death to record his teachings. Below them

> To the west of Griddhakuta Hill is Vaibhara Hill, at the foot of which are hot sulphur springs, crowded with people seeking a medicinal dip.

on the hill is the Pippala Watchtower, a curious rock and stone structure. It dates to the 5th century BC, when Rajgir was the capital of the Magadha Empire, ruled by King Bimbisara, who became a devotee of the Buddha. The remains of the great dry-stone wall he built can still be seen on Rajgir's hills.

Pawapuri, 20 km (12 miles) east of Rajgir, is sacred to Jains as the place where the founder of their faith, Mahavira, died in 500 BC. A lotus-filled lake, with the marble Jalmandir Temple in the middle of it, marks the site of his cremation.

---

⑪ Parasnath

🏛 Giridih district, Jharkhand; 179 km (111 miles) NE of Ranchi 🚌🚆 Madhuban

An important destination for Jain pilgrims, Parasnath is named after Parsvanatha, the 23rd Jain *tirthankara*, who is believed to have attained nirvana here. Clustered on top of Parasnath Hill, the highest peak in Jharkhand at 1,370 m (4,494 ft), are 24 Jain shrines and two temples, each dedicated to one of the Jain *tirthankaras*. The temple on the highest point is dedicated to Parsvanatha. Pilgrims begin their climb from Madhuban, a stopover at the foot of the hill, and it takes over three hours through forested slopes. Palanquins are available to carry those who do not want to walk. The views from the top are magnificent.

← Walking past one of the four gilded statues of the Buddha at Vishwa Shanti Stupa

↑ Monks carrying a statue of the Buddha in procession at Mahabodhi Temple

IN THE BUDDHA'S FOOTSTEPS

The Buddha was born in 566 BC as Siddhartha Gautama, prince of the kingdom of Kapilavastu. Though born in Lumbini, in Nepal, all the places associated with his life and his teachings are in Bihar and Uttar Pradesh. These are now part of a well-travelled circuit for Buddhist pilgrims, who follow in the Buddha's footsteps from Bodh Gaya, where he attained enlightenment, to Sarnath, where he preached his first sermon; and finally to Kushinagar, where he died in 486 BC.

RENUNCIATION

Renouncing his princely life, Prince Siddhartha left his palace and his family at the age of 30 to search for answers to the meaning of human existence and suffering.

SELF-MORTIFICATION

Emaciated by fasts and penances while he spent six years living with ascetics and wandering as a beggar, Prince Siddhartha found that such self-mortification gave him no answers.

ENLIGHTENMENT

The Buddha found enlightenment at Bodh Gaya, where, after meditating for 49 days under the Bodhi tree, he discovered that the cause of suffering is desire, and that desire can be conquered by following the Noble Eightfold Path.

TEACHING

His first sermon, delivered at Sarnath, contained the essence of his teachings: his path prescribed Right Understanding, Intention, Speech, Action, Livelihood, Effort, Mindfulness and Meditation.

DEATH

The Buddha died in 486 BC after eating wild mushrooms prepared by one of his followers. The grove of sal trees where he was cremated is marked by a stupa.

↑ A statue depicting the emaciated Buddha during his period of fasting and penance

↑ A giant statue of the Buddha at Kushinagar, marking the place where he died

12

Hazaribagh National Park

🏠 Hazaribagh district, Jharkhand; 135 km (84 miles) N of Ranchi; main entry point at Pokharia 🚉 Hazaribagh Rd Stn, 67 km (42 miles) S of Pokharia then bus 🚌 ℹ️ Tourist Office, near bus stand, Hazaribagh town, 16 km (10 miles) S of Pokharia; Divisional Forest Officer, Hazaribagh, (06546) 223 340 (permits)

Set on the undulating Chhota Nagpur Plateau at an average altitude of 615 m (2,018 ft), this national park is 16 km (10 miles) from Hazaribagh. The name of this quiet town means "Thousand Tigers", and this area was once famous for its tiger population. As a result of deforestation, most of the tigers are gone from the park; the heavy traffic on the Ranchi-Kolkata Highway has also driven away many animals. But there are plenty of wild boar, nilgai and sambar, and the tropical deciduous forests are a haven for birdlife.

13

Gaya

🏠 Gaya district, Bihar; 100 km (62 miles) S of Patna 🚉🚌 ℹ️ Bihar State Tourist Office, Railway Station; 94710 06727

Stretching along the banks of the Phalgu river, Gaya, along with Varanasi and Allahabad, is regarded as one of the

> **Did You Know?**
>
> The Barabar Caves were the inspiration for the Marabar Caves in EM Forster's novel *A Passage to India.*

↑ The picturesque waterfalls at Burha Ghagh, near Netarhat

three most sacred sites for performing Hindu funeral rites. It is believed that Vishnu himself sanctified Gaya, decreeing that prayers for departed souls performed here would absolve all their earthly sins. Dominating the religious life of the city is the Vishnupad Temple, which is closed to non-Hindus, but no such restrictions apply to the ghats and shrines along the river front.

The Barabar Caves, cut deep into a granite hill, are 30 km (18 miles) north of Gaya, along a bumpy jeep road. Dating to the 3rd century BC, these are the earliest examples of rock-cut caves in India. Of the four caves, the two most impressive are the Lomas Rishi Cave and Sudama Cave, which are remarkable for the lustrous polish on the stone, and for the way in which the caves have been shaped to imitate the rounded wood and bamboo dwellings that were common at that time.

The façade of the Lomas Rishi Cave is particularly fine, with delicately carved lattice work and a charming row of elephants paying homage to stupas. These caves were used

by the Ajivika sect of ascetics, who were contemporaries of the early Jain and Buddhist orders. It is unsafe to explore this wild and rugged area without reliable guides. Ask for guide recommendations at the Bihar State Tourism office.

14

Netarhat

🏠 Latehar district, Jharkhand; 160 km (99 miles) W of Ranchi 🚌

The only hill station in Bihar and Jharkhand, Netarhat is situated at an altitude of 1,071 m (3,513 ft) and lies deep within the forested Chhota Nagpur hills, just off the Ranchi-Hazaribagh Highway. There are several pleasant rambles in the hills around this little town, and fine views of the surrounding countryside from Magnolia Point. The scenic Burha Ghagh, or Burha Falls, makes an enchanting picnic spot. The sprawling wooden Swiss-style chalet here was built as the country retreat of the British governors of Bihar, and

→ The town of Ranchi seen from the top of Tagore Hill

the home of the Palamau Tiger Reserve. The sanctuary is dotted with bamboo, *sal* (*Shorea robusta*), *mahua* (*Madhuca indica*) trees from whose flower the area's tribal people (Oraons and Mundas) make a potent spirit, and grassland. It is inhabited by wild elephants, deer, leopards, tigers and several bird species.

16

Ranchi

🏠 Ranchi district, Jharkhand; 337 km (209 miles) S of Patna ✈ 5 km (3 miles) S of town centre 🚌🚕 ℹ Birsa Munda Airport; 9771334050

The capital of Jharkhand, Ranchi is a good base from which to explore the Chhota Nagpur Plateau. The town's main attraction is the 17th-century Jagannath Temple, perched on a hill in the south-western outskirts. Like the Jagannath Temple at Puri, this temple also holds an annual chariot festival.

The Chhota Nagpur Plateau is the home of the forest-dwelling Munda and Oraon tribes. The exhibits and artifacts in the **State Museum** provide a picture of their lifestyles and social structures. Hundru Falls, some 45 km (28 miles) east of Ranchi, is a picturesque picnic spot. This is the point where the River Subarnarekha drops down dramatically from the plateau in a 100-m (328-ft) waterfall. Sleepy McCluskieganj, 40 km (25 miles) northwest of Ranchi, was established as a settlement for Anglo-Indians, who felt they belonged neither to British nor to Indian society, and wanted a haven of their own. Today, only a handful of the original settlers remain, living in cottages often decorated with pictures of the British royal family.

State Museum
🕙 10:30am–4:30pm Tue–Sun
🚫 Public hols

is now a boarding school for boys. The school authorities usually welcome visitors.

15

Palamau Wildlife Sanctuary

🏠 Palamau district, Jharkhand; 170 km (106 miles) W of Ranchi; main entry point at Betla 🚉 Daltonganj, 24 km (15 miles) NW of Betla 🚌 ℹ Tourist Office, Betla, (06562) 256513; Deputy Director, Palamau Wildlife Sanctuary, Daltonganj (permits)

Set in hilly tribal country on the northwestern edge of the Chhota Nagpur Plateau, this wildlife sanctuary is known as

MADHYA PRADESH AND CHHATTISGARH

Covering a vast area of 308,252 sq km (119,017 sq miles), Madhya Pradesh and Chhattisgarh constitute the geographic heart of India – and have subsequently been in the path of most invading forces, who have left their mark in stone and mortar. The most significant early kingdom here was the Mauryan Empire. The legendary Mauryan emperor, Ashoka, who ruled in the 3rd century BC, expanded his territory until the kingdom stretched from modern-day Afghanistan to Bangladesh. Sickened by the human toll of war, he became a Buddhist and eschewed violence, promoting the religion across his empire and building Buddhist temples.

After the decline of the Mauryans, the area was controlled by numerous dynasties who founded smaller princely kingdoms and built fantastical palaces and graceful and soul-lifting religious structures, before most were conquered by the Delhi Sultanate and subsequently the Mughals. After the decline of the Mughals, the Hindu Marathas took power, until the British wrested control of the princely states in the early 19th century. The state of Madhya Pradesh was formed in 1956, nine years after independence; in August 2000 its southeastern districts were formed into Chhattisgarh, which seceded to become a new state later the same year.

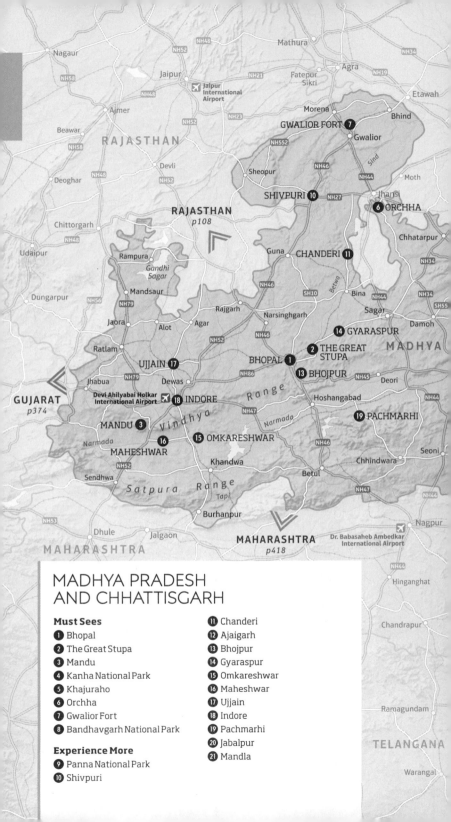

MADHYA PRADESH AND CHHATTISGARH

Must Sees
1 Bhopal
2 The Great Stupa
3 Mandu
4 Kanha National Park
5 Khajuraho
6 Orchha
7 Gwalior Fort
8 Bandhavgarh National Park

Experience More
9 Panna National Park
10 Shivpuri

11 Chanderi
12 Ajaigarh
13 Bhojpur
14 Gyaraspur
15 Omkareshwar
16 Maheshwar
17 Ujjain
18 Indore
19 Pachmarhi
20 Jabalpur
21 Mandla

↑ Praying in the monumental Taj-ul-Masjid mosque

museum displays jewellery, ritual objects, musical instruments, murals and costumes.

①

BHOPAL

Madhya Pradesh; 776 km (482 miles) S of Delhi ✈11 km (7 miles) W of city centre 🚌 ℹMP Tourism, Paryatan Bhavan, Bhadbhada Rd; www.mptourism.com

The capital of Madhya Pradesh, Bhopal was founded in the 11th century by Raja Bhoj. By the 1700s, it was held by a Muslim dynasty whose rulers included several women, the Begums of Bhopal. The city stretches along the shores of two artificial lakes. The old quarter, to the north, is a maze of narrow lanes, bazaars and mosques.

③

State Museum

Shyamla Hills, Banganga Marg ☎(0755) 266 1856 ⏱10am–5pm Tue–Sun

A collection of 12th-century Jain bronzes is the highlight

①

Taj-ul-Masjid

Hamidia Rd ⏱Daily ⏳To non-Muslims on Fri and on Muslim festivals

This pink-washed mosque was begun by Sultan Jehan Begum, a prodigious builder who also built hospitals around the city, in 1878. The mosque was only completed in 1971, almost a century later.

The enormous courtyard of the mosque has a *dukka* (water tank) for ritual ablutions, and a striking prayer hall with rows of pillars. The mosque is majestic rather than beautiful, surmounted by three white domes and flanked by two 18-storeyed minarets.

②

Indira Gandhi Rashtriya Manav Sangrahalaya

Shyamla Hills ⏱11am–6:30pm Tue–Sun (Sep–Feb: 10am–5:30pm) ⏳Public hols 🌐igrms.gov.in/en

Set in the hills overlooking the Upper Lake, this open-air museum, whose name translates as Museum of Man, re-creates the traditional homes of local communities. The Himalayan Village, Coastal Village and Desert Village feature actual-size dwellings. Among the highlights are 32 rock shelters decorated with prehistoric designs. An indoor

↑ Statue of the goddess Vamhasti at Bhopal's State Museum

of this museum, which also has a series of striking stone sculptures, mostly from the 6th to 10th centuries. Older pieces include a Standing Buddha in black granite.

④ 🏛 🍴
Bharat Bhavan

🏠 Shyamla Hills ⏰ 2–8pm Tue–Sun (Nov–Jan: 1–7pm) 🚫 Public hols 🌐 bharat bhawan.org

A cultural complex, Bharat Bhavan was established to promote India's tribal and folk art heritage. Its Tribal Art Gallery houses votive objects, terracotta figures, masks, wall paintings, woodcarvings and metal sculptures created by craftsmen from Bastar. A gallery across the courtyard has contemporary Indian art.

⑤
The Chowk

🏠 Bazaar ⏰ 10am–9pm Tue–Sun

In the old quarter of Bhopal is the Chowk (literally, main square). Streets radiate out from it, with each one special-izing in a particular type of goods – the *batuas* (beaded purses) for which Bhopal is famous, tussar silk, caps, drums and spices. *Havelis* line the streets, with wooden-fronted shops on the ground floor and elaborate wrought-iron balconies above. Dominating the area is the **Jama Masjid**, with its gold finials. Built in 1837 by Qudsia Begum, one of Bhopal's female rulers, it is now surrounded by shops selling silver jewellery.

South of the Chowk is the Moti Masjid ("Pearl Mosque"), built in 1860 by Qudsia Begum's daughter and successor. With its striped dome and tapering sandstone minarets, it looks like a smaller version of the Jama Masjid in Delhi *(p86)*.

Jama Masjid
⏰ 6:30am–7pm daily 🚫 To non-Muslims on Fri and festivals

⑥ 🏛
Van Vihar National Park

🏠 Shyamla Hills ⏰ 7am–7pm Sat–Thu

Van Vihar is closer to a zoo than a national park. Its most famous inhabitants are the white tigers. A good time to see these rare creatures is at about 4pm, when they are served their evening meal.

⑦ 🏛
Birla Museum

🏠 Near Lakshmi Narayan Temple 📞 (0755) 255 1388 ⏰ 9:30am–5pm daily

This museum displays stone sculptures dating from the 7th to 12th centuries. Particularly impressive is Vishnu in his boar (Varaha) incarnation.

Must See

EAT

Under the Mango Tree
A high-end restaurant specializing in Mughal-style cuisine: fragrant kebabs, rich curries and sumptuous biryanis.

🏠 Jehan Numa Palace Hotel, 157 Shyamla Hill 🌐 jehannuma.com

₹₹₹

Manohar Dairy and Restaurant
A popular spot, this canteen serves up tasty vegetarian fare, as well as delicious sweets and pastries.

🏠 MP Nagar 🌐 manohardairy.com

₹₹₹

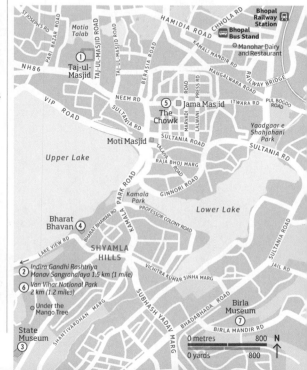

2 🗺️ 🍴

THE GREAT STUPA

📍 Raisen district, Madhya Pradesh; 46 km (29 miles) NE of Bhopal 🚌🚗 🕐 Daily 🏛️ Archaeological Museum, www.mptourism.com

The remarkable and well-preserved Great Stupa, commissioned by Mauryan emperor Ashoka in the 3rd century BC, is the crowning glory of Sanchi town.

🔍 HIDDEN GEM
Fine Fertile Form

Of the many sculptures on the Great Stupa, the serene *salabhanjika* (tree nymph), which effortlessly supports the weight of the East Gateway's lowest architrave, is a traditional fertility goddess and perhaps the finest sculpture on the stupa.

An early Buddhist convert, Ashoka was responsible for spreading the religion across his empire, and he is thought to have built the main hemispherical stone structure of the Great Stupa to hold the ashes of the Buddha.

The shape of the monument is variously believed to symbolize the upturned alms bowl of a Buddhist monk or an umbrella of protection for followers of the Buddhist dharma. The stupa has four intricately carved stone toranas (gateways), added in the 1st century BC. After Ashoka's reign, a number of other Buddhist monuments were also constructed around the Great Stupa.

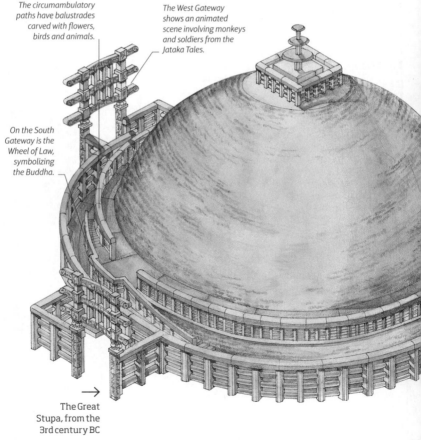

The circumambulatory paths have balustrades carved with flowers, birds and animals.

The West Gateway shows an animated scene involving monkeys and soldiers from the Jataka Tales.

On the South Gateway is the Wheel of Law, symbolizing the Buddha.

→ The Great Stupa, from the 3rd century BC

↑ Visitors admiring the West Gateway of the Great Stupa

On the North Gateway the village chief's daughter offers the Buddha kheer.

The East Gateway shows a royal retinue from when Buddha was a prince.

OTHER SITES AROUND SANCHI

From the 3rd century BC to the 7th century AD, Sanchi was a thriving Buddhist establishment of stupas and monasteries. The complex shows the development of Buddhist art across different periods, stretching out over 1,000 years. But by the 14th century, Buddhism was on the wane in India and Sanchi was deserted and half forgotten, until it was "rediscovered" in 1818 by General Taylor of the Bengal Cavalry. Between 1912 and 1919 it was restored by the Archaeological Survey of India, and declared a UNESCO World Heritage Site in 1989.

Stupa 3

Built in the 2nd century BC, this stupa has a single gateway, which contained the relics of two of the Buddha's closest disciples, Sariputra and Maudgalyayana.

Monastery 51

The 10th-century Monastery 51 is one of the more interesting here. Its courtyard is surrounded by a colonnade, behind which were the cells of 22 monks.

Temple 17

On the eastern side, Temple 17 dates to the 5th century AD. A flat-roofed structure with columns surmounted by double-headed lions, this is the earliest well-preserved example of an Indian stone temple. Its style considerably influenced the development of temple architecture.

Stupa 2

Located below the Great Stupa just outside the enclosure is Stupa 2, which was built in the 2nd century BC. Its railings are carved with lotus medallions and mythical beasts. Also depicted is a horse with stirrups.

Archaeological Museum

Near the Great Stupa is the remains of a polished stone Ashokan Pillar. The four-headed lion capital found here can now be seen in the Archaeological Museum, alongside displays including a pair of winged Mauryan lions, sculptural friezes from the gateways and statues of the Buddha and Bodhisattvas.

Udayagiri

This site, 20 km (12 miles) north of Sanchi, has magnificent examples of 5th-century AD rock-cut caves carved into the hillside. Most notable is Cave 5, with its sculpture of Varaha, the incarnation of Vishnu as a boar rescuing the earth goddess.

↑ The spectacular sculpture of Vishnu, here shown in his form as the boar, Varaha

The most well-known landmark
in Mandu, the Jahaz Mahal,
surrounded by gardens ↑

3 🏛️ 🍴

MANDU

🏠 Dhar district, Madhya Pradesh; 105 km (65 miles) SW of Indore
🚌 🕐 Sunrise-sunset daily 🛈 Malwa Resort; www.mptourism.com

Perched on a crest of the Vindhya Mountains is the deserted citadel of Mandu, one of India's most romantic and picturesque sites. Enclosed within its winding parapet walls, and surrounded by steep, wooded ravines, are palaces, mosques, lakes and pleasure pavilions, built between 1401 and 1529, by the sultans of Malwa, who referred to it as Shadiabad, the "City of Joy".

Mandu is spread over a 23-sq km (9-sq mile) area, but its major monuments are clustered in four groups – the Royal Enclave, Village Group, Sagar Talao Group and Rewa Kund Group.

Royal Enclave

Dominating the Royal Enclave are the Jahaz Mahal (p284) and the majestic Hindola Mahal ("Swinging Palace"), whose massive inward-sloping walls give the impression that the building is swaying. Built in the late 15th century as the royal assembly hall, it has an austere façade lightened by delicate tracery work on its arched windows. Next to it is a well, the Champa Baoli, which is connected to a series of subterranean rooms cooled by flowing

↑ The graceful arches and
sloping walls of Hindola Mahal

water, where the ladies of the harem spent summer days. The oldest of the monuments is Dilawar Khan's Mosque, built by the first Malwa sultan in 1405, using material from old Hindu temples.

Village Group

Located in the centre of the village, this group has three main sights. The first marble tomb to be built in India, Hoshang Shah's Tomb (1440) is perfectly proportioned; Malwa's most powerful sultan is buried here. Opposite it is the magnificent Jama Masjid (built in 1454) said to have been inspired by the Great Mosque at Damascus. Next to it is the Ashrafi Mahal madrasa with the ruins of a seven-storeyed Victory Tower, built in 1443 and said in contemporary accounts to be Mandu's finest structure.

Sagar Talao Group

Worth visiting here is the 1432 Malik Mugith's Mosque, with carved pillars from Hindu temples. In a pretty, wooded area to its south are the Dai ki Chhoti Bahen ka Mahal and Dai ka Mahal, built for two royal nurses. The octagonal-domed houses show traces of tilework.

Rewa Kund Group

Southeast is the Rewa Kund Group. Beside the Rewa Kund Stepwell, fed by an underground

↑ The lovely Rupmati's Pavilion, legacy of an epic romance between a sultan and a beautiful singer

stream whose waters are said to be sacred, is Baz Bahadur's Palace, built in 1508–9. Its most charming feature is an octagonal pavilion overlooking a garden. Just south is Rupmati's Pavilion, with lovely fluted domes, from where there is a great view of the countryside. A short distance west of Sagar Talao, a flight of steps leads to Neelkanth Mahal. This palace, with its many water channels and cascades, was built in 1574 for the Mughal emperor Akbar's Hindu wife.

> **The first marble tomb to be built in India, Hoshang Shah's Tomb is a perfectly proportioned.**

Mandu: Jahaz Mahal

The Jahaz Mahal ("Ship Palace") was built by the fifth sultan of Malwa, Ghiyasuddin (r 1469–1500). Lying on a long, narrow strip of land between two of the many man-made lakes, Munja Talao and Kapur Talao, the palace gives the impression of an anchored ship, especially during the monsoon, when the lakes are full. This pleasure palace was staffed entirely by the hedonistic sultan's harem of 15,000 women, who also served as his personal bodyguard.

The juxtaposition of conical and domed roofs over the pavilions adds great charm to the Jahaz Mahal's silhouette.

Blue and yellow tiles decorated the pavilions.

The most spacious part of the palace, the terrace, with its pavilions and kiosks, overlooks the lakes.

Entrance

① The terrace pool in the pleasure palace of Jahaz Mahal was fed by rainwater.

② Intricate water channels are found all over Jahaz Mahal, planned for both pleasure and practical purposes.

③ The palace was designed by the sultan, Ghiyasuddin, who wanted to enjoy a hedonistic retirement after decades of war. This beautiful bathing pool was fed by water channels and had plenty of space for reclining.

The intricate spiral designs of the water channels are characteristic of the simple elegance of Mandu's architecture.

The terrace pool, similar in design to the one on the ground floor, is fed by a water channel.

The beautiful bathing pool at the northern end is surrounded on three sides by colonnades.

↑ Jahaz Mahal, one of the pleasure palaces at Mandu

Narrow rooms lie at either end of the ground floor, with its three large halls.

BAZ BAHADUR AND RUPMATI

One day while out hunting, Sultan Baz Bahadur (r 1554–61) spotted a girl, Rupmati, singing as she bathed in the Narmada river. Bewitched by her beauty and her voice, Baz Bahadur asked her to live with him in Mandu. She agreed – as long as he built her a pavilion from where she could see the Narmada. Thereafter, Bahadur spent his time in the pursuit of love and music, leaving his kingdom vulnerable to attack. When Emperor Akbar's general, Adham Khan, attacked Mandu in 1561, he won an easy victory. Baz Bahadur fled, deserting Rupmati, who was captured. As the Mughal general waited outside her room to claim her, Rupmati committed suicide by swallowing poison.

4 🛡️ 📷

KANHA NATIONAL PARK

📍 Mandla district, Madhya Pradesh; 196 km (122 miles) SE of Jabalpur; entry points at Khatia, Kisli and Mukki 🚌 🕐 Oct–Jun 🛈 MP Tourism, Baghira Log Huts, Kisli; www.mptourism.com

The magnificent Kanha National Park is often described as India's finest game sanctuary and a model for wildlife conservation, as it protects a number of endangered species. The landscape here comprises grassy meadows and flat-topped hills with beautiful streams and lush deciduous forests.

The inspiration for Rudyard Kipling's famous *The Jungle Book*, Kanha is today an important Project Tiger *(p174)* Reserve. Along with Bandhavgarh *(p198)*, it is one of the best places to spot these elusive creatures, as there are now around 80 tigers in the park – one of the highest tiger densities in India. Park guides expertly track them through marks and the alarm calls of deer and langurs.

The glorious variety of wildlife found within this 1,954-sq-km (754-sq-mile) park – once the exclusive hunting ground of the British viceroys – includes deer, leopard, hyena, sloth bear, python and nearly 300 species of birds. Conservation efforts have increased the numbers of the rare Central Indian barasingha, or swamp deer, which was close to extinction 30 years ago.

→

A spotted deer in the misty Kanha landscape with the sun low in the sky

KIPLING'S JUNGLE BOOK

The English writer Rudyard Kipling (1865–1936) was born in Bombay (Mumbai), and though he spent little time in India, the country provided the setting for many of his books. Among his most enduring works is *The Jungle Book*, which features delightful stories of animal behaviour and the law of the jungle. Set in the Seonee Forests of Kanha, the book's endearing hero is the wolf-reared boy Mowgli; the story revolves around his adventures with the many enchanting - and at times, scary - animal characters, including Rikki-tikki-tavi the mongoose, Shere Khan the tiger, Kaa the python, and Baloo the bear.

→ Prowling through the park, this tiger is one of 80 in Kanha

STAY

Kipling Camp
A short drive from the park's Khatia gate, this well-run camp has charming cottages set around a forest clearing.

⌂ Morcha Village, Mandla District
🌐 kiplingcamp.com

₹₹₹

← A young elephant taking a mud bath – a common sight in Kanha

KHAJURAHO

🏠 Chhatarpur district, Madyha Pradesh; 275 km (171 miles) SE of Gwalior ✈️ 5 km (3 miles) S of temples 🚌 🕐 Kandariya Mahadev Temple: 5am–noon & 4–9pm daily; Son et Lumière: Oct–Feb: 6:30–7:25pm: Mar–Sep 7:30–8:25pm ℹ️ MP Tourism, Taj Chandela; www.mptourism.com

The magnificent temples at Khajuraho, a UNESCO World Heritage Site, were built between the 9th and 10th centuries by the Chandela dynasty, who dominated central India at that time. The surviving temples are monuments to the artistic flowering that took place under the patronage of these powerful rulers, who made Khajuraho their peacetime capital.

Thanks to Khajuraho's relative isolation, its temples were largely spared the ravages of Islamic raiders, but they were abandoned after the decline of the Chandelas in the 13th century. Hidden in dense forest for 700 years, the temples were "rediscovered" in 1838 by Captain T S Burt of the Bengal Engineers, though they may well have been secretly still in use for some time. There are 25 remaining temples here, although it is thought that there were originally around 85, and ongoing excavations have unearthed ruins in the vicinity. The temples are dedicated to Shiva, Vishnu and Ganesha as well as to Jain *tirthankaras*, showing the culture of acceptance among religious groups at the time.

EAT

Raja Café
A stalwart of the Khajuraho traveller scene, Raja Café offers superb views of the temples and a globe-trotting menu.

🏠 Opp Western Group
📞 (07686) 272307

₹₹₹

Mediterraneo
Authentic Italian with a first-floor terrace, serving wood-fired thin-crust pizzas, homemade pasta and excellent coffee.

🏠 Jain Temples Rd
📞 (07686) 272246

₹₹₹

Climbing the steps of one of Khajuraho's many temples

 INSIDER TIP
Mangeswara Temple

Just outside the Western Group, Mangeswara Temple is often over-looked, but witnessing sunrise and sunset prayers in its 1,000-year-old inner shrine is a magical experience.

Kandariya Mahadev

The most impressive and largest of the temples is Kandariya Mahadev, the pinnacle of north Indian temple architecture. It is remarkable for its grand dimensions, its harmonious composition and its exquisite embellishments. Over 800 sculptures cover the temple, depicting gods and goddesses, beasts and warriors, dancers and musicians, and the erotic scenes for which the Khajuraho temples are famous. The temple is designed to resemble Mount Kailash, the home of the gods: the main spire, 30 m (98 ft) high, is surrounded by 84 smaller ones, creating the impression of a mountain range.

↑ The mountainous Kandariya Mahadev, and *(inset)* a stone lion and warrior in battle

Exploring Khajuraho

The Khajuraho temples are divided into three groups. The most important are in the Western Group, which, as well as Kandariya Mahadev, includes the Lakshmana and the Vishwanath temples. The superb ceiling of the entrance porch and the female figures inside the Lakshmana Temple (AD 930) are worthy of special attention. The pair of street singers on the south façade, with their expressions of intense absorption, are also remarkable. Opposite is a pavilion with a magnificent statue of Varaha, the boar incarnation of Vishnu. In the Vishwanath Temple (AD 1002), the *apsara* (nymph) on the south façade is outstanding, as is the apsara (celestial nymph) playing the flute, which can be seen in the interior chamber. The Matangeshwar Temple (built AD 900), with its plain circular interior, is the only one still in everyday use. The Archaeological Museum, near the entrance to the Western Group, has a fine collection of sculptures from the area.

A short distance away is the Eastern Group of temples. The Jain Parsvanatha Temple (AD 950) is the most remarkable for the intricately carved ceiling pendants in its entrance porch. Three exquisite sculptures here show *apsaras* applying kohl around their eyes, painting their feet (both on the southern façade), and fastening ankle bells (on the northern façade).

The last phase of temple-building in Khajuraho is seen in the Southern Group. The Chaturbhuj Temple (built AD 1090) has a superb four-armed image of Shiva in the inner sanctum and is the only major temple in Khajuraho without any erotic sculptures.

→
Lakshmana Temple, one of the oldest and largest temples in Khajuraho

←
A shrine to Nandi the sacred bull, a common sight at temples devoted to the Hindu god Shiva

WHY ARE KHAJURAHO'S TEMPLES COVERED WITH EROTIC SCULPTURES?

There are several competing theories: some argue they were inspired by the ancient Sanskrit text of the Kama Sutra and designed to be used as a how-to guide; others believe they were made by a religious group that used sex as a form of worship. Alternative theories include the idea that they were produced to distract the gods and protect the temples from natural disasters, functioned as a meditation aid or represented Shiva and Parvati's wedding celebrations.

INSIDER TIP
Rhythm of the Night

Each night for a week in February, it's as if the sculptures step off the temple walls and onto the stage, when classical Indian dance and music *(p292)* are showcased at the Khajuraho Dance Festival *(khajuraho dancefestival.com)*.

↑ Looking up at the hundreds of carved figures on the walls of Kandariya Mahadev

CLASSICAL MUSIC AND DANCE

Indian music and dance are simultaneously modes of worship and a joyous celebration of life. Based on ancient codified texts, they originated as a form of worship in the temples, and gradually acquired a more secular character with royal patronage. Different regions of India have their own classical dance forms, while classical music is distinguished by two main styles – Hindustani, from north India, and Carnatic *(p529)*, specific to south India.

ORIGINS

The origins of Hindustani classical music date to about 3000 BC, with roots in Hindu Vedic literature – the Samaveda is the veda of chants, its verses written with notated melodies, not meant to be read but sung. The core of the ancient Indian conception of music consisted of *gita* (melody), *vadya* (instrumental music) and *nrtta* (dance), which were gradually codified into the *Natya Shastra*, a Sanskrit treatise on the performing arts, thought to have been compiled between 500 BC and AD 500. Royal patrons encouraged the development of music across the subcontinent, and by the 16th century great *gharanas*, or schools of music, were being founded; these have preserved their individuality by passing down knowledge orally from guru to *shishya* (disciple).

THE RAGA

The raga (melodic line) is the system of modes that underlies all Indian classical music. Each raga consists of at least five notes, and there is no written score, giving the singer great latitude to reorder the notes

↑ Kishori Amonkar, a doyenne of Hindustani vocal classical music

CLASSICAL DANCE

A range of gestures, postures, expressions and moods, codified in the *Natya Shastra*, constitute the "language" of Indian classical dance forms. Most scholars recognize eight styles: Bharat Natyam, Kuchipudi, Kathak, Odissi, Manipuri, Kathakali, Mohiniyattam and Sattriya. Their themes are mostly based on religious mythology, and percussion and music play an important role.

Did You Know?

The *Natya Shastra*'s nine moods *(navarasa)* range from the erotic and heroic to the wondrous and quiescent.

Types of Dance

Manipuri

Manipuri, from the northeast, enacts the legend of Radha and Krishna *(p180)*. Stiffened skirts and gentle swaying movements are typical of Manipuri dance.

Kathak

Kathak was a favourite dance at the royal courts of northern India. Complex footwork and multiple pirouettes characterize this dance form.

and compose and improvise within the framework of the raga. There are more than 100 ragas, each assigned to a time of day or season, according to the mood it evokes. Recitals usually begin with a leisurely *alap*, an evocation of the raga, followed by a slow- or medium-paced *bandish* (composition) and ending with a fast-paced piece.

HINDUSTANI VOCAL MUSIC

The most ancient and austere form of Hindustani vocal music is *dhrupad*, said to have developed from the chanting of Vedic hymns and accompanied only by the *tanpura* (drone) and *pakhawaj* (drum). The Dagars and the Gundechas are among its foremost exponents. *Khayal* developed from *dhrupad* and contains more embellishments and ornamentations. Mallikarjun Mansur (1910–92), Kishori Amonkar (1932–2017) and Bhimsen Joshi (1922–2011) were some of its best-known performers, while today you can attend recitals by Padma Talwalkar and Rashid Khan, alongside other eminent singers. *Thumri* and *dadra* are lighter, more romantic forms of classical music.

HINDUSTANI INSTRUMENTAL MUSIC

Instrumental recitals follow much the same pattern as vocal ones. The sitar and sarod are among the most prominent concert instruments, made popular by Ravi Shankar (1920–2012) and Amjad Ali Khan respectively. Bismillah Khan (1913–2006) played the *shehnai*, a ceremonial reed pipe, which he popularized into a concert instrument.

↑ Tabla virtuoso Zakir Hussain in concert

→ Amjad Ali Khan, one of India's top exponents of the sarod

Odissi

Odissi developed in the temples of Odisha as an offering to the deities. Sensuous and spiritual at the same time, Odissi has sinuous movements and highly sculptural poses.

Bharat Natyam

Bharat Natyam, from Tamil Nadu, has eloquent eye and hand movements *(mudras)*. Chiselled movements and symmetrical stances are typical of this dance form.

Kuchipudi

Kuchipudi is a highly dramatic dance form from Andhra Pradesh, which often enacts scenes from the great epics, the *Mahabharata* and the *Ramayana*.

6 🏛 🎟

ORCHHA

🏠 Tikamgarh district, Madhya Pradesh; 120 km (75 miles) SE of Gwalior 🚉 Jhansi, 19 km (12 miles) NW of Orchha, then taxi or bus 🚌 ⏱ Son et Lumière (Chaturbhuj, Jehangir Mahal & Raj Mahal): Mar–Oct: 7:30–8:30pm; Nov–Feb: 6:30–7:30pm 🛈 MP Tourism, Sheesh Mahal & Betwa Retreat; www.mptourism.com

Orchha is dramatically positioned on a rocky island, enclosed by a loop of the Betwa river. Founded in the 16th century, it was the capital of the Bundela kings until 1738, when it was abandoned for Tikamgarh. Crumbling palaces, pavilions, hammams, walls and gates, connected to the town by a 14-arched causeway, are all that remain today.

The most spectacular sights in the old town are the three main palaces: Raja Mahal, Jahangir Mahal and Rai Praveen Mahal (named after a royal paramour), all arranged together symetrically. There are also three beautiful temples – the Ram Raja, the Lakshmi Narayan and the Chaturbhuj. A unique blend of palace, fort and temple styles, the Chaturbhuj Temple is dedicated to Vishnu (its name literally means "he who has four arms") and has huge arcaded halls for massed singing, and a soaring spire.

Lying along the Betwa river, at the Kanchana Ghat stairs, are the 14 beautiful *chhatris* (cenotaphs) of the Orchha rulers. Built in the 17th century, they serve as reminders of Orchha's feudal history.

Jahangir Mahal

An excellent example of Rajput Bundela architecture, this palace was built by the Bundela king Bir Singh Deo, who commissioned and named it in honour of the Mughal emperor Jahangir, who spent one night here. The multilayered palace, a blend of Hindu and Islamic styles, has 132 chambers off and above the central courtyard and an almost equal number of subterranean rooms. The square sandstone palace is extravagantly embellished with lapis lazuli tiles, graceful *chhatris* and ornate *jali* screens. Its modest museum is worth a look, if only for the *sati* pillars – memorials to queens who sacrificed themselves (willingly or not) on their husband's funeral pyres.

→
Sunken baths in the central courtyard of Jahangir Mahal, overlooked by its domed pavilions

↑ The *chhatris* of Orchha
reflected in the waters
of the Betwa at sunset

1 Lakshmi Narayan Temple
is dedicated to Lakshmi, the
Hindu goddess of prosperity
and consort of Vishnu.

2 The vibrant orange-and-
pink Ram Raja Temple is the
only temple where Rama is
worshipped as a king – it was
converted from a palace when
an idol of Rama supposedly
refused to be moved to the
Chaturbhuj Temple.

3 Notable for the vibrant and
well-preserved murals in its
great halls, Lakshmi Narayan
Temple depicts a range of
religious and secular life.

GWALIOR FORT

N of Gwalior city centre, Madhya Pradesh; 344 km (213 miles) S of Delhi 14 km (8 miles) N of city centre 8am–6pm daily; Son et Lumière: Mar–Oct: 8:30pm daily, Nov–Feb: 7:30pm daily; museum: 10am–5pm Sun–Thu Fri & public hols Hotel Tansen Residency, 6 Gandhi Rd; www.mptourism.com

The massive Gwalior Fort stretches for nearly 3 km (2 miles) atop a 100-m- (328-ft-) high sandstone and basalt hill. Its formidable bastioned walls enclose a series of exquisite temples and palaces.

This spectacular fort has many and varied structures; of these, the Man Mandir Palace is the most worth visiting. Built between 1486 and 1516 by Raja Man Singh of the Tomar dynasty, the palace is regarded as one of the finest examples of Rajput secular architecture, embellished with superb stone carving and latticework. Brilliant blue, yellow and green tiles depicting parrots and peacocks, rows of ducks, elephants, banana trees and crocodiles decorate its façade.

Rounded bastions, topped with cupolas and decorated with tilework, and *(inset)* one of the fort's courtyards

Described by a 16th-century Persian chronicler as "the pearl in the necklace of castles of Hind", Gwalior Fort has had a turbulent history, beginning in the 8th century AD. It was successively ruled by Hindu dynasties, Delhi sultans, the Mughals and the Maratha Scindias, and was briefly in British hands in the 19th century.

The fort is best entered from the Urwahi Gate on its western side, where 21 colossal Jain sculptures (7th–15th century AD) depicting the *tirthankaras* are carved into the rock face.

Lying to their left is the richly carved Teli ka Mandir, the tallest temple in the fort. Built in the 9th century and dedicated to Vishnu, it has an unusual rounded *shikhara* (spire). To its north are two 11th-century Vishnu temples, the Saas-Bahu ("Mother-in-Law and Daughter-in-Law") Temples, whose *shikharas* were destroyed by Sultan Qutbuddin Aibak in the 12th century.

At the northeastern edge of the fort is the Archaeological Museum, whose fine collection of Jain and Hindu sculpture includes the celebrated statue of the *salabhanjika* (wood nymph), originally from the temple at Gyaraspur.

↑ Jain sculptures depicting the *tirthankaras* carved into the cliff on the approach to Gwalior Fort

Described by a 16th-century Persian chronicler as "the pearl in the necklace of castles of Hind", Gwalior Fort has had a turbulent history.

WHAT ELSE TO SEE IN GWALIOR

Apart from its fort, Gwalior's main attraction is the 19th-century Jai Vilas Palace, whose magnificent Durbar Hall holds two of the world's largest chandeliers. Before they were hung, the roof was tested by having elephants stand on it. North of the fort is the old town, which has two striking Islamic monuments – the Tomb of Mohammed Ghaus, a Mughal nobleman, and the Tomb of Tansen, a famous singer and one of the "nine jewels" of the Mughal emperor Akbar's court.

BANDHAVGARH NATIONAL PARK

📍 Shahdol district, Madhya Pradesh; 237 km (147 miles) SE of Khajuraho; main entry point at Tala 🚌 🚉 Umaria, 33 km (21 miles) SW of Tala 🕐 Oct–Jun ℹ️ White Tiger Forest Lodge, Tala (MP Tourism); www.mptourism.com

One of India's most important tiger reserves, Bandhavgarh National Park sprawls across an area of 625 sq km (241 sq miles). Apart from some 50 tigers, the park's wildlife includes 250 species of birds, leopard, deer, jungle cats and packs of *dhole* (Indian wild dogs).

Great rocky hills, lush deciduous forests, marshes and meadows make Bandhavgarh one of India's most scenic areas. Among the park's attractions is an ancient fort that dates back to the 1st century AD and whose ramparts are a good place for bird-watching. The Sheshasaya Statue, an 11-m- (36-ft-) long statue of the reclining Vishnu, guarded by a seven-headed snake, lies at the base. As well as tigers, look out for the dhole, a wild dog with a red coat, large upright ears, a bushy tail and a distinctive whistling call.

Did You Know?

It's said you have a 90 per cent chance of seeing a tiger in Bandhavgarh during a stay of more than three days.

↑ A curious leopard taking it easy on a tree branch after a hard-earned meal

EXPERIENCE MORE

9 ⊛ ⊛

Panna National Park

🏠 Madhya Pradesh; 25 km (16 miles) S of Khajuraho; entry points at Madla & Hinanta 🚉 Khajuraho ⏰ Mar–Jun: sunrise–11am & 4pm–sunset; Oct–Feb: sunrise–11am & 3pm–sunset 🌐 panna tigerreserve.in

In late 2009 Panna National Park's tiger population fell to zero as a result of poaching and mismanagement. Since then, however, the reserve has recovered dramatically. Now, following a successful reintroduction programme, its 543 sq km (210 sq miles) of forests, waterfalls, savannah grassland, plateaus and gorges are home to around 35 tigers. Despite being easily accessible from the famous temple complex of Khajuraho, the park receives only a fraction of the visitors of Madhya Pradesh's larger and better-known parks, Kanha and Bandhavgarh.

While tigers are of course the main draw, Panna is rich in other forms of wildlife too, including sloths, dhole, deer, langur monkeys, pythons and even the somewhat-elusive leopards. Panna is also a haven for bird-watchers, with more than 200 resident and migratory species, notably blossom-headed parakeets, white-necked storks and paradise flycatchers. Also scattered throughout the park are records of human history, including rock paintings thought to be around 2,000 years old, as well as ruins of the Gondwana kingdom (14th–18th century).

Hiring a guide is compulsory, but this can be arranged on entry. Travelling in small groups is ideal, and early mornings and late afternoons are the best times to catch a glimpse of the animals.

← Snap-happy safari-goers capturing the park's top attraction, and *(inset)* a family of elephants

❿ Shivpuri

🏠 Madhya Pradesh; 117 km (73 miles) SW of Gwalior 🚌🚗 ℹ️ Tourist Village, Shivpuri; (07492) 223 760/221 297

The summer capital of the Scindia rulers of Gwalior, Shivpuri was once a thickly forested region, and a favourite hunting ground of the Mughals. Today, the main attractions are the 19th-century white marble cenotaphs of Madhavrao Scindia and his mother, which stand facing each other in a formal Mughal-style garden. With their mix of *shikharas* (spires), domes and cupolas, they epitomize Indo-Islamic architecture. Madhavrao's cenotaph is decorated with *pietra dura* work in lapis lazuli and onyx. There are life-size statues of the ruler and his mother and, in accordance with family tradition, their favourite foods are left here every day. The colonial-style Madhav Vilas Palace has airy terraces overlooking the town. The 156-sq-km (60-sq-mile) Madhav National Park is nearby, and has a mixed deciduous forest with an artificial lake, surrounded by grasslands.

⓫ Chanderi

🏠 Madhya Pradesh; 227 km (141 miles) S of Gwalior 🚌 ℹ️ MP Tourism, Tanabana; www.mptourism.com

Built by the Pratihara kings in the 10th century, the medieval town of Chanderi is dominated by the Kirtidurga Fort, perched 200 m (656 ft) above the Betwa river and overlooking an artificial lake, Kirtisagar. After the Pratiharas, Chanderi fell to the sultans of Delhi, Malwa, the Mughal emperor Babur and then, finally, to the Marathas, becoming part of the Scindia kingdom of Gwalior.

The entrance to the fort is through the Khuni Darwaza

The summer capital of the Scindia rulers of Gwalior, Shivpuri was once a thickly forested region, and a favourite hunting ground of the Mughals.

("Bloody Gateway"), marking the point at which the Mughal emperor Babur broke through the 6-km- (4-mile-) long granite walls of the fort, when he conquered it in 1528. Most of the structures inside the fort are attributed to Sultan Mahmud of Malwa, and are executed in the graceful provincial Afghan style that distinguishes the buildings of Mandu (p282). The most ambitious edifice in the complex is the Koshak Mahal, built in 1445. The sultan originally planned it as a seven-storeyed palace, but he only managed to complete two storeys, each with balconies, rows of windows and the beautifully vaulted ceilings.

Chanderi was once a flourishing centre of trade, and an exploration of the town reveals large sandstone *havelis*, shops raised on plinths and ruined caravanserais lining

↓ The ornate cenotaph of Madhavrao Scindia at Shivpuri, and *(inset)* a niche with his statue

the winding lanes. The town is also famous for its gossamer muslin saris and brocades.

Deogarh Fort, the "Fortress of the Gods", is 25 km (16 miles) southeast of Chanderi. Within it is a splendid display of sculptures from a group of 9th- to 10th-century Jain temples. Below the fort, the 5th-century Vishnu Dasavatara Temple has fine sculptures and carved pillars topped by musicians. A statue of Vishnu asleep on Ananta, the cosmic serpent, is an early masterpiece of Indian art.

 Climbing the stone stairs to the imposing Bhojeshwar Temple in Bhojpur

⑫
Ajaigarh

🏠 **Panna district, Madhya Pradesh; 75 km (47 miles) E of Khajuraho** ⏰ **Daily**

A great Chandela citadel, built in the 9th century AD and perched 500 m (1,640 ft) above the plains, Ajaigarh is now a spectacular ruin. The steep path up to the top goes past gigantic sculptures carved into the sheer cliff face, including a particularly enchanting one of a cow and calf. Within the fort lie the ruins of once-magnificent palaces, broken fragments of statues and several poignant *sati* pillars, marking the self-immolation of countless Rajput widows. The fort also houses the Ajay Pal ka Talao, a famous lake and the ruins of a Jain Temple.

⑬
Bhojpur

🏠 **Madhya Pradesh; 28 km (17 miles) SE of Bhopal** 🚌 🛈 **MP Tourism, Bhopal; (0755) 276 6750**

Founded by the 11th-century Paramara king Raja Bhoj, who also established Bhopal (*p278*), Bhojpur is dominated by the monumental, though incomplete, Bhojeshwar Temple. Impressive sculptures

cover parts of its unfinished corbelled ceiling and its entrance doorway.

Inside, on a tiered platform, is a stone Shivalinga, 2.3 m (8 ft) high and 5.3 m (17 ft) in circumference. Etched on the paving stones and rocks in the forecourt are the architect's detailed plans for the finished temple, while on the northeast side are the remains of a massive earthen ramp used to haul stone up to the roof.

The Bhimbetka Caves, about 25 km (15 miles) south of Bhojpur, are a UNESCO World Heritage Site. Their prehistoric paintings date back some 12,000 years.

⑭
Gyaraspur

🏠 **Madhya Pradesh; 64 km (40 miles) NE of Bhopal** 🚌 🛈 **MP Tourism, Bhopal; (0755) 276 6750**

Built on a hillside at Gyaraspur, the ornately carved 9th-century Maladevi Temple is now in ruins. Partly carved out of a rock, much of the temple's superb sculpture has been pillaged. The exquisite statue of the *salabhanjika*, which is now the pride display of the Archaeological Museum at Gwalior Fort (*p295*), was salvaged from here.

THE BHIMBETKA CAVE PAINTINGS

In 1957, well-known Indian archaeologist VS Wakankar discovered over 1,000 rock shelters near Bhimbetka village. More than 500 of these were covered with paintings. The earliest, from the Upper Paleolithic period, are of large animals such as bison and rhino. Most of the paintings are from the Mesolithic period (8000 to 5000 BC) and depict vignettes of daily life and hunting scenes. Later caves (1st century AD) show battle scenes and Hindu deities.

15

Omkareshwar

⊙ Madhya Pradesh;
77 km (48 miles) SE of
Indore ▣▣▣ ℹ MP
Tourism, Narmada Resort;
www.mptourism.com

The island of Omkareshwar,
at the confluence of the
Narmada and Kaveri rivers,
is an enchanting pilgrimage
town. With jagged cliffs on its
southern and eastern sides,
the small island is dotted with
temples, sadhus' caves and
bathing ghats, and filled with
the sound of chanting. A
circumambulatory path leads
around the island, which is
linked to the mainland by a
concrete causeway, though
visitors can also arrive by
barge. Inside the towering
white *shikhara* of the **Sri
Omkar Mandhata** ("Bestower
of Desires") **Temple** is a
sacred Shivalinga, one of 12
jyotirlingas (natural rock lingas
said to have miraculously
emerged from light).

Did You Know?

The sacred island of
Omkareshwar is said
to be shaped like
the sacred Hindu
"om" symbol.

STAY

Ahilya Fort
Home of one of the
most celebrated female
rulers of the 18th
century, this stunning
historic fort is now
an atmospheric and
opulent place to stay.

⊙ Ahilya Fort,
Maheshwar
🌐 ahilyafort.com

₹₹₹

At the eastern end of the
island is the 13th-century
Siddhnath Temple, which
has beautiful sculptures of
apsaras. The northern end
has a cluster of Hindu and
Jain temples. Overlooking
them is a ruined palace,
part of a fortified township
that stood here until it was
sacked by Muslim invaders
in the 11th century.

**Sri Omkar Mandhata
Temple**
🕐 7am–6pm daily

Siddhnath Temple
🕐 5am–6pm daily

↑ Colourful boats at the
ghats on the Narmada
river, Maheshwar

16

Maheshwar

⊙ Madhya Pradesh; 90 km
(56 miles) SW of Indore
▣ Barwaha, 39 km (24
miles) E of town centre,
then taxi or bus ▣ ℹ MP
Tourism, Narmada Resort;
www.mptourism.com

Picturesquely sited on the
banks of the Narmada,
Maheshwar is an important
Hindu pilgrimage centre. It
was the site of the ancient city
of Mahishmati, which is mentioned in classical Sanskrit
texts. Maheshwar's beautiful
temples and ghats were
erected by Queen Ahilyabai
of the Holkar dynasty, in the
mid-18th century.
    The 1.5-km- (1-mile-) long
river front is dotted with
shrines, ghats and the cenotaphs of the Holkar rulers, and

← The pilgrimage town of
Omkareshwar, with boats
moored on the Narmada river

is usually thronged with pilgrims taking a dip. A fan-shaped stairway leads from the river front to Maheshwar Fort's royal enclosure and the Ahilyeshwar Temple, built in 1798. The richly carved courtyard, leading on to the palace, has an impressive statue of Ahilyabai. This benevolent queen, who also built the Vishwanath Temple (p178) in Varanasi, was described by a British colonial official, Sir John Malcolm, as "one of the purest and most exemplary rulers that ever lived".

Also within the fort is the Rehwa Weavers' Society, where the famous gossamer-fine Maheshwari cotton and silk textiles are woven.

---

⑰

Ujjain

🏠 Ujjain district, Madhya Pradesh; 56 km (35 miles) N of Indore 🚌🚃 ℹ️ MP Tourism, Shipra Residency; www.mptourism.com

On the banks of the Shipra river, Ujjain is one of India's seven sacred cities, and one of the four sites of the Kumbh Mela. During the 4th–5th centuries AD it was the second capital of the Gupta Empire, with the celebrated Sanskrit poet Kalidasa as one of its leading lights. Its glory was, however, eclipsed in the 13th century after it was sacked by the Delhi Sultans.

The focal point of the town is the Mahakaleshwar Temple (an 18th-century reconstruction on the site of the original), with its much-venerated Shivalinga. In the main square is the Gopal Temple, whose silver doors are believed to be from the Somnath Temple in Gujarat, ransacked by Mahmud of Ghazni in the 11th century. A similar pair of doors are at the Golden Temple in Amritsar (p204). Ram Ghat, the largest of the sacred ghats on the banks of the river, is the site of the Kumbh Mela (the next mela here is due in 2022).

On the opposite bank is the Chintaman Ganesh Temple, whose carved pillars, dating to the 11th century, are the only relics of the original temple. At the southwestern edge of the city is the Vedh Shala Observatory. Built in 1730 by Sawai Jai Singh II of Jaipur, the Mughal-appointed governor of Malwa, it is a smaller version of the one at Jaipur (p112). The charming, if a bit ramshackle, 15th-century Kaliadeh Palace, 8 km (5 miles) north of Ujjain, on an island in the Shipra, was built by the sultans of Malwa.

> ### THE HILL OF DEVI
>
> The celebrated British writer E M Forster (1879-1970) spent a number of months in the princely state of Dewas, just south of Ujjain, as secretary to its eccentric maharaja. His novel, *The Hill of Devi*, is an insightful look into life at court, with all of its festivities, complicated protocol and intrigues. Dewas was particularly interesting, as the tiny kingdom was split between two brothers who ruled separately, each with his own palace and army. Forster was at the court of the elder maharaja and the experience also provided him with material for his novel *A Passage to India* (1924).

The majestic façade of Indore's Rajwada Palace, all that remains of the building following a fire

18

Indore

Madhya Pradesh; 187 km (116 miles) SW of Bhopal 10 km (6 miles) W of town Tourist Reception Centre (MP Tourism), 42 Residency Area, opposite St Paul High School; www.mptourism.com

Until 1947, Indore was a princely state ruled by the Maratha Holkar dynasty. At the heart of the city, surrounded by a lively bazaar, is their former abode, Rajwada Palace, now just an imposing façade after a fire in 1984. Nearby is Kanch Mandir ("Glass Temple"), an opulent 19th-century Jain temple decorated with mirrors, chandeliers, and murals on glass.

On the southwestern edge of Indore is Lalbagh Palace, built in the early 20th century. Now a museum called the **Nehru Centre**, its gilded Rococo interiors house miniature paintings, medieval coins and tribal artifacts.

Nehru Centre
(0731) 247 3264
Tue-Sun

19

Pachmarhi

Madhya Pradesh; 210 km (130 miles) SE of Bhopal Piparia, 47 km (29 miles) N of Pachmarhi, then taxi or bus Tourist Motel, Pipariya, (07576) 22 2299; MP Tourism, Amaltas Complex Station; www.mptourism.com

This delightful hill station, at an altitude of 1,067 m (3,501 ft), lies in the verdant hills of the Satpura Range. Its attractions include waterfalls and pools, and caves with prehistoric art. Developed into a sanatorium and army station by the British in the mid-1800s, the town retains a genteel, Raj-era ambience.

Pachmarhi means "Five Houses", and the town takes its name from the five ancient Pandava Caves, set in a garden south of the bus stop. From the caves, paths lead to the scenic Apsara Vihar ("Fairy Pool"), the Bee Fall, which tumbles down for 35 m (115 ft), and the Rajat Prapat Waterfalls, a horsetail waterfall with a drop of 107 m (351 ft).

The wooded hills around Pachmarhi, home of the Gond and Korku tribes, are dotted with cave shelters, some of them with paintings dating back 10,000 years. The most accessible of them is the Mahadeo Cave, 6 km (4 miles) from the Jai Stambh ("Victory Pillar") in the centre of town. The Jatashankar Cave Temple, dedicated to Shiva, is a short excursion, 2 km (1.3 mile) from the main bus stop.

20

Jabalpur

Madhya Pradesh; 330 km (205 miles) E of Bhopal 14 km (8 miles) W of town centre MP Tourism, Railway Station & Kalchuri Residency; www.mptourism.com

The gateway to Bandhavgarh *(p298)* and Kanha *(p286)*, two of India's finest wildlife sanctuaries, Jabalpur was, from the 12th to 16th centuries, the capital of a powerful Gond tribal kingdom. The most

famous Gond ruler was Rani Durgavati, who defended her kingdom against the Mughals. In 1817 the British made it an army cantonment and administrative centre, to deal with the menace of gangs of highway bandits known as *thuggees*, who would rob travellers. In the 1830s, Colonel William Sleeman launched a campaign against the *thuggees*, and in a few years had wiped them out. The word thug (from *thuggee*), though, has found a permanent place in the English language. In the bazaar is the **Rani Durgavati Museum** with stone sculptures and Gond tribal artifacts. The ruined **Madan Mahal Fort**, built in 1116, overlooks the town from a hill to the west.

The spectacular Dhuandhar Falls are 22 km (14 miles) southwest of Jabalpur.

Rani Durgavati Museum
◈ ◷ 10am–5pm Tue–Sun
☒ Public hols

Madan Mahal Fort
◈ ☏ (0761) 267 7290
◷ 8am–6:30pm daily

INDIGENOUS ART IN MADHYA PRADESH

Madhya Pradesh is home to millions of indigenous people (referred to locally as *adivasi*, or tribal people), who maintain strong and distinctive traditions of arts and crafts. Among the most famous indigenous artists was painter Jangarh Singh Shyam, who came from a Gond community in eastern Madhya Pradesh and was internationally renowned. Bhopal's Museum of Man and Bharat Bhavan *(p279)* house many examples of indigenous paintings, sculptures, masks and other artworks, including several pieces by Shyam himself.

㉑

Mandla

⌂ Madhya Pradesh; 95 km (59 miles) SE of Jabalpur
▤▦ *ℹ* MP Tourism, Tourist Motel; (07642) 26 0599

This sleepy town sits on a loop in the Narmada river, which provides a natural moat for the 17th-century Gond Fort, now in ruins. Mandla is a sacred city for Gond people, whose warrior queen, Durgavati, committed suicide here in 1564 when she was defeated by the Mughal emperor Akbar's army. Temples and ghats line the river, where the Gonds perform their funeral rites. At the main bazaar, near the bus stand, shops sell tribal silver jewellery and bell metal.

←
Dhuandhar Falls, formed by the Narmada river in the vicinity of Jabalpur

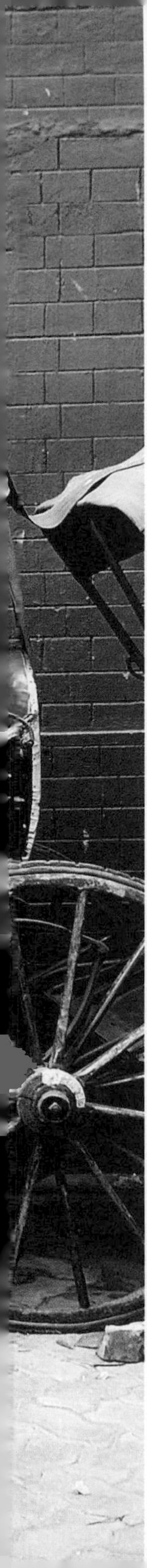

KOLKATA

One of the world's great cities, Kolkata, or Calcutta as it used to be known, has been through many incarnations. From an obscure village on the banks of the Hooghly river, it evolved into the capital of Great Britain's Indian empire. In 1690, an English merchant, Job Charnock, established a trading post in the riverside village of Sutanuti, which, together with neighbouring Govindapur and Kolikata, grew into the city of Calcutta. Over the next 200 years, the city became a flourishing commercial centre with imposing Victorian Gothic buildings, churches, and boulevards. Simultaneously, intellectual and cultural life bloomed, with a renaissance of Bengali art and literature, and the growth of a strong nationalist reform movement that led to the founding of the Brahmo Samaj, an off-shoot of Hinduism, and the establishment of Hindu – now Presidency – College, then the foremost centre of English education. The decision to shift the capital to New Delhi in 1911 and the urban decay of the 1960s diminished some of the city's affluence, but never quenched its effervescence. Today, this vibrant city with its distinct imperial flavour is the capital of the state of West Bengal.

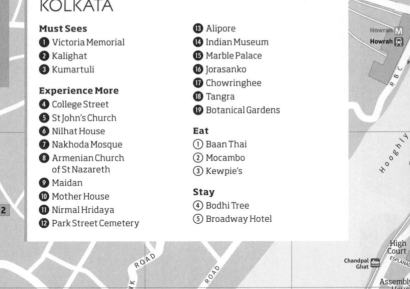

KOLKATA

Must Sees
1. Victoria Memorial
2. Kalighat
3. Kumartuli

Experience More
4. College Street
5. St John's Church
6. Nilhat House
7. Nakhoda Mosque
8. Armenian Church of St Nazareth
9. Maidan
10. Mother House
11. Nirmal Hridaya
12. Park Street Cemetery
13. Alipore
14. Indian Museum
15. Marble Palace
16. Jorasanko
17. Chowringhee
18. Tangra
19. Botanical Gardens

Eat
1. Baan Thai
2. Mocambo
3. Kewpie's

Stay
4. Bodhi Tree
5. Broadway Hotel

Hooghly

Millennium Par

High Court

Tow Ha

Chandpal Ghat

ESPLANADE ROW WE

Assembly House

Babu Ghat

Eden Gardens

Eden Gardens Park

EDEN GARDENS ROAD

GRAND TRUNK ROAD

UPPER FORESHORE ROAD

KONA EXPRESSWAY

DUKE ROAD

Hooghly

STRAND ROAD

Fort William

Vidyasagar Setu

Prinsep Ghat

Shalimar

9 Maidan

Beyond Central Kolkata

RAMRAJATALA

Hooghly

SOUTH DUM DUM

3 Kumartuli

HOWRAH

SHIBPUR

BIDHANNAGAR

BELEGHATA

Botanical Gardens
19

KOLKATA

Hooghly

area of main map

BALLYGUNGE

18 Tangra

TOPSIA

BHAWANIPUR

Alipore 13

11 Nirmal Hridaya

Kalighat 2

4

SANTOSHPUR

0 km   3
0 miles   3

N

KHIDIRPUR ROAD

CASUARINA AVE

Brigade Parade Ground

QUEEN'S WA

Race Course

HOSPITAL ROAD

1 Victoria Memorial

Polo Ground

ACHARYA JAGADISH

ALIPORE ROAD

DEBENDRA LAL KHAN ROAD

HARISH MUKHERJEE RD

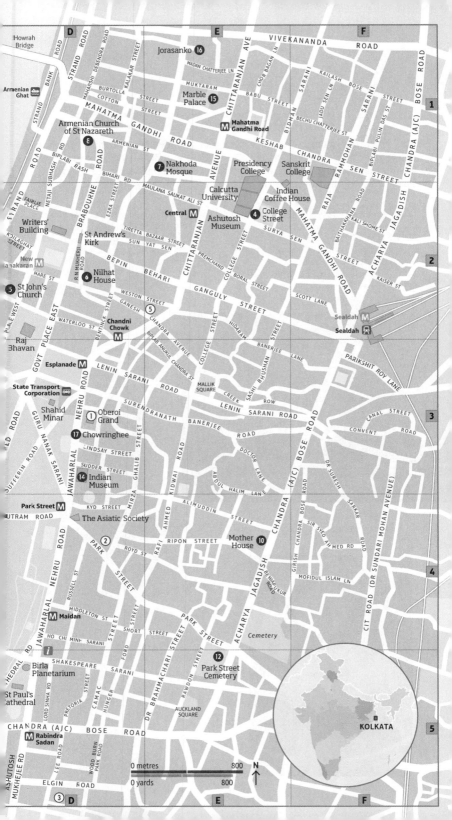

① ⑂ Ⓜ

VICTORIA MEMORIAL

📍C5 🏠1 Queen's Way ⏰Memorial: 10am–6pm Tue–Fri, 10am–8pm Sat & Sun; gardens: 5:30am–6pm daily 🚫Public hols 🌐victoriamemorial-cal.org

The city's most celebrated landmark, this monument to imperial self-confidence was the brainchild of Lord Curzon (1859–1925), one of British India's most flamboyant viceroys. The foundation stone of this impressive structure was laid by the Prince of Wales, later King George V, during his visit in 1906.

The domed Neo-Classical structure, completed in 1921, was constructed with marble from Makrana, which also supplied marble for the Taj Mahal, and financed by donations from princes and ordinary citizens. Designed by William Emerson, President of the British Institute of Architects, the building stands in spacious grounds dotted with ornamental palms, ponds and statues. Now a museum, its 25 galleries are spread over the ground and first floors. The collection, which covers a fascinating selection of Raj memorabilia, includes the Calcutta Gallery, with oil paintings and watercolours of the city's history.

↑ The ornamental and imposing white marble exterior of the Victoria Memorial

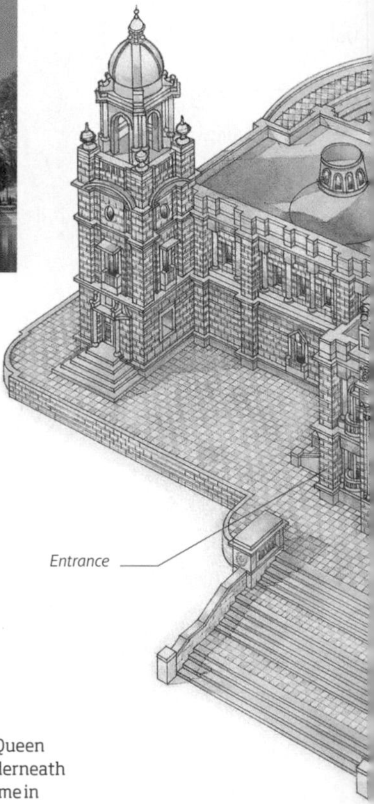

Entrance

← A statue of Queen Victoria underneath the main dome in the memorial

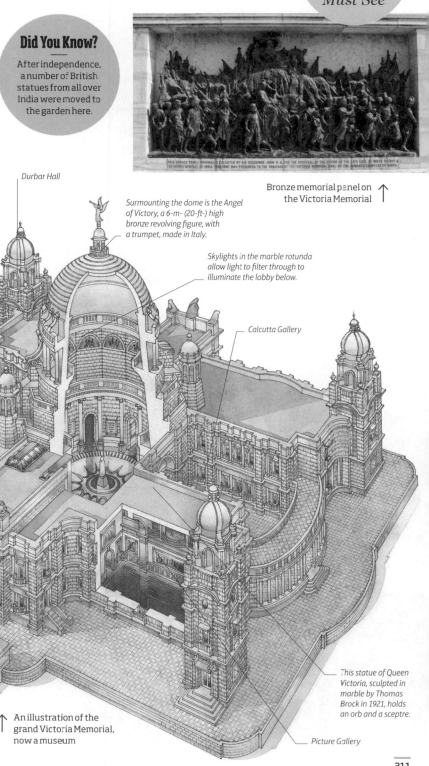

Did You Know?

After independence, a number of British statues from all over India were moved to the garden here.

Bronze memorial panel on the Victoria Memorial ↑

Durbar Hall

Surmounting the dome is the Angel of Victory, a 6-m- (20-ft-) high bronze revolving figure, with a trumpet, made in Italy.

Skylights in the marble rotunda allow light to filter through to illuminate the lobby below.

Calcutta Gallery

This statue of Queen Victoria, sculpted in marble by Thomas Brock in 1921, holds an orb and a sceptre.

↑ An illustration of the grand Victoria Memorial, now a museum

Picture Gallery

❷
KALIGHAT

📍 A5 🏛 Ashutosh Mukherjee Rd 🕐 5am–2pm & 5–10:30pm daily

Kolkata's oldest pilgrimage site, the temple complex of Kalighat finds mention in numerous medieval poems and ballads – and it is said that the city itself was named after the temple.

While the present Kali Temple dates to the early 19th century, this has been a sacred spot for much longer. One of the most famous myths associated with Kalighat is that of Shiva and Sati (*p269*). When Sati's body was chopped into 52 pieces by Vishnu's magic *chakra* (discus), her big toe landed in the spot where the temple was subsequently founded.

Although associated with Shiva and Sati, the main diety worshipped here is Kali, the Hindu goddess of death, as well as sex and violence. Primarily worshipped in south India, and particularly in West Bengal, Kali is a wild goddess, and the iconography at this temple reflects that. The image of the goddess in the dark inner sanctum is of an untamed figure, with tangled tresses and wide, ferocious eyes. Her extended tongue has a gold covering, which is changed every day.

Kalighat has, over the years, become known for Kalighat *pats*, a distinctive painting style adopted by the scroll-painters of Bengal. They use paper and water-based paints to depict contemporary subjects. A good collection of Kalighat *pats* is on display at the Indian Museum (*p319*). It is considered auspicious to visit the temple on Tuesdays as well as on Saturdays. Avoid long queues by visiting on another day.

Did You Know?

Kali is often depicted as a blue goddess with a row of human skulls around her neck.

① A woman walks through a Kolkata street that is lined with market stalls.

② An artist hard at work creating a relief artwork on a Kolkata street.

③ The Kali Temple in Kalighat displays some spectacular images of the goddess Kali.

↑ The Kali Temple, which was built on a sacred site in the 1800s

SHIVA AND SATI

In love with Shiva from a young age, Sati became such an outstanding ascetic that she won his admiration and his hand in marriage. Her father, King Daksha, was horrified and publicly insulted her husband. Sati threw herself onto a fire to immolate herself in protest, starting the notorious tradition named after her. Grief-stricken, Shiva went into a massive and very destructive rage until Sati was reincarnated as Parvati, who married her beloved once again.

A busy workshop, filled with rows of handcrafted clay gods and goddesses

③

KUMARTULI

 B4 **North Chitpur Rd, Kolkata**

Literally the "Area of the Potters", Kumartuli is a maze of alleys, where images of various Hindu gods and goddesses are sculpted. Hundreds of families, each with their own workshops, live and work here, making frames, kneading clay, shaping body parts or deftly applying paintwork to rows and rows of divine forms.

The best time to visit Kumartuli is late August and early September, when potters create the idols for the ten-day-long Durga Puja, west Bengal's favourite annual festival. Watching them at work, painstakingly moulding the clay to create images of the goddess Durga and other deities, is a fascinating experience.

Nearby is an ancient temple dedicated to Shiva, known as the Buro Shiva (Old Shiva Temple), famous as probably the only remaining terracotta temple in the city. Further away is the giant Rabindra Setu (formerly the Howrah Bridge), an airy, elegant mesh of steel that appears to float above the turgid Hooghly River *(p335)*. The sunset behind the bridge is one of the loveliest sights in the city. To its south is the impressive Vidyasagar Setu. This massive cable-stayed suspension bridge was opened in 1992 to connect south Kolkata with Shibpur and Howrah station.

↑ Potters applying the finishing touches to their handiwork

→ Detailed painting of the goddess Durga, often modelled on popular Hindi film actresses

← The ten-armed goddess Kali, the great protector, standing on the prostrate Shiva

←

Stallholders waiting for customers at the book market on College Street

the old British fort that stood on the site of the present General Post Office *(p323)* in 1756, he imprisoned over 100 British inhabitants in a small, airless cell. Only 23 people were found alive the next morning – the rest had died of asphyxiation and thirst.

EXPERIENCE MORE

④ College Street

♀ E2 **⚐ Bidhan Sarani, North Kolkata**

College Street is the heart of Bengali intellectual life. The pavements are crowded with stalls selling textbooks, exam guides, classics and second-hand books. Many of Kolkata's best bookshops are also here.

Presidency University was established in 1817 and was originally known as Hindu College. Started as an institution for the city's rich, who wanted their sons to receive a Western-style education, it is now a reputable insitution with alumni such as noted film director Satyajit Ray (1922–92) and economist Amartya Sen, who won the Nobel Prize for Economics in 1998.

Across the road is the dark, cavernous Indian Coffee House, the favourite haunt of the city's intelligentsia since it opened in 1942. Even today, waiters serve endless cups of strong coffee to teachers, students, writers and poets.

Down a lane opposite the university is the Sanskrit College, founded in 1824 to promote the study of ancient Indian languages, history and culture. Its ground floor has a small display of medieval Hindu sculpture and palm-leaf manuscripts. The buildings of Calcutta University, founded in 1857, are next to Presidency. On the ground floor, the excellent **Ashutosh Museum** specializes in the art of eastern India. The exhibits include terracottas, bronzes, old manuscripts and some exquisite examples of *kantha* (a quilting technique) and Kalighat paintings, or *pats*.

Ashutosh Museum

☎ (033) 2241 0071
🕙 10:45am–4:30pm Mon-Fri

⑤ St John's Church

♀ D2 **⚐ 2/2 Council House St** **☎ (033) 2243 6098**
🕙 8am–5pm daily

The first parish church in Kolkata, St John's was established in 1787. It features an impressive stained-glass panel of The Last Supper, in which the artist Johann Zoffany has given the 12 disciples the faces of British personalities famous in the city at the time.

A short distance away is the memorial to the victims of the Black Hole Tragedy, an event that became one of the most infamous horror stories of the Raj. When Siraj-ud-Daula, the Nawab of Bengal, captured

⑥ Nilhat House

♀ D2 **⚐ Behind Old Mission Church** **☎ (033) 2248 6201 (entry permits)** **🕙 Auctions: 9am–6:30pm Tue-Thu**

A tea auction centre, Nilhat House stands on the site of an indigo trading house (*nil* means indigo, while *hat* is market). It dates to 1861; only the tea auction houses in London are older. Tea has always played an important role in the state's economy, especially in the colonial era. Even today, the bidding for teas from Darjeeling and the Dooars in northern Bengal and Assam is brisk – although the bidding is now online for every tea except Darjeeling. Visitors can view these proceedings with prior permission.

⑦ Nakhoda Mosque

♀ E2 **⚐ 1 Zakaria St** **☎ 990 370 8808** **🕙 During prayers**

Located in central Kolkata, Nakhoda Mosque is the city's largest mosque and is based on the design of Akbar's tomb at Sikandra *(p165)*. Built in 1926, it is surmounted by a dome

→

People on the Maidan, with the imposing Victoria Memorial in the background

and faced with red sandstone, with minarets that rise to a height of 46 m (151 ft). It can accommodate over 10,000 people for prayer, but on major religious occasions, people spill out onto the street.

8 Armenian Church of St Nazareth

🚩 D1 🏛 Armenian St, near Brabourne Rd ⏰ Daily; ask the caretaker for access

Built by Armenian traders in 1724, the Armenian Church of St Nazareth stands on the site of the original 1688 wooden church, which burned down in 1707. Immigrants from Isfahan in Persia, the Armenians were among the earliest foreign traders to settle in Kolkata. Once a thriving community, today their numbers have dwindled. The church has a unique rounded spire, and its grounds house several graves with ornate tombstones.

9 Maidan

🚩 C4 🏛 Bounded by Strand Rd, AJC Bose Rd, Cathedral Rd & Eden Gardens Rd

In the heart of the city, this 400-ha (988-acre) park contains several interesting areas and buildings, such as Fort William, dating from 1781. To the north of the fort are the pleasant Eden Gardens, famous for hosting international cricket matches.

At the northern corner of the Maidan is the Burmese Pavilion, rising from a small lake. To its east is the Shahid Minar. It was originally called Ochterlony Monument after Sir David Ochterlony, who led the British armies to victory in the Anglo-Nepal War in 1816. The monument is a fluted Doric column, 48-m (157-ft) high with a cupola for a roof. To its south is the Maidan's most impressive building, the Victoria Memorial (p310).

Not far from the Memorial is **St Paul's Cathedral**, which was designed by Major WN Forbes in 1847. Its grounds are lined with trees, and the interior is notable for a superb stained-glass window designed by Edward Burne-Jones.

Kolkata Race Course, the largest in India, is on the southwestern corner of the Maidan. Racing is popular in Kolkata and races are held throughout the year. Polo is played here for a few weeks in the winter season.

St Paul's Cathedral

⏰ Church: 10am–6pm daily; services: 7:30am, 8:30am, 10:30am & 6pm Sun

---

⑩ Mother House

📍 E4 🏠 54A AJC Bose Rd
🕐 8am-noon & 3-6pm Fri-
Wed 🚫 Easter Mon, 22 Aug,
26 Dec 🌐 motherteresa.org

Kolkata is inextricably linked
to Mother Teresa. At first, she
was a teaching nun at Loreto
Convent, but the death and
devastation she witnessed in
the city during the famine of
1943 and the Partition of India
in 1947 (p209) made her leave
this cloistered world and dedi-
cate her life to the poor. The
Missionaries of Charity was a
new order she formed in 1950,
with the Mother House as its
headquarters. This simple
building is today also her final
resting place. Her grave, on
the ground floor, has no ornamentation, only a Bible placed
on it. On a board on the wall
are two words, "I thirst".

⑪ Nirmal Hridaya

📍 A5 🏠 251 Kalighat Rd
📞 (033) 2464 4223
🕐 8-11am & 3-5pm daily

Mother Teresa's home for the
destitute, Nirmal Hridaya
("Pure Heart") is near the Kali
Temple (p312). The site was

probably chosen because the
temple teems with people
who come here to die and
attain *moksha*. A large, clean
hall is full of beds for the sick
and dying, who are cared for
by nuns in their characteristic
white-and-blue saris. Visitors
who want to work as volunteers must first register at
Mother House.

⑫ Park Street Cemetery

📍 E5 🏠 Bounded by
Rawdon St & Park St
🕐 10am-6pm Mon-Fri

A romantic, overgrown haven
in the middle of the city, away
from the heat and crowds,
Park Street Cemetery was
opened in 1767 to receive the
body of John Wood, an official
in the Custom House of the
East India Company. From
then until the first half of the
19th century, it served as the
resting place of many important Europeans who died in
Kolkata. William Jones, the
great scholar and founder of
The Asiatic Society (p321), lies
under a pyramid-shaped
tomb. Visitors will also find the
graves of Henry Vansittart,
one of the first British governors of Bengal, and Henry
Louis Vivian Derozio (1809–

1831), a Eurasian teacher at
Hindu College in the mid-19th
century, who died at the age
of 23. Derozio was one of the
pioneers of what has come to
be known as the Bengal
Renaissance, a movement
which championed local
culture and social change.
The best-known tomb is that
of Rose Aylmer, an early love
of the poet Walter Savage
Landor. A spiralled obelisk,
it is inscribed with lines by
Landor. Also buried here is
Colonel Kyd, founder of the
city's Botanical Gardens (p321).

⑬ Alipore

📍 A5 🏠 Bounded by AJC
Bose Rd, Belvedere Rd &
Alipore Rd

The city's most fashionable
address, the suburb of Alipore
in south Kolkata is a world
of tree-lined avenues with

STAY

Bodhi Tree

Enjoy the beautiful
decor and artworks at
this quirky boutique
guesthouse in a quiet
neighbourhood.

🏠 48/44 Swiss
Park, Tollygunge
🌐 bodhitreekolkata.com

₹₹₹

Broadway Hotel

Barely changed since
1937, this hotel has big
rooms, an Art Deco bar-
restaurant and loads
of faded charm.

🏠 27A Ganesh Chandra
Avenue, Bowbazar
🌐 broadwayhotel.in

₹₹₹

↑ Taking in the tombs and mausoleums in the
verdant surrounds of Park Street Cemetery

palatial houses surrounded by well-kept lawns. **Alipore Zoological Gardens**, was established here in 1875 and has a large collection of birds and mammals. Nearby, the Belvedere Estate houses the **National Library**, with over two million manuscripts and books. The library has since expanded to the Bhasha Bhawan, another building in the same grounds. The Belvedere was built in the Italian Renaissance style and was once the residence of

Animal skeletons in the Indian Museum, and (inset) the grand museum building ↑

Bengal's lieutenant governors. The lush gardens of the **Agri Horticultural Society**, founded in 1820 by the missionary William Carey to develop and promote agri-culture and horticulture in India, are also found here. In the society's first 40 years, they imported seeds, bulbs and plants from England, South Africa and southeast Asia. Since then it has amassed a varied collection of rare flowering trees and herbs.

Alipore Zoological Gardens

🌐 🏠 2 Alipore Rd 🕐 9am-5pm Fri-Wed 🌐 kolkatazoo.in

National Library

🌐 🏠 Belvedere Road 🕐 9am-8pm Mon-Fri, 9:30am-6pm Sat & Sun 🚫 Public hols 🌐 nationallibrary.gov.in

Agri Horticultural Society

🏠 1 Alipore Rd 🕐 7-10am & 2-6pm Mon-Sat (only to members and guests)

14 ⊗ ⊗

Indian Museum

📍 D3 🏠 27 JL Nehru Rd
📞 (033) 2249 9902/9979
🕐 10am-5pm Tue-Sun
🚫 Public hols

The country's oldest and largest museum, the Indian Museum was founded in 1814. The imposing building was designed by Walter Granville, who was also the architect of the General Post Office (p323), and dates to 1878. Highlights of the collection include artifacts from the 2,500 BC Indus Valley civilization, sculpture from Gandhara, the superbly sculpted railings from the 2,000-year-old Bharhut Stupa, and a display of 5th-century Gupta coins, as well as fine paintings and miniatures. The Zoological Section exhibits stuffed birds from British zoological expeditions.

TOP 3 MODERN ART GALLERIES

Verandah Art Gallery
🌐 verandahart.com
This Sreepally gallery promotes the city's best emerging artists.

Chitrakoot Gallery
🌐 chitrakootart.com
Near the Museum of Modern Art, this has an unrivalled collection.

Experimenter Gallery
🌐 experimenter.in
Dynamic art shown in a space on Hindusthan Rd.

THE DURGA PUJA

Durga Puja is west Bengal's favourite annual festival. Usually held between September and October, it heralds the advent of autumn and the new harvest. Brightly illuminated *pandals* (bamboo structures), often shaped like famous monuments such as the Taj Mahal, are erected on roads and in parks, and an image of the goddess Durga is installed within. Presents are exchanged and great feasts are prepared. On the final day, the images are immersed in the Hooghly, to the beating of drums and cries of "Jai Ma Durga!" ("Hail to Mother Durga!").

Did You Know?

Rabindranath Tagore's prolific output includes over 2,000 songs, plus numerous poems and paintings.

Today, the old house has been expanded and turned into Rabindra Bharati University, which specializes in the study of Bengali cultural forms. The house itself has been preserved as the **Rabindra Bharati Museum**. Beginning with the room in which Rabindranath Tagore died, it traces the history of this illustrious family and contains a large collection of art and memorabilia.

Rabindra Bharati Museum
⊗ ☎ (033) 2269 6610
☐ 10am–5pm Mon–Fri, 10am–2pm Sat & Sun

15
Marble Palace

☐ E1 ☐ 46 Muktaram Babu St ☎ (033) 2269 3310, 2248 8271 (entry permits) ☐ 10am–3:30pm Tue, Wed & Fri

This opulent mansion was built in 1835 by Raja Rajendra Mullick, a wealthy *zamindar* (landowner). His descendants still live here, but most of the house is open to visitors. Rajendra Mullick travelled extensively in Europe and brought back an eclectic collection of Venetian chandeliers, Ming vases and Egyptian statuary that he housed in his Classical-fronted mansion, built around a colonnaded courtyard. Today, the Marble Palace – named for the nearly 100 varieties of marble on the floors – provides a glimpse into the life of a rich 19th-century Bengali household.

16
Jorasanko

☐ E1 ☐ 6/4 Dwarkanath Tagore Lane

A major centre of Bengali art and culture in the 19th century, Jorasanko is the ancestral home of Bengal's favourite son, Rabindranath Tagore. Built in 1785, this simple three-storeyed, red-brick structure housed the lively and cultivated Tagore family, many members of which were prominent intellectuals and social reformers. The lane on which the house is located is named after Dwarkanath Tagore (1794–1846), the poet's father and a wealthy entrepreneur.

→ Statue of the poet Rabindranath Tagore at Jorasanko, his home

17
Chowringhee

☐ D3 ☐ JL Nehru Rd

Now called Jawaharlal Nehru Road, Chowringhee was a fashionable promenade during the Raj. At its northern end is the Oberoi Grand, once considered "the most popular, fashionable and attractive Hotel in India". Behind it is New Market, built in 1874. Surmounted by a clock tower, shops here are placed along many interconnected corridors. One of the oldest is the Jewish confectionery and bakery, Nahoum's, which has a beguiling variety of cookies, fudge and spiced cakes.

At its southern end, on Park Street, is the **Asiatic Society**,

→ A store selling baskets at New Market, built in the 19th century on Chowringhee

founded in 1784 by Sir William Jones, a formidable Oriental scholar. He was the first to establish the common origins of Latin and Sanskrit, and called Sanskrit the "mother of all languages". The Society's museum and library have a collection of over 60,000 old and rare manuscripts in Sanskrit, Arabic and Persian, plus artifacts such as a 3rd-century BC stone edict, and 17th-century folios from the *Badshahnama*, Abdul Hamid Lahori's history of the Mughal emperor Shah Jahan's rule.

Asiatic Society

⌖ 1 Park St ⏲ Library: 10am–5pm Mon–Sat; museum: 10am–6pm Mon–Fri
🌐 asiaticsocietykolkata.org

---

⑱

Tangra

⌖ B5 ⏲ Off the Eastern Metropolitan Bypass

This eastern suburb is the city's new Chinatown. Chinese immigration to Kolkata began in the 18th century, and today large numbers of this still significant community have settled in the area. A Chinese newspaper and journal are published from here, and there are many excellent and tiny restaurants, mostly extensions of family kitchens. "Tangra Chinese", with its discernibly Indian flavour, is today as distinct a cuisine as Szechuan and Cantonese.

---

⑲

Botanical Gardens

⌖ A5 ⏲ W bank of the Hooghly river, Shibpur
🚢 From Babu Ghat ☏ (033) 6732 3135 ⏲ 6am–5pm daily

The Botanical Gardens, in the Shibpur suburb of Howrah, was established in 1787 by Colonel Kyd, an official of the East India Company. It has an astonishing array of flora including ferns, cacti and palms, as well as plants from every continent.
The chief attraction is the magnificent banyan tree *(Ficus bengalensis)*. Claimed to be the largest banyan

INSIDER TIP
Jamsteady

Jamsteady *(jamsteady. in)* is a regular live music night held in Kolkata's excellent Princeton Club. Usually held on a Friday – although sometimes on other nights too – it showcases the city's best independent sounds with a line-up of local artists.

tree in the world, it is more than 200 years old, and its branches, giving rise to nearly 300 aerial roots, spread over 60 m (197 ft). The central trunk was, however, struck by lightning in 1919 and was subsequently removed.
Although it has regular opening hours, if you wish to see the **Palm House**, be sure to plan a morning visit, since it may be closed in the afternoon for security reasons.

Palm House
⏲ 10am–5pm daily

A SHORT WALK
BBD BAGH

Distance 2.5 km (1.5 miles) **Nearest Metro**
BBD Bagh **Time** 40 minutes

The "heart" of Kolkata, this area was the site of the
original Kolikata, one of the villages from which the
city grew. In 1930, three young Indian freedom fighters,
Binay, Badal and Dinesh, shot the British inspector-
general of police inside the Writers' Building. The
square, now named after them, is ringed by British
colonial buildings dating to the 18th and early
19th centuries. This area is a stroll through Kolkata's
history as the centre of colonial India.

Did You Know?

Lal Dighi, or the "Red
Pool", is named after
the coloured tint it has
acquired from the
Holi festival.

*Job Charnock's Tomb can
be found here. Charnock is
believed to have laid the
foundations of the English
settlement in Kolkata.*

STRAND ROAD

HARE STR

*The design of St John's Church was
based on London's St Martin-in-the-
Fields. The construction engineers
wanted the spire to be higher, but
desisted, fearing the soggy sub-soil.*

KS RAY ROAD

High Court

COUNCIL H

ESPLANADE ROW

START

0 metres 100
0 yards 100

N

↑ St John's Church, set in
a peaceful garden in
the city centre

*The magnificent Neo-Classical Gates of
Raj Bhavan lead to the old Government
House, built in the mid-18th century. This is
now the residence of the state governor.*

Kolkata's General Post Office, housed in this building, has an impressive rotunda. Designed by Walter Granville and built in the 1860s, it stands on the site of the old mud fort.

Locator Map
For more detail see p308

KOLKATA

Around BBD Bagh

The hub of colonial India from 1777, the **Writers' Building** derives its name from the "writers" (clerks) of the East India Company who worked here.

Consecrated in 1818, **St Andrew's Kirk** has a soaring steeple, a magnificent organ and a beautifully carved pulpit.

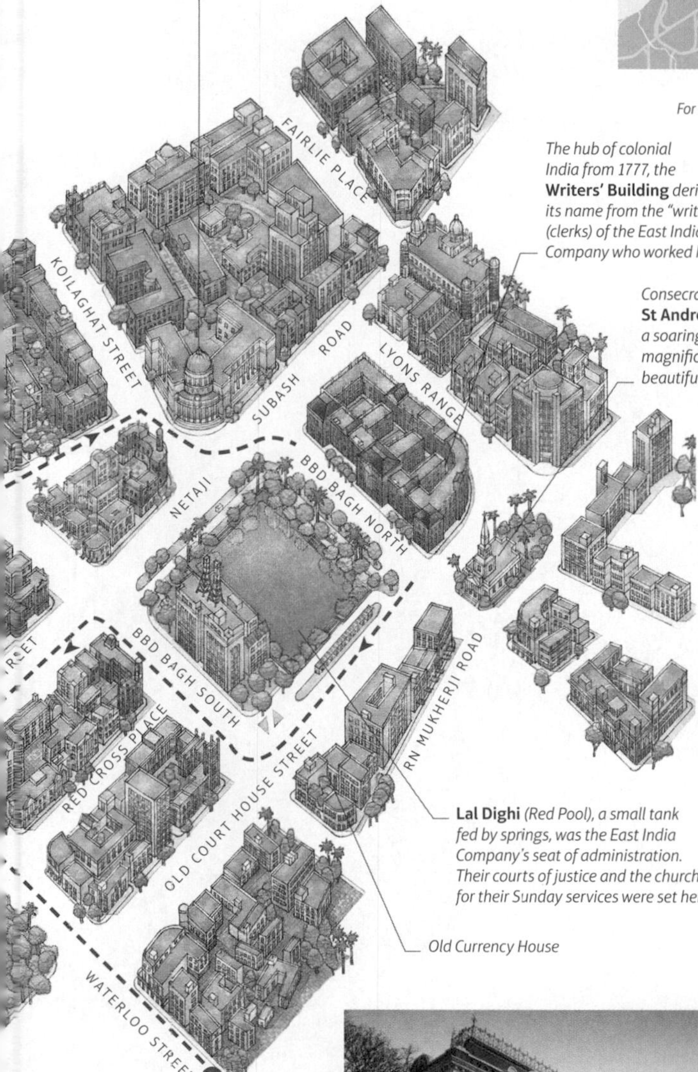

FAIRLIE PLACE

KOILAGHAT STREET

SUBASH ROAD

NETAJI

BBD BAGH NORTH

LYONS RANGE

BBD BAGH SOUTH

RED CROSS PLACE

OLD COURT HOUSE STREET

RN MUKHERJI ROAD

STREET

Lal Dighi (Red Pool), a small tank fed by springs, was the East India Company's seat of administration. Their courts of justice and the churches for their Sunday services were set here.

Old Currency House

WATERLOO STREET

FINISH

→ The Corinthian façade of the imposing Writers' Building

Workers on a tea plantation in Darjeeling

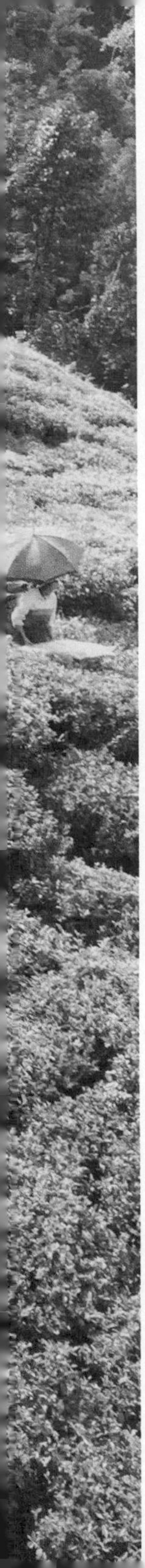

WEST BENGAL AND SIKKIM

The neighbouring states of West Bengal and Sikkim have wildly divergent histories that bely their geographic proximity. Remote Sikkim, which borders Bhutan, Nepal and China, is ringed by mountains, and has long been home to three main indigenous groups: the Lepcha, Limbu and Magar peoples. A Buddhist monarchy was established in the 17th century, when three lamas proclaimed Phuntsog Namgyal as Sikkim's first priest-king. The monarchy survived incursions by Nepal and Bhutan, as well as dominance by China, before the British Raj established control here – although the monarchy maintained nominal power. Sikkim's final priest-king only ceded the state to the Indian Union in 1975.

West Bengal, with its capital Kolkata, has long been the cradle of Bengali culture, even though it has been subject to numerous occupying forces over its long history, from the Mauryan Empire to the Delhi Sultanate. Kolkata was later capital of the colonial Raj, although many British residents escaped to the cooler hill station of Darjeeling, famous for its tea production, during summer. When India achieved independence in 1947, Bengal was split into east and west. The east section, once part of Pakistan, now forms the country of Bangladesh.

Jigme Dorji
National Park

H i m a l a y a s

Faro   Thimphu   Trongsa

Paro
International
Airport

BHUTAN   Mongar

Gelephu

WEST BENGAL
AND SIKKIM

13 JALDAPARA
WILDLIFE SANCTUARY

Madarihat

NH27

Alipurduar

NH17

Koch
Bihar

Nalbari   Rangia   ASSAM   Nagaon

ASSAM AND
THE NORTHEAST
p358

NH27

Guwahati   NH27

NH17   Lokpriya Gopinath Bordoloi
International Airport   NH27

Rangpur

NH6

MEGHALAYA   Shillong   Umrangso

N5

Tura   Nongstoin   NH106   Dauki   Haflong

Garo   Hills   NH6

Brahmaputra   Osmani International Airport   N2

Bogra   Sylhet   NH37

Silchar

Mymensingh

Sirajganj   N4   N3

BANGLADESH

Padma

Magura   N7   N8   N1

Hazrat Shahjalal
International Airport   Dhaka

Cormilla

Madaripur

N7   N8

Khulna

WEST BENGAL
AND SIKKIM

Must Sees
1 The Sundarbans
2 Shyama Raya Temple
3 Darjeeling

Experience More
4 Hooghly River
5 Dakshineshwar
6 Belur Math
7 Barddhaman
8 Shantiniketan
9 Murshidabad
10 Gaur
11 Pandua
12 Siliguri
13 Jaldapara Wildlife Sanctuary
14 Kurseong
15 Kalimpong
16 Gangtok
17 Yuksam
18 Tashiding Monastery
19 Pelling

Bay of Bengal

① ⊗ ⊗

THE SUNDARBANS

🏠 24 Parganas district, West Bengal; 168 km (104 miles) SE of Kolkata ⏰ All year; tours compulsory 🛈 Field Director, (03218) 255 280 (permits); Tourist Department, Kolkata; www.wbtourismgov.in

The vast Ganges–Brahmaputra Delta, an intricate network of waterways, creeks and alluvial islands, covers some 105,000 sq km (40,541 sq miles) and has the world's largest tropical mangrove forest, home to an abundance of wildlife.

The Sundarbans Reserve Forest, stretching across 4,230 sq km (1,633 sq miles), was created within the Ganges–Brahmaputra Delta and declared a Tiger Reserve in 1973 to protect the endangered Royal Bengal tiger. A part of the reserve also houses the Sundarbans National Park, a UNESCO World Heritage Site covering 1,330 sq km (514 sq miles). The wetlands abound with marine life, including crustaceans and dolphins, as well as reptiles such as Olive Ridley turtles and estuarine crocodiles. Hundreds of species of birds, including many waterfowl, can be seen here. Tours are compulsory, though rowboats with boatmen are available to hire from Sajnakhali. The best time to visit is between September and April.

The western boundary of the Sundarbans has a number of popular beaches and reserves, all of which can be reached by road or boat. Millions of pilgrims gather on Sagar Island at Ganga Sagar for the annual Ganga Sagar Mela during Makar Sankranti in January. Diamond Harbour is a popular picnic spot, while Bakkhali and Digha have beautiful beaches and are popular resorts. Bakkhali is also a haven for birdlife.

Spotted deer galloping through a mangrove forest, and *(inset)* visitors gliding quietly through the waters

TALE OF THE TIGER

The tiger plays a major role in India's cultural history as a symbol of power. In Hindu iconography, the goddess Durga is often portrayed riding a tiger, while Shiva wears its skin. Tiger images can also be seen in vibrant murals in Buddhist monasteries. In the Sundarbans, ritual offerings are made to the forest deity Banbibi, to seek protection from tigers. Yet statistics belie their mythic status. In 1900, India's tiger population was 40,000; by 1972 it had fallen to 1,800. Alarmed, the Indian government launched Project Tiger *(p174)*. India now has about 70 per cent of the world's tiger population, protected in 28 reserves across the country.

→ Several generations living in one of the Bangladeshi settlements in the Sundarbans

↑ The estuarine, or saltwater, crocodile ("saltie"), one of the world's largest reptiles

2

SHYAMA RAYA TEMPLE

⌂ Bankura district, West Bengal; 132 km (82 miles) NW of Kolkata 🚗🚌 ⏲ Daily

The elaborately adorned terracotta temples of Bishnupur, legacy of the once-powerful Malla dynasty, date from the 17th and mid-18th centuries. The most imposing of these was the Shyama Raya Temple, built in 1673.

Bishnupur was the capital of the Malla kings, a dynasty of oscillating power and influence who ruled for over a thousand years. At the time Shyama Raya Temple was constructed, Bishnupur was at the heart of a flourishing of Bengali culture, which saw developments in arts, culture and architecture, such as these temples. The well-preserved Shyama Raya, made of red clay bricks, stands out against the vibrant green and ochre colours of the landscape. It is richly decorated with scenes from Lord Krishna's life as well as episodes from the *Ramayana* and other motifs.

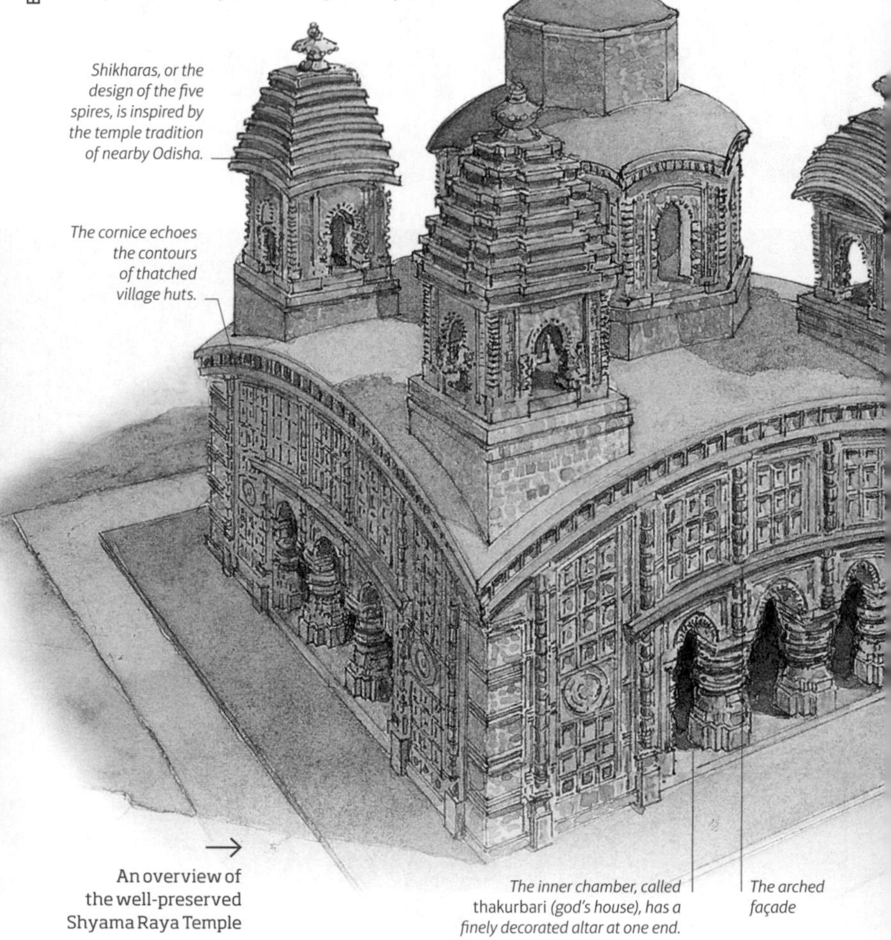

Shikharas, or the design of the five spires, is inspired by the temple tradition of nearby Odisha.

The cornice echoes the contours of thatched village huts.

→ An overview of the well-preserved Shyama Raya Temple

The inner chamber, called thakurbari (god's house), has a finely decorated altar at one end.

The arched façade

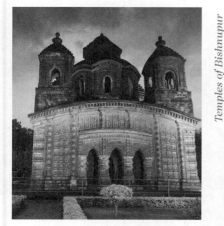

The intricately decorated façade of the Shyama Raya Temple

Scenes from the epics alternate with scenes from daily life on the friezes. Here, Krishna plays his flute for the gopis (milkmaids).

Temples of Bishnupur

Rasa Mancha Temple

▷ The Rasa Mancha Temple, built by the ruler Bir Hambir in the late 16th century, has 108 pillars and a pyramidal roof. Images of Krishna and Radha were displayed here for the Rasa Festival, a tradition that continues today.

Keshta Raya (Jor Bangla) Temple

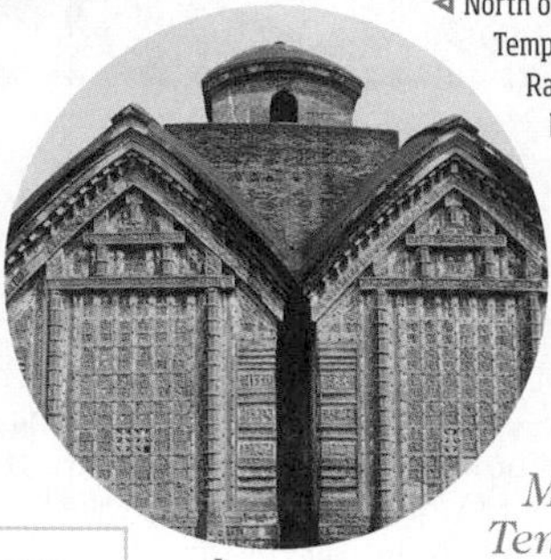

◁ North of the Rasa Mancha Temple is the large Keshta Raya (Jor Bangla) Temple, built in 1655. It has joined twin roofs, and floral motifs, scroll work and scenes from the *Ramayana* and *Mahabharata* embellish the friezes on the walls.

Madan Mohan Temple

▷ The Madan Mohan Temple, further north than Keshta Raya, is named after another name for the god Krishna. It was built in 1694 by King Durjana Singh Deva and has friezes showing events from the life of Krishna. Similarly to Shyama Raya Temple, it has a distinctive pyramidal roof structure.

Shridhara Temple

To the northwest of Madan Mohan Temple, Shridhara Temple was built later than many other temples here, in the 19th century. It was thought to have been built by a local family. This temple is also distinguished from the others by its design; it has nine spires or *nav ratna*. Shridhara Temple is one of the more popular temples here, mainly for its wonderful friezes. The frieze at the entrance shows the god Shiva dancing, and other remarkable carvings depict scenes from the famous epics of the *Ramayana* and *Mahabharata*.

BANKURA HORSES

The region around Bishnupur is known for its folk art, including a variety of clay handicrafts. The district's most famous product is the Bankura horse, a stylized animal with a long neck and elongated ears, in warm terracotta colours. Artisans have used the same techniques of hollow clay moulding and firing for generations. Sizes vary from palm-sized toys to gigantic creations over 1 m (3 ft) high. The horses are votive figures, usually placed in front of shrines.

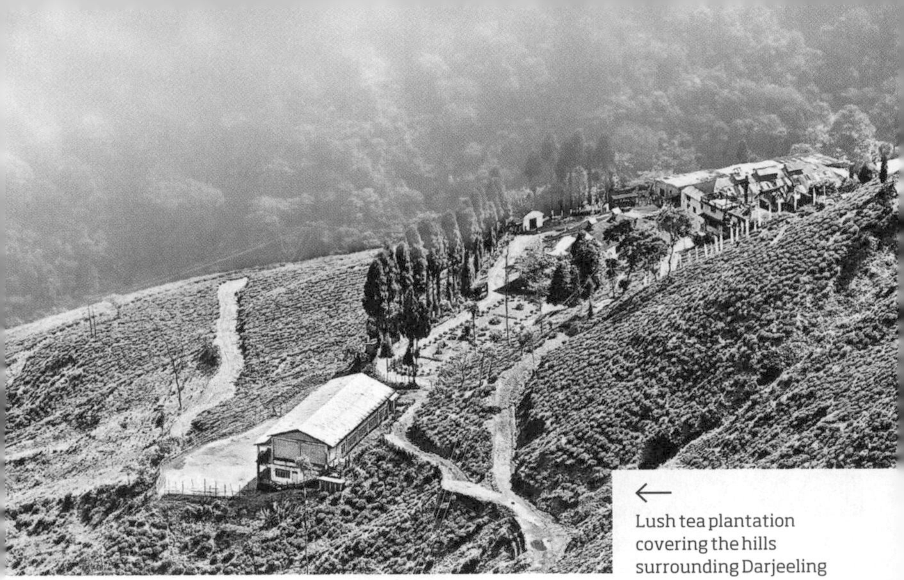

Lush tea plantation covering the hills surrounding Darjeeling

3

DARJEELING

Darjeeling district, West Bengal; 79 km (49 miles) NW of Siliguri Bagdogra, 90 km (56 miles) S of city centre, then bus or taxi Tourist Information Centre, 1 Nehru Road, Chowrasta; www.wbtourism.gov.in

The name Darjeeling derives from the monastery of Dorje Ling (meaning Place of the Thunderbolt) that once stood on Observatory Hill. In the mid-19th century, the British built a sanatorium here, and subsequently Darjeeling became Bengal's summer capital.

①

The Mall

Darjeeling's main hub, The Mall – otherwise known as Chowrasta Square (cross-roads) – is lined with shops selling teas, curios and souvenirs. On one corner of the Mall, the Tea Museum relates the local history of tea plantations.

②

Bhutia Busty Monastery

1 km (0.5 miles) E of the Mall Sunrise-sunset daily

Built in 1879, this monastery is where the cult text *The Tibetan Book of the Dead* was found, in the library attached to the shrine. It was translated into English in 1927. The murals in the temple are beautiful – but visitors are required to ask for permission before entering.

③

Observatory Hill

1 km (0.5 miles) NE of the Mall

Kanchenjunga, India's highest peak at 8,588 m (28,209 ft), dominates the town. Excellent views of the snow-clad range of the Eastern Himalayan peaks can be enjoyed from the windy, prayer flag-lined Observatory Hill.

STAY

Mayfair Darjeeling
A deluxe hotel with top service and great views.
Mall Road, Chauk Bazaar, Darjeeling mayfairhotels.com
₹₹₹

Glenburn Tea Estate
There are spacious suites and breathtaking scenery at this working tea plantation.
Off Rishi Road (Darjeeling-Kalimpong Road) glenburnteaestate.com
₹₹₹

Cedar Inn
A beautiful boutique hotel in a big old house - ask for a room with views of Kanchenjunga.
Jalpahar Road, below St Paul's School, Darjeeling cedarinndarjeeling.com
₹₹₹

④ 🗺️
Himalayan Mountaineering Institute

📍 Birch Hill Park, entrance on Jawahar Rd West
🕐 Institute: Mon-Fri; museum: Fri-Wed
🌐 hmidarjeeling.com

The Himalayan Mountaineering Institute is to the south of North Point on Birch Hill. Its Mountaineering Museum has a fascinating contour model of the Himalayan peaks, while the Everest Museum gives a history of the various attempts to climb Everest and other Himalayan peaks. The adjacent Himalayan Zoo is famous for its high-altitude fauna, including snow leopards, Siberian tigers and red pandas.

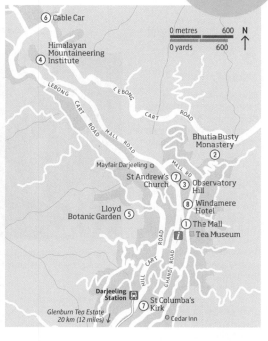

⑤
Lloyd Botanic Garden

📍 Chauk Bazaar 🕐 6am-5pm daily

This peaceful garden is home to an interesting and varied collection of Himalayan flora – the hundreds of species of orchids in its Orchid House are particularly lovely.

⑥
Cable Car

📍 North Point

In the northwest corner of town is a cable car connecting Darjeeling to Singla Bazaar in the Little Rangeet Valley. The hour-long journey provides a view of the mountains and the valley's tea gardens.

⑦
St Andrew's Church and St Columba's Kirk

📍 Chauk Bazaar

Darjeeling has some well-preserved colonial churches.

St Andrew's Church, west of Observatory Hill, was built in 1843, though the clock tower was added later. St Columba's Kirk, near the train station, was built in 1894 and is worth a visit for its magnificent stained-glass windows.

⑧
Windamere Hotel

📍 Observatory Hill
🌐 windamerehotel.com

Some of the best-preserved examples of Raj-era grandeur in India are Darjeeling's hotels and clubs. Just above Observatory Hill is potentially the most well known of this ilk, the rattan-and-chintz-decorated Windamere Hotel, which, in its heyday, was visited by British aristocrats and Indian royalty. Open fires heat the sedate lounge, which is decorated by old hunting prints. Tea here is a throwback to the Raj, with maids serving sandwiches and Darjeeling tea as a string quartet plays.

DARJEELING TEA

Darjeeling is known as the Champagne of teas. Its biscuity Muscatel flavour comes from the area's particular soil and elevation, and from its use of the small-leafed, Chinese variety of the tea bush. There are four seasonal "flushes", with the light first flush and the full-bodied second flush being the best. Darjeeling tea comes in various grades - from whole-leaf Flowery Orange Pekoe to Broken Orange Pekoe, fannings and dust. Purists drink it without milk.

EXPERIENCE MORE

4

Hooghly River

🏛 West Bengal; 24 km (15 miles) N from Kolkata to Shrirampur 🚉🚌🚢 ℹ Babu Ghat (near Eden Gardens) or Tourism Centre; www.wbtourism.gov.in

Upon entering the lower Gangetic Plains in West Bengal, the Ganges breaks up into many channels. The main distributary, the Hooghly (also known as Hugli), flows 260 km (162 miles) from Murshidabad to the Bay of Bengal.

Between the 15th and 19th centuries, this navigable river attracted Dutch, Portuguese, French, Danish and British traders. Their settlements transformed the river banks into a mini Europe – the remnants of which can be best explored today by taking one of the river cruises.

Up river from Kolkata is Shrirampur (Serampore), a Danish colony until 1845. Dr William Carey, the first Baptist missionary in India, set up a printing press here in 1799 and translated the Bible into several Indian languages, including Bengali, marking the beginnings of modern Bengali prose. He also founded the first theological college, today Shrirampur College, in 1818. Its library houses a priceless collection of 18th- and 19th-century books.

↑ Climbing up to an old house in Chandannagar, a former French settlement on the Hooghly river

On the east bank is the city of Barakpur (Barrackpore), the site of the British viceroys' once-gracious country house. The mansion, known locally as Lat Bagan ("Governor's or Lord's Garden"), was built by Lord Wellesley in the early 19th century.

Chandannagar (Chandernagore), a French settlement from 1673 until 1952, still retains a Gallic ambience, courtesy of the public benches on the waterfront, replicas of those found in Paris parks. The Église du Sacré Cœur has a statue of Joan of Arc and a Lourdes grotto.

North of Chandannagar is Chinsurah (Chunchura), an Armenian settlement taken over by the Dutch in 1625 and later by the British. The Armenian Church was built in 1697, though the steeple was added a century later.

Further upriver is Bandel, founded by the Portuguese in 1580. The Church of Our Lady of Bandel, consecrated in 1599, is the oldest in eastern India. People of all faiths still pray at the statue of Our Lady of Happy Voyages, an icon with an interesting history. In 1632, while the city was being sacked by the Mughal emperor Shah Jahan, the icon was lost in the river, but later reappeared miraculously on the banks in front of the church. Further north is Bansberia, site of several terracotta temples. The Ananta Vasudeva Temple, built in 1679, has a panel of warriors carved above the entrance, while the nearby Hanseshwari Temple, built in 1814, has a fabulous array of Kremlin-like onion domes and an elaborately carved façade.

5

Dakshineshwar

🏛 West Bengal; 12 km (7 miles) N of Kolkata 🚉🚌 🕐 5am-8pm daily ℹ www.wbtourism.gov.in

North of Kolkata, on the east bank of the Hooghly river, Dakshineshwar is one of Bengal's most popular pilgrimage spots. The temple, built in 1855 by a rich and pious widow, Rani Rashmoni, was initially opposed by orthodox religious interests, because Rashmoni was not a Brahmin (the highest Indian caste). No Brahmin was willing to be the temple priest. Only

Ramakrishna Paramhansa, then still a boy, agreed, and he spent many years there, preaching and developing his philosophy of the essential oneness of all faiths.

The whitewashed temple is set on a high plinth and topped by nine cupolas. The roof, with its line of rounded cornices, stands out against the sky. Inside the sanctum is an image of Bhabatarini, an incarnation of the goddess Kali. Within the large compound, strung along the river bank, are 12 smaller temples, each dedicated to the god Shiva. Crowds of pilgrims visit Dakshineshwar daily, lending the sprawling temple complex a cheerful and bustling atmosphere. Visitors should dress conservatively.

6

Belur Math

🏠 West Bengal; 10 km (6 miles) N of Kolkata 🚌🚆 Or taxi from Kolkata ⏰ Hours vary, check website 🌐 belurmath.org

On the west bank of the Hooghly river is Belur Math, the headquarters of the Ramakrishna Mission. The

→
The Dakshineshwar Temple, on the banks of the Hooghly river

RAMAKRISHNA PARAMHANSA

Ramakrishna was born in 1836. He became a priest at Dakshineshwar, where he began a life of prayer and meditation. His philosophy was lucid – there is an inherent truth in all religions, and a simple life is a pure life. His teachings were carried to the USA and to Britain by his main disciple Swami Vivekananda (1863–1902), who set up many Ramakrishna Mission centres abroad for religious studies.

order was established in 1897 by the reformist Hindu crusader Swami Vivekananda, Ramakrishna Paramhansa's foremost disciple. The modern temple within the sprawling complex was built in 1938 and embodies

Ramakrishna's philosophy, based on the unity of all faiths. The ground plan is in the shape of a cross, the windows have arches reminiscent of Mughal buildings, the gate shows Buddhist influence and Hindu architectural motifs decorate the façade. Visitors should dress conservatively.

7

Barddhaman

🏠 West Bengal; 125 km (78 miles) NW of Kolkata 🚌 🌐 www.wbtourism.gov.in

The rajas of Barddhaman (Burdwan) were once powerful landlords and great patrons of the arts. Today, the small, town is a gateway to some interesting sites. The rajas built several temples at Kalna, 50 km (31 miles) to the east, in the 18th and 19th centuries. The Shiva Temple, with 108 minor shrines, is the most impressive. Nabadwip, 20 km (12 miles) to the north of Kalna, was the birthplace of Sri Chaitanya (1486–1533), founder of the movement that revived the Krishna cult (p187). Nabadwip is a charming town, with a few old houses built of the narrow red brick, unique to pre-British Bengal. Many pilgrims throng the Gauranga Temple here.

Students of Shantiniketan's Kala Bhavan, the fine arts department, celebrating Holi

country's leading artists, such as Binode Bihari Mukherjee (1904–80), Nandalal Bose (1882–1966) and Ram Kinkar Baij (1910–80).

The university's excellent **Vichitra Museum**, open daily, has memorabilia from the poet's life, including his paintings, developed from the sketches he made in the margins of his written work. Excellent performances of Rabindra Sangeet (songs written and set to music by Tagore) can be heard at the campus every evening.

The nearby village of Kenduli is the birthplace of the medieval poet Jayadeva, who composed the *Gita Govinda*, a paean to Krishna. Every year in January the Bauls, a community of wandering mystic minstrels known for their soulful songs and saffron robes, gather here for Kendulimela, a three-day festival of music.

Visva Bharati University
⊘ 🕐 Hours vary, check website 🅦 visvabharati.ac.in

8

Shantiniketan

🏠 West Bengal; 213 km (132 miles) NW of Kolkata 🚉 Bolpur, 3 km (2 miles) S of Shantiniketan, then rickshaw 🚌 Bolpur 🅕 www.wbtourism.gov.in

This serene settlement was founded by Hindu philosopher Debendranath Tagore in 1863. In 1901, his son Rabindranath

started a school here, which became a university in 1921. Rabindranath's aim was to establish an institution that followed the traditional Indian *gurukul* system of instruction, where gurus would teach while sitting outside. The university specialized in all branches of the arts and humanities, with a special emphasis on Bengali culture.

Today the **Visva Bharati University**'s structure is more conventional, but certain traditions, such as open-air lessons, remain sacrosanct. Shantiniketan's association with contemporary Indian art is evident by the works on display by many of the

RABINDRANATH TAGORE

Born into a rich and cultivated family in 1861, Tagore was India's ultimate Renaissance man. He became a poet, lyricist, novelist, essayist, painter, choreographer, actor, dramatist and singer – as well as the author of India's national anthem. After the translation of his poem *Gitanjali* into English by WB Yeats, he was awarded the Nobel Prize in 1913. He was knighted by the British government, but returned the honour in protest against the massacre at Jallianwala Bagh *(p205)*. Tagore died in August 1941, but his memory is still deeply revered.

9

Murshidabad

🏛 West Bengal; 200 km (124 miles) N of Kolkata
🚉🚌

Murshidabad, the former capital of the nawabs of Bengal, was founded in 1704 by Nawab Murshid Quli Khan, governor of the Mughal emperor Aurangzeb. His grave lies beneath the stairs of the Katra Mosque, built in 1724 along the lines of Kartalab Khan's Mosque at Dhaka. The nawab chose this site because he wanted the footsteps of the faithful to pass over him.

Hazarduari ("A Thousand Doors"), the nawabs' palace, was built in the 1830s by General Duncan McLeod of the Bengal Engineers, who, inspired by Italian Baroque, gave it a banquet hall lined with mirrors and a striking circular Durbar Hall. The palace is now a museum with many fine exhibits, such as a gigantic chandelier, presented by Queen Victoria and hung directly over the nawabs' solid silver throne. The library has over 10,000 books, among them illuminated versions of the Qur'an. A collection of arms and armour is also on display. The town declined after Kolkata grew in importance.

Hazarduari

♿ 🕐 9am–5pm Sat–Thu

← The imposing architecture of the Katra Mosque at Murshidabad

10

Gaur

🏛 West Bengal; 328 km (204 miles) N of Kolkata
🚉 Malda, 12 km (7 miles) N of Gaur 🚌 🛈 www.wbtourism.gov.in

This abandoned city dates to the 15th and 16th centuries, though the area has a much older history. The Buddhist Pala kings ruled here from the 8th century until they were ousted by the Senas, Bengal's last Hindu dynasty, in the 12th century. Thereafter, it was ruled by a series of Muslim sultans. Gaur (also known as Gour) was sacked by Sher Shah Suri in 1539, and ravaged by plague in 1575, after which it became part of the Mughal Empire.

On the eastern bank of the Bhagirathi river are the ramparts of a fort, within which is a brick wall that once enclosed a palace. The northern gate, the Dakhil Darwaza, built in 1459, has corners embellished with carving. To its north are the remains of Sona Mosque, built in 1526, and Gaur's largest mosque. Other interesting buildings include the many-arched Qadam Rasul Mosque, built in 1530 to enshrine an impression of the Prophet Mohammad's footprint, and the Lattan Mosque with its colourful tiles.

11

Pandua

🏛 West Bengal; 360 km (224 miles) N of Kolkata
🚉 Malda, 18 km (11 miles) S of Pandua, then taxi or bus 🚌 🛈 www.wbtourism.gov.in

In the 1300s, Pandua replaced Gaur as the capital of Bengal's Muslim rulers. Its ruins lie on

↑ The remains of the Adina Mosque, built in the 14th century in Pandua

either side of a 10-km (6-mile) stretch of an old paved brick road. At the northern end, the Adina Mosque, built by Sultan Sikandar Shah, imitates the design of the great mosque at Damascus and contains Sikandar Shah's tomb. Further south is the early-15th-century Eklakhi Mausoleum, with the grave of Sultan Jalal-ud-din. The inner chamber, unusually, has an image of Ganesha carved over the entrance archway. The Qutb Shahi Mosque, to the south, is sometimes called the "Golden Mosque" as its minarets were once topped with yellow tiles.

12 Siliguri

🏠 West Bengal; 79 km
(49 miles) SE of Darjeeling
✈ Bagdogra, 12 km (7 miles)
W of Siliguri, then taxi or
bus 🚉 New Jalpaiguri,
60 km (37 miles) SE of
Siliguri, then taxi or bus 🚌
🛈 Tourist Office, Siliguri;
www.wbtourism.gov.in

Siliguri, in the foothills of the
Eastern Himalayas, was once
a calm provincial town, with
quiet streets and well-
equipped shops where tea
planters would come to stock
up on provisions. Today, much
of the town is a vast trucking
depot, though it has some
lively bazaars, such as the one
on Tenzing Norgay Road. The
Tibetan woollens on sale here
are good bargains, and cane
furniture, a speciality of the
area, is widely available. In
the winter, Siliguri hosts
international Buddhist
conferences and also serves
as the transit point for
travellers to the Jaldapara
Wildlife Sanctuary.

Clustered close to Siliguri
are New Jalpaiguri, the
railhead for the area, and
Bagdogra, which has the
airport. Along with Siliguri,
these towns act as gateways
to the hill stations of
Darjeeling, Kurseong and
Kalimpong, as well as to
Bhutan and Sikkim. The
drive between these towns
goes past beautiful green
expanses of tea plantations.

13 Jaldapara Wildlife Sanctuary

🏠 West Bengal; 200 km
(124 miles) SE of Siliguri
🚉 Madarihat, the entry
point, then taxi 🚌🚌
🕐 Mid-Sep–mid-Jun
🛈 www.wbtourism.gov.in

The region around the
Jaldapara Wildlife Sanctuary,
in the richly forested Dooars
Valley, was once the hunting
ground of the kings of Bhutan.
Today, it is one of the biggest
reserve forests in West
Bengal, covering an area
of 216 sq km (83 sq miles).
Established in 1941, the
reserve sprawls over lush
deciduous forests and dense
scrubland, with the Torsa river
flowing through it. This is one
of the few places in India
where the great Indian one-
horned rhinoceros (p362) can
be easily spotted. About 50 of
these magnificent animals live
in the sanctuary, protected
from poachers who hunt them
for their horns, which are
believed to be a powerful
aphrodisiac. The sanctuary

> **The sanctuary
> is also home to
> various other rare
> and endangered
> species, including
> the leopard, tiger,
> hispid hare, hog-
> badger, and sloths.**

is also home to various other
rare and endangered species,
including the leopard, tiger,
hispid hare, hogbadger, and
sloths. Bird species include the
lesser pied hornbill and the
Bengal florican, with its
mottled and streaked plumage.
In addition, there are eight
species of freshwater turtles
in Jaldapara's ponds.

The northern part of the
sanctuary, known as Totopara,
is located along the banks of
the Torsa river. It is home to
the Toto tribe, now only 1,300
strong, whose members have
consistently refused to adopt
modern-day comforts.

The sanctuary's waterholes,
where animals, including
elephants, come to drink in
the evenings are excellent
spots for wildlife sightings.
The best way to explore the
sanctuary is to take a jeep
safari through the park. The
elegant **Hollong Forest Lodge**
within the sanctuary offers
food and accommodation.

←

One of the Indian
rhinoceroses at Jaldapara
Wildlife Sanctuary

↑ Women working in a tea plantation in the vicinity of Kurseong

Hollong Forest Lodge
☎ (0353) 251 1974 (Tourist Office, Siliguri)

⓮
Kurseong

🏠 West Bengal; 50 km (31 miles) NW of Siliguri 🚗🚌 *i* www.wbtourism. gov.in

Halfway between Siliguri and Darjeeling, on the Darjeeling Himalayan Railway line, quiet Kurseong is charming and secluded. It is smaller than Darjeeling, with a milder climate because of its lower altitude. Set amid tea gardens, with lush vegetation and a picturesque lake, Kurseong is known for its natural beauty. According to local legend, the place got its name from *kurson-rip*, a beautiful wild orchid found in the area.

Kurseong is a walkers' paradise. The eight-hour trek from Mirik to Kurseong runs through tea estates, orange orchards, cardamom plantations and small villages, and provides spectacular views of the valley. Similarly, the five-hour walk to Ghoom is also beautiful, winding along a ridge that runs through a thick, but well-shaded, forest.

⓯
Kalimpong

🏠 West Bengal; 51 km (32 miles) E of Darjeeling 🚌 *i* www.wbtourism.gov.in

Kalimpong was once part of Sikkimese and then Bhutanese territory, before it became part of British India in the 19th century. It was at the head of the ancient trade route to Tibet and still has the feel of a frontier town. Its market sells a mix of the exotic and the mundane, from fern shoots to plastic buckets.

The Thongsa Monastery is Kalimpong's oldest monastery, built in 1692, and is a brisk hour's walk away. To the south of the town, the Zong Dog Palri Fo Brang Monastery, blessed by the Dalai Lama in 1976, has some fine mandalas. The town's many nurseries produce a large number of exotic orchids, gladioli, amaryllis lily and cacti.

BAULS, BENGAL'S WANDERING MYSTIC MUSICIANS

Bauls are Bengali minstrels, usually itinerant ascetics. Mixing Hindu and Islamic mysticism, Bauls can be from either religion, drawing ideas from both, as well as from Buddhism. Bauls have their own rituals and typically wear distinctive, multi-coloured clothes. Their favourite instrument is a one-stringed lute called *ektara*. There are often festivals of Baul music around the state, including in Kolkata and Kenduli, both held in January.

⑯

Gangtok

📍 East Sikkim, Sikkim;
110 km (68 miles) N of
Siliguri ✈ Pakyong,
28 km (17 miles) S of city
centre 🚉 Siliguri, 107 km
(66 miles) S of city centre
🚌 ℹ Sikkim Tourism, MG
Marg; www.sikkim
tourism.gov.in, sikkimpts.
azurewebsites.net
(permits)

The capital of Sikkim,
Gangtok reflects this tiny
state's extraordinary ethnic
diversity. In the crowded city,
Lepchas (the region's original
inhabitants) live alongside
Tibetans, Bhutias, Nepalis
and Indians from the plains.
Until 1975, Sikkim was a
kingdom, with the status
of an Indian Protectorate. It
was ruled by the Chogyals,
Buddhists of Tibetan origin.
However, the British Raj's
policies of importing cheap
labour from neighbouring
Nepal for Sikkim's rice,
cardamom and tea plantations
drastically changed Sikkim's
demography. Soon Nepali
Hindus constituted 75 per
cent of the state's population.
In 1975 Sikkim voted to join
the Indian Republic, ending
the rule of Palden Thondup
Namgyal, the last Chogyal.

At the town's northern edge
is the early 20th-century
Enchey Monastery, whose
large prayer hall is full of
murals and images representing the pantheon of Mahayana
Buddhist deities. At the
southern end is the **Namgyal
Institute of Tibetology**.
Established in 1958, it has a
rare collection of medieval
Buddhist scriptures, bronzes
and embroidered *thangkas*.

Saramsa Orchidarium,
14 km (9 miles) south of
Gangtok, displays many of the
450 orchid species found in
Sikkim. They flower from April
to May, and again in October.

Rumtek Monastery,
24 km (15 miles) southwest of
Gangtok, is the headquarters
of the Kagyupa (Black Hat)
Tibetan Buddhist sect, and the
seat of its head, the Gyalwa
Karmapa. The 16th Karmapa
fled Tibet in 1959 after the
Chinese invasion, and he built
this replica of his monastery
at Tsurphu in Tibet. Rumtek is
an impressive complex, its
flat-roofed buildings topped
with golden finials and filled
with treasures brought from
the monastery in Tibet.

Especially splendid is the
reliquary *chorten* of the 16th
Karmapa, behind the main
prayer hall, made of silver and
gold and studded with corals,
amber and turquoise. Since
the 16th Karmapa's death in
1981, there have been two
claimants to his title (and the
monastery's treasures). Until
this dispute is resolved, the
armed guards that surround
the monastery will remain to
protect the treasures.

Tsomgo Lake, about 34 km
(21 miles) northeast of Gangtok,
lies at an altitude of 3,780 m
(12,402 ft). Visitors to the lake
require a special permit from
the tourism office in Gangtok.
The lake is impressive both in
spring and summer, when it is
surrounded by alpine flowers,
and in winter when it freezes.

Enchey Monastery
🕐 9am–5pm daily
🌐 sikkimstdc.com

**Namgyal Institute of
Tibetology**
♿ 🕐 10am–4pm Mon–Sat
🚫 2nd Sat & public hols
🌐 tibetology.net

Rumtek Monastery
🕐 9am–6pm daily
🌐 rumtek.org

← Pristine alpine landscape surrounding Tsomgo Lake, near Gangtok

17

Yuksam

⌂ West Sikkim, Sikkim; 162 km (101 miles) W of Gangtok ⊞ *i* Pelling Information Centre; www.sikkimtourism.gov.in, sikkimpts.azurewebsites.net (permits)

Yuksam was the first capital of Sikkim. A stone throne and some *chortens* mark the historic spot where the first Chogyal of Sikkim was crowned in 1641. Below it is Kathok Lake. Dubdi Monastery, built in 1701, with its exquisite Buddhist images and meditation cave, is a steep half-hour climb above. Yuksam is the starting point for the trek to Dzongri.

18

Tashiding Monastery

⌂ West Sikkim, Sikkim; 145 km (90 miles) W of Gangtok ⊞ ◷ Daily ⊡ sikkimtourism.gov.in, sikkimpts.azurewebsites.net (permits)

Built in 1716, Tashiding Monastery stands on the

Did You Know?

Sikkim only became part of the Indian Union in 1975, after the population voted to abolish the monarchy.

summit of a heart-shaped hill, where Guru Padmasambhava is said to have shot an arrow and then meditated on the spot where it fell. Surrounded by *chortens*, *mani* stones (prayer stones), water-driven prayer wheels, and the Ratong and Rangeet rivers, with Mount Kanchendzonga looming behind the hill, this is a magical spot.

During the annual Bumchu Festival, large crowds descend on the monastery from all over Sikkim. At this festival, sacred water, said to have been put into a sealed jar by a 17th-century Buddhist saint, is mixed with river water and distributed as a powerful blessing to devotees. Miraculously, the supply of sacred water never runs dry.

Tashiding also has the Thongwa Rangdol Chorten, a mere glimpse of which is supposed to wipe away all a visitor's sins. The main temple, which was rebuilt in 1987, has large images of the Buddha and the Bodhisattvas.

19

Pelling

⌂ West Sikkim, Sikkim; 143 km (89 miles) W of Gangtok ⊞ Gezing, 9 km (6 miles) S of city centre, then local bus or taxi *i* Pelling Information Centre; www.sikkim tourism.gov.in, sikkimpts. azurewebsites.net (permits)

Situated on a ridge, at an altitude of 1,859 m (6,100 ft), with excellent views of the peaks and glaciers of the Kanchendzonga Range, Pelling is a convenient base from which to explore western Sikkim and embark on treks. This is the state's most beautiful and unspoilt region, with expanses of forest, green river valleys, superb trekking trails and Sikkim's oldest monasteries. Pelling is a day's drive from Gangtok, and is accessible from Darjeeling (72 km/45 miles south).

The monastic complex of Pemayangtse was built in 1705 on a ridge a half-hour's walk from the town. The austere three-storeyed main monastery is a treasure house of *thangkas*, murals and images, with a breath-takingly intricate model of Zangdopelri, the seven-storeyed celestial home of Guru Padmasambhava, on the top floor. Pemayangtse has an annual festival, with spectacular masked dances. Sikkim's second oldest monastery, Sangachoeling (built in 1697), is a steep 40-minute hike through thick forests above Pemayangtse. It has exquisite murals.

Khecheopalri Lake, 25 km (16 miles) north of Pelling, is sacred to both Buddhists and Hindus, who come here to make a wish.

← Buddhist monks wearing traditional red robes inside Tashiding Monastery

Intricate stonework on Konark's Sun Temple

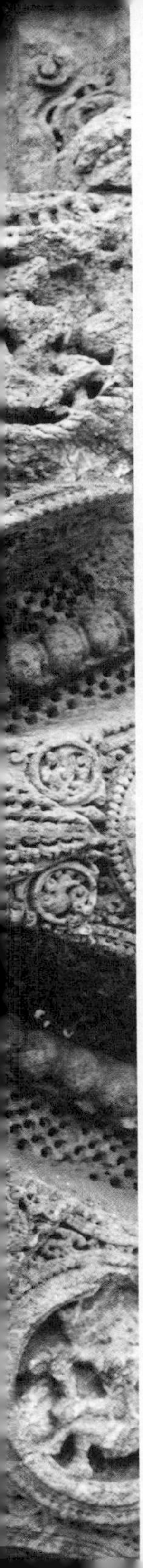

ODISHA

Bounded on the west by the thickly forested hills of the Eastern Ghats, and on the east by nearly 500 km (311 miles) of coastline on the Bay of Bengal, Odisha, also known as Orissa, covers an area of 156,000 sq km (60,232 sq miles). For millennia, this area was ruled by powerful Hindu dynasties. These were established after the fall of the Mauryan Empire – it was the bloody battle to control Odisha that turned the famous Mauryan emperor Ashoka into a Buddhist. The most prolific dynasty during this time were the Gangas, who ruled from the 11th to the 15th centuries; arts and architecture flourished during their rule, and monuments such as the magnificent Sun Temple at Konark, now a UNESCO World Heritage Site, were built. Even when most of India fell to Muslim invaders, Odisha remained a bastion of Hindu religion and culture – until King Mukunda was killed by his own people in 1568 and Afghans from Bengal conquered the territory, followed by Mughal emperor Akbar. Split into a group of princely states, Odisha was subsequently ruled by the Marathas before becoming part of the British Raj. After independence, princely kingdoms in the region joined the state of Orissa, which was integrated into the Indian Union in 1950.

ODISHA

Must Sees
1. Bhubaneswar
2. Konark Sun Temple

Experience More
3. Puri
4. Chilika Lake
5. Taptapani
6. Gopalpur-on-Sea
7. Cuttack
8. Ratnagiri
9. Bhitarkanika Sanctuary
10. Berhampur
11. Baleshwar
12. Baripada
13. Similipal National Park

MADHYA PRADESH
AND CHHATTISGARH
p274

ANDHRA PRADESH
AND TELANGANA
p564

JHARKHAND

Daltenganj

NH20

Dhanbad

Siu¬i

NH14

Ranchi

NH18

Asansol

NH19

Durgapur

Gumla

Puruliya

Bankura

Barddhaman

BIHAR AND
JHARKHAND
p258

NH43

NH20

Jamshedpur

WEST BENGAL

NH18

NH14

SH10

Rourkela

NH220

Kharagpur

NH16

NH143

Jashipur

NH49

BARIPADA
12

WEST BENGAL
AND SIKKIM
p324

NH49

Barakot

NH220

13
SIMILIPAL
NATIONAL PARK

NH53

NH49

NH20

Baitarani

NH18

11 BALESHWAR

Rengali
Reservoir

NH16

Ramapur

NH149

Anandadur

NH55

Anugul

Brahmani

Bhadrak

SH9

Chandbali

NH53

RATNAGIRI

Phulabani

SH23

Dhenkanal

NH16

8

9 BHITARKANIKA
SANCTUARY

Mahanadi

7 CUTTACK

Khordha

1 BHUBANESWAR

Paradwip

NH57

Nayagarh

SH13

NH57

NH316

2 KONARK
SUN TEMPLE

Pushikulya

Aska

NH16

4

3
PURI

CHILIKA
LAKE

Bay of
Bengal

BERHAMPUR

Chhatrapur

10

6 GOPALPUR-ON-SEA

ODISHA

0 kilometres   60

0 miles   60

N

❶

BHUBANESWAR

🏛 Bhubaneswar district; 480 km (298 miles) S of Kolkata
✈ 4 km (2 miles) NW of city centre 🚌🚕 ℹ Odisha Tourism,
BJB Nagar; www.odishatourism.gov.in

The capital of Odisha, Bhubaneswar is famous for its superb Hindu temples, mostly in the older, southern part of the city. The new town, with its administrative buildings and tree-lined avenues, is in the north.

①
Lingaraj Temple

🏛 Old Town ⏰ Sunrise-sunset daily ⛔ To non-Hindus

This magnificent 11th-century temple represents the high point of the Orissan style, where both sculpture and architecture have evolved in perfect harmony. Its grandeur lies in its towering 55-m-(180-ft-) high *deul* (spire) with dramatic vertical ribs, and in the consummate artistry with which each sculpture and embellishment is executed. The temple's large courtyard has about 150 smaller shrines.

The main deity here is Shiva as Tribhuvaneswar ("Lord of the Three Worlds"), from which the city takes its name.

②
Bindusagar Tank

🏛 N of Lingaraj Temple, Old Town ⏰ Daily

North of Lingaraj Temple is the large Bindusagar Tank, a reservoir with a pavilion in the middle. It is believed to contain water from every sacred river in India. The main deity of the Lingaraj Temple is brought here for a ritual bath every year.

③
Vaital Deul Temple

🏛 Old Town ⏰ Sunrise-sunset daily

This 8th-century temple west of Bindusagar features eerie interior carvings. The main deity here is an eight-armed Chamunda (a Tantric form of Durga), with a garland of skulls, seated on a corpse, and flanked by a jackal and an owl.

④
Parasurameshwar Temple

🏛 Old Town ⏰ Sunrise-sunset daily

Built in the 7th-century, this is the best preserved and most lavishly sculpted of the early temples. Set into the shrine's outer walls are images of Shiva and other deities, among them a potbellied Ganesha and his brother Karttikeya.

of frolicking monkeys. A unique feature of the *jagamohan* is the decorated ceiling, carved into a lotus with eight petals. The sculptures of female figures in this temple are remarkable for their expressive faces, with hairstyles and jewellery shown in exquisite detail.

---

⑥
Rajarani Temple

🏠 Tankapani Rd
🕐 Sunrise-sunset daily

Dating from the 11th-century, this temple is renowned for its fine sculptures of *dikpals* (the guardians of the eight cardinal directions) perched on lotus flowers. Of these, Agni, the God of Fire on a ram, and Varuna, God of the Oceans seated on a crocodile, are particularly impressive.

⑦
Odisha State Museum

🏠 BJB Nagar 🕐 10am–5pm Tue–Sun 🚫 Public hols
🌐 odishamuseum.nic.in

The highlight of this interesting state museum is its rich collection of Buddhist and Jain sculptures, coins and painted palm-leaf manuscripts, as well as jewellery and art.

↑ The enormous Lingaraj Temple, with vertically ribbed spire

50

The number of temples at Bhubaneswar, which was once called "Temple Town".

⑤
Mukteshwar Temple

🏠 Old town 🕐 Sunrise-sunset daily

The 10th-century Mukteshwar Temple is notable for its exquisite sculptures and elegant proportions. Its beautiful *torana* (gateway) is decorated with langorously reclining female figures. The *jagamohan* is illuminated by diamond-shaped latticed windows on the north and south walls, their outermost frames depicting enchanting scenes

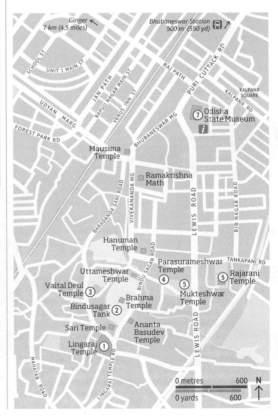

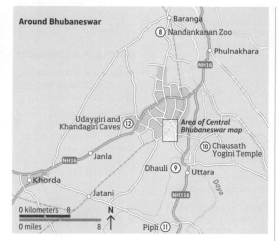

Around Bhubaneswar

Baranga
8 Nandankanan Zoo
Phulnakhara
NH16
Udaygiri and
Khandagiri Caves 12
Area of Central
Bhubaneswar map
10 Chausath
Yogini Temple
NH16 Janla
Dhauli 9 Uttara
Khorda
Daya
Jatani
NH316
0 kilometers 8
0 miles 8
N
Pipli 11

He won the war, but the carnage and misery the battle inflicted on the people filled the emperor with remorse and brought about a dramatic change of heart. He gave up *digvijaya* (military conquest) for *dharmavijaya* (spiritual conquest), embraced Buddhism, and publicized his new maxims in rock edicts, installed in different parts of his empire. One of these is here, at the base of Dhauli Hill, in which the emperor declares, "All men are my children", and enjoins his officials to ensure impartiality, non-violence, justice and compassion in administration. The top of the rock is sculpted into an imposing elephant's head, symbolizing the Buddhist dharma. This is one of the earliest sculptures found in the subcontinent. The huge white Shanti Stupa ("Peace Pagoda") at the top of the hill was built by Japanese Buddhists in the early 1970s.

AROUND BHUBANESWAR

8
Nandankanan Zoo

⌂ Nandankanan Rd
⏱ Hours vary, check website ⊕ nandan kanan.org

At this zoo – famous for its white tigers – the animals live in natural surroundings.

9
Dhauli

⌂ 8 km (5 miles) S of Bhubaneswar

A stark white Buddhist stupa in the middle of green paddy fields on the banks of the Daya river marks the site of the bloody battle of Kalinga, fought by one of India's greatest rulers, the Mauryan emperor Ashoka in 260 BC.

10
Chausath Yogini Temple

⌂ 15 km (9 miles) SE of Bhubaneswar

This 9th-century, circular temple is dedicated to the

A devotee praying at Chausath Yogini Temple, which is open to the sky

chausath yoginis or 64 manifestations of the goddess Shakti, who symbolizes female creative energy. All the images, each about 0.6 m (2 ft) tall and carved out of black chlorite stone, are placed in niches in the inner enclosure. The presiding deity, a graceful 10-armed yogini, is in the 31st niche. The temple is in the pretty village of Hirapur.

⑪

Pipli

📍 20 km (12 miles) S of Bhubaneswar

On the highway to Puri, Pipli is a village of artisans famous for their colourful appliqué-work fabrics. The craft originated to serve temples, providing intricately stitched awnings and covers for deities, and hangings in vivid hues for festival days. Today, garden umbrellas, cushion covers, wall hangings and bags are made in Pipli using the same techniques, in which cloth is cut into bird, flower, animal and other decorative shapes, and stitched on to fabric of a contrasting colour. Shops selling these line both sides of the highway as it passes through Pipli, enveloping it in a blaze of colour.

⑫ ✍

Udaygiri and Khandagiri Caves

📍 7 km (4 miles) W of Bhubaneswar

The twin hills of Udaygiri ("Sunrise Hill") and Khandagiri ("Broken Hill") were honey-combed to make retreats for Jain monks in the 1st century BC. Located just off the road from Bhubaneswar to Kolkata, the hills rise suddenly from the flat surrounding plains, and are separated from each other by the highway.

Coming from Bhubaneswar, Udaygiri, the hill on the right, is best explored first, as it has the more interesting caves. The most impressive of its 18 caves is the two-storey Rani Gumpha or "Queen's Cave" (Cave 1), with lavishly sculpted friezes of women dancing and playing music, kings and queens in courtly splendour, elephants, monkeys and foliage.

Other notable caves are Chhota Hathi Gumpha, or "Small Elephant Cave" (Cave 3), with six superb elephants flanking its entrance; Ganesh Gumpha (Cave 10), whose sculptures include an intriguing battle scene with a woman riding an elephant, while soldiers in kilts chase her; and Bagh Gumpha or "Tiger Cave" (Cave 12), its front ingeniously shaped like a tiger's head with the mouth open.

The most significant cave historically is Hathi Gumpha or "Elephant Cave" (Cave 14). On the rock above its entrance is an inscription from the 1st century BC. It records that the caves were carved by

↑ An artisan making a piece of appliqué fabric for which Pipli is famed

Kharavela, third king of the powerful Chedi dynasty, whose conquests included large parts of Bihar, the Deccan and south India. The inscription also states that King Kharavela rebuilt his capital, Kalinganagar, after it was destroyed by a cyclone.

Across the highway, on Khandagiri, are 15 caves with carvings of sacred Jain symbols. The Ananta Cave (Cave 3), with its figures of twin serpents above the doorways, is the most important and has superb ornamentation and lively friezes, which includes one of boys chasing lions, bulls and other animals. Another great carving in this cave shows the goddess Lakshmi in a lotus pool, being bathed with water from pitchers held by two elephants. Three of the caves – numbers 5, 8 and 9 – have impressive carved figures of the Jain *tirthankaras* in relief.

Unlike Buddhist caves such as those at Ajanta (*p424*) and Ellora (*p422*), most of the Udaygiri and Khandagiri caves are so low that it is impossible to stand upright in them. This was in keeping with the self-mortification and asceticism that Jain monks were expected to practise. The site attracts sadhus, who gather here in January every year to meditate in the caves.

117

The number of caves originally thought to have been carved at Udaygiri.

2 ✍ 🅼 🖵

KONARK SUN TEMPLE

📍 Puri district; 65 km (40 miles) SE of Bhubaneswar 🚌 🕐 Temple: 6am–8pm daily; archaeological museum: Fri–Wed 🌐 odishatourism.gov.in/visit/konark

One of India's great architectural marvels, this temple to the sun god, Surya, was conceived as a gigantic chariot, with 12 pairs of wheels to carry him on his daily journey across the sky.

Built in the 13th century by King Narasimhadeva of the Eastern Ganga dynasty, who ruled the Kingdom of Orissa, the temple is a remarkable feat, and testament to the cult of the sun god. The building is thought to have been constructed over 12 years, utilizing the skills of 1,200 artisans, including the master builder Bisu Moharana. While much of it is in ruins – only the base of the main temple shrine, which was destroyed in the 19th century, remains – visitors still get a sense of how grand this monument once was. The audience hall, with its distinctive tiered roof, is the most complete remaining part of the temple. One of the most spectacular aspects of the Sun Temple is the sculptures – which represent everything from gods and demons to kings and peasants, elephants and horses – which all jostle for space on the walls with dozens of erotic couples. This is related to the tantric beliefs that form part of the cult of the sun god. The complex at Konark is now recognized for its architectural significance, and is a UNESCO World Heritage Site.

The majestic image of the sun god stands on a chariot, flanked by his wives, and other deities.

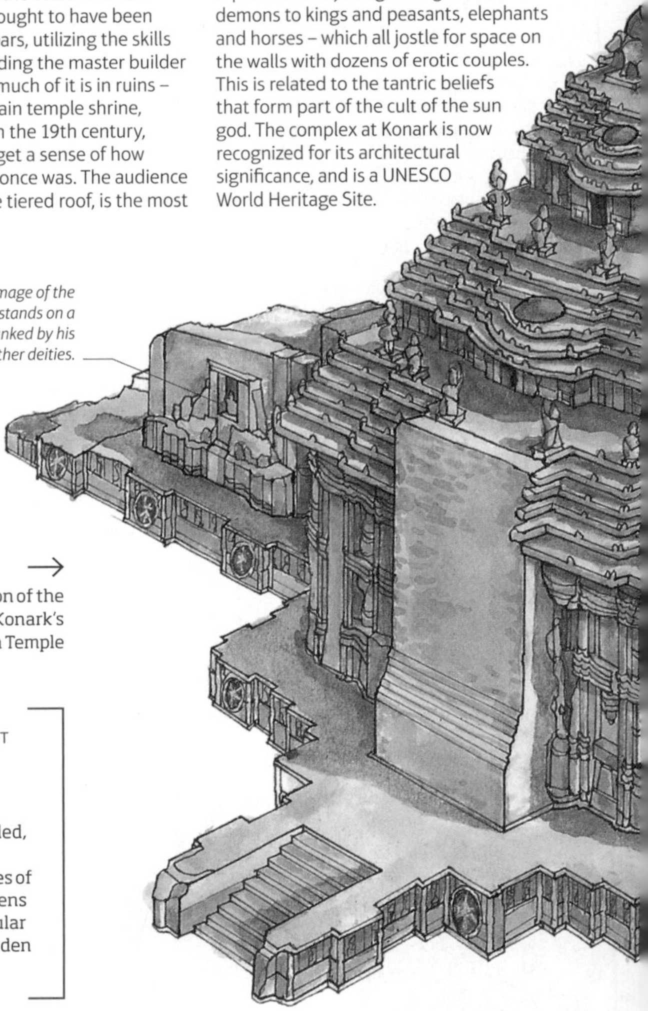

→

An illustration of the remains of Konark's Sun Temple

📷 PICTURE PERFECT
The Bird is the Word

The Sun Temple is covered with detailed, graceful and often sensuous sculptures of *alasa kanyas* (maidens at leisure): a particular highlight is the maiden with her pet bird.

1 One of Odisha's glories, the Sun Temple is well preserved.

2 The Sun Temple was dedicated to Surya, the sun god, here sculpted in stone.

3 The building was designed to represent Surya's chariot, with 24 carved wheels.

The Cymbal Player sculpture is in a row of wonderfully animated dancers, musicians and drummers on the terrace of the pyramidal roof.

The three-tiered roof is shaped like a stepped pyramid and crowned with a round fluted stone called an amalaka. The terraces between each are covered with sculptures.

A demure snake goddess provides a contrast to the amorous couple beside her. The erotic sculptures here are a celebration of life.

Main entrance

EXPERIENCE MORE

③
Puri

🏠 Puri district; 62 km (39 miles) S of Bhubaneswar
🚉🚌 ℹ️ Odisha Tourism, Station Rd; www.odisha tourism.gov.in/puri

One of the most important pilgrimage sites for Hindus in India, the seaside town of Puri is dominated by the towering Jagannath Temple. Early European sailors, for whom its 65-m- (213-ft-) high spire was an important landmark, called it the White Pagoda to differentiate it from Konark's Sun Temple, which they named Black Pagoda.

The **Jagannath Temple** was built in the 12th century by King Anantavarman of the

> INSIDER TIP
> **Take a Tour**
>
> Explore the medieval lanes, markets, temples and sacred bathing sites of Puri's old city, sampling some *chhena poda* en route, on a Grass Routes walking tour *(www.grassroutes journeys.com)*.

> **Local specialities include the colourful *pattachitra* paintings and round *ganjifa* playing cards painted with religious themes**

Eastern Ganga dynasty. Surrounded by a 6-m- (20-ft-) high wall, its main gate is guarded by a pair of brightly painted stone lions. Non-Hindus are not allowed within the temple, but they can get a good view of the complex, with its multitude of small shrines and its courtyard thronged with pilgrims, from the roof of the Raghunandan Library, just across the street from the main gate.

The temple is similar in design to the Lingaraj Temple in Bhubaneswar (p346): at both, there are three smaller shrines adjoining a tall sanctuary tower. The elegant stone column near the entrance, topped with the figure of Arun, charioteer of the sun god, was brought here from the Sun Temple at Konark in the 18th century. From Jagannath Temple,

Puri's main thoroughfare of Bada Danda runs through the town. It is crammed with pilgrims' rest houses and shops selling food, religious souvenirs and handicrafts. Local specialities include the colourful *pattachitra* paintings and round *ganjifa* playing cards painted with religious themes, as well as *chhena poda*, a delicious local cheesecake.

Puri's beach is the town's other principal attraction, although it is not always safe for swimming because of dangerous undercurrents. The long beach front is crowded with stalls and groups of pilgrims along Marine Parade. Sunbathers and swimmers should therefore head to the eastern end, which is cleaner and more secluded, or to the beaches attached to the better hotels. Local fishermen wearing conical hats serve as lifeguards on the beach, and also take visitors out to sea in their boats to watch the spectacular sunsets here.

Jagannath Temple
🕐 6am–10pm daily; check ritual times before visiting
🚫 To non-Hindus

← Crowds of Hindu pilgrims thronging the chariot of Lord Jagannath during a religious festival in Puri

④ Chilika Lake

◨ Puri, Ganjam and Khordha districts; 50 km (31 miles) SW of Puri ◨ Balugaon, then taxi or bus ◨ Balugaon & Satpada ◨ Odisha Tourism, Barkul; (06756) 211 078

A vast, shallow lagoon covering 1,100 sq km (425 sq miles), Chilika is separated from the Bay of Bengal by a sandy ridge, with just a narrow channel connecting it to the sea. Believed to be the largest brackish water lake in Asia, Chilika is recognized as one of the most important wetlands in the world because of the phenomenal variety of aquatic- and bird-life it supports. From November to February, the lake and its reed islands teem with nesting birds, including several winter migrants, such as the golden plover, flamingo, purple moorhen and osprey.

A major attraction at Chilika are dolphins, which are often spotted off Satpada Island, at the confluence of the lake and the sea. Nalabana Island, at the core of the lake, is the best place for bird-watching and is now a sanctuary. Visitors will need to hire private boats to get to both islands; these are available at Balugaon, Barkul, Satpada and Rambha. Boat trips can also be organized through Odisha Tourism. Kalijai Temple, built on a small rocky island, is a pilgrimage spot that attracts festive crowds during the Makar Mela in January. The lake also supports the local people who earn their living from its prawns, crabs and fish.

---

⑤ Taptapani

◨ Ganjam district; 51 km (32 miles) SW of Berhampur ◨ ◨ Odisha Tourism; (06814) 211 631

Picturesquely located on a forested hill in the Eastern Ghats, this spa is renowned for its hot springs. The boiling, sulphurous water bubbles out of a crevice in the hillside and is piped to a pool in a clearing. Apart from being beneficial for various chronic ailments, the hot springs are also believed to cure infertility. A tree with seed pods overhangs the pool, and women seeking the infertility cure are supposed to pick up seeds from the tree that have fallen to the muddy bottom of the pool – a difficult feat since the water is too hot for more than a quick dip. The Saora tribal women, whose villages are nearby, can often be seen taking the cure. The most comfortable way

to enjoy the hot springs is by renting a room in the Odisha Tourism rest house just below the pool, as it has hot water from the springs piped directly into its bathtubs.

---

⑥ Gopalpur-on-Sea

◨ Ganjam district; 172 km (107 miles) SW of Bhubaneswar ◨ Berhampur, 18 km (11 miles) E of town centre, then taxi or bus ◨ ◨ Odisha Tourism, Berhampur Pantha Niwas; (0680) 234 3931

This quiet seaside town was, in ancient times, a great seaport for Odisha's maritime trade with Indonesia. The British later developed it as a beach resort and it now has a sleepy charm, except during the Durga Puja holidays in October, when it swarms with tourists from Bengal. However, swimming in the sea is not safe because of treacherous undercurrents. The beach, lined with bungalows and dotted with casuarina groves, remains a good place to spend the day, even without swimming, as visitors can watch the fishing boats and the sunset.

↑ A boat on Chilika Lake, which supports a range of aquatic and winged residents

7
Cuttack

⌂ Cuttack district;
35 km (22 miles) N of
Bhubaneswar ⚐🚌
ℹ Odisha Tourism,
Arunodaya Market Bldg,
Link Rd; www.odisha
tourism.gov.in/cuttack

Situated on the Mahanadi
Delta, Cuttack is Odisha's
most populous city, and was
its capital from the 10th
century onwards until 1956,
when the capital was moved
to Bhubaneswar (p346). There
is little evidence today of the
city's historic past and the
gateway and moat of the
13th-century Barabati Fort,
in northwest Cuttack, are
all that remain of this great
citadel, which once had a
nine-storeyed palace.

The eastern part of town
is more interesting, with
silversmiths' shops in Balu
Bazaar and Nayasarak,
where Cuttack's famous
silver filigree jewellery is
made. Nearby, in the shops
on Jail Road, the full range
of Odisha's beautiful
handicrafts are available,
including ikat silk, carved
hornware and paintings.

In this area, a cluster of
green domes marks the
18th-century Kadam Rasul
Mosque, where the Prophet
Muhammed's footprints are
carved on a round stone.

8
Ratnagiri

⌂ Cuttack district;
70 km (43 miles) NE of
Cuttack 🚌 ℹ www.
odishatourism.gov.in/
visit/ratnagiri

The ruins of three major
Buddhist sites – Ratnagiri,
Udaigiri and Lalitgiri – are
situated close to each other,
and can be conveniently
visited on a day trip from
Cuttack or Bhubaneswar,
driving through a beautiful
landscape of low hills and
lush paddy fields. The most
impressive of the three sites
is Ratnagiri ("Hill of Jewels"),
which, between the 7th and
the 11th centuries, was a
major Buddhist university
and monastic establishment,
described by the 7th-century
Chinese traveller Hiuen Tsang.
Located on top of a mound,
crowned by a large stupa, the
best-preserved structure here
is a monastery with a central
courtyard and an impressive
colonnade around the monks'
cells. A beautiful 4-m- (13-ft-)
high image of the seated
Buddha can be seen inside,
together with other Buddhist
divinities, and the entrance
doorway is superbly

THE INDONESIAN CONNECTION

From the 4th century BC to the 14th century AD, the
power and wealth of successive kingdoms in Odisha
derived from their rich maritime trade, especially with
Bali, Java and Sumatra in Indonesia. With the trading
links came cultural influences, still visible in Odisha's
crafts. The intricate art of ikat weaving came from there,
as did the silver filigree work that is still being carried out
in Cuttack. Today, Odisha's old maritime links with Bali,
Java and Sumatra are commemorated in a festival called
Bali Yatra (Bali Journey). This is held in Cuttack during the
full moon of Kartik (October/November) and includes a
colourful fair held on the Mahanadi river.

170

species of bird can be spotted at the Bhitarkanika Sanctuary.

carved. There is also a small **Archaeological Museum** on-site that displays other sculptures found at Ratnagiri.

The nearby Udaigiri ("Sunrise Hill"), 10 km (6 miles) south of Ratnagiri, is still being excavated and seems to have better preserved sculptures. The western spur of the hill has a row of rock-cut sculptures, while the northern spur is covered with the ruins of brick stupas. A colossal sculpture of the Buddha here has an inscription dating it to the 8th century.

Lalitgiri ("Hill of Grace"), about 10 km (6 miles) south of Udaigiri (and directly connected by bus to Cuttack), is believed to be the oldest of the sites. The ruins, spread over two adjacent hills,

include a terraced stone platform, a gallery of life-size Bodhisattva figures and a domed temple. Some of the better preserved sculptures and a carved doorway have been incorporated into a modern Hindu temple. At the foot of a hill is a village of stone-carvers who keep alive Odisha's fine tradition of stonework.

Archaeological Museum

◉ ◷ 10am–5pm Sat–Thu Ⓦ asi.nic.in/museum-ratnagiri

---

9 ⟨⟩

Bhitarkanika Sanctuary

⌂ Kendrapara district; 106 km (66 miles) E of Cuttack; entry points at Chandbali and Rajnagar ◰ Bhadrakh, 50 km (31 miles) NW of Chandbali, then bus ▭▭ ◷ Mid-Oct–mid-Apr ℹ For permits and bookings, call Bhubaneswar (06786) 220 397 or Rajnagar (06729) 272 460

Famous as the nesting ground of the Olive Ridley turtle, this 145-sq-km (56-sq-mile) sanctuary and national park is situated on the delta of the Brahmani and Baitarani rivers on the Bay of Bengal. It also has the largest mangrove forests in the country after the Sundarbans in West Bengal (*p328*), with 63 of the 72 known mangrove species found here.

Encompassing 12 offshore islands, long sandy beaches and numerous rivulets and creeks, Bhitarkanika is home to an impressive range of fish, more than 170 species of birds, such as storks, sea eagles and kingfishers, and the largest number of estuarine crocodiles in the country. Bagagahana and Saribana are the spots to visit for bird-watching in Bhitarkanika. Accommodation is available at a forest rest house at Chandbali, as well as deep

↑ A kingfisher at Bhitarkanika Sanctuary

within the sanctuary at Dangmal, Habalikhati and Ekakula (all three are accessible by boat). Odisha Tourism in Bhubaneswar and Cuttack organize tours and the necessary Forest Department permits for Bhitarkanika.

10

Berhampur

⌂ Ganjam district; 170 km (106 miles) SW of Bhubaneswar ◰ ▭ ℹ Odisha Tourism, Railway Station; www.odisha tourism.gov.in/brahmapur

The main commercial centre in southern Odisha, Berhampur (also known as Brahmapur) is famous for its beautiful handwoven ikat silk, available in its bustling bazaar where weavers sit at their looms. The railhead for the seaside town of Gopalpur-on-Sea, Berhampur is also a convenient base for visiting Jaugarh, 35 km (22 miles) north of the city. Jaugarh has a 3rd-century BC rock edict erected by the Emperor Ashoka following the Battle of Kalinga, after which he renounced armed conflict and ceased expanding his kingdom. The emperor was famous for ruling an empire that stretched from modern Iran to Assam in the northwest, for promoting Buddhism and for his ethical edicts. The Biramchinarayan Temple, built in the 17th century, is a short distance away at Buguda. It has beautiful murals depicting scenes from the epic poem *Ramayana*.

← Visitors exploring the ancient Buddhist complex at Ratnagiri

← Colourful stalls at the weekly market in Chandipur, a small coastal village near Baleshwar

12

Baripada

🏠 Mayurbhanj district; 178 km (111 miles) NE of Bhubaneswar 🚉🚌
🌐 www.odishatourism. gov.in/baripada

The main market town of northeastern Odisha, Baripada is the headquarters of Mayurbhanj district, which is rich in forests and has a large population of tribal people. Baripada is also the gateway to Similipal National Park. The town holds a Rath Yatra (chariot festival) in June or July, which takes place around the Jagannath Temple. This festival is a small-scale version of the one held in Puri (*p352*), but is equally lively and vibrant, as the entire town joins in the procession. A unique feature in Baripada is that the chariot of the female deity, Subhadra, is pulled only by women.

Another colourful festival held here is Chaitra Parba (in April), at which tribal groups perform the vigorous Chhau dance wearing fabulous costumes. It was originally performed by warriors just before they went onto the battlefield. In the eastern part of town, **Baripada Museum** has fine sculptures, pottery, and coins found in the area.

Haripur, 16 km (10 miles) southeast of Baripada, has the evocative ruins of palaces and temples built by the rulers of the Bhanja dynasty, who made this their capital in the 15th century. The most impressive ruins are of the brick-built Rasikaraya Temple and the Durbar Hall of the Bhanja kings.

Baripada Museum
⊘ 🕐 Irregular hours

11

Baleshwar

🏠 Baleshwar district; 214 km (133 miles) NE of Bhubaneswar 🚉🚌
🌐 Odisha Tourism, SPA Complex, Station Square; (06782) 262 048

Once a bustling seaport, Balasore or Baleshwar was established by the British in 1642. It was later in the possession of the French and the Dutch, but had lost its importance by the 18th century, with the silting up of the port. Its colonial past is visible in the ruins of some Dutch tombs, and what are said to be the remnants of old canals that led to the sea. Today Baleshwar is a sleepy town, surrounded by paddy fields and villages. It is known for the hand-crafted lacquer boxes and brass fish made locally, and for the Akhada Arts Festival, which happens during Durga Puja (Sep/Oct).

The tranquil seaside village of Chandipur, 16 km (10 miles) east of Baleshwar, is easily reached by a short taxi or scooter ride from the town. Here, the sea recedes up to 5 km (3 miles) at low tide, leaving an expanse of clean white sand. Odisha Tourism offers accommodation in a picturesque old bungalow a short distance from the beach, with the day's fresh catch served at dinner. The only blot on this peaceful landscape is the Indian Army's test firing range for rockets, just outside the village, against which environmentalists and villagers have been campaigning for many years.

> 💬 INSIDER TIP
> ## Odissi Tribal Crafts
>
> Odisha has numerous indigenous groups, many of whom create textiles and jewellery. Grass Routes (*grass routes.co.in*) offers tours to village markets where these are for sale.

---

⑬ 🚶 🅜 Similipal National Park

📍 Mayurbhanj district; 320 km (199 miles) N of Bhubaneswar; entry points at Lulung and Jashipur 🏠 Baripada, 50 km (31 miles) E of the park 🚌 To Lulung and Jashipur 🕐 Nov-mid-June ℹ For bookings and permits, contact Field Director, Similipal Tiger Reserve, Baripada; (06792) 255 939

This extraordinarily beautiful park is located amid the hills and forests of northeast Odisha. Stretching over 2,750 sq km (1,062 sq miles), Similipal comprises dense sal (Shorea robusta) and rosewood forests, broken by lush grasslands. Many rivers, such as the Budhabalanga, Khairi, Salandi and Palpala, and cascading rapids traverse the forest, creating spectacular waterfalls similar to those at Joranda (150 m/492 ft) and Barehipani (400 m/1,312 ft).

Originally the maharaja of Mayurbhanj's private hunting ground, Similipal was declared a wildlife sanctuary in 1957. A total of 1,076 types of mammals, 230 species of birds and 29 species of reptiles reside here. One of the earliest tiger reserves in India, it is home to about 100 tigers, as well as an impressive range of other fauna including elephants, leopards, deer, gaur (Indian bison) and pangolins (or scaly anteaters). These curious-looking animals, covered with large overlapping scales, feed exclusively on termites and ants, tearing open anthills with their powerful claws and scooping up the insects with their long tongues.

The rare muggers (marsh crocodiles) can be spotted in rivers or basking on the banks, where they dig tunnels to keep cool. At Jashipur, the western entry point to the park, there is a crocodile sanctuary, where the reptiles can be observed at close quarters. One of the park's best spots for viewing wildlife is located in the grasslands at Bacchuri Chara – a favourite haunt of elephant herds. There is another good area for sightings at Manghasani Peak (1,158 m/3,799 ft), one of the highest in the park. Basic food and accommodation are available in forest rest houses at Lulung, Barehipani, Chahala, Joranda and Nawana.

Khiching, 20 km (12 miles) west of the western entry point of Similipal National Park at Jashipur, was the capital of the Bhanja kings in the 10th and 11th centuries, and has some of the finest examples of temple sculpture to be seen in Odisha. The main sight is the towering Khichakeshwari temple,

TRIBES OF ODISHA

More than 60 different tribes, descended from the original, pre-Aryan inhabitants, live in Odisha. The Saoras, near Taptapani (p353), live in beautifully painted mud houses decorated with carved doors. Further west are the Koyas, whose customs decree that their women must marry only younger men. The Kondhs are renowned for their knowledge of medicinal herbs and for their beautiful metal jewellery. Contact Odisha Tourism in Bhubaneswar for information about the necessary permits to visit some tribal areas.

reconstructed in the early 20th century entirely from the ruins of the original temple that stood here. It is adorned with superb images of several deities, including a vibrant dancing Ganesha.

A number of other temples, together with the ruins of two forts built by the Bhanja kings, dot this hamlet.

Among the highlights of the small **Archaeological Museum**, which can have irregular hours, are outstanding life-size statues of Shiva and his consort Parvati, and exquisite sculptural panels from now-fallen temples.

Archaeological Museum
⊛ 📍 Goddess Kichakeswari temple 🕐 Tue-Sun

←

A tiger near a pond in Similipal National Park, a wildlife sanctuary

A local fisherman on the lagoon at Majuli Island

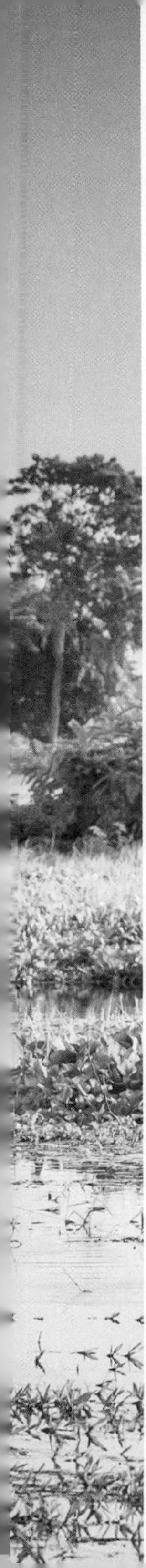

ASSAM AND THE NORTHEAST

Assam and the other six northeastern states, often called the Seven Sisters, make up the most geographically isolated and least-visited part of India. This region, which has international borders with China, Myanmar (Burma), Bhutan and Bangladesh, has an unusually rich diversity of ethnic groups, languages, religions, climates and landscapes, and a history that stretches back thousands of years. This culture remains strong, particularly as the region's various kingdoms resisted Mughal control. One of the most notable empires here was the Buddhist kingdom of Ahom, founded in the 13th century, which maintained dominance over the area now called Assam for 600 years. Ahom resisted multiple invasions until it was eventually conquered by the neighbouring kingdom of Burma. It was in Assam that the British East India Company encountered the world's only native tea plants outside of China, which led to India's establishment as the centre of the tea trade and the annexation of the territory by the British. Arunachal Pradesh, Meghalaya, Nagaland, Manipur, Mizoram and Tripura are home to more than 100 different indigenous groups, whose languages and culture are still an important part of everyday life.

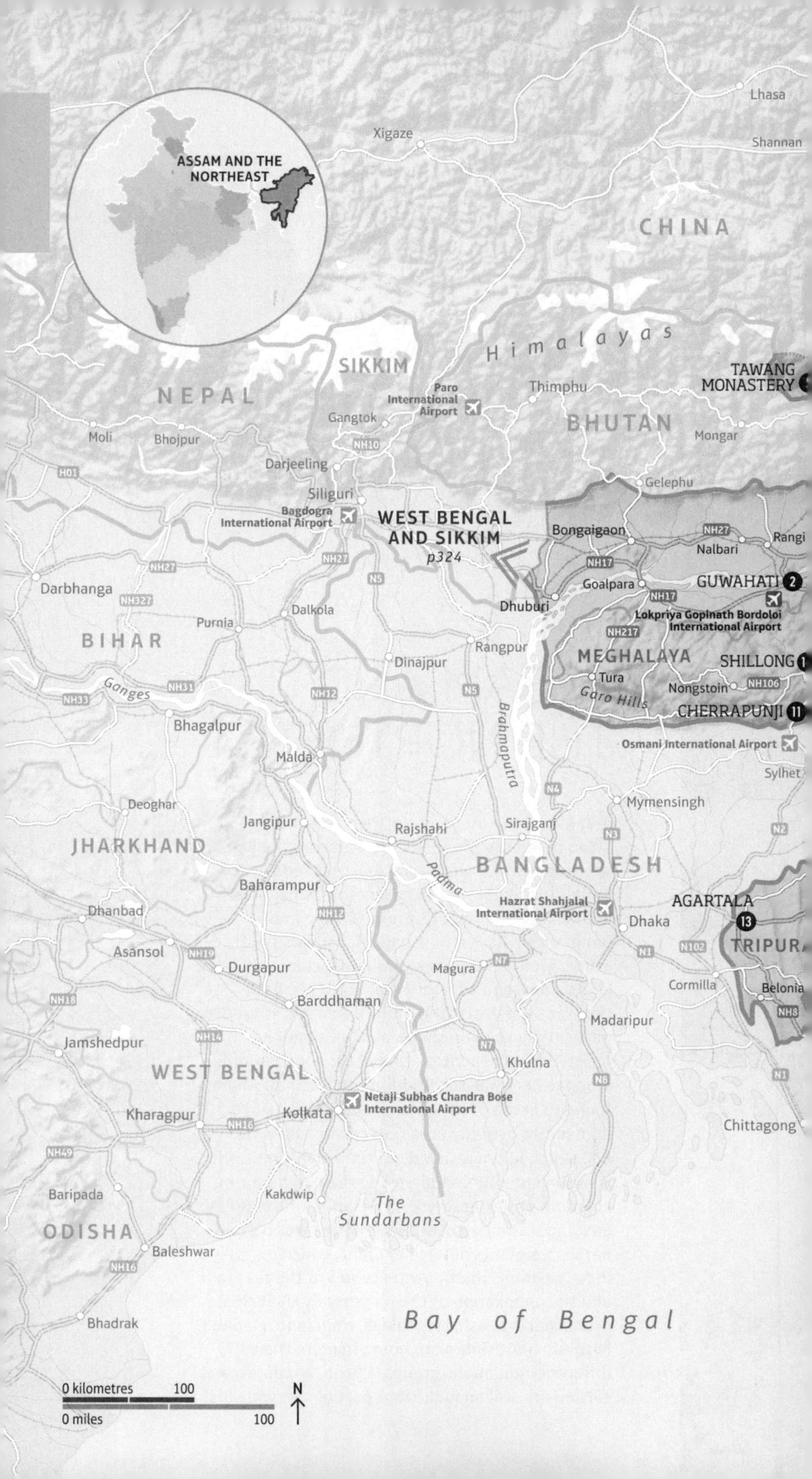

ASSAM AND THE
NORTHEAST

Xigaze

Lhasa

Shannan

CHINA

TAWANG
MONASTERY

Himalayas

NEPAL

SIKKIM

Moli

Bhojpur

Darjeeling

Gangtok

Paro
International
Airport

Thimphu

BHUTAN

Mongar

Siliguri

Bagdogra
International Airport

NH10

WEST BENGAL
AND SIKKIM
p324

Gelephu

Bongaigaon

Nalbari

NH27

Rangi

Darbhanga

NH327

Purnia

Dalkola

NH27

N5

Dhuburi

Goalpara

NH17

NH17

GUWAHATI

Lokpriya Gopinath Bordoloi
International Airport

NH217

BIHAR

Bhagalpur

Ganges

NH31

Dinajpur

NH33

Malda

N5

Rangpur

MEGHALAYA

Tura

Garo Hills

Nongstoin

SHILLONG

NH106

CHERRAPUNJI

Brahmaputra

Deoghar

Jangipur

Rajshahi

Sirajganj

Osmani International Airport

Sylhet

NH12

Mymensingh

N3

JHARKHAND

Baharampur

N4

BANGLADESH

Dhanbad

NH19

Durgapur

NH18

Asansol

Barddhaman

Magura

N7

Hazrat Shahjalal
International Airport

Dhaka

N1

NH102

AGARTALA

TRIPUR

Cormilla

Belonia

NH8

Jamshedpur

NH14

WEST BENGAL

N7

Khulna

Madaripur

N8

N1

Chittagong

Kharagpur

NH16

Kolkata

Netaji Subhas Chandra Bose
International Airport

NH49

Baripada

Kakdwip

The
Sundarbans

ODISHA

Baleshwar

NH16

Bay of Bengal

Bhadrak

0 kilometres   100

0 miles   100

N

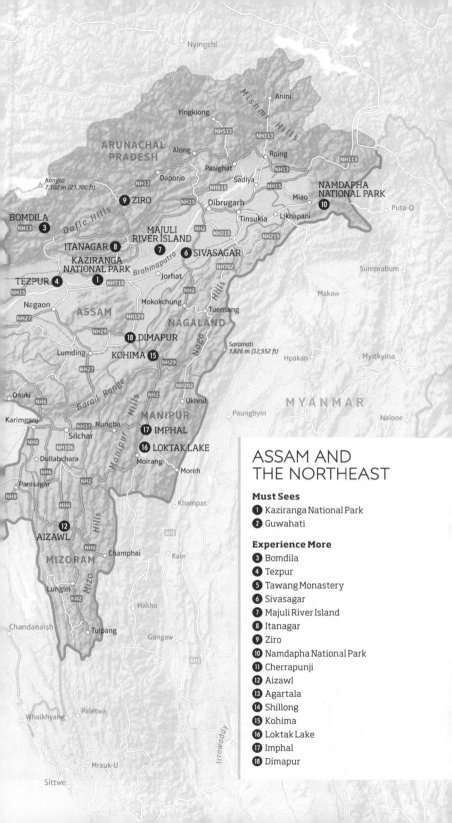

ASSAM AND THE NORTHEAST

Must Sees

1 Kaziranga National Park
2 Guwahati

Experience More

3 Bomdila
4 Tezpur
5 Tawang Monastery
6 Sivasagar
7 Majuli River Island
8 Itanagar
9 Ziro
10 Namdapha National Park
11 Cherrapunji
12 Aizawl
13 Agartala
14 Shillong
15 Kohima
16 Loktak Lake
17 Imphal
18 Dimapur

① ⊗ ⊗
KAZIRANGA
NATIONAL PARK

🏠 Golaghat district, Assam; 215 km (134 miles) NE of Guwahati ✈ Jorhat, 96 km (60 miles) NE of Kohora, the entry point, then taxi 🚉 Furkating, 75 km (47 miles) E of Kohora, then taxi 🚌 🕐 Nov–Apr ℹ Bonani Tourist Lodge, Kohora; (03776) 262 423

Assam's magnificent Kaziranga National Park, declared a World Heritage Site by UNESCO, is the home of the Indian one-horned rhinoceros. A rich variety of other wildlife can also be sighted in the park, including over 100 tigers, India's largest population of Asiatic buffalo, herds of wild elephants, Hoolock gibbons and pythons, and 300 species of birds, including the rare Bengal florican.

Kaziranga has relatively few visitors, but those who make the journey are highly rewarded for their efforts. Beautifully situated on the banks of the Brahmaputra, the park's landscape is characterized by vast grasslands and swamps, dotted with patches of semi-evergreen forest. The Mikir Hills, where many animals migrate for the monsoon, form its southern boundary.

Jeep safaris are easily arranged and are less restricted than those in central Indian parks, but elephant safaris have been suspended indefinitely.

STAY

IORA: The Retreat
Cosy rooms, a tea garden and a restaurant serving delicious Assamese cuisine.

⌂ Bogorijuri
🖥 kazirangasafari.com

₹₹₹

Diphlu River Lodge
Two daily safaris are included at this comfortable lodge built from natural materials.

⌂ Kuthuri, near Bagori Police Outpost
🖥 diphluriverlodge.com

₹₹₹

↑ A lone elephant, silhouetted by the sun, padding slowly through the park

→ A pair of Asiatic buffalo grazing among the park's tall grasslands

THE INDIAN ONE-HORNED RHINOCEROS

Kaziranga is one of the last refuges of the long-suffering Indian one-horned rhinoceros *(Rhinoceros unicornis)*, an endangered species that was perilously close to extinction at the beginning of the 20th century. A successful series of conservation measures have seen their numbers rise to 2,500 (across Assam and the foothills of Nepal), of which 1,500 are in Kaziranga alone. Once found extensively across the whole of the subcontinent, the rhino population dwindled dramatically because of widespread poaching for its horn, a prized ingredient in Chinese medicine. Actually a mass of closely matted hair, each rhino horn fetches an exorbitant price in Southeast Asia, where it is believed to have great medicinal and aphrodisiac properties.

↑ The Indian one-horned rhino, a conservation success story

② GUWAHATI

🏛 Kamrup (Metro) district, Assam; 1,081 km (672 miles) NE of Kolkata ✈ Lokpriya Gopinath Bordoloi International, 25 km (16 miles) W of city centre 🚉 🚌 ℹ Assam Tourism, Station Rd; (0361) 254 7102

The capital of Assam, Dispur lies in Guwahati city. Ringed by the Nilachal Hills, Guwahati stretches along both banks of the broad Brahmaputra river and is a busy commercial centre for Assam's tea and oil industries. Its outer fringes are dotted with betelnut palm trees.

Kamakhya Temple, one of India's most important pilgrimage sites ↑

① Umananda Temple

🏛 Peacock Island
⛴ Umananda Ghat, 1 km (0.6 miles) N of railway station ⏰ 5:30am–6pm daily

On the lush Peacock Island in the middle of the Brahmaputra, this 16th-century temple is dedicated to Shiva's wife. The island itself swarms with friendly monkeys and is an great place to watch the river.

② Navagraha Temple

🏛 Chitranchal Hill

Believed to mark the site of the ancient city of Pragjyotishpur,

the old name of Guwahati, Navagraha ("Nine Planets") Temple was built when the city was famous as a centre of astronomy. The temple has a striking red dome; underneath is a chamber with nine *lingas* representing the planets.

③ State Museum

🏛 GN Bordoloi Rd 📞 (0361) 254 0651 ⏰ Winter: 10am–4:30pm daily; summer: 10am–5pm daily 🚫 Mon, 2nd & 4th Sat of month

This museum, just east of the railway station, has reconstructions of tribal villages, a comprehensive collection of local handicrafts and a

gallery of medieval stone and bronze sculptures, which were excavated from Ambari, an archaeological site in the heart of the city.

④ Zoo and Botanical Gardens

🏛 RG Baruah Rd 📞 (0361) 220 1363 ⏰ 7am–4:30pm Sat-Thu

The well-maintained zoo is in the eastern part of the city. Clouded leopards, hornbills and the one-horned rhinos, can be seen in moated enclosures. The Botanical Gardens adjoin the zoo.

⑤ Hajo

🏛 32 km (20 miles) NW of Guwahati

Hajo is a pilgrimage site for Buddhists, Hindus and Muslims. The 16th-century Hayagriva Madhava Temple, on Monikut Hill, is sacred to Hindus and Buddhists, who believe that the Buddha died here. Fine bas-reliefs of scenes from the *Ramayana* decorate

THE MIGHTY BRAHMAPUTRA

This majestic river is named after the Son of Brahma, Creator of the Universe. Beginning near the holy mountain of Kailasa in Tibet, it sweeps around the eastern end of the Himalayas before plummeting through the gorges of upper Arunachal Pradesh. Just before the end of its 2,900-km (1,802-mile) course, the Brahmaputra merges with the Ganges to create the huge Bengal delta.

its walls. On another hill is the Poa Mecca ("Quarter of Mecca") Mosque, established by an Iraqi prince who visited Assam in the 12th century.

---

⑥
Madan Kamdev

🏠 50 km (31 miles) NW of Guwahati

Exuberantly erotic carvings of deities and celestial nymphs lie strewn on a small hillock at these temple ruins, which date from the 10th to 12th centuries.

---

⑦
Kamakhya Temple

🏠 Nilachal Hill, 8 km (5 miles) NW ⏲ 8am–1pm daily 🌐 kamakhyadham. com

This temple is one of India's most important pilgrimage sites. According to legend, as a furious and grieving Shiva carried the corpse of his wife, Sati (also known as Parvati) around the skies, parts of her dismembered body fell to the earth. Kamakhya is believed to mark the place where her vagina fell, and is therefore said to have special powers associated with energy and creation. In accordance with tantric rituals, a goat is sacrificed here every day, and offered to the goddess.

Buddhist prayer flags and a photo of the Dalai Lama in the mountains near Bomdila

EXPERIENCE MORE

❸

Bomdila

🏠 West Kameng district, Arunachal Pradesh; 140 km (87 miles) NW of Tezpur 🚌 ℹ️ Travel permits required

A pleasant town at an altitude of 2,530 m (8,301 ft), Bomdila is the headquarters of Arunachal's West Kameng district. It has Buddhist monasteries surrounded by apple orchards, with views of snowcapped peaks, terraced paddy fields and waterfalls. The Crafts Centre, opposite the Lower Gompa monastery, has displays on carpet weaving. The town's inhabitants belong largely to the Sherdukpen and Monpa tribes, who combine Tibetan Buddhism with their original animist beliefs.

 GREAT VIEW
Apple of Bomdila's Eye

Situated near the border with Bhutan, Bomdila has spectacular mountain scenery – and the best place to see this is from R.R. Hill, the town's highest point, with panoramic views.

---

❹

Tezpur

🏠 Sonitpur district, Assam; 180 km (112 miles) NE of Guwahati ✈️ Salonibari, 10 km (6 miles) N of town centre, then bus or taxi 🚍🚌 ℹ️ Tourist Office, Zenkins Rd; (03712) 221 016

A picturesque town on the Brahmaputra river, Tezpur is surrounded by green valleys covered with tea gardens. The town is a convenient take-off point for trips to other parts of Arunachal Pradesh.

Tezpur means "City of Blood", and this gory name is derived from its legendary past as the capital of the Hindu demon kings, the Asuras, said to have been vanquished here by Lord Krishna in a bloody battle. More recently, in 1962, Tezpur was involved in another battle when the invading Chinese army reached its outskirts before suddenly declaring a ceasefire and halting.

The ruins of the Da Parbatia Temple, 5 km (3 miles) west of the city, dating from the 5th to 6th centuries, bear testimony to Tezpur's ancient past. All that is left of the temple are some sculptures and an exquisitely carved

door frame, with images of the river goddesses Ganga and Yamuna on either side. Chitralekha Udyan, close to the Tourist Lodge, is Tezpur's prettiest spot, with a landscaped garden near a lake. It is embellished with 9th- and 10th-century sculptures.

Scenic Bhalukpong, 58 km (36 miles) northwest of Tezpur, is set in green foothills that mark the border of Assam and Arunachal Pradesh. The main attractions here are medicinal hot springs and an Orchid Centre located 7 km (4 miles) away at Tipi, with some 500 varieties of native orchids.

Nameri National Park covers 200 sq km (77 sq miles). The Jia Bhoroli river winds through its deciduous forests, which are home to clouded leopards, *mithuns* (Indian bison) and the rare whitewinged wood duck. For adventure activities, the **Potasali Eco-Camp** organizes whitewater rafting and *mahseer* fishing trips.

Orang National Park is often described as a miniKaziranga since it has a similar landscape of marshes, streams and grassland. This sanctuary is home to the one-horned

> **The road to the monastery reveals a stunning landscape of snowy peaks, Monpa hamlets, and juniper and dwarf rhododendron bushes.**

rhinoceros, who favour this habitat, as well as the Asiatic wild buffalo.

Nameri National Park
🎫 ♿ 📷 35 km (22 miles) N of Tezpur ⏰ Nov–Apr ℹ For permits, contact Divisional Forest Officer, Western Assam Wildlife Division, Dolabari, Tezpur; (03712) 268 054

Potasali Eco-Camp
📞 (09435) 145 563/250 025

Orang National Park
🎫 ♿ 📷 65 km (40 miles) NW of Tezpur ⏰ Oct–Apr ℹ For permits, contact Divisional Forest Officer, Mangaldoi, (03713) 230 022

---

⑤ Tawang Monastery
📍 Tawang district, Arunachal Pradesh; 325 km (202 miles) NW of Tezpur 🚌 🌐 tawang monastery.org

The famous Gaden Namgyal Lhatse, popularly known as Tawang Monastery, is India's largest Buddhist monastery.

It is situated in Arunachal Pradesh at an altitude of 3,050 m (10,007 ft). As the road ascends from Bomdila, the scenery becomes alpine, and lush with pine, oak and rhododendron forests, and a short, high-altitude bamboo, which is the favourite food of the red panda. Past the Dirang Valley with its old *dzong* (fort), the road climbs sharply to the Sela Pass. At 4,249 m (13,940 ft), this is the second-highest motorable pass in the world; the highest is in Ladakh.

Beyond a memorial to a valiant Indian soldier who held up the advancing Chinese army during the India-China conflict of 1962, the road descends to a wide valley. The monastery, on a spur surrounded by snowcapped peaks, dominates the valley. When the Dalai Lama fled Tibet in 1959, his route into India was through Tawang, and he still visits the area regularly to hold special prayer sessions.

Founded in 1645 by a lama from Merak in Bhutan, this Gelugpa (Yellow Hat) establishment has over 500 resident monks. It was also the birthplace of the sixth Dalai Lama. The three-storeyed *dukhang* (assembly hall) has a magnificent 8-m- (26-ft-) high statue of the Buddha. The ancient library, leading onto the main courtyard, has an excellent collection of *thangkas* and valuable Buddhist manuscripts.

The Bramdungchung Nunnery, associated with Tawang Monastery, is 12 km (7 miles) northwest of Tawang. The road to the monastery reveals a stunning landscape of snowy peaks, Monpa hamlets, and juniper and dwarf rhododendron bushes. Fluttering prayer flags and a long prayer wall mark the approach to the nunnery, guarded, as most in this region, by fierce Tibetan mastiffs. Note that a permit is required to travel into this region.

Tawang Monastery, and *(inset)* a statue of Buddha wearing the Gelugpa yellow hat ↓

6 Sivasagar

🏠 Sivasagar district, Assam; 370 km (230 miles) NE of Guwahati 🚉 Jorhat, 60 km (37 miles) S of city centre 🚌 ℹ️ Assam Tourism, near Shivadol Temple 🌐 sivasagar.nic.in

At the heart of Assam's tea and oil-producing region, Sivasagar is also the state's most historic city, as the seat of the Ahom dynasty, which ruled Assam for 600 years. Originally from Myanmar (Burma), the Ahoms converted to Hinduism and gradually adopted local customs and culture after conquering Assam in 1228. The Ahoms were defeated by the Burmese in 1817, and their kingdom became part of the British Indian Empire in 1826.

Dominating the town is the enormous 103-ha (255-acre) man-made Sivasagar Lake, with three temples on its banks. Especially impressive is the towering Shivadol Temple with its 33-m- (108-ft-) high gilded spire, built by an Ahom queen in 1734. About 4 km (2 miles) south of the town are the ruins of two 18th-century brick palaces, Kareng Ghar and Talatal Ghar. Both are seven storeys high, and the latter also has three underground floors and a warren of secret tunnels.

Did You Know?

Assam is the only area outside of China where native tea plants have been discovered.

---

7 Majuli River Island

🏠 Assam; 314 km (195 miles) NE of Guwahati 🚉 Neamati Ghat, 13 km (8 miles) N of Jorhat 🚢 From Neamati Ghat to Majuli, then bus to Garamur ℹ️ On arrival, foreigners must register with the Sub-Divisional Officer, Majuli, who also handles bookings

Perhaps the largest inhabited river island in the world, Majuli covers an area of 929 sq km (359 sq miles). It is easy to forget that Majuli is an island, holding within it hills, rivulets and little islands of its own. This amorphous landmass is constantly being sculpted into new dimensions and shapes by the Brahmaputra river. Every year, during the annual monsoon, the river submerges large tracts of land, forcing the inhabitants to move to higher ground. After the floods recede, leaving behind fertile, freshly silted land, the people return to cultivate the area.

The first *satras* (monasteries) in Majuli were founded in the 15th century by the reformer-philosopher Srimanta Sankardeva. These are rich repositories of Assamese arts and crafts, and regularly stage dance-dramas in praise of Vishnu. Majuli's main settlement is at Garamur, which has two *satras*. About 20 others are scattered across the island. Visitors can stay in the *satras*, and should offer to make a donation.

---

8 Itanagar

🏠 Arunachal Pradesh; 420 km (261 miles) NE of Guwahati 🚉 Lakhimpur, 60 km (37 miles) NE of town centre 🚌 ℹ️ Directorate of Tourism, Itanagar, (0360) 221 4745; apply for Inner Line Permits (ILP) online at www.arunachalilp.com

Until it became the capital of Arunachal Pradesh in 1971,

→ The remains of Talatal Ghar, an 18th-century palace constructed by the Ahoms at Sivasagar

Itanagar was a settlement of the Nishi tribe, one of the largest among the 26 major tribes that inhabit the state. A few traditional Nishi longhouses still remain, now all but swamped by Itanagar's newly constructed government buildings. The Nishi men traditionally wore the beak of a great hornbill on their cane headgear, but this practice is now being discouraged as the hornbill is a protected species.

The **Jawaharlal Nehru Museum**, near the Secretariat, offers a comprehensive look at the arts and crafts of all the tribes of Arunachal Pradesh. Cane and bamboo artifacts, textiles, jewellery and totem objects are on display here. A pretty but bumpy 6-km (4-mile) drive north from Itanagar leads to the lovely, emerald-green Gyakar Sinyi Lake, surrounded by dense forests. Many of the tall trees are festooned with orchids.

Jawaharlal Nehru Museum
 ⌂ Siddharth Vihar
☎ (0360) 221 2276
⊙ Sun–Thu

9

Ziro

⌂ Arunachal Pradesh;
150 km (93 miles) NE of Itanagar ⛟ ℹ Deputy Commissioner's Office, (03788) 224 255; apply for Inner Line Permits online at www.arunachalilp.com

The picturesque town of Ziro, in central Arunachal Pradesh, lies in a large, flat valley, surrounded by low pine-covered hills. This area, better known as the Apatani Plateau, is the home of the prosperous Apatani tribe who practise a unique system of cultivation that combines rice-growing with fish farming. The flooded paddy fields are stocked with fingerlings, the two staples of Apatani diet thus coming from the same plot of land. Like the Nishis,

the Apatanis wear their hair in a bun on their foreheads, held with a brass skewer, and the women sport noseplugs.

On a hilltop in Ziro sits Gompa Buddhist Temple with its yellow-roofed shrine and a tree planted by the Dalai Lama. Ziro is also the site of one of India's best outdoor music festivals.

Northeast of Ziro, three other areas – Daporijo, Along and Pasighat – are open to foreigners (with permits). The latter two are situated on the Brahmaputra river and are inhabited by the Adi tribe. The drive from Ziro to Pasighat (300 km/186 miles) is wonderfully scenic, through dense expanses of virgin forest and tribal villages.

SHOP

Craft Centre and Emporium
Run by the state's Industries Department, this Itanagar store offers a good selection of crafts from all over Arunachal Pradesh at reasonable prices.

⌂ Koloraing Road, Itanagar

10

Namdapha National Park

⌂ Arunachal Pradesh; 380 km (236 miles) NE of Itanagar ⛟ Margherita, 64 km (40 miles) SW of Miao, the entry point ⊙ Oct–Mar ℹ Director, Project Tiger, Miao, (03807) 222 253; apply for Inner Line Permits (ILP) online at www.arunachalilp.com

This wonderful park in the east of the state, bordering Myanmar (Burma), covers an epic 1,985 sq km (766 sq miles). Rising from the plains to 4,500 m (14,764 ft) in the Himalayas, it is the only reserve in India where all the four big cats of the Himalayas – tiger, leopard, clouded leopard and the snow leopard – are found. It was declared a Tiger Reserve in 1983. Other wildlife includes the great Indian hornbill and the red panda.

The legendary Burma Road (or Stilwell Road) begins at Ledo, 60 km (37 miles) southwest of Miao. This 1,700-km (1,056-mile) road, of strategic importance in World War II, connected Ledo, via jungles and mountains, to Kunming in China's Yunnan province. Supervised by the American General Joseph Stilwell and built at a huge human cost, it has fallen into disrepair, but is still used by locals travelling on foot.

↑ A clouded leopard, one of the four big cat species of the Himalayas, in Namdapha National Park

→

The double-decker root
bridge at Umshiang,
near Cherrapunji

STAY

**Cherrapunjee
Holiday Resort**
This family-run guest
house is located near
the root bridges.

⌂ Laitkynsew Village,
Cherrapunji
ⓦ cherrapunjee.com

₹₹₹

Pinewood Hotel
Set among the trees by
Ward Lake, this hotel
is a quiet retreat.

⌂ Rita Road, Shillong
☎ (0364) 222 3116

₹₹₹

Na La Ri Resort
A place to fish, swim,
birdwatch or just relax,
in cottages or tents.

⌂ Lawbyrwa, Sumer,
near Shillong
ⓦ oknortheast.com/
2017/08/
nalari-resort.html

₹₹₹

⑪
Cherrapunji

⌂ East Khasi Hills district,
Meghalaya; 143 km
(90 miles) S of Guwahati 🚌

Famous as one of the wettest
places on earth, Cherrapunji,
the former state capital, is a
writhing mass of jungle and
streams. By training the roots
of the rubber plant from one
side of a stream to another,
local residents have created
solid living bridges called *jing
kieng jri*, which strengthen
with age. The double-decker
root bridge at Umshiang is
the most well known.

---

⑫
Aizawl

⌂ Mizoram; 480 km
(298 miles) SE of Guwahati
✈ 35 km (22 miles) W of
town centre, then bus or
taxi 🚌 ⓘ Mizoram
Tourism, Bungkawn;
(0389) 233 3475; apply for
Inner Line Permits (ILP)
online at mizoram.nic.in/
more/ilp.htm

Perched along a ridge, Aizawl
is Mizoram's capital, and home
of the Mizo tribes, said to have
migrated here from Myanmar

300 years ago. Almost the
entire population of Mizoram
is now Christian, converted by
missionaries who first came
here in 1891. As a result of
the schools they started,
Mizoram has the second
highest literacy rate in India.
Blue jeans are more
commonly seen today than
tribal dress among the men,
but the women still wear their
elegant *puans* (long, narrow
skirts). Visitors can see these
being woven at the Weaving
Centre in Luangmual, 7 km
(4 miles) away.

---

⑬
Agartala

⌂ West Tripura district,
Tripura; 600 km (373 miles)
S of Guwahati ✈ 12 km
(7 miles) N of town centre,
then bus or taxi 🚌 ⓘ Swet
Mahal; (0381) 222 3893

The capital of Tripura, a
former princely state, Agartala
is a pleasant town dominated
by the sprawling **Ujjayanta
Palace**, built in 1901 in Indo-
Saracenic style. Now the State
Legislature, the opulent palace
interior includes a tiled Chinese
Room with a magnificent
ceiling. It is open to visitors
when the Assembly is not in

14

Shillong

East Khasi Hills district, Meghalaya; 127 km (79 miles) S of Guwahati **Meghalaya Tourism, 3rd Secretariat, Lower Lachumiere; (0364) 250 0736**

Capital of the tiny state of Meghalaya, Shillong, with its mist-shrouded hills, pine forests, lakes and waterfalls, is sometimes described as the "Scotland of the East". Lying at an altitude of 1,496 m (4,908 ft), it was chosen as the headquarters of the British administration in Assam in 1874 and soon developed into a popular hill station.

The town still retains a distinctly colonial ambience, with its mock-Tudor bungalows, churches, polo ground and golf course.

The sprawling and bustling **Bara Bazaar** offers a vivid glimpse of Khasi tribal society. The stalls are piled high with enticing produce from the surrounding villages – honey, pineapples, dried fish, wild mushrooms, raw betel nut and bamboo baskets. Most of the stalls are run by Khasi women dressed in their traditional tunic-like *jainsems*

session. Tripura is renowned for its exceptionally fine cane and bamboo work, freely available in the market.

Neermahal Water Palace, 55 km (34 miles) to the south, on an island in Rudrasagar Lake, was the summer home of the former maharajas of Tripura. Built in white marble and red sandstone, this palace has a profusion of pavilions, balconies, turrets and bridges.

Ujjayanta Palace
⏱ 5-7pm daily

PICTURE PERFECT
Ujjayanta Palace

Make your way to Agartala's Ujjayanta Palace come evening to capture a shot of its illuminated white edifice reflected in the surrounding lake - it makes a beautiful photo.

and tartan-checked shawls. North of the market, the small **Museum of Entomology** has a collection of rare butterflies and insects found in Meghalaya, including the giant yellow and black bird-wing butterfly and lovely iridescent beetles.

In the centre of town, the horseshoe-shaped **Ward Lake** has pleasant paths around it, paddle boats for hire and a café. A short distance to its south is **Lady Hydari Park**, with a pretty Japanese garden and a mini zoo which includes fauna native to Meghalaya's forests, such as hornbills and the ferret-like slow loris.

The beautiful Bishop and Beadon Falls are 3 km (2 miles) north of Shillong, just off the Guwahati-Shillong Highway. Further along the same route, Umiam Lake is a large artificial reservoir with facilities for angling, kayaking and water-skiing. The road to Mawphlang, 24 km (15 miles) southwest of Shillong, is a good place to see some of Meghalaya's rare species of orchids in their natural habitat.

Bara Bazaar
🏠 Bara Bazaar Rd
⏱ Mon-Sat

Museum of Entomology
🏠 Umsohsun Rd
⏱ 11am-4pm Mon-Sat

Ward Lake
⏱ 8:30am-7pm daily (to 5:30pm Nov-Feb)

Lady Hydari Park
⏱ 8am-5pm Tue-Sun

↑ Stalls heaped with colourful vegetables at the Bara Bazaar market in Shillong

15

Kohima

🏠 Nagaland; 339 km (211 miles) E of Guwahati 🚉 Dimapur, 74 km (46 miles) NW of Kohima, then taxi or bus 🚌 ℹ️ Nagaland Tourism; apply for Inner Line Permits (ILP) online at tourismnagaland.com

The capital of Nagaland, Kohima, at an altitude of 1,500 m (4,921 ft), is a small town surrounded by hills. The Naga people comprise the majority of the population in this state.

Kohima is famous in World War II history for the decisive battle fought around the tennis court of the British deputy commissioner's house that finally stopped the Japanese advance into India in April 1944. Those who fell in the battle are buried in the beautifully kept War Cemetery covering a terraced hillside. A poignant inscription at the base of one of the two large crosses here reads: "When you go home/ Tell them of us and say/ For your tomorrow/ We gave our today."

Kohima's main bazaar is the hub of this community, and local Naga people, wearing distinctive colourful woven shawls, come from surrounding villages to sell their produce. At the market, visitors can buy local delicacies that form staples of the Naga diet, such as bees' larvae.

The **State Museum**, 2 km (1 mile) north of the bazaar, has an excellent collection of Naga masks, textiles, jewellery and totem pillars from all the 16 Naga tribes. Particularly worth a look is a ceremonial drum that looks like a dugout canoe. The drum is engraved with stylized waves, and has gongs that look like paddles. This and other factors, such as the use of seashells in their costumes, has led some anthropologists to conjecture that the Nagas were originally a seafaring people, possibly from Sumatra. Today, a high percentage of Nagas are Christians, and a church can be found in almost every corner of the state.

On a hill overlooking the town, the original village of Kohima, Bara Basti, is a settlement of the Angami Naga tribe. Though now considerably modernized, it still has its ceremonial gate-way and a large traditional community house called the *morung*, with crossed horns surmounting its gable. A less modernized Angami Naga village is Khonoma, 20 km (12 miles) southwest of Kohima. It has wooden houses, a carved gateway and sur-rounding stone wall, and it is mainly agricultural – terraced paddy fields cover the hillside, irrigated by bamboo pipes.

State Museum

🧭 🏠 Upper Bayavü Hill 📞 (0370) 226 0133 🕐 10am–4pm Tue-Sun 🚫 Public hols

16

Loktak Lake

🏠 Manipur; 48 km (30 miles) S of Imphal 🚌 ℹ️ For bookings on Sendra Island, contact Manipur Tourism; (0385) 224 603/220 802; apply for Inner Line Permits (ILP) online at www.manipurtourism.gov.in

Almost two-thirds of this huge expanse of freshwater lake is covered by saucer-shaped islands of reed and decom-posing soil matter, known as *phumdi*, home to a community of fishermen. The southern part of the lake forms the Keibul Lamjao National Park, where *phumdi* form the hab-itat of the *sangai*, an endan-gered Manipur brow-antlered deer. These deer have divided hooves, adapted to their habitat. Sendra Island, at the heart of the park, has great views of the lake, its islands and its birdlife. Due to political instability, only day-trips to Loktak Lake are possible.

↑ The elegant buildings forming Imphal's Govindaji Temple complex, where dances take place on festival days

17

Imphal

🏠 Manipur; 484 km
(301 miles) SE of Guwahati
✈ 6 km (4 miles) S of centre
🚌 Manipur Tourism,
next to Hotel Imphal; apply
for Inner Line Permits (ILP)
online at www.manipur
tourism.gov.in

The capital of Manipur (the "Jewelled Land"), Imphal lies in a broad valley enclosed by forested hills. Its inhabitants mostly belong to the Meitei tribe. The liveliest part of the town is the Ima Keithel ("Mothers' Market"), where more than 3,000 women congregate daily to sell fresh produce, fish, grain, canework and handicrafts, including the elegant striped textiles worn by the Meitei women.

Imphal's main temple, the Govindaji Temple, stands east of the Bazaar, and on festivals associated with Lord Krishna the graceful Manipuri dance is performed here. Sagol Kangjei, Manipuri polo, is a favourite sport in Imphal (they claim to have invented the game), and an opportunity to see a match should not be missed – the polo ground is in the centre of the town. It is a fast and furious game, with the players dressed in dhotis and often riding bareback on the agile Manipuri horses. Two well-tended Commonwealth War Graves Cemeteries are on the northern and eastern outskirts of town. The men who died fighting the Japanese during the invasion of Manipur in World War II are buried here. An Orchidarium with various indigenous species is 12 km (7 miles) north of town.

Moirang, 45 km (28 miles) south of Imphal, with its ancient temple to the pre-Hindu god, Thangjing, is the spiritual home of the Meiteis, who celebrate Lai Haraoba. During World War II, Moirang was the headquarters of the Indian National Army (INA), which was led by Subhash Chandra Bose and fought against the Allies.

←

Distinctive reed islands known as *phumdi*, dotting lush Loktak Lake

18

Dimapur

🏠 Nagaland; 74 km
(46 miles) NW of Kohima
🚍🚌 ℹ️ Tourist Office; apply
for Inner Line Permits (ILP)
online at tourismnagaland.
com

A gateway to the rest of Nagaland, Dimapur was founded by the Kachari rulers, a Tibeto-Burmese people who were displaced from their territories in Assam in the 13th century by the invading Ahoms. Some of the ruins of their old capital can be seen. Most notable are 30 carved megaliths, believed to be fertility symbols.

> ### INDIGENOUS PEOPLES
>
> Northeast India is home to an extraordinary diversity of indigenous peoples. Arunachal Pradesh alone has 26 major groups, while Nagaland has 16. Many others inhabit Assam, Manipur, Mizoram, Meghalaya and Tripura. Geographically isolated from each other by steep mountain ridges, rivers and gorges, these groups have distinct cultural identities, customs, crafts, diets, history and languages.

Beautiful Jain temples crowning Shatrunjaya Hill in Palitana

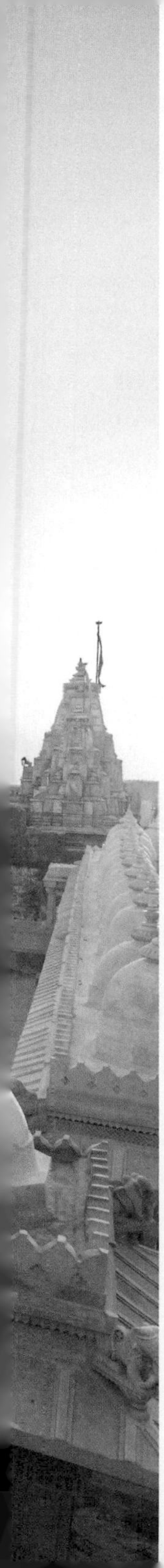

GUJARAT

The state of Gujarat has three distinct regions – a corridor running north to south which is the industrial mainland, a peninsula known as Saurashtra, and Kutch, which is partly desert and partly marshland. As with most Indian states, Gujarat does not have a history as a united province, but rather a potted ancestry of large empires or smaller princely states. It was one of the main areas that comprised the ancient Indus Valley Civilization, and was home to one of the world's first seaports – there is evidence of early trade with the world, as well as numerous remains from the Indus kingdom, particularly at Lothal. Subsequently ruled by the Mauryan and Gupta empires, Gujarat was passed between different dynasties for hundreds of years before becoming a part of the Delhi Sultanate, and subsequently the Sultanate of Gujarat in the 14th century. This rich and aggressive state successively repulsed multiple Mughal invasions before falling in the 16th century. Various European powers attempted to make inroads into Gujarat, attracted by the 1,666-km (1,035-mile) coastline, starting with the Portuguese, who wrested control of the northern area of Diu in the early 16th century. The area was eventually conquered by the British in the early 19th century, before becoming a united state after independence in 1947.

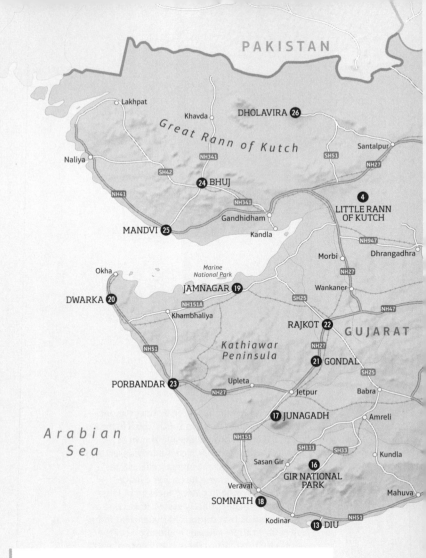

GUJARAT

Must Sees

1 Ahmedabad
2 Adalaj Vav
3 Modhera Sun Temple
4 Little Rann of Kutch

Experience More

5 Vadodara
6 Patan
7 Lothal
8 Nal Sarovar Sanctuary
9 Siddhpur
10 Champaner
11 Daman
12 Surat

13 Diu
14 Palitana
15 Bhavnagar
16 Gir National Park
17 Junagadh
18 Somnath
19 Jamnagar
20 Dwarka
21 Gondal
22 Rajkot
23 Porbandar
24 Bhuj
25 Mandvi
26 Dholavira

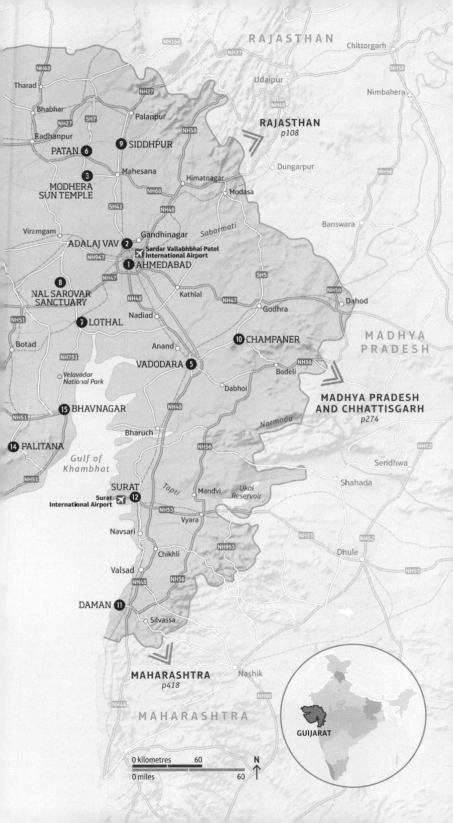

❶

AHMEDABAD

Ahmedabad district; 545 km (338 miles) NW of Mumbai 10 km (6 miles) N of city centre HK House, Ashram Rd; www.gujarattourism.com

Legend has it that this bustling city owes its foundation to Sultan Ahmed Shah (r 1411–42), who, while out hunting, encountered a warren of rabbits that turned on his hounds and defended their territory. The sultan built his new capital at the site and named it after himself – Ahmedabad.

①

The Old City

Bounded by Lady Vidyagauri Rd, Sardar Patel Rd & Kasturba Gandhi Rd

A maze of crowded bazaars, *pols* (large gateways, leading to residential quarters), exquisitely carved façades, temples, mosques and subterranean stepwells *(vavs)* mark the square that makes up the Old City. This area is best explored on foot, and the Ahmedabad Municipal Corporation organizes a daily **Heritage Walking Tour** through the atmospheric bylanes.

Heritage Walking Tour
Swaminarayan Temple
heritagewalk ahmedabad.com

STAY

House of MG
Situated in a beautiful heritage house that once played host to Gandhi, the House of MG has 38 rooms and two traditional restaurants (Green House and Agashiye). It also runs a number of walking tours that explorethe heritage of the city.

Lal Darwaja
houseofmg.com

₹₹₹

②

Bhadra Fort

Court Rd, Bhadra
9am-5pm daily

Built at the site of the original city, Bhadra Fort has panoramic views of the surrounding streets, and was renovated in 2004. Southwest of the fort is Ahmed Shah's Mosque, a simple place of worship which was built in 1414 on the site of an early-13th-century Hindu temple.

③

Jama Masjid

Manek Chowk, Mahatma Gandhi Rd 6am-8pm daily

Along Mahatma Gandhi Road, the Jama Masjid was built by Sultan Ahmed Shah in 1423 to enable the faithful to congregate for Friday prayers. The masons who constructed this yellow sandstone structure ingeniously used pieces retrieved from demolished Hindu and Jain temples – the black slab close to the main arch is said to be the base of an inverted Jain idol. The mosque's 15 domes are supported by 260 pillars covered with intricate carvings. The interior is illuminated by natural light that is filtered through latticework screens.

④

Sarkhej Roja

Sarkhej Makarba Road
9am-6pm daily

Southeast of the city is the Sarkhej Roja, a beautiful complex of tombs and pavilions around an artificial lake, built as a retreat for Gujarat's rulers between 1445 and 1461. Its tombs include that of Ahmed Shah's spiritual advisor, Sheikh Ahmed Khattu. Finely carved brass latticework is a unique feature of this site.

⑤

Calico Museum

Shahi Bagh, N of Delhi Gate Only via guided tours at 10:30am Thu-Tue calicomuseum.org/ contact-us

A major centre of India's textile trade and industry since the 15th century, this town is an appropriate spot for this outstanding museum. Its collection of rare textiles,

← Evening shoppers browsing stalls for items of interest

which spans the 17th and 18th centuries, includes royal tents, religious paintings, carpets and Kashmir shawls housed in a beautiful *haveli*. Bookings are required for guided tours and numbers are limited.

⑥
Tomb of Ahmed Shah

🅰 Manek Chowk, Mahatma Gandhi Rd 🕐 Daily

Outside the east entrance of the Jama Masjid is the Tomb of Ahmed Shah (Badshah no Hajiro), with elegant pillared verandahs, where the sultan, his son and grandson are buried. His queens are buried in the mausoleum of Rani no Hajiro, which echoes the layout of the sultan's tomb. Visitors must cover their heads.

> 💬 INSIDER TIP
> **Snack Food**
>
> *Patra* is a famous local snack of gram and tamarind butter spread on *arbi* leaves. Try it at the lovely Green House or Swati Snacks (*www. swatisnacks.com*), both of which serve a range of Gujarati food.

⑦
Sabarmati Ashram

🅰 Gandhi Smarak Sangrahalaya 🕐 8:30am–6:30pm daily 🌐 gandhi ashramsabarmati.org

A spartan colony of tiled houses, the Sabarmati Ashram was a second home to Mahatma Gandhi, from where he orchestrated the final struggle for India's freedom. The ashram now preserves his memory. His cottage, Hriday Kunj, has been kept much as he left it and contains items such as his round eyeglasses, books and letters.

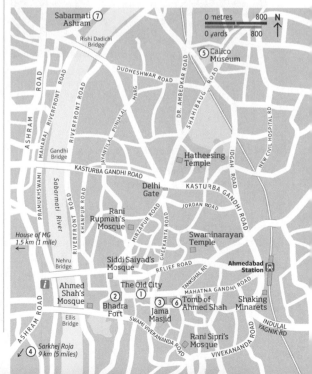

②

ADALAJ VAV

🏠 Gandhinagar district; 19 km (12 miles) N of Ahmedabad city centre
🚌 Buses available, but taxis and autos are the best options from
Ahmedabad ⏰ 24 hrs daily 🚩 www.gujarattourism.com

Adalaj Vav, perhaps Gujarat's finest stepwell, was built in 1499 by
Rudabai, the wife of a local Vaghela chieftain, to conserve water and
provide a cool and pleasant ambience for social interaction. Though
its well is no longer in use, it is still used for rest and recreation today.

The *vavs* (stepwells) of Gujarat are an ingenious answer to the water scarcity in
this arid region. Many of these elaborately ornamented underground wells are
dedicated to deities, acknowledging the hand of God in providing life-sustaining
water. A series of beautiful platforms and galleries are built into the sides of the
stepwell, all the way down to its subterranean depths. The main corridor leads
down five storeys to a depth of 30 m (98 ft), through pavilions whose walls,
pillars and niches are covered with sculptures. Adalaj is best viewed at noon,
when sunlight filters down to the bottom.

↑ Visitors looking down
onto the main well of
Adalaj Vav

←
One of the many
intricate Indo-Islamic
floral stone carvings
found inside the well

OTHER STEPWELLS IN GUJARAT

The 11th-century Rani ni Vav, a UNESCO World Heritage
Site in Patan *(p386)*, is among the most elaborately
carved stepwells in India, with some 800 sculptures.
Built in 1500, Dada Harir Vav in Ahmedabad is one of the
finest examples of a *vav* from the Muslim period in Gujarat.
The 15th-century Ambarpur Vav, 18 km (11 miles) from
Ahmedabad, is one of the few *vavs* still in use.

The galleries of Adalaj
Vav beginning to glow
as midday approaches

3 ⬡ Ⓜ ▢

MODHERA SUN TEMPLE

📍 Mehsana district; 100 km (62 miles) NW of Ahmedabad 🚉 Mehsana, 26 km (16 miles) away, then taxi or bus ⏰ 7am–6pm daily 🅘 gujarattourism.com

This magnificent temple complex was built in 1026 by King Bhima I of the Solanki dynasty to honour Surya, the sun god. The complex is laid out in an east-west direction, so that every day at high noon the sun's rays course through the chambers, striking the centre of the inner sanctum.

The Modhera Sun Temple is a feast for the eyes, a series of intricately carved halls and shrines. The complex is set beside a *kund*, a vast reservoir shaped like an inverted pyramid that is lined with 108 statues of gods and demi-gods. The juxtaposition of water against the Sun Temple is inspired by Vedic scriptures, which say that the sun was born from the depths of a primordial ocean. Off the impressive forecourt, the Entrance Hall leads through to the Sabha Mandapa, the assembly hall, once reserved for religious ceremonies. From here, visitors go through the Nritya Mandapa, the dance hall, to the Garbhagriha. The walls and pillars of this inner sanctum are richly carved with images of deities, in order of their celestial hierarchy – both these carvings and the ones on the exterior are extraordinarily detailed.

← Stone staircases rippling around the *kund*, a sacred reservoir

→ Visitors admiring the impressive Entrance Hall, with its 12 columns

↑ Carvings of Hindu deities and scenes from everyday life patterning the inner temple walls

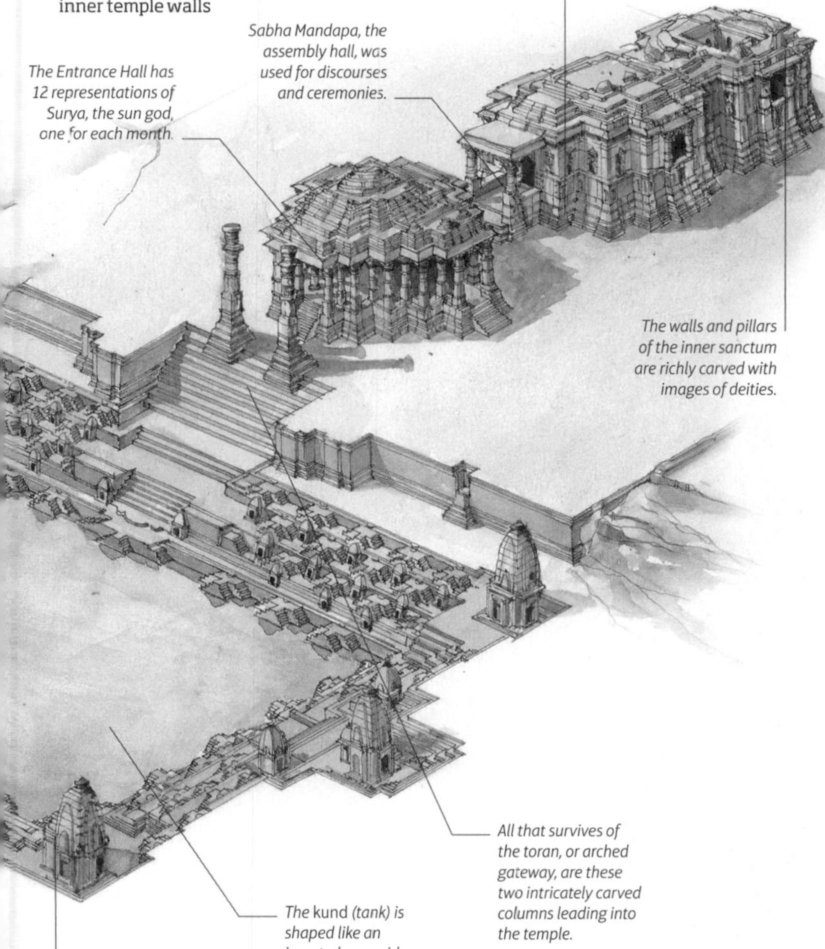

Must See

The Nritya Mandapa hall leads from the assembly hall towards the inner sanctum, and was used for dance performances.

Sabha Mandapa, the assembly hall, was used for discourses and ceremonies.

The Entrance Hall has 12 representations of Surya, the sun god, one for each month.

The walls and pillars of the inner sanctum are richly carved with images of deities.

All that survives of the toran, or arched gateway, are these two intricately carved columns leading into the temple.

The kund (tank) is shaped like an inverted pyramid. Flights of stairs create a ripple effect down to its base.

The magnificent tank is surrounded by miniature shrines, topped by curved shikharas.

↑ The 11th-century Modhera Sun Temple complex

Did You Know?

One of the earliest Vedic gods, Surya is said to be the creator of the physical universe.

383

An expanse of salt crystals
glittering in the sunlight, and
(inset) workers offloading
baskets of harvested salt ↑

4 🈁 🈂️

LITTLE RANN OF KUTCH

🏠 Kutch district; entry points at Dhrangadhra (130 km/81 miles SW of Ahmedabad) & Dasada (117 km/73 miles NW of Ahmedabad) 🚉 Dhrangadhra, 20 km (12 miles) S of park 🚌 Dhrangadhra & Dasada, then bus or jeep 🛈 For permits: contact Forest Office, Dhrangadhra; Gujarat Tourism, Ashram Rd, Ahmedabad; www.gujarattourism.com/destination/details/12/80

An expanse of salt flats and grasslands in northwest Gujarat, the Little Rann of Kutch has a stark and unforgettable beauty – in sunlight, the salt glitters like diamonds, while at night it bathes the landscape in an eerie blue haze.

Every year, during the monsoon, these salt flats are transformed into great marshy swamps, with patches of higher ground forming grassy islands. This unique ecosystem, which supports a variety of rare fauna, forms a sanctuary that is one of the last refuges of the Indian wild ass, known locally as *ghorkhur*. Dhrangadhra and Dasada are both interesting bases from which to visit the Rann and arrange accommodation. Dasada has a 15th-century fort and a village where potters and textile printers practise their craft. Dhrangadhra has a fine 18th-century palace and a bazaar with interesting colonial buildings. Tours of the sanctuary can be arranged through the Forest Office here.

STAY

Shaam-e-Sarhad
Magical resort with thatched roundhouses, promoting indigenous culture through sustainable tourism.

🏠 Hodka, Kutch
🌐 hodka.in

₹₹₹

Rann Riders
Eco-resort with tribal cottages among the wetlands. Fantastic local music every evening.

🏠 Dasada, Kutch
🌐 rannriders.com

₹₹₹

→ A master Kutch embroiderer displaying her work in the village of Dasada

↑ A herd of endangered Indian wild ass padding across the plains of Kutch

EXPERIENCE MORE

EXPERIENCE Gujarat

Vadodara

📍 Vadodara district;
112 km (70 miles) SE of
Ahmedabad 🚆 8 km
(5 miles) NE of town
centre 🚌🚕 🛈 www.
gujarattourism.com

Situated on the Vishwamitri
river, Vadodara owes much
of its splendour to Sayajirao
Gaekwad III (1863–1939),
a former ruler who trans-
formed his principality into
a progressive centre of
culture, education and
industry. Today Vadodara,
also known as Baroda, is
a vibrant city with many
interesting buildings,
museums and parks. The
Laxmi Vilas Palace, an Indo-
Saracenic pile, was designed
by the English architect Major
Charles Mant and completed
in 1890. It is still the residence
of the former ruling family.
The grounds host a golf club.
The **Maharaja Fateh Singh
Museum**, also within the
grounds, has a rare collection
of paintings by the famous
Indian artist Raja Ravi Varma
(1848–1906).

Sayaji Bagh, a beautiful
park in the heart of the
city, houses a zoo, a
planetarium and the
**Vadodara Museum
and Picture Gallery**,
which has an eclectic
collection of Mughal
miniatures, European
oil paintings and royal
artifacts. Pride of place

Did You Know?

The Vadodara-
Chandod line is the
oldest narrow-gauge
railway in the world.

goes to its collection of 68
striking bronzes from Akota, a
centre of Jain culture in the
5th century. Other notable
sights are the Kirti Mandir, the
samadhi(memorial) of
Vadodara's royal family; and
the Nyaya Mandir, an Indo-
Saracenic building that is now
a law court. The Maharaja
Sayajirao University's College
of Fine Art is an institute of
national eminence.

Not far from Vadodara,
the Amul Dairy is synonymous
with the "White Revolution"
that made India self-sufficient
in milk. It helped pioneer
India's dairy cooperative
movement, and now procures
one million litres of milk every
day from a thousand milk
cooperative societies.

Laxmi Vilas Palace
📞 (0265) 243 1819
🕐 10am–5pm Tue–Sun,
by appt

Maharaja Fateh
Singh Museum
📞 (0265) 242
6372 🕐 10am–
5:30pm
Tue–Sun

Vadodara Museum and
Picture Gallery
📞 (0265) 79 359
🕐 10:30am–5pm
Tue–Sun

Amul Dairy
📍 Anand, 38 km (24 miles)
NW of Vadodara 🕐 3–5pm
daily

Patan

📍 Mehsana district;
125 km (78 miles) from
Ahmedabad 🚌🚕 🛈 www.
gujarattourism.com

The town of Patan was the
capital of this region between
the 8th and 15th centuries,
before Sultan Ahmed Shah
moved his base to Ahmedabad
(*p378*) in 1411. The ruins of the
old capital, Anhilwada, include
the seven-storeyed Rani ni
Vav stepwell. Constructed in
the 11th century by Queen
Udaymati as a memorial to
her husband, it features some
800 sculptures and uniquely
has direct as well as lateral
series of steps leading to the
water's edge. At the base are
37 niches with the elephant
god Ganesha carved into them.
Nearby is the Sahastralinga
Talav, a water tank with 1,000
shrines dedicated to the god
Shiva, stands on the banks
of the Saraswati River.The
town is also known for
its production of
beautiful *patola*
saris (*opposite*).

7 Lothal

📍 Ahmedabad; 78 km (48 miles) SW of Ahmedabad 🚉 Lothal-Burkhi, 6 km (4 miles) SW of Lothal, then local transport 🚌 Burkhi 🕐 10am–5pm Sat–Thu ℹ www.gujarattourism.com

A remarkable city of the Indus Valley Civilization (p70) that existed 4,500 years ago, Lothal (literally, "Mound of the Dead") stood 6 km (4 miles) northwest of the confluence of the Sabarmati and Bhogavo rivers. A navigable estuary to the sea through the Gulf of Cambay (now Gulf of Khambat) made it a flourishing port that once traded with Egypt, Persia and Mesopotamia.

The foundations of a well-planned city are revealed with blocks of houses, paved drains, channels and wells, and 12 public baths. Lothal was surrounded by a mud brick embankment, to protect it from the perennial floods that, in all probability, were the cause of the city's destruction around 1900 BC.

Among the prize exhibits in the **Archaeological Museum** are a copper figurine and a

> In 2001, Indian oceanographers found the foundations of two cities under the sea, complete with streets, houses, temples and staircases.

PATOLA WEAVING

Patola is an intricate silk-weaving technique practised in Patan. Typical motifs include jewels, flowers, animals, dancing women and geometric forms. The craft is laborious – it takes a month to weave one sari length (5.5 m/6 yd) – and its product is highly prized, especially in a bridal trousseau.

gold-bead necklace.

In 2001, oceanographers found the foundations of two cities under the sea, complete with streets, houses, temples and staircases. Objects recovered from the seabed have been carbon-dated to 7,500 BC, suggesting that civilization may have started 5,000 years earlier than previously believed. The city may have been submerged as sea levels rose at the end of the Ice Age in about 8000 BC.

Archaeological Museum
♿ 🕐 10am–5pm Sat–Thu

8 Nal Sarovar Sanctuary

📍 Ahmedabad district; 60 km (37 miles) SW of Ahmedabad 🚉🚌 Viramgam, then taxi ℹ Conservator of Forests (02717) 223500; permits (079) 372 3500; www. gujarattourism.com

Nal Sarovar sanctuary is one of the largest bird sanctuaries in the country. The 115-sq-km (44-sq-mile) Nal Lake and the surrounding swamp forests are best visited between November and February,

← The grandiose Laxmi Vilas Palace, built in the late 19th century in Vadodara

when they attract as many as 250 species of waterfowl, including geese, flamingoes, cranes, pelicans, storks, ibis, cormorants and spoonbills. Winter migrants from as far as Siberia, such as the bluish-grey demoiselle crane, also gather here in their hundreds. Unfortunately, pressures on the habitat from the resident fishing communities, and from growing numbers of tourists, are slowly depleting the lake's rich range of birdlife.

9 Siddhpur

📍 Mehsana district; 114 km (71 miles) N of Ahmedabad 🚉🚌 ℹ www.gujarat tourism.com

The town of Siddhpur was once famous for the Rudra Mala Complex of Shiva temples, dating from the 10th century. It was destroyed by Muslim invaders in the 1200s. Historical accounts describe a three-storeyed complex, profusely carved in stone and supported by 1,600 pillars, with 11 smaller shrines and three gateways. Two porches and four columns from the main shrine are all that remain today, together with a well-preserved carved gateway with two columns. The town also has interesting wooden *havelis* and pillared mansions, built by Muslim traders in the 1800s.

⑩ Champaner

🏠 Vadodara; 50 km (31 miles) NE of Vadodara 🚌
ℹ️ www.gujarattourism.com

The atmospheric deserted city of Champaner, a UNESCO World Heritage Site, sits at the foot of Pavagadh Hill. Once the seat of a Rajput Chauhan dynasty, Champaner was conquered by the Muslim ruler Mahmud Begada in 1484. He spent 23 years rebuilding the citadel, adding mosques, palaces and tombs within its massive walls, guarded by huge gateways. Champaner remained the capital of Gujarat until 1535, when it was conquered by the Mughals. Thereafter, it fell into decline.

The remains of many old mosques and palaces reflect a blend of Islamic and Jain traditions. The Jama Masjid, built in 1523, is a large structure with a perfectly proportioned dome and a richly ornamented exterior with 172 pillars and 30-m- (98-ft-) high minarets.

The Pavagadh Fort, at the crest of the 820-m- (2,690-ft-) high Pavagadh Hill, is 4 km (2 miles) to the southwest of Champaner. It has a cluster of Muslim, Hindu and Jain shrines, and the ruins of an ancient fortification, reflecting its chequered past. On the way up the hill are the ruins of the Sat Mahal, the seven-storeyed palace of the Chauhan kings. The kings were slain when they refused to embrace Islam after the Muslim conquest, and their women and children committed *jauhar* (self-immolation).

🔍 HIDDEN GEM
Chhota Udaipur's Haat

To get a taste of Gujarati village life, visit the Saturday *haat* (market) at Chhota Udaipur (65 km/40 miles east of Champaner), where vendors sell vegetables, spices and crafts.

→

A vibrant display of spices and other flavourings at a street market in Surat

⑪ Daman

🏠 Daman Union Territory; 390 km (242 miles) S of Ahmedabad 🚉 Vapi, 10 km (6 miles) SE of Daman, then taxi or bus 🚌 ℹ️ daman.nic.in

Tucked away in the southern tip of Gujarat, adjoining Maharashtra, the tiny enclave of Daman was a Portuguese colony until 1961. The Damanganga river, which flows into the Arabian Sea, divides the town into two distinct parts – Nani Daman (Little Daman), which is dotted with hotels and bars, and Moti Daman (Big Daman), the old Portuguese township.

Moti Daman is enclosed within the massive Daman Fort, ringed by a moat linked to the river. Its ten bastions and two gateways date to 1559. The large Bom Jesus Cathedral, built in 1603, has a richly carved portal and an ornamental altar. The smaller Rosario Chapel, outside the fort walls, has exquisitely carved wooden panels depicting scenes from the life of Jesus. The lighthouse, to the north of the fort, offers views of the Gulf of Cambay.

St Jerome's Fort, in Nani Daman, houses the lovely chapel of Our Lady of the Sea, with a delicate Classical façade of 12 columns crowned with a cross.

Although Gujarat is a mainly dry state, alcohol is legal in a few former Portuguese enclaves, including Nani Daman. This area also has a great riverside fish market.

←

The pleasantly symmetrical Jama Masjid, a 16th-century mosque at Champaner

12

Surat

📍 Surat district; 234 km
(145 miles) S of Ahmedabad
🚌🚗 ℹ Athava Lines, Jilla
Seva Sadan - 2, Block A;
www.gujarattourism.com

Strategically located on the coast, Surat was once a prosperous port. At various times the Portuguese, Dutch, Mughals, Marathas and British held sway here, but its importance began to wane after 1837, when it was ravaged by flood and fire and many of Surat's Hindu and Parsi merchants left for Bombay (Mumbai). Today Surat is a major industrial centre.

The 16th-century Surat Castle is the town's oldest structure. Ordered by Sultan Mahmud III, the castle has 4-m- (13-ft-) thick walls and 12-m- (39-ft-) high battlements. Iron strips were used to bind its various elements and all of its joints were filled with molten lead to make it as impenetrable as possible. Especially noteworthy is the imposing gateway in its eastern wing, with a menacingly spiked exterior and a delicately carved interior.

Northeast of Surat Castle, just beyond Kataragama Gate, are the English, Dutch and Armenian cemeteries, which bear witness to the city's varied colonial past. Though now overgrown, they are worth exploring for the intriguing personal histories recounted on the tombs' epitaphs. Particularly impressive is the mausoleum of Sir George Oxinden, a governor of the Surat Port, and his brother, in the British cemetery. The elaborate tomb of Baron Adriaan van Reede, built in the 17th century, in the Dutch cemetery has an enormous double cupola.

Modern Surat is known for its flourishing textile industry, which produces the famous *tanchoi* (brocade) silk. It also specializes in jewellery and is a major diamond-cutting centre for suppliers from all over the world.

> **Northeast of Surat Castle, just beyond Kataragama Gate, are the English, Dutch and Armenian cemeteries, which bear witness to the city's varied colonial past.**

13 Diu

⌂ Diu Union Territory;
360 km (224 miles) SW of
Ahmedabad 🚉 Delwada,
10 km (6 miles) N of town
centre 🚌 ℹ Diu Jetty;
(02875) 252 653

The little island of Diu was
once known as the "Gibraltar
of the East". A Portuguese
colony from the 16th century
onwards, it was ceded to India
in 1961 and is today a Union
Territory administered by the
Central Government. The
majestic Diu Fort on the
eastern end of the island
dominates the town. Built in
1535, when the Portuguese
took control of Diu, it is worth
a visit for its impressive
double moat, its old cannons
and for the superb views of
the sunset it offers.

Diu town, sandwiched
between the fort to the east
and the city wall to the west,
retains a distinctly Portuguese
atmosphere in its churches
and mansions. The Nagar
Seth Haveli is particularly
outstanding, with carved
balconies and stone lions.
The Church of St Paul (built
in 1610) has a lovely carved
wooden altar, statues of saints
and a sonorous old organ.

Its impressive Gothic façade
was rebuilt in 1807. Nearby,
the St Thomas Church (built in
1598) houses a museum of
religious artifacts and stone
inscriptions.

The sandy beach at Nagoa,
7 km (4 miles) from the town,
is fringed with palm trees.
Other beaches nearby are
Jallandhar and Chakratirth,
which has a sunset viewpoint.
As a Union Territory, Diu is
not subject to Gujarat's
prohibition laws. This explains
the profusion of bars in the
town, and the crowds of
Gujaratis on weekends.

14 Palitana

⌂ Bhavnagar district;
52 km (32 miles) SW of
Bhavnagar 🚉🚌 ℹ www.
gujarattourism.com

An extraordinary cluster of
1,008 Jain temples crowns the
twin summits of Palitana's
Shatrunjaya Hill and covers
the saddle linking them. The
first Jain *tirthankara* (spiritual
teacher) Adinath is said to
have visited this hill, while his
chief disciple, Pundarika, is
believed to have attained
enlightenment here. Most of
the temples date to the 16th
century. They are grouped
into nine fortified clusters
called *tuks*, and named after
the wealthy devotees who
paid for their construction.
Each *tuk* has a main shrine
surrounded by several smaller
ones. The most impressive of
these is the 17th-century
Adinath Temple, on the hill's
northern ridge. Its ceilings,
walls and supporting brackets
are covered with carvings of
saints, dancers, musicians and
lotus blossoms. Many
images of Adinath are
enshrined inside.

Dominating the southern ridge is the 16th-century Adishvara Temple, with its richly ornamented spire. The main image within portrays Rishabhnath. It has eyes made of crystal and is adorned with necklaces and a magnificent gold crown.

The 4-km (2-mile) ascent to the summit of the hill takes about two hours. From the top, there is a panoramic view of the Gulf of Cambay and the countryside.

↑ Asiatic lions at Gir National Park, the only habitat outside of Africa for these big cats

---

15

Bhavnagar

🏠 Bhavnagar district; 175 km (109 miles) SW of Ahmedabad ✈ 8 km (5 miles) SE 🚉🚌 ℹ www.gujarattourism.com

A convenient base for exploring the magnificent temple town of Palitana, Bhavnagar itself is not without charm – its old bazaar, dotted with merchants' *havelis*, has shops specializing in tie-dye textiles and gold and silver jewellery. In the southeast corner of the city, on the road to the airport, is the semicircular **Barton Museum** (built in 1895). It houses the private collection of coins, weapons and *objets d'art* of a British officer, Colonel Barton, who served here in the 19th century.

The **Nilambagh Palace**, once the former rulers' residence, was built in 1859 and is now a luxury hotel with peacocks in the garden.

The flat grasslands of the 36 sq-km (14 sq-mile) **Velavadar National Park** (65 km/40 miles north of Bhavnagar) are home to over a thousand blackbucks. Blackbucks were protected by the Bishnoi community until the state took over this role. A walk through the park at dusk provides a glimpse of the wolves that hunt this Indian antelope and of the nilgai that congregate at the park's watering holes.

Barton Museum
⊘ 🏠 Gandhi Smriti, Crescent Circle 📞 (0278) 242 4516 🕙 10am–6:30pm Mon–Sat

Nilambagh Palace
🏠 Ahmedabad Rd 📞 (0278) 242 4241

Velavadar National Park
⊘⊘ ℹ Forest Dept, Bhavnagar; (0278) 288 0342 🕙 Mid-Oct–May

← Clusters of ornate Jain temples lining the ridges of Shatrunjaya Hill, in Palitana

---

💬 INSIDER TIP
Morning Safari

If you are planning to head out on an early morning safari at Gir National Park, be sure to dress up warm for the ride as temperatures are considerably cooler than later in the day.

16

Gir National Park

🏠 Junagadh district; 368 km (229 miles) SW of Ahmedabad; entry point at Sasan Gir 🚉🚌 🕙 Mid-Oct–mid-Jun 🌐 girlion.gujarat. gov.in

The Gir National Park is the lion's only habitat outside Africa. Asiatic lions are smaller than African ones, with a fold of skin along the belly. The males have shorter manes. The species was on the verge of extinction in the early 1900s, but thanks to conservation efforts Gir's 259 sq km (100 sq miles) of dry scrub forest is today home to about 320 lions.

A number of rivers wind through Gir, making it a haven for a range of wildlife, including the caracal, the *chausingha* (four-horned antelope), the blackbuck and the leopard.

17 Junagadh

🏙 Junagadh district;
320 km (199 miles) SW
of Ahmedabad 🚉🚌
ℹ Majevadi; www.
gujarattourism.com

Junagadh, meaning "Old Fort", takes its name from the fort of Uparkot, built in the 4th century on a plateau at the eastern edge of the town. The fort is surrounded by massive walls, over 20 m (66 ft) high in places, and a 90-m- (295-ft-) deep moat inside the walls. This once teemed with crocodiles that were fed on criminals and political enemies. An ornate, triple-arched gateway marks the entrance to the fort. Inside, a cobbled path leads past Hindu temples to the now deserted Jama Masjid, with carved stonework and pillars. Nearby is a cluster of Buddhist caves dating to the 2nd century. The fort also has two 11th-century stepwells.

In the mid-19th century, the nawabs of Junagadh moved

↑ A local family walking past a distinctive archway on Nagar Road, Junagadh

down from the old fort into new colonial-style palaces in the city. The **Durbar Hall** of the City Palace, built in 1870, houses a museum with the typical trappings of royalty – palanquins, silver thrones and old armour. A complex of royal mausoleums can be seen near the city's railway station, the most notable of which is the Mahabat Maqbara, also known as the Taj Mahal of Junagadh, with splendid silver doors.

Junagadh's main attraction, however, is Girnar Hill, 6 km (4 miles) east of the city. An extinct volcano, this has been a holy site for Buddhists, Jains and Hindus since the 3rd century BC. Over 4,000 steps lead to the top of the 1,080-m- (3,543-ft-) high hill. En route is an Ashokan Rock Edict, dating to 250 BC, which conveys Emperor Ashoka's message of non-violence. Halfway up the hill is a cluster of Jain temples, including the Neminath Temple, enshrining a black marble image of the 22nd Jain *tirthankara* who is believed to have died here. The 12th-century Amba Mata Temple, at the top, is popular with newly-weds, who come seeking blessings for conjugal bliss.

Durbar Hall

⊗ 📞 (0285) 262 1685
🕙 10am–6pm Thu-Tue
🚫 2nd & 4th Sat

THE NAWAB OF JUNAGADH AND HIS DOGS

The 11th Nawab of Junagadh (1900–59) had a passion for dogs, and his pedigreed pooches, 800 of them, were housed in luxury. On the eve of India's independence, when the princely states were given the option of either remaining in India or becoming a part of Pakistan, the Nawab's decision to accede to Pakistan was thwarted by popular protest. The Nawab, however, decided to leave Junagadh. He boarded the aircraft with his dogs, leaving behind his entire harem of concubines.

> The cycle of pillage and reconstruction at Somnath continued over the next seven centuries. The present temple, made of stone, was built in 1950.

18 Somnath

🏙 Junagadh district;
406 km (252 miles) SW
of Ahmedabad 🚌 ℹ www.
gujarattourism.com

Situated on the coast with a commanding view of the Arabian Sea, the Somnath Temple is revered as one of the 12 most sacred sites dedicated to Lord Shiva. The temple's legendary wealth made it the target of successive plundering armies, beginning in 1026 with ruler Mahmud of Ghazni, who is said to have made off with camel-loads of gold and precious gems, leaving the edifice in ruins. The cycle of pillage and reconstruction at

→

The Gomti river, with the Dwarkadhish Temple in the background, Dwarka

Somnath continued over the next seven centuries. The present temple was built in 1950.

East of the temple, at the confluence of three rivers, is Triveni Tirth. The ghats going down to the sea at this spot are said to mark the place where Lord Krishna's funeral rites were performed.

---

⑲

Jamnagar

◪ Jamnagar district; 308 km (191 miles) SW of Ahmedabad ↪10 km (6 miles) W ▣▭ ℹ www.gujarattourism.com

Founded by a local prince, Jam Rawal, in 1540, Jamnagar's old walled city is dominated by the **Lakhota Fort**, the original seat of its rulers, and the Ranmal Lake, which surrounds it. The fort was badly damaged during the earthquake in January 2001, though visitors are still allowed inside. The museum in the fort has fine sculptures from nearby excavation sites, dating from the 9th to 18th centuries. Close by is the Kotha Bastion, which once stored the rulers' arsenal.

In the heart of the old town is the circular Darbar Gadh, where the Jamsahebs (as the rulers were called) held public audiences. This structure was also damaged heavily in the 2001 earthquake, but the ground floor is safe for visitors.

The lanes leading off from here are worth exploring, as the city is famous for its tie-dye fabric and silver jewellery. In this area are two Jain temples, the Shantinath and Adinath Temples, entirely covered with mirrorwork, gold leaf, murals and mosaics. Close to them is the 19th-century Ratanbai Mosque, its doors inlaid with mother-of-pearl. In the early 20th century, Jamnagar was ruled by the famous cricketer KS Ranjit Sinhji (r 1907–33). The city acquired several elegant public buildings and parks under his able administration.

The **Marine National Park**, in the Gulf of Kutch, is located 30 km (19 miles) from Jamnagar. An archipelago of 42 islands, the park's marine life is best viewed from the island of Pirotan.

Lakhota Fort

⊛ ◐ Thu–Tue ⏰ 2nd & 4th Sat

Marine National Park

⊛ ▭ Jamnagar jetty ℹ For permits, contact the Park Director, Jamnagar; (0288) 255 2077

⑳

Dwarka

◪ Jamnagar district; 453 km (281 miles) SW of Ahmedabad ▣▭ ℹ www.gujarattourism.com

Legend has it that about 5,000 years ago, Lord Krishna forsook his kingdom at Mathura (p187) and moved to Dwarka, where he founded a glittering new city that was subsequently submerged by the sea. Excavations of the seabed have indeed established the existence of a submerged city near Dwarka.

Hindu pilgrims flock to Dwarka throughout the year. The city's main temple is the towering Dwarkadhish Temple, dating to the 16th century. Built of granite and sandstone on a plinth area of 540 m (1,772 ft), it is supported by 60 pillars and rises seven storeys to an impressive height of 51 m (167 ft).

21 Gondal

🏠 Rajkot; 218 km (136 miles) SW of Ahmedabad 🚉 38 km (24 miles) S of Rajkok 🚌🚐 ℹ️ www.gujarattourism.com

During the British period, Gondal was the capital of a progressive princely state. Some of its wide-ranging social and economic policies can still be seen: the town has plenty of trees and an underground electricity supply, and the surrounding villages are well connected and irrigated. Bhagwat Singhji, who headed the reforms, also made education for girls free and compulsory.

The focal point of the town is the 18th-century Naulakha Palace. Now a museum, it showcases artifacts, textiles, the royal wardrobe and a collection of classic cars. The Bhuvaneshwari Ayurvedic Pharmacy's factory gives an insight into the world of traditional Indian medicine.

22 Rajkot

🏠 Rajkot district; 216 km (134 miles) SW of Ahmedabad 🚉 1 km (0.6 miles) NW 🚌🚐 ℹ️ Bhavnagar House; www. gujarattourism.com

The headquarters of the Saurashtra region (southwest

Did You Know?

Artisans make patterns on Kutch's bandhni tie-dyed textiles by plucking it with their fingernails.

Gujarat) during the British Raj, modern Rajkot is a commercial and industrial town, and the centre of the region's groundnut trade.

Rajkot's many 19th-century buildings give it a distinctly colonial appearance. The **Watson Museum** has a fine collection of portraits of local rulers, tribal artifacts, archaeological finds from Harappan sites and a statue of Queen Victoria. The impressive Rajkumar College, established by the British for the sons of the Gujarat nobility, remains a prestigious public school.

Wankaner Palace, 39 km (24 miles) northeast of Rajkot, is an eclectic mix of Mughal, Italian and Victorian-Gothic styles. Though still inhabited by the former royal family, a portion is now a luxury hotel. Halvad, 125 km (78 miles) north of Rajkot, has a 17th-century lakeside palace.

Watson Museum
⊛ 🏠 Jubilee Bagh 📞 (0281) 222 3065 🕘 9am–1pm & 3–6pm Thu–Tue 🚫 2nd & 4th Sat

23 Porbandar

🏠 Porbandar district; 400 km (249 miles) SW of Ahmedabad 🚌🚐 ℹ️ www. gujarattourism.com

Porbandar is famous as the birthplace of Mahatma Gandhi. The house where he was born in 1869 still stands in a small alley, in the western part of the city. Next door is the Kirti Mandir Museum, with photographs from Gandhi's life, and extracts from his speeches and writings. The city has little else to attract visitors.

24 Bhuj

🏠 Kutch district; 217 km (135 miles) W of Ahmedabad 🚉 7 km (4 miles) N of city centre 🚌🚐 ℹ️ Tourist Information Bureau; www. gujarattourism.com

Until the 2001 earthquake reduced much of Bhuj to rubble, this was a fascinating walled city, with beautiful palaces and *havelis*, and a famous bazaar rich in handicrafts and jewellery. Bhuj was the capital of the prosperous princely state of Kutch, whose wealth derived from its trade with East Africa and the Persian Gulf ports.

The town's main attraction is the Darbargadh Palace complex, which houses the fabulous Aina Mahal or "Palace of Mirrors", built in 1752. The palace and its contents are linked to its Gujarati architect, Ramsinh Malam. Shipwrecked off the East African coast as a 12-year-old, he was rescued by a Dutch ship and taken to the Netherlands, where he spent the next 17 years. There,

← A fishing boat near the beach at Porbandar, Gandhi's birthplace

Expansive views from the Vijay Vilas Palace, Mandvi, and (inset) an elegant interior

he mastered Delft tile-making, glass-blowing, enamelling and clock-making. When he returned home, he was given the opportunity to display these skills. The Aina Mahal was thus decorated with Venetian-style chandeliers, Delft blue tiles, enamelled silver objects and chiming clocks – all made locally under Ramsinh's supervision. Local crafts, such as a superb ivory-inlaid door, jewelled shields and a marvellously detailed scroll painting of a royal procession, were also displayed. All these form a part of the palace museum.

The **Folk Arts Museum** houses Kutch textiles and local crafts, and a reconstructed village of Rabari *bhoongas*.

Folk Arts Museum
🖼️⊘ 🏠 Mandvi Rd 📞 (02832) 220541 🕙 10am-12pm, 3pm-6pm Tue-Sun 🗓️ 2nd & 4th Sat

> Until the 2001 earth-quake reduced much of Bhuj to rubble, this was a fascinating walled city, with beautiful palaces and havelis, and a famous bazaar

㉕
Mandvi

🏠 Bhuj district; 60 km (37 miles) SW of Bhuj 🚌
ℹ️ www.gujarattourism.com

This old port town has fine beaches, good swimming, and camel and horse rides along the shore. Close to the beach is the red sand-stone **Vijay Vilas Palace**, an impressive Indo-Edwardian structure built in the 1920s as a royal summer retreat. Its lovely, well-maintained garden, drawing room and rooftop terrace are open to visitors and provide beautiful views of the sea. In the town is the curious 18th-century Old Palace of the Kutch rulers (now a girls' school). Architecturally a blend of local and European styles, it has a façade decorated with cherubic Dutch boys holding wine goblets – Indian archi-tect Ramsinh Malam's salute to his adopted country.

Vijay Vilas Palace
⊘ 🕙 8am-6pm Thu-Tue

㉖
Dholavira

🏠 Bhuj district; 250 km (155 miles) NE of Bhuj 🚌
🕙 Daily ℹ️ Bhuj Super-intendant of Police; (02836) 280287 (permits); www.gujarattourism.com

Dholavira is a small village where archaeologists have unearthed extensive remains of a city that dates back to about 3000 BC. Lying on Khadir Bet island in the Great Rann of Kutch, it is – along with Lothal (p386) – the largest-known Indus Valley settlement in India. The site reveals evidence of a remarkable planned city with broad roads, a central citadel, a middle town with spacious dwellings, a lower town with open spaces for markets and festivities, and two stadia. The presence of large reser-voirs and a dam reflect the existence of sophisticated systems for harvesting water.

The distinctive skyline of Mumbai, with its soaring skyscrapers

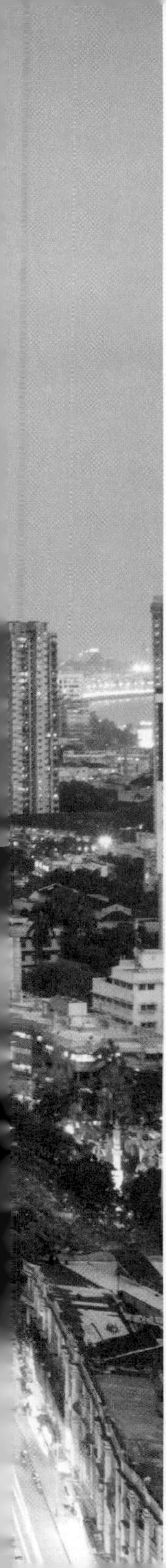

MUMBAI

Mumbai (formerly Bombay), capital of the state of Maharashtra, is India's most dynamic, cosmopolitan and crowded city. Consisting of seven swampy islands when the Portuguese acquired it in 1534, Bombay (from the Portuguese Bom Bahia or "good bay") came to the British Crown in 1661 as part of the dowry of Catherine of Braganza, when she married Charles II. Finding little use for the islands, the British leased them to the East India Company, which quickly realized the islands' potential as an excellent natural harbour in the Arabian Sea. The rise of Bombay began in the late 1600s, when the company relocated its headquarters here. By the 18th century, Bombay had become the major city and shipbuilding yard on the western coast, and by the 19th century, land reclamations had joined the islands into the narrow promontory that it is today. The promise of commercial opportunities lured communities of Gujaratis, Parsis and Baghdadi, or Sephardic, Jews to Bombay, giving the city its vibrant multicultural identity. In 1995, the city reverted to its local name, Mumbai, from Mumba-Ai (Mother Mumbai), the patron goddess worshipped by the Koli fishermen who were the original inhabitants of these islands. The city suffered a horrific four-day terror attack in 2008, but all its communities stood together in solidarity, and its population continues to grow as it welcomes migrants from all over the country, who flock to this "land of opportunities" in search of fame, fortune, or just a bit part in a Bollywood movie.

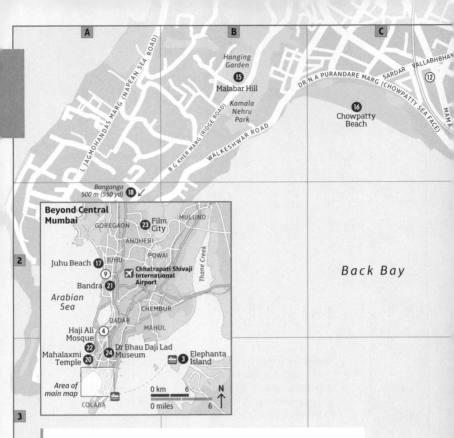

MUMBAI

Must Sees

1. Chhatrapati Shivaji Terminus
2. Chhatrapati Shivaji Maharaj Vastu Sangrahalaya
3. Elephanta Island
4. Gateway of India

Experience More

5. Kala Ghoda
6. General Post Office
7. Town Hall
8. Bombay Stock Exchange
9. Crawford Market
10. Horniman Circle
11. Colaba Causeway
12. Shahid Bhagat Singh Marg
13. Ballard Estate
14. Marine Drive
15. Malabar Hill
16. Chowpatty Beach
17. Juhu Beach
18. Banganga
19. Khotachiwadi
20. Mahalaxmi Temple
21. Bandra
22. Haji Ali Mosque
23. Film City
24. Dr Bhau Daji Lad Museum

Eat

1. Trishna
2. Kala Ghoda Café
3. The Table
4. The Bombay Canteen

Drink

5. Colaba Social
6. Leopold Cafe
7. Harbour Bar

Stay

8. Abode
9. Soho House Mumbai
10. Taj Mahal Palace

Shop

11. No-Mad
12. Playclan

① 🍴 🛍

CHHATRAPATI SHIVAJI TERMINUS

📍 F3 🏠 1 Dr Dadabhai Naoroji Rd, Fort 🌐 cr.indianrailways.gov.in

The most impressive example of Victorian Gothic architecture in India, Chhatrapati Shivaji Terminus Railway Station (formerly known as Victoria Terminus) is a rich extravaganza of domes, spires and arches. Designed by Frederick William Stevens and decorated by local art students and craftsmen over ten years, it was completed in 1888.

The railway station was originally named after Queen Victoria to commemorate her Golden Jubilee, and is now the headquarters of the Central Railway. Over 1,000 trains and three million passengers, including crowds of suburban commuters, pass through the station daily. When it was opened, the terminus became an icon of the city, which was even nicknamed "Gothic City" in honour of it. The station is remarkable for its design, which was one of the first to blend Indian and British architectural styles. In 2004, the station was declared a UNESCO World Heritage Site, and there is a heritage gallery open to visitors that explores the building's history.

The gables are crowned by sculptures representing Engineering, Agriculture and Commerce.

↑ An intricate stone peacock on the façade

Booking hall

← Travellers buying tickets in the grand Star Chamber booking hall

An overview of Mumbai's main station, the famous Chhatrapati Shivaji Terminus ↑

↑ Chhatrapati Shivaji Terminus's famous Gothic building

A 4-m (13-ft) statue representing Progress holding a torch crowns the colossal dome.

A majestic staircase of blue stone, with beautiful iron railings, sweeps up beneath the dome.

Gargoyles serving as water spouts jut out from the base of the large dome.

Set into the octagonal tower below the dome are brilliant stained-glass windows, decorated with a locomotive and foliage.

Studded into the façade are busts of Raj-era personalities, such as Sir Bartle Frere.

The station's gateposts are topped by stone sculptures of a lion and a tiger, for Britain and India.

An exquisite peacock carving, one of the many incredible sculptures here, decorates this window.

Did You Know?

Architect George Wittet went on to design another famous landmark, the Gateway of India *(p406)*.

↑ Palm trees swaying in the breeze in the immaculately maintained museum gardens

② 🔲 🔲 🔲

CHHATRAPATI SHIVAJI MAHARAJ VASTU SANGRAHALAYA

📍 F4 🏛 159-161 M G Rd, Kala Ghoda, Fort 🕐 10:15am-6pm daily 🗓 Public hols 🌐 csmvs.in

Housed in a grand Indo-Saracenic building, Chhatrapati Shivaji Maharaj Vastu Sangrahalaya ("King Shivaji Museum") is one of the best museums in India, renowned for its superb sculptures and miniature paintings.

The museum was originally named after the Prince of Wales (the future George V), who laid the building's foundation stone in 1905. During World War I, it served as a military hospital and was formally inaugurated in 1923. The dome is based on that of the Gol Gumbaz in Bijapur *(p475)*, while the finial is based on the Taj Mahal in Agra *(p166)*.

The museum has built a fine collection of over 60,000 rare art objects (mostly donated from private collections), comprising sculptures, terracottas, bronzes, excavated artifacts from the bronze-age Harappan sites, Indian and European paintings, and porcelain and ivories from China and Japan. There is also a natural history section.

GALLERY GUIDE

The museum's galleries are spread across three floors. The ground floor has sculpture (including Gandhara classics), the pre- and proto-history gallery, the natural history section and the Coomaraswamy Hall, which hosts seminars and exhibitions. On the first floor are miniature paintings, prints, coins, Indian decorative arts, Himalayan art, and the Khandavala and Roychand galleries. The second floor has European paintings and decorative arts, arms and armour, Chinese and Japanese art, Indian textiles and costumes, art from the Bombay School and the Nicholson Gallery. At the entrance to the building is the excellent museum shop.

1 A visitor looks closely at the incredibly detailed work on this gold sculpture of Hindu dieties.

2 A giant statue of the reclining Buddha's head greets visitors as they approach the museum through the gardens.

3 The museum has skilfully incorporated the original wooden pavilion of a *wada* (royal house) into the Circular Gallery on the first floor.

③ 🛹 Ⓜ 🛍

ELEPHANTA ISLAND

📍B3 🚗15 km (9 miles) NE of Mumbai (approximately 1 hr by ferry) ⛴9am–5:30pm, every 30 min from the Gateway of India (ferry may be suspended during the monsoon) 🕐9am–5pm Tue–Sun

Located on an island off Mumbai's eastern shore, the 6th-century AD Elephanta cave temples, chiselled into a rocky cliff and dedicated to the Hindu god Shiva, contain some great masterpieces of Indian sculpture.

The origins of the cave temples at Elephanta, a UNESCO World Heritage Site, are lost in obscurity, but in all probability date to the 6th century AD and represent the period of Brahmanical revival after Buddhism began to decline.

From the pier, visitors can take the ticketed miniature train or climb the flight of 125 steps to the Great Cave's main Northern Entrance, a huge square hall supported by two-dozen massive pillars. Here, in a deep recess against the rear (south) wall, is the huge triple-headed Shiva statue, the Maheshmurti, also known as Trimurti. This is the glory of Elephanta, and few visitors can fail to be moved by this compelling image, hailed by art historian Percy Brown as "the creation of a genius". The three faces represent Shiva in his different manifestations. The central face depicts the Preserver; the one facing west represents the Creator; the head facing east is the Destroyer. A *linga* (an abstract symbol of Shiva) is housed in the main shrine at the western end of the temple.

Contrasting images of peace and violence, joy and fury, can be seen throughout. Thus, one sculpture near the Western Entrance lyrically depicts the marriage of Shiva and Parvati, while opposite it is a powerful panel showing Shiva brutally impaling the demon Andhaka. The Eastern Entrance has Shiva and Parvati contentedly playing dice as the demon-king Ravana tries to destroy their home.

There are four other Hindu caves alongside the Great Cave on the western Gun Hill, and two Buddhist caves on the eastern Stupa Hill.

Every February, the caves serve as an atmospheric backdrop to the Elephanta Festival of classical dance and music.

←

The three-headed Maheshmurti, depicting Shiva as the Creator, Protector and Destroyer

Massive pillars holding up the entrance to the caves ↑

Did You Know?

The island was renamed Elephanta by the Portuguese after a stone elephant that once stood here.

Two gigantic *dvarapalas* (doorkeepers) flanking the temple's central shrine

④

GATEWAY OF INDIA

⬤ F5 ⌂ Apollo Bunder, Chhatrapati Shivaji Marg & P J Ramchandani Marg

Mumbai's most famous landmark, built in 1924, was the first sight to greet travellers to Indian shores during the British Raj. Ironically, it also became the exit point for British troops after India gained independence in 1947. The Gateway commands a spectacular view of the sea and is particularly impressive when illuminated at night, with the inky black sea stretching beyond it.

The Gateway was built to commemorate the 1911 visit of George V, and later became the ceremonial entrance to India for viceroys and governors. This 26-m- (85-ft-) high monument, with two large reception halls and embellishments inspired by 16th-century Gujarati architecture, is the heart of Mumbai's tourist district and is always teeming with with locals, visitors, vendors and boatmen, who provide regular services across the bay and to islands such as Elephanta (p404). Set in a pleasant garden facing the Gateway is an equestrian statue of Shivaji, Maharashtra's great warrior-hero. Around the Gateway are several majestic colonial-era buildings, including the old Yacht Club (now the Atomic Energy Commission), the Royal Bombay Yacht Club and the stately Taj Mahal Hotel. The eastern sea face stretching out in front of the Gateway is Apollo Bunder, one of Mumbai's favourite promenades. Today, astrologers and ear-cleaners hustle for business, while dozens of yachts, boats and ferries bob about in the waters beyond.

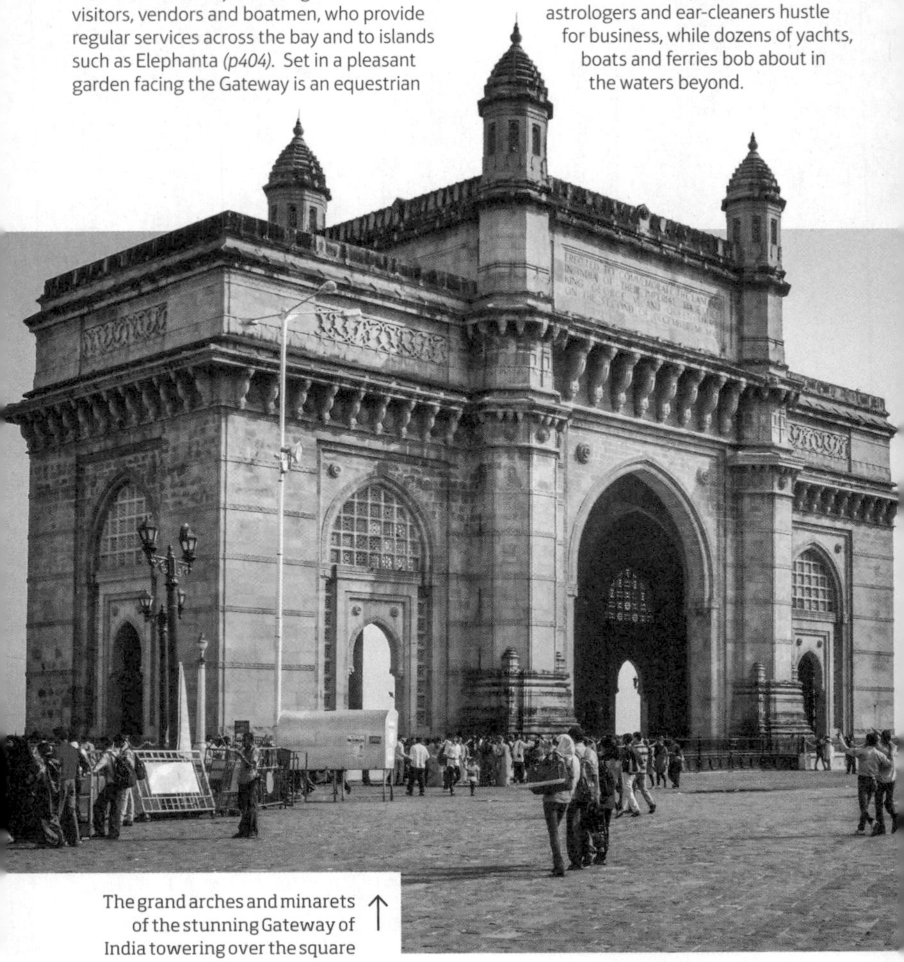

The grand arches and minarets of the stunning Gateway of India towering over the square ↑

TAJ MAHAL HOTEL

The iconic Taj Mahal Hotel was built in 1903 by Parsi industrialist Jamshedji Tata who, it is said, decided to erect a magnificent hotel when he was barred from the "Whites Only" Watson's Hotel. In 2008, this historic building was one of the sites of a terror attack. The Tatas spent £24 million to restore the hotel to its former glory and highlight its Florentine, Moorish and Oriental design.

↑ An array of intricate pinwheels on display in the street during the Kala Ghoda Arts Festival

Did You Know?

When George V visited the Gateway in 1911 he was met with a mock cardboard structure - it had yet to be built.

EXPERIENCE MORE

5 🍴 🖥 🏛

Kala Ghoda

📍 E4 🏠 Fort 🌐 www.kalaghodaassociation.com

Named after the black-stone equestrian statue of Edward VII that once stood opposite the Jehangir Art Gallery, Kala Ghoda is something of an artistic centre in Mumbai. This tight network of streets north of Colaba stretches from the Regal Circle at the southern end of Mahatma Gandhi Road to Mumbai University at the northern end, with the Oval Maidan to the west and the Lion Gate to the east. The district is home to small, independent galleries, local designer boutiques and hip cafés inside crumbling old mansions. Local artists tout their work outside the Jehangir Art Gallery, and every February the nine-day Kala Ghoda Arts Festival takes over the area.

Nearby, the Wellington Fountain, now in the middle of a traffic roundabout, is surrounded by magnificent colonial buildings, such as the old Majestic Hotel, with its mock minarets and the Art Deco Regal Cinema. Equally impressive are the National Gallery of Modern Art and the Indo-Saracenic building of the Chhatrapati Shivaji Maharaj Vastu Sangrahalaya *(p402)*.

6

General Post Office

📍 F3 🏠 Walchand Hirachand Marg ⏰ 9am–8pm Mon–Sat, 10am–5:30pm Sun

Completed in 1913, this fabulous composition of minarets, domes and arches was designed by John Begg and supervised by George Wittet. A prime example of the Indo-Saracenic style, the General Post Office (GPO) building combines elements of Indian architecture, most notably an Islamic dome inspired by the Gol Gumbad in Bijapur *(p475)*, with classical European traditions. Mumbai's main post office, the GPO has a lofty three-storeyed rotunda inside, leading to its various departments. Business is conducted from behind the delightfully old-fashioned wooden counters.

7

Town Hall

Q F4 **⌂** Shahid Bhagat Singh Marg, Fort **⏰** 10am–5pm Mon–Sat **⊗** Public hols **w** asiaticsociety.org.in

Designed by Colonel Thomas Cowper and completed in 1833, Mumbai's Town Hall is one of the finest Neo-Classical buildings in India, and one of the earliest surviving colonial buildings in the city. Its impressive façade of pedimented porticoes surmounts a row of fluted Doric columns. A grand flight of 30 steps leads into a magnificent Assembly Hall, the venue for public meetings during the British Raj.

The Town Hall, with its imposing high ceiling, teak-panelled walls and elegant cast-iron balustrades, now houses the **Asiatic Society**, founded in 1804 by Sir James Mackintosh. This institution's library has a priceless collection of 800,000 volumes, including a first edition of Dante's *Divine Comedy*, ancient Sanskrit manuscripts and old Bombay gazetteers. It also holds fragments of what is believed to be Gautama Buddha's begging bowl.

8

Bombay Stock Exchange

Q F4 **⌂** Dalal Street, Fort **⊗** To the public

The Bombay Stock Exchange towers above Dalal Street. This is Mumbai's Wall Street, and the presence of close to 50 banks on a short stretch underlines the frenetic pace of its commercial activity. Just before lunchtime, the area swarms with *dabbawalas* who

→
The bustling aisles of Crawford Market, built in the late 19th century

bring homemade lunchboxes to the thousands of office workers in the area.

9

Crawford Market

Q F2 **⌂** Dr Dadabhai Naoroji Rd and Lokmanya Tilak Rd **⏰** 9am–8pm Mon–Sat, 9am–12pm Sun

While the official name of this market is now Mahatma Jyotiba/Jyotirao Phule Market, everyone still calls it by its old name of Crawford Market. Located to the north of Chhatrapati Shivaji Terminus, the market was designed by William Emerson; completed in 1869, it was the first building in India to be lit up by electricity. This architectural extravaganza of Moorish arches and half-timbered gables, topped by a clocktower, consists of a central hall with two wings. The floor is paved with stone from Scotland, which remains cool through the day, and the lamp brackets are shaped like winged dragons. Above the entrance doors are marble bas-reliefs depicting scenes from market life, which were carved by Lockwood Kipling, father of the

---

EAT

Trishna

Go for the buttery king crab. Be sure to book.

Q E4 **⌂** Ropewalk Lane **☎** (022) 2270 3214

₹₹₹

Kala Ghoda Café

Lovely café at the front, wine bar at the back.

Q E4 **⌂** Ropewalk Lane **w** kgcafe.in

₹₹₹

The Table

Delightful afternoon tea in a stylish setting.

Q E5 **⌂** Apollo Bunder Marg **w** thetable.in

₹₹₹

The Bombay Canteen

Regional dishes with a twist include pork vindaloo tacos.

Q A2 **⌂** Kamala Mills **w** thebombaycanteen.com

₹₹₹

Britannia & Company

Iconic Irani café. Try the classic berry pulao.

Q F3 **⌂** 11 Sprott Rd

₹₹₹

writer Rudyard Kipling, as was the fountain in the courtyard decorated with Hindu river goddesses and animals. This is still where Mumbai comes to shop, and tiers of wooden stalls display nearly 3,000 tonnes of fresh produce, from fruit and flowers to fish and exotic birds. West of the market is Zaveri Bazaar, where diamond, gold and silver merchants have their stores. Northwest of the market, on Mutton Street, is Chor Bazaar ("thieves' market"), with its antiques and bric-a-brac shops.

10

Horniman Circle

F4 **Veer Nariman Rd, Fort**

The old Cotton Green, where traders used to buy and sell bales of cotton, was laid out as a public garden in 1872. It was renamed after independence in honour of Benjamin Guy Horniman, a former editor of the *Bombay Chronicle*, an active supporter of India's freedom movement. Today,

←

Bronze statue of a bull at the Bombay Stock Exchange, on Dalal Street

the garden is frequented by students and office workers and is the venue for open-air theatrical performances and cultural events in winter.

The elegant circle of Neo-Classical buildings around the garden was built in the 1860s, and was inspired by the Royal Crescent in Bath, among other places. Designed by James Scott, the buildings share a uniform façade with pedestrian arcades and decorative terracotta keystones from England, and represent Mumbai's earliest planned urban compositions.

Anchoring the western edge of the flower-filled green is

St Thomas' Cathedral, the city's oldest Anglican church, which was consecrated in 1718. It has an imposing bell tower, fine 19th-century stained glass and marble memorials to heroes. The monument to Raj Governor Jonathan Duncan depicts him being blessed by Hindus for his efforts to stop infanticide.

Near the cathedral, the Readymoney Mansion has detailed timberwork, carved balconies and Mughal arches.

St Thomas' Cathedral

7am-6pm daily
stthomascathedral mumbai.com

CHOR BAZAAR

Legend has it that if you have something stolen in Mumbai, you can buy it back at Chor Bazaar, or the "thieves' market". A bargain hunter's paradise, Chor Bazaar is a network of crowded streets lined with shops that sell everything from antique lamps to secondhand mobile phones. Bring your best bargaining skills and a poker face - prices are quite fluid and depend on how you negotiate.

⑪
Colaba Causeway

📍 E5 🚇 Colaba

Constructed by the British in 1838, Colaba Causeway was built to connect the main city with Colaba, its southernmost spur. Today, the posh road, part of Shahid Bhagat Singh Road, is an eclectic mix of shops, restaurants and residential enclaves. Among them is the charming Parsi housing colony of Cusrow Baug, built in 1934, where the distinct culture and lifestyle of this dwindling but still prominent community is preserved. The Causeway's many restaurants include one that has become an institution, the Leopold Café and Bar, one of the first Irani cafés in the city and still a popular meeting place.

1871

The year the popular Leopold Café and Bar opened – initially as an oil wholesale shop.

Further south are the Sassoon Docks, worth visiting early in the morning when they are buzzing with activity. This is when the fishermen bring in their catch and a wholesale fish market is set up by the lively, professional Koli fishwives. At the southern end of Colaba is the Afghan Memorial Church of St John the Evangelist (open daily), built between 1847 and 1858. This grand Neo-Gothic structure, with a 60-m (197-ft) bell tower and imposing front porch in buff basalt stone, was built in memory of the soldiers who died in the First Anglo-Afghan War (1839–42), and is full of memorial stones. It has superb stained glass, especially on its windows, where a panel depicts the Crucifixion.

---

⑫
Shahid Bhagat Singh Marg

📍 F3 🚇 Fort

This busy street is the bustling commercial hub of the Fort area. This historic structure was built by the East India Company in 1716, and while virtually no traces of it remain, the area still offers a fascinating glimpse into the continuities between colonial and present-day Mumbai.

The Reserve Bank of India, on the site of an old military barracks, is India's central banking institution. Designed by J A Ritchie and built in 1939, it has an Art Deco entrance flanked by two impressive columns. There are attractive cast-iron grilles in the window panels. The modern high-rise offices of the Reserve Bank, across the road, stand in the grounds of the old Mint. This is a majestic Classical-fronted

---

THE PARSI COMMUNITY IN MUMBAI

Mumbai's cosmopolitan, progressive culture owes a great deal to the contribution of the Parsi (meaning "Persian") community. Originally from Iran, where they followed the ancient Zoroastrian faith, they migrated to India in the 10th century AD when the advent of Islam brought with it the religious persecution of Zoroastrians. They settled along the west coast of Gujarat, absorbing many local traditions, and later moved to Mumbai, where they made their name as brilliant financiers and traders, and founded leading industrial houses. The Parsis are also renowned for their philanthropy across Mumbai.

The busy interior of the famous Leopold Café and Bar, on Colaba Causeway

building, designed and built in 1827 by Major John Hawkins of the Bombay Engineers' Regiment. Entry into the Mint is restricted, but the fantastic RBI Monetary Museum, on the ground floor of the neighbouring Amar Building, is free to enter and has displays on the history of notes and coins.

West of the Mint, occupying a corner site at the intersection of Pherozeshah Mehta and Shahid Bhagat Singh roads, is the imposing Gresham Assurance House. This Art Deco structure has an impressive basalt façade, with two grand pillars and a dome.

The Marshall Building, directly opposite, has a Florentine dome, and was constructed in 1898 to accommodate the warehouse and offices of a British engineering firm. Its façade, embellished with a medley of angels, portholes and pediments, blended contemporary European architecture with Indian design styles.

Drinking water fountains or *pyaos* were set up across the city by local philanthropists to provide respite from the hot Indian summer. At the point where Shahid Bhagat Singh Marg meets Mint Road is the Ruttonsee

Mulji Drinking Water Fountain designed by Frederick Williams Stevens, the leading architect of Bombay in the Victorian era, who also designed the Municipal Corporation Building and the Chhatrapati Shivaji Terminus (*p400*). This fountain was erected in 1894 by a local trader in memory of his only son. Made of limestone and red and blue granite, it is decorated with projecting elephant heads whose trunks spout water. The fountain also has a special trough from which animals can drink.

Further down Mint Road, just before its junction with Walchand Hirachand Marg, is another *pyao* and the Kothari Kabutarkhana. Literally "Pigeon House", the Kabutarkhana is an ornate stone structure, built in the 18th century by a Jain merchant, Purushottamdas Kothari, and added to in the 19th and early 20th centuries.

At the western end of Walchand Hirachand Marg is Bhatia Udyan, an oasis of green in the midst of swirling traffic. It has a statue of Sir Dinshaw Maneckji Petit, a baronet, captain of industry and leading Parsi philanthropist of the early 20th century. The statue was sculpted by Sir Thomas Brock, and the surrounding garden is a good place from which to view some of Mumbai's grand Victorian buildings, including the former

Victoria Terminus, the Mumbai Municipal Corporation building and the ornate General Post Office.

Shahid Bhagat Singh Marg eventually runs into D'Mello Road, which used to be known as Frere Road. This area lay under water until the 1860s, when it was reclaimed by the Port Trust. Today the road is lined with popular eateries.

DRINK

Colaba Social
Mumbai's young enjoy affordable Indian wines or craft beers in this dark, buzzy, industrial chic bar.

◉E5 ⬠B K Boman Behram Marg
ⓦsocialoffline.in

Leopold Café and Bar
Made famous in the hit novel *Shantaram*, this is a firm favourite of travellers to Mumbai. Its large menu is somewhat overpriced, but its location makes it a dynamic place for an evening pint.

◉E5 ⬠Colaba Causeway 📞91 22 2282 8185

Harbour Bar
One of the many excellent bars in the Taj Mahal Palace, this one has been serving fine wines and whisky since 1933. Be sure to try the signature From the Harbour cocktail.

◉F5 ⬠Apollo Bundar
ⓦtajhotels.com

The Ruttonsee Mulji Drinking Water Fountain, dating from 1894

13

Ballard Estate

F3 **Bounded by Shahid Bhagat Singh Marg, Walchand Hirachand Marg and Shoorji Vallabhdas Marg**

This entire area was part of the sea until it was reclaimed by the Bombay Port Trust and converted into a business district. Planned between 1908 and 1914 by George Wittet, architect of the Gateway of India, the area was developed according to the strict guidelines set by him, maintaining a restrained elegance in contrast to the over-ornamentation of the Victorian edifices in the Fort area. The district's broad pavements and neat tree-lined avenues feature stone buildings of uniform height and style, giving the estate an atmosphere of calm tranquillity, unusual in a business quarter.

A convenient point of entry into Ballard Estate is from Shoorji Vallabhdas Marg, near the imposing Marshall Building. Among the most impressive buildings on this street is the Customs House. Designed by Wittet himself, it has a grand entrance portico

in Renaissance style, framed by two columns rising to the height of the building. Next to it is the Mumbai Port Trust, also designed by George Wittet. Two striking ships in full sail are sculpted on its basalt façade. Further down the road, to the east, is the Port Trust War Memorial, honouring the memory of port officers who died in World War I. The memorial has a single fluted column shaft in stone, surmounted by a lantern. The Grand Hotel dominates the corner of Walchand Hirachand Marg and Ram Gulam Marg. Another of George Wittet's designs, it has a striking central atrium. The grandiose Mackinnon & Mackenzie Building has an impressive portico, columns and statues. This, and other beautiful Edwardian buildings, such as Darabshaw House and Neville House, make Ballard Estate a uniquely elegant business district. The renowned Irani café Britannia is also here.

> The buildings of Marine Drive are characterized by a strong Art Deco flavour, a style that was popular in Mumbai during the 1930s and 1940s.

14

Marine Drive

D3 **Back Bay, South Bombay**

Known as the "Queen's Necklace" after the glittering string of streetlights lining the road, Marine Drive (renamed Netaji Subhash Chandra Road) sweeps along a sea-facing promenade that runs from Nariman Point to Malabar Hill. Built on land reclaimed from the sea in the 1920s, it is also the main arterial link between the suburbs and the city's prime commercial and administrative centres, Nariman Point and the Fort area (p410). Situated at its eastern periphery is the Oval Maidan, now World Heritage listed, nursery of such legendary Indian cricketing heroes as Sachin Tendulkar and Sunil Gavaskar.

The buildings of Marine Drive are characterized by a strong Art Deco flavour, a style that was popular in Mumbai during the 1930s and 1940s. With the advent of electric lifts, and with concrete replacing the earlier stone and brick, the apartment blocks

on the seafront were built to a uniform height of five floors, making this the most fashionable residential area of the time. Real estate prices on this stretch remain very high. The most notable buildings here are the Oberoi and the National Centre for the Performing Arts (NCPA). The NCPA, at the southern tip of Marine Drive, is the city's most active venue for music, dance and theatre performances. Its Tata Theatre and Experimental Theatre stage works by international and Indian playwrights, while India's finest musicians and dancers perform regularly in its other auditoriums.

The best way to enjoy Marine Drive during the day is from the upper floor of a red double-decker bus, which provides panoramic views of the sea and the city's skyline. In the evening, the area swarms with people taking their daily walks, couples meeting after work and families gathering around the vendors selling coconut water and *bhelpuri*.

THE DABBAWALAS

Most office workers in Mumbai spend two hours commuting. Hot, home-cooked lunches would be an impossibility - if not for the *dabbawalas*. They pick up meals in *dabbas* (steel containers) from each house, colour-code addresses onto their lids, thread them onto poles and cycle off to hand them over to colleagues who deliver to the offices. Only 300 lunches are said to go astray each year.

picked clean by vultures. This, they believe, is one of the most environmentally friendly ways of disposing of the dead. A fall in Mumbai's vulture population, however, remains a cause of worry. A thick belt of trees surrounds the Towers, which are closed to visitors.

The Hanging Gardens, perched at the top of Malabar Hills, provide a pleasant open space with views of the city.

of the famous Ganesh Chaturthi festival which takes place every August/September, where tens of thousands of worshippers bring huge, elaborate Ganesh statues from across the city to immerse them in the ocean. It is an unmissable spectacle for any visitor.

---

⑮ Malabar Hill

◉ B1 ⬚ Bounded by Napean Sea Rd, Ridge Rd and Walkeshwar Rd

This posh residential area, once dotted with bungalows set in large, forested compounds, is today crowded with high-rise apartment blocks, home to Mumbai's rich and famous. The Parsi Towers of Silence are also located in this area. Parsis, who believe that the elements of earth, water, air and fire are sacred and should not be defiled, place their dead in these tall, cylindrical stone towers to be

←

Night falling on Marine Drive, a stretch known for its Art Deco buildings

---

⑯ Chowpatty Beach

◉ C1 ⬚ Bounded by Napean Sea Rd, Ridge Rd and Walkeshwar Rd

At the northern end of Marine Drive, Chowpatty Beach is where young and old come together every evening to watch the sunset, eat street food snacks on the sand or ride the fairground attractions that set up just behind it.

The ocean itself is not clean, so swimming is not advised, but this is a superb people-watching destination and a hive of activity at weekends.

One of the highlights here are the ubiquitous *bhelpuri* stalls, serving up portions of the classic Mumbai snack of puffed rice, tomatoes, onions and a tangy tamarind sauce. Chowpatty is also the location

---

SHOP

No-Mad
Brave the chaos of Mangaldas textiles market to seek out this designer fabric shop. Expect chai on arrival and air-con.

◉ E2 ⬚ 1st Floor, Mangaldas Market
Ⓦ no-mad.in

Playclan
A modern lifestyle store, Playclan sells clothing, stationery and accessories bearing whimsical designs inspired by Indian folklore.

◉ C1 ⬚ Opera House, Parmanand Marg
Ⓦ theplayclan.com

17

Juhu Beach

📍 A2 📌 N of Bandra

The sandy coastline of Juhu Beach lies north of the city centre. On weekends it is packed with families playing cricket, paddling in the water and enjoying the breeze. Vendors offering snacks, toys and fairground rides add to the *mela* (fair) atmosphere.

The Prithvi Theatre, on Juhu Church Road, stages plays in Hindi, Gujarati and English, and has a lively café, popular with Mumbai's arty crowd.

18

Banganga

📍 A2 📌 Walkeshwar, Malabar Hill

Hidden amid the skyscrapers of Malabar Hill is the small settlement of Banganga, set around a sacred tank. According to legend, Rama, the hero of the *Ramayana*, pausing here while on his way to rescue his abducted wife Sita, shot an arrow into the ground and a spring gushed forth. This is the origin of the tank, and devotees take regular ritual dips in it. The site has several temples, including Jabreshwar Mahadev, and rest houses (*dharamsalas*) for pilgrims.

STAY

Abode

Design-led rooms with vintage furniture and pretty, tiled floors

📍 E5 📌 M B Marg 🌐 abodeboutique hotels.com

₹₹₹

Soho House Mumbai

The hippest hangout for Mumbai's creative elite, Soho House overlooks Juhu Beach.

📍 A2 📌 Juhu Tara Rd 🌐 sohohousemumbai. com

₹₹₹

Taj Mahal Palace

This hotel with views over the Gateway of India has hosted Obama and the Dalai Lama.

📍 E5 📌 Apollo Bunder 🌐 tajhotels.com

₹₹₹

19

Khotachiwadi

📍 D1 📌 Bounded by Jagannath Shankarshet Rd and Raja Ram Mohan Roy Rd, Girgaum

The lovely old neighbourhood of Khotachiwadi (literally, "Headman's Orchard") grew as a suburban settlement in the 19th century, and retains the sleepy quality of a coastal village. The low, tile-roofed cottages have timber eaves and open verandahs with cast-iron balconies.

20

Mahalaxmi Temple

📍 A3 📌 Bhulabhai Desai Rd 🕐 6am–10pm daily 🌐 mahalaxmi-temple.com

Devotees throng this temple, dating to the 18th century and dedicated to Lakshmi, the goddess of wealth and prosperity. The approach to the temple is lined with stalls selling coconuts, flowers and plastic icons. Nearby, the Mahalaxmi Race Course has horse races every weekend from November to April.

↑ Crowds enjoying the open air amid vendors of assorted goods at Juhu Beach

21
Bandra

♦ A2 ⊠ N of Mahim Bay

The modern, prosperous Bandra, in the north of Mumbai, is linked to the city by the Mahim Causeway. The Portuguese, who retained Bandra until the late 1700s, built several Roman Catholic churches, including the **Mount Mary Basilica**. Outside the church is a market selling wax models of various body parts. Devotees with ailing limbs buy the appropriate model and solemnly place it on the altar before the Virigin Mary in the belief that she will effect a miraculous cure. A Portuguese fort, Castella de Aguada, also known as Bandra Fort, offers spectacular views of the sea and the hinterland. The Bandra-Worli Sea Link

→ The Bandra-Worli Sea Link, a modern bridge across Mahim Bay

connects Bandra in the western suburbs with Worli in southern Mumbai.

Mount Mary Basilica
♦ Mount Mary Rd ⊙ 6:30am-8:30pm Mon-Sat, 6:30am-7pm Sun ⊠ mountmary basilicabandra.in

22
Haji Ali Mosque

♦ A3 ⊠ Off Lala Lajpat Rai Marg ⊙ 6am-10pm daily ⊠ hajialidargah.in

This dargah (tomb) of a rich merchant, Haji Ali Shah Bukhari, is accessed via a long causeway, which gets submerged at high tide. Bukhari is known for giving up his wealth after a pilgrimage to Mecca. The dargah dates to the 15th century, but the neighbouring dazzling white mosque was built in the early 20th century and seems to float on its small island, off the coast of Worli.

23 Ⓜ
Film City

♦ A2 ⊠ Goregaon East 🛈 Maharashtra Film, Stage & Cultural Development Corporation; (022) 2840 1533

Built in 1978 to meet the needs of Bollywood, Film City sprawls over 140 ha (346 acres) in the city's northern outskirts. Bollywood produces some 800 feature films a year,

making it the world's largest film industry, rivalled only by south India's Telugu and Tamil equivalents. Film City is where many Bollywood blockbusters are shot, as are most Indian TV soaps and serials. Song-and-dance routines, dramatic scenes and action-packed fight sequences take place on Film City's dozen shooting stages, against outsized backdrops of medieval forts, dense jungles and opulent cardboard palaces.

24 Ⓒ Ⓜ Ⓒ Ⓒ
Dr Bhau Daji Lad Museum

♦ A3 ⊠ 91/A Ambedkar Road, Byculla East ⊙ 10am-6pm Thu-Tue ⊠ bdlmuseum.org

Worth visiting for its ornate 19th-century Renaissance Revival architecture alone, this little museum – which was the city's first, established in 1855 – displays maps, artifacts and photographs related to Mumbai's history.

> 💬 **INSIDER TIP**
> **Lower Parel**
>
> One of Mumbai's coolest neighbourhoods, Lower Parel, south of Juhu Beach, sits in the repurposed Mathurdas Mills Compound. Here you'll find glitzy malls, luxury hotels, and trendy bars and eateries.

A SHORT WALK
KALA GHODA

Distance 2 km (1 mile) **Nearest Station** Churchgate **Time** 30 minutes

Kala Ghoda, or "Black Horse", was named after an equestrian statue of King Edward VII that once stood at the intersection of Mahatma Gandhi Road and K Dubash Marg. Despite the original statue having been moved to the gardens surrounding the zoo, the name persists in public memory, thanks in part to the large mural and a new statue of a black horse that commemorates it. Stretching from Wellington Fountain, at the southern end of

Mahatma Gandhi Road, to Mumbai University at the north, and flanked by the Oval Maidan and the naval base at Lion Gate, this area is a hub of cultural activity. It houses a number of art galleries, museums, restaurants and boutiques, and hosts the famous annual Kala Ghoda Arts Festival in February.

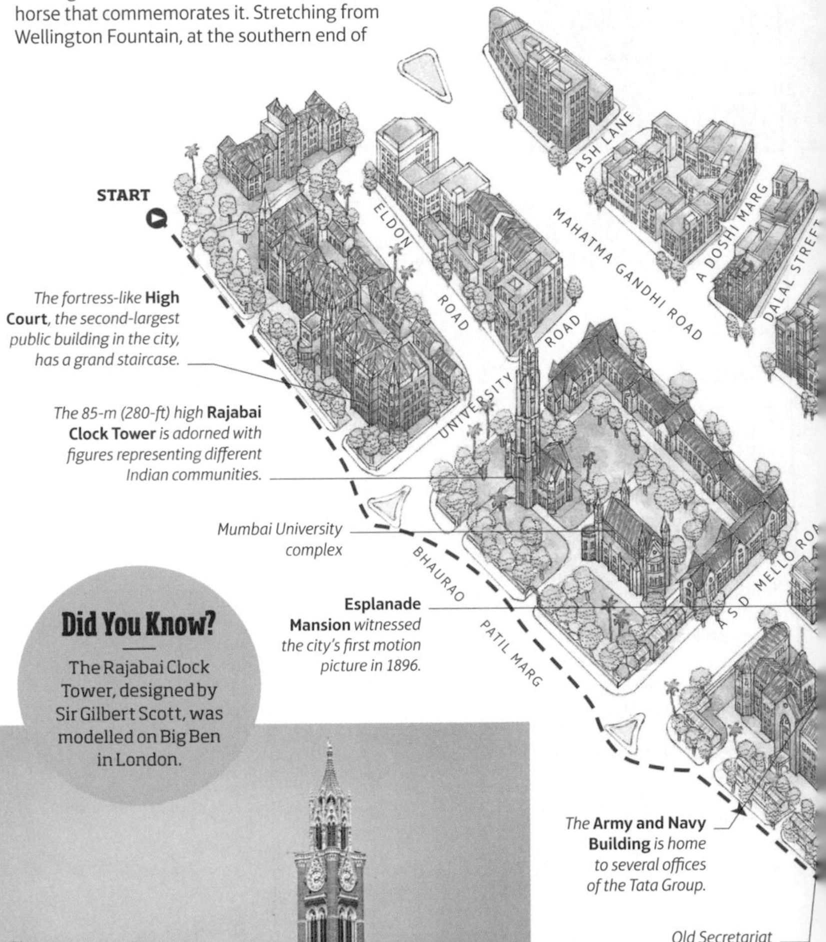

START

The fortress-like **High Court**, the second-largest public building in the city, has a grand staircase.

The 85-m (280-ft) high **Rajabai Clock Tower** is adorned with figures representing different Indian communities.

Mumbai University complex

Did You Know?

The Rajabai Clock Tower, designed by Sir Gilbert Scott, was modelled on Big Ben in London.

Esplanade Mansion witnessed the city's first motion picture in 1896.

ASH LANE

MAHATMA GANDHI ROAD

A DOSHI MARG

DALAL STREET

ELDON ROAD

UNIVERSITY ROAD

BHAURAO PATIL MARG

A S D MELLO ROAD

The **Army and Navy Building** is home to several offices of the Tata Group.

Old Secretariat

← Playing cricket with the Rajabai Clock Tower and High Court in the background

Locator Map
For more detail see p398

←
Visitors reading in the
elegantly designed
David Sassoon Library

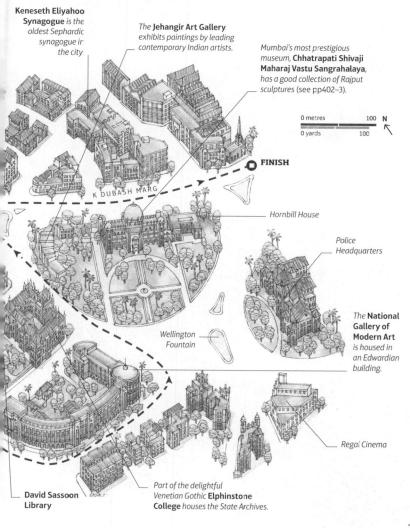

Keneseth Eliyahoo Synagogue *is the oldest Sephardic synagogue in the city*

The **Jehangir Art Gallery** *exhibits paintings by leading contemporary Indian artists.*

Mumbai's most prestigious museum, **Chhatrapati Shivaji Maharaj Vastu Sangrahalaya,** *has a good collection of Rajput sculptures (see pp402–3).*

0 metres 100 N
0 yards 100

K DUBASH MARG

FINISH

Hornbill House

Police Headquarters

The **National Gallery of Modern Art** *is housed in an Edwardian building.*

Wellington Fountain

Regal Cinema

David Sassoon Library

Part of the delightful Venetian Gothic **Elphinstone College** *houses the State Archives.*

MAHARASHTRA

Best known for its bustling capital Mumbai, Maharashtra is a state with a varied landscape of verdant hills, scenic coastal plains and busy industrial centres covering an area of 308,000 sq km (118,920 sq miles). The hills of the Western Ghats, source of many rivers, run parallel to the narrow Konkan Coast, while cradled in the centre is the Deccan Plateau, formed from black volcanic lava 70 million years ago. This area only became a state in 1960, a number of years after independence from the British Raj, as a result of political agitation for a united state for Marathi-speaking people.

Maharashtra first emerged in history as part of the Mauryan Empire in the 4th century BC. This empire was followed by other significant dynasties, including the Satavahanas, whose kings protected the state against Scythian invasion, and the Chalukyas, who successfully repelled early Arab incursions. From the 2nd century BC, this area saw a great flowering of art and architecture, most clearly represented in the famous UNESCO World Heritage sites of the Buddhist caves at Ajanta and the rock-cut temples at Ellora.

As with most other areas in India, Maharashtra was eventually conquered by the Mughals, who were subsequently repelled by the Marathas. This great Hindu dynasty then built a great empire that stretched across India, leaving behind monuments such as the massive forts around Pune. In the early part of the 20th century, the state saw a number of independence movements emerge, and it was in Mumbai in 1942 that the ultimatum was given to the British to quit India.

MADHYA PRADESH
AND CHHATTISGARH
p274

ANDHRA PRADESH
AND TELANGANA
p564

MAHARASHTRA

Must Sees
1 Ellora Caves
2 Ajanta Caves

Experience More
3 Alibag
4 Murud-Janjira
5 Ganapatipule
6 Kolhapur
7 Matheran
8 Mahabaleshwar
9 Pune
10 Lonavla
11 Ahmadnagar
12 Nasik
13 Pandharpur
14 Aurangabad
15 Daulatabad
16 Melghat Tiger Reserve
17 Nagpur
18 Lonar
19 Tadoba-Andhari Tiger Reserve
20 Sevagram Ashram

❶ ⟨⟩ ⟨⟩ ⟨⟩ ⟨⟩

ELLORA CAVES

🏛 Aurangabad district; 30 km (19 miles) NW of Aurangabad 🚌 From Aurangabad
🕐 9am–5:30pm Wed–Mon ℹ www.maharashtratourism.gov.in

The 34 caves at Ellora, built between the 6th and 9th centuries, are among the most splendid examples of rock-cut architecture in India. Ellora was sited on a lucrative trade route to the west coast, and it was the revenue from this route that sustained the 500 years of extraordinary excavation here.

The caves at Ellora are numbered from the southern end and fall into three groups – Buddhist, Hindu and Jain. The Buddhist Caves (1 to 12) date from the 7th to 8th centuries. The first nine are variations of *viharas* or monasteries, and are filled with Buddha figures, Bodhisattvas and mythological scenes. The most splendid is Cave 10, or Vishwakarma's Cave, named after the celestial carpenter. The Hindu Caves (13 to 29) were carved between the 7th and 9th centuries, and represent the peak of Ellora's development. Cave 14, or Ravana ki Khai, contains impressive sculptures of deities from the Hindu pantheon. The Jain Caves (30 to 34) date from Ellora's last stage, in the 9th century, and are simpler than the Hindu ones.

The Kailasanatha Temple

The finest of Ellora's rock-cut caves is the magnificent Kailasanatha Temple (Cave 16), a UNESCO World Heritage Site. Commissioned by the Rashtrakuta king Krishna I in the 8th century, this mammoth complex was carved out of a huge rocky cliff face. Sculptors chiselled through 85,000 cubic metres (about 3 million cubic feet) of rock, beginning at the top of the cliff and working their way down. The resulting marvel, embellished with huge sculptural panels, was meant to depict Mount Kailasa, the sacred abode of Lord Shiva.

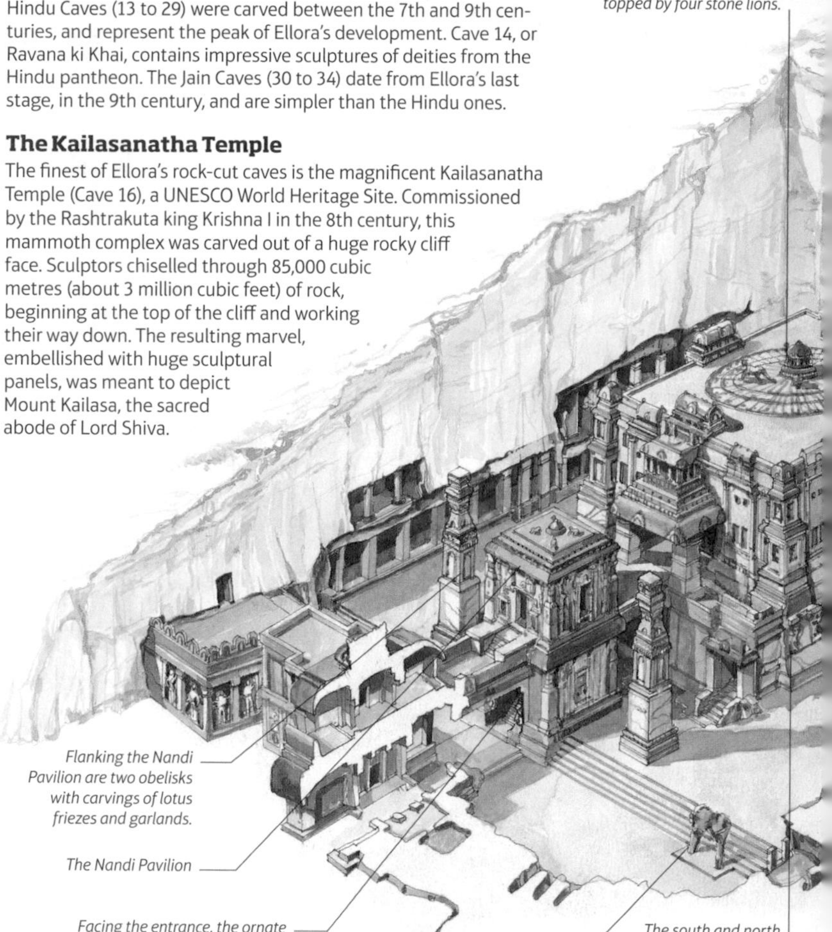

The mandapa *(assembly hall) roof is embellished by a lotus carved in rings, topped by four stone lions.*

Flanking the Nandi Pavilion are two obelisks with carvings of lotus friezes and garlands.

The Nandi Pavilion

Facing the entrance, the ornate Gajalakshmi panel in the Nandi Pavilion depicts Lakshmi being bathed by elephants.

Two life-size stone elephants flank each side of the courtyard.

The south and north walls have Ramayana and Mahabharata panels respectively.

Aerial view of the
Kailasanatha Temple, in
the Ellora Caves complex ↑

Rising 33 m (107 ft), the
shikhara (spire) was once
covered in white plaster to
look like snowy peaks.

↑ Marvelling at the
sculptures in the
Hindu Cave 29

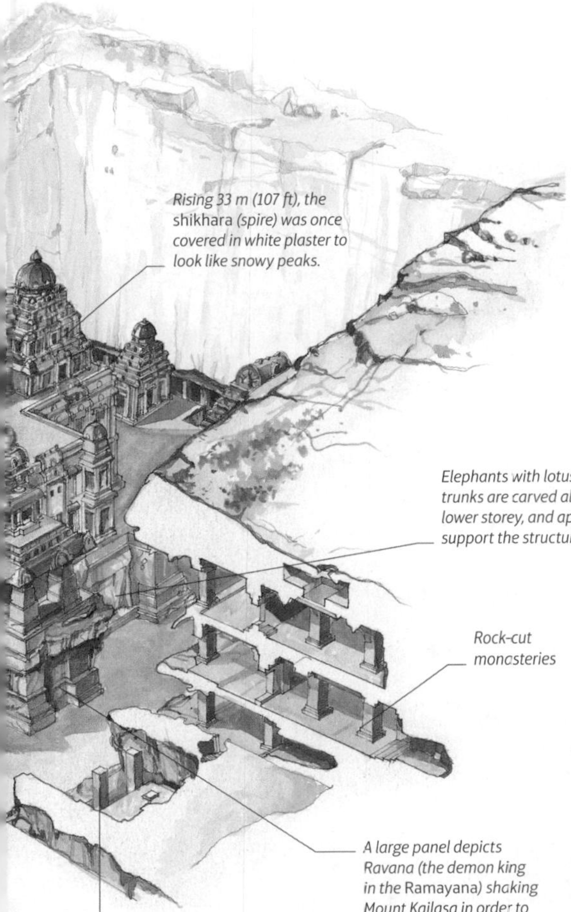

Elephants with lotuses in their
trunks are carved all along the
lower storey, and appear to
support the structure.

Rock-cut
monasteries

← An illustration of the
magnificent 8th-century
Kailasanatha Temple

A large panel depicts
Ravana (the demon king
in the Ramayana) shaking
Mount Kailasa in order to
disturb Shiva and Parvati
in their mountain home.

The Hall of Sacrifice contains
life-size images of Durga
and Kali, as well as of
Ganesha, Parvati and the
seven mother goddesses.

Did You Know?

The Kailasanatha
Temple is the largest
monolithic rock-cut
temple in the world.

2 (icons)

AJANTA CAVES

🏠 Aurangabad district; 110 km (68 miles) NE of Aurangabad 🚌 From Aurangabad
🕐 9am–5:30pm Tue–Sun 🛈 www.maharashtratourism.gov.in

The earliest and finest examples of Buddhist painting in India can be seen at the Ajanta caves, now a UNESCO World Heritage Site. The 30 rock-cut caves here, the earliest of which date to the 2nd century BC, are decorated in magnificent, detailed compositions recounting stories from Buddha's life. This reflected the religious purpose of the caves, which were used as prayer halls and monasteries.

The caves lie in a dramatic horseshoe-shaped enscarpment overlooking the Waghora river gorge. The first group – Caves 8, 9, 10, 12, 13 and 15 – were built from the 2nd to 1st centuries BC, in the austere Hinayana phase of Buddhism. Cave 10 is thought to be Ajanta's oldest cave and one of its finest *chaitya grihas* (prayer halls). The second group of caves are from the Mahayana period in the 5th to 6th centuries AD, when artistic expression was more exuberant. Of this group, Cave 1 is famed for its splendid murals, and the main shrine of Cave 2 has a magnificent painted ceiling. Of the final group (Caves 21 to 27, 7th century), Cave 26 displays the full magnificence of Ajanta's art. Especially remarkable are two splendid panels – a *Temptation of the Buddha by the Demon Mara*, and a 7-m (23-ft) image of the reclining Buddha. After this time, the caves faded into disuse and the jungle concealed them, until they were rediscovered, quite by accident, by an English soldier in 1819.

An aerial view of
the Ajanta Caves and
(*inset*) the interior of
Buddhist Cave 26

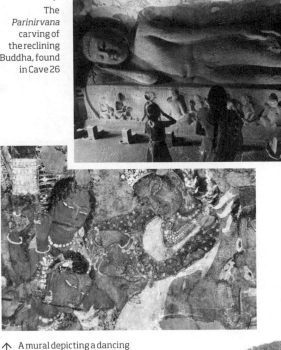

AJANTA'S MURALS

Village life and royal courts, warfare and Buddhist practices, Himalayan mountains and jungles full of wildlife – Ajanta's outstanding collection of murals provides a snapshot of life in India more than 2,000 years ago. They are also among the finest surviving examples of ancient art anywhere in the world. Above the verandah of Cave 1 are friezes of scenes from the Buddha's life, while its ceiling is supported by 20 carved and painted pillars. There is also a striking image of Padmapani, a figure who represents the compassion of the Buddha. A fantastic and emotive image – the *Dying Princess* – can be found in Cave 16.

→ The *Parinirvana* carving of the reclining Buddha, found in Cave 26

↑ A mural depicting a dancing scene, found in Cave 1

A couple walking by the water at Kihim Beach, near Alibag

EXPERIENCE MORE

❸
Alibag

🏠 Raigarh district; 108 km (67 miles) S of Mumbai
🚌🚢 From Gateway of India, Mumbai, to Mandve, 18 km (11 miles) N of Alibag, then bus

The port of Alibag, located just across the bay from Mumbai, was developed by the Marathas in the 17th century in an attempt to protect their kingdom from the Dutch, Portuguese and the increasingly powerful British. Alibag is today a quiet coastal town, popular with Bombayites as a location for holiday homes. Its most

Did You Know?

It is thought Alibag got its name from the orchards, or *bagh*, owned by a local man named Ali.

impressive sight is its beach, a lovely 5-km (3-mile) stretch of soft silver sand, lined with coconut and casuarina trees.

Kolaba Fort, constructed on an island in 1662 by the Maratha ruler Chhatrapati Shivaji, looms over the skyline. It is a forbidding grey mass of lead, steel and stone, built on a rock jutting from the sea, and can be reached on foot during low tide. Protected by its high ramparts are a temple dedicated to Lord Ganesha, and next to it a sweet-water well that must have been useful during sieges. There are two main entrances to the fort, one from the shore and another from the sea. The enormous shore-side doorway is decorated with sculptures of tigers, elephants and peacocks.

Kihim Beach, only 9 km (6 miles) north of Alibag, is a tranquil getaway, with woods brimming with birds and wild flowers. It was the favourite haunt of the famous Indian ornithologist Salim Ali (1896–1987), author of a fine book on Indian birds.

❹
Murud-Janjira

🏠 Raigarh district; 165 km (103 miles) S of Mumbai
🚢 From Gateway of India, Mumbai to Mandve, then bus; from Rajpuri to Janjira Fort ℹ️ www.maharashtra tourism.com

A sleepy coastal town with Indo-Gothic houses and meandering pathways, Murud has a picture-perfect beach for lazy, sunny afternoons. The little village of Rajpuri, 4 km (2 miles) south of the main Murud town, is the gateway to the Janjira Fort, the strongest island-fort in the Konkan, still enduring the surge and retreat of the Arabian Sea. Boats are available at Rajpuri to take visitors to the fort.

Also evocatively known as the Jazeere Mehboob or "Moon Fort", it was built in 1511 by the Siddis, who originally arrived in the Deccan from Abyssinia as part of the slave trade or as

→

The temple of Swayambhu Ganapati at Ganapatipule, honouring Lord Ganesha

soldiers. The fortress, with its high ramparts, 22 bastions and granite walls jointed with lead to withstand the onslaught of the sea, proved invincible against attacks by the Portuguese and British, and even against the great Maratha leader, Shivaji. The steps of the fort lead to a stone gate, where there is a stone engraving of a lion holding six elephants in captivity, which represents six successive Sidci victories. Rusty cannons point outwards through niches in the ramparts. The palaces, gardens and mosques lie in silent ruin. Luxurious vegetation grows around the palace of the Siddi ruler, Sirul Khan.

⑤
Ganapatipule

🏠 Ratnagiri district; 375 km (233 miles) S of Mumbai 🚉 Ratnagiri, then bus 🚌 ℹ️ www.maharashtra tourism.com

The small coastal village of Ganapatipule is named after the 400-year-old temple of Swayambhu Ganapati. Here, the self-originated idol of Ganapati (the local name of Lord Ganesha) is revered by Hindus as one of the eight sacred sites, or "Ashtha Ganapatis", in India. Devotees show respect to the deity by

performing a *pradakshina*, a walk around the hill near the temple. The beach has long stretches of pristine white sands and clear waters. Beyond the coast lie groves of fruit trees, including mango, banana, jackfruit, coconut and betel nut.

Ratnagiri, 25 km (16 miles) to the south, is famous for its groves of delicious Alphonso mangoes, locally known as *hapus*. Ratnagiri's fortress, Ratnadurg Fort, is situated along the coast, and is intact, with a notable Bhagavati temple within its walls.

GANESHA, THE REMOVER OF OBSTACLES

Lord Ganesha, the elephant-headed son of Shiva and Parvati, is the most popular deity in India, and especially beloved in Maharashtra. Images of the endearing, pot-bellied god are found in every household, on temple doorways and shop entrances. No task or enterprise is ever begun without invoking him, as he is the Lord of New Beginnings. Worshipped in many guises, he is Vighneshwara, the Remover of Obstacles, and Siddhidata, the God of Prosperity and Success. Ganesha is above all a friend, lovable and benign. According to legend, Ganesha gained his elephant head after Shiva, in a state of fury, cut his son's head off and then, in remorse, stuck on the head of a passing elephant. The deity's four arms hold his various attributes. Two of these always grasp his broken tusk and a round sweet-meat called *modaka*. His other two hands sometimes hold a lotus blossom, an elephant goad, an axe or prayer beads. His festival, Ganesha Chaturthi, crosses all social boundaries uniting the people of Maharashtra in a frenzied ten-day celebration.

6
Kolhapur

🏠 Kolhapur district; 237 km (147 miles) S of Pune ✈🚆🚌
ℹ Maharashtra Tourism; www.maharashtra tourism.gov.in

Situated on the Panchganga river, the city of Kolhapur is a thriving commercial centre, most known today for its dairy industry. It is also one of Maharashtra's most important pilgrimage sites, associated from early times with the worship of Shakti, the Mother Goddess. Ruled by the Hindu Yadava dynasty between the 10th and 13th centuries, it was later occupied by the Mughals. In 1659, Kolhapur was finally seized by the Maratha chief Shivaji, who ruled the powerful Hindu dynasty at the time, and was later inherited by his younger son. The state was ruled by the Bhonsles, one of the four Maratha princely families, until independence.

The Shri Mahalakshmi, or Amba Bai Temple, dedicated to the Mother Goddess, was built in the 7th century by the Chalukya king Karnadeva. The temple's idol is encrusted with diamonds and other precious stones, and is said to be a *swayambhu*, or naturally occurring monolith. The *mandapa*, or pavilion, has a finely carved ceiling. Behind the temple are the remains of the Old Palace or Juna Rajwada, where members of the former maharaja's family still live. There is a small museum and temple inside. Near the palace gates are the city's wrestling grounds, where young men practise traditional Indian wrestling, known as *kushti*. The **New Palace**, 2 km (1 mile) north of the city centre, was completed in 1881. Designed by Major Charles Mant, it merged European, Jain, Hindu and Islamic elements in a style that became known as Indo-Saracenic. Inside the palace, the **Shahaji Chhatrapati Museum** displays royal memorabilia, including garments, hunting photographs and one of the deadly-looking swords of Mughal emperor Aurangzeb.

Kolhapur is also famous for its hand-crafted leather slippers, known as *chappals*.

The fortress at Panhala, a hill station 19 km (12 miles) northwest of Kolhapur, is well protected by three impressive double walled gates and 7-km-(4-mile-) long ramparts. Within its walls stand two temples, one dedicated to Amba Bai and the other to Maruti, the Wind God, as well as huge stone granaries, the largest of which, Ganga Kothi, covers 948 sq m (10,204 sq ft). Established in the 12th century by Raja Bhoja II, the fortress fell successively to the Yadavas, the Adil Shahis of Bijapur, Shivaji, Emperor Aurangzeb and the British. There are many private homes in Panhala as well, including that of the famous Indian singer Lata Mangeshkar.

New Palace
💲 🕐 9am–1pm, 2:30–6pm Tue–Sun

Shahaji Chhatrapati Museum
🕐 9am–6pm Tue–Sun

> Near the palace gates are the city's wrestling grounds, where young men practise traditional Indian wrestling, known as *kushti*.

7
Matheran

🏠 Raigarh district; 118 km (73 miles) NW of Pune
🚆 From Neral Junction, take the toy train to Matheran (2 hrs) 🚌 ℹ Opposite the railway station; www. maharashtratourism.gov.in

The closest hill station to Mumbai, Matheran (meaning "Mother Forest" or "Forest on Top") lies at a height of 803 m (2,635 ft) above sea level. This picturesque town is situated in the forested Sahyadri Hills. In 1855, Lord Elphinstone, the governor of Bombay, visited

← Kolhapur's Indo-Saracenic New Palace, built in the late 1800s

← Stunning view from a lookout point in Mahabaleshwar

Matheran, and the town soon became fashionable. A railway line was laid in 1907, and a quaint toy train still winds its way slowly through hills and forests. All motor vehicles are completely banned within the limits of the town, making it uniquely peaceful, despite the burgeoning crowds of visitors that descend upon it, particularly on weekends.

Matheran has many lookout points: Porcupine Point, or Sunset Point, is known for its spectacular sunsets; Louisa Point has views of the ruined Prabal Fort; and from Hart Point on a clear day you can see as far as Mumbai.

---

⑧ Mahabaleshwar

📍 Satara district; 115 km (71 miles) SW of Pune
🌐 www.maharashtra tourism.gov.in

The largest hill station in Maharashtra, Mahabaleshwar sits 1,372 m (4,501 ft) above sea level. In 1828, Sir John Malcolm, Governor of Bombay, chose this spot as the site for a sanatorium. Soon after, the wooded slopes were covered with colonial structures, among them Government House, the Mahabaleshwar Club, and the polo grounds and race course. There are also several lookout points such as Mumbai Point, from where the sea can be seen on a clear day, and Arthur's Seat, which affords panoramic views of the Konkan Coast. In the old town is the sacred Krishna Temple, which is built on the legendary site of the Panchganga, or source of five rivers – the Koyna, Savitri, Venna, Gayatri and the mighty Krishna, along with temples dedicated to Hanuman and Rama. Nearby are several berry farms, where visitors can pick strawberries and raspberries.

The beautiful hill station of Panchgani, 18 km (11 miles) east of Mahabaleshwar, is the starting point for many scenic trekking trails. It is also dotted with some charming British and Parsi bungalows. The majestic hill-top forts of Pratapgarh and Raigad, 18 km (11 miles) west and 70 km (43 miles) northwest of Mahabaleshwar respectively, were both strongholds of the Maratha Empire. They offer commanding views of the surrounding countryside.

STAY

Dune Barr House
This converted 19th-century bungalow exudes a stately air, with genteel rooms and the wonderful Verandah in the Forest restaurant.

📍 Matheran
🌐 dunewellness group.com

₹₹₹

The Machan
The Machan is an eco-friendly hideaway with luxurious timber-and-glass treehouses overlooking the forest – some even have their own private plunge pools. There's also an on-site spa.

📍 Lonavala
🌐 themachan.com

₹₹₹

9

Pune

⊕ Pune district; 163 km (101 miles) SE of Mumbai ✈ 12 km (7 miles) NE of city centre, then shuttle bus or taxi 🚌🚋 ℹ Maharashtra Tourism, I Block, Central Bldg; www.maharashtra tourism.gov.in

The industrial city of Pune, at the confluence of the Mutha and Mula rivers, is bounded by the Sahyadris in the west. Its pleasant climate and proximity to Mumbai made it the perfect monsoon capital for the British in the 19th century. Then called Poona, it became an important administrative centre and military camp.

↓ A bustling scene in the city of Pune, with street vendors selling produce

1990

The year that Osho died at his ashram in Pune, aged 59.

Even today, the Indian army's Southern Command is still based here.

From 1750 until 1817, Pune was ruled by the Peshwas. In the old city are the remains of their Shaniwar Wada Palace, built in 1736 and razed in a fire in 1828. Only its outer walls and the main entrance with large spikes, designed to deter the enemy's elephants, survive. Further south is Vishram Bagh Wada, which is a beautiful Peshwa palace with an elaborate wooden façade.

For many visitors, Pune is synonymous with the internationally famous **Osho International Meditation Resort**. Founded by Bhagwan Rajneesh or Osho – the flamboyant pop mystic, or "sex guru" as he was called – had a meteoric rise in the West, and his ashram continues to attract devotees from Europe and America.

Housed in a traditional Maratha house or *wada*, is the charming privately owned **Raja Dinkar Kelkar Museum**. On display is a collection of beautiful everyday objects such as pots, lamps, pens, ink stands, nutcrackers and other utilitarian items. An interesting piece is a Maharashtrian Chitrakathi scroll painting, which was used in folk theatre performances. The **Tribal Museum**, east of the railway station, showcases the state's tribal cultures, especially from

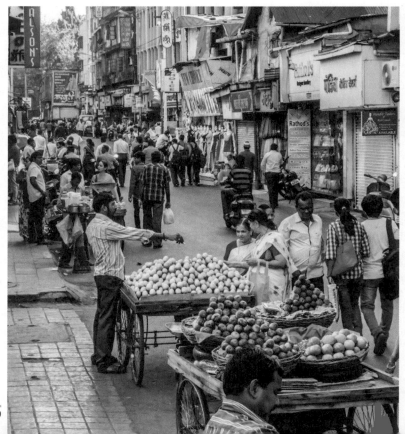

→
Visitors braving the rain at the Bhaja Caves complex, near Lonavla

the Sahyadri and Gondwana regions. The **Aga Khan Palace**, across the Mula river to the north of the city, is where independence leader Mahatma Gandhi was imprisoned by the British for two years; today, it is the Gandhi National Memorial. Gandhi's wife, Kasturba, died here and her ashes have been interred in a memorial in the gardens.

Other places of interest in the city include the rock-cut Pataleshwar Cave Temple, dating from the 8th century; the hilltop Parvati Temple; and fine gardens, such as Empress Botanical Gardens and Bund Gardens. Pune is the centre of Maratha culture, with a lively tradition of theatre, classical music and dance.

About 50 km (31 miles) southwest are the forts of Rajgad and Sinhgad (the "Lion Fort"). The latter is associated with Tanaji Malusare, leading general of Shivaji, a famous early Maratha Empire king. He is said to have conquered the fort by making domesticated monitor lizards climb the wall with strong ropes attached – which his warriors then used to scale the fortress.

Osho International Meditation Resort
⌂ 17 1st Lane, Koregaon Park
🌐 osho.com

Raja Dinkar Kelkar Museum
♿ ⌂ 1377-78 Shukrawar Peth 🕐 10am-5:30pm daily
🚫 Public hols 🌐 rajakelkar museum.org

Tribal Museum
♿ ⌂ 28 Queen's Garden, off Koregaon Rd 📞 (020) 2636 2772 🕐 10am-5pm Mon-Sat

Aga Khan Palace
♿ ⌂ Ahmednagar Rd
📞 (020) 2668 0250
🕐 9am-5:30pm daily

⑩ Lonavla

⌂ Pune district; 62 km (39 miles) NW of Pune 🚃🚌
🌐 www.maharashtra tourism.gov.in

On the main train line from Mumbai to Pune, Lonavla was once a sleepy hill station famous for its *chikki*, a type of caramelized sweet. It has now become a popular weekend getaway for city-dwellers from nearby Mumbai.

The town has a bustling main street, as well as many pleasant walks. It is also a convenient base for exploring the surrounding hills and towns.

Located 8 km (5 miles) northwest of Lonavla is Khandala, a pretty town with panoramic views of the Western Ghats. The famous Buddhist rock-cut **Karla Caves** near Lonavla date from the 2nd to 1st centuries BC. The splendid *chaitya griha* (prayer hall), the largest and best-preserved of the early Buddhist caves on the Deccan Plateau, is the most significant sight here. It has a magnificently sculpted courtyard, a towering 14-m- (46-ft-) high façade with a horseshoe shaped window, and a large pillared hall with a monolithic stupa. The 20-odd **Bhaja Caves**, also near Lonavla, are the oldest in the region, dating back to the 2nd century BC. Cave 12, a *chaitya griha*, still contains the remains of wooden beams on its ceiling. On either side of

the façade are carvings of multistoreyed structures with windows and balconies.

Karla Caves
♿ ⌂ 11 km (7 miles) E of Lonavala 🕐 9am-5pm daily
ℹ️ Maharashtra Tourism, Karla; (02114) 282 230

Bhaja Caves
♿ ⌂ 12 km (7 miles) SE of Lonavala 🕐 9am-5:30pm daily

⑪ Ahmadnagar

🏛 Ahmadnagar district; 120 km (75 miles) NE of Pune 🚉🚌 ℹ️ www.maharashtratourism.gov.in

Ahmadnagar was founded in 1490 by Ahmad Nizam Shah Bahri, the son of an Islamic convert, and the city became the seat of his Muslim kingdom. But by 1599, this sultanate was experiencing infighting after the death of the sultan with no clear successor. The Mughals, led by emperor Akbar, took advantage of this situation and invaded. However, the dead sultan's sister, Chand Bibi, successfully defended the city until she was assassinated by her troops and the Mughals seized the town. The kingdom attempted to resist, but was completely subdued by 1636.

Most of this fighting took place around the impressive Ahmadnagar Fort, 4 km (2 miles) northeast of the train station. It was built in 1490, and the stone walls were added in 1563. Its palace, the only surviving structure, consists of a large hall with several domes. It shows the distinctive architectural style of the Nizam Shahi dynasty, who were all prolific builders, unmistakably influenced by Persian style. The Jama Masjid dates to the same period, as does the nearby ornate Damri Mosque. Built in 1568, it has a trefoil parapet and finials topped by miniature pavilions.

Mughal Emperor Aurangzeb died in Ahmadnagar – then part of the Mughal Empire – in 1707, and his body rested briefly at the small Alamgir Dargah, near the cantonment, before being interred at Khuldabad (p435). To the west of the town lies Bagh Rauza, a walled garden. It contains the lavishly decorated mausoleum of the town's founder, Ahmad Nizam Shah Bahri. In 1942, the British imprisoned Jawaharlal Nehru (p76)

in the fort. It was here that he wrote his famous book, *The Discovery of India*.

⑫ Nasik

🏛 Nasik district; 187 km (116 miles) NE of Mumbai ✈️🚉🚌 ℹ️ Maharashtra Tourism; www.maharashtratourism.gov.in

The town of Nasik is one of India's most holy sites. A bustling temple town, built on both banks of the Godavari river, it has almost 200 shrines. The ghats that line the river front are the venue for the spectacular Kumbh Mela. Legend says that Rama, hero of the *Ramayana*, lived here during his 14-year exile. Ramkund, the centrally located tank and the town's focal point, is believed to mark the spot where Rama and his wife Sita bathed. The ashes of the dead are also immersed here.

← The ornate Damri Mosque, dating from the 16th century

Vineyards near the temple town of Nasik, and (inset) sampling Indian wine at a bar ↑

Most of Nasik's temples date to the 18th century. The Kala Rama Temple, east of Ramkund, is built in black stone. It supposedly marks the spot where Sita was abducted by Ravana. The Rameshwar Temple has carvings on the roof of its hall, while the Muktidham Temple, close to the station, carries inscriptions from the *Bhagavad Gita* on its walls.

Pandu Lena, 8 km (5 miles) south of Nasik, has 24 Buddhist caves dating to the 1st and 2nd centuries BC. The oldest is Cave 10, a *vihara* (monastery) which has splendid sculptures and inscriptions above its entrance. Cave 18, an early *chaitya griha*, has a beautifully carved exterior. Other fine caves include Caves 3 and 20. The sacred Trimbakeshwar Temple, 33 km (21 miles) west of Nasik, is built on the site of one of Shiva's 12 naturally occurring *jyotirlingas* (lingas of light). It is surrounded by a large paved platform and has a carved *shikhara*. Though the temple is closed to non-Hindus, visitors can still get a good view of the courtyard and the shrine leading off it.

About 88 km (56 miles) south of Nasik is the town of Shirdi, the site of the temple complex of the first Sai Baba, Maharashtra's most popular saint, who died in 1918.

NASIK WINERIES

While best known as a pilgrimage town, Nasik is emerging as India's most notable wine region, producing a wide variety of wine, from sparkling brut to shiraz. It is home to the country's largest and most recognized winery, Sula *(sulawines. com)*, as well as being the area where legendary French winery Chandon has set up its Indian vineyard. Most wineries are near Nasik town; the most popular are Sula, Soma *(www. somavinevillage.com)* and York *(www.york winery.com)*. These offer tastings and tours; Sula even has a one-day wine course. Many also offer accommodation.

13

Pandharpur

🏛 **Sholapur district; 250 km (155 miles) SE of Pune** 🚉🚌 ℹ **www.maharashtra tourism.gov.in**

The spiritual capital of Maharashtra, Pandharpur is situated on the banks of the Chandrabhaga river and is the site of the sacred shrine of Vithoba, one of several incarnations of Lord Vishnu. The temple was built in 1228 and is the focal point of a sacred pilgrimage that draws thousands of Varakaris (members of one of the most popular religious sects in the state) every July to attend the Ashadh Ekadashi fair. *Dindis* or group processions travel to Pandharpur from every village in the area, accompanied by devotional singing. The riverfront, lined with numerous bathing ghats, comes alive with crowds of people, who gather here for their ritual dip.

⑭ Aurangabad

🏛 **Aurangabad district; 337 km (210 miles) NE of Mumbai** ✈ **10 km (6 miles) E of town, then taxi** 🚍🚋 ℹ **Maharashtra Tourism, Station Rd East; www.maharashtratourism.gov.in**

The largest city in northern Maharashtra, Aurangabad is the nearest air-link to the splendid caves at Ellora and Ajanta (p424). It was founded in 1610 by Malik Ambar, prime minister of the Nizam Shahi rulers of Ahmadnagar (p432). In 1653 it became the headquarters of Aurangzeb, the last great Mughal emperor, who renamed it after himself.

The city's most famous monument is the Bibi ka Maqbara, an imitation of the Taj built in 1678 by Aurangzeb's son, Azam Shah, in memory of his mother Rabia Durrani. Standing in the middle of a large Mughal garden, it has four large minarets at the ends of its raised platform. Like the Taj, it uses white marble and stucco, but there is none of the fine *pietra dura* work that distinguishes Shah Jahan's creation (p166). Aurangzeb's walled city

makes up the central part of the city. On the left bank of the Khan river is the Dargah of Baba Shah Musafir, a Sufi saint who was Aurangzeb's spiritual guide. The complex contains a small mosque, a *madrasa* (theological college), a law court, the zenana (women's quarters) and a water mill (Panchakki), fed by a rectangular tank. Also within the old city, close to Zafar Gate, is the Himroo Factory. Aurangabad is famed for its ancient art of weaving brocade, using silk and gold threads. When the city's prosperity declined, the weavers began using less-expensive cotton and silver threads, producing *himroo*, which literally means "similar". The factory also produces rich Paithani saris, intricately woven with gold thread.

About 3 km (2 miles) north are the Aurangabad Caves, which can be divided into two groups. Of the five caves in the western group, the oldest is Cave 4, dating to the 1st century AD. It is a fine *chaitya griha* with a monolithic stupa. Carved on the rock face outside is a superb image of the Buddha, seated on a lion throne. The eastern group, nearby, comprises four caves. Cave 6 has delicately sculpted Bodhisattvas, surrounded

by flying figures. The most splendid of the caves is Cave 7, featuring large sculptures of Tara and Avalokitesvara. Its inner sanctum has a superb frieze of a female dancer accompanied by musicians.

⑮

Daulatabad

🏛 **Aurangabad district; 13 km (8 miles) NW of Aurangabad** 🚌 **Maharashtra Tourism organizes bus tours** 🕘 **9am–6pm daily** ℹ **www.maharashtratourism.gov.in**

Perched on a granite outcrop of the Deccan Plateau, this formidable fort has witnessed some of the greatest carnage in the region. Originally called Deogiri, it was captured in 1296 by Alauddin Khilji, the Deccan's first Muslim invader from Delhi.

Did You Know?

Bibi ka Maqbara is 30 per cent smaller than the Taj Mahal, on which it is modelled.

The overgrown ruins
of the imposing
fortress at Daulatabad

Alauddin was followed by Muhammad bin Tughlaq, who annexed the fort in 1328 and renamed the town Daulatabad ("City of Fortune"). When he decided to shift his capital here, he compelled Delhi's entire population to march across an epic 1,127 km (700 miles). Thousands died of starvation or disease along the way, and when the move failed, the sultan and his court marched back to Delhi. Daulatabad was later conquered by the Deccani Bahmani sultans, the Nizam Shahis, the Mughals, the Marathas and, finally, the Nizam of Hyderabad – each conquest proving more bloody than the last.

Four solid concentric walls protect the fort. The first of its three zones is Ambarkot, the outer fort. Within stands the 60-m- (197-ft-) high victory tower, Chand Minar, built in 1435 by Alauddin Bahmani to celebrate his conquest of the fort. In the nearby Jama Masjid, 106 pillars from Jain and Hindu temples separate the main hall into 25 aisles. A triple gateway studded with iron spikes provides access into Kataka, the inner fort. Gateways lead through fortified walls into the base of the citadel, known as Balakot, separated by a moat that was once infested by crocodiles.

A series of dark tunnels lead to the citadel's heart and end near the pillared Baradari, a late Mughal pavilion. The fort's ramparts offer sweeping views.

The small walled town of Khuldabad ("Heavenly Abode") is 10 km (6 miles) north of town. The Alamgir Dargah, dedicated to the Muslim saint Sayeed Zain-ud-din (d 1370), is its most famous monument. Also known as Rauza, this religious complex, established by Sufi saints in the 14th century, was considered so sacred that several Deccani sultans chose to be buried here. Emperor Aurangzeb, who died in the Deccan in 1707, is buried in a simple tomb in the courtyard. The beautiful tomb of Malik Ambar is a short distance to the north.

16

Melghat Tiger Reserve

Amravati district; 326 km (203 miles) NE of Aurangabad Amravati, 95 km (60 miles) SE of the entry point, Semadoh Maharashtra Tourism organizes buses & Jeeps from Amravati to the park Feb-mid-Jun: 7am-7pm; Oct-Jan: 7am-6pm daily www.maharashtra-tourism.gov.in

The Project Tiger (p174) reserve of Melghat, meaning "Meeting Place of the Ghats", spreads across the Gawilgarh Hills, which have a dense canopy of teak and bamboo forests, now threatened by rampant commercial exploitation for timber. Along with its elusive 70 tigers, the reserve is home to about 50 leopards, chausingha (four-horned antelope), dhole (Indian wild dog), jungle cats, hyenas and many birds. The sanctuary also supports the state's largest concentration of gaur, the endangered Indian bison.

The best time to visit is from December to May, when the park is pleasantly cool. Its five rivers, the Khandu, Khapra, Sipna, Garga and Dolar, dry out in summer, and the few remaining pools of rainwater are highly prized as watering holes.

Aurangabad's Bibi ka
Maqbara, and (inset) its
ornate stucco decoration

⑰

Nagpur

🏠 Nagpur district; 520 km (323 miles) NE of Aurangabad ✈ 10 km (6 miles) S of city centre, then bus or taxi 🚌🚂 ℹ Maharashtra Tourism; www.maharashtra tourism.gov.in

On the banks of the Nag river, Nagpur lies exactly in the centre of India. The capital of the Central Provinces until it became part of Maharashtra state after independence, it is a fast-developing industrial city and the country's orange-growing capital. Historically, it was the capital of the indigenous Gond people, until it was captured by the Maratha Bhonsles in 1743, and then by the British in 1861.

In October 1956, the city witnessed an event of great social importance, when Dr BR Ambedkar, writer of the Indian Constitution and a freedom fighter born into a lower-caste Hindu family, converted to Buddhism in a stand against the rigid Hindu caste system. Nearly 200,000 people followed him, and the movement gathered great momentum, resulting in about three million conversions.

Nagpur town is built around Sitabaldi Fort. In the eastern part of the city are the remains of the Bhonsle Palace, which was destroyed by fire in the 19th century. South of the old city lie the Chhatris, or memorials of the Bhonsle kings. A number of colonial buildings are situated in western Nagpur: among them are the High Court and the Anglican Cathedral of All Saints (1851).

Ramtek, 40 km (25 miles) northeast of Nagpur, is associated with the 14-year exile of Rama, Sita and Lakshman, as told in the epic *Ramayana*. It was the capital of the Vakataka dynasty between the 4th and the 6th centuries, and the fort on the Hill of Rama dates to this period. Its walls, however, were built in 1740 by the founder of Nagpur's Bhonsle dynasty, Raghoji I.

↑ Lonar Lake, created by the violent impact of a meteorite

⑱

Lonar

🏠 Buldana district; 130 km (81 miles) E of Aurangabad 🚂 Jalna, 83 km (52 miles) W of Lonar, then bus or taxi ℹ Maharashtra Tourism; www.maharashtra tourism.gov.in

The tiny village of Lonar is famous for its remarkable meteorite crater. Thought to be the only hypervelocity impact crater in basaltic rock in the world, the mammoth crater, which is 2 km (1 mile) in diameter and 700 m (2,297 ft) deep, is estimated to be about 50,000 years old. Scientists

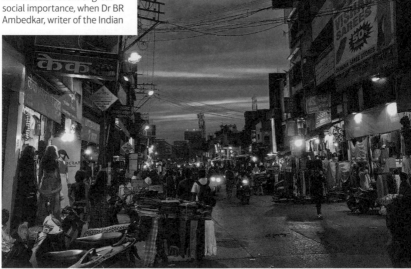

believe that the meteorite is still buried beneath the south-eastern edge of the crater. A lake fills the bottom, and the ruins of some Hindu temples stand on its shores. The crater is rich in birdlife, and monkeys and deer can also be seen. There are a few rest houses in the village that offer rooms and some eateries, too.

19
Tadoba-Andhari Tiger Reserve

⌂ Chandrapur district; 45 km (28 miles) N of Chandrapur ⏱ Hours vary, check website 🅦 tadoba nationalpark.in

In the far east of Maharashtra, 208 km (129 miles) south of Nagpur, the Tadoba-Andhari Tiger Reserve is the largest national park in the state. Known as "the Jewel of Vidharbha", it spans around 620 sq km (385 sq miles) of teak forests, lakes, valleys and grasslands. The park is home to an estimated 75 to 80 tigers (though there are plans to relocate some of these cats to other reserves), as well as sloth bears, barking deer, jackals and bison, and close to 200 species of birds. In addition to daytime safaris in the park itself, visitors can also go on fascinating night-time circuits through the buffer zone that surrounds the reserve.

←

Dusk on a shop-lined street in the city of Nagpur, in the geographical centre of India

20
Sevagram Ashram

⌂ Wardha district; 75 km (47 miles) SW of Nagpur 🚉🚌 To Wardha, then bus or auto 🅦 gandhi ashramsevagram.org

Mahatma Gandhi's historic ashram, east of Wardha, was established in 1936. Sevagram ("Village of Service") was based on Gandhi's philosophy of rural economic develop-ment. It became the head-quarters of India's National Movement, which led the fight for independence from Britain, and was where Gandhi lived and worked for many years. Spread over 40 ha (99 acres) of farmland, the ashram has numerous *kutirs*, or rural dwellings, and several research centres. Gandhi's personal effects, such as his spinning wheel and specta-cles, are on display. Khadi, the coarse home-spun cotton that Gandhi made famous as the symbol of India's freedom struggle, is on sale here. A photo exhibit opposite the main entrance depicts scenes from Gandhi's life, while a hospital catering to the needs of local villagers is located on the main road. Prayers, which visitors can attend, are held daily at 4:30am and 6pm under a pipal tree planted by Gandhi.

The ashram of Gandhi's famous disciple, Vinobha Bhave, is 10 km (6 miles) north of Sevagram at Paunar. Bhave started the Bhoodan move-ment that sought to persuade landowners to give portions of their holdings to the poor.

STAY

tigress@ghosri
On the edge of Tadoba-Andhari Reserve, this lovely boutique-hotel has stylish en-suites, smart service and a forest-fringed swimming pool.

⌂ Ghosri Village, Bhadravati
🅦 tigressghosri.com

₹₹₹

Svasara Jungle Lodge
As well as bright and breezy rooms, this lodge outside Tadoba-Andhari has a swimming pool, spa and even a mini "jungle cinema".

⌂ Near Kolara gate, Chimur
🅦 svasararesorts.com

₹₹₹

Vivanta
This sophisticated palace-style hotel, set in manicured gardens, offers well-equipped rooms, several fine places to eat and drink, a swimming pool and a spa.

⌂ Dr Rafiq Zakaria Marg, Rauza Bagh, Aurangabad
🅦 tajhotels.com

₹₹₹

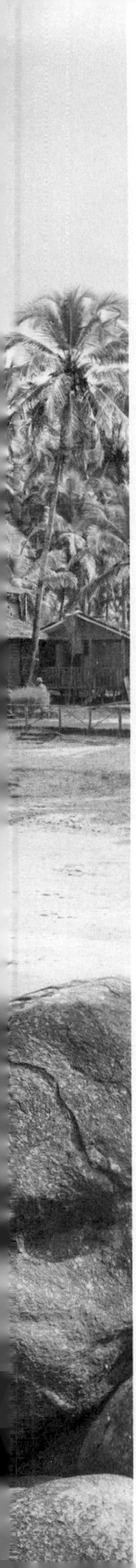

GOA

This tiny state along the Konkan Coast covers 3,702 sq km (1,429 sq miles) and consists of just two districts, North and South Goa. Although Goa was a part of some of India's most famous historical kingdoms, including the Mauryan Empire and the Bahmani Sultanate, it was the Portuguese, who invaded and annexed Goa in 1510, who had the biggest impact on the state's distinct culture.

After defeating the Bijapur Sultanate, the Portuguese established a small but powerful enclave that ruled here for 400-odd years, leaving its mark in food, language and architecture, particularly in the large number of churches in the former capital, Old Goa. During this time, the infamous Goa Inquisition suppressed – and sometimes executed – people who followed religions other than Catholicism, leading many to abandon the state for surrounding areas. But this was not only a time of internal unrest, as many other external powers attempted to capture Goa. This list includes the great Hindu dynasty, the Marathas, who the Portuguese only repelled with the help of the Marathas' bitter rivals, the Mughals. The Portuguese clung onto this enclave past even when the British left India, and Goa only became a part of the Indian Union after Indian soldiers invaded by sea, land and air in 1961, defeating Portuguese forces after a 36-hour battle.

GOA

Arabian Sea

GOA

Must Sees
1. Panaji
2. Old Goa
3. Braganza House

Experience More
4. Anjuna
5. Calangute
6. Vagator
7. Ashwem
8. Arambol
9. Terekhol Fort
10. Assagao
11. Tambdi Surla
12. Ponda
13. Margao
14. Rachol
15. Palolem
16. Majorda
17. Agonda
18. Tropical Spice Plantation
19. Reis Magos

PANAJI

🏛 North Goa district; 588 km (365 miles) S of Mumbai
✈ Dabolim, 30 km (19 miles) S of town centre, then
bus or taxi 🚌 Margao, 33 km (21 miles) SE of town
centre 🛈 GTDC Paryatan Bhavan; www.goa.gov.in

Goa's relaxed capital, Panaji, is reminiscent of a
provincial Mediterranean town – particularly in
Fontainhas, an old-world precinct characterized
by a jumble of painted, tile-roofed houses, where
many of the residents still speak Portuguese.

> The palace's strategic location made it a point of entry for ships and a stopover for viceroys and governors en route to Old Goa.

①
Old Secretariat

🏛 Avenida Dom Joao Crasto

The riverfront summer palace
of Yusuf Adil Shah, Goa's 16th-
century Muslim ruler, fell to
the Portuguese in 1510,
despite a formidable battery
of 55 cannons and a salt-water
moat that protected it.

Rebuilt in 1615, its strategic
location made it a point of
entry for ships and a stopover
for viceroys and governors
en route to Old Goa (p442).
In 1760, after Old Goa was
abandoned in favour of Panaji,
the palace became the official
residence of the viceroys –
until 1918, when the residence
moved to the Cabo Palace,

southwest of Panaji. Extensive
renovations have transformed
the original Islamic structure
into the colonial building it is
today, with a sloping tiled roof,
wide wooden verandahs and
cast-iron pillars – although
the emblem of the Indian
government, the Ashoka
Chakra, has now replaced the
Portuguese viceroys' coat of
arms above the entrance.

On the ground floor, the
State Museum houses a
modest collection of pre-
colonial artifacts, such as
statues, *sati* stones, antique
furniture and carvings from
ravaged Hindu temples, as
well as some Christian icons.

State Museum
📞 (0832) 243 4406 🕙 10am–
6pm Mon–Fri 🚫 Public hols

SUBODH KERKAR AND THE MUSEUM OF GOA

On arrival at Goa airport, visitors are greeted by stunning
black-and-white photographs of fishermen and huge
sculptures of chili peppers. To see more, head to
contemporary artist Subodh Kerkar's Museum of Goa in
Pilerne, 6 km (4 miles) north of Panaji *(www.museum
ofgoa.com)*. Through his art, Kerkar talks about Goa's
history - a Goan fishing boat is adorned with Chinese
soup spoons to illustrate the history of Chinese trade,
while the chili sculptures speak of the old spice route.

←

The Church of Our Lady of the Immaculate Conception, built in the early 17th century

② Church of Our Lady of the Immaculate Conception

🏠 Church Square 🕘 9am-12:30pm & 3:30-7:30am daily 🌐 icchurchpanjim.com

Overlooking Largo da Igreja or "Church Square", is the Church of Our Lady of the Immaculate Conception, the town's most important landmark. Portuguese sailors used to come to the original chapel, consecrated in 1541, to offer thanksgiving prayers after their voyage from Lisbon.

The present church, with its Baroque façade framed by twin towers, was built in 1619. Its most striking feature, the double flight of stairs leading up to the church, was added in 1871. The chapel in the south transept has a fine altar screen. The Baroque splendour of the church's altars is in contrast to its simple interior.

③ Menezes Braganza Institute

🏠 Malacca Rd 📞 (0832) 222 4143 🕘 Mon-Fri

The Institute Vasco da Gama was built to impart knowledge in the arts and sciences. It was later renamed after the journalist and philanthropist Luis de Menezes Braganza (1878–1938), whose family home is in Chandor (p448).

The superb mural in blue-and-white painted ceramic tiles (azulejos) was added to the entrance lobby in 1935, and depicts scenes from the epic Os Lusiadas, which recounts the history of the Portuguese presence in Goa.

④ Panaji Old Town

🏠 Between Ourem Creek and Altinho Hill

These old residential quarters were built in the 1800s and are characterized by a jumble of painted houses, streets lined with taverns serving Goan cuisine and bakeries.

EAT

Viva Panjim
Sample traditional Goan fare accompanied by fado music.

🏠 Fontainhas, Panaji 📞 (0832) 242 2405

₹₹₹

Martin's Corner
Try chicken cafreal and classic fish curries.

🏠 Betalbatim, nr Majorda 🌐 martinscornergoa.com

₹₹₹

Joseph Bar
Come here for the atmosphere, and stay for the drinks and sliders.

🏠 Gomes Pereira Rd, Altinho 📞 (0839) 0665 795

₹₹₹

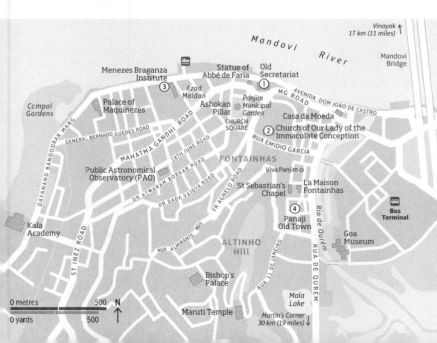

2

OLD GOA

🏠 North Goa district (Tiswadi taluka); 9 km (6 miles) E of Panaji 🚉 Karmali, 9 km (6 miles) S of Old Goa 🚌 From Panaji 🛈 GTDC, Old Goa Residency, behind Police Station, near M G Statue; www.goa.gov.in

A walk through Old Goa (also known as Velha Goa) – the Portuguese capital until the mid-1700s and now a UNESCO World Heritage Site – takes in two of Goa's most important religious monuments, the Basilica de Bom Jesus and the Sé Cathedral. Upon Holy Hill are some of Goa's oldest churches, in a range of European styles, from sober Renaissance to exuberant Baroque.

↑ Panoramic view of Old Goa famed for its churches, including *(inset)* Sé Cathedral

①
Church of St Cajetan

🏠 E of Viceroy's Arch
🕐 Daily

Built by Italian friars in 1651, this church is renowned for the exuberant woodcarvings on its high altar and pulpit. The distinctive dome and interior, laid out in the shape of a Greek cross, embody the majesty of Italian Baroque.

②
Sé Cathedral

🏠 Senate Square 📞 (0832) 228 4710 🕐 Daily

Ordered by the government in Portugal to build a church worthy of their empire, the viceroy Francis Coutinho envisaged a cathedral that would be the largest in Asia. This is the magnificent result. While it has many glories, the pièce de résistance is the gilded high altar with six panels depicting the life of St Catherine of Alexandria.

③
Church of St Francis of Assisi

🏠 W of Sé Cathedral
🕐 Daily

Built by the Franciscan friars in 1521, this is one of Old Goa's most important churches. A Baroque church, it has nautical items such as navigators' globes. Its gilded main altar depicts the crucified Jesus, four Evangelists, St Francis, and Our Lady with the Infant Jesus.

④ 🎨
Archaeological Museum

🏠 Convent of St Francis of Assisi 🕐 9am–5pm Sat–Thu 🌐 asigoacircle.gov.in

A bronze statue of the poet Luis Vaz de Camões holding his epic *Os Lusiadas* stands in

---

Did You Know?

The first printing press in India was set up at the Jesuit College of St Paul in Old Goa.

⑤

Church and Monastery of St Augustine

🅰 Holy Hill

Once India's largest church, this building is now in ruins. The 46-m- (151-ft-) high belfry is the most notable remain.

⑥

Church of Our Lady of the Rosary

🅰 Holy Hill · 🅲 Daily

This church was built on top of Holy Hill in 1526 by Alfonso de Albuquerque. He had watched Yusuf Adil Shah's defeat in 1510 from this very spot and vowed to build a church here.

⑦

The Church of Our Lady of the Mount

🅰 Off the Cumbarjua Road

Built in 1510 by Alfonso de Albuquerque after his victory over Yusuf Adil Shah, this church offers magnificent views over Old Goa's towers and turrets.

the museum, now housed in the converted convent of St Francis of Assisi, adjoining the church. The first-floor Portrait Gallery has 60 paintings of Goa's viceroys and governors.

THE GOA INQUISITION

At the request of Spanish priest Francis Xavier, a tribunal of Jesuits arrived in 1560 and took over Adil Shah's secondary palace, to the south of Sé Cathedral. Their mission was to curb the libertine ways of the Portuguese settlers and convert "infidels". During the Inquisition in 1567, Hindu ceremonies were banned, temples were destroyed and Hindus forcibly converted. Those who refused were locked in the dungeons of the "Palace of the Inquisition" (as Adil Shah's palace was known) to await trial. The condemned were burnt alive. Over the next 200 years, 16,000 trials were held and thousands were killed. It was not until 1812 that the Inquisition was finally dissolved.

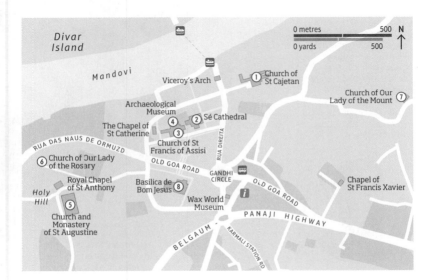

BASILICA DE BOM JESUS

⑧ ⌖

🏛 Rua das Naus de Ormuz, Old Goa 🕐 9am-6:30pm Mon-Sat, 10am-6:30pm Sun; mass held twice daily 🌐 bomjesus.org

Revered by Roman Catholics all over the world, the Basilica de Bom Jesus houses the remains of Goa's patron saint, Francis Xavier. In 1946, Pope Pius XII granted it the status of Minor Basilica, the first church in south Asia to receive this honour.

Built by the Jesuits in 1594, this grand Baroque structure blends Corinthian, Doric, Ionic and composite styles in its magnificent three-tiered façade. The Duke of Tuscany, Cosimo III, donated the elaborate tomb of St Francis in exchange for the pillow that lay under the saint's head. The tomb took the Florentine sculptor Giovanni Foggini ten years to build; it was finally assembled in 1698. It has four bronze plaques depicting scenes from the saint's life, and the silver reliquary containing the sacred relics is surmounted by a cross with two angels. The adjoining Professed House (1589) was used as the priests' quarters until it was damaged by a fire in 1633.

ST FRANCIS XAVIER (1506-1552)

Francis Xavier was sent to Goa by Portuguese king Dom Joao III. He arrived in May 1542 and converted nearly 30,000 people over the next few years. He died while on a voyage off the coast of China in 1552 and was temporarily buried on an island. A year later, when his remains were due to be enshrined in the basilica in Goa, his body was found to still be in pristine condition. This was declared a miracle, and in 1622 he was canonized.

The gilded main altar has statues of St Ignatius of Loyola and Infant Jesus.

Chapel of the Blessed Sacrament

Altar of Our Lady of Hope

↑ An illustration of the 16th-century Basilica de Bom Jesus

1

2

3

① The exterior of the Basilica de Bom Jesus is the most impressive in Goa and the only one with a distinctive red laterite façade.

② The gilded gold main altar features statues of saints and Jesus, as well as cherubs crafted by local artisans in the typically Hindu style.

③ This ornate golden statue of Mary and Jesus stands in the Basilica.

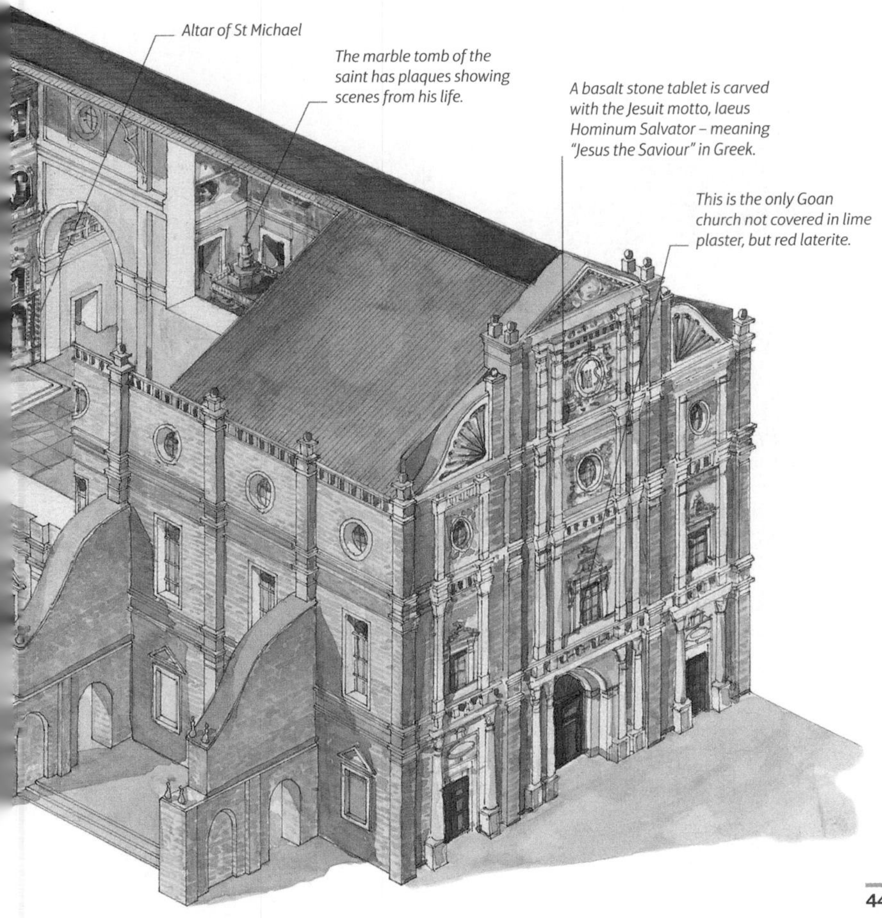

Altar of St Michael

The marble tomb of the saint has plaques showing scenes from his life.

A basalt stone tablet is carved with the Jesuit motto, Iaeus Hominum Salvator – meaning "Jesus the Saviour" in Greek.

This is the only Goan church not covered in lime plaster, but red laterite.

3

BRAGANZA HOUSE

⌂ Church Square, Chandor; 20 km (12 miles) E of Margao ▣▦ ⊙ Admission to both wings only by prior appointment; donations appreciated ⓦ www.goa. gov.in/places/braganza-house

Goa's countryside is dotted with grand colonial mansions, built by the wealthy Goan gentry who prospered in the 18th and 19th centuries. The homes of these local aristocrats were built in the traditional style of the region – and the most impressive of them all is Braganza House.

The awesome scale of Braganza House and the magnificence of its interior make it Goa's grandest colonial mansion. This 17th-century building is still occupied by two branches of the Braganza family. The descendants of Antonio Elzario Sant'Anna Pereira occupy the east wing, while Francisco Xavier de Menezes Braganza's descendants live in the west wing. Both men received royal titles and a coat of arms from the king of Portugal in the late 19th century. While the exterior of Braganza House was influenced by the traditional buildings of the region, the furniture and interior decor were largely European, as shown in the private apartments here. The top floors have the splendid ballroom, library and chapel, and fine collections of 18th-century furniture, portraits and Chinese porcelain.

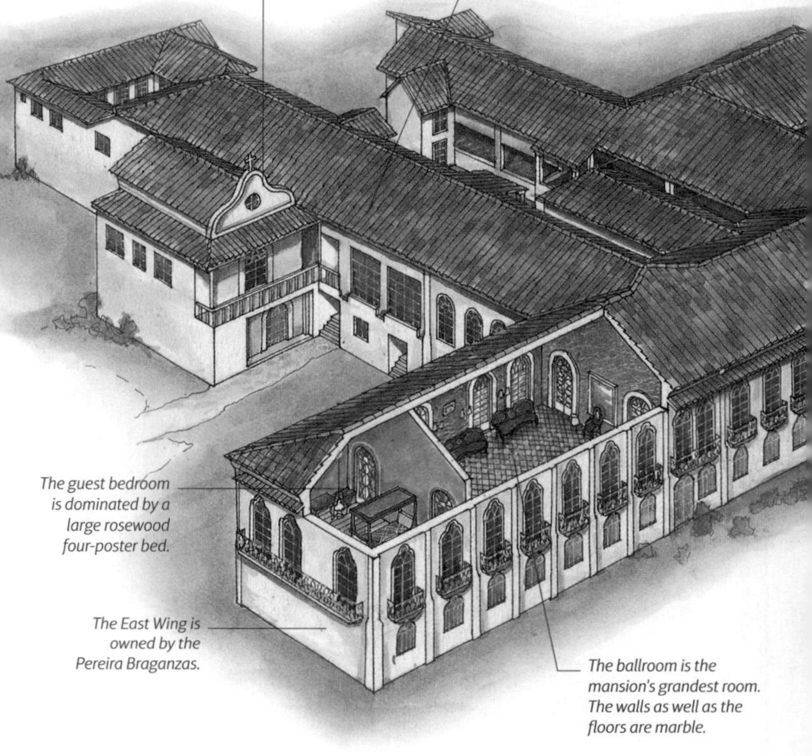

The Baroque-style chapel has a diamond-encrusted fingernail of St Francis Xavier on its altar.

A long table fills the first floor dining hall of this sprawling mansion.

The guest bedroom is dominated by a large rosewood four-poster bed.

The East Wing is owned by the Pereira Braganzas.

The ballroom is the mansion's grandest room. The walls as well as the floors are marble.

Colonial Mansion Highlights

↑ The entrance to Braganza House, designed in the traditional Goan style

The West Wing is occupied by the Menezes Braganzas.

Exquisite Chinese porcelain is displayed in one of the salons.

The library has Goa's finest private collection, with over 5,000 books.

A long and elegantly furnished hallway lies just behind the façade of the house.

Entrance

The monumental double staircase forms the core of the house, connecting the lower entrance level to the furnished top floors.

↑ An illustration showing the ornate Braganza House

Oyster-Shell Window Shutters

A unique feature of 16th- and 17th-century Goan architecture, oyster shells were used in place of glass panes and effectively kept out the heat and glare. While these feature in most Goan mansions, a particularly fine example is at Sat Burnzam Gor ("Seven Gables") in Margao, where oyster-shell shutters line the façade.

Pyramidal Balcao

▽ A typical pyramidal balcao, or porch, graces the entrance of the Figueredo House in Loutolim. Chairs were often placed under the balcao, as it was customary to socialize at the front door.

Antique Rosewood Carvings

While the exteriors of these mansions look more traditionally Goan, the interiors were more influenced by Europe - particularly the furniture. Carved rosewood furniture, crafted by local artisans and representing the local style of Indo-Portuguese Baroque, was a key feature.

European-Style Salons

▷ Most mansions in Goa featured European-style salons, like the ballroom at Braganza House. Another excellent example is the regal ballroom in Dr Alvaro Loyola Furtado Mansion in Chinchinim, built in 1833. It has glorious crystal chandeliers hanging from the ceiling and elegant European-style furniture.

EXPERIENCE MORE

❹
Anjuna

⌂ North Goa district (Bardez taluka); 18 km (11 miles) NW of Panaji
🚌 *i* www.goa-tourism. com/anjuna

Anjuna is a pretty, sprawling town with a lively beach-party scene and a popular flea market. Held on Wednesdays, the market is crowded with hawkers selling a range of items: Balinese batik, silver jewellery, papier-mâché boxes, Tibetan prayer wheels, Rajasthani mirrorwork and Kerala woodcarvings. Fluorescent rave gear and trendy beachwear round off the selection. Head to the great Artjuna café for great food and shopping.

❺
Calangute

⌂ North Goa district (Bardez taluka); 16 km (10 miles) NW of Panaji
🚌 *i* www.goa-tourism. com/calangute

The centre of the hippie scene in the 1960s and 1970s, Calangute is now Goa's most popular beach, crowded with visitors from all over India and the world, who are often drawn by the excellent paragliding and sunbathing. Its beach is wide and sandy, and extends in both directions along the coast. The stretch up to the neighbouring town of Baga, 3 km (2 miles) north of Calangute, and down to the lively hub of Candolim, 2 km (1 mile) south, is lined with beach-shack restaurants. Those looking for traditional Goan flavours should head to Souzo Lobo in Calangute, where they serve delicious food and a range of cocktails, or Britto's in nearby Baga. Voted among India's best restaurants, Bomras is tucked away on the main road between Candolim and Fort Aguada, 2 km (1 mile) further south, and is known for its Burmese fusion food.

Baga is also popular with visitors, and has a good market near the resort called the Saturday Night Bazaar, which sells crafts and other goods from all over India.

Around 2 km (1 mile) inland from Calangute, Saligao has beautiful churches, including the Church of Mae de Deus, designed in the Neo-Gothic style, plus antiques shops and the Paperboat Collective shop and café.

SHOP

Rangeela
In a beautiful building with a courtyard, this plant-filled shop sells a range of upscale clothes, textiles and homewares.

⌂ 13 Saunta Vaddo, Anjuna-Mapusa Road
🖥 rangeelagoa.com

Alchemy
Ethically sourced clothes for glamorous nomads can be found at this store inside the Sublime restaurant.

⌂ 481 Bouta Waddo Anjuna-Mapusa Road
🖥 alchemygoa.com

People Tree
This collective offers eco-conscious clothes, bags made from recycled tyres and fair trade toys.

⌂ 6 Saunta Vaddo, Anjuna-Mapusa Rd
📞 (0832) 226 8228

↑ Anjuna's famous flea market, under the swaying palm trees on the beach

[1] Thalassa restaurant on Vagator beach is always a popular place to eat.

[2] The peaceful river at Mandrem is lined with huts.

[3] The beautiful beach at Palolem often attracts visitors for its nightlife.

[4] A fishing boat at Colva.

GOA'S BEACHES

Goa is famous for its spectacular beaches, which stretch 106 km (66 miles) from Querim in the north to Galjibag in the south. Each of these beaches has its own character: the central beaches are the busiest, but there are quieter beaches to the north and south.

QUIET BEACHES

More known for its party beaches than peaceful stretches of sand, Goa still has a number of places where there are only a handful of beach shacks and even fewer people. Querim, close to Fort Terekhol, is a lovely stretch of beach with only a few shacks. Below a deep cliff, little Vagator beach is family friendly and has a few beach shacks. Mobor is a stretch of paradise – pass through the crowds of neighbouring Cavelossim to find this beautiful patch of sand. Galjibag is a turtle-nesting reserve, with a peaceful vibe and a number of little shacks.

> Goa still has a number of places where there are only a handful of beach shacks and even fewer people.

PARTY BEACHES

Palolem is a crescent-shaped beach with a party vibe popular with expats. One of the most crowded beaches in Goa, Colva has a long stretch of sand backed by shady palms. Baga, an extension of Calangute, Goa's most developed beach, has numerous bars, resorts and some lively night venues. For those seeking beach clubs blasting out Goan trance music, head to Anjuna beach.

ACTIVE BEACHES

Goa is one of the yoga capitals of India and attracts a range of devotees, from those seeking high-end yoga schools to others who want to vinyasa flow on the beach to the sound of a drum circle. Arambol is an idyllic, peaceful beach; as is Mandrem, where you can find a number of beach-front yoga schools. It has a long stretch of beach also known for kite-surfing, and stand-up paddle-boarding (SUP) classes are offered on its river.

STAY

Fort Tiracol Heritage Hotel

There are seven elegant rooms in this renovated fort. The dinner menu is devised by Chris Saleem of Sublime.

⌂ Terekhol Village, north of Ashwem
🌐 forttiracol.in

₹₹₹

Beach Street

Stay in beach cabanas near the palace of the Deshbrabu family, and swim in the lovely pool.

⌂ Junas Wadda, Mandrem
🌐 beachstreet.in

₹₹₹

Siolim House

This grand mansion near Morjim offers suites as well as yoga and Ayurvedic treatments.

⌂ Siolim
🌐 siolimhouse.com

₹₹₹

⑥ Vagator

⌂ 17 km (11 miles) N of Panaji 🚌 Chapora village
🛈 www.goa-tourism.com/vagator

A beautiful bay sheltered by rocky outcrops at both ends, Vagator consists of a number of small beaches fringed by shady coconut palms.

The southernmost cove of Ozran lies below a steep cliff, where a freshwater stream empties into a clear pool, ideal for swimming. Little Vagator, to the north, is popular with families. Big Vagator beach is dominated by the red laterite Chapora Fort on top of a hill at its northern tip. Now in ruins, this fort was built by the Portuguese in 1717 on the remains of an older bastion erected by the Adil Shahi sultans. Its name, Chapora, is derived from "Shahpura", or "Town of the Shah", as the village was once known. In 1739, Sambhaji, the son of the Maratha chief Shivaji, occupied the fort for a short time until it was returned to the Portuguese in exchange for Bassein, near Mumbai. Its ramparts, now desolate, offer sweeping views of the coast. Chapora village, below the fort, has many pleasant cafés.

⑦ Ashwem

⌂ 30 km (19 miles) N of Panaji 🚌 🛈 www.goa-tourism.com/ashwem

Despite development, Ashwem Beach, the sandy stretch running from the mouth of the Mandrem river to the rocky outcrop at the start of Morjim Beach, still has a lot of charm. **Vaayu Waterman's Village** hotel, at the mouth of the river, offers stand-up paddleboarding and surfing lessons. The people who run it aim to preserve the beauty of Goa with regular beach clean-ups. There is also a shack-free bit of beach outside the beautiful eco-conscious Elsewhere resort. To the south is a lovely stretch of sand and laterite rocks with beach cabanas at Palm Grove and Anahata, where beach-goers can enjoy sundowners at the many beach shacks.

Morjim, 3 km (2 miles) south, has another cluster of lovely resorts popular with visitors. There is a Olive Ridley turtle-nesting area here, so motor-boats are banned.

Vaayu Waterman's Village
⌂ Ashwem Beach Rd, Ashwem Beach 🌐 vaayuvision.com

Tourists relaxing with a drink at a casual, tree-shaded restaurant in Arambol

8

Arambol

🏠 50 km (31 miles) N of Panaji 🚌 🚆 Every half hour from Siolim 🛈 www. goa-tourism.com/arambol

With its festival vibe, Arambol is a magnet for musicians, yoga practitioners and designers. It is also popular with daytrippers, who come to check out the sunset drum circle and the evening bazaar that springs up on the sand. The main street is filled with stalls selling colourful

The palm-fringed beach at Vagator as seen from Chapora Fort

fabrics, musical instruments and crystals. A vibrant beach carnival takes place every March, and there is also an annual juggling convention.

Live music and performances are an essential part of the nightlife at Arambol. ASH is the place for alternative and global fusion music, while Jungle Dance Café has a huge stage and curates excellent dance performances, as well as hosting workshops.

Further north is Sweet Lake and another pretty beach, which is only accessible on foot. This is a fantastic spot from which to watch the many paragliders take off from the hill between Querim and Arambol.

9

Terekhol Fort

🏠 42 km (26 miles) N of Panaji 🚌 🚆 Every half hour from Querim 🛈 www. goa-tourism.com/tiracol

Across the Terekhol river from Querim is the little hamlet of Terekhol, with Terekhol (Tiracol) Fort on a plateau above it. The early-18th-century fort was captured by the Portuguese

in 1776 from the Bhonsles, a Maratha clan. It was the scene of an uprising in 1954, when a group of *satyagrahis* (freedom fighters) hoisted the Indian flag on its ramparts in an act of civil disobedience against Portuguese colonial rule. The fort's high battlements face the sea, looking across the waters to Fort Aguada, Arambol and Chapora. The tiny chapel within the fort, with a statue of Christ in the courtyard, is usually closed, but the atmospheric Fort Tiracol Heritage Hotel offers some excellent views.

10

Assagao

🏠 North Goa district (Pernem taluka); 17 km (10 miles) N of Panaji

Assagao is a beautiful inland neighbourhood full of Indo-Portuguese houses, a number of which have been restored to their former glory and transformed into restaurants, hotels and shops. Many windows are shaded by antique shutters filled with traditional oyster shells, while pink bougainvillea, delicate frangipani flowers and mango trees fill the gardens of these houses or spill over their porches. Most people visit for the food, and there is a relaxed atmosphere in little courtyard restaurants like Villa Blanche and at the award-winning Sublime restaurant. Project Café Goa has beautiful rooms to rent, all curated by different interior designers from across India.

Did You Know?

The Portuguese government only ceded Goa in 1961 – 14 years after the British left.

↑ Bucolic landscape at the Dudhsagar Waterfalls, near the temple of Tambdi Surla

⑪ Tambdi Surla

⌂ 73 km (45 miles) E of Panaji 🚌 To Panaji or Ponda, then taxi *ℹ* www.goa.gov.in/what_to_see/temples

Hidden away in the forests of Tambdi Surla, the oldest existing Hindu temple in Goa dates from the Kadamba period (between the 11th and 13th centuries). Built in black basalt and dedicated to Shri Mahadeva (Shiva), the temple is made of stone slabs fitted neatly into each other, without using mortar. The entrance hall has ten pillars, and the *shikhara* (spire) above the sanctum has a miniature relief and fine carvings of Brahma, Vishnu, Shiva and his consort Parvati.

The **Bhagwan Mahaveer Sanctuary** is home to deer, leopard and the Indian bison. The 600-m- (1,969-ft-) high Dudhsagar Waterfalls on the Goa-Karnataka border are its main attraction. The small **Bondla Wildlife Sanctuary,** also nearby, is known for its variety of birds.

Bhagwan Mahaveer Sanctuary

🌀 ⌂ 20 km (12 miles) SE
🕘 8am–5:30pm daily

Bondla Wildlife Sanctuary

🌀 ⌂ 30 km (19 miles) E
🕘 9am–5pm Tue–Sun

⑫ Ponda

⌂ 28 km (17 miles) SE of Panaji 🚌 *ℹ* www.goa.gov.in/what_to_see/temples

The town of Ponda is a busy commercial centre, and its main sight is the small Safa Shahouri Mosque, 2 km (1 mile) to the west. Built by Ibrahim Adil Shah (a successor of Yusuf Adil Shah) in 1560, it is a white rectangular structure, with window arches, topped by a slanting tiled roof. A ritual tank to the south has the same designs as those on the *mihrabs* (arched niches).

Ponda also lends its name to the *taluka* (sub-district) of the same name, which is renowned for its numerous Hindu temples, tucked away in thick forests. As the Portuguese expanded their territory in central Goa, they destroyed over 550 temples. Hindu priests fled with their religious artifacts to regions that lay outside Portuguese control, especially the area around Ponda town, where they built new temples in the 17th and 18th centuries.

→

The silver screen at Ponda's Shri Ramnath Temple, and *(inset)* the temple's exterior

Goan temples are a fascinating blend of European Baroque, Muslim and Hindu architectural styles. Their basic plan remains Hindu, but often Muslim domes replace the usual *shikharas* (spires) over the main sanctum, and prayer halls are decorated with ornate European chandeliers.

The Shantadurga Temple, 3 km (2 miles) southwest of Ponda at Kavlem, is Goa's most popular shrine. The temple has an unusual pagoda-style roof, dominated by a five-storeyed octagonal lamp tower, unique to Goa. Grand chandeliers hang from the gilded roof in the huge central hall, and embossed silver screens shield the main sanctuary, which holds the

silver deity of Shantadurga (a form of Shiva's consort Parvati). Also of interest are the huge *rathas* (chariots) that are used during the Jatra festival in January. The Shri Ramnath Temple, a short walk away, is noted for the grand silver screen embossed with animal and floral motifs in front of its sanctum.

The Shri Nagueshi Temple, 4 km (2 miles) west of Ponda at Bandora, dates to 1780. Built for the worship of Nagesh (Shiva as Lord of the Serpents), it is one of the oldest temples in this region. Its entrance hall has carved wooden friezes depicting scenes from the famous epics *Ramayana* and *Mahabharata*.

The 18th-century Shri Lakshmi Narasimha Temple is situated in Velinga village, 5 km (3 miles) northwest of Ponda. Surrounded by forest, it is one of Goa's most attractive temples. A tower standing close by houses the temple's musicians during the annual Jatra festival, held here in May.

About 10 km (6 miles) to the northwest of Ponda, at Priol, lies one of Goa's wealthiest temples: the ornate 18th-century Shri Mangesh Temple, which is dedicated to Shiva. The courtyard has a sacred *tulsi* (basil) plant growing in a bright green urn, a typical Goan feature. There is a large sacred tank and a white lamp tower, whose seven storeys give it the appearance of a wedding cake. Dance-dramas are performed here during the Jatra festivities in April and May. A vividly painted elephant on wheels stands at the entrance to the white and yellow temple. Inside, 19th-century Belgian chandeliers hang from the ceiling, while the main sanctum has a linga transferred from Mormugao.

About 4 km (2 miles) northeast of Ponda town, near the village of Khandepar, is a cluster of Hindu rock-cut caves from the 10th–13th centuries, with carved lotus decorations on the ceiling and simple door frames.

13

Margao

⌂ South Goa district
(Salcete taluka); 33 km
(21 miles) SE of Panaji
🚌🚐 🛈 www.goa.gov.in/
places/margao

Goa's second most important
city after Panaji, Margao
(Madgaon) is the admin-
istrative and commercial
capital of the South Goa
district. This bustling town,
known for its vibrant four-day
Carnival, also serves as the
area's main trading centre for
local fish and farm produce.

The town square, Praça
Jorge Barreto, has the large,
colonial Municipal Building,
which houses the library.
Just behind the Municipal

> **Did You Know?**
> ———
> Held before the
> beginning of Catholic
> Lent, the riotous
> Carnival in Margao is
> the biggest in India.

| From the intersection east of the church, a road winds up to Monte Hill, from where the views across Margao's rooftops of the entire southern coast are spectacular.

Building, to the south, are
Margao's bazaars, selling the
day's catch of fish and fresh
fruit and vegetables. The
Covered Market close by sells
just about everything, from
piles of soap flakes and flower
garlands to pulses, dried fish
and spicy pork sausages. A
row of shops to the north sells
locally made wines, and the
lane just outside the market
has several cloth merchants.

Lined with well-preserved
colonial mansions, Abbé de
Faria Street winds north from
the town square and leads to
Margao's old Latin Quarter. Its
central square, Largo de Igreja,
is also surrounded by colourful
18th- and 19th-century town
houses, with tiled roofs,
wrought-iron balconies and
balustrades. In the centre of
the square is a monumental
16th-century cross, overlooked
by the towering Baroque
Church of the Holy Spirit.
Built in 1565 on the site of
a ravaged Hindu
temple, the

church and the adjoining
Jesuit College of All Saints
were ransacked numerous
times by Muslim raiders.
While the seminary was
moved to Rachol, the
church was rebuilt in 1675.
Its whitewashed façade is
flanked by two towers topped
by domes and embellished
with lanterns, though its
side walls have been left
unusually bare of lime-plaster.
The grand interior has a
stucco ceiling, a gilded pulpit
decorated with carvings of
the apostles, a Rococo altar
and elegant Baroque altar-
pieces in the transepts. Just
behind this church, Agostinho
Lorenço Street leads east to
the imposing mansion called
Sat Burnzam Gor, or "Seven
Gables", named after the
seven gables or pyramidal
crests on its roof. Built in
1790 by Ignacio da Silva,
the viceroy's
secretary, the

→ Street procession
of colourful floats
at the Carnival
in Margao

house has huge salons filled with richly carved rosewood furniture and priceless porcelain. From the intersection east of the church, a road winds up to Monte Hill, from where the views across Margao's rooftops of the entire southern coast are spectacular.

The pretty villages around Margao have a number of colonial country mansions, dating to the prosperous period from the 18th to the 19th centuries, when local landlords began to profit from Portugal's control over the maritime trade routes from Africa to Malacca (in Malaysia). Many of these homes were also owned by Goans, who held high posts in the Portuguese government.

Loutolim, 10 km (6 miles) to the northeast, was once an important Portuguese administrative centre, and has a cluster of stately homes, including the stunning **Figueiredo Mansion**, with its charming collection of antiques. Benaulim, 6 km (4 miles) southwest of Margao, also has fine mansions, with typical Goan *balcaos* (porches) and terracotta-tiled sloping roofs. The ethnographic collection at the **Goa Chitra Museum** sheds light on the area's architectural and agricultural past. Further south is the village of

Quepem, with the **Palácio do Deão** – or Priest's House – and its beautiful gardens. As well as a restaurant, the palace offers a cultural space showcasing Goan crafts, pottery, dance and music.

Sat Burnzam Gor
🚫 🅾 By prior appointment only; contact Mrs de Silva

Figueiredo Mansion
🏠 Loutolim ⏰ 10am-1pm & 2-5:30pm daily 🌐 www. figueiredohouse.com

Goa Chitra Museum
🎟 🏠 Benaulim ⏰ 9am-6pm daily 🌐 goachitra.com

Palácio do Deão
🏠 Quepem
⏰ 10am-5pm daily
🌐 palaciododeao.com

🔟4
Rachol

🏠 52 km (32 miles) SE of Panaji 🚌 ℹ️ www.goa-tourism.com/rachol

The small hamlet of Rachol occupies the site of an old fortress built by the Bijapur sultans (p474) and ceded to the Portuguese in 1520. A laterite archway and a dry moat are the only remnants of the bastion – once fortified with 100 cannons – that used to guard this spot, which was the southern border of the Portuguese territories. The pretty Church of Nossa Senhora das Neves (Our Lady of the Snows), in the village, was built in 1576.

Today, Rachol Seminary, built in 1606, is probably the most important of Goa's seminaries. First established in Margao in 1574, and known as the College of All Saints, the seminary was relocated here after the Margao institution was destroyed in a Muslim raid in 1579. Spectacularly located on the summit of a hill, the building has a grand façade, flanked by imposing,

↑ Inside the Church of St Ignatius Loyola, Rachol

fort-like watchtowers. The seminary's vast entrance hall is covered with impressive murals and opens onto a central courtyard, surrounded by cloistered rooms made of solid teak, each one with an adjoining wood-panelled study. The grand staircase is adorned with Hindu sculptures, excavated from the ancient Hindu temple on the site of which the seminary was constructed.

Attached to the seminary is the Church of St Ignatius Loyola. It has an ornately carved-and-gilded altar with a painting of St Constantine, the first Roman emperor to convert to Christianity. According to legend, a few bone fragments and a vial of his blood were brought to Rachol in 1782, and are supposedly enshrined near the entrance.

EAT

Palácio do Deão
Indo-Portuguese lunch dishes served on the verandah - the stuffed crabs are a must.

🏠 Opposite Holy Cross, Quepem
🌐 palaciododeao.com

₹₹₹

 The crescent-shaped beach at Palolem, with fishermen starting work

15
Palolem

🏠 37 km (23 miles) S of Margao 🚌 *i* www.goa-tourism.com/palolem

Southern Goa is for the most part isolated and unspoilt by mass tourism. Thanks to its remote location away from the crowded beaches of central and northern Goa, Palolem is the ideal spot for a quiet beach holiday. Famous for its spectacular sunsets, this bay is enclosed by a rocky outcrop at one end, and Canacona Island, which is known for its good campsite, at the other. Among its attractions – apart from watching the sunset – are the boat rides offered by local fishermen, who take visitors out to sea to look for dolphins, as well as other animals.

16
Majorda

🏠 10 km (6 miles) NW of Margao 🚌 *i* www.goa-tourism.com/majorda

The beach at Majorda, which stretches up to the neighbouring town of Utorda, is one of the most peaceful in South Goa, and offers a respite from nearby Colva, one of this region's most developed beach resorts. The beach is pristine, too, as cleaners sweep the sand daily; it is great for walks and leisurely sundowners. The small town itself is lovely, with some elegant mansions.

The area has a few great luxury hotels, namely Alila Diwa or, for those seeking something more intimate,

the boutique 100-year-old Vivenda dos Palhacos. Tourism from Colva has also spilled over to Varca Beach, 5 km (3 miles) south of Colva, which has many plush hotels, as well as a church with an imposing façade.

17
Agonda

🏠 7 km (4 miles) N of Palolem 🚌🚖 *i* www.goa-tourism.com/agonda

The village of Agonda is even quieter than Palolem, and is known for its beaches and nesting turtles. Galgibaga, 8 km (5 miles) south of Palolem, has a beautiful stretch of sand shaded by eucalyptus trees. The remote Cotigao Wildlife

> **Majorda Beach is great for walks and leisurely sundowners. The small town itself is lovely, with some elegant mansions.**

Sanctuary, 18 km (11 miles) west of Palolem, is worth visiting for its tranquil beauty.

⑱ Ⓨ
Tropical Spice Plantation

📍 Keri, North Goa district (Bardez taluka); 6 km (4 miles) N of Ponda 🚌 ⏰ 10am–4pm daily 🌐 tropicalspiceplantation.com

One of several plantations close to Ponda, Tropical Spice Plantation offers guided tours around the grounds, with an expert who illustrates the health benefits of several indigenous spices, plants and herbs, from cardamom and coriander. Herbs and spices have long been key elements of both India's 5,000-year-old traditional medical system and the country's cuisine. There is also a butterfly garden and a great restaurant serving up traditional meals.

---

⑲
Reis Magos

📍 North Goa district (Bardez taluka); 8 km (5 miles) NW of Panaji 🚌

Reis Magos Fort was built in 1551 by Don Alfonso de Noronha, the fifth viceroy, as a second line of defence after the forts at Aguada and Cabo (the tip of Dona Paula). It once housed a prison, which was moved to Mormugao in 1996. Adjacent to the fort is the Reis Magos Church. Built in 1555, this is one of Goa's earliest churches, and has the royal Portuguese coat of arms on its façade. Fort Aguada, 4 km (2 miles) west of Reis Magos, was built in 1612 as a defence against the Marathas and the Dutch. Its church, dedicated to St Lawrence, the patron saint of sailors, was built in 1630, while the huge lighthouse dates to 1864. The local beach, Sinquerim, is known for its luxury resorts.

The 16th-century Reis Magos Church, nestled amid a lush palm grove ↓

STAY

Vivenda dos Palhaços
In a restored building from the late 1920s, this hotel has elegant rooms, a pool and a communal dinner table.
📍 Majorda
🌐 vivendagoa.com
₹₹₹

Mateus
Stay in stylish rooms in a renovated 19th-century Portuguese mansion in the heart of the old town.
📍 432 Rua 31 de Janeiro, Panjim
🌐 mateusgoa.com
₹₹₹

Cassoi by Ciarans
Timber huts with thatched roofs housing large mosquito-covered beds are hidden amid the foliage on the sand – it is an enchanting and relaxing retreat.
📍 Galjibag
🌐 cassoibyciarans.com
₹₹₹

A woman selling lemons in a Bengaluru market

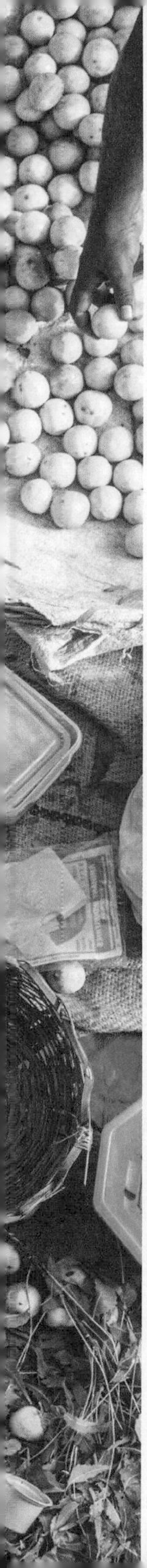

KARNATAKA

Extending from the Arabian Sea and the fertile forested ridges of the Western Ghats, Karnataka's history is written on its landscape through its epic collection of historical monuments. The most famous is, perhaps, the ruins of Hampi, the site of the great citadel of the Vijayanagar empire, which dominated from the 14th to 17th centuries. Similarly striking are the Hindu temples at Badami, Aihole and Pattadakal, which are some of the earliest found in south India, and speak to the art and architecture that flourished in the reign of the early Chalukya dynasty. One of the most memorable sites in the state is Tipu Sultan's 18th-century European-style island fort at Srirangapattana, the location of his final stand against the invading British forces. The kingdom of Mysore, which he ruled, was a significant thorn in the side of the British, but in the Fourth Anglo-Mysore War, Tipu Sultan and his forces were overwhelmed; Tipu died defending a gateway of his city. After the fall of the Vijayanagar empire, northern Karnataka became a series of sultanates at Bijapur, Gulbarga and Bidar, with their walls enclosing mosques, audience halls and royal tombs, and princely states. A number of these agitated against the British Raj in the 19th century, and the state was also the home of some of India's leading freedom fighters. The maharaja of Mysore ceded his kingdom to the Indian Union after independence in 1947; other small areas joined it to form what is now the state of Karnataka in 1973.

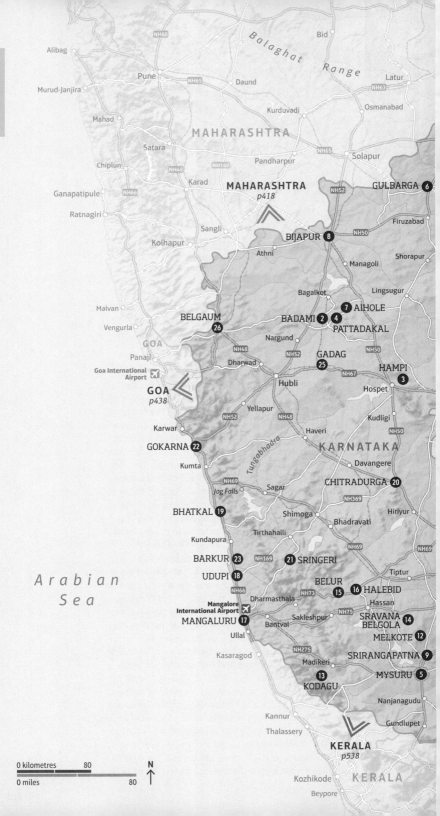

KARNATAKA

Must Sees
1. Bengaluru
2. Badami
3. Hampi
4. Pattadakal

Experience More
5. Mysuru
6. Gulbarga
7. Aihole
8. Bijapur
9. Srirangapatna
10. Talakad
11. Somanathapura
12. Melkote
13. Kodagu
14. Sravana Belgola
15. Belur
16. Halebid
17. Mangaluru
18. Udupi
19. Bhatkal
20. Chitradurga
21. Sringeri
22. Gokarna
23. Barkur
24. Bidar
25. Gadag
26. Belgaum

❶
BENGALURU

🚗1,033 km (642 miles) S of Mumbai ✈40 km (25 miles) NE of city centre, then bus or taxi 🚌🚕 ℹ️KSTDC, Yeshwantput Circle Bus Stand; www.karnataka tourism.org/tour-item/bangalore

Often described as Asia's Silicon Valley, Bengaluru is India's fifth-largest and fastest-growing city. Established in the 16th century, it now has a population of young professionals, giving it a vibrant, cosmopolitan air.

① Vidhana Soudha

📍Dr Ambedkar Rd ⏰2:45–5:30pm Mon–Fri with prior permission only

This imposing building houses the Secretariat and the State Legislature of Karnataka. Constructed in 1956 after the transfer of power from the ruling Wodeyar dynasty to the central government, it was designed by the then-chief minister Kengal Hanumantaiah, who intended it to "reflect the power and dignity of the people". It is capped by a 20-m (66-ft) dome surmounted by the four-headed Ashokan lion, symbol of the Indian state. With Rajasthani jharokhas, Indo-Saracenic pillars and other decorative elements, the Vidhana Soudha is an excellent example of post-independence architecture. The woodwork inside is noteworthy, especially the sandalwood door to the Cabinet Room, and the Speaker's Chair. The best time to visit is 6–8:30pm, when the building is illuminated by lights.

② Attara Kacheri

📍Opposite Vidhana Sabha ⏰10am–5pm Mon–Fri

This graceful, two-storeyed building was completed in 1864 and housed the Public Offices from 1868 until 1956. These were later moved to the Vidhana Soudha, and this building became the High Court. On the ceiling of its Central Hall is a portrait of Sir Mark Cubbon, commissioner of Mysuru from 1834 to 1861.

③ Cubbon Park

📍Cantonment ⏰6am–6pm Tue–Sun 🚫Mon, 2nd Tue of the month

Laid out in 1864 by Richard Sankey, the chief engineer of Mysuru, Cubbon Park extends over 135 ha (334 acres). Its landscaping integrates natural rock outcroppings with groves of trees and giant bamboos. The park is liberally dotted with statues, such as that of

> 🔍 HIDDEN GEM
> **Cheerful Chai**
>
> The restaurant under the shady banyan tree at the old-fashioned Airlines Hotel *(4 State Bank of India Rd; (080) 2227 3783)* is a surprising retreat. Order the masala chai or the great variety of south Indian snacks.

←

The imposing Vidhana Soudha, the seat of the government of Karnataka

the 19th-century ruler Chamarajendra Wodeyar (r 1868–94), overlooking the pond near an octagonal, cast-iron bandstand. In the middle of the park, Sheshadri Iyer Memorial, a red Neo-Classical building, houses a library.

---

④

Government Museum

🏛 Kasturba Gandhi Rd
☎ (080) 2286 4483
🕐 Museum: 10am-5pm Tue-Sun; Venkatappa Art Gallery: 10am-5pm Tue-Sun

Established in 1866, this is one of the oldest museums in the country. Housed in a red stucco Neo-Classical building, it has three sections, with a fine collection of wooden sculptures and paintings.

The Venkatappa Art Gallery forms one wing of this museum. In addition to a number of works by K Venkatappa, after whom this gallery is named, it

has numerous watercolours and paintings made in the Mysore style. These works still retain a greenish coating, imparted by a finishing rub with jade. The gallery also has sculptures from different eras.

---

⑤

St Mark's Cathedral

🏛 M G Rd 🕐 7am-7pm daily
🌐 saintmarks.in

This simple cathedral was completed in 1812 and consecrated by the Bishop of Calcutta in 1816. An elegant, cream-coloured structure, it has an imposing portico in front and an apsidal recess at the rear.

---

⑥

Bengaluru Palace

🏛 N of Vidhana Soudha
☎ (080) 2336 0818
🕐 Mon-Sat

Built in 1880 at the exorbitant cost of one million rupees, the Bengaluru Palace was modelled on Windsor Castle, complete with fortified towers

and turreted parapets amid undulating lawns. It is now rented out as a popular venue for wedding functions.

STAY

Leela Palace
This palatial hotel has sumptuous rooms, four restaurants, a café and a bar.

🏛 Old Airport Rd
🌐 www.theleela.com

₹₹₹

The Park
A heritage hotel set in lush grounds not far from M G Rd, offering great-value apartments and cottages.

🏛 2 Clapham St 🌐 www.casacottage.com

₹₹₹

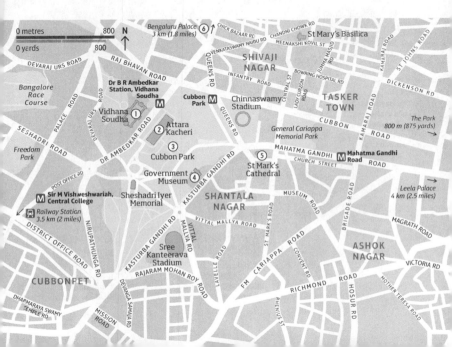

BADAMI

📍480 km (298 miles) NW of Bengaluru 🚌🚉 🕐Cave
temples: sunrise-sunset daily; museum: Sat-Thu
ℹ️Karnataka Tourism, Hotel Mayura Chalukya;
www.karnatakatourism.org/tour-item/badami

Dramatically situated within a horseshoe of red
sandstone cliffs, overlooking the green waters of
Agasthya lake, the historic town of Badami is home to
several rock-cut and structural monuments, the most
richly decorated of which are its famous cave temples.

Situated in the north of Karnataka in Bagalkot, Badami (once
known as Vapati), was the capital of the powerful Chalukya kings,
who ruled this area during the 6th and 7th centuries AD. These
rulers also held sway at Pattadakal *(p470)* and Aihole *(p474)*.
Although this site contains a number of buildings, the four cave
temples (three devoted to Hindu deities, and the fourth to
Jainism) are the undoubted star attractions here. Carved out of
the sandstone hills and connected to each other by stairs, the
caves are numbered in order of
their creation: Cave 1 is dedicated to Shiva, Caves 2 and 3 to
Vishnu, and Cave 4, thought to
be at least 100 years older
than the others, to the
Jain saints, showing
the changing influ-
ences of the day.

AROUND AGASTHYA

Agasthya Lake is
surrounded by the
remains of this historic
town. Apart from the
caves, the most notable
sites here include Badami
Fort and Yellamma
Temple, with its multi-
storey tower. Sculptures
and other finds from the
site can be seen at the
Archaelogical Museum.
Plan for at least a full
day and hire a driver if
you want to take in all
of the sites.

↑ Buthanatha Temple, one of the
buildings from historic Badami
surrounding Agasthya Lake

A flight of stairs leading up to the verandah at the entrance to Cave 1

Scaling the cliffs of Badami, a popular site for sport climbing and bouldering

Cave 1

A flight of steps in this cave on the northwest part of the hill leads up to a pillared verandah, behind which is a square, columned hall with a small sanctuary in the rear wall. The highlights here are the carved panels on the ceiling and the Nataraja panel, an 18-armed depiction of the dancing Hindu god Shiva expressing many different symbolic hand gestures. It is one of the earliest and finest depictions of the Nataraja in Karnataka.

Cave 2

▶ Sixty-four steps above and to the east of Cave 1, this cave is dedicated to the Hindu god Vishnu, depicted in the form of Trivikrama (a giant who crosses the universe in three steps). It also features a superb frieze of Varaha (an incarnation of Vishnu as a boar who rescues Bhudevi, the goddess of earth, from the depths of the cosmic ocean) on one end of the porch. The ceiling is adorned with images of celestial couples, the lotus motif encircled by fish and symbols of the swastika (a sacred symbol for Hindus).

Cave 3

◀ A further 60 steps up from Cave 2, the verandah of this large and beautiful cave has an enormous four-armed figure of Vishnu seated on Adisesha, the serpent whose five hoods spread protectively over his crown. At his feet is the bird Garuda, his mount. This is the only cave with an inscription, dated AD 578.

Cave 4

▶ Immediately next to Cave 3, *tirthankaras* (literally "ford-makers", the 24 spiritual masters of Jainism) cover the walls and columns of Cave 4, on top of a cliff. Although the cave is thought to have been built around 100 years after the others, some elements were added in the 11th and 12th centuries, when this part of Karnataka was governed by a later line of Chalukya rulers.

Did You Know?

The 7th-century Virupaksha Temple is believed to be the oldest functioning temple in India.

Virupaksha temple sitting amid the boulders and ruins of Hampi ↑

HAMPI

🏠 364 km (226 miles) NW of Bengaluru 🚉 Hospet, 13 km (8 miles) W of Hampi ✉ ℹ Bazaar St (foreigners must register at the police station); www.karnatakatourism.org/tour-item/hampi

Covering an area of over 20 sq km (8 sq miles), the ruins of the fabled city of the Vijayanagar kings are one of India's most incredible sites – not least for the surreal surrounding landscape of barren hills and giant boulders.

Vijayanagar, or the "City of Victory", on the banks of the Tungabhadra river, was the capital of the powerful Hindu rulers for more than 200 years. The middle of the city was called Hampi, and is now the name by which the site is known. Vijayanagar reached its zenith under Krishnadeva Raya (r 1510–29) and Achyuta Raya (r 1529–42), two of the dynasty's greatest rulers.

The site is split into the Sacred and Royal Centres, separated by an irrigated valley. The grandest of all the religious monuments in the Sacred Valley is the Vitthala Temple, the pinnacle of Vijayanagar art and architecture. Other notable temples include the Virupaksha Temple, dedicated to Shiva, and the Temple of Achyuta Raya, one of the major Hindu temples, dating from 1534. The Royal Centre is enclosed by fortified walls, and the remains of palaces, baths and a 100-columned audience hall can be explored, as can the majestic, domed Elephant Stables and the lovely Lotus Mahal.

← Taking a coracle ride along the boulder-lined Tungabhadra river

↑ The well-preserved stepwell in the Royal Centre, surrounded by ruins

💬 INSIDER TIP
Surreal Sunrise

Join the throng that climb up Matanga Hill, with the small temple on the peak, to watch the sunrise across the Virupaksha Temple, Hampi Bazaar and other-worldly landscape.

A visitor amid the complex of ancient temples at Pattadakal

④ 🏛️

PATTADAKAL

📍 22 km (14 miles) NE of Badami 🚉 Badami, 24 km (15 miles) SW of town 🚌
ℹ️ www.karnatakatourism.org/tour-item/pattadakal

Situated on the banks of the Malprabha river, the UNESCO World Heritage Site of Pattadakal is a sacred complex of 8th-century temples that reveal the artistic achievements of the Chalukya kings, as seen in nearby Badami (p466) and Aihole (p474).

Unlike Badami and Aihole, which were important ancient settlements, Pattadakal was mainly used for royal festivities and coronation ceremonies. There are nine Hindu temples here, and one Jain sanctuary; the architecture across these is unique, as some of the temples were built in the north Indian temple style, with curved towers (shikharas), and others in the south Indian, with stepped pyramidal-form towers (vimanas). These spectacular structures reveal a great deal about the evolution of temple architecture in south India. The most impressive is Virupaksha, which is remarkably well preserved.

Did You Know?

The temple of Virupaksha, dedicated to Shiva, is still an operating Hindu shrine.

North Indian-Style Temples

▼ Notable for their curved towers over the inner sanctum, north Indian-style temples are exemplified in the Kadasiddeshvara and Jambulinga temples situated near the entrance. These are unassuming sandstone structures with damaged wall sculptures and curving tiered towers. The larger but incomplete Galaganatha Temple nearby has a well-preserved tower with sharply cut tiers of horseshoe-shaped motifs and a ribbed finial. The Kashi Vishvanatha Temple, to the west, dates from the mid-8th century and further illustrates the developments in the north Indian temple style.

South Indian-Style Temples

▼ South Indian temple towers rise in a stepped pyramid form, as in the Sangameshwara Temple, the earliest in the complex. It was erected by the Chalukya king Vijayaditya, who died in AD 733 before the structure was completed. Its multistorey tower is capped with a square domed roof.

The largest temples are the twin Virupaksha and Mallikarjuna temples to the south. Both are dedicated to Shiva and were constructed in AD 745 by two sister queens of the powerful Chalukya king Vikramaditya II, to commemorate his victory over the Pallava rulers of Tamil Nadu. These temples are said to be based on the Kailasanatha Temple in Kanchipuram *(p525)*.

Jain Temple

▶ To the west of the village is a 9th-century Jain Temple built by the Rashtrakuta rulers, who succeeded the Chalukyas in the middle of the 8th century. A spacious open porch with peripheral lathe-turned columns is overhung with angled eaves. Some remarkable carvings of life-size elephant torsos are placed beside the doorway that leads into the inner hall.

↑ A Nandi guardian bull, protecting the Kadasiddheshwara Temple

EXPERIENCE MORE

⑤ Mysuru

🏠 140 km (87 miles) SW of Bengaluru ✈ 10 km (6 miles) S of city centre 🚉🚌 *i* KSTDC, Hotel Mayura Yatrinivas, 2 Jhansi Laxmi Bai Rd; www.karnatakatourism.org/tour-item/mysore-3

📷 PICTURE PERFECT
Light and Bright

Once a week on Sunday evenings, Mysuru's Amba Vilas Palace is lit up like an enormous Christmas tree with thousands upon thousands of lightbulbs, making for quite a breathtaking spectacle.

Situated among fertile fields, and skirted by wooded hills, Mysuru was the capital of the Wodeyar rulers, who governed southern Karnataka when the Vijayanagar kings were in power here. The Wodeyar dynasty ruled almost uninterrupted from 1399 until independence, except for the 38-year rule of the Muslim warlord Haider Ali and his son Tipu Sultan, in the 18th century. Modern Mysuru is the creation of Tipu Sultan, who, in 1793, levelled the old city and built the present town. Today, Mysuru remains an important cultural centre, with the largest university in Karnataka. The town is also renowned for its ivory work, silk-weaving, sandalwood incense and carvings.

Several elegant public buildings, erected under the Wodeyars, enhance the wide, tree-lined streets. In the heart of the town is the late-19th-century Indo-Saracenic Amba Vilas Palace, a magnificent treasure house of exquisite carvings and works of art from all over the world. To its west is ornate Jaganmohan Palace, built in 1861 to mark the coronation of Krishnaraja III. It partly hides a Neo-Classical structure, now the Chamarajendra Art Gallery, which houses an interesting collection of disparate objects including antique furniture, ceramics and ivory. On its top floor is a splendid collection of musical instruments, as well as magnificent paintings by 19th-century Keralan artist Raja Ravi Verma.

Near the northwestern corner of Amba Vilas Palace is Krishnaraja Circle, where a statue of Krishnaraja Wodeyar stands beneath a pavilion. Sayyaji Rao Road leads out from this circle, and is the main shopping strip in the town. A short distance away is Government House, the seat of the British Residents from 1805. Nearby, the Cathedral of St Philomena, with a stained-glass interior, is a Neo-Gothic structure that was completed in 1959.

In the western part of the city is the Neo-Classical Manasa Gangotri, the campus of the university at Mysuru. The Oriental Research Institute here houses a collection of Sanskrit manuscripts, while the Folklore Museum has one of the most important ethnographic collections of south Indian toys, puppets and household objects, as well as two wooden chariots. On the way to Chamundi Hill, 8 km (5 miles) southeast of Mysuru, is the gleaming white Lalitha Mahal Palace, built in 1930 by the Wodeyars. Formerly a private royal guesthouse, it is now a hotel. About halfway up the hill is a Nandi bull sculpture, dating to 1659. Carved out of a single boulder, it is 7.5-m (25-ft) long and 5-m (16-ft) high. The richly decorated guardian is depicted crouching. The Chamundeshvari Temple, at the summit of the hill, was built in the 17th century by the Wodeyars and was later refurbished. It houses a beautifully decorated idol of Chamundeshvari, the family deity of the Wodeyar kings.

> **The Wodeyar dynasty ruled almost uninterrupted from 1399 until independence, except for the 38-year rule of the Muslim warlord Haider Ali**

↑ Amba Vilas' opulent interior and *(inset)* its Indo-Saracenic façade

❻ Gulbarga

🏛 160 km (99 miles) NE of Bijapur 🚉 🚌 ℹ Gulbarga Tourist Office; (08472) 220 644

This small provincial town contains some of the earliest examples of Islamic architecture in Karnataka, dating from the 14th and 15th centuries.

The Dargah of Gesu Daraz, which dates to around 1422, is to the northeast of the present town. It is one of south India's holiest Muslim shrines. Khwaja Gesu Daraz, or Bande Nawaz, as he was affectionately known, was a Sufi mystic from the Chishti sect. He fled from north India and sought refuge here at the court of Firuz Shah Bahmani, a pious and enlightened ruler.

His simple tomb stands in the middle of a sprawling complex that comprises a group of lesser tombs, mosques and *madrasas,* and is a major pilgrimage centre. A complex of seven royal tombs, the Haft Gumbad, lies west of the dargah. Firuz Shah Bahmani, who also died in 1422, is buried here in the most elaborate mausoleum. Immediately west of the city are the desolate ruins of the forbidding fort, almost circular and protected by a wide moat. To the rear of the fort is the 14th-century Bazaar Street, lined with chambers that have been converted into dwellings. To the west of the fort are the derelict tombs of the early Bahmani sultans. The most interesting structure, however, is the nearby Jama Masjid. Built in 1367 to commemorate Gulbarga's status as the capital, this is one of south India's earliest mosques, the only one without an open courtyard . Another 14th-century monument is the Shah Bazaar Mosque, to the north of the fort. Its domed entrance chamber leads into a courtyard with a prayer hall beyond. A street from here proceeds westwards to an arcaded portal flanked by minarets.

EAT

Kamat Madhuvan
Traditional and simple pure vegetarian place.

🏛 Nanjangud Rd, Mysuru 📞 99800 04507

₹₹₹

New Shilpashri
North Indian favourites are offered at this breezy rooftop spot.

🏛 Gandhi Square, Mysuru
📞 (0821) 244 8558

₹₹₹

Parklane
Rooftop dining at a fine old hotel, with tasty curries and live music.

🏛 Sri Harsha Rd, Mysuru
📞 (0821) 243 0400

₹₹₹

← Perennially popular with tourists, the colonnaded Durga Temple at Aihole

⑦ Aihole

🚗 44 km (27 miles) NE of Badami 🚉 Badami, 46 km (29 miles) SW, then bus or taxi 🌐 www.karnataka tourism.org/tour-item/ aihole

Time seems to have stood still in this small, dusty town, situated on the Malprabha river, about 14 km (9 miles) downstream from Pattadakal (p470). Fortifications encircle much of the town. Within are ancient sandstone temples of varying types, some of which were used as dwellings and are named after their former inhabitants. The temples are associated with both the early and later Chalukya rulers of Badami (p466), and date from the 6th to the 11th centuries.

Most visitors begin their tour of Aihole at the Durga Temple. This monument is elevated on a lofty plinth, with steps at one end leading to a porch with elaborate carvings on its columns. Other sculptural masterpieces – of Shiva with

Nandi, Narasimha, Vishnu with Garuda, Durga and Harihara – stand in the niches lining the colonnade. The temple is in fact misnamed, as the identity of the image that was once worshipped here is unknown.

Nearby is a small complex containing the Ladkhan Temple. This building is recognizable by the tiers of sloping slabs that form the roof of the spacious hall as well as the adjoining entrance porch. River goddesses and amorous couples are carved on the columns of the porch, while images of deities can be seen on the side walls of a small chamber at the rooftop level. The adjacent Gaudar Gudi comprises a small sanctuary set within an open mandapa, with balcony seating on four sides. The ruined Chakra Gudi is near the stepped tank. The Kunti Group, a quartet of temples conceived as open columned halls with interior sanctuaries, lies to the south. The temple to the southeast, probably the first to be built, has superbly carved ceiling panels portraying the Hindu Trinity of Brahma, Vishnu and Shiva. A similar trio of ceiling panels can be seen in the Hucchapayya Math, lying a short distance beyond.

A stepped path leads to the top of the hill southeast of the

town, passing by a two-storeyed Buddhist temple. At the summit of the hill stands the serene Meguti Temple, built in AD 634, the earliest dated structural monument in Karnataka. The temple's clearly articulated basement, plastered walls and eaves show the south Indian style of temple architecture in its earliest phase. An impressive seated Jain figure is installed in the sanctuary. Prehistoric megalithic tombs are located to the rear of the temple.

The road, going downhill, follows the curving fortifications and passes the Jyotirlinga Group, until it ends at the Durga Temple. To the north of the Durga Temple is the Chikki Gudi, with exquisitely carved columns, beams and ceiling panels. A path to the right leads to the small Hucchimalli Gudi, with a north Indian-style tower and an unusual icon of Karttikeya, Shiva's son, carved on the ceiling of the front porch.

Nearby lies the rock-cut Ravala Phadi Cave, dating to the late 6th century. Inside are splendid carvings of Hindu divinities. These include a Dancing Shiva in a subshrine; Ardhanarishvara, Harihara and Shiva with Ganga on the walls of the main hall; and Varaha and Durga in the antechamber of the small linga sanctuary. Tiny shrines and a fluted column stand in front.

→ The Ibrahim Rauza mausoleum, where Ibrahim II and his wife are buried

Did You Know?

The dome at Gol Gombaz forms a whispering gallery, and any sound is amplified within the complex.

Bijapur

🏛 530 km (329 miles)
NW of Bengaluru 🚉🚌
ℹ Karnataka Tourism,
Station Rd; (080) 2235
2828

After the fall of the Bahmanis,
the Adil Shahi sultans emerged
as the principal rulers of the
Deccan in the 16th and 17th
centuries. Their capital, the
fortified city of Bijapur, was
protected by ramparts with
prominent bastions, and
many of the original cannons
are still in place. The Malik-i-
Maidan ("Lord of the Plain"),
reputedly the largest cannon
of the period in India, still
guards the western entrance.
Within the fort's walls are
several splendid mosques,
palaces and tombs that were
built by a succession of
enlightened rulers.

Bijapur's most celebrated
building, the monumental
tomb of Muhammad Adil Shah
(r 1627–56), second son and
successor of Ibrahim II, is
commonly known as the
"Round Dome", or Gol
Gumbaz. The slightly bulbous
dome, the largest in the world
after St Peter's in Rome, rises
on a base of petals to form a
fitting climax to the whole
composition. Completed in
1656, the tomb stands in the
middle of a formal garden.
On the west side is a small
mosque with five arches
flanked by slender minarets.

The Citadel, in the heart
of the city, is defined by its
fortified walls and surrounded

DECCANI PAINTING

The Muslim rulers of the
Deccan, especially of
Golconda (p527) and
Bijapur, during the 14th
and 15th centuries,
encouraged art and
established a Deccani
School of Painting. This
was influenced first by
direct contact with
Central Asia and Persia,
and later by the Mughals.
At the court of Bijapur,
elements of European
Renaissance and Persian
art were added to the
Indian tradition to create
the Deccani style.

by a wide moat. The south
gate, the only one surviving,
leads into what was the
palace complex. To its northwest stands the Sat Manzil,
the seven-storey pleasure
palace, from the top of which
the whole city could once
be seen. Only five storeys
now remain. It overlooks an
exquisitely ornamented
miniature pavilion called the
Jal Mandir. A short distance
to the north are the Gagan
Mahal, the audience hall of Ali
Adil Shah I, and the Anand
Mahal, or the "Palace of Joy",
where the ladies of the
seraglio lived. Other fine
structures include the Mecca
Masjid, a charming little
mosque to the east of the
Citadel, and Karimuddin's
Mosque near the south gate.

The walled city, outside the
Citadel, is scattered with
monuments built by

the Adil Shahi sultans. To the
east of the Citadel is the two-
storey Asar Mahal, built in
1646 as the hall of justice and
later converted into a sacred
reliquary to house two hairs
of the Prophet. A short distance away is the elegant
Mihtar Mahal, from the period
of Ibrahim II (r 1580–1626)
entered through a triple-
storeyed gateway.

The grandly conceived
Jama Masjid, to the southeast,
was begun by Ali Adil Shah I in
1576, but never finished. The
marble floor of the capacious
prayer hall has been divided
into some 2,250 rectangular
bays to resemble prayer mats.

The exquisite Ibrahim Rauza
mausoleum, often described
as the finest Islamic building
in the Deccan, was built by
Ibrahim II for his wife. However,
he died before her and
is also buried here.

⑨ Srirangapatna

🚗 16 km (10 miles) N of Mysuru 🚌🚆 From Mysuru
🌐 www.karnataka tourism.org/tour-item/ srirangapatna

Known to the British as Seringapatam, this island fortress in the Kaveri river enjoys historical significance as the site of the battles between the British and Tipu Sultan, the "Tiger of Mysuru", in the 18th century. The British finally stormed the citadel in 1799, killing Tipu and consolidating their power in south India. Today, none of the structures within the fort survive, barring the bridges across the Kaveri river, from which the bathing ghats and the ramparts can be seen.

To the east and the south, a broad moat surrounds polygonal bastions and turreted parapets. The Mysuru Gate and Elephant Gate, to the south, are flanked by guardrooms. Sultan Battery, the dungeons where Tipu used to keep British prisoners, is to the north; nearby is the Water Gate, where Tipu was killed.

The large Sri Ranganatha Temple, which gives the island its name, was substantially restored in the 19th century. The inner sanctum enshrines an image of the reclining Vishnu and is approached through pillared halls and a gilded open courtyard.

The **Daria Daulat Bagh**, Tipu Sultan's summer palace, built in 1784, stands in the middle of a beautiful garden near the river, a short distance south of the fort. Each of its sides has three arched openings in the centre and the whole palace is surrounded by a pillared verandah. The east and west walls of the

→

The Daria Daulat Bagh, a fine example of Mughal architecture

> The large Sri Ranganatha Temple, which gives the island its name, was substantially restored in the 19th century. The inner sanctum enshrines an image of the reclining Vishnu.

verandah are both covered with murals, restored in 1855. On the west wall are scenes of battle, one of which illustrates Haidar Ali's victory over the British at Pollilur (1780), while the east wall depicts courtly scenes. The carved woodwork and the elegant painted floral designs on the wall reveal Mughal influence. The palace is now a museum, with maps, paintings and Tipu memorabilia on display. Further south is the Gumbaz – the tombs of Haidar Ali and Tipu Sultan. The walls of the chambers are decorated with the tiger-stripes motif *(bubri)* that were favoured by Tipu.

Daria Daulat Bagh

📷 📞 (08326) 252 045
🕒 8:30am–5:30pm daily

⑩ Talakad

🚗 45 km (28 miles) SE of Mysuru 🚌

The historic city of Talakad, situated on the north bank of the Kaveri river, now lies partly buried under shifting sand dunes. From the 5th to the 10th centuries it was the capital of the Ganga dynasty, but only two modest temples survive from that period.

The largest edifice at this site is the 12th-century Vaidyanatheswara Temple, dedicated to Shiva. Nearby is the more modest Kirti Narayana Temple, where the 3-m- (10-ft-) high image of Vishnu is still worshipped. A festival, the Panchalinga Darshana, is celebrated here at intervals of 12 years.

⑪ Somanathapura

🚗 36 km (22 miles) E of Mysuru 🚌

A beautiful representation of Hoysala architecture, the **Keshava Temple** is the

↑ Visitors at the Keshava Temple in the village of Somanathapura

highlight of the little village of Somanathapura. Built in 1268 by Somanatha, a general of King Narasimha III, its design is attributed to the sculptor and architect Janakacharya. The temple is accessed from the east, through a doorway with an open portico, where a slab records Somnatha's generous donations. Unlike the other Hoysala temples at Halebid and Belur, this is well preserved and has complete towers. The temple has three star-shaped shrines that lead off a pillared hall; both the shrines and the hall stand on a high plinth. The basements of the inner

sanctums and hall are carved with animal and floral patterns, while images of deities under foliage canopies occupy the walls above. The interior of the hall is remarkable for its splendid columns and the elaborate ceilings, which display lobed motifs, pendant buds and looped bands.

Also in Somanathapura is the ruined Panchalinga Temple, built in 1268 in honour of Somnatha's family.

Keshava Temple
◈ ⏰ Daily

⑫
Melkote

🏠 54 km (34 miles) N of Mysuru 🚌 ℹ️ Tourist Office; (08232) 238 377

A picturesque hill town of shrines and monasteries, Melkote is a major pilgrimage centre for devotees of Vishnu; it is also associated with Ramanuja, the renowned Hindu philosopher and social reformer who died in 1137. Ramanuja is worshipped along with Vishnu in the Narayana Temple, which is located in the southern part of town.

South of the temple is a solitary gopura, while perched on the summit of a hill to the northeast of the town is the small Narasimha Shrine, which

overlooks the large Kalyani Tank. The tradition of religious learning for which the town is known – first introduced by Ramanuja – survives in Melkote's many institutions, of which the Academy of Sanskrit Research is the most famous.

TIPU SULTAN: THE "TIGER OF MYSURU"

Tipu Sultan was a shrewd diplomat, expert soldier and excellent scholar who dreamed of a modern industrial state. His main adversaries were the British, who had conquered part of his father's territory in the first two Mysuru Wars (1767-9 and 1780-84). Tipu waged two more wars against them, ending with the 1799 fall of Srirangapattana, where he died fighting.

Did You Know?

Legend has it that the first coffee plants were smuggled to India from Mecca in Saudi Arabia by a Muslim pilgrim.

13

Kodagu

📍 120 km (75 miles) SW of Mysuru 🚌 📘 www. karnatakatourism.org/tour-item/madikeri

Picturesquely set amid the forested mountains of the Western Ghats, the district of Kodagu (or Coorg) was an independent state until it was incorporated into the newly formed state of Karnataka in 1956. Madikeri, the district headquarters, situated 1,500 m (4,921 ft) above sea level and surrounded by rolling coffee and orange plantations, is a charming hill town, and a convenient base from which to explore Kodagu.

Madikeri (or Mercara) was once the capital of the Hindu Lingayat kings, who ruled for over 200 years from 1600, except for a brief period when Tipu Sultan *(p477)* seized power. The fort, at the centre of the town, was built by the third Lingayat king in 1812. Within its stone ramparts, it contains the simple palace of the Lingayat rulers, along with a temple, an old church, a museum and the local prison.

The famous Omkareshvara Shiva Temple, situated in a hollow east of the Fort, was built by Linga Raja II in 1820 and dedicated to Vishnu and Shiva. The temple complex consists of brick buildings in the Indo-Saracenic style set in courtyards surrounded by pillared verandahs. Other notable monuments in Madikeri are the Royal Tombs of Raja Dodda Vira, his wife and his son, Linga Raja II. Curiously, these display a distinct Islamic influence, with onion-shaped domes, minarets and trellises.

Kodagu remains pleasantly cool all year round, and the hills are at their most lush after the heavy monsoon showers, when they make for delightful hiking territory. The walk up to Abbey Falls, 8 km (5 miles) from Madikeri, is popular and takes trekkers through forests and coffee plantations. Kodagu is renowned for its sprawling coffee plantations, first introduced in the mid-19th century by the British. The Kodava people bought back their land after independence, but several estates still retain their British names. Kodagu produces some of the world's finest varieties of mild coffee; in fact, it is Karnataka's richest district because it accounts for the majority of coffee exports from the state. Coffee bushes are grown in the benevolent shade of large trees such as oak and rosewood, and in mixed plantations with crops of oranges, pepper vines and spices like cardamom.

Nisargadhama, 27 km (17 miles) from Madikeri, is a beautiful forest retreat on a riverine island on the Kaveri. The bamboo cottages built here by the forest department are ideal for viewing wildlife.

Talakaveri, 45 km (28 miles) southwest of Madikeri, at an altitude of 1,276 m (4,186 ft), is the source of the Kaveri, one of India's nine sacred rivers; there is a small shrine built around the spring. Its height also offers incredible views. At Bhagamandala, 36 km (22 miles) southwest of Madikeri, the Kaveri meets its two tributaries, Kanike and Sujoythi. Several shrines dot the area near the confluence, which is also the site of the Bhagamandala temple, built in the Keralan style.

→

Sravana Belgola's statue of Gommateshvara, carved from a single block of stone

INSIDER TIP
Blue Tokai

The famous eco-conscious brand Blue Tokai sources much of its coffee from the hills of Kodagu – and all of its beans from Karnataka. It is possible to visit a plantation here and sip some at the source.

Panorama of the surrounding mountains seen from beside Talakaveri shrine, Kodagu

⑭
Sravana Belgola

🏠 140 km (87 miles) W of Bengaluru 🚌 ⓕ www.karnatakatourism.org/tour-item/belur

This small town between two granite hills, Indragiri and Chandragiri, is the most important Jain site in south India. It is dominated by the colossal 17.7-m- (58-ft-) high statue of Gommateshvara, also known as Bahubali, son of the first Jain *tirthankara*. On the summit of the 143-m- (469-ft-) high Indragiri Hill, the north-facing statue of the naked saviour stands on an anthill staring impassively ahead. Entwined around his legs and arms are creepers, indicating the length of time he stood immobile in meditation. An inscription at the base records its consecration in AD 981 by Chamundaraya, the powerful minister of Rajamalla IV, a Ganga king.

The town, which lies at the base of the hill, has a large tank as well as a number of Jain temples (*bastis*). Perhaps the most interesting of these is the *matha*, near the steps leading to Indragiri Hill. The walls of its courtyard

have a series of vivid 18th-century murals illustrating the past and present births of Parsvanatha, the 23rd *tirthankara*, as well as scenes from the annual fair held here. Some fine Jain bronzes are displayed in the sanctuary that opens off the courtyard. On Chandragiri Hill, to the north of the town, is another cluster of *bastis* established by the 10th- to 12th-century Ganga kings and their powerful ministers. The Neminatha Basti, commissioned by Chamundaraya,

enshrines an image of the 22nd *tirthankara*, Neminatha. The adjoining Chandragupta Basti has fine miniature panels and a 5-m- (16-ft-) high sculpture of Parsvanatha is enshrined in another nearby *basti*.

Every 12 years, Jainism's most important festival, the Mahamastaka-bhisheka (head-anointing ceremony), is held here. The festival commemorates the consecration of the Bahubali monolith, and attracts thousands of monks, priests and pilgrims. A special scaffold is erected behind the statue so that priests can ritually bathe the god with milk, water from the holy rivers, ghee, saffron, sandalwood paste, vermilion and flower petals.

The village of Kambadahalli, 15 km (9 miles) east of Sravana Belgola, is another Jain settlement. The 10th-century Panchakuta Basti houses a trio of *tirthankaras* in three separate shrines.

THE KODAVAS

The people of Kodagu, known as Kodavas, are a distinct ethnic group and have their own language, Coorgi. The Kodavas were traditionally an agricultural people known for their skill in martial activities, and family groups lived in huge four-winged homes called *ain mane*. Many Kodavas now live in towns, but continue to follow cultural traditions, festivals and events. Weddings are unique in that there are no priests and they are solemnized by elders. At these events, the men dress in *kupyas*, long black coats belted with a tasselled sash, while women wear saris with pleats at the back. Their cuisine includes tangy pork curry served with rice dumplings.

⑮

Belur

🏠 17 km (11 miles) SW of Halebid 🚉 Hassan, 34 km (21 miles) SE, then bus or taxi 🚌 ℹ️ www.karnatakatourism.org/tour-item/belur

Belur was the capital of the Hoysala Empire before it moved to Halebid, and has a number of buildings from this period. The most impressive is the **Chennakeshava Temple**, built in 1117 to commemorate the Hoysala triumph over the Cholas. At the end of the town's main street, a towered *gopura*, erected by the kings of Vijayanagar in the 16th century, marks the entrance to the temple. Inside is a court-yard surrounded by shrines and colonnades. In the centre is the main temple, a single star-shaped sanctuary opening onto a columned hall fronted by a screened porch.

The surface of the structure is covered with richly textured relief carvings. The lintels have foliate frames running between aquatic monsters; the stone grilles that filter light into the porch are raised on friezes of elephants, lotus stems, and couples. Brackets fashioned as female dancers, musicians and huntresses support the eaves.

Chennakeshava Temple

📞 (08177) 222 218
🕖 7:30am–7:30pm daily

⑯

Halebid

🏠 213 km (132 miles) W of Bengaluru 🚉 Hassan, 34 km (21 miles) S, then bus or taxi 🚌 ℹ️ www.karnatakatourism.org/tour-item/halebeedu

Set amid a lush agricultural landscape, isolated Halebid was the Hoysala capital in the 12th and 13th centuries. While the palace has yet to be excavated, the stone ramparts that once surrounded the city can still be seen. Outside these ramparts, to the east, is the vast tank known as Dorasamudra, which was also the city's original name.

Today, the main attraction of Halebid is the unfinished Hoysaleshvara Temple, which was begun in 1121 by King Vishnuvardhana. This structure comprises a pair of identical temples, each with its own east-facing linga sanctuary opening onto a hall and a screened porch. Each temple is also preceded by a pavilion with a huge statue of the bull

108

The number of Vishnu temples in India. This is considered a holy number.

Nandi, steed of Shiva. The outer walls are elevated on friezes of naturalistic and fanciful animals, interspersed with carvings of scenes from the *Ramayana* and the *Mahabharata*. Among the finest wall panels here are those of Shiva dancing on the outstretched skin of the elephant demon he had slain, Krishna playing the flute and Krishna holding up Mount Govardhan, on the south face of the southern sanctuary. On the north face of the northern sanctuary is a splendid Nataraja (Shiva as the Lord of Dance) and a panel depicting a crouching multiarmed, multiheaded Ravana creeping up on Shiva and Parvati seated on Mount Kailasa. Set on the plinth on which the temple is raised is a three-dimensional composition of a warrior plunging his sword into a leonine beast, interpreted as the dynastic

← The elaborately carved entrance to Belur's Chennakeshava Temple

symbol of the martial Hoysala rulers. The landscaped garden in front of the Hoysaleshvara Temple now serves as an **Archaeological Museum**. A panel here shows a majestic seated Ganesha. South of the complex is a group of 12th-century Jain *bastis*.

Archaeological Museum
◉ ⏰ 8am–5pm Sat-Thu
ⓦ asi.nic.in/museum-halebid

---

❼

Mangaluru

🏠 357 km (222 miles) W of Bengaluru ✈ 20 km (12 miles) N of city centre, then taxi or bus 🚉 🚌
🅹 www.karnataka tourism.org/tour-item/murdeshwar-mangalore

This thriving port on the estuary of the Netavati and Gurpur rivers is the largest city in Dakshina (South) Kannada, the coastal district famous for its coffee, cashew nut and pepper plantations. Rich harvests of these crops have attracted traders throughout the ages. Arab merchants first came here in the 13th and 14th centuries, and were later followed by the Portuguese and the British.

Mangaluru today presents a panorama of terracotta-roofed houses, whitewashed churches, lovely temples and mosques, nestling amid groves of coconut palms. Among its historic monuments is the old watchtower, known as Sultan's Battery, built in 1763 by Haider Ali of Mysuru (*p472*).

Mangaluru's 19th-century churches include the domed Church of the Most Holy Rosary and the Jesuit College of St Aloysius. At the foot of Kadiri Hill, 3 km (2 miles) north of the city, is the 17th-century Manjunath Temple, with some superb bronze images of the Buddha dating to the 10th–11th centuries. Numerous Jain temples and monasteries dot the villages

↑ Hindu pilgrims worshipping in the Krishna Temple on Udupi's main square

around Mangaluru. The finest is the elaborate 15th-century Chandranatha Basti, located at Mudabidri, 35 km (22 miles) to the northwest. Dominating the summit of a hill at Karkala, 18 km (11 miles) further north, is the 13-m- (43-ft-) high Gommateshvara monolith (1432), an obvious imitation of the larger and earlier one at Sravana Belgola. The 16th-century Chaturmukha Basti, a perfectly symmetrical temple with a central chamber enshrining 12 *tirthankaras*, stands at the base of the hill. The pilgrimage town of Dharmasthala, 75 km (47 miles) to the east, is well-known for its Shiva temple.

---

❽

Udupi

🏠 58 km (36 miles) N of Mangaluru 🚉 🅹 Room 303, 2nd Fl, A-Wing, Rajatadri, Manipal; www.karnataka tourism.gov/tour-item/udupi

All roads in the bustling pilgrim town of Udupi lead to the large open square in the centre, where the Krishna Temple is located. The famous 13th-century Vaishnava teacher Madhava is believed to have founded the temple

by installing an image of Krishna he had rescued from a shipwreck. Parked outside the temple are the festival chariots with dome-like towers made of bamboo and covered with colourful textiles. After passing through the entrance gate, pilgrims bathe in the tank before entering the main sanctuary with its silver doors and viewing window. Surrounding the square are other temples and the eight *mathas* associated with the Krishna Temple, built in the traditional Kanara style with wooden verandahs and sloping roofs.

Udupi also lends its name to a type of inexpensive eatery serving traditional south Indian vegetarian food, such as the *masala dosa* and *idli*. These restaurants, which originated here, are now found all over India.

In Manipal, 4 km (2 miles) to the east, the **House of Vijayanath Shennoy/ Heritage Village Museum** is worth a visit, as it contains several examples of typical local homes, as well as a fine collection of everyday objects.

House of Vijayanath Shennoy/Heritage Village Museum
⏰ 10am–5pm Mon-Sat
ⓦ indiaheritagevillage.org

The magestic Jog Falls near Bhatkal, during monsoon season ↑

STAY

SwaSwara
Stay in timber villas at this luxurious resort with a pool and Ayurvedic centre.

🏠 Om Beach
🌐 swaswara.com

₹₹₹

Gokarna International Beach Resort
Among the palms near the beach, the cottages and rooms here have kitchenettes and verandahs.

🏠 Kudlee Beach
🌐 gokarnabeach resort.com

₹₹₹

Matthuga Homestay
Homely rooms and cottages in the middle of a peaceful plantation, plus a vegetarian menu.

🏠 Talavata, 8 km (5 miles) from Jog Falls
🌐 matthuga.in

₹₹₹

19
Bhatkal

🏠 165 km (103 miles) N of Mangaluru 🚌

The many Jain and Hindu stone temples at Bhatkal date from the 16th and 17th centuries, when the town was an important port. On the main street are the Parsvanatha and Chandranatheshvara *bastis*, while 2 km (1 mile) to the east, on the other side of the highway, is the Khetapai Narayan Temple, built in 1540. Its sanctuary and hall are enclosed within stone screens fashioned to imitate wood. Finely sculpted guardian figures flank the doorway.

India's highest waterfalls, the impressive Jog Falls, lie 60 km (37 miles) northeast of Bhatkal. They can be seen at the head of the Sharavati river, framed by jagged pinnacles of rock.

20
Chitradurga

🏠 200 km (124 miles) NW of Bengaluru 🚌 🚍 🛈 Kamana Bhavi Extension, 8th Ward Fort Rd; (08194) 234 466

Located at the base of a rugged chain of hills, this town was a prominent outpost of the Vijayanagar Empire. Later, in the 17th–18th centuries, it became the headquarters of a line of local chiefs known as Bedas, until it was occupied by Haider Ali in 1799 and then by the British.

The **fort**, expanded by Haider Ali and defined by walls of huge granite blocks, rises above the town. A series of three gates leads to the irregular inner zone, strewn with striking granite boulders. There are several small temples here, as well as a number of ceremonial gateways erected by the Bedas. The platforms and pavilions within the compound of the Sampige Siddheshvara Temple mark the spot where the Bedas were crowned. The remains of rubble- and-mud-built granaries and residences, and a large circular well can be seen nearby.

The local **Government Museum** displays a range of artifacts from surrounding sites. On the main street of town, the 17th-century Ucchalingamma Temple should not be missed.

Fort
♿ 🕐 Sunrise-sunset daily

Government Museum
📞 (08194) 224 202
🕐 9am-5pm Tue-Sun

㉑
Sringeri

🏠 100 km (62 miles) NE of
Mangaluru 🚌 🚐

The small settlement of
Sringeri, tucked away in
the forested ranges of the
Western Ghats, is today an
important pilgrimage centre
and one of the most powerful
seats of orthodox Hinduism in
south India. This was where
Shankaracharya, the great
9th-century philosopher and
social reformer, established
the first of his four *mathas*; the
other three are at Joshimath
in the Himalayas *(p191)*, Puri
(p352) to the east and Dwarka
(p392) to the west. Today,
his successors, who are also
known as Shankaracharyas,
still wield a tremendous
influence in both religious
and temporal matters. Two
temples overlook the Tunga

🔍 HIDDEN GEM
Take a Hike

Don't miss the path that
starts beside Gokarna's
Shri Mahaganapati
Temple and traces its
way across the scrubby
headland of reddish
rock to the picturesque
arc of Kudlee Beach, just
outside of town.

BEACHES AROUND GOKARNA

There are many beaches around Gokarna. The main
stretch of sand here gets crowded with Indian tourists
and pilgrims, who perform ablutions in the sea; it is also
home to a fishing community. To the south there are four
beaches that attract visitors. The closest and most
attractive is perfectly curved Kudlee Beach, with guesthouses and restaurants under the palms. Across the next
headland is busier Om Beach, whose shape resembles the
holy symbol. Only the hardy make the trek to Half Moon
and Paradise beaches, which have no facilities.

---

river, which is crammed with
sacred fish. The smaller one
is dedicated to Sharada, a
popular form of the goddess
Saraswati. Next to it, at the
16th-century Vidyashankara
Temple, the Shankaracharya is
worshipped in the form of a
linga. This stone temple is set
on a high platform and is laid
out on an almost circular star-
shaped plan. Friezes depicting
Shiva and Vishnu embellish its
walls. The main hall has massive piers carved as rearing
yalis (mythical leonine beasts).

㉒
Gokarna

🏠 200 km (124 miles) N of
Mangaluru 🚌 ℹ️ Main Rd,
Karwar; (08382) 221 172

Spectacularly situated by the
Arabian Sea, this charming
little town with clusters of

traditional tile-roofed brick
houses is a favourite with
visitors in search of sun, sea
and sand. More than just a
beach town, Gokarna is also
an important centre of
Sanskrit learning. At the
western end of the main
street, the Mahabaleshvara
Temple was destroyed by the
Portuguese in 1714 and later
rebuilt. In the sanctuary is a
stone linga, encased in brass
and placed on a coiled stone
serpent. The floor of the
hall in front has an intricate
engraving of a giant tortoise.
Shiva's birthday (Feb/Mar) is
celebrated here with great
fanfare. The two great temple
chariots lead a procession
through the town's narrow
streets, while priests chant
hymns in praise of Shiva.

㉓
Barkur

🏠 71 km (44 miles) N of
Mangaluru 🚌

A flourishing port in the 15th
and 16th centuries, until its
river silted up, today Barkur is
known for its many temples
with their sloping terracotta-
tiled roofs. The largest is the
Panchalingeshvara Temple,
at the southern end of town.
Devotees gather at the
stepped tank nearby for a
ritual bath before worshipping
at the two east-facing linga
shrines. The other temples
include one dedicated to both
Shiva and Ganesha, and the
smaller Someshvara and
Somanatheshvara temples.

↑ Fishermen's boats on the sandy beach
in Gokarna, on the Arabian Sea

㉔

Bidar

🏛 120 km (75 miles) NE of Gulbarga 🚌 *ℹ* www.karnatakatourism.org/tour-item/bidar

> To the left of Bidar Fort is the Rangin Mahal, an exquisite palace built by Ali Shah Barid in the 16th century, adorned with magnificent tile mosaics.

This city was included in the World Monuments Fund in 2014, and has a long history. It became the Bahmani capital in 1424, when Firuz Shah's brother and successor, Ahmad Shah, moved his court here. With the collapse of the Bahmani dynasty at the end of the 15th century, control of the region passed into the hands of the Baridis.

Bidar's Fort, built in 1428 by Ahmed Shah Bahmani, occupies a promontory that is defended by double rings of walls and a moat partly carved out of the bedrock. A trio of arched gates, one with polychrome tilework, another with a prominent dome, leads into what was once the royal enclave. To the left is the Rangin Mahal, an exquisite palace built by Ali Shah Barid in the 16th century. The hall, with its original wooden columns displaying ornate brackets and beams, and the rear chamber adorned with magnificent tile mosaics and mother-of-pearl inlay, are especially striking.

Nearby is the unusual Solah Khamba Mosque, with massive circular columns, built by the Tughlaqs in 1327.

In front is the Lal Bagh, a walled garden with a central lobe-fringed pool. A short distance to the south is the ruined Diwan-i-Am, the Public Audience Hall, and the Takht Mahal, a monumental portal with traces of hexagonal tiles decorated with tiger and sun emblems in the spandrels.

The sizeable old walled town sprawls beneath the ramparts of the fort. On one side of the main north-south street is the Takhti-i-Kirmani, a 15th-century gateway embellished with bands of foliate and arabesque designs. Further south is the magnificent late-15th-century Madrasa of Mahmud Gawan, named after the erudite prime minister who was the virtual ruler of the Bahmani kingdom. This used to be a famous theological college, and at one time it featured a huge library that was well-stocked with scholarly manuscripts. A superb example of Central Asian-style architecture, it has four arched portals that stand against a background of domes facing a central court. A pair of minarets flank its façade. Tile mosaics on the exterior still

survive, including a finely worked calligraphic band in rich blue and white. Further south, the Chaubara is a circular tower marking the intersection of the city's two principal thoroughfares.

The mausolea of the Baridi rulers lie west of Bidar. The largest is the Tomb of Ali Shah Barid (1577). This lofty, domed chamber, open on four sides, stands in the middle of a symmetrical four-square garden. Blank panels above the arches once contained tile mosaic, well-preserved examples of which can still be seen inside. The black polished basalt sarcophagus is still in situ.

Bidar is also known for a special type of encrusted metalware, often mistaken for damascening, known as *bidri*. Introduced in the mid-17th century by artisans from Iran, the craft flourished under court patronage. The style, characterized by intricate floral and geometric designs inlaid in gold, silver or brass onto a matt black surface, was used to embellish various objects, including platters, boxes, *huqqa* bases and trays. Today, the finest pieces are housed in museums, and only a handful of artisan families still practise this skilled craft in the city of its origin.

The Bahmani necropolis stands in the open countryside near Ashtur, a small village 3 km (2 miles) northeast of Bidar. The oldest and grandest of the tombs here is the early-15th-century Tomb of Ahmad Shah, where splendid murals embellish the interior walls as well as the huge dome, clearly showing a Persian influence. The adjacent tomb of Alauddin Ahmad II, his successor, has coloured tile mosaics. Just outside is the Chaukhandi, the modest tomb of the saint Khalil Allah (d 1460), which has superb calligraphic panels over the doorways.

WILDLIFE SANCTUARIES OF KARNATAKA

The Nilgiri Biosphere Reserve, encompassing six contiguous wildlife sanctuaries, spans the states of Karnataka, Kerala and Tamil Nadu. Created to protect the extraordinary biodiversity of the last surviving tracts of tropical evergreen and deciduous forests of the Western Ghats, this reserve forms one of the most important migratory corridors for animals such as the Asian elephant and the Indian bison. These parks are within convenient reach of Bengaluru *(p464)* and Mysuru *(p472)*.

㉕
Gadag

⌂ 450 km (280 miles) NW of Bengaluru 🚉🚌 🛈 Keshav Clarks Inn, Hubli Rd, Mulgund Naka; (0837) 222 0765

The sleepy little town of Gadag comes to life during the height of the cotton season in May and June, when the local cotton market hums with activity.

A number of late Chalukyan monuments (11th–12th centuries) in the town indicate its historic past. Standing to the south is the Trikuteshvara Temple, remarkable for its three sanctuaries facing a common, partly open hall. Inclined slabs that serve as balcony seats are decorated with figurative panels, and are overhung by steeply angled eaves. Inside the hall, the columns have figures arranged in shallow niches. The east sanctuary accommodates three lingas, while the one to the south is dedicated to the goddess Saraswati.

In the middle of the town stands the Someshvara Temple. Though abandoned and now in a dilapidated state, its intricate carvings are fairly well preserved. Look for the doorways to the hall – these have densely carved figures and foliation.

The small village of Lakkundi, 11 km (7 miles) southeast of Gadag, has temples dating from the 11th–12th centuries, built of grey-

←

The large dome topping the 15th-century Madrasa of Mahmud Gawan, Bidar

green chloritic schist. Jain Basti, the largest, has a five-storeyed tower. Its basement is adorned with friezes of elephants and lotus petals. The nearby Kashi Vishvanatha Temple has a pair of sanctuaries facing each other across a common porch.

㉖
Belgaum

⌂ 502 km (312 miles) NW of Bengaluru 🚉🚌 🛈 Tourist Office, Ashoka Nagar; (0831) 247 0879

This bustling city, on the border with Maharashtra, was an important garrison town under the British. Earlier, in the 16th and 17th centuries, Belgaum was a provincial centre under the Adil Shahi rulers of Bijapur *(p475)*, the Marathas of Pune, as well as the Mughals when they occupied this part of Karnataka. The fort to the east is unusually elliptical in layout and its stone walls were built using a number of reused temple blocks. The Safa Mosque nearby was built in the first half of the 16th century by Asad Khan, the governor of Belgaum.

Colourful boats on Chennai's long Marina Beach

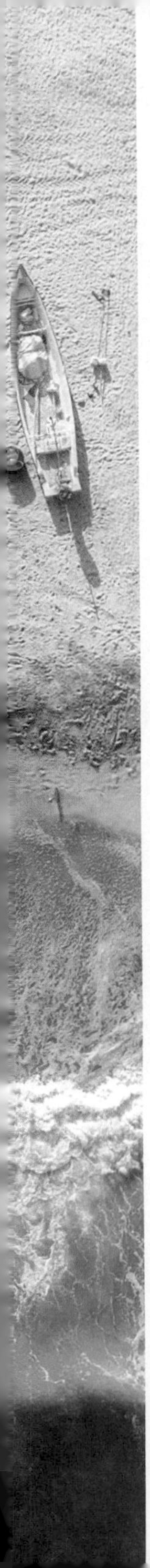

CHENNAI

Formerly known as Madras, Chennai is the state capital of Tamil Nadu. The city was once a group of villages set amid palm-fringed paddy fields, until two British East India Company merchants, Francis Day and Andrew Cogan, established a factory-cum-trading post here, a fortified settlement that came to be known as Fort St George. Outside its walls was George Town, whose crowded lanes, each devoted to a particular trade, serviced the British colonists. Colonial rule linked the various villages, including the settlement founded in the 16th century by the Portuguese at San Thomé, the sacred site associated with St Thomas the Apostle. Several centuries before the Europeans arrived, the great 7th-century Pallava port was in Chennai's Mylapore neighbourhood; its Kapaleeshwarar Temple, along with the Parthasarathi Temple at Triplicane, bear testimony to the city's antiquity. Colonial rule marked the beginning of the city's growth as a major commercial centre. Today, Chennai is a dynamic mix of the old and the new, its stately colonial structures juxtaposed with modern high-rises.

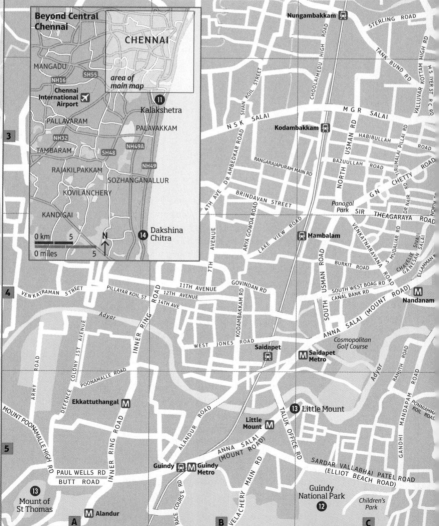

CHENNAI

Must See
1. The Marina

Experience More
2. Fort St George
3. George Town
4. St Andrew's Kirk
5. Egmore
6. Government Museum Complex
7. Anna Salai
8. Triplicane
9. Adyar
10. Mylapore & San Thomé
11. Kalakshetra
12. Guindy National Park
13. Little Mount and Mount of St Thomas
14. Dakshina Chitra

Eat
1. Amethyst
2. Annalakshmi
3. Ente Keralam
4. The Raintree

Stay
5. Footprint B&B
6. Marina Inn
7. Taj Connemara

THE MARINA

📍 F3 🏠 Between Fort St George and San Thomé Basilica 🚇 Fort 🚌

Described as "one of the most beautiful marine promenades in the world", the Marina, which winds along the coast next to one of India's largest urban beaches, is the perfect spot to escape the humid heat of the city and enjoy the sea breezes.

The promenade connects Chennai's Fort St George with San Thomé Basilica. On one side is the beach; on the other, a haven of tree-lined cobbled streets and spectacular colonial and Indo-Saracenic buildings. At the northern end is the Anna Samadhi, a memorial erected in honour of CN Annadurai, the former chief minister of Tamil Nadu, who brought significant political and social reforms to the state. Further south is the MGR Samadhi, a commemorative garden with gateways and pathways, which was built in honour of MG Ramachandran, a popular Tamil film icon and politician. Across Kamarajar Salai is a series of imposing red-brick buildings, built in a combination of architectural styles. The idiosyncratic Senate House was designed by Robert Chisholm in a harmonized blend of Byzantine and Saracenic styles. Further south is the impressive *Triumph of Labour* statue by Debi Prasad Roy Chowdhary, who became the first Indian principal of the Madras School of Arts and Crafts in 1929. West of the main road, off Annie Besant Road, is the Ice House, a circular building with a stone pineapple perched on its roof that was once a storehouse for ice imported from the United States. An imposing lighthouse marks the southern end of the Marina.

1

1. The *Triumph of Labour* statue reimagines the famous *Raising the Flag on Iwo Jima* from World War II as a team of inspiring labourers.

2. The grandiose Ice House, which looks like an ornate and fanciful cruise ship, now hosts exhibitions.

3. A memorial bust of CN Annadurai, the former chief minister of Tamil Nadu, is known as Anna Samadhi and located in a garden.

2

3

← The Marina's expansive beach, and *(inset)* happy families strolling near the water

ROBERT CHISHOLM'S LEGACY

Robert Chisholm (1840–1915) was among the most talented architects in India in the 19th century. In 1864, his designs for the Senate House and Presidency College won a competition, and he was made consulting architect to the Madras government. The next 15 years saw considerable activity on the Marina, and many innovative buildings were erected. Chisholm's designs blended Italian and Saracenic features, harmonizing with Chepauk Palace, already on the Marina and former home of the nawabs. For many years he was the head of the School of Industrial Art, now the Government College of Fine Arts.

EXPERIENCE MORE

2

Fort St George

F2 **Bounded by North Beach Rd and EVR Rd**

This was Britain's first bastion in India. The nucleus from which its Indian empire grew was established in a banana grove owned by a farmer called Madrasan. The official grant for the land, however, was given by Venkatadri Nayak, the deputy of the Raja of Chandragiri. The first factory within the enclosure was completed on St George's Day, 23 April 1644, and named Fort St George. This was the East India Company's main settlement until 1772, when Calcutta, now Kolkata, was declared the seat of the government.

The sloping ramparts were designed by Bartholomew Robins in 1750, after the original walls were destroyed by the French army in 1749. These ramparts form an irregular pentagon, further reinforced by a ring of earthen walls that slope down to a moat surrounding the entire complex. The drawbridges that once led to the fort's five main gates have been replaced by roads. Most buildings in the fort have limited access; only St Mary's Church and the Fort Museum are open to the public.

The first building to be seen on entering the fort through the Sea Gate is the Neo-Classical Secretariat, which is today the seat of the government of Tamil Nadu. Behind it lie the Legislative Council Chambers. With their handsome Classical lines and façades embellished with gleaming black pillars, these impressive buildings (erected 1694–1732) are said to be among the oldest surviving British constructions in India. The 45-m- (148-ft-) tall flagstaff was erected by Governor Elihu Yale in 1687 to hoist the Union Jack for the first time in India. Today, the Indian tricolour flies in its stead. Yale began his career as a clerk with the East India Company and later founded Yale University in the USA.

Standing to the south of the Legislature building is St Mary's Church, the oldest

ROBERT CLIVE

One of British India's most flamboyant figures, Robert Clive was only 19 when he began his career as a clerk for the East India Company at Fort St George. Later he became a soldier and fought at the Carnatic Wars, which established the Company's rule in South India. Clive was given the stewardship of Fort St George and later become Governor of Bengal. The wealth he amassed in India led to his trial, in England, on charges of corruption. Clive committed suicide in 1774.

Airy gallery at the Fort Museum, and (inset) the museum building, in the former Public Exchange ↓

Anglican church in Asia. It was built between 1678 and 1680 by Streynsham Master, then the governor of Madras. Memorials, paintings, antique Bibles (including one printed in 1660) and silver are displayed in the church, and speak of its vibrant history. Both Elihu Yale and Robert Clive were married in this church, and the three daughters of Job Charnock, the man said to have founded Kolkata, were baptized here before the family moved to Bengal.

To the north is the Parade Ground, formerly Cornwallis Square, which was laid out in 1715. Magnificent parades and rallies were held here. To its east are ministerial offices, and barracks for regiments. Near the southeast corner of the Parade Ground is the **Fort Museum**. A treasure trove of colonial memorabilia, the museum is housed in what was built to be the Public Exchange. It has paintings of British royalty, 18th-century weaponry, emblems and other relics from the British era. Among its prized possessions are a scale model of the fort and a painting of King George III and Queen Charlotte. There are lithographs on the second and third floors that provide fascinating views into old Madras and other parts of south India.

Near the museum's southern end, and overlooking its cannon, is the Cornwallis Cupola, which originally stood in the Parade Ground. This large domed

↑ The distinctive Indo-Saracenic architecture of the High Court building, in George Town

pavilion was built to house the statue of the governor-general, Lord Cornwallis. Sculpted in 1800, it shows him accepting the two young sons of Tipu Sultan as hostages.

Fort Museum
☎ (044) 2567 1127 ⏰ 10am–5pm Sat–Thu 🚫 Public hols

3

George Town

📍 E1 🏛 Bounded by Rajaji Salai (North Beach Rd) and NSC Bose Rd

In the 1640s, weavers and dyers from Andhra Pradesh were settled in this enclave to manufacture cloth for the East India Company's textile trade. The British referred to the settlement as "Black Town", while its inhabitants called it Chennapatnam, from where Chennai gets it name. When the entire area was rebuilt 100 years later, it was renamed George Town. During this time, most of the city's commercial activity was concentrated within this 5-sq-km (2-sq-mile) area. It still remains a busy hive of activity with public institutions in the south, trade and commercial premises in the centre, and residential quarters in the north.

The red-brick High Court, designed by Robert Chisholm in the Indo-Saracenic style, with stained glass and carved furniture, was opened in 1892. The nearby General Post Office, with its archways and square towers, is another fine Indo-Saracenic building.

Parry's Corner, at the junction of NSC Bose Road and Rajaji Salai, is named after Parry and Company. Founded by Thomas Parry in 1788, it is the oldest British mercantile company still operating in Chennai.

Today, each street in George Town is dominated by a particular trade. The area's longest street, Mint Street, gets its name from the authorized mint that was set up here in 1841 to produce gold coins. The mint buildings are now part of the government printing press. The 17th-century houses lining George Town were once the residences and business centres of Indian, as well as Portuguese, Armenian and other foreign, traders. Armenian Street is named after the many Armenians who lived here, while Coral Merchant Street housed a small Jewish community that traded in corals. Anderson Street specializes in paper, grain merchants operate from Audiappa Naicken Street, and textile wholesalers have their warehouses on Govindappa Naicken Street and Godown Street. Kasi Chetty Street and Narayanamudali Street are lined with shops selling imported bric-a-brac.

💬 INSIDER TIP
Nadi Astrology Reading

If you fancy a glimpse into your future, look for a practitioner of ancient Nadi astrology during your time in Chennai. A select few astrologers define personality traits and predict your future using palm leaves.

4
St Andrew's Kirk

9 D2 **🚇** Egmore
🕐 Daily; services at
6am, 9am & 6pm Sun
🌐 thekirk.in

A magnificent Neo-Classical church, St Andrew's Kirk was consecrated in 1821. Inspired by St Martin-in-the-Fields in London, it was designed by Major Thomas de Havilland and Colonel James Caldwell of the Madras Engineers. The body of the church is a circle, with rectangular compartments to the east and west. The circular part is topped by a dome coloured a deep blue, painted with golden stars and supported by 16 pillars.

5
Egmore

9 D2 **🚇** Bounded by Periyar EVR High Rd and Pantheon Rd **ℹ** Egmore Railway Station; (044) 2819 4579

The entire area south of Periyar EVR High Road and the curve of the Cooum river is known as Egmore. Originally a small village acquired by the East India Company in the late 17th century, Egmore was also an early residential locality, where wealthy Company merchants built palatial homes surrounded by lush and luxurious gardens.

The Government College of Arts and Crafts, founded in 1850, stands on EVK Sampath Salai. This striking Gothic building and its art gallery were built by Robert Fellowes Chisholm, who was also appointed its superintendent (principal) in 1877. Today the college is one of India's foremost art schools. Its gallery puts on regular exhibitions of contemporary painting and sculpture by artists and students.

To its west is the Egmore Railway Station, another of Chisholm's architectural gems. It was constructed in Indo-Saracenic style, with unconventional flattish domes and pointed arches.

Today Egmore is the upmarket commercial heart of Chennai, a concrete jungle of offices, department stores, boutiques and hotels.

> ### Did You Know?
>
> The Royal Enfield bullet motorcycle is an iconic image of India – and it is made in Chennai.

EAT

Amethyst
This peaceful garden café rustles up international fare such as bangers and mash.

9 D3 **🚇** White's Rd
🌐 amethystchennai.com

₹₹₹

Annalakshmi
Profits from this Sivananda restaurant with Ayurvedic menus go to the community.

9 D2 **🚇** 18/3 Rukhmani Lakshmipathy Rd
📞 (044) 2852 5109

₹₹₹

Ente Keralam
A Keralan restaurant offering delights such as *karimeen pollichattu* (backwater fish).

9 D3 **🚇** 1 Kasturi Estate, Poes Garden
🌐 entekeralam.in

₹₹₹

The Raintree
Dine on expertly prepared Chettinad fare, bursting with the taste of tamarind.

9 D2 **🚇** Taj Connemara Hotel, Binny Rd
🌐 tajhotels.com

₹₹₹

↑ The distinctive Indo-Saracenic architecture of Egmore Railway Station

SHIVA, THE COSMIC DANCER

Bronze sculptures depicting gods and goddesses are the glory of south Indian art. Strict iconographic guidelines determine the proportions of each image and the symbolic meaning of every stance, hand gesture, weapon and adornment. Master sculptors working within these rules were able to create images of individuality, power and grace. Among the most remarkable sculptures are those of Shiva as Nataraja, and his wife Parvati.

The sculpture below represents Shiva as Nataraja, the Cosmic Dancer, who symbolizes the cycle of evolution and transmutation. There are a number of Nataraja figures in the Government Museum *(p496)*, which were made during the Chola period, from the 9th to the 13th centuries.

↑ A bronze sculpture depicting the marriage of Shiva and Parvati

An open palm grants freedom from fear.

Ganga is shown among Shiva's flying locks, as he eased her descent to earth.

A tiny crescent moon, a symbol of the passage of time, balances in Shiva's hair.

The drum in his right hand shows the rhythm of creation.

The fire in the left hand represents destruction.

The ring of flames symbolizes the cosmos.

The left palm pointing to the foot symbolizes salvation from ignorance.

The left leg is lifted up in an animated dance movement.

The right leg tramples Apasmara, who stands in for ignorance.

→ A spectacular scupture of Shiva, represented here as Nataraja

6 Government Museum Complex

D2 **Pantheon Rd** **9:30am–5pm Sat–Thu** **govtmuseumchennai.org**

This complex of cultural institutions housed the Public Assembly Rooms in the 18th century, but now has some of Chennai's best museums.

The Indo-Saracenic Government Museum, with its faded red walls and labyrinth of staircases and galleries, spreads over five sections, each with a specific collection of objects. The 30,000-odd exhibits range from rocks and fossils to books and sculptures.

The Archaeological Section, in the main building, is noted for its collection of south Indian antiquities, including stone and metal sculpture, woodcarvings and manuscripts. Its rare collection of Buddhist antiquities numbers over 1,500 pieces. A major section comprises artifacts from Amravati (*p580*), that were brought here in the early 1800s by Colonel Colin Mackenzie. On display are sculptural reliefs, panels and free-standing statues. Objects include a 2nd-century votive slab with a rendering of a stupa, and numerous stone panels with momentous episodes from the Buddha's life depicted in low relief.

The Numismatics Section has a large collection of coins, particularly south Indian and Mughal ones. There are also some gold Gupta coins with Sanskrit inscriptions.

The Anthropology Section, in the front building, has a good collection of prehistoric antiquities, including cooking implements and hunting tools, among them the first stone utensil, or palaeolith, in India, discovered in 1863 by Bruce Foote. The Zoological Section, in the main building, is one of the largest sections of the museum. Although its scope is limited to south Indian fauna, a few non-indigenous animals and birds, such as the macaw, mandarin duck and golden pheasant, have been added to enrich the collection. There is also an 18.5-m- (61-ft-) long whale skeleton on display. The adjoining Museum Theatre, a semi-circular structure also built in Indo-Saracenic style, hosts public performances.

Some of the finest examples of south Indian bronze casting are on display in the Bronze Gallery. Its superb collection of almost 700 bronzes, specifically from the Pallava and Chola periods – a period when local artisans and arts flourished between the 9th and 13th centuries – have been retrieved from temples and sites in the region. There are also many impressive sculptures of the Nataraja, which is the depiction of Shiva performing his cosmic dance of creation (*p495*). Another outstanding piece is an 11th-century Chola Ardhanarisvara, a composite figure with Shiva and his consort Parvati joined together to form a holistic

← A gallery displaying the Government Museum's collection of bronzes

STAY

Footprint B&B
In a classy apartment block, Footprint blends Indian and European styles in its rooms.

D4 **Off TTK Rd** **footprint.in**

₹₹₹

Marina Inn
Conveniently located near Egmore Station, this modern hotel offers compact rooms and a global restaurant.

D2 **55/31 Gandhi Irwin Rd** **marinainn.in**

₹₹₹

Taj Connemara
Rooms at this wonderful Raj-era building have Victorian decor and verandahs looking across the pool.

D2 **Binny Rd** **tajhotels.com**

₹₹₹

↑ Vehicles driving past colourful movie posters along Anna Salai, Chennai's main shopping street

entity. Bronzes of other gods and goddesses in the Hindu pantheon, including Rama, Sita and Ganesha, also make up part of the collection here. Aside from Hindu gods, the museum displays various Buddhist bronzes from Amravati, a Chola Tara and Maitreya Avalokitesvara, and 11th-century images of various Jain *tirthankaras*.

Opposite is the imposing **Connemara Public Library**, inaugurated in 1896. This structure, with its profuse stucco decoration, woodwork and stained-glass windows, is one of India's four national libraries and contains every book published in the country. Its most prized possession is a Bible, dated 1608.

The **National Art Gallery** is perhaps the finest building in the complex. Designed by Henry Irwin, it was constructed in 1909 in Neo-Mughal style with a pink sandstone finish. Its immense door echoes the monumental gateways of Fatehpur Sikri *(p170)*. The collection offers more Chola

bronzes, including two fantastic images of Rama and Sita, and a superb 11th-century Nataraja.

Nearby, the Contemporary Art Gallery has works by south Indian artists, including Raja Ravi Varma.

Connemara Public Library
☎ (044) 2819 3751 ⏰ 8am-8pm daily ⏳ Public hols

National Art Gallery
☎ (044) 2533 3444
⏰ 9:30am-5pm Sat-Thu

Anna Salai

📍 D2 🅰 From Cooum Island to Little Mount

Leading from north Chennai to Little Mount at its southern end, Anna Salai (or Mount Road) is the city's main thoroughfare, a modern commercial stretch lined with hoardings depicting film stars and multistoreyed buildings. Anna Salai begins on an island

in Cooum Creek, just south of Fort St George. The site is watched over by the statue of Sir Thomas Munro, governor of the Madras Presidency from 1819 to 1827. Nearby, in an expanse of greenery, is the prestigious Gymkhana Club. Until 1920, its membership was restricted to garrison officers only, and, even today, the club grounds belong to the armed services.

The Old Government Estate, southwest of the Gymkhana Club, houses the mansion where the governors of Madras once lived in regal splendour. Though the main building is falling apart, its banqueting hall, built in 1802 and modelled after a Greek temple, retains its grandeur – and has been visited by numerous luminaries. Named **Rajaji Hall** after the first Indian governor-general, C Rajagopalachari, popularly known as Rajaji, the vast hall has beautiful panelling and chandeliers.

Anna Salai then enters its commercial stretch, with some of the city's oldest commercial landmarks, including one of India's largest bookshops, Higginbotham's, Spencer's, an international department store, and the Taj Connemara, one of the city's finest hotels.

Further south is St George's Cathedral, planned by James Lillyman Caldwell and built by Thomas de Havilland in 1814. Its distinctive 42-m-(138-ft-) tall spire is one of Chennai's major landmarks.

Rajaji Hall
☎ (044) 2533 3635

💬 INSIDER TIP
Walking Tours

For a fascinating glimpse into local history, lore and cuisine, take a walking tour of areas such as George Town or Mylapore. For details, contact Storytrails *(www.storytrails.in)*.

8

Triplicane

E3 **Off Kamarajar Salai (South Beach Rd)**

This crowded suburb, one of the first villages acquired by the British East India Company in the 1670s, derives its name from the sacred lily tank *(tiru-alli-keni)* that once stood here. One of the main sites is the historic **Parthasarathi Temple**, which was built in the 9th century and dedicated to Krishna (or Partha) in his role as Arjuna's divine charioteer *(sarathi)* in the epic, the *Mahabharata*. The temple festival, in December, attracts thousands of devotees.

At one time, the residences of the priestly Brahmin caste were clustered in the narrow lanes around the temple. Among them were the homes of the mathematical genius Srinivasa Ramanujan (1887–1920) and the early-20th-century nationalist poet Subramania Bharati (1882–1921). Triplicane was once part of the kingdom of Golconda, and as a result this quarter has the largest concentration of Muslims in the city. The Nawab of Arcot, Muhammad Ali Wallajah (r1749–95), an ally of the British in their struggle for power against the French, contributed generously to the construction of a large mosque here in 1795. Known as the Wallajah (Big) Mosque, this beautiful grey granite structure with graceful, slender minarets sits on Triplicane High Road. The adjoining graveyard contains the tombs of various Muslim saints.

Parthasarathi Temple
Sunrise–sunset daily

↑ Under the canopy of the 450-year-old banyan tree in the grounds of the Theosophical Society, Adyar

9

Adyar

D5 **S of San Thomé, across Adyar river**

Named after the river that flows through it, Adyar is one of Chennai's most rarefied areas – and few places in the city offer greater serenity than the sprawling gardens of the **Theosophical Society**, an organization that professes the unity of all humankind. Founded in New York in 1875, the society moved here seven years later, when it acquired Huddlestone Gardens on the banks of the Adyar river. Built in 1776 by John Huddlestone, a wealthy civilian, this large mansion is today the headquarters of the society. Its magnificent 108-ha (268-acre) estate comprises several 19th-century buildings, one of which was the home of its founder, Colonel Henry S Olcott.

The main building houses the Great Hall, almost spartan in its simplicity, where prayer meetings are held. Bas-reliefs, representing different faiths, and engravings of verses taken from the holy books of all world religions can be seen here. There are also marble statues of the founders, Colonel Olcott and Helena Petrovna Blavatsky, as well as one of Annie Besant, who became president in 1907. The Adyar Library and Research

Centre, founded here by Olcott in 1886, is one of the finest libraries in India. Its collection of 165,000 books and 20,000 palm-leaf and parchment manuscripts has made it a valuable repository for Indological research. The surrounding tranquil gardens have shrines dedicated to various faiths. The greatest attraction here, however, is the 450-year-old banyan tree, whose spreading branches cover an immense area of 4,180 sq m (44,993 sq ft). Over the decades, many of the society's meetings and spiritual discourses were held under its canopy. In 1989, unfortunately, a terrible storm destroyed its main trunk.

Brodie Castle, north of the Theosophical Society, is an imposing white structure on the banks of the Adyar. Now known as Thencral, it houses the prestigious Government Music College. Built in 1796 by James Brodie, an employee of the East India Company, it is said to be among the first

INSIDER TIP
Besant Nagar

The area around the spacious grounds of the Theosophical Society, in the quiet suburb of Besant Nagar (named after Annie Besant), is full of lovely cafés and interesting little boutiques.

"garden-houses" built in the city. These spacious, airy houses with broad pillared verandahs, set in sprawling wooded gardens, were typical of colonial Chennai.

Further north of Brodie Castle is the Madras Club, built by George Moubray, who came to India as an accountant in 1771. He acquired 42 ha (104 acres) of land on the banks of the Adyar, and built a house with a central cupola, surrounded by a beautiful garden. Known as Moubray's Cupola, this was once the exclusive preserve of the city's European population. Indians were only allowed membership in 1964, after the Madras Club merged with the Adyar Club.

Theosophical Society
📞 (044) 2491 2474
🕐 8:30-10am & 2-4pm Mon-Fri & Sat am

🔟
Mylapore and San Thomé

📍 E4 🚇 S of Triplicane

The site of the great port of the Pallavas in the 7th and 8th centuries, Mylapore is today one of the busiest parts of the city. This traditional quarter, with its religious organizations, tiny houses and lively bazaars, is dominated by the **Kapaleeswarar Temple**, the largest in Chennai. The main deity, Shiva, is symbolized as

a peacock (mayii), thus giving the area its original name, Mayilapura, the "Town of the Peacocks". According to legend, Shiva's consort, Parvati, assumed the form of a peahen to worship Shiva, represented here by his linga. A sculptural panel in a small shrine in the courtyard depicts the legend. The present temple was built after the original was destroyed by the Portuguese in the 16th century.

Mylapore's links with Christianity date to the 1st century AD, to the time of St Thomas, one of the apostles. In the 10th century, a group of Nestorian Christians from Persia (Iran) discovered the saint's burial site and built a church and tomb here. The Portuguese, also following the trail of the saint, established the settlement of San Thomé in the early 16th century. The present **Basilica of San Thomé**, built over the tomb of the saint, is a Gothic-style structure from 1898. It has an ornate interior with stained-glass windows and a towering steeple. The crypt is said to contain a small bone from the saint's hand and the weapon that killed him. Nearby, the Luz Church, built in 1516 by a Franciscan monk, is the oldest Catholic church in Chennai.

Kapaleeswarar Temple
🕐 5am-noon & 4-9pm daily

Basilica of San Thomé
🕐 Sunrise-sunset daily

← The Wallajah (Big) Mosque, built in the late 18th century in Triplicane

↑ Praying under a banyan tree at Kalakshetra, and (inset) dancers practising Bharat Natyam moves

⑪ Kalakshetra

⊙ A3 ⌂ Thiruvanmiyur, East Coast Rd 🚌 ⏰ 8:30–11:30am Mon-Sat 🔒 College hols 🌐 kalakshetra.in

This pioneering institution for classical dance, music and the fine arts, established in 1936, was the brainchild of Rukmini Devi. A protégée of Annie Besant (p498), she was deeply influenced by the progressive views of the Theosophical Society (p498). At 16, she scandalized conservative society by marrying George Sydney Arundale, the 40-year-old Australian principal of the society's school. The couple's travels exposed Rukmini to Western culture, especially dance, inspiring her to study ballet under the great Russian ballerina Anna Pavlova. Back in Chennai, she again defied tradition by learning and performing the classical *dasi attam*, hitherto the domain of *devadasis* (temple dancers). The International Centre for the Arts, which she set up for the revival of this dance form, now called Bharat Natyam, is today Kalakshetra, which means the "Temple of Art".

⑫ ✎ Guindy National Park

⊙ C5 ⌂ S Chennai, Sardar Vallabhbhai Patel Rd 🚇 Guindy 🚌 ⏰ 9am–5:30pm Wed-Mon ℹ www.tamilnadutourism.org/wildlife/wildlifemain.aspx

Once a distant suburb, Guindy has been engulfed by the fast-growing metropolis of Greater Chennai. Originally part of the private forest surrounding Guindy Lodge, a portion was officially declared the Guindy National Park in 1977. This mainly dry deciduous scrub jungle of acacia is interspersed with larger trees such as sandalwood (*Santalam album*), banyan (*Ficus bengalensis*) and jamun (*Syzygium cumini*). Its most famous residents are the herds of endangered blackbuck (*Antelope cervicapra*), introduced in 1924. Among its 130 species of birds are raptors such as the honey buzzard and the white-bellied sea eagle. Winter is the best time for bird-watching, when migrant birds visit the forest. A children's park and play area at the northeast corner has a collection of animals and birds. Also within the park is the Madras Snake Park, established in the 1970s by the American zoologist Romulus Whitaker. Today, the park houses king cobras, vipers and pythons, as well as crocodiles, turtles and lizards. Large boards provide information on the habitat and behaviour of the various species. For those who are interested, there are live

> **The couple's travels exposed Rukmini to Western culture, especially dance, inspiring her to study ballet under the great Russian ballerina Anna Pavlova.**

demonstrations of venom extraction; the venom is used as an antidote for snake bites.

The historic 300-year-old Guindy Lodge, to the west of the Park, is now the Raj Bhavan, the residence of the governor of Tamil Nadu. Built as a weekend retreat for the city's British rulers, this handsome white building was renovated and expanded in the mid-1800s by the then governor Grant-Duff.

13

Little Mount and Mount of St Thomas

C5 **SW Chennai Near Marmalog Bridge** **St Thomas Mount station**

A rock-hewn cave on Little Mount is believed to be the place where, in AD 72, the mortally wounded St Thomas, who had been called to India to spread Christianity, sought refuge. Near the modern Church of Our Lady of Good Health is the older Blessed Sacrament Chapel, built by the Portuguese over the cave. Inside the cave is the opening through which the fleeing saint is said to have retreated, leaving behind a still visible imprint of his hand near the entrance. At the rear end of the cave is the Masonry Cross before which St Thomas is said to have prayed. By the Church of the Resurrection is a perennial spring with curative powers. Legend claims that the spring originated when St Thomas struck the rock with his staff to provide water for his thirsty congregation.

About 3 km (2 miles) south-west of Little Mount is the 95-m- (312-ft-) high Mount of St Thomas or Great Mount. A flight of 132 steps leads to the summit and the Church of Our Lady of Expectations, built by the Portuguese in the 16th century. The most important relic here is the ancient stone cross that is embedded into the wall of the altar. Said to have been engraved by the saint himself, this is the legendary "bleeding cross" that miraculously bled between 1558 and 1704.

Below the eastern flank of the Mount is the Cantonment area, with its shady streets lined with 18th-century Neo-Classical bungalows.

14

Dakshina Chitra

A3 **Chingleput district; 26 km (16 miles) S of Chennai** **10am-6pm Wed-Mon** **dakshinachitra.net**

This heritage village, on the Coromandel Coast, provides a fascinating glimpse into the homes and lifestyles of the people of south India. The village features reconstructions of traditional houses, including, so far, five from Tamil Nadu, four from Kerala, two from Andhra Pradesh and two from Karnataka. The handsome Chettiar mansion (*p522*) on view, with its elaborately carved wooden door, reflects the wealth of the Chettiar merchant community, while the homes of priests, farmers, weavers and potters are simple yet elegant structures. Within the complex is an Ayyanar shrine and an open courtyard, where folk and classical dance performances and craft demonstrations are held.

ST THOMAS IN INDIA

According to legend, St Thomas, one of the 12 apostles, came to south India after Jesus died to spread the Gospel. It is said that one day in AD 72, while praying, he was mortally wounded by a lance, and fled to Little Mount, where he died. His body was carried to San Thomé, where he was buried in the crypt of the small chapel he had built. This is today the Basilica of San Thomé. The saint holds a special place in the hearts of Indians, and was decreed the Apostle of India in 1972.

↑ Artifacts on display in one of the houses in the heritage village of Dakshina Chitra

Watching the sun rise over Thiruvalluvar Statue at Kanyakumari

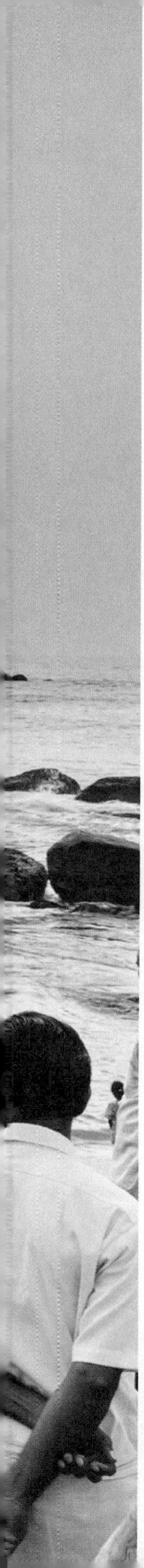

TAMIL NADU

A soulful state awash with religious cities and temples, Tamil Nadu was the cradle of ancient Dravidian culture, whose language forms the basis of many of the main south Indian languages today. It extends from the Coromandel Coast in the east to the forested Western Ghats in the west, and at its heart is the fertile Kaveri valley, a land of rice fields and spectacular temples. This valley was the site of ancient Cholamandalam, where the Chola kings built magnificent temples at Thanjavur and championed a renaissance of religious Hindu art, particularly sculptures.

Many towns in Tamil Nadu have the prefix "tiru", which means sacred, and indicates the presence of a major religious site. Great temples stand at Madurai and Chidambaram, which witnessed a flourishing of dance, music and literature under their enlightened rulers, as did the 7th-century port-city of Mamallapuram, which has spectacular rock-cut temples. Unlike many states, Tamil Nadu was subject to both French and British colonial forces – the French ruled in Puducherry from the 17th century, and Tamil Nadu's capital Chennai was one of the most important cities for first the British East India Company and then the Raj.

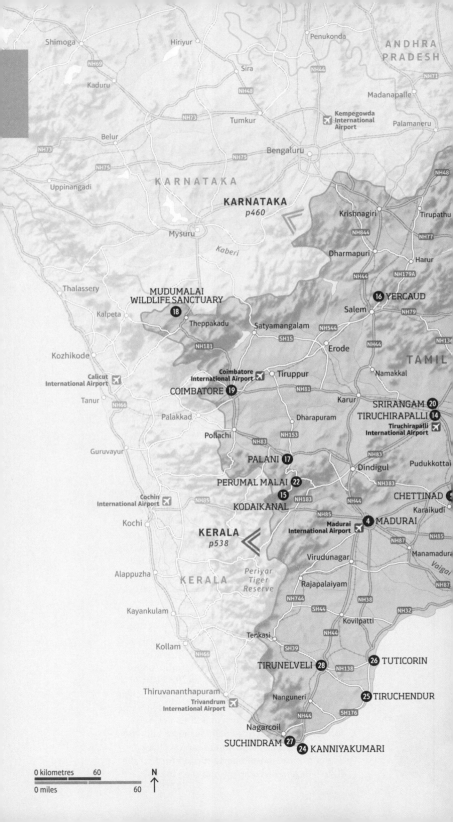

ANDHRA PRADESH
AND TELANGANA
p564

Chennai
Chennai
International Airport

⑩ VELLORE
⑧ KANCHIPURAM
Chengalpattu

① MAMALLAPURAM

TIRUVANNAMALAI
⑦ ⑥
GINGEE
FORT
Tindivanam

② PUDUCHERRY

Cuddalore

Kiranur

⑨ CHIDAMBARAM

N A D U
⑪ GANGAIKONDA CHOLAPURAM

KUMBAKONAM ⑬
Karaikal

⑫ TIRUVAIYARU
③ THANJAVUR
Nagappattinam

Kollidam

Adirampattinam

Palk Strait

Jaffna

Tondi

㉑ RAMANATHAPURAM
㉓
RAMESHVARAM
Mankulam

Mannar

Anuradhapura

S R I
L A N K A

Puttalam

TAMIL
NADU

TAMIL NADU

Must Sees
① Mamallapuram
② Puducherry
③ Thanjavur
④ Madurai
⑤ Chettinad

Experience More
⑥ Gingee Fort
⑦ Tiruvannamalai
⑧ Kanchipuram
⑨ Chidambaram
⑩ Vellore
⑪ Gangaikonda Cholapuram
⑫ Tiruvaiyaru
⑬ Kumbakonam
⑭ Tiruchirapalli
⑮ Kodaikanal
⑯ Yercaud
⑰ Palani
⑱ Mudumalai Wildlife Sanctuary
⑲ Coimbatore
⑳ Srirangam
㉑ Ramanathapuram
㉒ Perumal Malai
㉓ Rameshvaram
㉔ Kanniyakumari
㉕ Tiruchendur
㉖ Tuticorin
㉗ Suchindram
㉘ Tirunelveli

❶ MAMALLAPURAM

📍 **Kanchipuram district; 58 km (36 miles) S of Chennai** 🚌
ℹ **Covelong Rd; www.tamilnadutourism.org**

This coastal town was a major port city during the 7th century, and the spectacular and well-preserved rock-cut caves, monolithic shrines, structural temples and huge bas-reliefs from this period are the main reason people come to Mamallapuram– although there is a growing surfing community attracted by the waves.

① 🖐
Shore Temple

🕐 **Sunrise– sunset daily**

The spectacular Shore Temple, perched dramatically on a promontory by the sea, has survived the ravages of time. It was built by Mamalla for Vishnu, while the two Shiva shrines were added by Mamalla's successor Narasimha Varman II, more popularly known as Raja Simha. The temple has a low boundary wall, with rows of seated Nandis surrounding it. Placed inside are a reclining Vishnu, a 16-faceted polished linga and reliefs of Somaskanda – a composite form of Shiva with his consort Parvati and sons.

②
Bhagiratha's Penance

🕐 **Sunrise– sunset daily**

In the village centre is the bas-relief Bhagiratha's Penance, also known as Arjuna's Penance, or the Descent of the Ganges. Carved on a large rock with a natural vertical cleft, symbolizing the Ganges, the panel depicts in great detail the story of the sacred river's descent from the sky. This divine act, made possible by the penance of the sage Bhagiratha, is witnessed on the panel by celestial beings, ascetics and animals. The symbolism is best understood during the monsoon, when rainwater flows down the cleft and collects in the tank below.

Nearby are the unfinished Panch Pandava Cave Temple and Krishna's Butter Ball, a natural boulder perched precariously on a slope.

South of Bhagiratha's Penance is the Krishna Mandapa, a huge bas-relief showing the god lifting Mount Govardhan to protect the people from torrential rains, as well as performing his tasks as a cowherd. The Olakkanatha Temple, above the *mandapa*, was once used as a lighthouse.

← Sculpted monkeys on Bhagiratha's Penance

← Dusk falling on the Shore Temple, set in a dramatic location by the sea

The Trimurti Cave Temple, northwest of Bhagiratha's Penance, is dedicated to Shiva, Vishnu and Somaskanda. The shrines are guarded by statues of graceful doorkeepers. A sculpture of Durga standing on Mahisha's head is on an outer wall.

The two-storeyed Ganesha Ratha, further south, is attributed to Parameshvara Varman I (r 669–90). The temple, which was originally dedicated to Shiva, has beautifully carved inscriptions listing the royal titles of Parameshvara Varman.

③ Cave Temples

🕐 Sunrise–sunset daily

Near Bhagiratha's Penance are three cave temples. The Mahishasuramardini Cave Temple has a graceful portrayal of Goddess Durga on her lion mount, subduing the buffalo-headed demon Mahisha, on the northern wall. This movement-filled panel contrasts with the one on the southern wall, where Vishnu reclines in deep meditation before creating the earth. Nearby, the Varaha or Adi Varaha Cave Temple has beautifully moulded lion pillars, while the relief sculptures of Lakshmi, Durga and Varaha, the boar incarnation of Vishnu, are among the masterpieces of Pallava art.

> 🔍 HIDDEN GEM
> ### The Cat of Bhagiratha's Penance
> Look closely at the Bhagiratha's Penance bas-relief: there is a cheeky upright cat figure surrounded by mice, parodying the pose of the sage.

④
Archaeological Museum

📍 West Raja St 🕐 10am–5pm daily

This small museum displays a diverse assortment of sculptures and fragments excavated from the site.

Must See

STAY

Green Woods Resort
This friendly guesthouse is spread around a leafy courtyard.
📍 12 Othavadai Cross St
📞 (044) 2744 3318
₹₹₹

Mamallaa Heritage
Enjoy air-conditioned rooms, a swimming pool and a top restaurant.
📍 104 East Raja St
📞 9840260672
₹₹₹

Radisson Blu Resort Temple Bay
All rooms and chalets have a patio or balcony.
📍 57 Kovalam Rd
🌐 radissonblu.com
₹₹₹

⑤ 🏛 🏯

PANCH RATHAS

📍 1.5 km (1 mile) S of Mamallapuram village 🕐 6am–6pm daily
ℹ Covelong Rd; www.tamilnadutourism.org

The 7th-century complex of monolithic rock-cut shrines known as the Panch Rathas forms part of the UNESCO World Heritage Site at Mamallapuram, a remarkable ancient city built by Pallava king, Narasimha Varma I. These shrines, along with the rest of the city, are considered the greatest examples of Pallava art.

The Panch Rathas (five processional temple chariots) are named after the five Pandava brothers, heroes of the epic *Mahabharata*, and their queen and common wife, Draupadi. While the Panch Rathas have no connection to the famous epic, the name has stuck. Each structure here is shaped like a temple chariot and crafted from a single huge boulder, and contains the shrine of a different Hindu god.

The Panch Rathas are unfinished, and are believed to have never been consecrated as shrines – supposedly as Narasimha Varma I died before they could be completed. Yet, these buildings (still commonly referred to as temples) are a tribute to the genius of the stone-cutters who carved these large boulders in situ. In an ambitious experiment, the styles and techniques of wooden architecture were imitated in stone, to create a variety of forms that later influenced south Indian temple design. The stone elephant next to the Nakul Sahdeva Ratha is particularly spectacular.

Did You Know?

The Panch Rathas survived being battered by a tsunami in the 13th century and in 2004.

The two-storeyed temple of Arjuna Ratha has a graceful portrayal of Shiva leaning on his mount, the bull Nandi. Royal couples and other elegantly carved figures in the niches embellish the outer walls.

Nandi, carved out of a single rock, faces the Arjuna Ratha.

A four-armed Durga is carved on the rear wall of Draupadi Ratha, with kneeling devotees in front. One of these is shown in the process of cutting his head off, as an act of self-sacrifice.

Draupadi Ratha, a stone replica of a thatched tribal shrine, is the smallest ratha of the group.

The standing lion – Durga's mount – is placed in front of the Draupadi Ratha.

The spectacular temples of Panch Rathas, shaped like temple chariots →

Dharmaraja Ratha, an imposing three-storeyed ratha, is crowned by an octagonal domed roof.

The Pallava king Narasimha Varman I, the patron of this complex, is shown wearing a crown, a silk garment and jewellery.

> **INSIDER TIP**
> **Stone Souvenirs**
>
> This is a region long famous for its stone sculptures – plan to visit towards the end of your tour of Tamil Nadu in order to stock up on stone carvings from the many artisans' stalls around the village.

Niche figures on the lower level include beautiful sculptures of Harihara, a composite form of Vishnu and Shiva.

The gigantic Bhima Ratha has a barrel-vaulted roof and unfinished lower level, and is named after the brother famed for his strength.

← An overview of the unfinished Panch Rathas temples

Named jointly after the Pandava twins, Nakul Sahdeva Ratha is unique for its gajaprishta form, which looks like the back of an elephant.

↑ A stone carving of the goddess Ganga, representing the Ganges

2

PUDUCHERRY

⌖ 160 km (99 miles) S of Chennai ⛟🚌 ℹ Goubert Salai; www.pondytourism.in

The former capital of French territories in India, Puducherry is laid out in a grid pattern. Its main promenade, Goubert Salai, runs along the Bay of Bengal, and forms part of the French Quarter, with its elegant mansions, leafy boulevards, parks and cafés.

①

Puducherry Museum

⌖ 49 Rue St Louis
☏ (0413) 233 6203 (Director Art & Culture) 🕐 10am–5pm Tue–Sun

Located in the lovely old Law Building, near Government Park, the Puducherry Museum has an outstanding collection of artifacts from the French colonial period. The museum also displays rare bronzes and stone sculptures from the Pallava and Chola periods. Among the artifacts excavated from nearby Arikamedu, an ancient port that had trade links with Imperial Rome, are amphorae, coins, oil lamps, funerary urns and fragments of pottery and china. Inside the same compound is the

Romain Rolland Library, set up in 1872. It has a collection of more than 300,000 volumes, including many rare editions. The reference section, on the second floor of the library, is open to the public.

Romain Rolland Library
☏ (0413) 233 6426 🕐 9am–12:30pm & 4-7pm daily

②

Basilica of the Sacred Heart of Jesus

⌖ South Boulevard 🕐 Daily

A serene atmosphere cloaks this 18th-century Neo-Gothic basilica, which has stained-glass panels depicting the life of Jesus Christ, and handsome arches spanning the nave.

③ 🔖

Botanical Gardens

⌖ South Boulevard
🕐 10am–5pm daily

Designed in the formal French style, the Botanical Gardens has over 1,500 species of

---

EAT

La Terrasse
This restaurant, with its pleasant courtyard, is renowned for its prawn dishes, pizzas and quality coffee.

⌖ 5 South Boulevard
☏ 0413 234 1430

₹₹₹

Madame Shantés
Lively rooftop restaurant offering a range of delicious Indian, Chinese and French dishes.

⌖ 40A Rue Romain Rolland
☏ 0413 222 2022

₹₹₹

←

The colourful Basilica of
the Sacred Heart of Jesus
in the French Quarter

plants, including unusual trees
and shrubs from all over India.
An aquarium displays some
spectacular marine species
from the Coromandel Coast.

SRI AUROBINDO GHOSE

The Bengali poet-philosopher Aurobindo Ghose, who
joined the struggle for freedom in the early 1900s, was
known for his extremist views. To escape from the
British, he took refuge in French Puducherry, where he
studied, wrote about and popularized the principles of
yoga. His disciple, Parisian Mirra Alfassa, known later
as The Mother, came to the town during World War I. Sri
Aurobindo's philosophy so inspired her that she stayed
on and helped set up the ashram.

④
House of Ananda Rangapillai

🏠 109 Rangapillai St
☎ (0413) 233 5756 for appt
🕐 10am–6pm daily

This lavishly furnished house
was once the home of 18th-
century Indian nobleman
Ananda Rangapillai, French
Governor-General Dupleix's
favourite courtier and dubash
(translator). Now a museum, it
offers a fascinating glimpse
into a vanished lifestyle.

⑤
École Française d'Extrême-Orient

🏠 16 & 19 Rue Dumas
☎ (0413) 233 2504
🕐 Mon–Sat

The 19th-century École
Française d'Extrême-Orient is
noted for its research in Asian
history, archaeology and soci-
ology, and holds exhibitions.

⑥
Aurobindo Ashram

🏠 Rue de la Marine ☎ (0413)
223 3604 🕐 8am–6pm daily

Puducherry's best-known
landmark, the Aurobindo
Ashram was founded by Sri
Aurobindo in 1926. Set around
tree-shaded courtyards, it
is a peaceful retreat with a
flower-festooned memorial of
Sri Aurobindo and The Mother,
Mirra Alfassa, his spiritual
collaborator, in the garden.

⑦
Auroville

🏠 8 km (5 miles) NW of
Puducherry 🌐 auroville.org

Designed by French architect
Roger Anger in 1968, Auroville
was conceived by Mirra Alfassa
as a futuristic global city where
people from different castes,
religions and nations could
live together in harmony. Today
there are 550 residents living
in Auroville's International
Commune, which is overseen
by a foundation. The com-
mune has 40 settlements with
names such as Grace, Serenity
and Certitude; two of these,
Fraternité and Harmonie, sell
handicrafts made by locals.
The centre of the community
is the golden Matri Mandir, a
spherical meditation centre. It
has a marble chamber with a
crystal placed inside it that
reflects the sun's rays. The
light acts as a focal point to
aid meditation.

Did You Know?

Indira Gandhi was
introduced to Mirra
Alfassa in 1955, and
the Mother considered
her a "blessed child".

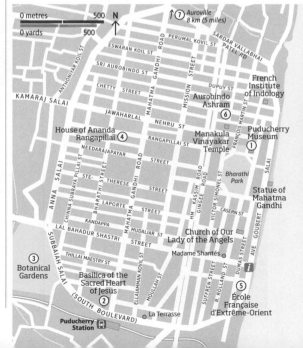

A SHORT WALK
PUDUCHERRY

Distance 2 km (1 mile) **Nearest Station** Puducherry
Time 25 minutes

The former capital of French territories in India, Puducherry was established in 1674 by François Martin, the first director of the French East India Company. The town is laid out in a grid pattern, with parallel streets cutting across each other at right angles. Its main promenade, the 3-km- (2-mile-) long Goubert Salai running along the Bay of Bengal, formed part of the French Quarter, with its elegant colonial mansions, tree-lined boulevards, parks, bars and cafés. Beyond this was a canal, now dry, that demarcated the Tamil Town, where the local populace once lived.

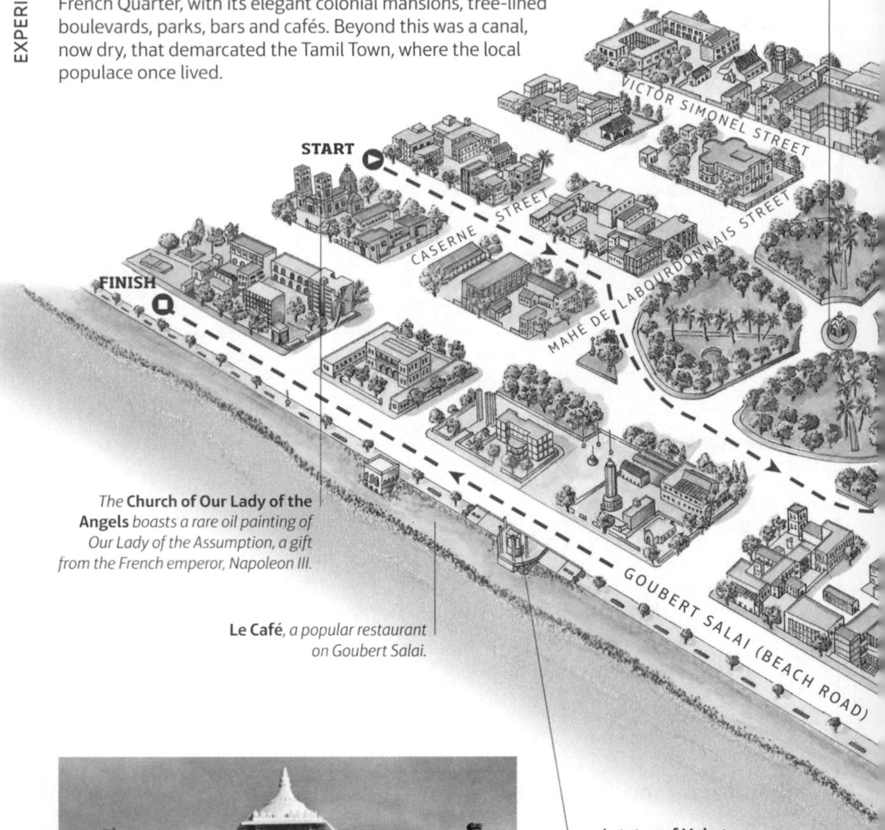

A pavilion stands in the centre of the tree-lined **Government Square**.

VICTOR SIMONEL STREET

START ▶

CASERNE STREET

FINISH ◻

MAHÉ DE LABOURDONNAIS STREET

The **Church of Our Lady of the Angels** *boasts a rare oil painting of Our Lady of the Assumption, a gift from the French emperor, Napoleon III.*

Le Café, *a popular restaurant on Goubert Salai.*

GOUBERT SALAI (BEACH ROAD)

A **statue of Mahatma Gandhi**, *4 m (13 ft) high, stands on a pedestal surrounded by eight stone pillars.*

← Admiring the statue of Mahatma Gandhi located on Puducherry pier

Strolling past the colourful colonial mansions along the streets of the French quarter →

General Hospital

A harmonious fusion of French and Indian styles of architecture, Dupleix's palatial home, **Raj Nivas**, is now the Lieutenant Governor's official residence.

Dedicated to Ganesha, **Manakula Vinayakar Temple** has a golden spire, and walls portraying 40 different forms of Ganesha.

MANAKULA VINAYAKAR

KOIL STREET

FRANÇOIS MARTIN STREET

Named after Sri Aurobindo, the serene **Aurobindo Ashram** (p511) organizes regular meditation sessions, to which all are welcome.

CAMPAGNIE ST

LAW DE LAURISTON STREET

MARTIN STREET

MARINE STREET

Did You Know?

It wasn't until 1954 that the French administration merged with the Republic of India in Puducherry.

Goubert Salai, the boulevard along the Bay of Bengal, is lined with grand colonial buildings.

Puducherry Museum's collection ranges from ancient Roman artifacts and Chola bronzes to beautiful snail shells.

| 0 metres | 100 | N |
| 0 yards | 100 | ↘ |

THANJAVUR

Thanjavur district; 350 km (218 miles) SW of Chennai
Hotel Tamil Nadu Complex; www.tamilnadutourism.org

The city of Thanjavur, or Tanjore, lies in the fertile Kaveri Delta. For nearly a thousand years, this great town dominated the political history of the region as the capital of three powerful dynasties. Today, Thanjavur's culture extends beyond temples and palaces to encompass classical music and dance. It is also a flourishing centre for bronze sculpture and painting.

① Royal Palace

East Main Rd **9am–5:30pm daily**

Resembling the shape of a flying eagle, this palace was built originally by the Nayaka rulers as their royal residence, and was later remodelled by the Marathas. A large quadrangular courtyard leads into the palace complex, at one end of which is a pyramidal, temple-like tower. Outside the palace complex stands the seven-storeyed, arcaded observation tower, although now without its capping pavilion.

The splendid Maratha Durbar Hall, built by Shahji II in 1684, has elaborately painted and decorated pillars, walls and ceiling. A wooden canopy embellished with glittering glass pieces and supported by four wooden pillars stands above a green granite slab, on which the royal Maratha throne once stood. The other buildings include the Sadir Mahal, which is still the residence of the erstwhile royal family, and the Puja Mahal.

The **Rajaraja Museum and Art Gallery** (better known as the Thanjavur Art Gallery), in the Nayaka Durbar Hall, was established in 1951 and has an impressive collection of bronze and stone idols dating from the 7th to the 20th centuries. Particularly of note are the images of Shiva, such as the Kalyanasundaramurti, showing the wedding of Shiva and Parvati, and the Bhikshatanamurti, which depicts Shiva as a wandering mendicant, carrying a begging bowl and travelling with a dog.

Next to the Rajaraja Museum is the **Saraswati Mahal Library**, constructed by the Maratha rulers. This is one of the most important reference libraries in India, with a fine collection of rare palm-leaf manuscripts and books collected by the versatile and scholarly Serfoji II. An adjoining museum displays some of these valuable works.

HIDDEN GEM
Wedding Art

One of the treasures at the Rajaraja Museum is the set of statues depicting the wedding of Shiva and Parvati, witnessed by Vishnu and Lakshmi. Note the diminutive antelope in Shiva's left hand.

The magnificent and colourful Royal Palace of Thanjavur

The **Royal Museum** occupies part of the private quarters of the Maratha Palace, and exhibits the personal collection of Serfoji II. Nearby is the Sangeeta Mahal (Music Hall), built by the Nayakas, and specially designed with acoustic features for musical gatherings.

Rajaraja Museum and Art Gallery
⊗ ☐ 9am–1pm & 3–6pm Mon–Sat ☒ Public hols

Saraswati Mahal Library
☐ Museum: 10am–5pm Thu–Tue; library: 10am–5pm daily

Royal Museum
⊗ ☐ 9am–5pm daily

---

② Shivaganga Fort

☐ Off Hospital Rd
☐ Daily

The quadrangular Shivaganga Fort, southwest of the old city, was built by the Nayaka ruler, Sevappa Nayaka, in the mid-16th century. Its battlemented stone walls, which enclose 14 ha (35 acres), are surrounded by a partly rock-cut moat. The square Shivaganga Tank in the fort was excavated by Rajaraja I, and later renovated to provide drinking water for the city. The fort also contains the great Brihadishvara Temple, Schwartz Church, and an amusement park.

---

③ Schwartz Church

☐ Off West Main Rd
☐ Daily

The 18th-century Christ Church or Schwartz Church, a legacy of Thanjavur's colonial past, stands to the east of the

Shivaganga Tank. This church was founded by the Danish missionary Reverend Frederik Christian Schwartz in 1779. When Schwartz died in 1798, the enlightened Maratha ruler Serfoji II donated a striking marble tablet to the church. This tablet, made by John Flaxman, has been placed at the western end of the church. It depicts the dying missionary blessing his royal patron, while surrounded by ministers and pupils from the school that he established.

---

④ Thiruvarur

☐ 55 km (34 miles) E of Thanjavur

The town of Thiruvarur, one of the old capitals of the Chola dynasty, is famous for its Thyagaraja Temple dedicated to the Somaskanda form of Shiva. The temple has four gopuras. Its ceiling is covered with 17th-century paintings of scenes from the Shiva legend.

THANJAVUR PAINTINGS

A distinctive school of painting emerged during the rule of the Marathas, patronized by Serfoji II. This style was characterized by vibrant colours as well as decoration with gold leaf and precious and semiprecious stones. The themes are mostly religious, and each deity is depicted in a specific colour from the symbolic palette of red, black, blue and white.

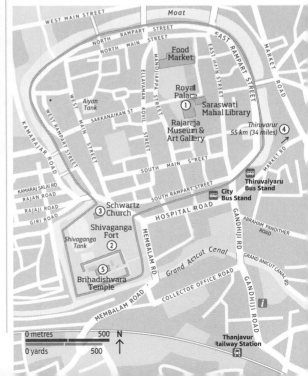

⑤ 🏛 🗺

BRIHADISHVARA TEMPLE

🏠 Thanjuvur, W of bus stand ⏰ 6am–8:30pm (central shrine 8:30am–12:30pm & 4–8:30pm) daily 🛈 tamilnadutourism.org

This dramatic monumental temple, the finest example of Chola architecture, is now a UNESCO World Heritage Site. Completed in AD 1010 and dedicated to Shiva, it was built as a symbol of the unrivalled power of one of the longest-reigning dynasties in Indian history.

Widely known among locals as the "Big Temple", Brihadishvara is built entirely from granite. Having entered through one Maratha-era and two original *gopuras* (gateways), you will find a shrine to Nandi, Shiva's sacred bull. Beyond that, in the middle of the rectangular court, is the entrance to the main tower, the *vimana*, which houses the central linga shrine and numerous sculptures, inscriptions and frescoes. Dotted around the temple are a series of subsidiary shrines to other gods and an archaeological museum, which displays, among other things, photographs of the temple before its restoration.

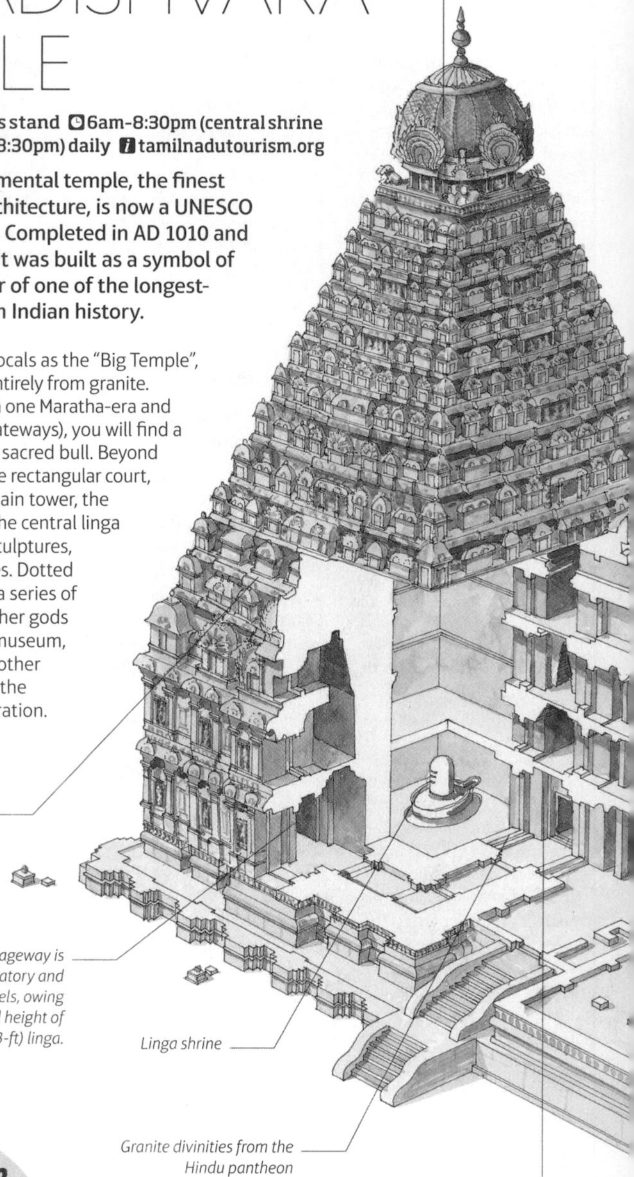

The cupola was carved out of a block of granite weighing 80 tonnes.

The 66-m- (217-ft-) high pyramid-shaped *vimana* has 13 storeys, and its gilded finial was presented by the king.

The passageway is circumambulatory and built on two levels, owing to the colossal height of the 4-m (13-ft) linga.

Linga shrine

Granite divinities from the Hindu pantheon occupy the wall niches of the sanctum.

Chola-era frescoes adorn this passage. They were discovered when the 17th-century Maratha paintings covering them began to disintegrate.

Did You Know?

The huge Nandi bull outside the temple was carved out of a single block of granite weighing 25 tonnes.

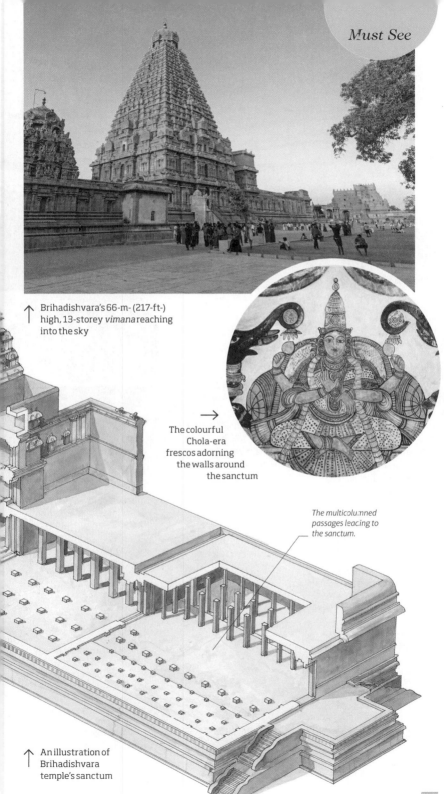

↑ Brihadishvara's 66-m- (217-ft-) high, 13-storey *vimana* reaching into the sky

→ The colourful Chola-era frescos adorning the walls around the sanctum

The multicolumned passages leading to the sanctum.

↑ An illustration of Brihadishvara temple's sanctum

④

MADURAI

🏛 Madurai district; 498 km (309 miles) SW of Chennai
✈ 12 km (7 miles) S of city 🚌🚆 ℹ Tourist Office, West Veli
Road; www.tamilnadutourism.org

One of south India's great temple towns, Madurai is
synonymous with the celebrated Minakshi Temple.
This ancient city on the banks of the Vaigai river has,
over the centuries, been a rich repository of Tamil
culture. Today, religion and culture remain a vibrant
part of the city's daily life.

① ✍

Thirumalai Nayakar Palace

🏛 1.5 km (1 mile) SE of
Minakshi Temple ⊙ Palace:
9am–5pm daily; Son et
Lumière: 6:45pm daily

The power and wealth of the
Nayakas is evident from the
remains of this once-grand
palace, built by Thirumalai
Nayaka in 1636. The building,
with its interesting Islamic
influences, was partially
restored in the 19th century
by Lord Napier, governor of
Madras between 1866 and
1872. Today, only the spacious
rectangular courtyard called
the Swarga Vilasam ("Heavenly
Pavilion") and a few adjoining

buildings survive. Measuring
3,900 sq m (41,979 sq ft), the
courtyard is surrounded by
massive circular pillars. To its
west lies the Throne Chamber,
a vast room with a raised,
octagonal dome. This room
leads to the Dance Hall, which
now houses a display of
archaeological objects.

---

②

St George's Church

🏛 Off W Masi St ⊙ 7am–
8pm daily

An excellent example of
Neo-Gothic architecture,
this church was designed by
Robert Fellowes Chisholm,
and consecrated in 1881.

③

Koodal Alagar Temple

🏛 1 km (0.6 miles) SW
of Minakshi Temple
⊙ 5:30am–12pm & 4–9pm
daily 🚫 To non-Hindus

One of the 108 most sacred
Vaishnavite shrines, this
glorious temple has three

STAY

Heritage Madurai
This period property
has vast modern rooms,
as well as a restaurant,
spa and bar.

🏛 11 Malakkal Main
Road, Kochadai
🌐 heritagemadurai.com

₹₹₹

←
Thiruparankundram temple, and *(inset)* the niche over its entrance

superimposed sanctuaries, of diminishing size, housing Lord Vishnu. From bottom to top, the images show Vishnu in the seated, standing and reclining position. The outer wall has beautiful sculptures and stone screens.

---

④ Thiruparankundram

📍 6 km (4 miles) SW of Madurai

Thiruparankundram is a small town known for its sacred granite hill. Regarded as one of the six sacred abodes of Murugan, the son of Shiva, the hill was the site of his marriage to Devayani, the daughter of Indra. There is a rock-cut temple here, built by the Pandyas in the 8th century. The temple is approached through a series of 17th- and 18th-century *mandapas*, at ascending levels, linked by stone steps. The entrance mandapa has typical Nayaka-period pillars with horse and yali riders, while portraits of Nayaka rulers are carved on the columns. The temple's main sanctum contains five shrines.

The 14-day temple festival, in March/April, celebrates the victory of Murugan over the demon Suran, his coronation, and his subsequent marriage to Devayani.

---

⑤ Tombs of the Madurai Sultans

📍 N of the Vaigai river
🕐 Daily

The sultans of Madurai ruled the city after the invasion in 1310 by Malik Kafur, a general of Alauddin Khilji. They lie buried to the north of the city. The complex includes the Goripalayam Mosque, with its flat-roofed prayer hall and tapering octagonal towers, and the tomb of a local Sufi saint, Bara Mastan Sada, built in the 16th century.

⑥ Alagarkoil

📍 20 km (12.5 miles) N of Madurai

The temple at Alagarkoil is dedicated to Kallalagar, a form of Vishnu who is regarded as Minakshi's brother. According to legend, when Kallalagar went to give his sister in marriage to Sundareshvara he stayed on the riverbank during the ceremony.

On the summit of the hill is Palamudircholai, the last of the six abodes of Murugan, marked by a shrine.

> 💬 INSIDER TIP
> **Colour Fabric**
>
> The Tailor's Market, also called Pudhu Mandapam, is near the entrance of Minakshi Temple. It is a riot of cloth and fabric in all conceivable hues. You can order made-to-measure clothes quickly and cheaply.

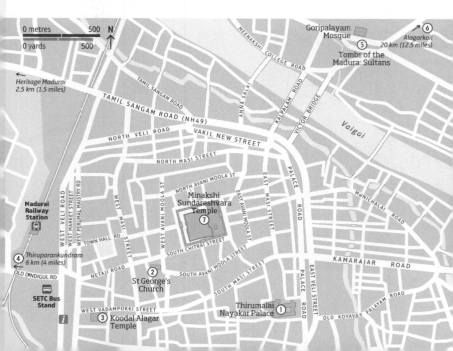

⑦ ⊛ ⊛

MINAKSHI SUNDARESHVARA TEMPLE

🏛 Chitrai St 📞 (0452) 234 4360 🕐 5am–12:30pm & 4–9:30pm daily 🚫 To non-Hindus (sanctum)

This enormous temple was first built by the Pandyas in the 7th century and extensively added to by successive dynasties. Especially impressive are its 14 soaring *gopuras*, covered with figures of deities, mythical animals and monsters painted in vivid colours.

One of the most spectacular examples of the uniquely south Indian Dravidian style of architecture, this temple complex is within a high-walled enclosure, at the core of which are two sanctums dedicated to Shiva, known here as Sundareshvara ("Handsome God"), and his consort Parvati or Minakshi ("Fish-Eyed Goddess"). These are surrounded by a number of smaller shrines and grand pillared halls.

The 14 *gopuras* indicate the entrance to the temple complex at the four cardinal points, while lesser *gopuras* lead to the sanctums of the main deities. The gateways were built by successive rulers to show both their devotion and power: the seven-storeyed Chitra Gopura, adjacent to the Ashta Shakti Mandapa (Hall of Eight Goddesses), is the tallest tower in the complex. To the east of here is the riotously coloured 16th-century Thousand-Pillared Hall, which displays bronze and stone images and has a set of pillars which produce the seven notes of Carnatic music. The Kalyana Mandapa, to the south, is where the marriage of Shiva and Parvati is celebrated every April during the Chithirai Festival, which culminates in a crowded, fun parade.

The stucco figures of deities on the tower are repaired, repainted and ritually reconsecrated every 12 years.

↑ Pilgrims making their way through the colourful Thousand-Pillared Hall

→ Vibrant stuccowork of gods, animals and monsters covering the temple's 14 *gopuras*

Fierce monster images, with protruding eyes and horns, mark the arched ends of the vaulted roofs.

↑ *Gopuras* of varying sizes soaring into the sky above the complex

← An illustration of a *gopura*, gateway to the Minakshi Sundareshvara Temple complex

Pyramidal gates (gopuras) rise to a height of more than 50 m (164 ft) and mark the four cardinal points of a temple complex.

Openings in the middle of the long sides allow light to enter the hollow chambers at each level.

MADURAI'S FERTILITY CULT

There is a thriving fertility cult surrounding the great Minakshi Sundareshvara Temple, connected with the coupling of the goddess Minakshi and Lord Shiva. According to myth, Minakshi appeared out of a sacrificial fire after the Pandyan King Malayadvaja prayed for a son. Initially shocked that his new daughter was female and had three breasts, the king was assuaged by a prophecy that she would lose the third breast on meeting her future husband, who later turned out to be Shiva himself.

5

CHETTINAD

⌂ Chettinad district; 82 km (51 miles) NE of Madurai 🚌 🚍
ℹ tamilnadutourism.org

In dusty, arid Chettinad, the streets of the region's
74 towns are lined with the unexpected sight of huge,
ornate mansions decorated with opulent treasures.

The Chettiar mansions, as they are known,
were built by the Chettiars, a wealthy Hindu
banking and trade clan, between 1850 and
1950 as their ancestral homes. While these
buildings originally housed multiple generations, many of them now sit empty for
most of the year, only used for large family
gatherings. The mansions were meant to
showcase the Chettiars' wealth, much of which
had been accummulated overseas. As a result,
the mansions are decorated with chandeliers
made of Murano glass from Venice, clocks from
Switzerland and tiles from England. Visitors
can visit a number of these houses (permission
often required). One of the best is the Raja's
Palace in Kanadukathan; walking through the
wildly colourful and fantastically ornate
interior is a jaw-dropping experience.

STAY

The Bangala
Converted mansion in leafy grounds with a swimming pool and excellent restaurant.

🏠 Devakottai Rd, Karaikudi
🌐 thebangala.com

₹₹₹

Chettinadu Mansion
Many original design features have been preserved in this 1902 mansion.

🏠 Kanadukathan
🌐 chettinad mansion.com

₹₹₹

Visalam
Beautiful house, with a large pool, Ayurvedic treatments, lavish rooms and a restaurant.

🏠 Kanadukathan
🌐 cghearth.com

₹₹₹

← Raja's Palace in Kanadukathan, Chettinad, and *(inset)* a figure of Lakshmi in front of the villa

Mansion Features

Long Verandah

▼ The typical long verandah with wooden pillars leads to a series of open courtyards, surrounded by rooms for the growing family.

Formal Reception

▼ The reception area has marble floors, stained-glass windows, painted cornices, teak and rosewood furniture and ornate chandeliers.

First Pillared Hall

▲ With each pillar made from an entire tree trunk of Burma teak, this hall is reserved for the men of the house to receive guests and conduct business.

Marble Floors

▲ Along with well-polished doorways, carved wooden beams, granite pillars and more, the marble floors display the skills of the Tamil craftsmen.

The ramparts of Gingee Fort dominating the hills and skyline

EXPERIENCE MORE

6

Gingee Fort

⌂ Viluppuram district; 37 km (23 miles) E of Tiruvannamalai 🚌 ⏱ 9am–4:30pm daily

A remarkable example of military engineering, Gingee (locally called Senji) Fort, has three citadels dramatically perched atop three hills – Krishnagiri to the north, Rajagiri to the west and Chandrayandurg to the southeast. These are enclosed by solid stone walls to form a vast triangular-shaped area extending more than 1.5 km (1 mile) from north to south. Built by the local Nayaka governors, feudatories of the Vijayanagar kings, in the 15th and 16th centuries, the fort was occupied by Bijapur's Adil Shahi Sultans, the Marathas, the French and finally the British. This once-great fortress city is dotted with dilapidated arcaded chambers, mosques, *mandapas*, small shrines, tanks and granaries. Many temples, mostly dedicated to Vishnu, survive as well. These include the deserted temple in the main citadel on the 242-m- (794-ft-) high Rajagiri Hill. The most prominent, however, is the great Venkataramana Temple, in the foothills of the outer fort, near Puducherry Gate. This was constructed by Muthialu Nayaka in the 17th century. Its original pillars were removed by the French and used in the Government Square at Puducherry *(p510)*. Near the gateway are panels depicting scenes from the famous epic *Ramayana* and the *Vishnu Purana*.

The fort's finest monument is the Kalyana Mahal, a square hall built for the ladies of the court. The building has a central eight-storeyed pyramidal tower with a single large room on each floor.

There are also traces of a network of natural springs and tanks that provided water to the citadel. One of the tanks, Chettikulam, has a platform where Raja Thej Singh, a brave 18th-century Rajput chief and vassal of the Mughal emperor, was cremated. Tamil folk songs glorify Gingee and Raja Thej Singh, who was killed in a heroic battle against the Nawab of Arcot.

7

Tiruvannamalai

⌂ Tiruvannamalai district; 85 km (53 miles) S of Vellore 🚉 🚌 ❢ www.tamilnadu tourism.org

One of the most sacred cities of Tamil Nadu, this pilgrim town is the place where Shiva is believed to have appeared as a column of fire in order to assert his supremacy over Brahma and Vishnu. Arunachala Hill (the "Red Mountain"), which forms a backdrop to the town, is said to be the site where the fire manifested itself, and is thus perceived as the light of god himself. On the day of the Karthigai

> 💬 INSIDER TIP
> ### Turn About the Temple
>
> At Tiruvannamalai at full moon, you can join thousands of pilgrims on a nocturnal circumambulation of holy Mount Arunachala – it is a truly unforgettable experience.

Deepam festival, an enormous *deepa* (lamp), using 2,000 litres (440 gallons) of ghee and a 30-m- (98-ft-) wide wick, is lit on the hill, and burns for days.

Arunachaleshvara Temple, the town's most important structure, is one of the five elemental shrines of Shiva, where the linga, encased in gold, represents fire. Covering 10 ha (25 acres), this is also one of the largest temple complexes in India, parts of it dating to the 11th century.

Tiruvannamalai is also where Sri Ramana Maharshi, the famed 20th-century saint, spent 23 years in meditation. The Sri Ramana Maharshi Ashram, near Arunachala Hill, attracts devotees from all around the world.

Arunachaleshvara Temple

☉ Sunrise-sunset daily
🚫 To non-Hindus

8

Kanchipuram

🗺 Kanchipuram district; 76 km (47 miles) SW of Chennai 🚌🚆 🛈 Hotel Tamil Nadu, 78 Kamakshi Amman Sannathi St; www.tamil nadutourism.org

The small temple town of Kanchipuram, or Kanchi, as it is popularly known, is one of the seven sacred cities of the Hindus. From the 6th to the 8th centuries, it was the capital of the Pallavas. Royal patronage from the dynasties that followed – Chola, Pandya and Vijayanagar – consolidated the city's reputation as a religious and commercial centre.

Kanchipuram is sacred to Shaivites (devotees of Shiva) as well as to Vaishnavites (worshippers of Vishnu). The town is thus divided into two distinct zones, with the Shaivite temples to the north and the Vaishnavite temples to the southeast.

It also has an important Devi (goddess) temple, the Kamakshi Temple, situated northeast of the bus stand.

The Kailasanathar Temple is the oldest, grandest structure in the town. Built in the early 8th century by Rajasimha, the last great Pallava king, this Shiva temple is surrounded by 58 smaller shrines, each with splendid carvings of the various representations of Shiva. The frescoes here are the earliest in south India. The sanctum has a circum-ambulatory passage with symbolic meaning – seven steps (indicating seven births) lead to a dark passage (for the journey of life) and a narrow outlet (indicating death). The great Ekambareshvara

↑ A Nandi statue at the Kailasanathar Temple in Kanchipuram

Temple on Car Street, which was constructed originally by the Pallavas, has a 16-pillared *mandapa* in front of it, a later addition by the Vijayanagar kings. This is one of the five *panchalinga* shrines and houses a linga made of earth (*prithvi*). Legend says that the goddess Kamakshi, as part of her penance for disturbing Shiva's meditation, created this linga with earth taken from under a mango tree. Lingas abound in the corridors of the temple complex, while on the western side of the shrine stands a sacred mango tree, said to be 3,000 years old.

The Vaikuntha Perumal Temple, located near the railway station, is one of the 18 temples dedicated to Vishnu. Erected by the Pallava king Nandi Varman II (r 731–96), this unique structure has three main sanctums, built one on top of the other. Each of them enshrines an image of Vishnu.

The Varadaraja Temple, on Gandhi Road, is the town's main Vishnu temple. The chief deity is a form of Vishnu known as Varadaraja (the "King who Bestows Benediction").

Kanchipuram, famed for its silk, is the seat of one of the four Shankaracharyas, who are head priests of the long-standing *mathas* (religious centres or monasteries) that were founded by the 9th-century philosopher-saint Adi Shankaracharya.

↑ Crowds outside Tiruvannamalai's Arunachaleshvara Temple for the Karthigai Deepam festival

A colourfully decorated *gopura* at the Nataraja Temple, in Chidambaram

9

Chidambaram

🏛 Thanjavur district; 60 km (37 miles) S of Puducherry 🚉🚌 🛈 Hotel Tamil Nadu, Railway Feeder Rd; www. tamilnadutourism.org

Sacred Chidambaram, where Shiva is believed to have performed his cosmic dance, the *tandava nritya*, is a traditional temple town where history merges with mythology to create a deeply religious ambience. All ancient Hindu beliefs and practices are zealously observed here, manifested in an endless cycle of rites and rituals.

The focal point of the town is the awe-inspiring **Nataraja Temple**, built by the Cholas in the 9th century to honour their patron deity, Shiva as Nataraja, the "Lord of Dance" (*p495*). The temple has an unusual hut-like sanctum with a gold-plated roof, the huge, colonnaded Shivaganga Tank, and four colourful *gopuras*. The most interesting is the eastern *gopura* which features detailed sculptures of the 108 hand and feet movements of Bharat Natyam, which are considered a veritable encyclo-paedia of this classical temple dance style.

Within the temple's three enormous enclosures are five major halls (*sabhas*), each conceived for a special purpose. In the outer enclosure, next to the Shivaganga Tank, is the Raja Sabha ("Royal Hall"), a beautiful thousand-pillared hall, built as a venue for temple rituals and festivals. Many Chola kings were crowned here in the presence of the deity. In the central enclosure is the Deva Sabha ("Divine Hall"), where the temple bronzes are housed, and administrative functions performed. The adjacent Nritya Sabha ("Dance Hall") has a superb collection of sculptures, the finest being the Urdhava Tandava.

The innermost enclosure, the holiest part of the complex, contains the Chit Sabha or Chitambalam ("Hall of Bliss"), from which the town derives its name. This is the main sanctum, housing one of the five elemental lingas of Shiva, the *akasha* linga, which represents ether, the all-pervading element central to human existence. The inner sanctum containing the linga is hidden behind a black curtain, symbolizing ignorance, which is removed only during prayer time. There is a certain aura of mystery to this veiled sanctum and it is often called the Sacred Secret of Chidambaram (Chidambara Rahasyam). Finally, the fifth hall, in front of the Chit Sabha, is the Kanaka Sabha ("Golden Hall"). This is where Shiva is supposed to have performed his cosmic dance.

Other areas of interest in the complex include the Govindaraja Shrine, housing the reclining Vishnu, the Shivakamasundari Shrine,

Imposing ancient Shiva temples at the once grand Gangaikonda Cholapuram

which is dedicated to Shiva's consort, Parvati, and the Subramanyam Shrine, in which Murugan is worshipped.

Religious traditions in the temple are preserved by hereditary priests known as *dikshitars*, whose ancestors came here 3,000 years ago. Chidambaram's other claim to fame is the modern Annamalai University, located to the east. Founded over 50 years ago, it is Tamil Nadu's first residential university, specializing in south Indian studies.

Nataraja Temple
🕉️⊘ 🏠 Near bus stand
🕐 6am–noon & 5–10pm daily

🔟
Vellore

🏠 Vellore district; 145 km (90 miles) W of Chennai 🚆 Katpadi, 5 km (3 miles) N of town centre, then bus 🚌 *i* www.tamilnadu tourism.org

Surrounded by a deep moat, the 16th-century Vellore Fort dominates the heart of this town. This formidable structure has withstood many battles, including an ill-fated mutiny led by the son of Tipu Sultan in 1806 against the British East India Company. Today, part of the fort houses some government offices, including the Archaeological

Survey of India (ASI), district courts and a prison. A museum inside the building has a small collection of historical objects. The only major structure to survive in the fort is the **Jalakanteshvara Temple**, constructed by the Nayakas, governors of the region under the Vijayanagar kings, in the mid-1500s. This Shiva temple is located near the fort's northern wall. In the outer courtyard is the ornate Kalyana Mandapa. Its pillars are carved with magnificent horses and *yali* riders.

Jalakanteshvara Temple
🕐 6am–1pm & 5–8:30pm daily

1️⃣1️⃣
Gangaikonda Cholapuram

🏠 Tiruchirapalli district; 40 km (25 miles) SW of Chidambaram 🚌 From Chidambaram or Kumbakonam

Grandly titled Gangaikonda Cholapuram, "The City of the Chola Who Took the Ganges", this now modest village was the capital of the powerful Chola dynasty during the reign of Rajendra I (r.012–44). A great military commander like his father Rajaraja I, Rajendra I was the first Tamil ruler to venture northwards. He built this city to commemorate his

🔍 HIDDEN GEM
Carved Planets

In the northeast corner of the Brihadishvara Temple at Gangaikonda Cholapuram is a stone block carved with the *navagraha* (the nine planets), which hold auspicious astrological significance.

successful campaign across the Ganges. According to an inscription, he then ordered the defeated rulers of other kingdoms to carry back pots of sacred Ganges water on their heads to fill the Chola-Ganga tank, a victory memorial.

Except for the magnificent **Brihadishvara Temple**, little remains of the capital city. Built as a replica of Thanjavur's Brihadishvara Temple *(p516)*, the towered sanctum of this granite Shiva temple is shorter than the one at Thanjavur. Adorning the lower walls, columns and niches are many remarkable sculptural friezes. One of the most outstanding is the panel depicting Shiva blessing Chandesha, a pious devotee sculpted to resemble Rajendra I himself. The sculptures of the *dikpalas* (guardians of the eight directions), *ekadasas* (the 11 forms of Shiva), Saraswati, Kalyanasundara and Nataraja are also splendid examples of Chola art.

Brihadishvara Temple
🕐 6am–12:30pm & 4:30–8pm daily

Tiruvaiyaru

📍 Thanjavur district; 13 km (8 miles) N of Thanjavur 🚌

The fertile region watered by the Kaveri river and its four tributaries is called Tiruvaiyaru, the sacred *(tiru)* land of five *(i)* rivers *(aru)*.

For nearly 2,000 years the Tamil people have regarded the Kaveri as the sacred source of life, religion and culture, and many scholars, artists, poets and musicians subsequently settled in this region under the enlightened patronage of the rulers of Thanjavur *(p514)*. Among them was Thyagaraja (1767–1847), the greatest composer-saint of Carnatic music, who refined features now essential to the genre, indelibly linking the history of this small town with the growth and development of south Indian classical music. The little Thyagaraja Temple was built to commemorate the last resting place of the

↑ A crowded festival event at Thyagaraja Temple, Tiruvaiyaru

celebrated composer-saint, and a musical festival is held here every year on the anniversary of his death, which falls, according to the Tamil calendar, in January. Hundreds of musicians and students of Carnatic music gather in the town and sing Thyagaraja's songs from morning till midnight for a whole week. As dawn breaks over the river, a procession of musicians makes the short journey from his house to the temple – singing all the way – where eager music lovers wait at the shrine, seated on the mud floor of the thatch-roofed auditorium. To the chants of priests, the stone image of Thyagaraja is bathed with milk, rosewater, sandalwood and honey while the five songs known as the *pancha ratna* ("five gems") of Thyagaraja, which are considered unequalled masterpieces of Carnatic music, are sung in a grand chorus by all the assembled musicians. This ceremony is an annual reaffirmation of devotion to the composer and to a great tradition of music. For music lovers from all over India, it can be a magical experience.

Also in the town is the 9th-century Aiyarappar Temple, built by the Cholas. Dedicated to Shiva, the shrines of Uttara (north) Kailasha and Dakshina (south) Kailasha, on either side of the main temple, were built by the wives of Rajaraja I and Rajendra I. The temple's huge *prakara* (boundary) walls, pillared *mandapas* and the Mukti Mandapa are immortalized in the songs of the Nayannars, a sect of 7th-century poet-saints.

Pullamangai village, 12 km (7 miles) northeast of Tiruvaiyaru, is noted for the 10th-century Brahmapurishvara Temple, with elegant depictions of various deities.

THANJAVUR BRONZES

The Thanjavur region's artistic traditions include the creation of bronze images using *cire perdue*, or the "lost-wax" technique. A model of the image is made in wax and coated with layers of clay to create a mould, which is heated to let the melting wax flow out through a hole at the base. A molten alloy of five metals *(panch loha)* is then poured in. When the metal cools, the mould is broken and the image is finished. Even today, traditional artisans, known as *sthapathis*, create these images according to a fixed set of rules laid down in the Shilpa Shastra, an ancient treatise on art. The main centre for bronze casting in Tamil Nadu is Swamimalai *(p531)*.

EXPERIENCE Tamil Nadu

CARNATIC MUSIC

The classical music of south India is known as Carnatic music. It is almost exclusively devotional in character, uses instruments different from those used in Hindustani music, has a structured melody and lays more emphasis on rhythm. Some of the greatest Carnatic music was composed between 1750 and 1850 by the musical trinity of Thyagaraja, Syama Sastri and Muthuswami Dikshitar, who, between them, wrote over 2,500 songs.

VIOLIN

Traditional Indian instruments are used alongside Western ones. A string instrument of Western origin, the violin is played in a seated position.

MRIDANGAM AND GHATAM

In Carnatic music, the double-sided *mridangam (left)* is the main percussion instrument, but even the *ghatam* – a simple clay pot – can produce fabulous rhythms in the hands of an accomplished player.

NADASVARAM

This double reed wind instrument is a must at temple festivals and auspicious occasions. The accompanying *thavil* (drum) player improvises complex rhythms.

VEENA

Resembling the more widely seen sitar, the veena is a long-necked lute-style string instrument that is beautifully handcrafted in south India.

TOP 3 **FORMS OF CARNATIC MUSIC**

Kriti
The major vocal genre of Carnatic music, *kritis* have three parts. These include a refrain and two verses, and generally have a religious theme.

Varnam
One of the most complex forms of Carnatic vocal music, *varnams* encapsulate the main features of the underlying raga, or melody.

Padam
Often sung during Bharat Natyam dance performances, *padams* are classical love songs in the Carnatic tradition, often inspired by eroticism.

This musician plays a *ghatam*.

Bombay Jayashri is one of the leading vocalists of the genre.

The tanpura *is a string instrument that supports the melody.*

↑ A Carnatic *sabha* in progress, with Bombay Jayashri and her accompanists

13

Kumbakonam

📍 Thanjavur district; 74 km (46 miles) SW of Chidambaram 🚉🚌
ℹ️ www.tamilnadu tourism.org

Like Kanchipuram (p525), Kumbakonam is one of the most sacred cities in Tamil Nadu. Located on the southern bank of the Kaveri river, this ancient city is the legendary spot where Shiva's arrow shattered the cosmic pot (kumbh) containing the divine nectar of creation (amrit), a myth that gave Kumbakonam both its name and sanctity. Today, the city represents the traditional cultural values of the Tamil heartland. It is also the region's main commercial and craft centre, famous for its textiles, jewellery, bronze casting and its locally grown betel leaves.

It is believed that when the divine nectar emerged from the pot, it filled the Mahamaham Tank. This is Kumbakonam's sacred centre and the site of the great Mahamaham Festival, held every 12 years (the last one was held in 2016). At the auspicious time, thousands of devotees enter the tank for their holy dip when the purifying power of the water is said to be at its height. The devout believe that all of India's sacred rivers (Ganges, Yamuna, Saraswati, Sarayu, Godavari, Narmada, Kaveri, Payokshini and Kanniyakumari) also bathe in the tank to cleanse themselves of the sins of humanity accumulated in their waters.

The tank has steps at the four cardinal points, and 16 ornate pavilions in honour of the 16 mahadanas (great gifts bestowed by a ruler on a spiritual centre). There is art from the Nayaka dynasty – a relief depicting a king being weighed on a balance against gold (a ceremony known as tulapurushadeva) – carved on the roof of a 16-pillared mandapa that stands at the northwest corner of the tank, giving a clue to its age. To the north is the Kashivishvanatha Temple, which has a small shrine facing the water; this is dedicated to the nine sacred rivers, which are personified as goddesses. A shrine that represents the Kaveri river occupies the central position.

To the east of the tank, the 17th-century Adikumbheshvara Temple is built on the place where, in legend, Shiva shattered the pot. A unique feature here is the depiction of 27 stars and the 12 zodiac signs carved on a large block of stone in the Navaratri Mandapa. It also has a superb collection of silver vahanas (vehicles) which are used during festivals to carry the

temple deities. The grand, 12-storeyed Sarangapani Temple, to the east is the most important Vaishnavite shrine in the city.

Nearby is the 9th-century Nageshvara Temple, a fine example of early Chola dynasty architecture. The town's oldest temple, this is the site of an annual festival that celebrates the worship of the linga by the sun. Niches on the sanctum walls contain exquisitely carved figures depicting the forms of Shiva and scenes from the Ramayana.

Some 4 km (2 miles) west of Kumbakonam, the spectacular Airavateshvara Temple at Darasuram was built by the Chola king, Rajaraja II (r 1146–73). This temple is dedicated to Shiva, who is known here as Airavateshvara, the "Lord of Airavata". Legend claims that after Airavata, the white elephant of the God of the Heavens, regained his lost colour, he worshipped Shiva at this spot.

The four-tiered temple has a sanctum and three halls, of which the finest is the Raja-gambira Mandapa, conceived

←

A colourful procession during the Mahamaham Festival in Kumbakonam

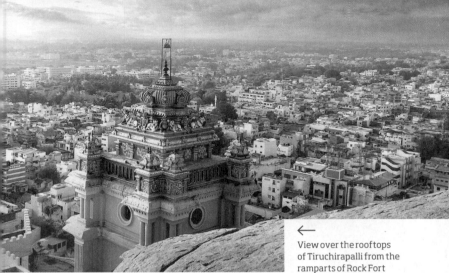

View over the rooftops of Tiruchirapalli from the ramparts of Rock Fort

as a stone chariot drawn by caparisoned horses, with Brahma as its driver. About 8 km (5 miles) west of the town is Swamimalai, one of the six sacred shrines devoted to Lord Murugan, who, says the legend, propounded the meaning of "Om", the sacred mantra, to his father Shiva, and thus assumed the title Swaminatha ("Lord of Lords"). The temple, situated on a hill, has an impressive statue of Murugan in the sanctum; interestingly, he has an elephant as his vehicle instead of the typical peacock.

14

Tiruchirapalli

Tiruchirapalli district; 60 km (37 miles) W of Thanjavur 7 km (4 miles) S of town centre, then bus or taxi Hotel Tamil Nadu, 101 Williams Rd; www. tamilnadutourism.org

Situated at the head of the fertile Kaveri Delta, this city is named after the fierce three-headed demon *(tirusira)* who attained salvation after being slain by Shiva. The town's history is interwoven with the political fortunes of the Pallavas, Cholas, Nayakas,

Did You Know?

Tiruchirapalli used to be famous for its cigars, which were smoked by Winston Churchill.

and finally, the British, who shortened its name to Trichy. Today, Tiruchirapalli is Tamil Nadu's second-largest city.

Dominating the town is the massive **Rock Fort**, perched dramatically on a rocky outcrop that rises 83 m (272 ft) above the flat plains. This impregnable fortress was constructed by the Nayakas of neighbouring Madurai, who made Tiruchirapalli their second capital during the 16th and 17th centuries. They also expanded the Shiva temple, where the god is worshipped as Thayumanavar (the "God who became a Mother"). Legend says that when a flash flood prevented a mother from coming to her pregnant daughter's aid, Shiva assumed her form and helped in the childbirth. Further up, on the summit, is a small Ganesha Temple, from where there are spectacular views of the sacred island of Srirangam.

At the base of the southern rock face is the first of the two cave temples. The lower one dates to the 8th century, and the upper one to the reign of the great Pallava ruler, Mahendra Varman (r 600–630). This contains one of the great wonders of Pallava art, the Gangadhara Panel, depicting Shiva holding a lock of his matted hair to receive the River Ganga as she descends from the heavens. Much of the present town dates to the 18th and 19th centuries, when the British constructed the cantonment and numerous civic buildings and churches. Many of these buildings are located around the large Teppakulam Tank at the base of the fort – a busy area that is surrounded by fruit, vegetable and flower markets.

At Kallanai, 24 km (15 miles) northeast of Tiruchirapalli, is a 300-m- (984-ft-) long earthen dam across the Kaveri river, the Grand Anicut. This formed part of the hydraulic system created by the Cholas to divert water from the river into a vast network of irrigation canals. The original no longer exists, and the dam in operation today was rebuilt by the British in the 1800s.

Rock Fort

6am–8pm daily

↑ Kodai Lake, created by the construction of a dam in Kodaikanal

🄯 Kodaikanal

🏛 Madurai district; 120 km (75 miles) NW of Madurai 🚌 Palani, 65 km (40 miles) N of town centre, then bus or taxi 🚌 ℹ️ www.tamil nadutourism.org

Lush green valleys, terraced plantations and a pleasant climate make Kodaikanal one of Tamil Nadu's most popular hill stations. American missionaries were the first Westerners to move to Kodaikanal, or Kodai as it is commonly called, in the 1840s, when they set up a sanatorium-cum-retreat here. They also established Kodai's International School in 1901.

This picturesque town spreads around Kodai Lake, created by the dam built by Sir Vere Henry Levinge in 1863. A 3-km (2-mile) trail around the lake makes for a pleasant walk. East of the lake is Bryant Park, famous for its plant collection (including over 740 varieties of roses) and its annual flower show, held in May.

Beyond the city centre are a number of scenic areas, such as Pillar Rocks, Silver Cascade and Green Valley View, which offer enchanting picnic spots and views of the deep valley.

Kodai also has many options for cycling, riding and long, rambling walks. A short trail following the hillside, called Coaker's Walk, provides a panoramic view of the hill station. The walk ends at the Church of St Peter, which was built in 1884, and has fine stained-glass windows.

Some 3 km (2 miles) north-east of the lake is the Kurunji Andavar Temple, dedicated to Murugan. It is named after the beautiful purple-flowering *kurunji* plants, associated with the god. The Chettiar Park nearby, laid out along the hillside, is where the *kurunji* blooms every 12 years (the next one will be in 2030).

🄰 Yercaud

🏛 Salem district; 32 km (20 miles) NE of Salem 🚌 Salem, then bus 🚌 ℹ️ Hotel Tamil Nadu, Yercaud Ghat Rd; www. tamilnadutourism.org

This attractive hill station, situated in the Shevaroy Hills, was established in the early 1800s by the British, who introduced the coffee plant here. Today, its surrounding slopes are entirely covered with plantations of coffee, tea, jackfruit and plantains.

The man-made Yerikadu Lake and the Killiyur Falls are two of the area's most scenic spots, while Lady's Seat, near the lake, offers delightful views of the surrounding countryside. The town and its environs have several apiaries that produce delicious honey. The Horticultural Research Station has an interesting collection of rare plants.

🄱 Palani

🏛 Madurai district; 120 km (75 miles) NW of Madurai 🚌 Madurai, 119 km (74 miles) SE of town centre, then bus or taxi 🚌🚌

A major pilgrimage centre, Palani is situated on the edge of the great Vyapuri Tank. Its hilltop Subrahmanyam Temple is the most famous of the six abodes of Murugan, the son of Shiva, who is said to

→

Gigantic statue of Lord Shiva at a yoga centre in Coimbatore

have come here disguised as a mendicant after quarrelling over a fruit with his brother, Ganesha. Popularly known as Dandayutha Pani ("Bearer of the Staff"), Murugan is depicted with a clean shaven head, holding a stick. His image is made of medicinal herbs, mixed together to create a wax-like substance. During the Thaipoosam festival, the temple attracts thousands of pilgrims, many of whom shave their heads as an expression of devotion. An electric cable car takes devotees up the 600 steps to the hill shrine. Palani is also a base for some fantastic hikes in the surrounding hills.

18 🚏 🅼

Mudumalai Wildlife Sanctuary

🏛 Nilgiris district; 64 km (40 miles) **W** of Udhagamandalam 🚌 Theppakadu, the main entry point 🕙 7–9am & 3–6pm daily 🅸 Tourist Office, Theppakadu, (0423) 244 3977; for bookings, contact Wildlife Warden's Office, (0423) 244 5971

Mudumalai or "Ancient Hill Range", at the base of the Nilgiri Hills, is separated from Karnataka's Bandipur National Park by the Moyar river.

This sanctuary is an important constituent of the 5,500-sq km (2,124-sq mile) Nilgiri Biosphere Reserve of the Western Ghats. Along with adjacent Bandipur and Nagarhole, it provides one of the most important refuges for the elephant and the Indian gaur in India. The park covers 322 sq km (124 sq miles) of undulating terrain, and rises to 1,250 m (4,101 ft) at Moyar Betta. The lowest point of the sanctuary is at the picturesque Moyar Waterfalls. Its topography is as varied as the vegetation, which ranges from dense deciduous forests of teak, laurel and rosewood in the west, to scrub jungle towards the east, interspersed with grassland, swamps and bamboo brakes. The sanctuary provides a habitat for a rich diversity of wildlife, including the Nilgiri tahr, sambar, tiger, leopard, spotted deer, flying squirrel, Malabar civet and Nilgiri langur. Over 120 species of birds, including the scops owl and the crested hawk eagle, can be seen here as well.

19

Coimbatore

🏛 Coimbatore district; 502 km (312 miles) SE of Chennai ✈ 10 km (6 miles) NE, then bus 🚉🚌 🅸 Hotel Tamil Nadu, Dr Nanjappa Rd; www.tamilnadutourism.org

Tamil Nadu's third largest city, Coimbatore is a major industrial centre and the state's commercial capital. It is also a convenient base for visiting the Nilgiri hill stations. The city has two famous temples: the Perur Temple, on

THE NILGIRIS

The picturesque *nila giri* or "Blue Mountains", at the junction of the Eastern and Western Ghats, are so named because the shrub *kurunji (Strobilanthes kunthianus)* turns the hills blue with its blossoms every 12 years. The Nilgiris are home to 18 tribal groups and several hill stations. The century-old Blue Mountain Train terminates at Ooty, or Udhagamandalam. To its east is Kotagiri, in the shadow of Dodda Betta, the Nilgiris' highest peak. Coonoor, to the south, is surrounded by hills and verdant plantations of tea and coffee.

the Noyyal river, and the Muruga Maruthamalai Temple, on top of a hillock, dedicated to Lord Shiva and his son Murugan respectively. The world's largest bust statue – depicting Shiva – was unveiled near here in 2017. The Siruvani Waterfalls are beautiful, and its water famed for its purity and taste.

20

Srirangam

🅐 Tiruchirapalli district; 9 km (6 miles) N of Tiruchirapalli 🚌

The sacred 3-km- (2-mile-) long island of Srirangam, formed by the Kaveri and Kollidam rivers, is one of the most revered pilgrimage sites in south India. At its core is the majestic **Ranganatha Temple**. Dedicated to one of the forms of Vishnu, this is one of the largest temple complexes in Tamil Nadu and covers an enormous area of 63 ha (156 acres). The complex has evolved over a period of four centuries. Extensive reconstruction first took place in 1371, after the original 10th-century temple was destroyed by the Delhi Sultan, Alauddin Khilji. Its present form also includes extensions added in the 17th century by the Nayaka rulers, whose second capital was in neighbouring Tiruchirapalli. The last addition was in 1987, when the southern gateway was finally completed.

Dominated by 21 *gopuras* (gateways), the complex has seven *prakara* (boundary) walls defining its seven enclosures. The outer three comprise residences for priests, hostels for pilgrims, and small restaurants and shops selling religious books, pictures and temple offerings.

The sacred precinct begins from the fourth enclosure, beyond which non-Hindus are not allowed. This is where the temple's most important shrines are located. Among these are the spacious Hall of 1,000 Pillars, where images of Ranganatha and his consort are enthroned and worshipped during one of the temple's many festivals, and the Seshagirirayar Mandapa, a magnificent pavilion carved with rearing stone horses with mounted warriors attacking animals and *yalis* (mythical leonine beasts). A small museum close by has a good collection of stone and bronze sculptures. The core of the complex is the sanctum, with its gold-plated *vimana*, where an image of Vishnu as Ranganatha, reclining on the cosmic serpent Adisesha is enshrined. This temple is also the place where the great 11th-century philosopher Ramanuja developed the bhakti cult of personal devotion into a formalized mode of worship. Today, a constant cycle of festivals glorifying Vishnu are celebrated throughout the year.

East of the Ranganatha Temple is the mid-17th-century **Jambukeshvara Temple** in the village of Tiruvanaikka. The main sanctum contains one of the five elemental lingas, representing Shiva as the manifestation of water. Legend says that the linga was created by Shiva's consort, Parvati, and in homage to her, the priest wears a sari when performing the *puja*. Non-Hindus can view the outer shrines in the complex, but not the main sanctum.

Ranganatha Temple
🕑 ⊘ 🄲 (0431) 243 2246
🕐 Temple and museum: 6am–9pm daily

Jambukeshvara Temple
⊘ 🕐 6am–9pm daily

21

Ramanathapuram

🅐 Ramanathapuram district; 117 km (73 miles) SE of Madurai 🚌 🚌

This ancient town is associated with the Setupatis, local rulers who rose to prominence in the late 17th century under the Madurai Nayakas. They gained their prestige and income by controlling the isthmus that led to Rameshvaram Island. A century later, their rule came to an end with surrender to the British East India Company in 1792.

To the west of the present town is the palace complex of the Setupatis. Though little remains, the 17th-century Ramalinga Vilas, on the north side of the palace complex, still has well-preserved and varied wall paintings. These depict the epics as well as battle scenes, business transactions and royal ceremonies. The upper chambers depict more private royal scenes, including family gatherings, music and dance recitals, as well as hunting expeditions.

On the outskirts of the town, the 400-year-old Erwadi Dargah houses the tomb of Ibrahim Syed Aulia, a Muslim saint. It attracts devotees from all over India, as well as from Sri Lanka, Malaysia and Singapore during its annual festival in June/July.

↑ One of several elaborately carved gateways at Ranganatha Temple in Srirangam

↑ Finely decorated temples at the sacred island of Rameshvaram *(inset)*

22
Perumal Malai

🏔 Dindigul district; 100 km (62 miles) NW of Madurai 🚌

A popular trekking destination in the Western Ghats, Perumal Malai is a 2,440-m (8,005-ft) peak. The ridges immediately below it are home to a settlement that sprawls near the hilltop Sri Mariamman Temple, a popular pilgrimage site,. The chilly Palar River immediately to the west of the village is ideal for an invigorating dip.

23
Rameshvaram

🏔 Ramanathapuram district; 163 km (101 miles) SE of Madurai 🚉🚌
ℹ Tourist office, East Car Street; www.tamil nadutourism.org

A major pilgrimage site, the sacred island of Rameshvaram juts out into the Gulf of Mannar, the narrow body of water separating Tamil Nadu from Sri Lanka.

The Ramanathaswamy Temple, in the middle of the island, is dedicated to Shiva. It houses the linga that Lord Rama, the hero of the epic *Ramayana*, is said to have installed and worshipped after his victory against Ravana in Lanka. Founded by the Chola rulers but then extensively expanded during the Nayaka period in the 16th to 18th centuries, this massive temple is enclosed within a high wall with five *gopuras*. The most remarkable feature of this temple is the Sokkattan Mandapa, so called because it resembles a *sokkattan* (dice) in shape. It surrounds the core of the temple on four sides in a continuous corridor, and is the largest and most elaborate of its kind, with 1,212 pillars extending 197 m (646 ft) from east to west and 133 m (436 ft) from north to south. The complex also has a staggering 22 *tirthas* (tanks) for ritual ablutions; it is believed that a dip in the Agni Tirtha, in front of the temple, removes all sins. The installation ceremony of the linga by Rama and Sita is celebrated every year.

Standing on Gandamadana Hill, the highest point of the island, 3 km (2 miles) northwest of the Ramanathaswamy Temple, is a two-storeyed *mandapa* that is said to shelter the footprint of Rama.

Dhanushkodi ("Rama's Bow"), the southernmost tip of Rameshvaram, about 18 km (11 miles) from the main temple, has a spectacular beach and a temple.

GUARDIAN DEITIES

Huge figures made of burnt clay can be seen on the outskirts of villages in Tamil Nadu's southern districts. Worshipped as the guardians of the villages, these deities include Ayyanar, a mustachioed god with prominent eyes, whose horse stands by his side so that he can ride through the night, keeping evil spirits at bay. Other deities are Munisami, who rides a lion, and Karuppusami, the nocturnal avenger who punishes thieves.

24 Kanniyakumari

🏠 Kanniyakumari district; 235 km (146 miles) SW of Madurai 🚌🚉 ℹ️ Tamil Nadu Tourism, Beach Rd; www. tamilnadutourism.org

The southernmost tip of the Indian subcontinent, where the Indian Ocean, the Arabian Sea and the Bay of Bengal meet, Kanniyakumari enchants visitors with its spectacular views, especially at sunrise and sunset. The most breathtaking of these occurs on Chaitra Purnima (the full-moon night in April), when both sunset and moon-rise occur at the same time.

Kanniyakumari is believed to be the abode of Kumari, the Virgin Goddess, who is said to have done penance here so that she could marry Shiva. The marriage, however, did not take place, since it was deemed that she remain a virgin in order to save the world. Her temple, the **Kumari Amman Temple**, a popular pilgrimage centre on the seashore, was built by the Pandya kings in the 8th century and was renovated by the Chola, Vijayanagar

Did You Know?

The statue of Tiruvalluvar, whose epic *Tirukural* was 133 chapters, is 40.5 m (133 ft) tall.

and Nayaka rulers. The magnificent structure has a Navaratri mandapa with a beautifully painted panel of Mahishasuramardini (Durga killing the demon Mahisha). An 18th-century shrine within the temple contains the foot-prints *(sripadaparai)* of Kumari, who performed her penance at this spot.

The Gandhi Memorial, near the temple, is where Mahatma Gandhi's ashes were kept before immersion. The building is designed so that every year on 2nd October (Gandhi's birthday), at midday, the rays of the sun fall on the exact spot where his ashes were placed.

Just off the coast, on a rocky island, the **Vivekananda Memorial** marks the spot where the great Indian philosopher, Swami Vivekananda

meditated before attending the World Religious Conference in Chicago in 1893. Near the memorial is the imposing statue of Tiruvalluvar, the 1st-century BC Tamil poet who wrote *Tirukural*, an epic tome on virtues and morality, often referred to as one of the classics of Tamil literature.

Kumari Amman Temple
🕓 4:30am–12:30pm & 4–8pm
🚫 To non-Hindus (sanctum)

Vivekananda Memorial
♿ 🚤 🕓 8am–4pm daily

25 Tiruchendur

🏠 Tuticorin district; 210 km (130 miles) S of Madurai 🚌🚉 From Madurai, Tirunelvelli, Tuticorin and Nagercoil

This beautiful coastal town, one of the six sacred abodes of Shiva's son Murugan, is known for the Subramanyam Temple, dating from the 9th century. The temple, entered through the towering Mela *gopura*, is built on a rocky promontory overlooking the Gulf of Mannar, and provides lovely

views. On the seashore here, there are many caves and rock-cut sculptures.

Manapad, 18 km (11 miles) south, has the Church of the Holy Cross. Built in 1581, it preserves a fragment of the "True Cross", brought from Jerusalem.

---

26 Tuticorin

🏛 Tuticorin district; 148 km (92 miles) S of Madurai 🚉🚌 ℹ www.tamilnadutourism.org

Tamil Nadu's second-largest natural harbour, Tuticorin (also known as Thoothukodi) is the main port of call for ships from Southeast Asia, Australia and New Zealand. It is also a major industrial centre.

The city's other important commercial activity is pearl fishing. Ancient Tamil literature mentions a flourishing trade with the Romans, who bought Tuticorin pearls in exchange for gold and wine. Today the government strictly regulates pearl fishing, in order to protect the oyster beds – sometimes pearl fishing is allowed only once in ten years. The pearl fishers still use traditional methods, diving to a depth of up to 70 m (230 ft) without oxygen. Most divers can remain underwater for more than a minute; their only safeguard against accidents or natural danger is to dive in pairs.

Tuticorin was occupied by the Portuguese in the 17th century and later by the Dutch and the British. Its colonial past is visible in two elegant churches, the Dutch Sacred Heart Cathedral, built in the mid-19th century, and the beautiful 17th-century Church of the Lady of the Snows, built by the Portuguese.

← The Vivekananda Memorial, on a rocky island off the shore of Kanniyakumari

↑ Famous Courtallam Falls, renowned for its waters' medicinal properties

27 Suchindram

🏛 Kanniyakumari district; 247 km (153 miles) S of Madurai 🚉 Nagarcoil, 5 km (3 miles) NW of town centre, then bus 🚌

This small temple town is closely linked with the legend of Kumari, the Virgin Goddess (an incarnation of Parvati). It is believed that Shiva rested at this quiet spot by the banks of the Pelayar river, while the goddess Kumari performed her penance at Kanniyakumari.

Suchindram's unique Thanumalayan Temple is dedicated to the Hindu Trinity of Brahma, Vishnu and Shiva. The rectangular complex has enormous, brightly coloured *gopuras*, which date from the 17th and 18th centuries, and depict stories from the great epics. One of the two main shrines, built in the 13th century, contains the sthanumalaya linga, which symbolizes Brahma, Vishnu and Shiva. The other is dedicated to Vishnu, whose image is made of a special kind of jaggery and mustard.

The temple also features a set of musical pillars made from single blocks of granite. When tapped, each pillar produces a different musical note. A special *puja* is held here every Friday evening, with music and a procession.

28 Tirunelveli

🏛 Tirunelveli district; 154 km (96 miles) SW of Madurai 🚉🚌 ℹ Tamil Nadu Tourism, Tirunelveli Junc, www.tamilnadutourism.org

Situated by the Tamaraparani river, Tirunelveli is dominated by the colourful and imposing Kanthimathi Nellaiyappar Temple, parts of which date to the 13th century. This complex of twin temples, dedicated to Shiva and Parvati, has two huge rectangular enclosures linked by a long corridor. The Shiva temple is to the north, while the Parvati temple is to the south. The elaborate *mandapas* here include the Somavara Mandapa, with two pillars carved like *gopuras*; the Rishaba Mandapa, with carved sculptures of Manmatha, the God of Love, and his consort Rathi; and the Mani Mandapa, with stone pillars that produce the melodic notes of Carnatic music (*p529*) when tapped.

Every summer, the temple's wooden chariots are led in procession through the town during the Chariot Festival.

Courtallam (Kuttalam) Falls, at an elevation of 170 m (558 ft), are 59 km (37 miles) northwest of Tirunelveli. This picturesque spot is famed for its exotic flora and the medicinal properties of its waters.

KERALA

Nestled between the Western Ghats and the Arabian Sea, Kerala is an enchanting mosaic of coconut groves and paddy fields, wide beaches and labyrinthine backwaters, verdant hills and rainforests. The state has been a major centre for the spice trade since 3000 BC, and was where the ancient Romans and Greeks came to purchase items such as pepper. Its history as a trading power has meant that Kerala has always had a heterogeneous population. Its diverse culture is enriched by the three great religions, which have ancient roots here. Hinduism is the faith of the majority, practised with a rare rigour that prohibits non-Hindus from entering most temples. Politically, too, the state has mainly been ruled by a series of Hindu dynasties. Christianity, followed by a quarter of the population, was brought to Kerala by the Apostle St Thomas in the 1st century AD, while Islam was introduced by Arab traders in the 7th century. Kerala's trading history made it particularly attractive to colonial empires, and the French, Portuguese, Dutch and British all tussled for power and established footholds here. After independence in 1947, this area joined the Indian Union; the current state of Kerala was formed in 1956. A politically conscious state where power alternates between Left and Centrist parties, Kerala boasts the highest literacy rate in India.

Mangalore
International Airport

Mangaluru

Uppinangac

KASARAGOD DISTRICT ㉒

Bekal

Neeleshwaram

NH66

Taliparamba

Kannur

A r a b i a n
S e a

❺
LAKSHADWEEP

KERALA

Must Sees

❶ Kochi
❷ Thiruvananthapuram
❸ Padmanabhapuram Palace
❹ Periyar Wildlife Sanctuary
❺ Lakshadweep

Experience More

❻ Kovalam
❼ Varkala
❽ Ponmudi
❾ Aranmula
❿ Agasthyakoodam
⓫ Kottayam
⓬ Sabarimala

⓭ Mannarasala
⓮ Alappuzha
⓯ Kaladi
⓰ Kodungallur
⓱ Munnar
⓲ Eravikulam National Park
⓳ Silent Valley National Park
⓴ Thrissur
㉑ Palakkad
㉒ Kasaragod District
㉓ Thalassery
㉔ Kozhikode
㉕ Wayanad District

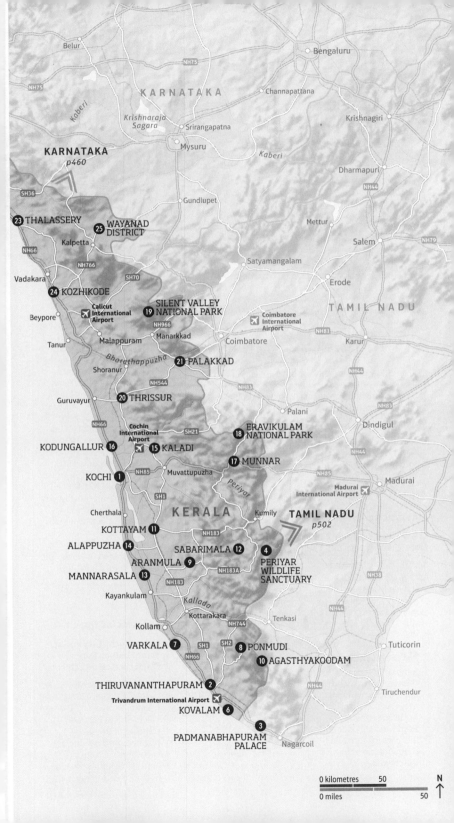

KOCHI

 Ernakulam district; 386 km (240 miles) S of Mysuru
✈ 36 km (22 miles) E of city centre, then bus or taxi 🚍
ℹ Tourist Information Centre, near Ernakulam jetty;
www.keralatourism.org/kochi

Kerala's most cosmopolitan city, Kochi is also its main trading centre for spices and seafood. Its harbour, surrounded by palm groves, green fields and backwaters, has charmed visitors for centuries.

① Mattancherry Palace

🏠 Jew Town ☎ (0484) 222 6085 ⏰ 10am–5pm Sat–Thu

Built by the Portuguese in the mid-1550s, this palace was given to the ruler of Kochi as a token of goodwill in exchange for trading rights.

> INSIDER TIP
> **Ferry Ride**
>
> Jump on a passenger ferry and get a cheap boat tour from the port at Matancherry to Fort Kochi and on to Vypin Island and Ernakulam - and back again. Avoid commuter times to miss the crowds.

The two-storeyed structure is today a museum with a rare collection of murals and royal artifacts. In the central Durbar Hall is the portrait gallery of the Kochi rulers. The adjacent bedrooms and chambers are renowned for their murals, representative of Kerala's temple art, which depict religious and mythological themes as well as episodes from the *Ramayana*.

② Paradesi Synagogue

🏠 Jew Town ☎ (0471) 232 1132 ⏰ 10am–noon & 3–5pm Sun–Thu

In a cul-de-sac at the end of a narrow lane in the heart of Jew Town is India's oldest synagogue. The first Jewish settlers reached Kodungallur in the 1st century AD, but persecution by the Portuguese in the early 16th century forced them to migrate to Kochi, where they settled on land given by the raja and built a synagogue in 1568. In 1940, there were 2,500 Jews in Kerala, but today only a few families remain, as the rest have migrated to Israel. The present synagogue, with its tiled roof and clock tower, was rebuilt in 1664 with Dutch help, after it was destroyed by the Portuguese in 1662. Its treasures include beautiful silver and gold Torah scrolls and crystal chandeliers. The floor is covered with exquisite blue willow-pattern tiles.

③ St Francis Church

🏠 Fort Kochi ⏰ Mon–Sat, after 11:30am Sun
🌐 stfranciscsichurch.com/

Established in the early 1500s by the Portuguese (who called it Santo Antonio), this is one of India's earliest European churches, with a simple façade that became the model for later churches. After the Portuguese, it was taken over by the Dutch and the British.

↑ High-rise apartment blocks dotting the lush landscape of Kerala

④ Willingdon Island

Named after the viceroy, Lord Willingdon, this man-made island was created in the 1920s out of silt dredged to deepen Kochi port. Situated between Mattancherry, Fort Kochi and Ernakulam, it has some good hotels, as well as the main harbour, the Port Trust building and the customs house. It is also an important naval base.

⑤ 🍴 Bolgatty Palace

⌂ Bolgatty Island
ⓦ bolgattypalacekochi.com

A narrow strip of land, this beautiful island with breathtaking views of the bay is the location of Bolgatty Palace. Set in 6 ha (15 acres) of lush green lawns, this palatial structure was built by the Dutch in 1744 and was later the home of the British Resident. It has now been converted into a hotel, and is also open to non-residents.

⑥ Hill Palace

⌂ Thripunithura, 10km (6 miles) SE of Ernakulam
☎ (0484) 278 1113 ⓣ 9am–4:30pm Tue–Sun

Built in 1895, the hill palace at Thripunithura was the official residence of the former rulers of Cochin, an early Keralan kingdom. The palace, set in spacious grounds, is now a museum with a fairly good collection of paintings, manuscripts and royal memorabilia.

Must See

EAT

Malabar Junction
Delicious fusion food at the stunning Malabar House boutique hotel.

⌂ 1/269 Parade Rd, Malabar Junction
ⓦ malabarhouse.com

₹₹₹

Caza Maria
Authentic Keralan specialities – try the fish moilee and rice.

⌂ 6/125 Jew Town, Mattancherry
☎ (0484) 222 5601

₹₹₹

Ethnic Passage
Small café with good coffee.

⌂ Bazaar Rd, Mattancherry
☎ (0484) 222 5601

₹₹₹

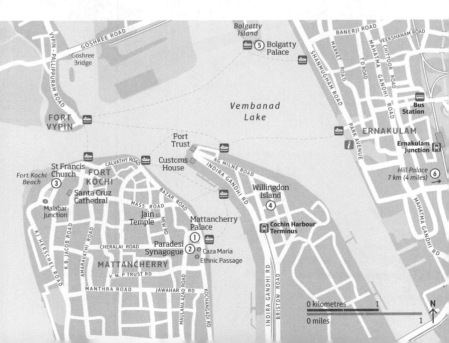

A SHORT WALK
FORT KOCHI

Distance 1.5 km (1 mile) **Nearest Ferry** Fort
Kochi Ferry Terminal **Time** 15 minutes

Kochi's natural harbour, created by a massive flood in 1341,
attracted imperialists and merchants from all over the world.
In the 16th century, the Portuguese built a fort here, which was
later occupied by the Dutch and then the British. Today, this
quarter, with its mixture of architectural styles, encapsulates Fort
Kochi's tumultuous history. One of the most famous sites here is
that of the Chinese fishing nets, which are thought to have been
brought over by Chinese explorers in the 15th century. This area
has now been declared a Heritage Zone.

Built in 1887, **Santa
Cruz Cathedral** *has
impressive murals
on its ceiling.*

This charming **Kashi
Art Café,** *in an old
Dutch building, houses
an art gallery.*

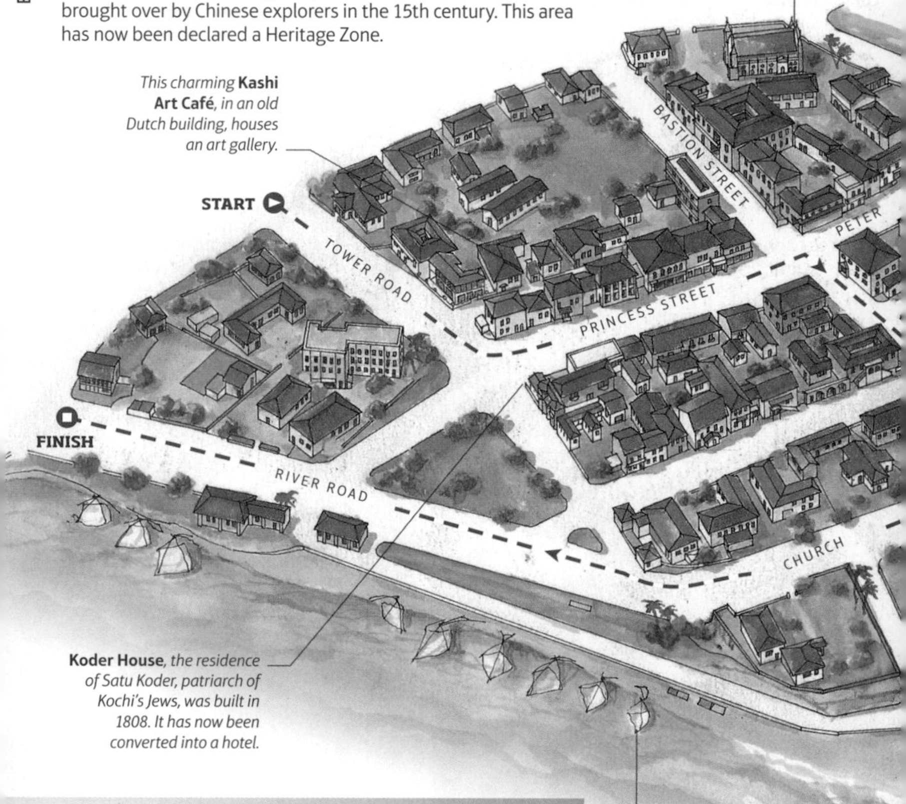

START

TOWER ROAD

BASTION STREET

PETER

PRINCESS STREET

FINISH

RIVER ROAD

CHURCH

Koder House, *the residence
of Satu Koder, patriarch of
Kochi's Jews, was built in
1808. It has now been
converted into a hotel.*

*First erected between
1350 and 1450, these
cantilevered* **Chinese
Fishing Nets** *indicate
trade links with China.*

←

Huge Chinese fishing
nets looming over the
sea as the sun sets

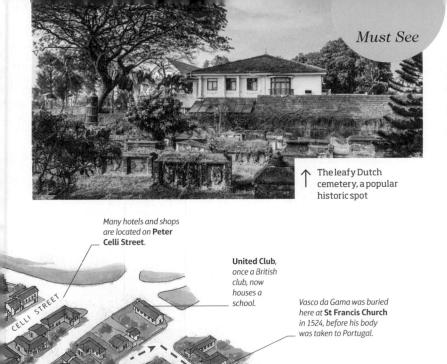

↑ The leafy Dutch cemetery, a popular historic spot

Many hotels and shops are located on **Peter Celli Street**.

United Club, once a British club, now houses a school.

Vasco da Gama was buried here at **St Francis Church** *in 1524, before his body was taken to Portugal.*

The historic **Malabar House Residency** *is now a wonderful hotel.*

The Dutch cemetery

CELLI STREET

RIDSDALE ROAD

PARADE ROAD

ROAD

NEW SEA WALL

Did You Know?

The name Kochi can be interpreted as "co-chin" which translates to "like China".

| 0 metres | 80 | N |
| 0 yards | 80 | ↓ |

②

THIRUVANANTHAPURAM

⌂ Thiruvananthapuram district; 205 km (127 miles) SE of Kochi ✈ 6 km (4 miles) W of city centre, then bus or taxi ▣▣ ℹ Tourist Information Centre, Museum Rd; www.dtpcthiruvananthapuram.com

Kerala's capital, known until 1991 as Trivandrum, was the seat of the former royal family of Travancore from 1750 to 1956. The Sree Padmanabhaswamy Temple has given the city its name, which means the "Holy City of Anantha", the sacred thousand-headed serpent on whom Vishnu reclines. The old quarter clusters around the temple, while along busy Mahatma Gandhi Road are mansions and modern high-rises.

①
Sree Padmanabha-swamy Temple

⌂ Fort area ⌚ Hours vary, check website 🚫 To non-Hindus ⓦ sreepadmanabhaswamytemple.org

Located in the fort encircling the old town, this is the only temple in the state with a towering seven-storey *gopura*, which is commonly seen in Tamil Nadu's temple architecture. A flagstaff encased in gold stands in the huge courtyard. The main corridor, around four sides of the courtyard, has 324 columns and two rows of granite pillars, each embellished with a woman bearing a lamp *(deepalakshmi)*. The hall also has mythological animal sculptures. Rich murals adorn the outer walls of the inner shrine, where the 6-m- (20-ft-) long reclining Vishnu resides, with his head towards the south and feet to the north.

②
Government Arts and Crafts (Napier) Museum

⌂ Museum Rd ⌚ 10am-4:45pm Tue–Sun (from 1pm Wed) ⓦ napiermuseum.org

Located in a well-planned compound is a complex of museums and the city's zoo. The Government Arts and Crafts Museum, earlier known as the Napier Museum after John Napier, a former governor of Madras, is in a red-and-black brick Indo-Saracenic structure, designed by Robert Fellowes Chisholm in the 19th century. It exhibits a rare collection of bronzes, stone sculptures, exquisite ivory carvings and a temple chariot, which were all fashioned in the territories of the former kingdom of Travancore.

The striking red-and-white Kanakakunnu Palace, where the Travancore royal family once entertained their guests, is adjacent to the complex, on top of a hill, and now hosts cultural events.

③
Shri Chitra Art Gallery

⌂ Museum Rd ⌚ 10am-4:45pm Tue–Sun (from 1pm Wed) ⓦ napiermuseum.org

In the northern part of the museum compound is the Shri Chitra Art Gallery, housed in a beautiful building. The pride of its collection are the works of Raja Ravi Varma (1848–1906) and his uncle Raja Raja Varma, pioneers of a unique academy style of painting in India. Raja Ravi Varma was considered the finest Indian artist of his time, and his paintings have inspired the popular religious prints that can be found in many homes.

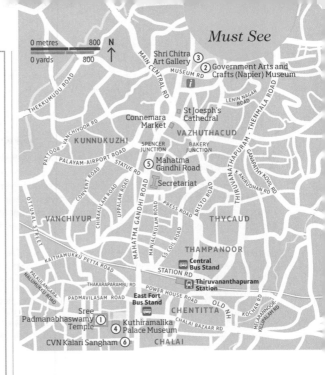

AYURVEDA THERAPY

Ayurveda means the science of life; it is a holistic medical system developed in India that dates back over 5,000 years. The focus is preventive medicine, using diets and herbs to avoid disease and promote longevity. As the sister science to yoga, *asana* (poses) and *pranayama* (breathing exercises) were as likely to be prescribed as herbal medicine. In modern Ayurveda, a physician will be trained as both a Western and Ayurvedic practitioner. The Government Ayurveda College in Thiruvananthapuram, founded in 1889, is one of the oldest in Kerala.

---

④ ⑮ ⑯

Kuthiramalika Palace Museum

🏛 Fort area 📞 (0471) 247 3952 🕐 8:30am-1pm & 3-5:30pm Tue-Sun

This interesting museum (also known as Puthen Malika) is housed in an 18th-century palace built by Raja Swathi Thirunal Balarama Varma, a statesman, poet, musician and social reformer. A fine example of Kerala architecture, this wooden palace has a sloping tiled roof. The wood carvings are particularly noteworthy, especially the 122 horses lining the eaves of the building. On display are artifacts from the royal collection, including a solid crystal throne given by the Dutch, and another carved out of ivory.

---

⑤

Mahatma Gandhi Road

The city's main road runs from the Sree Padmanabhaswamy Temple to the Victoria Jubilee Town Hall. Among the impressive buildings that line this road are the Secretariat, the headquarters of the state government; the University College; and the Public Library. The latter, founded in 1829, holds more than 250,000 books and documents in Malayalam, Hindi, Tamil and Sanskrit. To the north, beyond the Connemara Market, are the Jama Masjid, St Joseph's Cathedral and the Neo-Gothic building of Christ Church.

---

⑥ ⑮ ⑯

CVN Kalari Sangham

🏛 East Fort area 🕐 For lectures and performances 🌐 cvnkalari.in

This training centre for *kalaripayattu* was established in 1956 to revive Kerala's martial arts tradition. Each morning, students gather at the gymnasium (*kalari*) to perform a series of exercises that help develop combat skills. The centre also has a shrine to the deity of martial arts, Kalari Paradevata.

← Sree Padmanabhaswamy Temple, Kerala's most recognizable temple

3 ⌖ ⌖

PADMANABHAPURAM PALACE

🏠 Kanniyakumari district, Tamil Nadu; 52 km (32 miles) SE of Thiruvananthapuram
📞 (04651) 250 255 🕐 9am–5pm Tue–Sun 🚌

Set amid lush hills, verdant paddy fields and perennial rivers, Padmanabhapuram Palace is the finest example of Kerala's distinctive wooden architecture. The importance the region places on this style of building is evident in the folkloric figure of the master carpenter Perumthachan, who was said to have built many temples.

Laid out in a sequence of four adjoining walled compounds, comprising public and private zones, the palace has richly carved wooden ceilings, sculpted pillars, slatted windows and pagoda-like tiled roofs. It features many of the distinctive elements of wooden architecture: sloping tiled roofs to drain away the heavy monsoonal rains; decorative gables; and ornate wooden pillars. From 1590 to 1790, Padmanabhapuram was the centre of the former princely state of Travancore, which straddled parts of present-day Tamil Nadu as well as Kerala. In the 18th century, the capital of Travancore moved to Thiruvananthapuram, and the palace lost its importance. By a quirk of fate, this beautifully kept palace now falls in Tamil Nadu but is maintained by the government of Kerala.

← The Padmanabhapuram Palace, with distinctive tiled rooftops

VASTU SHASTRA

A traditional system of architecture within India, Vastu shastra is similar to feng shui and takes into account spatial geometry and layout. The focus is to integrate the structure with nature and the four directions: for example, it is said that sleeping with the legs towards the east improves reputation; towards the west brings mental harmony; towards the north increases prosperity – but never to the south as this brings bad dreams and negative thoughts. The Padmanabhapuram Palace is designed according to the principles of vastu. The doors and windows of the palace were placed to encourage energy flow.

The 16th-century Padmanabhapuram Palace ↑

→
The king's council chambers with carved wooden beams

The Lady's Chamber houses two large swings, a pair of enormous Belgian mirrors and a royal bed.

The Bath House is a small, airy room where the male members of the royal family were given a massage before they bathed.

The prayer hall, on the third floor of the King's Palace, has exquisite murals on its walls.

Built in 1550, the Mother's Palace is the oldest building in the complex. It contains intricate wooden pillars.

The clock tower's chimes could be heard from a distance of 3 km (2 miles).

Horse lamp

The king's council chamber has wooden louvres to let in light and air. The gloss on the floor was achieved using a mix including sand and egg white.

The dining hall, laid out over two storeys, could seat 2,000 guests.

The entrance hall has a profusely carved wooden ceiling with 90 different inverted flowers.

The main gate to the palace complex entrance is reached after crossing a large courtyard.

The palace museum houses artifacts including furniture, weapons, and utensils.

Did You Know?

The horse lamp in the entrance hall hangs from a chain that keeps it perfectly balanced, despite the wind.

Thick wisps of early morning
mist drifting over the placid
waters of Periyar Lake ↑

4 (⚐)(🏔)

PERIYAR WILDLIFE SANCTUARY

🏠 Idukki district; 190 km (118 miles) N of Kochi 🚌🚆 🕐 6am–6pm daily
ℹ️ keralatourism.org/ecotourism/destinations

A dense tropical evergreen and deciduous forest set high in the Western Ghats, Periyar's scenic beauty and rich biodiversity are due to the 100-year-old lake at its heart, which provides a permanent source of water for herds of elephants and other animals.

The construction of the Mullaperiyar Dam across the Periyar river at Thekkady in 1895 submerged large tracts of land and created a lake, which now forms the nucleus of the ecosystem of the 925 sq km (357 sq miles) wildlife sanctuary. The sanctuary was declared a Tiger Reserve in 1978 and is currently home to around 35 tigers, plus many playful elephants and numerous varieties of rare flora and fauna. As well as jeep safaris within the park itself, it is possible to go on short treks close to Periyar. There are many hotels near the sanctuary – the Forest Canopy has a glass-walled restaurant so you feel immersed in the trees. They can also arrange bamboo rafting.

150

The number of varieties
of orchid at Periyar,
though some are as
elusive as tigers.

THE WILDLIFE OF PERIYAR

As an important tiger and elephant reserve, Periyar is a firm favourite for wildlife enthusiasts. Depending on your budget and your sense of adventure, there are several ways to seek out the fauna, be it by boat, by jeep or on foot. The best time to visit is October to June.

① Tigers
In 1978, Periyar became the tenth Tiger Reserve in India and the first in Kerala. Although catching sight of the elusive tiger in his jungle abode is not unusual, it is by no means a sure thing.

② Elephants
The year-round water of the lake and abundant grassland make the sanctuary an ideal habitat for elephants, which now number approximately 800. Two-hour boat cruises on the mist-shrouded lake offer excellent opportunities for spotting them.

③ Indian Giant Squirrel
Found in Periyar's deciduous and evergreen forests, this huge maroon-coloured acrobat can leap 6 m (20 ft). Unlike his smaller cousins, who bury their food under the ground, this squirrel hides its nuts in caches high up in the trees.

④ Lion-Tailed Macaque
The Western Ghats are one of the few places to see the endangered lion-tailed macaque. They are shy but adept communicators – they have 17 different calls.

⑤ Birdlife
Birds include the majestic great hornbill and Malabar grey hornbill, as well as kites, parakeets and flycatchers.

One of Lakshadweep's
many pristine beaches,
lined with palm groves

5

LAKSHADWEEP

🏠 Union Territory of Lakshadweep; 200–450 km
(124–280 miles) W of Kochi ✈ From Kochi to Agatti
⛴ From Kochi & between the islands ℹ Permits
(mandatory) take at least two months to procure, see
lakshadweep.gov.in; trips are only possible as part of
a package tour, see www.lakshadweeptourism.com

An archipelago of 36 coral islands, with untouched
beaches and verdant coconut groves, the Lakshadweep
Islands lie off the Kerala coast in the Arabian Sea. Only
two islands – Bangaram and Kadmat – are open to
foreign visitors, while Indian visitors have a choice
of six; all offer superb snorkelling and scuba diving.

① Kavaratti Island

🏠 450 km (280 miles) W of
Kochi 🕐 To Indian passport
holders only

Lakshadweep's administrative
headquarters, Kavaratti is the
busiest island and home to a
large number of mainlanders,
most of whom work for the
government. It has beautiful
white beaches, and its crystal-
clear lagoon is popular with
water sports enthusiasts. Fifty-
two mosques on the island
cater to the predominantly
Muslim population. The Ujra
Mosque (restricted entry) has

an ornate ceiling carved
from driftwood. The island
also has a Marine Aquarium,
which displays a variety of
tropical fish and corals.

② Agatti Island

🏠 55 km (34 miles) NW of
Kavaratti 🕐 To Indian
passport holders only

Lakshadweep's only airport
is on Agatti Island. It has a
fine lagoon and offers easy
access for day visits to the
uninhabited islands of
Bangaram, Tinnakara and

Parali I and II. Although all
visitors arriving by plane
must go through Agatti,
the island itself is not open
to foreign visitors.

③ Bangaram Island

🏠 58 km (36 miles) NW
of Kavaratti

The uninhabited Bangaram
Island, covered with dense
groves of coconut palms, has
lovely sandy beaches. Its
lagoon, rich with corals and
tropical fish, is excellent for
scuba diving and snorkelling.
The Bangaram Island Resort
has about 30 rooms, as well as
a restaurant and bar. Visitors
can choose from the variety of
water sports available,
including sailing. A health
certificate from a doctor is
required for diving.

Did You Know?

Lakshadweep, which
means "100,000
islands", is the smallest
Union Territory
in India.

④ Kadmat Island

🏝70 km (43 miles) N of Kavaratti Island

Thickly covered with palm trees, Kadmat Island has two fine lagoons. The **Water Sports Institute** offers canoeing, kayaking and glass-bottomed boat rides, while the **Lacadives Dive School**, on the same premises, offers snorkelling and scuba diving.

Water Sports Institute
📞 (0484) 235 5387

Lacadives Dive School
🖥 lacadives.com

---

⑤ Kalpeni Island

🏝125 km (78 miles) SE of Kavaratti Island 🛂 To Indian passport holders only

The shallow lagoon of Kalpeni Island is the largest in the island group. With excellent reefs, Kalpeni is ideal for diving and snorkelling. Coral debris, deposited by a storm in 1847, has formed raised banks on the eastern and southern shores.

⑥ Minicoy Island

🏝258 km (160 miles) S of Kavaratti Island 🛂 To Indian passport holders only

Lakshadweep's southernmost island, Minicoy has a unique culture influenced by the neighbouring Maldives. Mahl, spoken here, is a dialect of the Maldivian Dhivehi, which is related to the Indo-Persian languages with a script written from right to left. Minicoy is often referred to as "Women's Island", as its ten villages are matrilineal. It is also rich in the performing arts; the traditional Lava dance is performed on festive occasions. Tuna fishing has become an important activity, with the establishment of a tuna-canning factory. Minicoy has a grand lagoon, and is the only island in the archipelago with a stretch of mangroves along its shores. A large lighthouse, built by the British in 1885, commands an impressive view of the sea.

MARINE LIFE IN THE CORAL REEFS

The complex and fragile reef ecosystem of the Lakshadweep islands is alive with an extraordinary range of marine life. Over 600 species of reef fish, such as clown fish and parrot fish, giant clams, delicate sea fans and sea anemones, ink-blue starfish, dolphins, harmless sharks and marine turtles, make up the spectacular diversity of the underwater world.

Cherbaniani Reef

Byramgore Reef

Chetlat Island

Bitra Island

Kiltan Island

Perumulappara

④ Kadmat Island

Amindivi Island

Bangaram Island ③

Agatti Island ② Pitti Island

Androth Island

① Kavaratti Island

Suheli Island

Kalpeni Island ⑤

0 km   60
0 miles   60

⑥ Minicoy Island

EXPERIENCE MORE

⑥
Kovalam

⌂ Thiruvananthapuram district; 16 km (10 miles) S of Thiruvananthapuram
✉ 🌐 dtpcthivuvanan thapuram.com

Until the 1960s, Kovalam was just a sleepy fishing village with wide courtyards for drying fish. However, once its spectacular beach and shallow, crystal-clear waters were discovered by Westerners, it became a favourite with hippies and backpackers, and over the years acquired the reputation of being a shabby, downmarket resort. Today it also attracts the rich and famous, who come here in private planes. As a result, the beaches are dotted with luxury and budget resorts, as well as cafés and government-approved Ayurveda centres that offer anything from a simple massage to three-week treatments.

Kovalam's sheltered natural bay is ringed by two rocky headlands. Its three beaches – Grove Beach, Eve's Beach and Lighthouse Beach, all within short walking distance of each other – provide visitors with their fill of sun, sea and sand. While the beaches to the south of the promontory are more crowded, the

> **The beaches are dotted with both luxury and budget resorts, as well as cafés and government-approved Ayurveda centres.**

ones to the north offer ample secluded space for sunbathing, safe swimming in the placid blue waters, catamaran trips and water sports.

---

⑦
Varkala

⌂ Thiruvananthapuram district; 40 km (25 miles) N of Thiruvananthapuram
✉ 🌐 www.keralatourism.org/varkala

This beautiful little beach town is better known among locals as a major pilgrimage centre. According to legend, the wandering Hindu sage Narada flung a cloth made from the bark of a tree into the air, and it landed at the spot where the small town of Varkala now stands. Narada then directed his disciples to pray for salvation at the newly created beach, which came to be known as Papanasham Beach or the "Beach of

Redemption". Since then, this beach has been associated with ancestor worship, as Hindus immerse the ashes of their dead here.

At the heart of the town is the sacred Janardhana Swamy Temple, which attracts many pilgrims. It is believed to be more than 2,000 years old.

Varkala's other pilgrimage centre is the hilltop Memorial of Sree Narayana Guru (1856–1928) at Sivagiri. Every day, countless devotees flock to the memorial of this great saint and social reformer, who was an advocate for "one caste, one religion, one god for mankind".

Now a popular resort and spa, the town is famous for its natural springs with therapeutic qualities, and is also a centre for Ayurvedic treatment and yoga.

Lighthouse Beach at Kovalam, and *(inset)* the lighthouse staircase

←

Snake boats on the Pampa river for the annual boat race festival at Aranmula

⑧ Ponmudi

🏠 Thiruvananthapuram district; 61 km (38 miles) NE of Thiruvananthapuram 🚌 𝒊 www.keralatourism. org/ecotourism/ destinations

Ponmudi, literally "Golden Crown", rises to a height of 915 m (3,002 ft) from the base of a thick tropical forest. Surrounded by tea estates and forested hills, this hill station still feels like an escape, refreshingly cool and mist-shrouded for most of the year. Its narrow winding paths offer pleasant walks.

---

⑨ Aranmula

🏠 Pathanamthitta district; 125 km (78 miles) NW of Thiruvananthapuram 🚌🚢 From Alappuzha 𝒊 www.keralatourism.org

This picturesque village on the banks of the Pampa river is famous as the venue for Kerala's magnificent snake boat races. The boat race festival has its origins in the legend of a devotee who once gave food to a Brahmin, believed to be Vishnu in disguise. However, the Brahmin, before disappearing, advised him to send his offering to the town of Aranmula instead.

Since then, during the festival, a ceremonial boat, carved out of a single block of wood, carries a consignment of food from a nearby village to the temple at Aranmula. On the last day of Onam, this ceremonial boat leads a procession of about 30 snake boats to the temple.

The Parthasarathy Temple, one of the state's five most important temples, is dedicated to Krishna in the form of Parthasarathy, the Divine Charioteer in the great epic, the *Mahabharata*. The image was brought here on a raft made of six bamboos, which is how the town got its name: in Malayalam, *aaru* means six and *mula*, bamboo.

Aranmula is also known for its mirrors made from an alloy of silver, bronze copper and lead, traditionally used in the arrangement of auspicious objects during Vishu, the Malayali New Year.

---

⑩ Agasthyakoodam

🏠 Thiruvananthapuram district; 60 km (37 miles) NE of Thiruvananthapuram 𝒊 Permits from Wildlife Warden, Thiruvanantha-puram, (0471) 236 0762; www.keralatourism.org

At an elevation of 1,890 m (6,201 ft), Agasthyakoodam is the highest peak in southern Kerala. It forms part of the Western Ghats and the Agasthyavanam Forest, named a sanctuary in 1992. The mountain is revered by both Buddhists and Hindus, as it is believed to be the abode of the Bodhisattva Avalokitesvara, as well as of the sage Agastya, a disciple of Shiva. The hills are rich in medicinal herbs and harbour many species of birds and wildlife. Trekking to the top takes two days and is permitted only from December to April. The summit provides fine views of the lake created by the Neyyar Dam. Permits are required to climb, and only 100 people are allowed on the mountain per day.

Scenes from the life of the Virgin Mary at the Cheria Palli Church, Kottayam →

⑪

Kottayam

⌖ Kottayam district; 160 km (99 miles) N of Thiruvananthapuram
🚍🚆 ⓘ www.discover kottayam.com

Enclosed by the blue waters of Vembanad Lake and the paddy fields of Kuttanad to its west, and by the lush hills of the Western Ghats to its east, Kottayam is one of Kerala's most beautiful districts. Its climate and landscape have combined to make the region prosperous. Kottayam town is surrounded by extensive plantations of rubber, and other valuable cash crops such as tea, coffee, cardamom and pepper. It is also the birthplace of Kerala's publishing industry and home to many Malayalam newspapers and magazines. A popular writers' co-operative society, the Sahitya Pravarthaka Sahakarana Sangham, which was set up here in 1945, has played a cardinal role in fostering the growth of Malayalam literature.

Kottayam also has an old Christian tradition that has been preserved by its large Syrian Christian population. It was one of the first towns to be patronized by St Thomas (p500) in the 1st century AD. Of the many fine churches and seminaries that dot the landscape, the best known are the two Syrian Orthodox churches, Valia Palli and Cheria Palli, both dating back to the mid-16th century. The churches stand on a hillock, about 2 km (1 mile) north of the town centre, and have colourful frescoes adorning their walls. Cheria Palli has lovely painted panels behind its main altar, depicting scenes from the life of the Virgin Mary.

Mannanam, 8 km (5 miles) north of Kottayam, is associated with the Syrian Catholic saint and social reformer Father Kuriakose Elias Chavara (1805–71), and was the seat of the first seminary of the Malabar Church in 1833.

A large temple dedicated to Shiva at Ettumanur, 12 km (7 miles) north of Kottayam, has beautiful murals, similar to those found at Mattancherry Palace in Kochi (p542). The 11th-century Mahadeva Temple at Vaikom, 40 km (25 miles) northwest of Kottayam, is famous for its

EAT

Chakara
This smart rooftop restaurant serves a particularly delicious Alleppey fish curry.

⌖ Raheem Residency, Beach Rd, Alappuzha
🌐 raheemresidency.com

₹₹₹

Saravana Bhavan
This friendly place is the best spot here for south Indian vegetarian food.

⌖ MG Rd, Munnar
📞 (0486) 230 418

₹₹₹

A houseboat navigating the backwaters around verdant Alappuzha →

elephant pageants and traditional dance performances between November and December.

12

Sabarimala

🏛 Pattanamthitta district; 191 km (119 miles) N of Thiruvananthapuram
🚌 To Pamba, then by foot
🌐 sabarimala.kerala.gov.in

One of India's most famous pilgrimage centres, Sabarimala lies in the Western Ghats at an altitude of 914 m (2,999 ft). The final 14-km (9-mile) approach from Pamba, through dense forest, is made on foot.

The temple dedicated to the popular deity Ayyappa is the focus of devotion here. The temple is open from November to mid-January, in April and during the first five days of each month of the Malayalam calendar. People of all religions can worship here – but women between the ages of 10 and 50 are restricted from entering. The final 18 sacred steps (each representing a sin that a devotee renounces on setting foot on it) are sheathed in *panchaloha*, an alloy of five metals, and lead to the inner sanctum. Only those who have observed 41 days of penance (celibacy, wearing black and not shaving) are entitled to undertake the pilgrimage.

---

100 per cent

Kottayam is the first town in Kerala to achieve 100 per cent literacy.

13

Mannarasala

🏛 Alappuzha district; 132 km (82 miles) NW of Thiruvananthapuram
🌐 mannarasala.org

The custom of worshipping snakes in Kerala reaches a climax at Mannarasala, the best known of the four main Naga temples in the state. According to legend, a woman from a family of great Naga devotees gave birth to two sons, one of whom was a serpent-child, an incarnation of Nagaraja, King of Snakes. He grew up within the family, but eventually asked his family to worship him before vanishing. The temples at Mannarasala, dedicated to Nagaraja and his consort, Sarpayakshini, are situated in a thick grove of tall trees and dense bushes, surrounded by thousands of stone serpents of various styles and sizes.

In Kerala, the ancestral home *(tharavad)* of every upper-class Namboothiri and Nair family is supposed to have a *sarpa-kavu* or snake-grove, housing a *nagakal* or snake stone. If a *tharavad* cannot afford to maintain its own shrine, the snake stones are offered to this temple.

The holy rites at Mannarasala are conducted by a priestess *(amma)*, a vestal virgin, who lives on the premises and is supported in her religious duties by her family.

Childless couples place a bell metal vessel *(uruli)* face down in front of the deities, to seek their blessings.

14

Alappuzha

🏛 Alappuzha district; 53 km (33 miles) S of Kochi
ℹ www.dtpcalappuzha.com

Alappuzha is a small town peppered with canals, backwaters, lagoons and beaches. The backwaters are largely untouched and have a rare serenity to them – this town is a popular launching point for backwater tours, but the slow ferry to Kottayam is the most affordable way to experience them. For your own backwater experience, you can book a houseboat in Alappuzha or Fort Kochi. The boats come with a chef, and you can take a day cruise or moor overnight.

The Nehru Trophy Boat Race is held here every August; competing boats include the impressive snake boat *(chundan)*, which is nearly 30 m (100 ft) long.

15 Kaladi

🏠 Ernakulam district; 35 km (22 miles) NE of Kochi 🚌 ℹ️ www.keralatourism.org

This quiet town on the Periyar river is the birthplace of the great Hindu saint Adi Shankaracharya *(p72)*. Two shrines, built in 1910 on the riverbank, honour his memory. One is dedicated to him and the other to the goddess Sharada. The old Shri Krishna Temple, not far from the Sharada Temple, has an image of the deity, said to have been installed by Shankaracharya himself. On the road to the Krishna Temple is a 46-m- (151-ft-) tall, nine-tiered octagonal tower, the Shri Adi Shankaracharya Kirti Stambha Mandapa. Each of its floors commemorates the life and works of Shankaracharya.

The 1,000-year old rock-cut Kalill Temple, 22 km (14 miles) southeast of Kaladi, was originally a Jain temple. It is now dedicated to the mother goddess. Unlike at other temples, a female elephant is used in all ceremonial rituals.

16 Kodungallur

🏠 Thrissur district; 32 km (20 miles) N of Kochi 🚌 ℹ️ www.keralatourism.org

Known as Cranganore to the Europeans, Kodungallur was the historical capital of the Cheraman Perumals, monarchs of the Chera Empire. Situated at the mouth of the Periyar river, this was the Malabar Coast's main port until a flood tide in 1341 silted up the harbour. After this catastrophe, Kochi *(p542)* became the main port.

The town is today a major destination for Hindus, Christians and Muslims alike. The Bhagavati Temple, in the town centre, is the venue of a three-day festival of erotic song and dance. This temple was originally the shrine of a Dravidian goddess. It was then taken over by either the Buddhists or the Jains. The festival marks the reclaiming of the site for the goddess.

St Thomas *(p500)* is said to have landed here in AD 52. The Marthoma Pontifical Shrine houses a sacred relic that was brought from the Vatican in 1953 to celebrate the anniversary of the saint's arrival 1,900 years earlier.

The Cheraman Mosque, near the city centre, resembles a Hindu temple in its design and was built in AD 629 by Malik Bin Dinar, who introduced Islam to Kerala.

17 Munnar

🏠 Idukki district; 130 km (81 miles) E of Kochi 🚌 ℹ️ www.keralatourism.org/munnar

The picturesque little town of Munnar lies at a height of about 1,800 m (5,906 ft) in a part of the Western Ghats that is known as the High Ranges. The name Munnar (which means "Three Rivers" in Tamil) is derived from the town's location at the

↑ Music and dancing at the annual festival in the Bhagavati Temple, Kodungallur

↑ Peaceful view over the tea plantations surrounding the town of Munnar

GREAT VIEW
Best Views

Enjoy wide-ranging vistas of misty hills and rolling plantations from Top Station. At 1,700 m (5,577 ft), this is the highest point in Munnar, right on the border between Kerala and Tamil Nadu.

confluence of three mountain streams: Nallathanni, Kundala and Mudrapuzha.

Located amid sprawling tea estates, Munnar was once a summer resort for the British government in south India. The most important plantation today belongs to Tata Tea, which oversees almost every local public facility.

A popular destination for visitors from Tamil Nadu and Kerala, Munnar and its environs offer a large number of hotels, restaurants and shopping malls. However, areas further away from the city centre remain relatively unspoilt, and the gentle hills offer excellent cycle rides and walks.

→

The Nilgiri tahr goat, inhabiting the rocky slopes of Eravikulam National Park

Mattupetty Lake, 13 km (8 miles) north of Munnar, is surrounded by semi-alpine scenery. A cattle-breeding centre is located nearby, and it is also possible to go boating.

18

Eravikulam National Park

☐ Idukki district; 16 km (10 miles) NE of Munnar ☐ From Munnar to the entry point, Rajamalai, ☐ Apr-Jan ☐ www. keralatourism.org/ ecotourism/destinations

The rolling high-altitude grasslands, a striking contrast to the dense *sholas* or tropical montane forests of the valleys, are unique to the mountain landscape of the Western Ghats. Easily the best-preserved stretch of

this extraordinarily beautiful landscape is the Eravikulam National Park, spread across a large area of 97 sq km (37 sq miles) at the base of Anaimudi Mountain. With a height of 2,695 m (8,842 ft), this has the distinction of being the tallest peak south of the Himalayas. Anaimudi, which means "Elephant Head", not surprisingly resembles one. The peak and its environs provide good hiking territory.

The park, on the border of Kerala and Tamil Nadu, was established in 1978 with the specific aim of conserving the endangered Nilgiri tahr, a rare breed of mountain goat. Today, the park is home to about 3,000 tahr, the single largest population of this slate-grey goat in the world. The park is also home to macaques, leopards and packs of *dhole*, the rare Indian wild dog. Its streams contain trout, and there are also more than 90 species of birds, including song birds such as the laughing thrush.

Eravikulam is also famous for the *kurinji (Strobilanthes kunthianus)*, the blue flowers that suddenly bloom en masse every 12 years and transform the rocky land-scape into a sea of blue. The *kurinji* is next expected to bloom here in 2030.

A lion-tailed macaque in Silent Valley National Park, and *(inset)*, the lushly forested hills of the Western Ghats

19
Silent Valley National Park

🏠 Palakkad district; 88 km (55 miles) NE of Kochi 🚌 Mannarkkad, the entry point 🛈 For permits and reservations (compulsory), contact the Wildlife Warden; www.silentvalley.gov.in

The Silent Valley National Park, spread over an area of 238 sq km (92 sq miles), preserves what is perhaps the country's last substantial stretch of virgin tropical ever-green forest. An important part of the Nilgiri Biosphere Reserve, the park is renowned for its rare plants and herbs, which include over 100 species of orchids, plus wildlife such as tigers, elephants, the Nilgiri langur, the sloth bear, the slender loris and the endange-red lion-tailed macaque. A variety of birds, as well as 100 species of butterflies, are also found here.

Accommodation is available at the forest lodge in Mukkali, just outside the park.

> An important part of the Nilgiri Biosphere Reserve, the park is renowned for its rare plants and herbs, which include over 100 species of orchids.

20
Thrissur

🏠 Thrissur district; 80 km (50 miles) N of Kochi 🚉🚌 🛈 www.dtpc thrissur.com

This town, radiating from an elevated area called The Round encircled by a road, was planned during the reign of Raja Rama Varma, the ruler of Cochin (Kochi) in the 1700s. In the heart of The Round is the Vadakkunnathan Temple, built in the 9th century and featuring superb wood-carvings and murals. North-east of the temple is the State Museum, with murals, woodcarvings and sculpture. The 18th-century Shakthan Thampuran Palace houses the archaeological museum, with stone sculptures and old weapons among its murals. The town suffered political upheaval for centuries, having been successively ruled by the Zamorins of Kozhikode, Tipu Sultan of Mysuru and the rulers of Kochi. The Dutch and the British have also made their presence felt, evidenced by the many impressive churches around the town.

Guruvayur, 29 km (18 miles) west of Thrissur, has Kerala's most popular temple. Legend has it that the 16th-century Shri Krishna Temple was created by Guru ("Instructor of the Gods") and Vayu ("God of the Winds"). The temple's elephant sanctuary is within the compound of an old palace nearby. It houses more than 40 elephants that belong to the deity – it is customary to present an elephant as an offering here.

The **Kerala Kala Mandalam**, founded in 1930 by the poet Vallathol Narayan Menon, offers intensive training in several dance and music forms. The complex also arranges performances.

Kerala Kala Mandalam

Cheruthuruthy (04884) 262 418 Open for tours Mon–Fri; bookings required Public hols, Apr/May

---

㉑
Palakkad

Palakkad district; 99 km (62 miles) N of Kochi www.dtpc palakkad.com

At the base of the Western Ghats, Palakkad (Palghat) derives its name from the dense forests *(kadu)* of *pala (Alsteria scholcris)* trees that once covered the land. Today, however, paddy fields and coconut plantations have taken their place.

Tipu's Fort, in the heart of the town, was built by Haider Ali of Mysore in 1766; it was subsequently occupied by the British after they defeated Ali's son, Tipu Sultan, some 30 years later. This sombre granite structure now houses various government offices.

The large Vishwanath Temple, on the banks of the Kalpathy river, is famous for

its chariot procession. On the outskirts of town are the extensive Malampuzha Gardens, laid out above a huge irrigation dam built across the Malampuzha river.

Thrithala, 75 km (47 miles) west of Palakkad, has the Kattilmadam Temple, a granite Buddhist monument dating from the 9th–10th centuries.

㉒
Kasaragod District

400 km (249 miles) NW of Kochi www. dtpckasaragod.com

Kerala's northernmost district, flanked by the Western Ghats to the east and the Arabian Sea to the west, is a fertile region of thickly forested hills and meandering rivers. It is named after its main town,

Kasaragod, a bustling centre of the coir and handloom industries. About 8 km (5 miles) north of Kasaragod, the beautiful Madhur Temple overlooks the Madhuvahiri river.

Situated 16 km (10 miles) south of Kasaragod is Bekal Fort, the largest and best-preserved fort in Kerala. This enormous circular structure is built with large blocks of laterite, and its outer wall rises majestically from the sea to a height of 39 m (128 feet). Inside is a concealed tunnel that leads directly to the sea. Bekal Fort's origins are shrouded in mystery, though it is thought to have been built in the mid-1600s by local chieftain Shivappa Nayak.

Many beautiful beaches lie to the north and south of the fort. About 6 km (4 miles) north of Bekal, Kappil Beach is a secluded area ideal for swimming. Kodi Cliff, at one end of the beach, is a scenic spot that offers wonderful views of the sunset on the Arabian Sea.

The Chandragiri Fort, on the banks of the Chandragiri river, is 10 km (6 miles) north of Bekal. This 17th-century fort is also attributed to Shivappa Nayak, who built it to defend his kingdom against the Vijayanagar rulers. The imposing Malik Dinar Mosque, nearby, is said to have been founded by Malik Ibn Dinar, a disciple of the Prophet Muhammad, who introduced Islam to Kerala in about AD 664.

The prettily situated 9th-century Ananthapura Temple, 30 km (19 miles) north of Bekal, is the only temple in Kerala in the centre of a lake. It is said to be the original abode of Ananthapadmanabha, the presiding deity of the Anantha Padmanabhaswamy Temple located in the state capital, Thiruvananthapuram *(p546)*.

The small hill station of Ranipuram is 80 km (50 miles) east of Kasaragod. Set amid acres of rubber and spice plantations, it offers good opportunities for trekking.

KERALA'S THEYYAM DANCE-RITUAL

This dance-ritual begins with the singing of the *thottam* (song) in praise of a deity, followed by a dance, the steps of which hint at Kerala's martial arts heritage. Drums and cymbals provide the accompaniment. The performers, all male, wear masks, body paint, colourful costumes and imposing headgear. A Theyyam is performed at Parassinikadavu Temple, 70 km (44 miles) south of Bekal, every day.

㉓

Thalassery

🏠 Kannur district; 255 km (158 miles) N of Kochi 🚌🚈
ℹ️ www.keralatourism.org

Fishing and agriculture are the major occupations in Thalassery (once known as Tellicherry), and the bartering of the day's catch is a lively event. The British East India Company established one of their first trading posts at Thalassery at the end of the 17th century. In 1708, they built the enormous laterite fort on the coast. An old lighthouse still stands on its ramparts, and there are also two secret tunnels, one of which leads into the sea.

The Thalassery Cricket Club, founded in 1860, is one of the oldest in India; cricket was introduced here in the late 18th century.

This region is one of the main centres of *kalaripayattu*, a type of martial arts, a fact that has made it a training ground for circus artistes as well. It is a common sight to see young men in the *kalari* (gymnasium) exercising to tone their muscles and practising with wooden weapons. Many images of deities adorn the *kalari*, giving it a sacred character.

㉔

Kozhikode

🏠 Kozhikode district; 254 km (158 miles) N of Kochi ✈️ Karipur, 25 km (16 miles) S of city centre 🚌🚈 ℹ️ District Tourism Promotion Council; www. dtpckozhikode.com

This busy commercial town, also known as Calicut, was the capital of the Zamorin kingdom, during which time it prospered as a major centre of the Malabar trade in spices and textiles. It was from Calicut that the word calico originated as the term for white, unbleached cotton.

Dominating the city centre is the large Mananchira Tank, flanked by the Town Hall and the Public Library, both fine examples of traditional architecture. A striking Roman Catholic cathedral also stands near the Mananchira Tank.

The town's Muslim heritage is indicated by its numerous mosques, remarkable for their large size and elaborate wood carvings. The Mishqal Palli, near the port, is the most impressive, with a five-tiered tiled roof. Note that this mosque is open only to Muslims.

The **Pazhassi Raja Museum** exhibits precious wood and metal sculptures and reconstructions of megalithic monuments. The Art Gallery next door has paintings by Raja Ravi Varma, the 19th-century painter who belonged to a princely family from Travancore. Kozhikode's busy shopping area, the quaintly named Sweetmeats Street – or SM Street, as it is popularly known – was once lined with shops selling *halwa*, a brightly coloured sweet made of flour and sugar. Court Road, leading off SM Street, houses the town's bustling Spice Market. Kozhikode is today the storage and trading centre for hill produce from Wayanad; spices such as cloves, cardamom, pepper, turmeric and coffee are sorted and packaged in the old ware-houses along the waterfront.

An 18-km (11-mile) drive north of the city leads to the village of Kappad, where a stone plaque on the beach marks the spot where Portuguese explorer Vasco da Gama is supposed to have landed in 1498. At the shipbuilding village of Beypore, 10 km (6 miles) south of Kozhikode, artisans still follow the traditional methods of their forefathers.

→

Kozhikode's Mishqal Palli Mosque, with its distinctive five-tiered roof

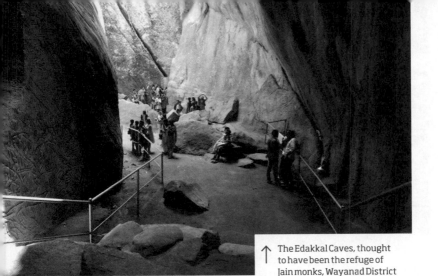

The Edakkal Caves, thought to have been the refuge of Jain monks, Wayanad District

The type of dhows that were built here for Arab merchants over 1,500 years ago are still in demand in west Asia. Visitors should make reservations.

Thusharagiri, around 50 km (31 miles) from Kozhikode, is a plantation town that grows rubber, pepper and spices. It is also a well-known trekking and rock-climbing destination.

Pazhassi Raja Museum
⌂ East Hill ☎ (0495) 238 4382
🕑 9am–4:30pm Tue–Sun

㉕
Wayanad District

⌂ 280 km (174 miles) NE from Kochi to Kalpetta 🚌
🌐 wayanadtourism.org

A region of virgin rainforests and mist-clad mountain ranges, Wayanad provides the ideal climatic conditions for Kerala's plantations of cardamom, pepper, coffee and rubber. Relatively untouched by modernization, this is the homeland of large tribal communities, such as the Cholanaikens and the Paniyas. It is also the favoured habitat of animals such as the Nilgiri langur, wild elephants and the giant Malabar squirrel. In the south, Kalpetta, the district headquarters, was

once a major Jain centre. The Ananthanatha Swamy Temple is at Puliyarmala, 6 km (4 miles) away, while on the slope of Vellarimala Hill, 20 km (12 miles) to the south, is the Glass Temple of Koottamunda, dedicated to Parsvanatha. The tallest peak in the area is Chembara (2,100 m/6,890 ft), situated 14 km (9 miles) southwest of Kalpetta and an excellent spot for trekking and birdwatching.

Sulthan Bathery (Sultan's Battery), 10 km (6 miles) east of Kalpetta, derives its name from Tipu Sultan of Mysuru (*p476*), who built a fort here in the 1700s. The **Edakkal Caves** have carvings of human and animal figures that are said to date to prehistoric times. The caves' environs abound in megaliths. The **Wayanad (Muthanga) Wildlife Sanctuary** is part of the Nilgiri Biosphere Reserve.

Edakkal Caves
🎫🎫 ⌂ 27 km (17 miles) E of Kalpetta 🕑 Sunrise–sunset Tue–Sun

Wayanad (Muthanga) Wildlife Sanctuary
🎫🎫 ⌂ 16 km (10 miles) E of Sultan Bathery 🕑 7–10am & 2–5pm daily 🛈 Permits from Wildlife Warden; (04936) 262 0454

ANDHRA PRADESH AND TELANGANA

This region formed south India's largest state until 2014, when a number of areas broke away to form a new state, Telangana. This is an area rich in trade, culture and natural resources, and its monuments tell of a long history of occupation. One of the first of many dynasties to gain a foothold here was the famous Mauryan Empire, known for both its epic conquests and for spreading Buddhism. The long-time capital of this region, Hyderabad, was founded in 1591 by Sultan Muhammad Quli Qutb Shah, an enlightened ruler whose city was a centre of trade and culture, where visitors rubbed shoulders with merchants, scholars and artisans from different lands. This was when the area's distinctive handicrafts flourished, including superb woven ikat textiles, pearl jewellery and inlaid metal bidri work. The state remained a cosmopolitan place under the following dynasty, the Asaf Jahi Nizams. This fabulously wealthy royal family ruled Hyderabad after the decline of the Mughals until Indian independence in 1948. Allegedly the richest rulers in India, the Nizams had a legendary collection of jewels – it was in Andhra Pradesh that the Kohinoor diamond was mined. The Nizams retained control of much of the state when the British arrived, and only the presence of the Indian army forced the Nizams to join this state with the Indian Union after independence in 1947.

0 kilometres 100

0 miles 100

N

Bhanupratapur

NH30

Umerkote

NH26

ODISHA

ODISHA
p342

Gopalpur

Kondagaon

CHHATTISGARH

Kotapad

Parvatipuram

Tekkali

MADHYA PRADESH
AND CHHATTISGARH
p274

Salur

NH16

SRIKAKULAM
DISTRICT

BORRA
CAVES

7

NH26

9

8 RAMATHEERTHAM

Vizianagaram

Visakhapatnam Airport

Anakapalle

6 VISAKHAPATNAM

Kottagudem

NH516E

NH16

Godavari

EAST GODAVARI
DISTRICT

10

NH30

Rajahmundry

Peddapuram

Eluru

NH16

Kakinada

Ryali

NH216

Mouths of
the Godavari

13 KONDAPALLI

12 VIJAYAWADA

NH65

Antarvedi

11 MACHILIPATNAM

NH216

Mouths of
the Krishna

Bay of
Bengal

ANDHRA PRADESH
AND TELANGANA

Must Sees

1 Hyderabad

2 Golconda Fort

Experience More

3 Warangal

4 Pochampalli

5 Palampet

6 Visakhapatnam

7 Borra Caves

8 Ramatheertham

9 Srikakulam District

10 East Godavari District

11 Machilipatnam

12 Vijayawada

13 Kondapalli

14 Amaravati

15 Nagarjunakonda

16 Srisailam & Krishna Gorge

17 Alampur

18 Tirupati

19 Sri Kalahasti

20 Chandragiri

21 Puttaparthi

22 Penukonda

23 Lepakshi

❶

HYDERABAD

📍 Ranga Reddy district, Telangana; 633 km (393 miles) N of Chennai ✈16 km (10 miles) N of city ✈22 km (14 miles) S of city 🚉🚌 ℹ️ telanganatourism.gov.in

The fifth largest city in India, Hyderabad was founded in 1591 and has now grown well beyond the confines of the original walled city. The sights include the grand palaces of the Nizams, as well as bazaars and mosques.

① Ⓜ
Falaknuma Palace

📍 Engine Bowli, Falaknuma
🌐 tajhotels.com

The most opulent of the Nizams' many palaces, Falaknuma Palace was built in 1872. The front façade is in Palladian style, while the rear is a jumble of Indo-Saracenic domes and cupolas. The lavish interior has tooled leather ceilings created by Florentine craftsmen, furniture and tapestries ordered from France, and Italian marble.

The Nizams' most important guests stayed here, but after the death of the sixth Nizam here in 1911 after a bout of drinking, the palace fell into disuse. Acquired by the Taj Group in 1995, it is now part of the luxury hotel chain.

←
The opulent Jade Room at the Falaknuma Palace, now a luxury hotel

②
Charminar

📍 Charminar Rd, Old City

In the heart of the Old City, Charminar ("Four Towers") is Hyderabad's signature landmark, a mosque and monument built in 1591 by King Muhammad Quli Qutb Shah of the Qutb Shahi dynasty. According to legend, it marks the spot where he first saw his lover, the beautiful Hindu dancer Bhagmati. Another story says he built it as thanksgiving at the end of a deadly plague epidemic. Today, a busy commercial area also known as Charminar surrounds the monument, with bazaars selling everything from cabbages to computers.

---

③
Purani Haveli (Nizam's Museum)

📍 Near Mir Alam Mandi Rd
🕙 10am–4.30pm Sat–Thu
🌐 thenizamsmuseum.com

A group of mid-19th-century Neo-Classical buildings, this

← Charminar's illuminated minarets seen from Shah Ali Banda Road

sprawling complex was the main residence of the sixth Nizam, Mahbub Ali Pasha. A glimpse of his lavish lifestyle can be seen in the eastern wing of the main building, in the Massarat Mahal. This has the Nizam's gigantic wardrobe, a 73-sq-m (786-sq-ft) room with closets on two levels, and a mechanical lift affording access to the upper tier.

Purani Haveli also houses the Nizam's Museum, which displays china, silver objets d'art and several fascinating photographs that capture the legendary opulence of the Nizam and his court.

④ ⊗ ⊗

Salar Jung Museum

📍 Near Naya Pul 🕙 10am–5pm daily 🚫 Public hols 🌐 salarjungmuseum.in

This eclectic collection of over 40,000 objects once belonged to Salar Jung III, prime minister

of Hyderabad between 1912 and 1914. Salar Jung's highly individual taste ranged from objects of sublime beauty to some bordering on kitsch.

The pride of the museum is the outstanding Mughal jade collection, which includes an exquisite, translucent leaf-shaped cup. Miniature paintings are also well represented, as are Indian stone and bronze sculpture and inlaid ivory objects.

European art is represented by 19th-century statuary plus paintings by the likes of Guardi, Canaletto and Landseer.

⑤

Osmania General Hospital

📍 Afzal Gunj 🌐 osmania generalhospital.org

This spectacular stone building with soaring domes was built in 1919 as part of the seventh Nizam's moderniza-tion plan after a catastrophic flood in 1908. Opposite it, across the river, are the Boys' High School and the High Court, built in pink granite and red sandstone.

Must See

EAT

Sodabottle-openerwala
This branch serves excellent Irani dishes.

📍 Road No 1, Jubilee Hills 🌐 soda bottleopenerwala.in

₹₹₹

Fusion 9
Upstairs bistro with global offerings.

📍 6-3-249/A Road no 1, Banjara Hills 🌐 fusion9.in

₹₹₹

Paradise Food Court
Chain eatery serving biryanis and kebabs.

📍 Mayur Marg, Begumpet 🌐 paradise foodcourt.in

₹₹₹

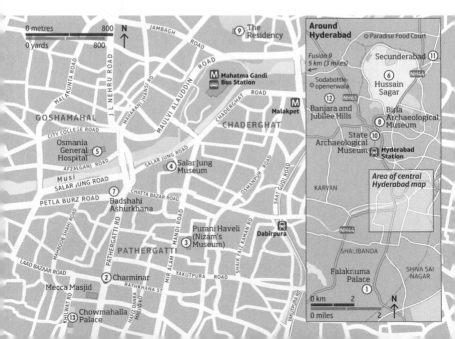

Did You Know?

Hyderabad's last nizam is said to have used the legendary 184.5-carat Jacob Diamond as a paperweight.

is a rock, on which stands a 17-m- (56-ft-) high monolithic statue of the Buddha weighing 350 tonnes. This was completed in 1986, but sank to the bottom of the lake when the ferry carrying it capsized. It was finally salvaged (intact) seven years later and installed on the rock in 1994.

⑥ Badshahi Ashurkhana

🏛 Patthergatti Rd ⏰ Daily, with permission of the caretaker

The historic Ashurkhana, or "Royal House of Mourning", was built in 1594 by Muhammad Quli Qutb Shah, the fifth Qutb Shahi ruler, as a congregation hall for Shias during the month of Muharram. It is one of the oldest Muslim buildings in the city, and houses beautiful silver and gold *alams* (ceremonial standards) that area studded with precious stones. These are carried in procession during Muharram. Exquisite mosaics adorn the central niche and the western wall, in glowing yellow, orange and turquoise.

⑦ Hussain Sagar

This huge lake, created in 1562, lies off Mahatma Gandhi Road. At the centre of the lake

⑧ Birla Archaeological Museum

🏛 Opposite Ravindra Bharathi, Saifabad ⏰ 10:30am–8pm daily 🌐 birlasciencecentre.org

Housed in a large complex on Naubat Pahad, this museum has a number of galleries that display bronze artifacts, arms and armour, sculptures, art and objects from excavation sites, including items found at Vaddamanu that date as far back as 100 BC. The complex also houses a science museum, planetarium, modern art gallery and the Birla Mandir temple.

⑨ The Residency

🏛 Koti Rd ⏰ 10am–5pm Mon–Fri, 10am–noon Sat

This elegant Palladian mansion, now the University College for Women, was built

in 1805 by the third Nizam as a gift for the British Resident at his court, James Kirkpatrick. It was decorated in Georgian style, with a painted ceiling and mirrors and chandeliers from Brighton Pavilion in England. The pediment above the portico still bears the East India Company's lion-and-unicorn coat of arms.

⑩ 🏷 State Archaeological Museum

🏛 Assembly Rd, N of Railway Station ⏰ 10:30am–5pm Sat–Thu 🌐 heritage. telangana.gov.in/museums

Two large Norman-style gateways mark the entrance to the Nampally Public Gardens, which contain the State Archaeological Museum. It has a large collection of Buddhist art, some fine Chola bronzes, Roman coins and even an Egyptian mummy. There are also replicas of murals and sculptures from the Ajanta and Ellora caves (*p422*).

⑪ Secunderabad

Northeast of Hussain Sagar along the Tank Bund Road, Secunderabad was estabished in 1806 as a cantonment to house British troops. It has since grown into a teeming

↑ The impressive and imposing Chowmahalla Palace and *(inset)* one of its opulent rooms

Falaknuma Palace *(p568)* for himself. Legend has it that the palace proved too expensive for him to maintain, so he gifted it to the Nizam, who promptly paid him a huge sum.

⑫
Banjara Hills and Jubilee Hills

As Hyderabad grew into "Cyberabad", these two leafy suburbs sprang up to house the bright young things of nearby HITEC City. The trendy Western clothes, smart boutiques and buzzing nightlife – not to mention the excellent eateries – here are in stark contrast to the traditional Muslim flavour of the Old City.

⑬
Chowmahalla Palace

🏛 Motigalli, Khilwat
🕐 10am-5pm Sat-Thu

Modelled on the Shah's palace in Tehran, Chowmahalla Palace was completed in the 1860s as a place for the Nizams to receive dignitaries. It is made up of four separate palaces and other grand buildings, spaced around landscaped gardens and formal courtyards. The most impressive structure is Khilwat Mubarak (Durbar Hall), which contains massive chandeliers, an array of furniture and ornaments, and historical displays.

THE NIZAMS OF HYDERABAD

Hyderabad was India's biggest and richest princely state, as large as England and Scotland together. The fabulous wealth of its rulers, the Nizams, came from their legendary hoard of emeralds and their diamond mines near Golconda, and many tales are told of their extravagance and eccentricities. The seventh and last nizam, Osman Ali Khan, was the world's richest man during his reign, but, unlike his ancestors, he was a notorious miser who smoked cigarette butts and wore the same set of shabby, patched clothes for weeks on end.

---

city that is an extension of Hyderabad. At its centre is the Parade Ground, overlooked by St Andrew's Church and the imposing colonial-style Secunderabad Club. The Neo-Gothic Holy Trinity Church (built in 1848) is 6 km (4 miles) north of the Parade Ground, and has beautiful stained-glass windows, elegant steeples on its square tower and a British cemetery.

The walled compound of the Paigah Palaces, where the Hyderabadi aristocracy lived, is 2 km (1 mile) west of the Parade Ground. The most imposing palace is Vicar Manzil, built by the leading nobleman at the sixth Nizam's court, Sir Vicar-ul-Umra; he had built the magnificent

←

The huge Hussain Sagar lake, dominated by a monolithic Buddha statue

2

GOLCONDA FORT

📍 Hyderabad district, Telangana, 11 km (7 miles) W of Hyderabad 🚇 🕐 Fort: 9am–5pm daily; museum & tombs: 10:30am–5pm Sat–Thu 🌐 telanganatourism.gov.in

Sprawling across a boulder-strewn plateau, Golconda Fort was a splendid city of grand palaces, mosques and gardens ruled over by the Qutb Shahi dynasty, which ruled the Hyderabad region from 1518 to 1687. It was famous for its great hoard of diamonds, including the celebrated Kohinoor diamond, now part of the British Crown Jewels.

This fortress is protected by three formidable lines of defence, the first of which encircles the citadel and its entire township. The middle wall surrounds the base of the hill, while the inner wall follows the contours of the highest ridge. Visitors enter through the Fateh Darwaza ("Victory Gate"), on the east side. Beyond the archaeological museum and the bazaar inside are the two massive arches of the Habshi Kaman Gate, which lead to the middle wall.

To its north is the austere, domed Jama Masjid, built in 1518 by Sultan Quli Qutb Shah, the founder of the dynasty; he was murdered here while at prayer by his son Jamshed in 1543.

Beyond is the Bala Hisar Gate, decorated with various Hindu motifs, including *yalis* (fantastic leonine beasts). This is the entrance to the inner citadel, known as the Bala Hisar Complex, where the royal palaces, assembly halls, workshops and an armoury are located. North of here is a walled enclosure known as Naya Qila, an extension to the fort. Hathion ka Jhaad ("Elephant Tree") is an extraordinary 700-year-old baobab tree imported by the sultans' Abyssinian guards.

The Grand Portico behind Bala Hisar is a good place to test the remarkable acoustics built into the fort's defences. A soft handclap here can be heard in the king's chambers at the summit.

Did You Know?

Golconda means "Shepherd's Hill". Legend has it a shepherd boy found an idol of a god here.

QUTB SHAHI TOMBS

This royal necropolis, where seven Qutb Shahi rulers are buried, is laid out in gardens with water channels, pools and tree-lined pathways. The tombs, built by each king in his lifetime, display a distinct and eclectic architectural style. The tomb of Muhammad Quli Qutb Shah, founder of Hyderabad, is the most impressive. It is surrounded by a spacious terrace, where poetry, music and food festivals are occasionally held, and traces of brilliant turquoise and green enamelled tiles still remain.

Qutb Shahi Palaces and the Summit

West of the Grand Portico are the ruins of the palaces. The most impressive is the Rani Mahal, a vaulted hall on a raised terrace, decorated with striking floral arabesques. Hollows in these carvings were once inlaid with precious stones. To the west of the Rani Mahal, a steep flight of 200 steps winds past royal baths, granaries, treasuries, water tanks and gardens to the summit, where you will find the three-storeyed Durbar Hall ("Throne Room") and a rooftop pavilion. Make the hike for the stunning views of the entire fort and its surroundings.

↑ The sprawling ruins of Golconda, and *(inset)* the acoustically precise inner chambers

EXPERIENCE MORE

3

Warangal

🏛 Warangal district
Telangana; 148 km (92
miles) NE of Hyderabad
🚂🚌 𝒊 telanganatourism.
gov.in

A major durrie (rug) weaving
centre today, Warangal was
described by the 13th-century
Venetian traveller Marco Polo
as one of the principal cities of
south India. It was the capital of
the Hindu Kakatiya kings, who
dominated this region until the
beginning of the 1300s.

An ancient fort at the edge
of the modern town is all that
remains of a once-grand city.
Built during the reign of the
Kakatiya queen Rudramadevi
(r 1262–89), its striking circular
plan, with three concentric
rings of walls, is still intact.
The innermost ring is made
of stone, with four massive
gateways at the cardinal
points. At its geometric centre,
four ornate and beautiful
toranas (gateways), of

remarkable size, show that this
was the sacred precinct, and
are the only remains of a great
Shiva temple.

A short distance to the
west is the Khush Mahal, an
audience hall built by Muslim
invaders in the 14th century.
Massive angled walls with slit
windows define a lofty interior
with vaulted arches, though
the roof is quite damaged. It
is very similar to the Hindola
Mahal in Mandu *(p282)*.

Hanamkonda, the site of the
first Kakatiya capital before it
moved to Warangal, is 3 km
(2 miles) northwest of Warangal.
The magnificent Thousand-
Pillared Temple here, dedicated to Shiva, was erected in
1163 by Rudradeva (r 1158–95),
the first great Kakatiya king.

This grey-green basalt
temple, known as the *trikuta*
or triple shrine, consists of a
trio of shrines dedicated to
Shiva, Vishnu and Surya. They
are connected to a *mandapa*,
now roofless, by a platform
with a magnificently polished
Nandi bull. A ceiling panel

Did You Know?

The warrior queen
Rudramadevi repelled
an uprising by nobles
who objected to
female rule.

carved with an image of
Nataraja covers the central
bay. The temple's gardens hold
several small linga shrines.

4

Pochampalli

🏛 Nalgonda district
Telangana; 41 km (26 miles)
E of Hyderabad 🚌
𝒊 telanganatourism.gov.in

Andhra Pradesh's ikat belt,
where intricate tie-dyed
textiles are woven, borders
Hyderabad. Pochampalli, the
name by which most of the
state's ikat fabric is known, is

the largest centre for this craft. The technique in its present form was introduced in the 19th century in Chirala, in Guntur district, from where the fabric was exported to Africa.

Pochampalli's main street is lined with busy workshops where the various stages of production take place. Ikat weavers first tie the yarn according to the pattern and then dye them in great vats. A special oil-based technique restricts the dye to the parts of the yarn that need to be coloured. The dyed yarn is then dried in the sun and finally woven on large hand-operated looms to produce a cloth called *telia rumal*.

The neighbouring village of Choutuppal, 20 km (16 miles) southeast of Pochampalli, produces mainly cotton ikat fabrics. Narayanpur, another major weaving centre, is about 36 km (22 miles) further down the Vijaywada Highway, again to the southeast.

↑ Hindu worshippers visiting the Ramappa Temple in the village of Palampet

---

⑤
Palampet

🏠 Warangal district, Telangana; 70 km (44 miles) NE of Hyderabad 🚍
ℹ️ telanganatourism.gov.in

This village is dominated by the Ramappa Temple, the best-preserved example of Kakatiya architecture. Dedicated to Shiva, it was built in 1213 by Recherla Rudra, a general of the ruler Ganapatideva (r 1199–1262). Like the Hanamkonda temple, the Ramappa Temple has a spacious *mandapa* with beautifully sculpted black basalt columns. This *mandapa*, which is cruciform in plan, also has porches with balcony seats on three sides. The eaves sheltering the peripheral

← The Kirti Torana stone gateway at the remains of the fort at Warangal

columns are supported by angled struts, many fashioned as three-dimensional maidens with graceful bodies in dancing poses. Other similar but smaller relief figures, as well as scenes from the epics, are seen in the central ceiling panel within the *mandapa*.

The sanctuary's exterior, in contrast, is devoid of any carvings, its simple ornamentation typical of the elegance of Kakatiya art. A stone pavilion sheltering a Nandi, which is smaller in size than the one at Hanamkonda, stands in front of the temple.

South of the Ramappa Temple is Ramappa Cheruvu, a vast artificial lake created by Recherla Rudra, and surrounded by picturesque hills. More Kakatiya temples can be seen at Gana Puram, a little village 13 km (8 miles) northwest of Palampet. The largest consists of a pair of Shiva shrines, both with *mandapas* and balcony seats. The main shrine has delightful female *dvarapalas* (doorkeepers) and finely carved brackets.

TRADITIONAL ANDHRA DURRIES

Although lustrous silk and wool carpets from Persia and Turkey were used to furnish the palaces of the Nizams of Hyderabad, Andhra Pradesh has long had a tradition of carpet weaving in Warangal and Eluru. Commonly known as durries, the carpets are made in cotton or wool, in a variety of designs and colours. The cotton durries from Warangal are usually woven into geometric patterns, while the woollen carpets of Eluru (274 km/170 miles southeast of Warangal) sport floral designs that hint at a Western influence. The more expensive *shatranjis*, with their chequered design, are made using heavy cotton thread.

→ Fishing boats and trawlers in the port at Visakhapatnam

6

Visakhapatnam

Visakhapatnam district, Andhra Pradesh; 354 km (220 miles) NE of Vijayawada 12 km (7 miles) W of town centre, then bus or taxi goandhrapradesh.com

India's second-busiest port after Mumbai, Visakhapatnam, also known as Vizag, is rapidly becoming the largest ship-yard in the country. It is an important industrial town and naval base as well. The town makes a convenient point from which to visit some of the beautiful beaches along the Bay of Bengal and the many picturesque temple towns of the northern coastal districts of Andhra Pradesh.

Named after Visakha, the Hindu God of Valour, this town was once part of the Mauryan emperor Ashoka's vast empire. Later, it was ruled by the Andhra kings of Vengi, and other south Indian dynasties, including the Pallavas, Cholas and Gangas. In the 15th century, Vizag became part of the Vijayanagar Empire. It came into British hands in the 17th century, after which it was developed into a major port.

Looming above the port is a hilly ridge with three crests, each with a religious shrine. On the southernmost one, Venkateshvara Konda, is a temple dedicated to Balaji (Krishna); in the middle is Ross Hill, with a mid-19th-century church; the third, Dargah Konda, has a shrine to a Muslim saint, Ishaque Madina.

Along the southern coast-line is Dolphin's Nose, a 358-m- (1,175-ft-) long rocky outcrop that rises 175 m (574 ft) above the sea. On it stands a light-house with a beam that can be seen 64 km (40 miles) out at sea. Vestiges of the city's colonial past are visible here in an old Protestant church, a fort, barracks and an arsenal, all dating to the 18th century.

Idyllic beaches, set on the fringes of the Eastern Ghats and bounded by forested hills and rocky cliffs, include the Ramakrishna Mission Beach

Idyllic beaches, set on the fringes of the Eastern Ghats and bounded by forested hills and rocky cliffs, include the Ramakrishna Mission Beach, now being developed as a tourist resort by Andhra Pradesh Tourism, Rishikonda Beach and Lawson's Bay.

Towards the north of the town, beyond Lawson's Bay, is Kailasagiri, a forested hill that has several lookout points for a panoramic view of the city and harbour. The twin town of Waltair, once a health resort for British officers, is north of the bay. Andhra University, one of the largest campuses in the state, is also situated here, along with a number of pretty 19th-century churches.

Simhachalam, the "Lion's Hill" Temple, is dedicated to Lord Varaha Narasimha, an incarnation of Vishnu. It stands at the summit of the thickly forested Ratnagiri Hill, 16 km (10 miles) northwest of Visakhapatnam. A flight of steps leads to the northern gateway, an elaborately decorated *gopura* that is the main entrance to the temple. Inside the compound is a tall *dvajasthambha* (flagpole). Similar in style to Konark's Sun Temple *(p350)*, the temple was constructed in the 9th or 10th century and was extensively

PICTURE PERFECT
Bay Shadows

Snap some shots from the rooftop Infinity restaurant of Novotel hotel, Visakhapatnam, as the amber sunset casts long mountain shadows over the nearby Bay of Bengal.

rebuilt during the 13th century. It is believed that the presiding deity was originally Shiva, but he was replaced by this incarnation of Vishnu after the reformer-saint Ramanuja visited the site in the 11th century.

7

Borra Caves

🏛 Visakhapatnam district, Andhra Pradesh; 90 km (56 miles) NW of Visakhapatnam 🚌
🕙 10am–5pm daily
ℹ goandhrapradesh.com

Close to the northern border of Visakhapatnam district, these magnificent limestone caves were discovered in 1807 by William King of the Geological Survey of India. The underground chambers, lined by stalactites and stalagmites, are now being developed by the state tourism department as a major attraction for visitors. Some smaller stalagmites are

worshipped as lingas, with Nandi bulls placed in front of them. The local people believe that the water trickling from the roof of the caves is from a mountain spring, that is the source of the Gosthani river.

About 33 km (20 miles) northeast of Borra is Araku Valley, home of several tribal communities, the state's original inhabitants. The valley, with its woods and waterfalls, offers pleasant walks.

8

Ramatheertham

🏛 Visakhapatnam district, Andhra Pradesh; 72 km (45 miles) NE of Visakhapatnam 🚌

Ruins from the Ikshvaku period (3rd to 4th centuries AD), when Buddhism flourished in this area, can be seen

at Ramatheertham. Set just outside the village is a group of structures on a hill known as Gurubhaktakonda ("Hill of the Devoted Disciple"). On a narrow rocky ledge about 165 m (541 ft) above the surrounding plains are the ruins of a stupa, monasteries, and prayer halls enclosing smaller stupas. Nearby, on a hill called Durgakonda, is a similar set of ruins, along with carvings of Jain *tirthankaras* (spiritual teachers) that date from the 8th and 9th centuries.

9

Srikakulam District

🏛 Andhra Pradesh; 108 km (67 miles) NE of Visakhapatnam 🚌

The headquarters of Andhra Pradesh's northernmost district, Srikakulam is on the banks of the Swarnamukhi river. On the outskirts of the town, at Arasavalli, is a sun temple built at an angle that makes the sun's rays fall on the deity's feet twice a year.

The Sri Kurmanadha Temple at Srikurman, 13 km (8 miles) east of Srikakulam, is dedicated to Kurma, the tortoise incarnation of Vishnu. It was built by the Chalukya kings in the 10th century but was substantially rebuilt by rulers from the Chola dynasty in the 12th and 13th centuries. The colonnade around the main shrine has 19th-century murals of Krishna and Vishnu.

Mukhalingam, 48 km (30 miles) north of Srikakulam, was the first capital of the Eastern Ganga kings, before they moved to Odisha (p344). The temples here date from their reign (the 9th to 13th centuries). The best preserved is the magnificent 9th-century Madhukeshwara Temple.

←

Heading deep into the Borra Caves, which are lined with stalactites and stalagmites

10

East Godavari District

Andhra Pradesh; 398 km (247 miles) E of Hyderabad to Rajahmundry 10 km (6 miles) from Rajahmundry Rajahmundry

The Godavari, one of south India's most sacred rivers, swells to a wide torrent (at places 6 km/4 miles across), just north of Rajahmundry town, where lush paddy fields and sugarcane plantations characterize the countryside.

Rajahmundry, the largest town in East Godavari district, is best known for the many Chalukya-era temples in its vicinity, and for the 2,743-m- (8,999-ft-) long bridge that spans the river. The lookout points on Dowleswaram Dam (built 1848–52), 10 km (6 miles) downstream, offer spectacular views of the river. Every 12 years, the Dakshina Pushkaram festival – the Kumbh Mela equivalent in the south of India – takes place here.

Peddapuram, famous for its fine handwoven silk and cotton, is 43 km (27 miles) northeast of Rajahmundry, on the road to Visakhapatnam.

Annavaram, 81 km (50 miles) northeast of Rajahmundry, is the site of the Satyanarayana Temple, on Ratnagiri Hill. It is renowned for its 4-m- (13-ft-) high statue of the Hindu Trinity and its ancient sundial.

The Godavari Gorge begins 80 km (50 miles) north of Rajahmundry. A drive or boat ride along the Gorge, which cuts through the hilly Eastern Ghats, offers views of spectacular scenery, with a series of lakes that many find reminiscent of Italy and Scotland.

Ryali, 37 km (23 miles) south of Rajahmundry, has a Chalukya temple dedicated to Vishnu. It houses a stone image of Goddess Ganga, from which flows a continuous trickle of water.

Draksharamam, located 46 km (29 miles) southeast of Rajahmundry, is famed for its 10th-century Bhimeswara Swamy Temple, which combines the Chalukya and Chola styles of architecture, and houses a 5-m- (16-ft-) high linga. The Godavari is said to have been split into seven streams by the Saptarishis (seven great sages) of Hindu mythology and three of these streams are believed to have gone underground here. Close to the town is an old Dutch cemetery, locally known as Ollandu Dibba ("Holland Mound"), with gravestones dated between 1675 and 1728, some with elaborate designs.

Antarvedi, on the banks of Vashishta river, a branch of the Godavari, is 112 km (70 miles) south of Rajahmundry. It is best reached by boat from Narsapur on the south bank. The Sri Laxmi Narasimha

Swamy Temple (built in 1823), with its brightly painted tower, stands on the river bank and is usually thronged with pilgrims who come for a dip in the holy river.

11

Machilipatnam

Krishna district, Andhra Pradesh; 340 km (211 miles) SE of Hyderabad

One of the first European settlements on India's eastern coast, Machilipatnam ("City of Fish") was a thriving port and textile centre in the 17th and 18th centuries. It was also where the British East India Company had their headquarters on the Coromandel Coast. The French and the Dutch briefly established themselves here as well. The Dutch cemetery, with its ornate tombstones, is all that remain from that period.

Machilipatnam was hit by a giant tidal wave in 1864, which drowned more than 30,000 people. It was caused by a volcanic eruption at Mount Krakatoa, some 5,000 km (3,107 miles) away. After that the town lost its importance as a port, but it remains famous for its *kalamkari* artisans.

---

⑫ Vijayawada

🏛 **Krishna district, Andhra Pradesh; 267 km (166 miles) SE of Hyderabad** 🚉🚌 ⓘ
goandhrapradesh.com

↑ Eluru Road, one of Vijayawada's two main streets and full of shops and offices

The second-largest city in the state, Vijayawada is a busy commercial town with one of the largest railway junctions in the country. In a pretty spot on the northern bank of the Krishna river, it is bounded on three sides by the Indrakiladri Hills. The area around the river banks is a pleasant contrast to the noisy, crowded town.

Within the city limits, on a low hill to the east, is the Kanaka Durga Temple, dedicated to the goddess Durga. The **Bapu Museum**, on M G Road, houses a fine collection of Buddhist and Hindu relics from the 2nd and 3rd centuries. Especially impressive are the white limestone Standing Buddha from the nearby Buddhist site of Alluru (3rd or 4th century), and the powerful depiction of Durga slaying the buffalo demon Mahisa (2nd century).

On the outskirts of town is the 1-km- (0.6-mile-) long Prakasam Barrage, first built in 1855 and extensively reconstructed in 1955. It irrigates nearly 1.2 million ha (3 million acres) of land, which has turned the Krishna Delta into the richest granary in Andhra Pradesh. Bhavani Island, a

←

A riverboat cruise carrying people to the Papi Hills, in the East Godavari District

scenic picnic spot, is just upstream, reached by launch from the river bank.

Mogalrajapuram, 3 km (2 miles) east of Vijayawada, and Undavalli, 4 km (2 miles) to the south, on the other side of the river, are famous for their rock-cut temples dating from the 5th to 7th centuries.

Mangalgiri, 12 km (7 miles) south of Vijayawada, is a textile village specializing in fine cotton saris and fabrics. It also has the impressive 14th-century Lakshmi Narasimha Temple complex, with a small Garuda shrine in front of it.

Bapu Museum
🏛 M G Road 🕐 10:30am–5pm Sat–Thu

---

⑬ Kondapalli

🏛 **Krishna district, Andhra Pradesh; 20 km (12 miles) NW of Vijayawada** 🚌
ⓘ www.goandhrapradesh.com

This pretty village, famous for its painted wooden toys, is dominated by the 8th-century hill fort built by the Eastern Chalukya dynasty. Encircled by ramparts and towers, the fort was an important stronghold in the Krishna Valley under the Qutb Shahis of

Hyderabad *(p568)*, in the 16th century. At the crest of the hill, a steep climb up, is the ruined Tanisha Mahal palace. The path descends past a deep tank, the granary and the armoury, to the Golconda Gate, which faces northwest towards Hyderabad.

KONDAPALLI TOYS

The craft of toy-making has been passed down for many generations in Kondapalli. Artisans fashion light, flexible poniki wood into distinctive figures of gods and goddesses, fruits and vegetables, to adorn Andhra homes during festivals. The various whittled parts are assembled using a tamarind-seed glue, before being painted in vivid colours.

→

An example of the brightly painted toys of Kondapalli

⑭ Amaravati

📍 Guntur district, Andhra Pradesh; 37 km (23 miles) W of Vijayawada 🚌 From Guntur ⓘ goandhra pradesh.com

The newly created capital of Andhra Pradesh, Amaravati is fast changing beyond all recognition as it expands, with administrative buildings and gleaming skyscrapers erected at a hectic pace. For centuries Amaravati was renowned mainly for its Maha Chaitya, or "Great Stupa", built by the Satavahanas in the 3rd and 2nd centuries BC. Today, little remains of this stupa apart from a low earthen mound, but in its day it was reputed to be the largest and most elaborate in south India.

The Maha Chaitya was enlarged several times by the Ikshvaku kings, reaching its final form between the 3rd and 4th centuries AD. Clad in the local white limestone, the structure was an earthen mound about 45 m (148 ft) in diameter and more than 30 m (98 ft) in height, including its supporting drum and capping finial. It was surrounded by a 6-m- (20-ft-) high railing and cross pieces, and lofty entrance gateways at the cardinal points, all exuberantly carved.

In the 5th century, when south India saw a revival of Hinduism, the stupa was abandoned, and remained so until a British official,

Colonel Colin Mackenzie, began excavating the site in 1796. Unfortunately, by the time a thorough investigation of the ruins began in the mid-1800s, most of the limestone portions had been pillaged.

Nevertheless, a great deal of fine sculpture remains at the site, and is on display at the **Archaeological Museum**, next to the Maha Chaitya. Unlike the stupa at Sanchi (p280), where the Buddha is represented through symbols such as the Bodhi tree or footprints, the Amaravati sculptures show him in human form. On display are large Standing Buddha images, some more than 2 m (7 ft) high, with natural poses and elegantly fluted robes that suggest the influence of late Roman Classical art. The second gallery has a remarkable

life-sized ceremonial bull, reconstructed from fragments discovered in 1980. A part of the stupa's railing, decorated with scenes from the Buddha's life, was rebuilt and is now in the courtyard.

Just north of the museum is the Amaralingeswara Swamy Temple, a colourful complex with four *gopurams*. Built during the 10th and 11th centuries, it was renovated in the 18th century by a local chief whose statue stands in the outer hall. A basement is believed to conceal the remains of a stupa, suggested by the pillar-shaped linga in the sanctuary, which was probably part of the stupa's dome.

Archaeological Museum
📍 Museum Rd 🕙 10am–5pm Sat-Thu 🌐 asi.nic.in/museum-amaravati

THE AMARAVATI SCULPTURES

The surviving limestone carvings from the Maha Chaitya are now divided between the Archaeological Museum at Amaravati, the Government Museum in Chennai (p496) and the British Museum in London. These reliefs testify to the vitality of early Buddhist art traditions in south India. Posts and railings show ornate lotus medallions, friezes of garlands carried by dwarfs, and Jataka Tales illustrated with vivid scenes of crowds, horse riders and courtiers. Drum panels are adorned with pots filled with lotuses, model stupas with serpents wrapped around the drums, and flying celestials above the umbrella-like finials.

← Remains of the Maha Chaitya of Amaravati, south India's largest stupa in its day

Did You Know?

A huge statue of the meditating Dhyana Buddha, which took ten years to complete, is at Amaravati.

15

Nagarjunakonda

📍 Guntur district, Andhra Pradesh; 189 km (117 miles) W of Vijayawada 🚇 Macherla, 22 km (14 miles) SE of site, then bus to Vijayapuri 🚌🚉 From Vijayapuri

Nagarjunakonda, also known as "Nagarjuna's Hill", is on the banks of the Krishna river. It was named after Nagarjuna Acharya, the 2nd-century Buddhist theologian and founder of an influential school of philosophy. Established in the 3rd and 4th centuries, when the region flourished under the rule of the powerful kings of the Ikshvaku dynasty, Nagarjunakonda was a sophisticated Buddhist settlement, with large monasteries and stupas, wide roads and public baths.

Nagarjunakonda was ruled by a succession of dynasties, culminating with the rulers of the Vijayanagar Empire, who built a fort around the Buddhist ruins. When the empire declined, the area was abandoned. It was rediscovered only between 1954 and 1961.

In the early 1960s, when the huge Nagarjuna Sagar Dam was being built across the Krishna, a number of these ancient Buddhist settlements were threatened with submersion. The Archaeological Survey of India reconstructed many of them, brick by brick, on top of the hill where the citadel once stood. Today, most of the hill has been submerged by the waters of the Nagarjuna Sagar lake, and the hilltop, jutting out like an island, is accessible by boats leaving regularly from the small village of Vijayapuri.

On the island, the path from the jetty leads first to the Simha Vihara 4. This comprises a stupa built on a high platform with a pair of *chaitya grihas* (prayer halls) adjoining it. While one of the *chaitya grihas* houses a second stupa, the other enshrines a monumental sculpture of the Standing Buddha. The Bodhishri Chaitya, opposite it, has a raised stupa contained within a semicircular-ended brick structure. To its west is the Maha Chaitya stupa which, with a diameter of 27.5 m

(90 ft), was one of the largest at Nagarjunakonda. Its internal rubble walls radiate outwards like the spokes of a wheel, and are filled with earth. Just ahead of it is the Swastika Chaitya, named after the Indian swastika emblem formed by its rubble walls.

Near the citadel walls is a stone megalith, some 2,000 years old. To its east is the **Archaeological Museum**, which houses superb sculptures from the ruins of Nagarjunakonda. They include limestone reliefs and panels carved with seated Buddhas, flying celestial beings and miniature replicas of stupas. Friezes from the railings that surrounded the stupas depict scenes from the Buddha's life. Among the sculptures are dignified Buddha figures dressed in elegant robes.

Archaeological Museum
🕙🕙 🕙10am–5pm Sat-Thu 🌐asi.nic.in/museum-nagarjunakonda

→ Relief of the Buddha in the gateway of a stupa, Nagarjunakonda

↑ The monumental dam at Srisailam, surrounded by thickly forested hills

16

Srisailam and Krishna Gorge

🏠 Kurnool district, Andhra Pradesh; 213 km (132 miles) S of Hyderabad 🚌 From Hyderabad 🌐 srisailam online.com

The pretty temple town of Srisailam, in the wooded Nallamalai Hills, overlooking the deep Krishna Gorge, is a popular pilgrimage spot. Dominating the town is the Mallikarjuna Swamy Temple, whose white-tiered *gopuras*, standing atop fortress-like walls, are visible from afar. The temple, which houses one of the 12 *jyotirlingas* (naturally formed lingas said to contain the light of Shiva), is believed to date to pre-Vedic times, though the present structure was built in the 15th century. The carvings on the walls represent Shiva in his many forms. A pillared hallway leads to the inner shrine, guarded by a monolithic Nandi.

Further up the hill is the Hatakesvara Temple, where the philosopher-saint Adi Shankaracharya is said to have written one of his treatises. A small Shiva temple at the top, Sikharam, offers breathtaking valley views.

The dammed waters of the Krishna power a huge hydro-electric project at Srisailam. When the waters are high enough, a luxury launch, the *Zaria*, ferries visitors from the reservoir at Nagarjuna Sagar to Srisailam Dam. For almost half the distance between the reservoir and Srisailam Dam, the river passes through a thick forest reserve, habitat of the tiger, panther and hyena. The river, which runs very deep at Srisailam, is known here as the Patal Ganga ("Underground Ganges") – according to legend, it springs from an underground tributary of the Ganges. On the ghats close to the dam, boatmen offer enchanting rides on their basin-shaped reed and bamboo boats.

17

Alampur

🏠 Mahboobnagar district, Andhra Pradesh; 215 km (134 miles) S of Hyderabad 🏠🚌

This village on the northern bank of the Tungabhadra river is the site of the earliest Hindu temples in Andhra Pradesh. Constructed by the Chalukya dynasty from Badami (*p466*) in the 7th and 8th centuries, the nine red sandstone shrines are collectively known as the Navabrahma Temples, and are dedicated to Shiva. The layout conforms to a standard scheme – each temple faces east, has an inner sanctum and a pillared *mandapa*, and is surrounded by a passage. The tower over the inner sanctum, capped by an *amalaka* (circular ribbed stone), shows the influence of north Indian temple architecture.

The later temples in the group have porches with perforated stone screens on three sides of the passage-ways, as in the Svargabrahma Temple, built in AD 689. This beautiful temple has outstanding sculptures, including a complete set of *dikpalas* (guardian figures) in the corner niches, and icons of Shiva in various forms. Some columns in the interior have been elaborately carved, such as those in the Padmabrahma Temple, but the Balabrahma Temple is the only one of the group still in use.

Next to the complex, the **Archaeological Museum** has a fine collection of early Chalukya sculptures. Just outside the village is the reconstructed Sangameshvara Temple, removed from a site that was submerged by the damming of the Krishna, 15 km (9 miles) to the north. Standing on a high terrace, it is similar to the Navabrahma group, except that the sculptural details have eroded.

Just to the southwest of the Navabrahma Temple complex are the Papanashanam Temples from the 9th and 10th centuries. These temples have imposing multitiered pyramidal roofs but little external decoration, though the interior columns are ornately carved. One of the temples has a ceiling panel of Vishnu's incarnations, and another has an image of Durga.

Archaeological Museum
◈ 🕐 10am–5pm Sat–Thu

18

Tirupati

📍 Chittoor district, Andhra Pradesh; 558 km (347 miles) S of Hyderabad ✈ 12 km (7 miles) S of the city centre, then taxi 🚆🚌

The most popular destination for Hindu pilgrims in India, Tirupati is the site of the **Shri Venkateshvara Temple**, situated in the Tirumala Hills, 700 m (2,297 ft) above the town. The seven "sacred hills" of Tirumala are believed to symbolize the seven-headed serpent god Adisesha, on whose coils Vishnu sleeps. The temple dates to the 9th century, although it has been expanded and renovated numerous times from the 15th century onwards. The aura that surrounds Lord Venkateshvara (a form of Lord Vishnu) as the "Bestower of Boons" has made his temple one of the most visited and the richest in India. The gold *vimana* and flagpole, and the gold-plated doorway into the inner sanctum, proclaim the temple's wealth. The jet-black stone image, 2-m (7-ft) high, is adorned with rubies, gold and diamonds. The deity also wears a diamond crown, believed to be one of the most precious ornaments in the world. He is flanked by his consorts, Sridevi and Bhudevi.

The entire complex is built to accommodate the huge influx of pilgrims, who come to seek favours from Lord Venkateshvara. This is one of the few temples in south India where non-Hindus are allowed into the inner sanctum. Devotees wait patiently in long queues for a special *darshan*, and make offerings of money, gold and jewellery.

The complex includes a ritual bathing tank and a small museum with images of deities, musical instruments and votive objects. Surrounding it are green valleys and the Akash Ganga waterfall, which is the source of the holy water used for bathing the deity. A unique feature at Tirupati is that many devotees offer their hair to the deity. It is believed that since hair enhances a person's appearance, shaving it off sheds vanity as well. This offering is usually made after the fulfilment of a wish.

In Tirupati town, the Govindarajaswamy Temple dates to the 16th–17th century and is dedicated to both Krishna and Vishnu. Built by the Nayakas, the successors to the Vijayanagar rulers, it is approached through a massive grey outer *gopura* that dominates Tirupati's skyline, and is carved with scenes from the *Ramayana* epic. An exquisite pavilion in the inner courtyard has carved granite pillars, an ornate wooden roof and sculptures of crouching lions. The temple has a magnificent image of the reclining Vishnu, called Ranganatha, coated with bronze armour. A short distance north of the temple, the Venkateshvara Museum of Temple Arts displays temple models and ritual objects.

Shri Venkateshvara Temple

🕐 Temple: 2:30–1:30am Sat-Thu, 2:30am–10:30pm Fri; darshan: hours vary, check website

🌐 tirumala.org

Entrance to the popular Shri Venkateshvara Temple, in Tirupati

GREAT VIEW
Kannappa Temple Views

For magnificent views of the Chittoor district, climb about 300 steps up a rocky outcrop to the Kannappa Temple at Sri Kalahasti, along with the many pilgrims who flock to the holy shrine.

19

Sri Kalahasti

Chittoor district, Andhra Pradesh; 41 km (25 miles) NE of Tirupati ⬜ From Tirupati

Located between two steep hills on the southern bank of the Svarnamukhi river, Sri Kalahasti is one of the most important pilgrimage centres in Andhra Pradesh. Dominating one end of the bustling main street is a 36.5-m- (120-ft-) high free-standing *gopura*, erected in 1516 by Emperor Krishnadeva Raya of the Vijayanagar Empire, which once ruled across southern India. The royal emblems of the dynasty, depicting the boar and the sword together with the sun and the moon, are carved on to the walls of this seven-storeyed towered gateway.

Nearby, similar but smaller *gopuras* provide access to the Kalahastishvara Temple, the town's main attraction, which is surrounded by a paved rectangular compound. A doorway to the south leads into a crowded enclosure of halls, pavilions, lamp columns and altars, all connected by a jumbled maze of colonnades and corridors. Some of the columns are carved as rearing animal figures.

In the north corridor is a set of bronzes of the 63 Shaivite saints called Nayannars. The inner sanctum, opening to the west, enshrines the *vayu* (air) linga (a symbolic representation of Shiva), one of the five elemental lingas of Shiva in south India. It is a curiously elongated linga protected by a cobra hood, made of brass. According to a local legend, a spider, a cobra and an elephant worshipped the linga in their own ways. The spider first spun a web around it to protect it from the sun's rays. The cobra, when he reached the shrine, was so upset to see the linga covered with dirty cobwebs that he cleaned and covered it with little stones. The last to arrive was the elephant, who removed the stones and decorated the linga with flowers. This continued for some time until the three devotees, each sure that his way of worship was the purest and that the others had committed sacrilege, decided to confront each other. In the ensuing fight, they collapsed, and Lord Shiva, pleased by their devotion, blessed them and named the shrine after them – Sri (spider), Kala (cobra) and Hasti (elephant).

Sri Kalahasti is also linked to the legend of Kannappa, the hunter, through its Kannappa Temple. One of the 63 Nayannars, Kannappa plucked out his eye in a frenzy of devotion and offered it to Shiva. A shrine commemorating him stands on the summit of the hillock that rises to the east.

→
Villagers riding a wooden cart across the river as the sun rises, Puttaparthi

---

KALAMKARI FABRICS

Deriving their name from the word *kalam* for pen and *kari* for work, these brightly coloured cotton fabrics are produced at Machilipatnam *(p578)* and Sri Kalahasti. Using a mixture of painting and dyeing techniques, figures are first drawn on the fabric, and then painted with a "pen" made of a bamboo stick padded at one end with cotton cloth. The traditional natural colours of ochre, soft pink, indigo, madder red and iron black are characteristic of *kalamkari* textiles. *Kalamkaris* from Sri Kalahasti depict mythological themes, with gods, goddesses and other celestial beings, while the ones from Machilipatnam display a distinct Persian influence.

Worshippers have thronged to this temple for generations in order to seek relief from the "evil effects" of Saturn. Some pilgrims also come here with their unmarried daughters in the hope that a special *puja* at the temple will help them find good husbands.

⑳ Chandragiri

⌂ **Tirupati district, Andhra Pradesh state; 18 km (11 miles) SW of Tirupati** 🚌 **From Tirupati**

This small village was once an important outpost of the Vijayanagar kings. It later became the capital of the Aravidu ruler, Venkatapatideva (r 1586–1614), whose reign saw the decline of the Vijayanagar Empire.

Chandragiri's once glorious past is reflected in the massive walls of its late-16th-century fortress and some abandoned palaces. The most important of these is the Raja Mahal, which has an arcaded Durbar Hall and a domed pleasure pavilion. It was here that Sir Francis Day of the East India Company was granted land in 1639, in order to set up a factory in what later came to be known as Madras. Nearby is the Rani Mahal, with its striking pyramidal towers and its façade decorated with leaves and geometric motifs.

㉑ Puttaparthi

⌂ **Ananthapur district, Andhra Pradesh; 437 km (272 miles) S of Hyderabad** ✈ **6 km (4 miles) SW of ashram, then taxi** 🚉 **Dharmavaram, 40 km (25 miles) N of Puttaparthi, then bus** 🌐 **sathyasai.org**

As the birthplace of Sri Sathya Sai Baba, the "godman" who preached religious tolerance, universal love and service to others, Puttaparthi has a special significance for his vast number of devotees from all over the world. The late Sai Baba's ability to produce *vibhuti* (sacred ash), seemingly miraculously out of thin air, is considered by his devotees to be a symbol of his god-like status and powers. From a very young age, Sai Baba, who was born Satyanarayana Raju in this village on 23 November 1926, claimed divine powers. When he was only 14, he declared that he was the reincarnation of a celebrated saint, Sai Baba from Shirdi in Maharashtra, who died in 1918. Sai Baba passed away in 2011. It is believed that he will return after his death as another saint called Prem Sai Baba. In 1950, Sathya Sai Baba established an ashram for his followers, whose numbers had swollen to a gigantic figure. Known as Prasanthi Nilayam, or the "Abode of Highest Peace", it is today a large complex with guest-houses, dormitories, kitchens and dining halls. Over the years, several buildings have appeared around the ashram – schools, colleges, residential complexes, hospitals, a planetarium, a museum and recreation centres – transforming this tiny village into a cosmopolitan township. Outside the ashram, at the lower end of the village, rural life continues, seemingly unaffected by the ashram's activities. The countryside around it is very fertile, with stretches of well-irrigated fields.

> **Did You Know?**
>
> The five elemental lingas representing Shiva each have their own temple in south India.

㉒

Penukonda

🏛 **Anantapur district, Andhra Pradesh; 425 km (264 miles) SW of Hyderabad** 🚌

A strategic Vijayanagar citadel from the 14th to the 16th centuries, Penukonda rises up the sides of a rocky hill to form an almost triangular fort. It was the capital of the succeeding Aravidu rulers until it was captured, first by the Qutb Shahis, then by the Mughals followed by the Marathas.

At the foot of the hill is the walled city, with its main gateways in the northern and eastern sides. To the south is a large tank. The main monuments are situated along the city's north–south road. The Parsvanatha Jain Temple contains a remarkable sculpture, from the Hoysala period (12th–13th centuries), of the Jain saint Parsvanatha standing in front of a serpent.

Further south are two granite temples dedicated to Rama and Shiva. The pilastered façade walls of the Rama Temple feature carvings depicting episodes from the *Ramayana* and the Krishna legend, while scenes from Shiva mythology are sculpted on the walls of the Shiva Temple. The adjacent Gagan Mahal is a palatial structure dating to the Vijayanagar period. An arcaded verandah leads to a vaulted hall with rear chambers. The domed pavilion above is topped by a pyramidal octagonal tower. A similar, smaller tower tops the adjoining staircase.

A short distance north of the walled city is the Dargah of Babayya, the shrine of a 16th-century Muslim saint. A popular pilgrimage place, it holds a fair every December.

㉓

Lepakshi

🏛 **Anantapur district, Andhra Pradesh; 478 km (297 miles) SW of Hyderabad** 🚌

An enormous monolith of Nandi, Shiva's bull, stands 1 km (0.6 miles) east of Lepakshi, welcoming visitors to this important pilgrimage town.

Lepakshi's top attraction is the Virabhadra Temple, set on a rocky outcrop. It was built in the mid-16th century, under the patronage of two brothers, Virupanna and Viranna, governors of Penukonda under the Vijayanagar empire. The temple is an important repository of the styles of sculpture and painting that evolved during this period.

Dedicated to Virabhadra (Shiva in his ferocious form), the temple stands in the middle of two concentric enclosures, built on three levels. It is entered through a *gopura* on the north side. On either side of the inner entrance are figures of the river goddesses Ganga and Yamuna, with a background of foliage. Among the other notable sculptures here are the carvings on the massive pillars that define the central space in the open hall; the deities, guardians and sages carved onto the piers of the unfinished Kalyana Mandapa; and the imposing monolithic seven-headed *naga* (serpent) sheltering a granite linga, to the southeast of the main shrine. Paintings in vibrant vegetable and mineral colours cover the ceilings of the two adjoining *mandapas* (one open and the other walled in), the walls of the Ardha Mandapa and some subsidiary shrines. Gods and goddesses, groups of donors and worshippers, and scenes from myths and legends bear witness to the superb pictorial art of the Vijayanagar empire.

← Virabhadra Temple, set on a tortoise-shaped granite outcrop in Lepakshi

LEPAKSHI PAINTINGS

The glory of Lepakshi lies in the magnificent frescoed ceilings of the Virabhadra Temple, where a series of exquisite paintings illustrate episodes from the epics and the Puranas. The figures are shown in profile, with prominent eyes and sharply chiselled noses and chins, and wearing beautiful costumes with hairstyles, textiles and jewellery rendered in exquisite detail. Some of the most beautiful paintings are on the ceiling of the open mandapa.

Ravana — Nandi — Shiva — Parvati — Brahma officiating as the priest —

Lepakshi's most spectacular fresco, showing the wedding of Shiva and Parvati ↑

As these examples demonstrate, many of the most spectacular paintings here are scenes from the life of the god Shiva, painted in a muted palette of white, green, black and various shades of ochre and brown, applied to a stucco surface specially treated with lime.

1 PARVATI AND SHIVA

Painted with her maids, Parvati is shown getting ready for her wedding to Shiva. Flat figures in stylized poses, often arranged in rows, characterize these paintings.

2 DAKSHINAMURTI

This painting shows Shiva as a Divine Teacher. Here, he is depicted seated on a hillock, expounding on mysticism and philosophy to sages gathered at his feet.

3 THE BOAR HUNT

This colourful work shows a wild boar charging at Arjuna and Shiva, who are preparing to shoot him.

Lush palm trees on Havelock Island

ANDAMAN AND NICOBAR ISLANDS

An archipelago of 572 idyllic islands in the Bay of Bengal, about 1,000 km (621 miles) from the mainland, the Andamans and the neighbouring Nicobar Islands are the peaks of a submerged mountain range that extends from Myanmar to Indonesia. They encompass three distinct ecosystems – tropical forests, mangroves and coral reefs – which support a staggering variety of plant and animal life. These islands are home to a number of indigenous peoples, and include some of the only uncontacted communities in the world. A few of these groups have always been fiercely independent; their hostility was probably why Marco Polo described the islands as being inhabited by cannibals when he journeyed to the region in the 13th century.

The Andaman and Nicobar Islands avoided the invasion and occupation that plagued the rest of the country, until Denmark colonized the islands in the 18th century. The Danes did not stay for long – they sold the islands to the British in the late 19th century. The Andamans acquired the sinister name Kala Pani ("Black Waters") in the 19th century, when the British established a harsh penal colony here. The islands became a part of independent India in 1950. More recently, the region was devastated by the Indian Ocean tsunami in December 2004. Thousands of visitors and locals lost their lives, although the indigenous peoples survived, thanks to traditional oral knowledge that warned them to flee to higher ground. Today, most of the island communities are well on the way to recovery.

ANDAMAN AND NICOBAR ISLANDS

Must See

❶ Mahatma Gandhi Marine National Park

Experience More

❷ Mount Harriet National Park
❸ Ross Island
❹ Ritchie's Archipelago
❺ Port Blair
❻ Cinque Island
❼ Chidiya Tapu
❽ Middle Andaman
❾ North Andaman

Kolkata,
Visakhapatnam,
Chennai

Bay of Bengal

ANDAMAN AND
NICOBAR ISLANDS

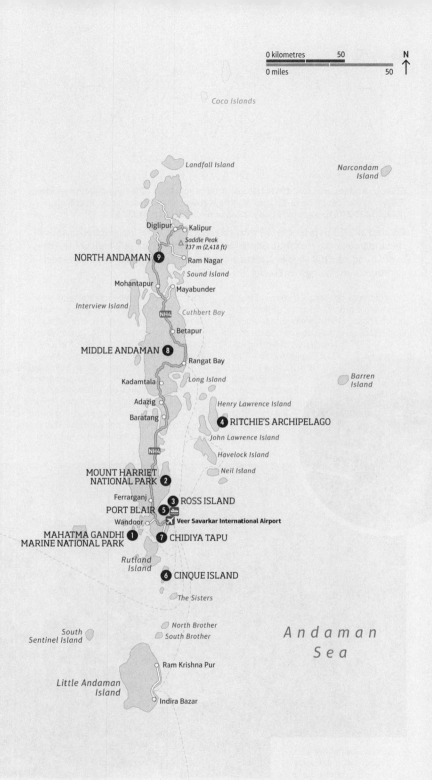

0 kilometres   50

0 miles   50

N

Coco Islands

Landfall Island

Narcondam Island

Diglipur · Kalipur

△ Saddle Peak
737 m (2,418 ft)

NORTH ANDAMAN ❾ · Ram Nagar

Sound Island

Mohantapur · Mayabunder

Interview Island   NH4   *Cuthbert Bay*

· Betapur

MIDDLE ANDAMAN ❽ · Rangat Bay

Kadamtala ·   *Long Island*

Barren Island

Adazig ·

Baratang ·   *Henry Lawrence Island*

❹ RITCHIE'S ARCHIPELAGO

John Lawrence Island

NH4   *Havelock Island*

MOUNT HARRIET
NATIONAL PARK ❷   · *Neil Island*

Ferrarganj ·   ❸ ROSS ISLAND

PORT BLAIR ❺

Wandoor ·   ✈ Veer Savarkar International Airport

MAHATMA GANDHI
MARINE NATIONAL PARK ❶   ❼ CHIDIYA TAPU

Rutland Island

❻ CINQUE ISLAND

The Sisters

A n d a m a n
S e a

South Brother

North Brother

South Sentinel Island

Little Andaman Island   Ram Krishna Pur ·

· Indira Bazar

↓ *Nicobar Islands*

MAHATMA GANDHI MARINE NATIONAL PARK

South Andaman Island; 29 km (18 miles) SW of Port Blair ⏱**Daily, subject to weather** **From Wandoor village** ℹ**Chief Wildlife Warden, Van Sadan, Haddo, Port Blair, (03192) 233 270; tours to Jolly Buoy & Redskin islands (03192) 232 694**

Created in 1983 to preserve the tropical ecosystems of 15 uninhabited islands in the Andamans, the Mahatma Gandhi Marine National Park at Wandoor stretches over 281 sq km (108 sq miles). It encompasses myriad lagoons, bays, coral reefs, rainforests and mangrove creeks.

Most of the islands are protected and thus inaccessible, but visitors can tour the marine park by boat. Ferries from Wandoor village skirt lagoons with kaleidoscopic sea beds, and are often chased by schools of playful dolphins. The coasts of the islands, meanwhile, reveal a fascinating transition from towering tropical canopies to silted mangroves. The park is most known for its coral reefs, which are often referred to as the rainforests of the sea and support an amazing array of marine life. Unfortunately, the 2004 tsunami caused widespread coral reef destruction in Jolly Buoy Island (open 15 November–15 May).

The islands in the park contain an impressive variety of plant life, with multilayered tropical rainforests of giant trees and over 120 types of fern, as well as mangrove forests. The only islands that allow visits are Jolly Buoy Island, ideal for snorkelling, and Redskin Island (open May–November), which has a nature trail.

Visitors swimming with grouper fish and *(inset)* a ferry to the national park

Angelfish
The angelfish is one of the reef's most vividly coloured fish. Its bright hues help to camouflage it as well as to advertise its territory.

Lion or Scorpion Fish
Measuring up to 40 cm (16 in), this ornate fish has venom in its rays, which can be fatal.

Giant Robber Crab
One of the largest and rarest crabs in the world, the giant robber has powerful claws that help it to climb trees and to break coconut shells.

Grouper Fish
The commonly found groupers can change their colour to match the rocks and reefs.

EXPERIENCE MORE

Mount Harriet National Park

🏝 South Andaman Island; 55 km (34 miles) N of Port Blair 🚢 From Chatham Wharf or Phoenix Bay Jetty (Fisheries Jetty) in Port Blair to Bambooflat Jetty, then taxi; day tickets available 🛈 Park permits from Chief Conservator; (03192) 230152

Some of the Andamans' highest peaks are in Mount Harriet National Park, lying across the inlet from Phoenix Jetty in Port Blair. Mount Harriet, at 365 m (1,198 ft), is surrounded by evergreen forests that support a remarkable biodiversity, mainly birds such as the great black woodpecker and the green imperial pigeon.

Well-marked hiking trails include the 2-km (1-mile) walk to Kalapathar, and the 16-km (10-mile) trail to Madhuban Beach, where visitors might see elephants. Beware of leeches during the monsoon.

The Forest Guest House, on top of Mount Harriet, offers fine views of Port Blair and Ross Island. Visits and overnight stays are possible with a permit.

---

3 Ross Island

🏝 Ross Island; 2 km (1 mile) E of Port Blair 🚢 From Aberdeen Jetty 🛈 Travel permits required; www.andamantourism.gov.in

A short ferry ride from Port Blair leads to Ross Island, which was the home of the indigenous Great Andamanese. In 1858 the British commandeered the island as a base for the administrators of the penal colony in neighbouring

↑ A tourist in the grounds of the ruined Anglican church on Ross Island

Port Blair, and set to work establishing a complex of swimming pools and bungalows, built through the efforts of convict labour. Within 20 years of British occupation, diseases such as syphilis and measles had virtually wiped out the Great Andamanese, whose numbers dropped from 5,000 to just 28.

The bleak modern history of the island continued in World War II, when the Japanese converted the site into a prisoner of war camp, and built war installations, remnants of which can still be seen. Ross Island now lies deserted, and the few extant signs of its colonial past, such as the chief commissioner's house and the Anglican church, are dilapidated and overgrown.

The area is now under the administration of the Indian Navy, whose museum, Smritika, records the lives of those imprisoned here. It is only possible to visit Ross Island on a day trip.

4

Ritchie's Archipelago

⌂ 20–40 km (12–25 miles) E of South Andaman 🚢 From Port Blair and Rangat Bay (Middle Andaman) ℹ Travel permits required; www.andamantourism.gov.in

Most of the islands in this tiny cluster are protected as a national park to preserve their biodiversity, and only three islands are open to visitors.

Of these, Neil Island, 42 km (26 miles) northeast, is the closest to the capital and is inhabited by settlers from Bengal. The interior is lush with paddy fields and plantations, and the beaches offer superb snorkelling opportunities.

Havelock Island, 69 km (43 miles) northeast of Port Blair, is the most popular among visitors, with a bazaar and guesthouses. **Coastal Cruise** and **MV Makruzz** both run ferry services there, and once on the island the best way to explore is by scooter or bike. Accommodation is available at Radhanagar Beach, where dolphins and turtles can be spotted.

The northernmost island in the archipelago, Long Island, 82 km (51 miles) north of Port Blair, attracts few visitors, perhaps because of the six-hour journey to get there (Long Island ferries do not run on Thursdays and Sundays). It nevertheless has attractive beaches. There is just one rest house and no public transport, although bicycles can be hired. North Passage Island, 55 km (34 miles) south of Port Blair, has a beautiful sandy beach at Merk Bay.

Barren Island, 132 km (82 miles) northeast of Port Blair, has India's only active volcano. Rising sharply from the sea, its vast crater spews smoke and the occasional lava flow. There is no public ferry; only chartered ferries make the 20-hour journey from Port Blair. Landing on the island is not permitted, so divers are the only visitors.

Coastal Cruise
w coastalcruise.in

MV Makruzz
w makruzz.com

Mangroves, and *(inset)* a natural rock arch at a beach on Neil Island

---

SNORKELLING AND SCUBA DIVING

Snorkels can be hired from numerous tour operators. For diving, there are several registered centres on Havelock Island, like Barefoot Scuba *(www.barefootscuba.in)*, Dive India *(diveindia.com)* and Andaman Bubbles *(andamanbubbles.com)*, which also runs diving courses, as does Scubalov *(scubalov.in)*. Lacadives *(www.lacadives.com)* is based in Chidiya Tapu. Coral reefs are sensitive, and even the gentlest touch can kill them. Do not touch or tread on them, and be very careful with your fins.

⑤

Port Blair

📍 South Andaman Island; 1,360 km (848 miles) E of Chennai ✈ 3 km (2 miles) S of town centre, then bus or taxi 🚌 ℹ️ www.andaman tourism.gov.in

↑ Leaving Port Blair's Aberdeen Jetty on a craft hired from the Rajeev Gandhi Water Sports Complex

The capital Port Blair, located in the southeast of South Andaman Island, is a good base from which to travel around the archipelago, and offers hotels, banks, tour operators and sports complexes.

The town's history began in 1789, when Lieutenant Archibald Blair of the British East India Company chose this site as a safe harbour for the Company's vessels. Fifty years later the islands became a penal colony. Those incarcerated were political activists involved in the War of Independence of 1857. In 1896, the construction of the **Cellular Jail** began; it soon became a symbol of colonial oppression. Designed specifically for solitary confinement, it earned the Islands the dreaded name of Kala Pani or "Black Waters", reflecting the atrocities that awaited the prisoners. Of the original seven wings laid out around a central watchtower, only four remain; three have been converted into a hospital and are lined with cells. The Japanese, who occupied the islands during World War II, destroyed part of the prison. In 1945, the British moved back and closed the jail. It is now a memorial to the political prisoners; a moving sound and light show is held here every evening.

The town's other places of interest are scattered around Aberdeen Bazaar, on the east side of town. West of the bazaar, the **Anthropological Museum** sheds light on the islands' tribal inhabitants and has a collection of rare photographs taken in the 1960s. The aquarium, also known as the **Fisheries Museum**, at the eastern end of M G Road, showcases hundreds of species of unusual fish, corals and shells. Next door, the **Rajiv Gandhi Water Sports Complex** hires out rowing boats, jet skis and paddle boats. The **Samudrika Naval Marine Museum**, run by the Indian Navy, has five galleries devoted to the history, geography and anthropology of the islands, and has a superb display on marine life.

Chatham Sawmills on Chatham Island, 5 km (3 miles) north, is one of the oldest and largest saw mills in Asia. Established by the British in 1836, this is where many of the islands' trees, including the towering *padauk* (Andaman redwood), are processed.

Viper Island, named after a 19th-century British shipping vessel that was wrecked off its shore, can be reached via a cruise from Port Blair. Its sinister history involves the local prison, which was built in 1867 and whose macabre gallows and torture posts can still be seen. Only daytime visits are allowed as the island has no inhabitants. About 14 km (9 miles) from Port Blair lies Sippighat Farm, where many varieties of spices and indigenous plants are grown.

Cellular Jail
♿ 🕐 9am–12:30pm & 1:30–4:45pm daily

Anthropological Museum
📞 (03192) 232 291 🕐 9am–4:30pm Tue–Sun 🚫 Public hols

Fisheries Museum
♿ 🕐 9am–1pm & 1:30–4:30pm Tue–Sun 🚫 2nd Sat of month, public hols

Rajiv Gandhi Water Sports Complex
📞 (03192) 232 694 🕐 10am–6pm daily

Samudrika Naval Marine Museum
♿ 📞 (03192) 248 327 (ext 2437) 🕐 9am–noon & 2–5pm Tue–Sun

Chatham Sawmills
🕐 10am–2pm Mon–Sat

⑥

Cinque Island

🏝 Cinque Island; 26 km (16 miles) S of Port Blair 🚤 Motorboats from Port Blair & Wandoor 🛈 Travel permits required; www.andamantourism.gov.in

The volcanic Cinque Island is perhaps the most beautiful of the entire Andamans group, as it has had little human interference over the years and is mostly uninhabited. Comprising two islands, North and South Cinque, connected by a sandbar, it was declared a sanctuary in 1987. The surrounding reefs of rare coral and varied marine life offer some of the best snorkelling and scuba diving in the Andamans. The sandy shores are also among the last refuges of the hawksbill and green sea turtles, which nest here annually in their hundreds. Visitors may only come for day trips.

Tiny groups of islands known as the Sisters and the Brothers, lying 12 km (7 miles) and 32 km (20 miles) south of Cinque respectively, can be visited only with a professional diving group. Large tracts of the remote southern island of **Little Andaman**, 120 km (75 miles) and eight hours by ferry from Port Blair, are a reserve for the 112 surviving members of the Onge tribe. It is not advisable to try and make contact with them. Part of northern Little Andaman is open to visitors.

Little Andaman

🚤 Check website for schedule 🛈 www.andamantourism.gov.in

---

⑦

Chidiya Tapu

🏝 South Andaman Island; 17 km (10 miles) S of Port Blair 🚍🚤 From Port Blair; taxis also available

The fishing village of Chidiya Tapu ("Bird Island"), at the southernmost tip of South Andaman Island, is an hour's drive from Port Blair. Its white beaches, skirting a large bay, make it a popular day trip with visitors.

Forest trails through the surrounding tropical undergrowth are a birdwatcher's delight, as they teem with an incredible variety of species, including rare sunbirds, kingfishers, woodpeckers and eagles. The beaches of Chidiya Tapu's, especially the picturesque Munda Pahar Beach, are excellent for snorkelling, and there are good camping facilities available on the island as well.

INDIGENOUS PEOPLES

Until the 18th century, the Andaman and Nicobar Islands were inhabited by a dozen distinct groups of indigenous tribes. Now, overwhelmed by the immigrant population and threatened by disease and loss of land, their numbers have fallen from 5,000 to just 800. The Mongoloid Nicobarese and Shompen tribes of the Nicobars probably came from Myanmar, while the origins of the four Negrito tribes – the Great Andamanese, Jarawas, Onges and Sentinelese – baffle anthropologists. Of these tribes, only the Nicobarese have partially integrated into the mainstream, while the Great Andamanese and the Onges live in tribal "reserves". The Sentinelese of North Sentinel Island are still hostile, fending off strangers with arrows. The Shompens are as wary of outsiders.

↑ A boat passing Baratrang Island en route to Middle Andaman

8
Middle Andaman

🏠 Middle Andaman Island; 170 km (106 miles) N from Port Blair to Rangat 🚢 From Port Blair 🛈 www.andamantourism.gov.in

Large tracts of the interior of this island are part of the highly protected Jarawa Tribal Reserve, home to the traditional hunter-gatherers, the Jarawa people. With the welfare of the Jarawas in mind, there is restricted public transport on the Andaman Trunk Road, which winds along the island's spine. Rangat Bay is the point of departure for ferries to Port Blair and Havelock and Long Islands. Just 15 km (9 miles) away, Cutbert Bay is a sanctuary for hundreds of marine turtles, which arrive here annually to nest. At the northern tip of the island, Mayabunder, 71 km (44 miles) from Rangat, is a beautiful spot and worth visiting.

🔍 HIDDEN GEM
Sunrise at Karmatang

Few foreign tourists venture as far as the unspoiled golden strand of Karmatang Beach at Mayabunder on Middle Andaman, but those who do are likely to be rewarded with a spectacular sunrise.

←

A peaceful landscape scene with a sunset over the beach at Chidiya Tapu

9
North Andaman

🏠 North Andaman Island; 290 km (180 miles) N from Port Blair to Diglipur 🚢 From Port Blair 🛈 www.andamantourism.gov.in

This is the least populated of the three large islands, and Diglipur, in the northeast, is one of the few places with accommodation. It is known for its beaches – in particular, Ram Nagar and Kalipur – and also has the islands' highest peak, Saddle Peak (737 m/ 2,418 ft), which is a national park. A scenic trail leads to the peak's summit.

EAT

Mandalay
Enjoy quality Indian and European food or sip a cocktail while admiring the fine views of the bay. There is a buffet some evenings.

🏠 Fortune Resort, Marine Hill, Port Blair 📞 (03192) 234 101

₹₹₹

Gyan Garden
One of the simplest but friendliest places to eat, where the locally caught fish and home-grown vegetables are as fresh as can be.

🏠 Main Rd, Neil Island 📞 (0) 99332 93078

₹₹₹

Anju-Coco
This large terrace restaurant serves everything from fish and chips to Tibetan *momos*. Ask for a flamboyant Waterfall cocktail.

🏠 Beach no 5, Havelock Island 📞 (0) 94760 76405

₹₹₹

Full Moon Café
This is one of the area's nicest seaside resort restaurants, serving spicy curries, fresh fish and seafood and a range of drinks.

🏠 Island Vinnie's, Beach no 3, Havelock 📞 (03192) 282 222

₹₹₹

NEED TO KNOW

BEFORE
YOU GO

Forward planning is essential to any successful trip. Be prepared for all eventualities by considering the following points before you travel.

AT A GLANCE

CURRENCY
Indian rupee (INR)

AVERAGE DAILY SPEND

SAVE	SPEND	SPLURGE
₹2,500	₹10,000	₹20,000

BOTTLED WATER	COFFEE	BEER	DINNER FOR TWO
₹50	₹75	₹300	₹1,000

ESSENTIAL HINDI PHRASES

Hello / Good bye	Namaste
Thank you	Dhanyavad
Good/Agreed	Accha
Do you speak English?	Kya aap angrezi bolte hain?
I (female) don't understand	Main samjhi nahin
I (male) don't understand	Main samjha nahin

ELECTRICITY SUPPLY

Power sockets are type C, fitting two-pin plugs, or type D or M for three-pronged plugs. Standard voltage is 230 bolts.

Passports and Visas

Almost all nationalities require a visa. Tourist visas are valid for six months and may be single- or multiple-entry. Consult **Indian Visa Online** to find out where you can apply. Note that within India, certain areas require special permits.
Indian Visa Online
🇼 indianvisaonline.gov.in

Travel Safety Advice

Visitors can get up-to-date travel safety information from the **UK Foreign and Commonwealth Office**, the **US Department of State**, and the **Australian Department of Foreign Affairs and Trade**.
Australia
🇼 smartraveller.gov.au
UK
🇼 gov.uk/foreign-travel-advice
US
🇼 travel.state.gov

Customs Information

An individual is permitted to carry the following within India for personal use:
Tobacco products 100 cigarettes, 25 cigars, or 125g tobacco.
Alcohol 2 litres of wine or spirits.
Cash If you plan to enter or leave India with foreign currency over US$10,000 – or US$5,000 in cash – you must declare it to the customs authorities. Indian currency may not legally be imported or exported by non-residents.
Telephones Satellite phones are banned.

Insurance

It is wise to take out an insurance policy covering loss of belongings, medical problems, delays and cancellations.

Vaccinations

Visitors arriving from some African and South American countries need a yellow fever

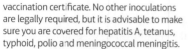

vaccination certificate. No other inoculations are legally required, but it is advisable to make sure you are covered for hepatitis A, tetanus, typhoid, polio and meningococcal meningitis.

Chloroquine-resistant malaria is a substantial risk in India, especially in parts of Karnataka, Odisha, Chhattisgarh, Jharkhand and the northeast. The usual preventative is mefloquine (Lariam), which is available at many Indian pharmacies; proguanil or doxycycline are alternatives. These should not be used without medical advice. Mosquitoes can spread diseases such as dengue and zika; visitors should bring and use high-DEET or PMD mosquito repellent.

Money

ATMs are widely available, except in more remote areas. Major credit and debit cards are accepted in many hotels and in some upmarket shops and restaurants, but note that credit card fraud is common. Be careful not to accept torn banknotes as these cannot be used.

Booking Accommodation

India offers a variety of accommodation, including luxury five-star hotels, family-run guesthouses and budget hostels. Many rail stations have retiring rooms which can be rented by passengers. Look out for heritage hotels, which may be anything from a *haveli* (mansion) to a maharaja's palace.

Travellers with Specific Needs

India can be a challenge for people with limited mobility, but things are slowly changing. New metro systems in Delhi, built by **Delhi Metro Rail**, are wheelchair accessible and have tactile paths for people with visual impairment. Ramps are becoming more common, and popular sites are making an effort to be more wheelchair-friendly. Hotels are unlikely to have wheelchair-adapted rooms, and those that do tend to be at the top of the market; you can find some hotels listed on **Disabled Access Holidays.** Mayfair, Ginger and Ibis are chains whose hotels often cater for people with limited mobility. In the UK, **Disabled Holidays** offer package tours to India for people with disabilities.

Delhi Metro Rail
W delhimetrorail.com/differentlyable.aspx

Disabled Access Holiday
W disabledaccessholidays.com/disabled-holidays/
Disabled Holidays
W disabledholidays.com

Language

India has over 500 languages and Indian banknotes are printed in seventeen of them. Most people speak local languages at home but use Hindi or English outside their own region.

Hindi and English are official languages in India. Hindi is widely spoken across northern India and is written in Devangari script. Indian English is widely used, and many books, newspapers and magazines are published in it. Around one in three people know at least some English and it is preferred to Hindi in the south and the northeast.

Urdu, the language of India's Muslims, is very similar, but written in Arabic-type script. Most north Indian languages are related to Hindi and Urdu; the most important are Bengali, Punjabi, Gujarati, Marathi and Assamese.

The main languages spoken in south India are different from those spoken in the north. The most important are Tamil, Kannada (spoken in Karnataka), Malayalam (spoken in Kerala) and Telugu (spoken in Telangana and Andhra Pradesh).

Closures

Sundays Most shops close.
Public holidays Each state has its own holidays. Only Republic Day, Independence Day and Gandhi Jayanti are national holidays.

MAIN PUBLIC HOLIDAYS	
1 Jan	New Year's Day
26 Jan	Republic Day
Mar/Apr	Holi
1 May	Labour Day
May/Jun	Id ul-Fitr
Jul/Aug	Bakr-Id
Aug	Krishna Janmashtami
15 Aug	Independence Day
2 Oct	Gandhi Jayanti
Oct/Nov	Diwali
Nov	Guru Nanak's birthday
25 Dec	Christmas Day

GETTING AROUND

Whether you're visiting for a short city break or travelling around the country, discover how best to reach your destination and travel like a pro.

AT A GLANCE

PUBLIC TRANSPORT COSTS

DELHI METRO

₹40

One-way New Delhi to Qutb Minar

DELHI-MUMBAI TRAIN

₹2,700

One-way 2nd class sleeper

DELHI-MUMBAI FLIGHT

₹5,000

One-way typical economy fare

SPEED LIMIT

NATIONAL HIGHWAYS

100 km/h (60mph)

EXPRESS-WAYS

120 km/h (75mph)

SECONDARY ROAD

70 km/h (40mph)

URBAN AREAS

50 km/h (30mph)

Arriving by Air

Most major international airlines fly to one or more of the airports at India's four main cities – Indira Gandhi International in Delhi, Chhatrapati Shivaji Airport in Mumbai, Chennai International Airport in Chennai and Netaji Subhash Chandra Bose Airport in Kolkata. Some may also fly to Hyderabad, Thiruvananthapuram, Bengaluru or Goa.

International airports offer a range of facilities that include left-luggage services, duty-free shops, currency exchange counters, restaurants, business centres and rest rooms with disabled access. In addition, there are counters for pre-paid taxis and car rentals.

For information on getting to and from India's main airports, see the table opposite.

Domestic Air Travel

Although more expensive than travelling by train, air travel in India is the most comfortable and convenient mode of long-distance inter-city travel. There are over eighty domestic airports in India – including in major tourist towns – and the main cities of Chennai, Delhi, Kolkata and Mumbai are connected to most of them. The national carrier **Air India** offers the largest number of routes across the country, but private airlines such as **IndiGo** and **SpiceJet** connect most cities and sometimes offer lower fares.

Air India
W airindia.in
IndiGo
W goindigo.in
SpiceJet
W spicejet.com

Train Travel

International Train Travel

Train travel in and out of India is not as extensive as the country's domestic network. There is a twice-weekly train connection on the Samjhauta Express from Delhi to Lahore, Pakistan, changing trains at the border. However, this train service is frequently disrupted by political events. To

GETTING TO AND FROM THE AIRPORT

Airport	Distance to city centre	Average journey time
Bengaluru: Kempegowda International Airport	40 km (25 miles)	45-60 mins
Chennai: Chennai International Airport	16 km (10 miles)	30 mins
Delhi: Indira Gandhi International (Terminal 3)	20 km (12 miles)	45-60 mins, metro 20 mins
Goa: Dabolim International Airport	29 km (18 miles)	50 mins
Hyderabad: Rajiv Gandhi International Airport	26 km (16 miles)	30-90 mins
Kolkata: Netaji Subhash Chandra Bose Airport	20 km (12 miles)	30-60 mins
Mumbai: Chhatrapati Shivaji Airport	30 km (19 miles)	50 mins
Thiruvananthapuram: Trivandrum Airport	8 km (5 miles)	20-40 mins

Bangladesh, the Maitree Express from Kolkata to Dhaka runs six times weekly, and the Bandhan Express from Kolkata to Khulna once weekly. Nepal and Bhutan have no rail systems, and there are no rail lines across the border to China, Tibet or Myanmar (Burma).

Domestic Trains

The Indian rail network runs the length and breadth of the country and is one of the most scenic ways to get around. Many cities have two or more main stations, so it is important to confirm which station your train is leaving from. Each train is known by its name and number. Air-conditioned express trains such as the Rajdhani Express or Shatabdi Express have fewer stops and offer better facilities and services than ordinary trains, providing punctual connections between many of India's most important cities.

Trains have first- and second-class chair-cars, and two- and three-tiered sleeper coaches (with berths that fold back during the daytime to provide seating). Air-conditioned trains are more expensive but meals and mineral water are included in your fare. Food and drinks are otherwise sold by vendors at stations, and meals are offered by rail catering services. Printed timetables ("Trains at a Glance") are available in most station bookshops, or you can check **Indian Rail** and **IRCTC**. Be aware that trains can often be hours late and stations are often very crowded. Trains may close boarding earlier than advertised departure times.

Try to book well in advance as trains are always crowded. Tickets are available at ticket counters at railway stations or from most travel agents. Buying rail tickets involves filling in a

form and giving your age and gender, which will appear on your ticket, along with the coach and seat number. It is possible to travel without a reservation, but not advisable for journeys of any length. If reserved tickets are unavailable, you can get an RAC (Reservation Against Cancellation) ticket which allows you to board the train and find seating space; you may get a berth (apply to the train's ticket collector), but there is no guarantee of this.

Stations at Delhi, Mumbai, Kolkata and Chennai as well as other major cities have special booking counters for foreign visitors. At New Delhi Railway Station, the International Tourist Bureau is located upstairs from the main hall – beware of touts trying to misdirect you.

Indian Rail
W indianrail.gov.in
IRCTC
W .irctc.co.in

Unique Trains

In Rajasthan in particular, you can travel in style on board some of India's luxury trains such as the **Palace on Wheels**, the **Royal Rajasthan on Wheels** or the **Fairy Queen** – all are seasonal. India's quaint "toy trains" are mainly narrow-guage railways up to hill stations, including the Darjeeling-Himalayan Railway, the Kangra Valley Railway and the Nilgiri Mountain Railway.

Fairy Queen
W royalindiantrains.com/fairy-queen
Palace of Wheels
W thepalaceonwheels.com
Royal Rajasthan on Wheels
W royalindiantrains.com/royal-rajasthan-on-wheels.html

Travelling By Bus

India has an extensive bus and coach network, offering frequent and fast connections to most cities as well as to the remotest parts of the country. Buses and coaches offer a wider choice of timings, stops and itineraries than trains. Most tourists do not choose to travel long-distance on ordinary buses. Deluxe buses are more comfortable; if travelling in summer, the best option is the deluxe air-conditioned coach. Unlike most normal bus services, deluxe buses for certain routes do require booking; you can reserve tickets through travel agencies such as **redBus**, **Cleartrip** and **MakeMyTrip**.

The various states' Road Transport Corporations run substantial interstate bus services across the country. Terminals can often be chaotic places, so arrive early and check at the enquiry counter for where to buy tickets to specific destinations. In more mountainous regions, buses are often the only public transport option; shared jeeps also accompany some services to remote areas.

Cleartrip
W cleartrip.com
MakeMyTrip
W makemytrip.com
redBus
W redbus.in

Ferries

Short ferry services are common across India's river network, with options ranging from small cruises to more rustic chain pontoons. The city of Alappuzha in Kerala is known for its houseboat cruises but these can be expensive; for a cheaper, but just as scenic option, take the local ferry along the backwaters.

For travel to the Andaman and Nicobar Islands, and the Lakshadweep islands, it is advisable to book ahead. Scheduled **Andaman ferries** depart from Visakhapatnam, Chennai and Kolkata, and travel to Port Blair, the capital of the Andaman Islands, once or twice a month. Connections to the Lakshadweep archipelago are more limited. Ferries run from mid-September to mid-May from Kochi (Kerala) but few tickets are available. The best way to get here is by package tour.

To travel by sea from Mumbai to Goa (or vice versa), catch the overnight **Angriya Cruise** – ships depart three times a week either side of the monsoon season.

Day and overnight boat tours operate in the mangrove forests of the Sundarbans – this is the only way to see the delta region.

Andaman Ferries
W andamans.gov.in
Angriya Cruise
W angriyacruises.com

Local Transport

Most large cities have reliable bus, taxi, rickshaw and autorickshaw services. Delhi has a large and reliable metro service, and other cities have smaller metro or light rail systems. In Delhi and Mumbai, the anti-pollution drive has seen the introduction of vehicles run on Compressed Natural Gas (CNG). Taxis and autos that have converted to CNG usage have a green band across the usual yellow-and-black body.

Metro and Suburban Train Systems

Mumbai has the best suburban train network in India, providing efficient and affordable connections. Delhi also has an extensive and efficient metro system whereas Kolkata's is older and smaller. Others cities such as Chennai, Lucknow, Jaipur and Hyderabad have metro systems, and more urban areas are following suit. Most metro systems and some suburban trains have "ladies only" compartments which women are advised to use, especially during commuting hours and at night. Try to avoid rush hour travel as serious overcrowding can occur, particularly in Mumbai.

Each system has its own norms for buying tickets or tokens. Most metro systems have smart cards, which may offer discounts or daily or weekly fares, and save queuing. Day passes are sometimes available (Delhi offers 1- and 3-day tourist cards), and multi-journey tickets exist on some systems; fares are so low that saving money isn't an issue, but these do save queuing, which can take a long time at some stations during rush hour.

Cycle Rickshaws

Cycle rickshaws are slow but cheap. Agree the price before setting off. Drivers ("rickshaw-walas") are among the poorest workers, and many tourists like to be generous with their tips. In some major tourist spots, such as Agra and Varanasi, rickshaws touting for business can be a nuisance. As a rule of thumb, avoid drivers touting for business – they often seriously overcharge and operate commission scams – and flag one down yourself.

Autorickshaws

The ubiquitous autorickshaws (popularly called autos) are the most common mode of transport in most places. They are essentially a motor-scooter with a couple of seats mounted on the back. Autos are more economical than taxis, but be prepared for some hair-raising drives. All autos have a meter, but drivers ("auto-walas") are usually unwilling to use it, and are notorious for over-charging tourists. Haggle for a good price before getting in. Carry some small change, as drivers may claim not to have any. Pre-paid auto booths with fixed prices exist at some transport terminals.

Taxis

Metered taxis (usually black with a yellow top) operate in most cities. They can be hailed in the street or hired at local taxi stands, although it is best to ask your hotel to organize a taxi for you. Taxis are available for point-to-point service or for a fixed rate for half a day (four hours or 40 km/25 miles); or a full day (eight hours or 80 km/50 miles). Radio cabs have been introduced in some cities such as Delhi and Mumbai, and are air-conditioned but more expensive than ordinary cabs. Adding extra charges for baggage are rare, but more likely when you take a pre-pay auto cab from a railway station. Taxis often charge a higher rate at night; in Delhi, for example, that applies from 11pm until 5am and is around 20 per cent. Airports may charge an access fee for vehicles which cab passengers will have to pay. Car-sharing services **Uber** and **Ola Cabs** operate in bigger cities and can be accessed with a smartphone.

Ola Cabs
W olacabs.com
Uber
W uber.com

Driving

Driving in India is potentially hazardous. Cows, cyclists and pedestrians appear oblivious of traffic, while cars and motorcycles weave in and out rather unpredictably, and are very likely to do things like overtake on the wrong side, turn and change lanes without indicating, or drive at night with no lights. Road conditions can also be poor and hazards are often unmarked. Accidents can attract an angry mob, especially if pedestrians or cows are involved, and it is advisable in such cases to leave the scene and go to the police to report the accident.

Hiring a Car
Most car rental firms offer a car with driver, and this is the option most tourists take as it is comparatively affordable if you are in a group. Remember to check if your driver speaks English and has a working knowledge of the region – try to meet them and inspect the car before you pay. Note that your driver will expect a tip at the end of each day.

If you are keen to self-drive, there are many Indian companies you can choose from. **Hertz** also has representatives in India. Be aware that hire cars are not always licensed to drive beyond their origin state and travelling outside these boundaries can often add an extra charge.

Hertz
W hertz.com

Rules of the Road
Driving is on the left, and there are no standard speed limits, even within individual states. On average, you may travel 40 km/h (25 mph) to 50 km/h (30 mph) on highway roads; however on more remote dirt tracks you may only reach around 10 km/h (6 mph). Seat belts are compulsory for drivers and front-seat passengers, and although this is rarely enforced, it is extremely advisable for everybody in a car to use a seat belt if possible. Try to avoid driving in the dark.

Motorbikes
Often the best way to explore smaller towns and cities, and their environs, is by motorcycle. Some places also have motorcycle taxis. If you prefer to travel independently, motorcycles are available for hire on a daily basis. Towns such as Puducherry, Hampi, Belur and Halebid can be explored by motorbike, available for rent at reasonable rates. Check the bike runs smoothly before paying. Some visitors, if in the country for a while, buy an Indian motorbike – usually the classic Enfield Bullet – and sell it again before they leave. However there is a lot of bureaucracy and paperwork involved in this process. It is also possible to rent motorbikes from firms such as **Lalli Singh** in Delhi, who offer organized tours, and well-known international firms such as **Blazing Trails**, who specialize in more adventurous tours.

Blazing Trails
W blazingtrailstours.com
Lalli Singh
W lallisinghadventures.com

Cycling

Cycling through areas of India is a worthy adventure, although it does come with its own set of challenges. A tourist on a bicycle may attract a lot of attention in rural India, including large crowds of onlookers, and sometimes unwanted attention from children or dogs. Some tourists bring bicycles from abroad, but be aware that spare parts for these may be hard to come by. It is easy to buy bicycles locally, and in most towns it easy to rent a bicycle for local use. Operators such as **Spice Roads** and **Art of Bicycle Trips** offer cycling package tours of varying degrees of difficulty.

It is advised that you bring your bike into your room with you overnight as a safety precaution.
Art of the Bicycle
W artofbicycletrips.com/destinations/india
Spice Roads
W spiceroads.com/destinations/india

PRACTICAL
INFORMATION

A little local know-how goes a long way in India. Here you will find all the essential advice and information you will need during your stay.

AT A GLANCE

EMERGENCY NUMBERS

GENERAL EMERGENCY

112

AMBULANCE

102

FIRE SERVICE

101

POLICE

100

TIME ZONE
IST (India Standard Time). There is no daylight saving time.

TAP WATER
Best avoided. Bottled water is widely available, or bring a filter or purifying tablets.

TIPPING

Waiter	10-15 per cent
Hotel Porter	₹50 per bag
Rickshaw-wala	20 per cent
Concierge	₹200
Taxi Driver	10-15 per cent

Personal Security

Travelling in India is relatively safe, but it is recommended that you follow a few simple precautions. If travelling with valuables, wear a money belt under your shirt and be discreet with your camera and phone. While shopping, ensure that shopkeepers make out a bill and process your credit or debit card in front of you. Never accept food or drink from strangers, especially on public transport. Keep your baggage close at transport terminals and beware of staged distractions; always padlock your luggage to the chain beneath your seat during train journeys.

Female Travellers

Although "eve-teasing" (sexual harassment) is a punishable offence, women – both Indian and foreign – face unwanted male attention on a daily basis, and there have been incidents of rape and violence against female travellers. Avoid walking alone in isolated places and in the rougher parts of cities. When hiring a car or taxi, ask your hotel to book it for you (or go to a cab rank) and note the licence plate number. When queuing for train or cinema tickets, use the "ladies' lines", and use the "ladies only" seats or compartments on buses and trains, if available.

LGBT+ Safety

Laws banning homosexuality have been overturned as unconstitutional, but same-sex marriages are not allowed. Hijras, who may be transwomen or intersex, are semi-accepted as a third sex, but face much discrimination. Kissing and cuddling in public is taboo for everybody.

Health

Seek medical supplies and advice for minor ailments from pharmacies. Wash, dress and cover all cuts and grazes, even if you would not bother at home. Larger cities have reasonably good hospitals, with 24-hour services equipped to handle casualty and emergency cases. Contact your embassy for their list of approved

hospitals, clinics, doctors and dentists. Try to avoid food, even fruit, that is not freshly cooked. In case of stomach upsets, drink plenty of fluids and stick to plain boiled food until the sickness subsides, or consult a doctor.

Smoking, Alcohol and Drugs

Gujarat, Bihar, Nagaland and Lakshadweep are alcohol-free (although some hotels serve alcohol to foreign tourists with permits), as are some religious sites and temple towns, such as Haridwar, Rishikesh and Pushkar. Many other states are partly dry or have numerous dry days. Smoking is banned in public places, including restaurants, bars, hotels and offices. India produces hashish and marijuana bud, but both are illegal with harsh penalties in force for possession. Bhang (marijuana leaf) is legally sold in licensed shops in some cities.

ID

There is no requirement to carry or show ID in India, and passports can usually be left in a hotel safe. It is nonetheless a good idea to keep a photo of your passport on your phone. You will need your passport to make train reservations.

Local Customs

Eat with your right hand only, as the left hand is reserved for practical usages, like going to the toilet. It is normal to take off shoes (with the left hand) before entering a house. Putting feet up on furniture will be considered bad manners, as is touching someone inadvertently with your feet. If sitting on the floor, keep feet tucked underneath rather than stretched out.

Living in close quarters with family and neighbours gives Indians a different sense of "personal space" than many Westerners. If crowded or jostled, particularly while travelling, be tolerant as space is often at a premium.

Indians tend to dress conservatively and keep the body well covered. Wearing shorts is considered uncouth, and women wearing clothes that display their legs, arms or stomachs will draw stares and unwanted male attention.

The famous Indian head wobble is ambigious: it can mean "yes", it can mean "no", it can mean "I'm thinking about it". It is best to clarify meaning.

Visiting Places of Worship

When visiting a temple or mosque, you should be covered from below the elbow to below the knee (women preferably to the wrist and ankle). Remove your shoes on entry and if sitting, keep feet facing away from the main shrine. Men may be asked to cover their heads with a handkerchief or scarf, and in a few south Indian Hindu temples they may also be required to change their shirts for dhotis. Jain temples do not allow leather items inside, even wallets and watch straps. A few Hindu temples also ban entry for non-Hindus. Women are sometimes banned from Jain and Hindu temples. This is controversial and some of these restrictions are being challenged in court.

Mobile Phones and Wi-Fi

National and international calls made from STD/ISD booths – very common and identified by signs – are much cheaper than at hotels. SIM cards for mobile phones are widely available, but you will need your passport to buy one. It is worth putting them on "do not disturb" mode to ban spam calls. Most hotels offer free Wi-Fi, but sometimes only in the lobby area. Internet cafés can be found in the shopping areas of most cities and towns.

Post

Mail sent abroad from India may take one–three weeks to arrive. Post offices are open Monday to Friday between 10am and 5pm, and on Saturdays until noon. Some services, such as Poste Restante (general delivery), may close earlier. Parcels sent overseas cannot exceed 20 kg (44 lb), and must be specially packed – check for details at the post office. Book Packet is a cheaper option for printed material.

Taxes and Refunds

GST (Goods and Services Tax) is levied on all goods and services, typically at 18 per cent for non-essential items. It is included in displayed prices. While GST on souvenirs should be refundable to foreign residents on leaving the country, no mechanism for this has, as yet, been put in place.

INDEX

Page numbers in **bold** refer to main entries.

PHRASE BOOK

India has 18 major regional languages, many with their own scripts. While Hindi, spoken by 30 per cent of the people and widely understood throughout India, is the official national language, other languages enjoy predominance in their respective regions. There are five major languages, four of them spoken in India's four largest cities and their surrounding regions: Hindi (spoken in Delhi); Bengali (spoken in Kolkata); Marathi (spoken in Mumbai); and Tamil (spoken in Chennai). The fifth language, Malayalam, is spoken in Kerala. While Hindi, Bengali and Marathi are Indo-European languages, descended from Sanskrit, Tamil and Malayalam are Dravidian languages, unrelated to the Indo-European group, though influenced by Sanskrit over the centuries. English is widely spoken and understood throughout the country and serves as a link language between the different regions. One can get by with English almost anywhere in India, but most Indians appreciate if a visitor makes an attempt to speak their language. Our phrase book covers two of these major languages: Hindi and Tamil.

HINDI

IN AN EMERGENCY

Help!	Bachāo!
Stop!	Roko!
Call a doctor!	Doctor ko bulāo!
Where is the nearest telephone?	Yahān phone kahān hai?

COMMUNICATION ESSENTIALS

Yes	Hān
No	Nā/Nahīn
Thank you	Dhanyavād/Shukriā
Please	Kripayā/ Meherbanī sé
Excuse me/Sorry	Kshamā karen/ Māf karen
Hello/Goodbye	Namasté
Stop	Rook jāo
Let's go	Chalo
Straight ahead	Sīdhā
Big/Small	Badā/Chhotā
This/That	Yeh/Voh
Near/Far	Pās/Door
Way	Rāstā
Road	Sadak
Yesterday	Kal
Today	Āj
Tomorrow	Kal
Here	Yahān
There	Wahān
What?	Kyā?
Where?	Kahān?
When?	Kab?
Why?	Kyon?
How?	Kaisé?
Up	Ūpar
Down	Nīché
More	Aur zyādā
A little	Thodā
Before	Pehlé
Opposite/Facing	Sāmné
Very	Bahut
Less	Kum
Louder/Harder	Zor sé
Softly/Gently	Dhīré sé
Go	Jāo
Come	Āo

USEFUL PHRASES

How are you?	Āp kaisé hain?
What is your name?	Āpkā nām kyā hai?
My name is...	Merā nām... hai
Do you speak English?	Kyā āp ko angrezi āti hai?
I understand	Samajh gayā (male)/ gayī (female)
I don't understand	Nahīn samjhā (m)/ samjhī (f)
What is the time?	Kyā bajā hai?
Where is...?	...Kahān hai?
What is this?	Yeh kyā hai?
Hurry up	Jaldi karo
How far is...?	...Kitnī door hai?
I don't know	Patā nahīn
All right	Achhā/Thīk hai
Now/Instantly	Abhī/Isi waqt
Well done!	Shābāsh!
See you	Phir milengé
Go away!	Hat jāo/Hato
I don't want it	Mujhe nahin chāhiye
Not now	Abhī nahīn

USEFUL WORDS

Which?	Kaun sā?
Who?	Kaun?
Hot	Garam
Cold	Thandā
Good	Achhā
Bad	Kharāb
Enough	Bus/Kāfī hai
Open	Khulā
Closed	Bundh
Left	Bāyān
Right	Dāyān
Straight on	Sīdhā
Near	Pās/Nazdīk
Quickly	Jaldī
Late	Der sé
Later	Bād mein
Entrance	Pravesh
Exit	Nikās
Behind	Pīchhé
Full	Bharā
Empty	Khālī
Toilet	Shauchālaya
Free/No charge	Nihshulk/Muft
Direction	Dishā
Book	Kitāb
Newspaper	Samachār patra

SHOPPING

How much does this cost?	Iskā kyā dām hai?
I would like...	Mujhe... chāhiye
Do you have...?	Kya āp ké pās... hai?
I am just looking	Bus dekh rahen hain
Does it come in other colours?	Yeh doosré rangon main bhī ātā hai kya?
This one	Yeh wālā
That one	Voh wālā
Black	Kālā
Blue	Nīlā
White	Safed
Red	Lāl
Yellow	Pīlā
Green	Harā
Brown	Bhurā
Cheap	Sastā
Expensive	Mehengā
Tailor	Darzī

BARGAINING

How much is this?	Yeh kitné kā hai?
How much will you take?	Kitnā logé?
That's a little expensive	Yeh to mehengā hai
Could you lower the price a bit?	Dām thodā kam kariyé
How about ...rupees?	...rupeye laingé?
I'll settle for ...rupees	...rupeye mein denā hai to dijiyé

STAYING IN A HOTEL

Do you have any vacant rooms?	Āpké hotel mein khāli kamré hain?
What is the charge per night?	Ek rāt ka kirāyā kyā hai?
Can I see the room first?	Kyā mein pehlé kamrā dekh saktā hoon?

USEFUL WORDS (continued)

Key	Chābī
Soap	Sābun
Towel	Tauliyā
Hot/Cold water	Garam/Thandā panī

EATING OUT

Breakfast	Nāshtā
Food	Khāna
Water	Pānī
Ice	Baraf
Tea	Chai
Coffee	Coffee
Sugar	Chīnī
Salt	Namak
Milk	Doodh
Yoghurt	Dahī
Egg	Andā
Fruit	Phal
Vegetable	Subzī
Rice	Chāval
Pulses (lentil, split peas etc)	Dāl
Fixed price menu	Ek dām menu
Is it spicy?	Mirch-masālā tez hai kyā?
Make it less spicy please	Mirch-masala thodā kam
Knife	Chhurī
Fork	Kāntā
Spoon	Chammach
Finished	Khatam

NUMBERS

1	Ek
2	Do
3	Tīn
4	Chār
5	Pānch
6	Chhé
7	Sāt
8	Āth
9	Nau
10	Dus
11	Gyārah
12	Bārah
13	Terah
14	Chaudah
15	Pandrah
16	Solah
17	Satrah
18	Athārah
19	Unnīs
20	Bīs
30	Tīs
40	Chālīs
50	Pachās
60	Sāth
70	Sattar
80	Assī
90	Nabbé
100	Sau
1,000	Hazār
100,000	Lākh
10,000,000	Karod (crore)

TIME

One minute	Ek minute
One hour	Ek ghantā
Half an hour	Ādhā ghantā
Quarter hour	Paunā ghantā

Half past one	Derh
Half past two	Dhāi
A day	Ek din
A week	Ek haftāh
Monday	Somwār

Tuesday	Mangalwār
Wednesday	Budhwār
Thursday	Guruwār
Friday	Shukrawār
Saturday	Shaniwār

Sunday	Raviwār
Morning	Subah
Afternoon	Dopahar
Evening	Shām
Night	Rāt

TAMIL

IN AN EMERGENCY

Help!	Udhaivi véndum!
Stop!	Nillu!
Call a doctor!	Doctor koopiddunga!
Where is the nearest phone?	Pakkatatillé phone engu irrukku?

COMMUNICATION ESSENTIALS

Yes	Aama/Seri
No	Illai/Véndaam
Thank you	Nanri
Please	Daivusaidhu
Excuse me/Sorry	Mannikavum
Hello/Goodbye	Vannakkam/ Paankalaam
Stop	Nillu
Let's go	Pohalaam
Straight ahead	Néré
Big/Small	Perisu/Chinannadu
This/That	Idhu/Adhu
Near/Far	Pakkatilai/Dooram
Way	Vazhi
Road	Theruvu
Yesterday	Nétru/Néthiku
Today	Inru/Innikki
Tomorrow	Naallai/Naallaiku
Here	Ingé
There	Angé
What?	Ennai?
Where?	Engé?
When?	Eppo?
Why?	Ain?
How?	Eppiddi?
Up	Mélai
Down	Kizhai
More	Unnum konjam
A little	Konjam
Before	Minaalai
Opposite/Facing	Edhirai
Very	Romba
Less	Kammi
Louder/Harder	Perisa/Unnum ongi
Softly/Gently	Molla
Go	Pongo/Po
Come	Vaango/Vaa

USEFUL PHRASES

How are you?	Neenga eppudi irukénga?
What is your name?	Onge peyar enna?
My name is...	Enodia peyar...
Do you speak English?	English pése theriyuma?
I understand	Ennakku puriyum
I don't understand	Ennakku puriyadu
What is the time?	Ippo ena mani?
Where is...?	...Enga irrukku?
What is this?	Idhu ennadhu?
Hurry up	Seekrama vaango
How far is...?	...Evallavu dooram?
I don't know	Ennaku theriyadu
All right	Seri
Now/Instantly	Ippovai
Well done!	Shabash!
See you	Apram parkalaam
Go away!	Poividu!
I don't want it	Ennaku véndaam
Not now	Ippo illai

USEFUL WORDS

Which?	Edhu?
Who?	Yaaru?
Hot	Soodu
Cold	Kulluru
Good	Nalladhu
Bad	Kettadhu

Enough	Porum
Open	Thirandurikku
Closed	Moodirukku
Left	Edudhu
Right	Valadhu
Straight on	Nérai
Near	Pakkatillai
Quickly	Seekrama
Late	Nerama
Later	Apram
Entrance	Varuvu
Exit	Velivaasal
Behind	Pinalai
Full	Rombiruku
Empty	Kaali
Toilet	Kaizhupu arai
Free/No charge	Ilevasaasam
Direction	Disai/Pakkam
Book	Pustagam
Magazine	Patrigai
Newspaper	Samachara patrigai

SHOPPING

How much does this cost?	Idhodiya vilai ennai?
I would like...	Ennakku idhu venum...
Do you have...?	...onga kitta irrukka?
I am just looking	Naan summa paakaren
Does it come? in other colours	Idh vera colouril kidaikuma?
This one	Idhu
That one	Adhu
Black	Karuppu
Blue	Neelam
White	Vellai
Red	Seguppu
Yellow	Manjhal
Green	Pachchai
Brown	Kappi niram
Cheap	Maluvu
Expensive	Vilai jasti
Tailor	Theyalkaran

BARGAINING

How much is this?	Idhu enna vilai?
How much will you take?	Neengu evalave edithipél?
That's a little expensive	Adhu konjam vilai jasti
Could you lower the price a bit?	Vilai konjam kurrakkai mudduyuma?
How about xx rupees?	xx rubaai seria?
I'll settle for xx rupees	xx rubaai tharuven

STAYING IN A HOTEL

Do you have any vacant rooms?	Kaali arai irruka?
What is the charge per night?	Oru raatriku evaluvu caasu?
Can I see the room first?	Naan mudulai araiya parrakalama?
Key	Chaavi
Soap	Soapu
Towel	Thundu
Hot/Cold water	Soodu/Jillu thanni

EATING OUT

Breakfast	Kaalai chittrundi
Food	Saapadu
Water	Thanni/Jalam
Ice	Ice
Tea	Chai
Coffee	Coffee
Sugar	Shakarai
Salt	Uppu
Milk	Paal
Yoghurt	Thairu
Egg	Muttai
Fruit	Pazham
Vegetable	Kayagiri
Rice	Arusi
Pulses (lentils, etc)	Paruppu
Fixed price menu	Ore vilai menu
Is it spicy?	Naraya masala irukka?
Make it less spicy please	Masala seriya irukka?
Knife	Kaththi
Fork	Fork
Spoon	Spoon/Theikarandi
Finished	Mudivu

NUMBERS

1	Onru/Onu
2	Erundu
3	Moonru
4	Naangu/Naalu
5	Anju/Aindhu
6	Aaru
7	Yezhu
8	Ettu
9	Ombodhu
10	Pathu
11	Pathinonru
12	Panandu
13	Pathimoonru
14	Pathinaalu
15	Pathinainthu
16	Pathnaaru
17	Pathinezhu
18	Pathinettu
19	Pathombadhu
20	Iravadhu
30	Mupaddu
40	Napadhu
50	Aimbadhu
60	Aravadhu
70	Yezhuvadu
80	Yenbadhu
90	Thonnuru
100	Nooru
1,000	Aayiram
100,000	Latcham
10,000,000	Kodi

TIME

One minute	Oru nimisham
One hour	Oru manéram
Half an hour	Ara manéram
Quarter hour	Kaal manéram
Half past one	Onre mani
Half past two	Erendarai mani
A day	Oru naal
A week	Oru vaaram
Monday	Thingakazhamai
Tuesday	Sevvaikazhami
Wednesday	Budhankazhami
Thursday	Viyaikazhami
Friday	Vellikazhami
Saturday	Nyaayatrikazhami
Morning	Kaalai
Afternoon	Madhyanam
Evening	Sayankaalam
Night	Raatri

ACKNOWLEDGMENTS

The publisher would like to thank the following for their kind permission to reproduce their photographs:

Key: a-above; b-below/bottom; c-centre; f-far; l-left; r-right; t-top

123RF.com: Nilanjan Bhattacharya 331bl; Mohammed Anwarul Kabir Choudhury 199cra; dinodia 267cra; Rupa Ghosh 263tr; meinzahn 92clb; milosk 42tl; Marina Pissarova 34-5ca, 468-9t, 556-7b; Dmitriy Tereshchenko 593tr; Richard Whitcombe 592-3b.

4Corners: Giordano Cipriani 20t, 274-5; Maurizio Rellini 8cl, 8-9; Reinhard Schmid 106bl, 107tl.

akg-images: Jean-Louis Nou 495tr.

Alamy Stock Photo: age fotostock 139clb, 232-3t; 329ca, 523crb, / Dinodia 101bl, / V. Muthuraman 493tr; Leonid Andronov 112-3t; 124-5b; 407cl; 424-5b; 435tr; Idris Ahmed 282-3t; Archivart 285br; Archive Pics 168br; Andrey Armyagov 219clb; Art Directors & TRIP 266bl; Abir Roy Barman 272-3t; John Bennet 472cr, 551tr, 551crb; Jens Benninghofen 450b; Sourabh Bharti 128-9t; Arunabh Bhattacharjee 428-9t, 478t; Frank Bienewald 51br, 58-9t, 178br, 231t, 315cra, 479b; BIOSPHOTO 175cla; Shashank Birla 149br; Anders Blomqvist 405; Florian Blümm 498-9b; Goran Bogicevic 416bl; Koushik Borah 368b; Cavan Images 467cla, 490cl; Charles O. Cecil 164b; Suman Chakraborty 331cra; Biplab Roy Chowdhury 256-7b; Chronicle 75t; chtn 156-7t; Classic Image 71cla, 71cb, 73tr, 74tl, 75bl; Gary Cook 548clb; Craft Images 72-3t; Daily Travel Photos 36tr; David Gee 5 389t; Francesco Dazzi 251t; dbimages 52-3t, 78-9, 171cra, 281br, 282br, 424cr, 425tr, 469clb, 491cla, 573tl, / Betty Johnson 197t; Deepu Sg 293clb; Design Pics Inc 84br, 115cra, 403bl; Roop Dey 48crb, 84crb, 133cra, 594clb, 596b, 597tl; dianajarvisphotography.co.uk 328cl; Dinodia Photos 32crb, 48tl, 69cr, 70t, 72br, 75br, 76cr, 76-7t, 121cl, 145br, 148bc, 167br, 171br, 176tr, 180clb, 191b, 193br, 194br, 211bl, 212cb, 212-3b, 265cra, 268bc, 269bc, 281tl, 292cra, 293tr, 294br, 300clb, 301tr, 310bl, 315bc, 320bc, 336tl, 348-9b, 349tr, 351cra, 408br, 411bl, 414-5t, 432bl, 435cb, 447cra, 467tl, 471br, 477br, 485tr, 492b, 501br, 515tr, 518t, 523bc, 525b, 528tr, 535t, 555tl, 578b, 583b, 584bl, 587cr, 587br; dpa picture alliance archive 226crb; Sandipan Dutta 370-1t; Eagle Visions Photography / Craig Lovell 137cla; Oscar Elias 354-5b, 356tl; Ephotocorp 143cr, 278crb, 293cb, 587crb, / Sangram Khot 426t, / Rajan Lakule 595tr, / Shashank Mehendale 496bl, / Shrikrishna Paranjpe 273b, / Dr. Suresh Vasant 475tr; Exotica 190tr, 453tl; EyeEm 28bl; Jorge Fernandez 188-9t; Fernando Quevedo de Oliveira 61tr, 469br; fabio formaggio 12clb; Stuart Forster 72cr; FotoFlirt 54-5t; Chris Fredriksson 129cb; Full Bloom 363tr; David Gabis 251cra; Tim Gainey 68cla; Anil Ghawana 28cr, 58bl, 175tl; Dara Gilroy 364bl; Tim Graham 180b; Granger Historical Picture Archive 168bl, 286br; Renato Granieri 413tr; Nigel Greenstreet 298cr; Marcel Gross 299tr; Andy Guest 72tl, 471bl; Chloe Hall 46-7bl; Hans-Joachim Aubert 333br; Martin Harvey 174bl; Alexander Helin 182-3b; hemis.fr / Fabrice Dimier 357bl, / Franck Guiziou 37tl, 545tl, 562b, / Francis Leroy 199b, 278t, 295bc, 331crb, 574b, 575tr, / Alain Schroeder 297br, 454-5b, / Paule Seux 38cra, 522-3t, / Soularue 449c; Christina Hemsley 147clb; Historic Images 74tr; History and Art Collection 76clb; The History Collection 247tr, 313br; Hornbil Images 551br; Peter Horree 512bl, 581br; imageBROKER 11br, 13t, 30tr, 68cra, 117br, 120b, 289tl, 522crb,

523cb, / Gilles Barbier 253tr, / Frank Bienewald 191cl, / Hans Blossey 36cra, / Joachim Hiltmann 477t, / Olaf Krüger 156bc, 157br, 302-3t, 305tr, 316tl, 497tl; ImageDB 63crb; India view 181tr, 240bl; IndiaPicture 43tl, 74bc, 219cra, 220bl, 292crb; 331c, 467cb, / V. Muthuraman 533tr, / Amit Pasricha 195br, 387tr, / Shalini Saran 236tc; Indiascapes 549tr; INTERFOTO 207bc; Parvesh Jain 192b; Manish Jaisi 50tr; Bhaven Jani 139br; Aviral Jha 464t; John Elk III 525tr; John Warburton-Lee Photography 301bc, 449br, 551cra, / Nigel Pavitt 318bl; Norma Joseph 380clb; JS 491tl; Premraj K.P 537tr, 561bl; Vignesh Kamath 406-7b; Samyak Kaninde 228cra; Joseph Manuel Kaninken 403br; Kettik Images 253bl; Andrey Khrobostov 211cr, 304tl; Ladi Kirn 457tr; Claudine Klodien 187br, 524t; Abhishek Kumar 125tl; Manish Lakhani 241cla; fabio lamanna 284clb, 284crb; Catherine Leblond 535cla; Lebrecht Music & Arts 74crb; Paul Lee 32bl; Martin Leitch 319t; Look 35tr, 62-3t, / Hauke Dressler 480b, / Holger Leue 394bl, / Andreas Strauss 96tl; Guillem Lopez 167bc; manu m 67cla; Ingemar Magnusson 121tl; Kumar Mangwani 470-1t; Saji Maramon 90-1; Marco Polo Collection / Balan Madhavan 560t; Maroš Markovic 172tl; J Marshall - Tribaleye Images 31tr; mauritius images GmbH 520bl; Aliaksandr Mazurkevich 238t; Neil McAllister 40cra, 385crb, 494br, 592cl, 594b; McPhoto / Nilsen 287cb; Cathyrose Melloan 529clb; Melting Spot 46tl; MichaelGrant 155c; John Michaels 401t; Philip Mugridge 385br; Sugato Mukherjee 335tr; Nature Picture Library / Sandesh Kadur 369tr; Newscom 293crb; Chetchai Ngampattaravorakul 266-7b; Nikreates 400clb; Sérgio Nogueira 447tl; Novarc Images 289cr, 290c; Octavio Global 220-1; christian ouellet 472-3t; Pragadeeswaran P 526-7b; Pacific Press 52bl, / Shaukat Ahmed 152t, / Saikat Paul 77crb; Anne-Marie Palmer 42tr, 510t; Roger Parkes 69tl; Dave Pattison 311tr; Paul Springett 06 513tr, 517t; david pearson 99br, 168cb, 410t, 451cla, 498tr; photoff 133t; PhotosIndia.com LLC 137tc, 571cla, / Exotica 402tr, / ImageDB 304-5b; PhotosIndia.com RM 10 207bl; Pictorial Press Ltd 76tl; The Picture Art Collection 89tl; Marina Pissarova 30-1ca, 458-9t; Leonid Plotkin 271br; Graham Prentice 145cra, 174-5b, 523bl; Prisma by Dukas Presseagentur GmbH 34tl, 74cla; Hira Punjabi 474tl, 553cr; Paul Quayle 321b; R Ramana Reddy Battula 292cb; Daniel J. Rao 22t, 358-9t, 366tl; mohamed abdul rasheed 558bl, 563t; Primo Dul Ravel 417tl; Really Easy Star / Tullio Valente 447ca; Simon Reddy 451cra; Fredrik Renander 573cr; Juergen Ritterbach 169crb; Robert Preston Photography 57br, 70br, 136clb; robertharding 34tr, 49tl, 92b, 169clb, 423cra, 445cla, 451tl, 509bc, / Richard Ashworth 556t; Pep Roig 59br, 234tr, 536b; Rolf_52 28crb; Anubhab Roy 577bl; Dmitry Rukhlenko - Travel Photos 219bl; Oleksandr Rupeta 38crb; Andrii Rybalka 346-7t; Santosh Saligram 11cr; sanjeevi v 491cra; Jan Schuler 32t, 136-7b; Sejpal 56tr, 395t, 395cra; Sfm Gm World 329tr; Sham 125c; Mahesh Dutt Sharma 103br; shoults 227bl; Sanjay Shrishrimal 175tr; Eitan Simanor 220clb; Abhishek Singh 364-5t; Aditya "Dicky" Singh 144-5b; Paramvir Singh 467cra, 467br; Raj Singh 71br; Aliaksei Skreidzeleu 116-7t; Igor Smoljan 232bl; Pradeep Soman 526tl, 534bl, 559bc; Vijaykumar Soni 382clb; Steve Speller 290clb; srijanrc landscapes 332t; Alexey Stiop 248-9t, 250b; Stockimo / Azhar Khan 100t, / ritwikmittal 436b; SuperStock 587ca, / V. Muthuraman 560cra; Trevor Thompson 220cra; Tiger Chaser 298-9b; TMI 430b; travelib asia 271crb; travelib india 219c, 323br; Tuul and Bruno Morandi 43cla, 55bl, 315crb; Leisa Tyler 59cla; UtCon Collection 209tr; Muthuraman Vaithinathan 54br; Vinicius Valle 204c; Lucas Vallecillos 50br, 98-9t, 101tc; Ivan Vdovin 466-7b;

photography 146tl; tropicalpixsingapore 27t, 564-5; Manjunath Undi 482t; VasukiRao 474-5b; Vivek_Renukaprasad 38bl, 183tr; VladimirSklyarov 6-7; VuCongDanh 119br; webguzs 44tl; yogesh_more 454cr; yuliang11 139t; ZU_09 446br.

Rutuja Kadam: 407tr.

Los Angeles County Museum of Art: The Ciechanowiecki Collection; Gift of The Ahmanson Foundation (M.2000.179.13). 71tr.

National Gallery of Modern Art, New Delhi: 94bl.

Patna Likes: 262t.

Picfair.com: Stockimo 21tl, 324-5.

Robert Harding Picture Library: Stuart Black 521tr; Matthew Williams-Ellis 35tl; Ephotocorp 226-7t, 425ca, 551cr; Michele Falzone 65clb; C. Huetter 129bc; Olaf Kruger 2-3; Peter Langer 297tr; Ben Pipe 18t, 200-1; Paul Porter 105t; Jose Fuste Raga 471crb; Alex Robinson 23t, 396-7; Aditya Singh 363cra.

Shutterstock: Ultimate Travel Photos 18bl, 214-5.

Front Flap
AWL Images: Peter Adams bl; **Getty Images:** Photographer's Choice / Adrian Pope tc; **iStockphoto.com:** eROMAZe 44 cb; Alexander Reshnya br; **Picfair.com:** Stockimo cra; **Robert Harding Picture Library:** Alex Robinson cla.

Cover images:
Front and spine: **Getty Images:** John Harper.
Back: **4Corners:** Maurizio Rellini tr; **Getty Images:** John Harper b; **iStockphoto.com:** lena_serditova cla, powerofforever c.

For further information see: www.dkimages.com

The information in this DK Eyewitness Travel Guide is checked regularly.
Every effort has been made to ensure that this book is as up-to-date as possible at the time of going to press. Some details, however, such as telephone numbers, opening hours, prices, gallery hanging arrangements and travel information, are liable to change. The publishers cannot accept responsibility for any consequences arising from the use of this book, nor for any material on third party websites, and cannot guarantee that any website address in this book will be a suitable source of travel information. We value the views and suggestions of our readers very highly. Please write to: Publisher, DK Eyewitness Travel Guides, Dorling Kindersley, 80 Strand, London, WC2R 0RL, UK, or email: travelguides@dk.com

Penguin Random House

Main Contributors Victoria McCulloch, Nick Edwards, Lottie Gross, Daniel Jacobs, Shafik Meghji, Roshen Dalal, Partho Datta, Divya Gandhi, Premola Ghose, Ashok Koshy, Abha Narain Lambah, Annabel Lopez, Sumita Mehta, George Michell, Rudrangshu Mukherji, Meenu Nageshwaran, Rushad R Nanavatty, Ira Pande, Usha Raman, Janet Rizvi, Ranee Sahaney, Deepak Sanan, Darsana Selvakumar, Sankarshan Thakur, Shikha Trivedi, Lakshmi Vishwanathan

Senior Editor Ankita Awasthi Tröger
Senior Designers Tania Da Silva Gomes, Bess Daly
Project Editor Lauren Whybrow
Project Art Editor William Robinson
Designers Hansa Babra, Bharti Karakoti, Jaileen Kaur, Nidhi Mehra, Ian Midson, Ankita Sharma, Priyanka Thakur, Stuti Tiwari Bhatia
Factcheckers Saumya Ancheri, Jo Caird, Edwina D'souza, Maria Edwards, Shiladitya Sarkar, Georgia Stephens
Editors Elspeth Beidas, Matthew Grundy Haigh, Rachel Laidler, Lucy Sara-Kelly, David and Sylvia Tombesi-Walton
Proofreader Debra Wolter
Indexer Helen Peters
Senior Picture Researcher Ellen Root
Picture Research Sophie Basilevitch, Sumedha Chopra, Sumita Khatwani, Lakshmi Rao, Rituraj Singh, Harriet Whitaker, Ravi Yadav
Illustrators Avinash Ramsurrun, Dipankar Bhattacharya, Danny Cherian, R Kamalahasan, Surat Kumar Mantoo, Arun P, Suman Saha, Ajay Sethi, Ashok Sukumaran, Gautam Trivedi, Mark Warner
Senior Cartographic Editor Casper Morris
Cartography Uma Bhattacharya, Simonetta Giori, Mohammad Hassan, Suresh Kumar, Kishorchand Naorem, Animesh Pathak
Jacket Designers Maxine Pedliham, William Robinson
Jacket Picture Research Susie Peachey
Senior DTP Designer Jason Little
DTP Vijay Kandwal, Mohd. Rizwan
Junior Producer Kariss Ainsworth
Managing Editor Hollie Teague
Art Director Maxine Pedliham
Publishing Director Georgina Dee

First edition 2002
Published in Great Britain by Dorling Kindersley Limited, 80 Strand, London, WC2R 0RL
Published in the United States by DK Publishing, 1450 Broadway, Suite 801, New York, NY 10018
Copyright © 2002, 2019 Dorling Kindersley Limited
A Penguin Random House Company
19 20 21 22 10 9 8 7 6 5 4 3 2 1

All rights reserved.
No part of this publication may be reproduced, stored in or introduced into a retrieval system, or transmitted, in any form, or by any means (electronic, mechanical, photocopying, recording, or otherwise), without the prior written permission of the copyright owner.
A CIP catalog record for this book is available from the British Library.
A catalog record for this book is available from the Library of Congress.
ISSN: 1542 1554
ISBN: 978 0 2413 6883 1
Printed and bound in Malaysia.
www.dk.com